D0579920

The coat of arms of
AMBASSADOR JOHN L. LOEB JR.

bestowed by

HER MAJESTY, THE QUEEN OF DENMARK,
MARGRETHE II

with the Grand Cross of the Order of Dannebrog

August 31, 1983

JOHN L. LOEB JR.

REFLECTIONS, MEMORIES AND CONFESSIONS

Produced by Scout Books & Media Inc

President Susan Knopf

Art Direction and Design Andrij Borys, Andrij Borys Associates, LLC

Editorial and Photo Manager Brittany Schachner

Editorial Coordinator Chelsea Burris

Copyeditor Peter Jaskowiak

Proofreader Karen Hammonds

Indexer Arc Indexing, Inc.

Special thanks to Valerie Tomaselli, president of MTM Publishing, for her support and guidance, and to Dirk Kaufman for his assistance, as well.

Special thanks to Ann Powell and Patricia Synan in Ambassador Loeb's office for their tireless and always cheerful assistance, and to Eugenie Pliakis and Bob Johnson for their support. And to Kathy Plotkin, whose notes make everything sound better.

ISBN #: 978-0-9762043-1-2
Printed in Canada
Fourth Printing

Photo Notes

Most of the photos and artwork in the book are from Ambassador John L. Loeb Jr.'s personal family collection. Sources have been included where the information was available.

Special thanks to the photographers who provided photos for this book, including Jan van Steenwijk, Annie Watt, Lou Manna Photography, Bachrach, and Karsh; Bill Orcutt for his photography of my art and homes; Mallory Sampson for our beautiful wedding photos; John Taylor for his photographs of my home in Purchase; Houlihan Lawrence and Lisa Teisch for their photographs of 170 Anderson Hill Road; North Wind Picture Archives; New York City Parks Photo Archive; Getty Images; and Alamy Stock Photo.

©2017 John L. Loeb Jr.

All rights reserved. No part of this book may be reproduced or utilized in any form or by any means, electronics or mechanical, including photocopying, recording, or by any information storage and retrieval system, without permission in writing from the publisher.

Published by John L. Loeb Jr.
P. O. Box 670
Purchase, New York 10577

Dedication

My mother wrote the following in her personal memoir: "The saga of the Lehmans, the Lewisohns, the Loebs and the Moseses is not over, and with all these people and their progeny it becomes a brilliant kaleidoscope. It is a never ending and always changing mosaic of human beings for whom I have an abiding love."

I have the same feeling as my mother, and therefore I am dedicating this book first of all to my dearest wife, Sharon, who has helped and counseled me with this memoir; and then to my children, Alexandra and Nicholas, and Alexandra's husband, Joe Driscoll; to my grandchildren, Aidan and Allegra; to my dear brother, Arthur, with whom I have an enduring bond; to my late sister Ann and my late brother-in-law Edgar Bronfman Sr., whom I greatly admired, and their children: Samuel, who helped me with my wine, Sonoma-Loeb; Matthew, who served on the Board of the George Washington Institute for Religious Freedom (GWIRF); Adam; Edgar Jr.; and Holly; to my late sister Judy and her late husband, Richard Beaty, a World War II hero, who was one of the fighter pilots who saved England before the U.S. entered the war; and their children: Richie, John, Anne, Frannie, Charlie, Nancy and Susan; and to the late Marco Chiara, Judy's second husband, and their daughter Daniela; to my sister Debby and her husband, James Brice, and to her first husband, Sir David Davies, and their son, Taran; and to my former wives, Nina Sundby and the late Meta Harrsen.

And to my Loeb first cousins, their children and all subsequent generations, including Tom Kempner and his wife, Ann Bernhard, and his former wife, the late Nan Schlesinger; the late Alan Kempner Jr. and his wife, Rosemary Smith, and his late wife, Sandra Stark; the late Carl L. Kempner and his wife, Doris Coleman, and their son, Michael Kempner, who has worked with me on a number of projects and also served on the board of GWIRF; John Levin, who was a brilliant former partner of mine at Loeb, Rhoades, and his wife, Betty Loeb; the late Peter Loeb and his wife, Jeanette Winter (the first woman partner at Goldman Sachs), and his former wife, Nancy Carol First; Jean Loeb and her husband, Raymond S. Troubh, and her former husband, the late Benet Polikoff Jr.; Constance Loeb and her husband, Dr. George L. Cohn; and Carl M. Loeb III and his wife, Hadassah Savetsky.

And to my Lehman first cousins, their children and all subsequent generations, including:

The Bernhards: William and his late wife, Catherine Cahill—he became a very close friend of mine and was best man at my marriage to Sharon; and Robert and his wife, Joan Mack Sommerfield, and his former wife, Frances Wells.

The Buttenwiesers: Peter and his wife, Terry Marek, and his former wife, Elizabeth Werthen; Lawrence and his wife, Ann Lubin; and Dr. Paul and his wife, Catherine Frum. Paul has helped me with GWIRF and introduced me to Margo Stern Strom, the founder of Facing History and Ourselves.

Finally, I dedicate this memoir to all others from the Lehman, Loeb, Lewisohn and Moses families whom I have not mentioned, and to all their unborn descendants.

And, of course, to my late parents, John Langeloth Loeb and Frances (Peter) Lehman Loeb, without whom much would not have been possible.

Acknowledgments

It has taken several years to bring this book to fruition and finally to print. Over these years, I have sought counsel, information, verification, photographs and knowledge from family members and many friends.

First and foremost, I want to thank Kathy Plotkin, who started me on this project years ago. She has encouraged me in every aspect of the project, most recently with the pictures. With regard to the pictures, Kathy has been working with Ann Powell and Robert Pack, who have been extraordinarily helpful.

I wish I could talk about each one of the people who has helped me, but that would turn into a book itself. They include Richard V. Allen; William Lehman Bernhard; Ambassador Stuart Bernstein; Sally Breckenridge from the Harvey School; Dr. Paul Buttenwieser; Dana Catalano; Mary Louise Chelbina; David Patrick Columbia; Maerita Cooper; John Cremin; Priscilla DeVargas; Anna DeVito; Ken Emerson; Harold Epstein; Michael Feldberg, PhD; Francis "Shorty" Fraenkel; Karen Franklin; Mario Gabelli; Julian and Irene Gingold; Jessica Goldsmith; David Kass; Susan Knopf, my publisher at Scout Books & Media, as well as her team, including Brittany Gialanella and Andrij Borys; Wendy Lehman Lash and Stephen Lash; Oscar Lewisohn; Lou Manna; Domingos Melo; Sandi Mendelsohn; Susan Mesinai; Monica Multos; Bill Orcutt; Judith W. Ringer; Ambassador Gilbert A. Robinson; Ellen Scordato; James T. Skay Jr.; Jon Sternfeld; Gloria M. Stevens; John Taylor; Valerie Tomaselli; Jan Van Steenwijk; Ben Vaughn; Annie Watts; and last but not least, my excellent and devoted office staff, including Robert Johnson, Eugenie Pliakis and Trish Synan.

Table of Contents

Dear Reader

For those of you who are armchair historians or genealogists, **Part One: Heritage** *will be a good place to start. There you will learn about my family heritage and the background that had an enormous influence on who I became.*

If you just want to get into the meat of my life and jump right in, you may find **Part Two: Starting Out** *a more intriguing place to begin. There you will find the story of my life—who I am, what I have experienced and what I have accomplished.*

For those who prefer to see the movie before reading a book, you will find an interesting DVD on the inside back cover.

Prologue

> *These German Jewish families are more than a collective American success story.*
> *At the point in time when they were a cohesive, knit, and recognizably distinct part*
> *of New York society, they were also the closest thing to Aristocracy—Aristocracy*
> *in the best sense—that the city, and perhaps the country, had seen.*
>
> —Stephen Birmingham, Our Crowd

I am a *Lehman* and a *Loeb*, which means I was born with two silver spoons in my mouth. It took me decades to understand the origins of those spoons and the winding path my family took to put them there. I come from generations of families that built America, families that tower and spiral back to our country's founding and beyond. They came and worked and built all that they could in this land that promised opportunity, in the most wild and expansive sense of the word.

Of course, we were rich; that much is known.

I remember asking my mother how it all began, and she said she didn't know, that "we always had money." I then asked, "But how do you know?" And she said, "As far as I know we *always* had money." It turned out she was right.

Money surrounded us like air—as necessary to our lives as the oxygen we breathed, and just as invisible. It was not who we were, but how could it be ignored? Yet there is so much more, as there always is. My family's story flows into the larger American story—of religion and politics and history, and of the revolutionaries who founded this nation and the immigrants who helped build it.

I am one of the few remaining scions of the families depicted in Stephen Birmingham's 1967 bestseller *Our Crowd*, a cultural history of New York's wealthy German-Jewish families. I am a descendant of four of them: Lehman, Loeb, Lewisohn and Moses.* More than most men, my story cannot be told without telling the story of others—not just my direct antecedents and family, but the network of families who made New York their own at the time of America's rise in the world. My story is their story, and their stories are, in a sense, everyone's.

Our Crowd was an ambitious book, attempting to define and frame our families beyond their money. Birmingham writes, "Their accomplishments and their contributions to the special spirit and élan ... of New York City make the fact of their wealth seem secondary." I can only hope this observation to be true, and my experience bears this out.

The book details a New York that once was, but also a New York that still is. It crackles under the pavement and stretches to the skies—both as a ghost of the past and a fact of the present. The New York built by the Loebs and Lehmans is an immovable part of the tapestry, but, like so much, it is being painted over by the twenty-first century's obsession with the new. History can never be entirely subsumed, but perhaps the reality of what those men and women accomplished fades in the telling.

I must admit that one of my interests in writing this book is to rage against the dying of the light—both my own flickering light and that of a family who chose not to write much down. "Due to a persistent reticence and unwillingness to boast," Birmingham wrote, the people of *Our Crowd* were "little understood as human beings." That is what I am trying to do here—bring the humanness down from the mountain.

It's strange how my family can be so well known and so mysterious at the same time, but that's how they wanted it. My hopes push against that family habit of privacy and reticence. "When a writer is born into a family," the Polish poet Czeslaw Milosz wrote, "that family is doomed." I hope this is not true.

Quite simply, I would like my children, grandchildren and their yet unborn children to know something of who their family was and what they did in America. Perhaps they would like to take the baton and explore even further. Consider this book only a relatively small part of their considerable legacy.

Nathaniel Hawthorne argued that families are always rising and falling in America, and perhaps that's true, but our family never dipped far enough for me to brag. My grandfather

---

* The Moseses were a Sephardic Jewish family who arrived in America in 1697; they were not a member of "Our Crowd."

used to say, "You only need to brag when you are down and out."

I was born in York House, a private maternity hospital on East 74th Street, on May 2, 1930, to John Loeb and his wife, Frances, better known as "Peter." ("I was a sick child," she once said, "and they called me Peter Pan, hoping that I would live forever.") At my birth my mother asked my father, "Does he have every little thing?" (She was so isolated from boys that the male appendage seemed a miracle.) He assured her that I did. Nature had given me all the requisite parts—toes, fingers and the like. My parents would take care of the rest.

But outside the walls of that hospital, things were bleak. The country had been in a tailspin during my nine months in the womb, and President Hoover was still claiming that the previous fall's market crash was a temporary setback. He assured a worried nation that the economy would bounce back. (It would, but not until twelve years later and under a different president.) We never suffered what so many others did in that Great Depression, but it was a dangerous and uncertain time. No one felt entirely safe. Owing to prenatal influence, I believe, I never quite shook the anxiety I had about money, even when all signs pointed away from danger.

My adolescence was a mix of ambition and angst, characterized by the colossal footprint left by my ancestors, about whom I remained constantly curious. A family friend once asked my mother how that kind of history might weigh on my siblings and me. "My husband and I have often talked about it," she responded. "But we've decided it's *their* problem." Indeed it was.

Both of my grandfathers, Carl M. Loeb and Arthur Lehman, were financial giants of their day—of any day, really. The expectations of success had been in my family's DNA for quite some time. I treated this with the reverence and appreciation that one would expect from a boy who wanted to please. Among my impressive ancestors were also Goliaths of public service: my great-uncle Irving Lehman was chief justice of the highest court in New York State, while my great-uncle Herbert Lehman left the firm that bore his name to serve first as governor and then U.S. senator from our home state.

Uncle Herbert, who was governor of New York during my childhood, left me enthralled as a young boy. His presence instilled in me a feeling that service could bring both duty and glamour. Uncle Herbert traveled with motorcycle escorts and, most impressively, once introduced me to Shirley Temple. My father was magic as well, disappearing every morning to some place called Wall Street—the name itself evoking a confusing picture in my young brain, a place where he "made money." I, of course, took this literally. When I asked for more details, I was told that the family business would be taught to me in due course. This was the stock answer I always received.

I got an MBA from Harvard and started to work for my father at Loeb, Rhoades & Co. at age twenty-seven. During the time I worked for the firm, however, I never entirely broke through the barrier that my father put up. I simply learned the family business because it was in the air; I breathed it in as I did the social aspects of their world: golf and tennis at the country club, fascinating and important people, bridge and word games, Westchester parties that swirled with conversation and cigarette smoke. A life of sportsmanship, culture and charitable giving (my parents never failed to give).*

There were no storm signals in my early life. During a fairly carefree early childhood, I was secure in the love—if not a superabundance of personal attention—of my parents and grandparents. I enjoyed the companionship and affection of siblings, countless cousins and visiting childhood friends, along with the doting attention of servants and hovering nannies. (When I was born, the Loeb household had a live-in staff of seven.)

At the age of nine I was sent to boarding school in my parents' hopes that it would "make a man" out of me. It did, but not in the exact ways my family intended. Boarding school opened my eyes to a few harsh realities, none greater than this: no amount of achievement or family wealth could insulate me from the anti-Semitism that raged even in the most educated circles of American life in the 1930s and 1940s. I have spent many years thinking about the measure of men, about how we measure a life of worth in this culture. The seeds of that thinking were planted in those boarding school years.

Bigotry came as a shock to me, the way things can to a young boy who is sheltered among his own. I thought we were immune to such ugliness and insulated from hate, ignorance and pain. I learned we quite certainly were not. Though we were Jews, I was brought up with no religion—we never went to synagogue, there were no bar mitzvahs in my family and I attended only one Passover Seder during my entire childhood.

Jewishness was not something I ever thought about—it was only when I experienced others' thoughts of it that it began to weigh on me. The memories of what I witnessed— particularly the cruel, anti-Semitic responses of my callous schoolmates after viewing newsreel footage of the Holocaust—have fueled a lifelong passion of mine: championing religious freedom and working to educate others on our country's history in this regard. I often speak of the need to go beyond religious tolerance, for the word "tolerance" itself seems half-hearted to me.

"Toleration is not the opposite of intoleration," Thomas Paine wrote, "but is the coun-

---

* My parents gave over $200 million to charity, including $150 million to Harvard University, at the time the largest gift in its history.

terfeit of it." Tolerance implies superiority—a granting of permission—rather than a wide acceptance, an embracing of differences, which is part of America's founding principles and enshrined in the Constitution and Bill of Rights.

As an adult, I would soon learn that social values and definitions of success were changing. Making it to the top of "Our Crowd" didn't matter as much—to me, to my parents, or to the world. When I grew up, we were comfortably ensconced, maybe insulated, among our own. There were Catholics, Protestants and Jews in New York—and each had their own leaders, networks and hierarchies. But even with New York's economic overlapping, these groups rarely met with one another socially.

In the postwar world of the 1950s and 1960s, things changed. Achieving social stature in the wider world of WASPs—"their crowd," as it were—would be the new measuring stick for my family and friends. There were no longer signs reading, "No Dogs. No Jews. No Consumptives." I became as welcome in the formerly "No Jews" social clubs—like the Knickerbocker Club—as I was anywhere else. This did not happen overnight, nor did it happen on its own. In fact, my parents were among those in the vanguard who made this assimilation possible.

Our story is by no means a pure Horatio Alger tale of hard scrabbling and pulling of bootstraps, and I cannot pretend it to be. America is a patchwork, after all, stitched together through everyone's stories, and my family's is no different. Ours is the American story, the immigrant story, the founders' story, the German story and the Jewish story. Among my ancestors are soldiers in the American Revolution, cattle dealers forbidden from owning land in their home country, salesmen who went down to Alabama and came back as cotton magnates, friends of the original Goldman and the original Sachs. Some were immigrants who came here and made a name for themselves; others were born into that name and did what they could with it. I am a product of all of this, as are my children, grandchildren and the unborn who will share the names that adorn these pages.

P.S. KRØYER 1851–1909
Self-Portrait, Sitting by His Easel at Skagen Beach (1902)
(Ambassador John L. Loeb Jr. Danish Art Collection)

The Joy of
My Danish Art
Collection

One of the great joys of my life as I walk through my home in Purchase, the townhouse in Manhattan, and my flat in London's Eaton Square is seeing the beautiful Danish paintings I've collected over the years. When I enter a room and see one of the paintings, I stop and look anew at the exquisite artwork. In order to share this experience with you, my reader, I am including some of these pieces in the pages that follow. Between each of the parts of this book, you will happen upon a selection of paintings. I hope you, too, will take a moment to look at and find joy in them.

—John L. Loeb Jr.

The history of my family in America begins in the late seventeenth century. The remarkable story of my ancestors provides insight into American history, and American Jewish history, over the generations since then. This photograph shows my "granny" Adeline and grandfather Carl Loeb, who were my father's parents.

PART ONE

Heritage

I am standing here beside an oil painting of my great-grandfather Mayer Lehman, which has hung behind my office desk ever since the 1970s. That was when I commissioned an artist to copy it from a photograph that once hung in the Lehman Brothers office.

The Lehman Story,
1720–1984

The Lehman Brothers firm that fell into bankruptcy in 2008 was not, as erroneously and extensively reported, the Lehman Brothers founded by my ancestors in 1844. In 1977, Lehman Brothers merged with the financial firm Kuhn, Loeb & Co. (no relation). In 1984, my ancestors' Lehman Brothers/Kuhn, Loeb company was bought by and folded into the American Express Company. Ten years later, in 1994, American Express formed a new company led by Richard Fuld, an employee of the original Lehman Brothers. Recognizing the value of the Lehman Brothers name, Fuld took it for this new company.

When American Express's *new* "Lehman Brothers" company collapsed fourteen years later in 2008, I received calls from concerned friends who thought I must have lost a great deal of money. I assured everyone that neither I nor any members of my family had any connection with the current Lehman Brothers. All of my family's financial interest in the original Lehman Brothers ended with the death of my grandfather Arthur Lehman in 1936.*

---

* I am not exploring the Emanuel Lehman side of the family here. Emanuel and Mayer built Lehman Brothers. Our family has written a book on the Lehman family titled *Lots of Lehmans*. It should be noted that the great art collection of Robert and Philip Lehman resides in the Metropolitan Museum of Art. They were the son and grandson of Emanuel.

Philip Isles, who is a great-grandson of Emanuel and a grandnephew of Robert, is the chairman of the Robert Lehman Foundation and is on the board of the Metropolitan Museum of Art. Philip is an outstanding individual; he worked at Lehman Brothers for years and has four children. His sister Tina Barney is a famous photographer and has had many of her works exhibited in, and some owned by, the Museum of Modern Art.

An interesting fact that is not widely known is that Mayer's oldest son, Sigmund, married one of Emanuel's children, Harriet Lehman. A descendant of this union was a great hero in World War II, Orin Lehman. He lost a leg in the war, the other was severely damaged, and his face was shattered. He cofounded Just One Break, an organization that brings together leading employers and qualified applicants with disabilities. His sister, Ellen Lehman McCluskey, was a famous interior decorator. Her daughters are Lady Sharon Sondes and Maureen McCluskey, and her son is Orin McCluskey. Another well-known descendant is Robin Lehman. Robin won two Academy Awards for documentary shorts (one for producing and one for directing) and is a well-known Hollywood cinematographer. There really should be a book about this side of the family.

From the Lehman collection: El Greco's *Christ Carrying the Cross*, El Greco's *St. Jerome*, and Rembrandt's *Gerard de Lairesse*. Courtesy of my cousin Philip Isles, nephew of Bobby Lehman, president of the Robert Lehman Foundation and board member of the Metropolitan Museum of Art.

Stephen Birmingham opens *Our Crowd* with a comment made by my great-aunt Hattie Lehman Goodhart, wife of the wealthy Philip J. Goodhart and the sister of future New York governor Herbert Lehman. In the 1930s, Hattie Lehman Goodhart held court in her home on West 81st Street in Manhattan, which her father (my great-grandfather Mayer Lehman), built for her and Philip. According to *Our Crowd*, Hattie frequently pronounced that there were only two kinds of people: "People we visit and people we *wouldn't* visit."[1] Such fastidiousness might have sounded grand to her father's ears. He was one of four surviving sons of a prosperous—but not elite—Bavarian cattle dealer, Abraham Løw,* and his wife, Eva. One has to wonder if Aunt Hattie would have considered her Bavarian relatives "people we visit."

In most small German towns in the 1800s, only one son of any given Jewish family, usually the eldest, was permitted to stay in town, marry and earn a living there. His sib-

---

* The family name Løw would later become Lehmann, but the final "n" was dropped, and the name became Lehman sometime after the three younger brothers emigrated to America.

House of Mayer and Babette Lehman at South Court Street in Montgomery, Alabama.
(Robert M. Morgenthau)

lings, including his sisters, were forced to leave home and find a way to survive elsewhere. This was one of the many challenges facing young nineteenth-century Jews in Germany. Seligman, the oldest Lehman brother, was allowed to remain at home in Rimpar, a small town near Würzburg. Henry, the youngest of the three brothers, left Germany at the age of twenty-one, going first to Mobile, Alabama, then moving on to Montgomery. He arrived in 1844, and Emanuel followed him in 1847. Their youngest brother, my great-grandfather Mayer Lehman, came to these shores in 1850.

When Henry first arrived in 1844, he peddled foodstuffs, kitchenware and general merchandise. By the time Mayer arrived six years later, Henry and Emanuel had founded a prospering general store called H. Lehman & Bro. Young Mayer started his new life in America as a hardworking clerk in his brothers' bustling store, for a time even sleeping in the store's back rooms. The three brothers began to barter their merchandise for cotton—Montgomery's prime commodity—in which Mayer became a proficient trader. By 1858, he was sufficiently solvent to marry another Bavarian, Babette Neugass.

Babette was the first child of Friederike and Isaak Neugass, a weaver in Rieneck, a town not far from Rimpar. Mayer supposedly met Babette at his oldest brother's wedding when she was only eleven and Mayer was eighteen. When Babette arrived in America, she was staying with relatives in New Orleans, where Mayer frequently made business trips. It was in New Orleans that my Lehman great-grandparents married, on January 6, 1858. When Babette became his bride, she was twenty, and he was three days shy of twenty-eight.*

Before the Civil War, the prospering young Mayer Lehmans "entered into social life very well"[2] and enjoyed a good life in a large home in Montgomery, Alabama. They were well respected in both civic and Jewish religious affairs. Mayer, a devout and generous Jew, was a member of the Montgomery Masonic Lodge, "a definite seal of civic approval."[3] Although the Masons are a fraternal organization, they incorporate Christian ideas and ideals in their rituals, so the induction of an observant Jew is indeed noteworthy.

Four of Babette and Mayer's eight children were born in Montgomery: Sigmund, Harriet ("Hattie"), Lisette ("Settie") and Benjamin, who died in infancy. Babette was an exacting matriarch whom her grown sons were expected to visit every day after work. She would insist that they "tell mother everything" before they went to their own homes, according to Great Uncle Herbert's memories.[4]

Mayer's older brother Henry died in 1855, at the age of thirty-three, of yellow fever while on a business trip to New Orleans. His death left his two younger brothers, Emanuel and Mayer, to run the business. Three years later, in 1858, shortly after Mayer's marriage, Emanuel moved to New York City to handle the financial aspects of their growing cotton trade at a new office at 119 Liberty Street. The gregarious Mayer, who had more expertise in cotton than Emanuel, remained in Alabama to run the store and the trading business and to maintain their strong relationship with the cotton planters. The saying in our family is that "Mayer made the money, and Emanuel conserved it." Despite their disparate personalities, or perhaps because of them, their business thrived.

In spite of the onset of the Civil War in 1861, the Lehman business continued, though obviously not as usual. Montgomery was the Confederacy's first capital, and much of the Lehman business had been taking place in New York. When war broke out, a devastated Emanuel scribbled on a pad *Alles ist beendet!*[5] (All is finished!) But it wasn't; the war never completely stopped the cotton trade, as both sides needed it for their war efforts. Even with Lincoln's blockade of the South, a trickle of cotton was

---

* Babette's sister Esther married Isaias Hellman, who began as a buyer and seller of banks in Los Angeles. He was president of the Nevada National Bank, which he merged with Wells Fargo Bank. He then became president of Wells Fargo. His cousin Francis Dinkelspiel tells his story in *Towers of Gold: How One Jewish Immigrant Named Isaias Hellman Created California*.

Mayer Lehman after moving to New York City, c. 1870. (Henry Morgenthau III)

Babette Neugass Lehman in New York City, c. 1870. (Henry Morgenthau III)

The Mayer Lehman Family in Tarrytown, NY, c. 1888. Front row, kneeling: Herbert (left) next to Irving. In the second row, seated (left to right): Hattie Lehman Goodhart holding daughter Helen, Mayer Lehman with grandson Howard Goodhart, Babette with grandson Allan Lehman, Settie Lehman Fatman with daughter Margaret. Back row (left to right): Philip J. Goodhart, Harriet Lehman (Sigmund's wife), Sigmund M. Lehman, Clara Lehman (later Clara Lehman Limburg), Morris Fatman, Arthur Lehman. (Herbert H. Lehman Suite & Papers, Columbia University)

smuggled up to New York or from New Orleans to Liverpool, England. Thus, the Lehmans most likely survived the Civil War by running the blockade.

Any cotton the Lehmans owned that they couldn't get out of Montgomery was housed in a warehouse co-owned by the Lehmans and a partner named John Wesley Durr. Sadly, much of the warehoused cotton was deliberately burned in 1865 by retreating Confederate troops to keep it out of Union hands. The burning did not bankrupt the prospering Durr-Lehman partnership, because a good deal of their profits had been invested in gold.[6] Believing that even Yankees would not be so uncivilized as to inspect a lady's petticoats, the gold was hidden in the skirts of Mrs. John Durr. When the Union troops left Montgomery, the gold was retrieved and divided between the two partners.

Even though rebuilding their business after the Civil War was painful, the Lehmans were solvent. In 1867, they lent $100,000 to the bankrupt state of Alabama, an amount equivalent to approximately $2.5 million today.[7] Mayer started another partnership with his wife's younger brother, Benjamin Neugass, in New Orleans, which underwent a succession of names and partners.

With the Lehman companies safely in family hands in the South and the war over, Mayer felt free to leave Montgomery and join Emanuel in New York City. In 1868, he moved to New York to share the new offices on Pearl Street off Hanover Square, the center of the cotton trade. Babette and the children soon followed him to New York. Mayer had owned seven slaves, and at least two of them, though free by then, came to New York to work for the Lehmans.

By 1876, the family was enjoying a comfortable life in a five-floor brownstone at 5 East 62nd Street. Babette bore Mayer four more children in Manhattan: Clara, Arthur, Irving and Herbert. The three youngest boys would become the most well known of Mayer's offspring. Arthur would help to increase the family financial success at Lehman Brothers, the intense and religious Irving would become chief justice of the New York State Court of Appeals, and the secular Herbert would be the only one to enter politics. Herbert would become governor of the state of New York (1933–1942), the first director general of the United Nations Relief and Rehabilitation Administration, (1943–1946) and a U.S. senator (1950–1957).*

In 1870, Mayer and Emanuel spearheaded the formation of the New York Cotton Ex-

---

* Among his many accomplishments, Uncle Herbert was one of the few members of Congress brave enough to offer early and vigorous objections to McCarthyism. *The New York Times* quoted Lehman as calling McCarthy "a threat to freedom" on a par with the threat from Communism itself. (*The New York Times*, December 14, 1954)

Herbert being sworn in for his second term as lieutenant governor on January 1, 1930, by his brother, New York State Appeals Court Judge Irving Lehman, while Governor Franklin D. Roosevelt and Herbert's wife, Edith, look on. (*The New York Times*)

My mother's father, Arthur Lehman (right), senior partner of Lehman Brothers, with his brothers—Herbert (middle), governor of New York, and Irving, chief justice of the New York State Court of Appeals, the highest court in the state—on December 31, 1934, the day Irving swore in Herbert for another term as governor of New York. In his memoir, *All in a Lifetime*, my father described them as "three of the most different men I'd ever known. Arthur was a hardheaded banker. Herbert was a great humanitarian. Irving was a leading jurist and a deeply religious man. They were all outstanding in their particular fields." (John L. Loeb Jr.)

change, where Mayer served on its first board of governors and headed its first finance committee. When he died at the age of sixty-seven, on June 21, 1897, after an unsuccessful abdominal surgery, the Exchange closed for an hour during his funeral, the first observance of this type for that institution. Emanuel retired not long after, and the Lehman fortune was passed on to the next generation. For many years, if someone's last name was not "Lehman," including my father, they were not allowed to join the firm.

After her husband's death, the widowed Babette moved to an apartment at the corner of 58th Street and Seventh Avenue. The West Side of Manhattan had by then become more chic than East 62nd Street where my grandfather Arthur Lehman grew up. As a boy, Arthur could look up Fifth Avenue at 70th Street—where the Frick Museum is today—and see a farm with goats feeding on grass.

My mother remembered her grandmother Babette as a seventy-year-old woman who looked ninety, always dressed in black. Each year, Babette visited the Arthur Lehmans for a month at Ridgeleigh, their summer home in Westchester County, north of the city. During Babette's visits, Adele Lehman found it convenient to lunch anywhere without her mother-in-law, thus partially avoiding Babette's criticism—specifically that she was not strict enough with her three daughters. Despite this "serious omission of discipline," they turned out very well.

The founding Lehman brothers had dealt primarily in basic tangible commodities; with the next generation of Lehmans in charge, the firm entered into large financial ventures, both for the firm and for its clients. The young lions were Mayer's sons Sigmund, Arthur and Herbert; Henry's son Meyer; and Emanuel's son Philip. With the increase in their stock and bond transactions, the firm bought a seat on the New York Stock Exchange in 1887. The "boys" bought companies and helped to finance railroads, textile mills and iron plants for the recovering South. They organized large banks and trusts and underwrote securities for such firms as F.W. Woolworth and sold stock for Sears Roebuck.* They were on a roll.

In the 1920s, my grandfather Arthur Lehman and Emanuel's son Philip were the two principals in the firm. Irving, never a major figure in the company, followed a career in law.[8] Herbert spent seventeen successful years with the Lehman Brothers Company until 1928, when he was elected New York's lieutenant governor under Governor Franklin D. Roosevelt.

Under my grandfather's and his first cousin Philip's earlier leadership, the company grew from a moderate-sized commodity business into a major investment banking house. At a 1925 Lehman Brothers anniversary celebration, it was noted that the company had done almost $2 billion in business that year (approximately $21 billion in today's money).[9] The firm pioneered what were then new industries: department store chains, food chains, mail order houses, electric power and light companies, automobile companies, aviation and motion picture companies. Arthur Lehman helped organize the Marine Midland Trust Co. and the Southern States Land and Timber Corporation, which acquired and reclaimed approximately one million acres of land in the upper Everglades, opening up lower Florida.[10]

The experience of the Lehmans during the Depression was unlike that of most other underwriters. Arthur and Philip successfully guided their company through the perils of the stock market crash in 1929 and the Depression that followed. The firm had been successful up to that point, and the investment world considered Lehman Brothers a first-rate firm. The Lehmans were among those in a position to help Wall Street recover and, at the same time, continue to make money themselves. When Philip died in 1947, the firm was passed on to Philip's son Robert "Bobbie" Lehman and the next generation.

In 1901, Arthur Lehman married Adele Lewisohn, one of three daughters of the famously wealthy copper and real estate magnate Adolph Lewisohn and Emma Cahn Lewisohn. The financial and Jewish social worlds saw the alliance of the two families as a wonderful merger of both wealth and social prestige. But, according to my mother, the Lewisohns—

---

* These were the kinds of companies that the old guard—like Kuhn, Loeb and J.P. Morgan—considered too "low-class" and risky to touch.

Governor Herbert Lehman and his wife, Edith Altschul Lehman, with President Roosevelt and his wife, Eleanor, having tea together. Herbert and Edith not only became great friends of the Roosevelts, they also enthusiastically supported the ideas of Roosevelt's New Deal.

especially Emma—were not thrilled. "Somehow my grandmother felt such a marriage was beneath her daughter," wrote my mother in her memoir. "Grandma Emma Cahn attempted to postpone the marriage by taking my mother to Europe for the summer, but Mother won out in the end, as she always won out in everything."[11]

Arthur Lehman died suddenly from an embolism on May 16, 1936, at the age of sixty-three. I was six years old, and my memories of him are slim. The family tells of his support of the Federation of Jewish Philanthropies of New York (of which he was a founder), the New School, the Museum of the City of New York and Harvard University. On the thirtieth anniversary of his graduation from Harvard, he gave his alma mater a new administration building, Lehman Hall. He was a proponent of the financial benefits of daylight savings time and a lover of the arts, leaving a huge collection of fifteenth- and sixteenth-century tapestries, paintings and illuminated books. He also built one of New York's greatest townhouses at 45 East 70th Street. Estée Lauder bought it from my grandmother Lehman's estate. He is also remembered for never being without a big black cigar and for wearing a fresh carnation in his lapel every day, clipped from the Lehman greenhouse.

My Lehman grandparents had three daughters: Dorothy, Helen and the youngest, my mother Frances, born in 1906. My grandmother Adele and her daughters were never involved in the Lehman business, but each carved out a social standing. Like her husband, Adele gave money to and raised money for Jewish philanthropies, museums, hospitals and the New York Philharmonic Orchestra. In spite of her well-known shyness, she agreed to hold offices in many of the nonprofit organizations in which she was involved, including the League of Women Voters. Though she and Arthur enjoyed playing cards, Adele also played both tennis and golf at a championship level. In 1947, she took up painting simple

ARTHUR LEHMAN'S HOME AT 45 EAST 70TH STREET
House is featured in the book *Great Houses of New York, 1840–1940*, pp. 259–263.

Much to my dismay, after the death of Grandma Lehman, my aunt Helen Buttenwieser sold the Manhattan home of my grandparents to Estée Lauder for a half million dollars. My father wanted to buy it, but my mother didn't want to live in her parents' home. Unfortunately, it was never shown to me, because I certainly would have bought it. A few years ago, my cousin Billy Bernhard and I attended a charity event on the house's ground floor and found that the downstairs—the foyer, the ballroom, including all the tapestries—looked exactly the same as it did when we were children. It's likely worth close to $40 million today.

Arthur Lehman
(1873–1936)

Adele Lehman
(1882–1965)

but charming still lifes and florals, a few of which I still have. Adele died on August 11, 1965, at the age of eighty-three.

My aunt Dorothy married the investment banker Richard Bernhard in 1923. Deeply involved in philanthropy, she received the first Child Welfare Award from Eleanor Roosevelt in 1962. However, she is best remembered in our family for administering the Mayer Lehman Charity Fund, established to help distant relatives escape from the Holocaust in Germany. She personally oversaw finding them homes and jobs and providing direct assistance in resettlement. All those who claimed to be family were accepted, even if they couldn't prove they were related. She sent affidavits for over a hundred families of which, sadly, only seventy-five were used. The families that did not use them believed the Hitler period would pass. Dorothy and Richard Bernhard had two sons, Robert and William, whom I also count as close friends. Billy was best man at my wedding to Sharon Handler in 2012. A loving aunt, Dorothy regularly wrote me cheerful and upbeat letters when I served in the Air Force at the end of the Korean War.

In 1929, my aunt Helen married Benjamin Buttenwieser, a partner in the investment banking firm Kuhn, Loeb. Benjamin was the deputy to the U.S. High Commissioner for Germany, John McCloy, after World War II. Helen was impressive in her own right. Though she had great difficulties in school as a child, she would become the only one of her sisters to earn a college diploma, from Connecticut College. She became a champion of nontraditional education and was an early supporter of Manhattan's prestigious Dalton School.*

Aunt Helen practiced law in Manhattan for fifty years and she was among the first women admitted to the New York County Bar Association. Her *New York Times* obituary noted, "Her two passions were the law and civil liberties. They merged when she became the first chairwoman of the Legal Aid Society, which she served for more than 50 years."[12]

---

* Mrs. Alger Hiss was a teacher at Dalton, and when Alger went on trial for treason, Helen was one of his defense lawyers. This act would put both Buttenwiesers on Nixon's infamous "enemies list" and kill my Uncle Ben's political hopes.

Adele with her three married daughters (from left): Frances ("Peter") Loeb, Dorothy Bernhard, and Helen Buttenwieser. They were her three greatest achievements. (American Jewish Historical Society)

A brilliant advocate for the causes she believed in, she was extremely outspoken, but her hallmark was a wonderfully self-deprecating humor that neutralized her frankness. She and Benjamin had three sons, my dear cousins Lawrence, Peter and Paul.

My mother Frances was known by almost everybody as "Peter," a nickname that stemmed from J.M. Barrie's *Peter Pan*. A sickly baby, Mother was called Peter because her parents wanted her to live forever, though for a while it did not appear she would last very long at all. The nickname stuck with her through adulthood. "Peter" was involved in politics from early on in her marriage in 1928 to my father John Loeb, though she never ran for office herself.

On November 21, 1930 (roughly six months after I was born), Governor Franklin D. Roosevelt wrote to Mother on New York State stationery from Warm Springs, Georgia:

> *I did not have an opportunity at the close of the campaign to thank you in person for all the splendid work and cooperation which you gave and I am therefore sending you these few lines of personal appreciation, and under separate cover a photo with the hope that we shall all of us always remember the most successful campaign which has been conducted in our State so far! Again, many thanks.*
>
> *Very sincerely yours,*
> *Franklin D. Roosevelt*

I think both Mother's strength and beauty were captured by Simon Elwes, a noted portraitist and a favorite of British royals.

My birth did not keep my mother from her outside commitments, too legion to enumerate. She took the most satisfaction from her twelve-year service as New York City Commissioner for the United Nations and the Consular Corps under the administrations of Mayors Abraham Beame and John Lindsay, from 1966 to 1978. She directed a staff of fifteen employees and many volunteers to ease culture shock in the foreign diplomatic community. The banner headline of her lengthy obituary in *The New York Times* in May 1996 read, "Lifesaver to Foreign Diplomats." Not only did my mother manage the commission's scant budget, she also wheedled, coaxed and bulldozed friends and relatives to commit tens of thousands of dollars to the cause of helping UN foreigners. Like her sisters, she was outspoken and was sometimes found to be abrasive at board meetings. Her hand was not always in its velvet glove, but she got things done. My mother was a natural politician, and had she been born in today's world, she would have been a senator at least. I'd like to think she could even have been president.

The Lehman fortune from my mother's side of the family accounts for the first of my two silver spoons, as well as for the legacy of a family well entrenched in politics, philanthropy and public service. The Lewisohn legacy, also from Mother's side, though a rich one, surprisingly enough did *not* provide a silver spoon. That story begins with my astounding great-grandfather Adolph Lewisohn.

Adolph Lewisohn was a man
of stature, financially speaking.
However, he stood only five feet
three. He frequently appeared in
his silk top hat, which made him
look taller. Gregarious by nature,
he became famous not only for
his great wealth, extraordinary
philanthropy and Lewisohn Stadium,
but also for the extravagant parties
he gave at his mansion on Fifth
Avenue in New York.

The Lewisohn Story,
1660–1939

Mother always said that my great-grandfather Adolph Lewisohn was the most interesting relative in our family. He didn't exactly tap dance his way through life, though he did tap dance, a rather quirky hobby he took up in his eighties. "Good exercise," he said. This charming idiosyncrasy was only one of the internationally famous American copper magnate's eclectic pursuits.[13]

At one time, Adolph was thought to be like royalty, as he was among America's wealthiest men. His early investments in copper, his canny eye for New York City real estate and his business relationships with such financial notables as the Rothschilds—all provided a fountain of funds for his lavish spending. He lived life to the hilt and could well afford whatever he fancied—and he fancied life on a grand scale. He also built up an enormous amount of influence over his lifetime, building relationships with fourteen U.S. presidents.[14]

Adolph was almost mythical in my mind when I was a child. He was of enormous importance, not just to my world, but to the *whole* world. I judged him so because of the respect and awe he was accorded by my parents, my parents' parents and my parents' friends.

There was practically nothing in the world that did not at some time engage Adolph Lewisohn's fervent attention, from raising prize-winning chrysanthemums to collecting fine art and rare editions of great books (including four Shakespeare folios). He spoke out passionately on behalf of prison reform, New York City's workhouses and women's suffrage. His lighter side bore an unbridled enthusiasm for chess, German *lieder* (art songs) and race cars—all well documented by wall-to-wall press coverage and his relentless avalanche of letters to *The New York Times*.

Adolph Lewisohn (1849–1938)

He pelted editors with letters endlessly on topics that ranged from scolding the owners of the *Titanic* for not having enough lifeboats aboard to pleading for more humane conditions in America's prisons—perhaps his most controversial stand. On the matter of America's penal system, he was more than ahead of his time. He devoted one full chapter in his unpublished autobiography to this subject, which had captured his attention as a child reading German translations of Charles Dickens's books and Victor Hugo's *Les Misérables*. Adolph's philosophy might be summed up by the 1968 book by Karl Menninger, *The Crime of Punishment*, which argues that our current penal system is based on vengeance, not rehabilitation.

To the dismay of family and friends, Adolph frequently visited prisons. They preferred his hosting President and Mrs. Calvin Coolidge at Prospect Point (which he did) to his dining with Sing Sing prisoners (which he also did). A compassionate and visionary man, he memorably observed that "too few jailers realize that they are physicians of broken men and damaged souls."

Adolph Lewisohn was born in 1849 into a financially comfortable Orthodox Jewish family of Hamburg, Germany. His father was known as "der Reiche [rich] Lewisohn," a man who contributed generously both to Jewish and non-Jewish causes.[15] Originally, the family surname was "Levy," segueing to Levysohn (Levy's son), until finally becoming Lewisohn.

As an avid genealogist, I was intrigued by the history of how Levy became Lewisohn. Adolph's great-great-grandparents Nacham Joachim Levy and Hanna Jacob Levy came from Rendsborg in the former duchies of Schleswig and Holstein, which were once part of Denmark but are now the single state of Schleswig-Holstein in northern Germany. In the 1700s, German authorities encouraged Jews to change their names from Jewish ones like Levy to secular ones. One of Nacham and Hanna's five sons, Calmer (originally spelled "Kalmer"), changed his last name to Hamburg. Upon his engagement to a Danish woman, he crossed the border into Denmark. After his marriage, the Danish authorities misspelled his name and changed it from Hamburg to Hambro. Thus, the famous Hambro banking family is descended from Calmer Joachim Levy and his wife, Toba Levi. Calmer's brother, Philip Joachim Levy, and his wife, Fanny Brie Levy, had a son, Lyon. Lyon Levy and his wife, Fanny Haarbleicher, Adolph's grandparents, were the couple who changed their name to Lewisohn.

Adolph was the youngest son of Samuel Lewisohn and his first wife, Julie Nathan Lewisohn. They produced four boys and three girls before Julie died at the age of forty-five. My great-grandfather first attended a private school, learning French and English there, and later noting that, by six, he was asked to "explain things" to his slower classmates. His later education was at the Hamburg Gymnasium, a German secondary school where classics, history, mathematics and modern languages were taught. The school was, in Adolph's words, "the nearest Hamburg came to having a university."* The gymnasium provided a liberal education that served him well for the rest of his long and intellectually curious life.

Adolph described his early life in Germany as happy, even though his mother died when he was six, and his father's fierce religious observance brought the boy back-handed slaps and boxed ears for even slight omissions and misdemeanors. From early on, he was an independent thinker, but he wisely kept his religious skepticism to himself—to keep the slaps to a minimum.

Partly to escape his domineering father, Adolph came to the United States in 1867 at the age of eighteen. He wrote that his education had made him "well-equipped for the future that lay before me in a new land."[16] Upon arriving in New York, he joined two of his three brothers in a branch of the family's international business, trading in ostrich feathers, horsehair, wool and pig bristles (considered kosher for Orthodox Jews because they are not edible). Healthy profits from these soft products eventually enabled the brothers to enter the more profitable field of metals. By 1879, when the Lewisohn brothers were trading lead, zinc and copper, they bought some copper mines in Montana. These were the genesis of the huge fortune Adolph would amass.

He and his even more financially savvy brother, Leonard, organized the United Metals Selling Company, which at one time sold 55 percent of all the copper produced in the United States. Adolph was president and a principal stockholder in the Tennessee Copper and Chemical Corporation, the Miami Copper Company and the South Amer-

---

* Adolph Lewisohn became one of forty-six founders of the Hamburgische Wissenschaftliche Stiftung (Hamburg University), which was finally completed after World War I.

ican Gold & Platinum Company, which owned mines in Colombia. He was the senior member of Adolph Lewisohn & Sons, a brokerage and investment house, and a prescient investor in Manhattan real estate during the booming 1900s. In short, he became extremely wealthy.

A tiny, roly-poly man, all of five feet three but taller in his silk top hat, he was once described as "short and animated, with a shrewd, philosophical air, a humanitarian outlook and an equable temper."[17] In a 1960 novel, *Portrait of a Father*, written by one of his granddaughters, Joan Lewisohn Simon (now Crowell), the main characters are thought to be based on the aging Adolph and his son Sam. The elderly man in the novel is described as looking like a "turtle walking," an unflattering but quite accurate description of Adolph Lewisohn as I remember him.

Adolph would never become religiously observant, but he would become a great humanitarian. He was perfectly at ease with being Jewish, but he was "not in sympathy with Jewish people (or with any others) who think themselves better than other people," he wrote. "The idea of 'the chosen people' does not appeal to me."[18]

Adolph Lewisohn's wife, Emma Cahn, looked regal as she posed for this portrait.

Although Adolph was a lifelong religious skeptic, he had a healthy respect for the Jewish traditions so rigorously instilled in him in his early life, especially his father's emphasis on philanthropy and *mitzvahs* (good deeds). He knew Hebrew well and ultimately joined Temple Emanu-El, the preeminent Reform congregation in New York, where he was a generous, if skeptical, member.

In June 1878, at the age of thirty, Adolph married Emma Cahn. Emma came from a prestigious Philadelphia Jewish family, and the marriage brought Adolph comfortably into the social arena of "Our Crowd."[19] Their wedding was held at her mother's home at 226 E. 48th Street in New York City. "Although I was not a believer in religious forces," he wrote, "we were

RESIDENCE AND ROSE GARDEN
ADOLPH LEWISOHN, ARDSLEY, N. Y.
C. 1920

This 40-room mansion of stone was built by my great-grandfather Adolph Lewisohn on his almost 400-acre estate, "Heatherdell Farm," in Ardsley, New York. It was ready for occupancy in about 1908. President Taft was a luncheon guest of Adolph Lewisohn's at the elegant home in 1912. It was ultimately torn down, and today the Ardsley High School sits on the mansion site. I am indebted to Westchester County historian and Ardsley village justice Walter M. Schwartz for this postcard from his personal scrapbook of Adolph Lewisohn memorabilia. (Archives of Judge Walter Schwartz)

married under the traditional Orthodox canopy." Adolph describes their European honeymoon trip as "one of the happiest chapters of my life," but strangely, as an article in *The Westchester Historian* notes, in "over 230 typewritten pages [of his autobiography] he never mentions his wife again."[20]

I never met my Great-Grandma Emma, who died in 1916, but I do know that she had been active in the women's groups of Temple Emanu-El.[21] Whenever a benefit was being held, especially if it supported women, Mrs. Adolph Lewisohn was sure to be one of the patronesses. Although she suffered a heart problem, she went on frequent walks, and my mother spoke of being fascinated by the little pedometer Emma wore on a chain at her waist so she could measure her distance.[22]

One of Adolph's homes was a nearly four hundred-acre estate in Westchester County called "Heatherdell Farm," which was a working farm located just outside the village

ADOLPH LEWISOHN'S MANHATTAN HOME

Adolph's Manhattan home on Fifth Avenue.

This is my great-grandfather's art gallery at his Fifth Avenue house in 1910, three years before the New York Armory show, which put Impressionist art in America on the map. On the right side of the mantel is van Gogh's *L'Arlésienne*, and to its left, Cézanne's *Portrait of Madame Cézanne*, which my parents bought in 1956.

of Ardsley.[23] My mother remembered that as a child she thought his Tudor-style manor, where she learned to milk cows, was like Mr. Rochester's house in *Jane Eyre*. Adolph named his huge home in Elberon, New Jersey, "Adelawn" for his daughter Adele. Adolph bought his Manhattan home at 881 Fifth Avenue from E.H. Harriman, a well-known railroad tycoon of the period. That famous mansion just north of 69th Street cost Adolph $800,000 in 1909, which would be around $30 million today. The house on Fifth Avenue has since been torn down and, together with the house next door, has been replaced by a large apartment building.

According to Adolph and Emma's granddaughter Joan Lewisohn Crowell, Adolph was absolutely devastated when Emma died in 1916.[24] Grieving and not wanting to live alone in his cavernous Fifth Avenue house without Emma, Adolph somehow persuaded his son Sam and his new young wife, Margaret Seligman Lewisohn, to live with him in his museum-like home. He only asked for a year, but that one year turned into twenty. Only when Adolph died would Sam and Margaret and their four daughters—Marjorie, Joan, Elizabeth and Virginia—have their own home. All of them except baby Virginia were born in Adolph's palatial mansion.

My only clear memories of Adolph Lewisohn center on his Christmas parties in the Manhattan mansion and at Prospect Point, the enormous camp that the renowned designer William L. Coulter built on four thousand acres on New York State's Upper Saranac Lake. It took all of 1903 and 1904 to complete the camp, and, when finished, it was so impressive it warranted eight pages in Harvey Kaiser's 1982 classic book *Great Camps of the Adirondacks*.[25]

In all, there were twenty-eight buildings, including a main lodge and three slightly more modest lodges, each named for, and used by, the families of his three daughters. Grandma Adele Lehman's cabin housed my family until 1937, when my parents bought "Gull Bay" across the lake. Adele's sisters, Florence Reckford and Clara Rossin, also had cottages designated for them and their families.*

The buildings at Prospect Point included the dining lodge, the boathouse and numerous smaller service and guest cottages. All were connected by paths of crushed stone, rustic bridges and covered walkways. The walkways were so long that guests were grateful for the wooden benches along the paths where they could stop for rest or conversation. Stuffed bears and multi-antlered deer heads were the decorative focal points in the main

---

* Adolph's son Sam, his wife, Margaret Seligman Lewisohn, and their four girls always stayed at an equally enormous camp belonging to Margaret's family, Fish Rock. It, too, was located on Upper Saranac Lake and was designed by William Coulter.

Adolph Lewisohn's Prospect Point house on Upper Saranac Lake.

A large boathouse stood below the main house, a welcoming sight when returning from a day's fishing or a cruise around the lake.

The Adirondack Mountains are faintly visible behind the pine-structured boathouse at Prospect Point. Barely visible, my Great-Grandfather Adolph stands on the deck, admiring the view.

Visitors docking at Prospect Point had this view of the main "cottage," sitting high above the pier.

lodge, and calculated rusticity was the design scheme throughout the camp—except for the grand pianos. The camp could accommodate eighty to ninety guests and about the same number of servants. At the height of the "season," there were often as many as 150 people on the premises at any one time.

Hardly a week passed in the early part of the 1900s in which Adolph and Emma were not mentioned in the New York City papers, especially when they set out for the Adirondacks on their private train. This was their annual summer migration from one of three grandiose homes. The retinue accompanying the Lewisohns to Prospect Point usually numbered at least forty, including Adolph's omniscient and omnipresent major domo, Mr. Meyer; his barber (who also played pinochle and golf with him); his chess teacher; two chauffeurs and his famous singing coach, J. Bertram Fox, a well-known lyricist and composer, known as a specialist in *lieder*. Adolph broke into these German art songs whenever he could round up a captive audience—though he also sang French, Italian and Hebrew songs with equal gusto. There were also the chef, the cooks, the guides, the house cleaners, the groundskeepers and the boat personnel likely awaiting Adolph and Emma's arrival. Soon to join them would be a raft of relatives, friends and hangers-on.[*]

Adolph slowed down in his late years, but only slightly. A "Talk of the Town" columnist noted the following in the June 23, 1934, *The New Yorker*:

> *Last year he sent out only three hundred invitations for New Year's. He has, however, entertained as many as five hundred on these occasions, and an estimated two hundred crashers. (The last couple of years, admission has been by card only.) About once a month he gives a formal dinner in his home for twenty-four or more, with a red carpet across the sidewalk.*

Adolph did not begin to sing publicly until he was sixty-nine, but thereafter he began a tradition of singing to his guests, especially at his well-publicized birthday parties "in a thin and quavery voice" and "looking like an elderly choir boy," according to Stephen Birmingham,[26] but in "a rich baritone," according to *The New York Times*.[27] For his eighty-ninth birthday he chose operatic arias, and "reporters seeking interviews had to wait while he finished an aria from *La Traviata*."[28]

---

[*] Prospect Point was sold for $38,000 to a Swedish restaurateur after Adolph's death in 1938. It has been sold several times since then and turned into such operations as a honeymoon lodge and a Jewish girls' camp, attended by two of my nieces. Since 1969, it has been owned and operated as a popular camp by a born-again Christian national organization called "Young Life."

MEMORIES OF LEWISOHN STADIUM The Doric columns of the Lewisohn Stadium pictured here were long remembered by anyone who ever visited the amphitheater in its glory days. At a ceremony held in May 1985, Adolph Lewisohn's descendants and other grateful New Yorkers recalled its affordable summer concerts and beautiful architecture. In 1972 the New York City Council had named the site of the stadium Adolph Lewisohn Plaza in honor of my great-grandfather. Thirteen years later, a bust of him and a memorial plaque were unveiled at Lewisohn Plaza. Those who attended the ceremony reminisced both about Adolph Lewisohn's gift of the stadium to City College, and about Minnie Guggenheimer, the stadium's beloved program emcee and tireless fundraiser for the public concerts and star-studded performances enjoyed there.

respectable living. The story in his autobiography of his forty-year involvement with this particular philanthropy is especially moving. He writes that, even as a boy, he ached for children in institutions:

> *In Hamburg as a little boy, I stood with my playmates and our nurses and watched the procession of orphaned children pass by. They seemed to be kindly treated but, as I remember, they wore a sort of uniform and each child carried a collection box at the end of a stick so that the children looking on could drop in small coins. As soon as I was able to comprehend such matters at all, I felt that this was not the right way to treat such children.*[37]

His passion for music found a philanthropic outlet when he funded the Lewisohn Stadium for the City College of New York. According to his granddaughter Dr. Marjorie

AN ARCHITECTURAL GEM A Greek tragedy, *The Trojan Women*, produced by British impresario Granville Barker, marked the opening of City College of New York's classically designed Lewisohn Stadium in May 1915. Located on the CCNY campus on Manhattan's Upper West Side, the concrete amphitheater and athletic facility had a seating capacity of 8,000. The arena was filled in the summertime by enthusiastic New Yorkers, drawn by a wide range of both popular entertainers and classical concerts, starring such varied performers as Leopold Stokowski, Jascha Heifetz, Louis Armstrong, Ella Fitzgerald, Frank Sinatra, Jack Benny and George Gershwin. Tickets were subsidized, with prices as low as 25 cents apiece. The stadium stood for fifty-eight years until it was razed in 1973.

Lewisohn, when asked why he made this huge gift, he was brief: "They asked me."* An outdoor facility for sports and entertainment, the stadium was an ideal summer home for America's oldest symphony orchestra, the New York Philharmonic. Perfect for outdoor music and theater presentations, the Lewisohn Stadium was designed along the lines of the ancient Roman and Greek amphitheaters.

He called it "a favorite child" of his and was thrilled when the prestigious British impresario Granville Barker presented *The Trojan Women* at the opening of the stadium on May 30, 1915. Droves attended the summer outdoor concerts that followed for many years. "Subways cost only 5 cents, tickets to the concerts only 25 cents, and even poor people could afford to attend," Marjorie Lewisohn said. "For some, it was the first

---

* "[The stadium] was born over a luncheon in the spring of 1912 attended by Mr. Lewisohn, Joseph L. Buttenwieser and John H. Finley, who was president of City College of New York." (*The New York Times*, May 18, 1965)

A picture of Adolph Lewisohn in a cap is a rarity, because he usually wore hats that made him look taller.

time they had ever heard music performed live in a concert of classical as well as popular music, made affordable by these summer performances."[38]

Thousands were enthralled the night a young, not-quite-famous George Gershwin played for the crowd. Dr. Lewisohn remembered with nostalgia the music of such celebrities as the operetta king Victor Herbert and pianist José Iturbi. In 1925, Marian Anderson, after winning a citywide talent search, made her debut at the stadium. In the 1940s, "bobby-soxers" screamed with youthful hysteria, sometimes fainting at the sight of their idol, Frank Sinatra, as he crooned to a standing-room-only audience.

Adolph's friend, the irrepressible Minnie Guggenheimer, was the stadium's biggest fan, program overseer and heftiest fundraiser. Thanks to Minnie, the subsidized tickets remained extremely affordable throughout their existence. Audiences of up to fifteen thousand adored Minnie Guggenheim in her role as the nightly emcee. "HELLO, EVERYONE," she roared at every performance. "HELLO, MINNIE," the crowd would roar back.

A beloved "Mrs. Malaprop," Minnie once announced that her favorite composer of all time was "that fine boy, Rodgers Hammerstein." Noted one author, "Her flair for showmanship made her the joy of the stadium-goers, the idol of newspapermen and a scandal of grammarians."[39]

Alas, the Lewisohn Stadium met the wrecker's ball in 1973, after fifty-eight years. The headline in *The New York Times* on April 5, 1973, read, "Farewell to Lewisohn: It Gave New Yorkers a Lot of Night Music." All that is left of Lewisohn Stadium is a yellowing page in New York's history. Sadly, with each passing year, fewer people remember it. The stadium's site between 136th and 138th Streets and Amsterdam and Convent Avenues was named the "Adolph Lewisohn Plaza" in 1972 by the New York City Council. There is also a bust of Great-Grandpa Adolph placed there now, and there was a re-dedication of the Lewisohn Plaza in May 1985.

Among the many, many press notices about him when he died, my favorite is a line from *The New York Times* editorial on August 19, 1938:

> *How many men of 89 or any other age have had the equable temper, the animation, the gayety of Adolph Lewisohn? He diffused sunshine. It was the radiation of the kindness that ruled his life.*[40]

My rich legacy from my great-grandfather Lewisohn was not money, but his philosophy: Give generously to those in need, support good and righteous causes (even if unpopular) and throw lavish parties—especially on your birthday.

Isaiah Moses
(1772–1857)

Always religious, Isaiah was a staunch traditionalist, known as a leader in the fight against reforms to the service of the Sephardic Beth Elohim.

Portrait by Theodore Sidney Moïse, born 1808; oil on canvas, undated but thought to be c. 1830–1835. (Cecil A. Alexander Jr. Collection)

The Moses-Loeb Story, 1697–1955

Like the one from my Lehman side, my second silver spoon came from the financial acumen of German immigrants attracted to America by the promise of a better life. Some of my father's Moses-Loeb ancestors were Sephardic Jews; most were Ashkenazi, like the Lehmans. All of them settled first in the pre-Civil War southern United States, later moving north in incremental stages, before finally settling permanently in New York.

The Moses-Loebs were a little behind the Lehmans in accumulating significant wealth, and, alas, my entrepreneurial grandfather Alfred Huger Moses was not successful in hanging on to it. But by the time my father died in 1996, the Loebs were financially equal to the Lehmans.

In the 1790s, my father's great-great-grandfather Isaiah Moses emigrated from his hometown of Bederkese, near Hanover, Germany, to England, where he married and sired four sons. When his wife died, he crossed the ocean to make his home in Charleston, South Carolina, a city known to have a thriving Jewish community. It was there that he became financially successful as a dry goods merchant.

In 1807, Isaiah remarried a fifth-generation American, Rebecca Phillips, who was almost sixteen. With Rebecca, Isaiah had eight more children.[*] By 1813, Isaiah was able to purchase a 794-acre plantation in Goose Creek called "The Oaks," seventeen miles from Charleston. With the help of his thirty-five slaves, Isaiah vainly tried to wrest profitable crops from the overworked land, depleted by former owners—among them a socially

---

[*] Rebecca's father and mother, Hannah Isaacks and Jacob Phillips, had been married in Newport, Rhode Island, the home of Touro Synagogue. It seems that having built the Loeb Visitors Center at Touro Synagogue was almost preordained in my genes.

Rebecca Phillips Moses (1792–1872)

Rebecca was born on a brigantine, a sailing ship captained by her father, Jacob Phillips, while her parents were en route from Columbia, South Carolina, to St. Eustatius, a Dutch West Indies island. It was a trip they made frequently. Married at the age of fifteen (almost sixteen), Rebecca was the mother of eight children and four stepchildren. Her oldest daughter, Hannah, commissioned this portrait of her mother when Rebecca was fifty-one. This second wife of Isaiah Moses was a passionate supporter of the Confederacy, and according to family legend, she suffered a stroke when she heard of General Robert E. Lee's surrender to the Union in April 1865. Her grandfather, Jacob Isaacks, was one of the founders of the Touro Synagogue in Newport, Rhode Island. C.W. Uhl, oil on canvas, 1843. (Cecil A. Alexander Jr. Collection) prominent family named Middleton who had owned it from 1678 until 1794 and still reside in Charleston.[41] In 1840, the plantation house burned to the ground, and Isaiah sold the property at a loss the next year.[42] All that was left of that page in family history was a wide pair of gates, a long avenue of oak trees and the slave quarters.

Because Rebecca Phillips's father, Jacob Phillips, had served in the South Carolina militia in the Revolutionary War, his male descendants, including me, were granted membership in the Sons of the American Revolution and the Sons of the Revolution in the State of New York. (It also means that those in his female line, including my daughter, Alexandra Loeb Driscoll, could become members of the Daughters of the American Revolution.)

It is also through Rebecca Phillips that I can claim a Sephardic ancestry. A few of Rebecca's ancestors were among the very earliest Jews to arrive in America, some coming from Emden, Germany, in 1697 and 1698. While they didn't arrive in 1654 on the *Sint Katrina*,* known as the "Jewish *Mayflower*," their early citizenship provided fuel for the tales of family legacies regaled to her grandchildren by our southern grandmother, Adeline Moses Loeb. Grandma Adeline's artistry is captured in colorful stories. In a musical southern cadence, she enthusiastically embellished her stories for her young audience, telling us about our important ancestry and her privileged early life in Montgomery, Alabama.

Adeline's grandfather Levi Moses (who was one of Rebecca and Isaiah's eight children) served the Hebrew Orphan Society in Charleston, South Carolina, as secretary-treasurer for eighteen years. During the Civil War, Jewish circles were grateful for how he miraculously saved the society's assets from the devastating onslaught of General Sherman's troops. They sent him a handsome silver goblet as a token of their gratitude, along with "a very flattering letter written upon parchment bound with ribbon and which I shall have framed."[43]

Adeline's father, Alfred Huger Moses, was more ambitious than his father and became an entrepreneur. A graduate of the College of Charleston, he left the city to study law in Montgomery, Alabama. During the Civil War he served in the Confederacy, reaching the rank of captain. He was almost hanged (or shot) when Union officials caught him destroying Confederacy papers in the Atlanta statehouse at the end of the war.[44] Captain Moses was among the many Confederate officials who would receive pardons from President

---

* The name of this ship has been long debated. It is also referred to in various sources as the *St. Charles* or the *St. Cathrien* (or *Sainte Catherine*).

Until 1841, the Oaks Plantation of Goose Creek, South Carolina, was owned by Isaiah and Rebecca Phillips Moses. Destroyed by fire in 1840, it was rebuilt into something very much like its original form and for many years served as the Oaks Golf & Country Club. (John L. Loeb Jr.)

In 1992, the annual meeting of the Southern Jewish Historical Society was held in Montgomery, Alabama, and was highlighted by the dedication of the Alfred Huger Moses room at the House of the Mayors. Pictured here are the attendees Rabbi Malcom Stern (author of the genealogical breakthrough book *Americans of Jewish Descent, 1654–1988*), his wife, Louise, and Ambassador John L. Loeb Jr. A portrait of Captain Moses is in the background. (John L. Loeb Jr. Collection)

Andrew Johnson and be reinstated as U.S. citizens. His official document of pardon now hangs in the office of my cousin Tom Kempner, Aunt Margaret's youngest son.

After the Civil War, Alfred returned to Montgomery and started Moses Brothers with his younger brother Mordecai. It would become the largest real estate, banking and brokerage business in Alabama. In 1871, Alfred married Jeanette Nathan, a nice Jewish girl from Louisville, Kentucky, with German ancestry.

The Alfred Moses family lived appropriately for their station in a huge federal style mansion on Perry Street—what might then have been considered the Fifth Avenue of the South. Infected with the boomtown fever of the early 1880s, Alfred Moses and Col. Walter S. Gordon bought three thousand acres of land across from the Tennessee River near Florence, Alabama, in 1883. They intended to found a town they would name Sheffield, after the great industrial city of northern England, and they bought another thirty thousand acres in counties immediately to the south. The area was known to have large deposits of iron and coal, and they planned to make Sheffield the iron manufacturing center of the South. Streets were graded, lots laid out and an iron furnace planned for the Sheffield Land, Iron and Coal Company. Railroad officials promised to lay tracks for trains to connect the fledgling town with big cities like Birmingham, Mobile and Chicago.[45]

A year later, with the panic of 1884, banks in New York began to fail, including those that would have funded trains to Sheffield. Fortunately, the young company had enough assets to rally, and Alfred Moses pushed ahead. By 1886, the "Iron City" was well on its way to becoming a reality, with real estate speculators making money and two banks established. By 1888, the company was a resounding success, and Alfred turned the reins over to others.

To make a long and sad story short, the subsequent management became too ambitious, its investors were overextended, and pig iron prices declined. The wonderful dreams of my great-grandfather also collapsed with the death of the Moses Brothers banking firm. The convergence of a banking crisis in England and a New York stock market panic in 1891 caused the Moses Brothers' banks in both Montgomery and Sheffield to fail. Being honorable men, the brothers allowed a run instead of closing the banks: clients withdrew most of their money, effectively causing the Moses family to lose everything. The brothers refused to declare bankruptcy, and eventually all the depositors were paid back and all debts settled. Sheffield still exists, but it never became the city of Alfred Huger Moses's dreams.

My Lehman great-grandfather, Mayer Lehman, and my Loeb great-grandfather, Alfred

Alfred Moses
(1840–1918)

Adeline's adored father is shown here in an 1886 or 1887 photograph. The photograph was taken around the peak of his success, shortly after he founded the city of Sheffield, Alabama, and became its first mayor. His brother-in-law Judge Nathan's family still lives in Sheffield. (John L. Loeb Jr.)

Jeanette Nathan Moses
(1849–1919)

Adeline's mother, Mrs. Alfred Huger Moses, was thirty years old in 1879, when this photo is thought to have been taken. She was a "great belle, slim, nice-looking rather than beautiful," according to her granddaughter Margaret Loeb Kempner. "She was very musical, played the piano beautifully, loved to sing and act in amateur theatricals, and generally played the female lead." Without doubt, the musically talented Adeline was given her first piano lessons by her mother. (Thomas L. Kempner Collection)

"This home—once a residence of the Alfred Moses family—is located on South Perry Street in Montgomery, Alabama. Now part of a historic district and one of seven homes included in Montgomery's Old House Revived Tour, it was restored in 2005 and is known as the Moses-Haardt house. Dating from the nineteenth century, it now houses local businesses." (*Montgomery Advertiser*, April 23, 2005)

In 1886, Alfred Moses built an imposing home on Montgomery Avenue overlooking the Tennessee River in the boomtown of Sheffield. But the family had only a short time to enjoy the home before investment failures forced them to move to St. Louis, Missouri. The house was ultimately destroyed by fire. (Sketch restored by Ardeth Abrams; from *Sheffield, City on the Bluff, 1885–1985*, published by Friends of the Sheffield Library)

The House of Mayors on South Perry Street in Montgomery, Alabama, was home to Mordecai Moses (Alfred's younger brother) from 1885 to 1893. The first Democrat to be elected after Reconstruction, Mordecai served that city as mayor for three terms. (Ambassador John L. Loeb Jr. Collection)

Huger Moses, were fellow Montgomery residents and friends. A family relative, Adeline Moses Wolff, once wrote my Aunt Margaret Loeb Kempner that the Lehman brothers "always regretted not having saved the Moses brothers."[46] The Lehman/Moses-Loeb families would one day merge through the 1926 marriage of my parents in New York City, a marriage that would never have come about if the Moses brothers' enterprises hadn't imploded in Alabama thirty-five years earlier.

After the firm's collapse and nearly broke, Alfred and Jeanette moved with their five children north to St. Louis, as did most of Alfred's brothers and sisters. Alfred Moses's favorite was his youngest child, my grandmother Adeline, who was fifteen at the time of his devastating losses. Alfred began a long, hard climb back to solvency in the insurance business, but he never again achieved the

Always proud of sewing her own clothes, a financial necessity in her teenage years, Adeline Moses Loeb no doubt designed and made the balloon-sleeved gown in which she posed for a picture in 1894. This was shortly before she met Carl Loeb at the boarding house of her aunts, Rose and Grace. Adeline and Carl married in 1896, when she was nineteen and he was twenty-one. (Thomas L. Kempner)

success of earlier days. Adeline took the change in fortune and lifestyle in stride, pitching in where she could. She learned how to sew her own dresses, how to type and gave piano lessons as well, walking to and from her students' homes because she had no money for the trolley. She is remembered as having enormous brown eyes, a proud bosom, a lovely singing voice and a lot of charm—which in the South has always gone a long way.[47]

My grandfather Carl M. Loeb was the son of Minna and Adolph Loeb, a successful German dry goods merchant. Carl arrived in New York City from Frankfurt in 1893, newly graduated from a gymnasium, where he'd learned English as a second language. He had followed his brilliant older brother, Julius, who had won a prestigious prize at Metallgesellschaft AG, the largest metal company in Europe, controlled by a Jewish family named Merton. The Merton family held a contest each year for Jewish boys in Frankfurt, with the winner of the prize receiving a job at Metallgesellschaft. Julius won the prize and was sent to New York City, where the American Metal Company, a subsidiary of Metallgesellschaft, was being formed.

Julius's younger brother, eighteen-year-old Carl, then talked his way into his own job at Metallgesellschaft. Carl was soon sent off to be an assistant to the manager of the recently opened St. Louis office. Once there, he found a genteel boarding house operated by none other than the sisters of Alfred Moses. Grace and Rose Moses, my Grandmother Adeline's maiden aunts, had become as impecunious as the rest of the family.

The dashing and ambitious Carl Loeb and the charming Adeline Moses soon met at her aunts' boarding house. They fell in love and were married in 1896, when Carl was twenty-one and Adeline was nineteen. A little over a year later another piece of good fortune came my grandfather's way: Jacob Langeloth, the president of the company, based in New York, fired the head of the St. Louis branch. The venerable Jacob sent word to Carl to "hold the fort" until a replacement could be found, since he was much too young to become the permanent manager and had not acquired "the necessary experience which we must expect from the man to whom we entrust our agency."[48]

Carl Loeb and Adeline Moses posed in a St. Louis, Missouri, studio on April 21, 1896, for what was probably the couple's engagement photograph. They would be married on November 12 of that year. The photo is a forecast of Carl Loeb's lifelong taste for sartorial elegance and Adeline's taste for large and commanding hats. (Thomas L. Kempner)

Never one to hide his shining light, Grandfather wrote back brashly. He admitted his youth but added that he had already been running the branch office for quite some time, and that if Mr. Langeloth planned to "depose" him, he would like to be transferred to "some other field quickly." He did not want to be "mortified" by having the managerial post yanked away from him without being given a fair trial.[49] Amazed by young Carl's audacity, the nettled Jacob Langeloth traveled to St. Louis, found the company running smoothly, was charmed by Adeline—and Carl kept the job. Under the hand of "C.M.," as he became known, the subsidiary turned into a major operation, and Loeb's young family thrived as well.

The Loebs' first baby, Margaret, was born in 1899; my father, John Langeloth, followed in 1902; Carl M. Jr. was born in 1904; and Henry arrived in 1907. In 1905, C.M. was made the vice president of American Metal, and the family moved to New York City. By 1910, Carl had bought a five-story home at 41 West 85th Street between Central Park and Columbus Avenue. In 1914, Jacob Langeloth died unexpectedly, and my grandfather was named president of American Metal. He was not yet forty.*

Granny Adeline Loeb never called her husband anything but "Mr. Loeb"—unless she was angry. Only then did she call him Carl. Southern to her well-corseted bones, she treated her grandchildren, whom she called "beaus and belles," to an annual Saturday matinee on Broadway. This was followed by a memorable trip to the Persian Room at the Plaza Hotel, where, dressed in Bergdorf Goodman elegance, she educated my siblings and me about our family.

Sometime around 1909, Adeline and Carl lined up their offspring for a family photo. In the stair-step order are Margaret (born 1899), John Langeloth (born 1902), Carl M. Jr. (born 1904) and Henry (born 1907). (John L. Loeb Jr. Collection)

As we entered the Plaza, she always bristled at the commanding gold statue of William Tecumseh Sherman on horseback. The statue never failed to enrage her. Granny Loeb was a passionate daughter of the Confederacy, and with good reason. Hadn't her daddy—Alfred Moses—served in the Confederate army? Hadn't her grandmother Rebecca Phillips suffered a stroke when a newsboy shouted that General Lee had surrendered? I learned this fascinating history while downing succulent petits fours at the Plaza, acquiring an early taste for both family genealogy and grand hotels.

According to my aunt Margaret Loeb Kempner, the only daughter of C.M. and Adeline, the Loebs lived quite formally, with an enviably pampered lifestyle. They rode in a Pierce Arrow driven by a liveried chauffeur, their house was filled with a staff out of *Downton Abbey*, and there were formal five-course gourmet dinners every night. C.M. loved really good food; in fact, he insisted on it. He always led the family dinner conversation, usually a discussion of a topic he'd chosen at random from the encyclopedia just before the family sat down to eat.

C.M. and Adeline had separate bedrooms, and Aunt Margaret, who could have been a professional writer, tells the best story of all:

---

* When C.M. first came to New York, Adolph Lewisohn invited him to lunch, but he refused because he knew he wouldn't be able to reciprocate.

Mother had the habit of putting on her prettiest nightgown, fixing herself up and putting on perfume when Father planned to visit her. . . . Father would push a note under her door. After one of their dinner parties, Mother saw the note, got herself all fixed up, and then read the note. It said, "Fire the cook."[50]

I have my own memories of Adeline's spirited arguments with my grandfather. "Family is more important than money," she insisted. "Not so," he said loudly, perhaps reminding her of the Moses family's lean days in St. Louis. He was fond of saying, "Happiness can't buy money." In my youth, I tended to side with my grandfather; today, with my intense interest in family and genealogy, I believe my grandmother was right.

The irony is that my mother's Lehman family felt Frances was marrying "down" when

Carl M. Loeb
(1875–1955)

Adeline Moses Loeb
(1876–1953)

By the early 1920s, when these two complementary portraits are thought to have been painted, Carl was well along in his career, though by no means as financially successful as he would eventually become. In the tradition of Adeline's forebears, sitting for a prominent artist denoted having "arrived." Given Carl's taste for elegance, it is not too surprising that the British painter Gerald Brockhurst (regarded as a young Botticelli by the age of twelve and profoundly influenced by da Vinci as well) was chosen to memorialize the couple. Portraying them in a painterly style evocative of earlier eras, Brockhurst clearly saw both Loebs as handsome, strong-willed and important, with Adeline the more approachable. Both portraits by Gerald L. Brockhurst, 1890–1978. (John L. Loeb Jr. Collection) she became engaged to my father, John Loeb, in 1926. If money was the only yardstick, perhaps she was. Carl M. Loeb's financial success at American Metal did not yet hold a candle to the Lehman wealth. He had started humbly in St. Louis, squirreling away his first earned money—a hundred dollars in gold pieces—in an old cigar box. The Lehmans were not terribly interested in genealogy, so the southern heritage of my father's father meant little to them. They also could not predict that C.M. and my father would prove to be incredibly successful on Wall Street. Although they had no money to leave, the Moses family gave me a legacy of a wonderful southern gentility and a sense of tradition that I treasure.

With the onset of World War I, the German-based company Metallgesellschaft transferred an owner's proxy to their American subsidiary, American Metal, and their new president, C.M. Loeb. When America entered the war, the U.S. government took control of the Metallgesellschaft shares, but the Alien Property Custodian (APC) agents did not interfere with Carl's running the business. After winning the war, U.S. officials sold off the confiscated shares, and C.M. bought a large amount. At the same time, he expanded the company's ownership of mining, smelting and refining facilities all over the world. Eventually, American Metal became a public company, and my grandfather built it into the largest nonferrous metals company in America.*

Carl would go on from success to success at American Metal until 1929, when, after too many clashes over his prickly and autocratic management style, it became almost impossible for him. The board's meddling became disruptive, despite C.M.'s successes. He offered his resignation to a fractious board of directors, which had become increasingly unhappy with him. His resignation ("in the interest of harmony") was accepted with unflattering alacrity. He "retired" in 1929, at the age of fifty-four, already a very wealthy man.

Thanks to one of the smartest moves he ever made, C.M. would become even wealthier in 1931, just when the effects of the Depression were being deeply felt. As part of his agreement to leave American Metal, he had negotiated a "put," which meant he had a right, for a stipulated number of years, to sell his shares in American Metal to its board members at the price the shares were at when he left. When C.M. left the company in 1929, his stock in American Metal Company was worth $80 a share. Less than two years later, that same stock would be worth around $1. The money C.M. made from that put would not only set the course for the next chapter of his life, but it would also set up my father's and my own as well.

---

* American Metal was also one of the founders of the Climax Molybdenum Company. In the thirties, Climax Molybdenum became one of the really hot stocks, eventually merging with the American Metal Company to become American Metal Climax.

My grandfather C.M. around the time of the founding of Carl M. Loeb and Company.

That next chapter was the beginning of Loeb, Rhoades & Co. There are two versions of how it all began. There is the version shared by my grandmother and my father. In this version, my grandmother complained to my father that C.M. was too much of a presence at home after his retirement. After a lengthy round-the-world trip with Adeline, the relatively young C.M. had become increasingly restless. My grandmother claimed she was living with a caged lion and implored my father to find something for my grandfather to do.

Father, a Harvard graduate who had majored in English and history, not finance (he received a C in statistics), had nevertheless started a financial career. Since his last name was not Lehman, he wasn't considered eligible to be taken on at Lehman Brothers—even though he was married to a Lehman. Arthur Lehman helped facilitate a position for my father at the up and coming Wertheim & Co.

Having had a taste of the financial world and blessed with an abundance of self-confidence, my father audaciously proposed to C.M. that the two of them found a financial firm, even though the Depression showed no signs of abating. My grandfather agreed, since he thought Wall Street was being run by "idiots," and the two of them could certainly do better. My grandfather's version of Loeb, Rhoades's genesis is simpler: concerned that my father was turning into a playboy, he thought that forming a new company would rescue his son from such a fate. There is probably some truth to both stories.

The fact that my father was not popular at Wertheim may have added to his enthusiasm for escaping to a new, if potentially perilous, venture. Like most tyros in financial firms, my father had started out as a "runner," a type of messenger boy, despite his Harvard degree. There was—and still is—a real caste system on Wall Street, and you were expected to know your place. A runner would arrive in the elevator and immediately be pushed to the rear—if he didn't have the sense to step there himself. One day after Father had just started at Wertheim, a severe rainstorm started unexpectedly. Innocent of the implications, my mother sent the family chauffeur to take my low-ranking father a raincoat and galoshes. That flouting of the caste system was perceived as unacceptable chutzpah by his cohorts. Though he did move up in the hierarchy, my father certainly never won any popularity contests at Wertheim.

Plans for the formation of Carl M. Loeb and Company began to brew sometime in 1930. While still working at Wertheim, Father would meet with his friend Teddy Bernstein, and he soon persuaded him to join him in the new venture. He also invited Teddy's father, Theodore Bernstein Sr. (known as "T.B."), to join the company as a major player and a "rainmaker." Both Theodores left the financial firm of Hirsch Lilienthal and accepted the new offer. Teddy Bernstein was to handle the back office, my father would be the floor broker, and C.M.'s firm hand would be at the helm.

Carl M. Loeb and Company was officially born on January 1, 1931, festively celebrated with champagne. By that time the stock on C.M.'s original "put"—from eighteen months earlier—had dropped from $80 a share to $1. The next question that arose was to what extent C.M. should exercise his put against the individual directors of American Metal. After all, the Depression caused an enormous collapse of the financial world. Over a few years, with some difficulty, C.M. was able to fully exercise that put, which made him a multimillionaire and nearly bankrupted two of American Metal's directors.

Though the new company was well financed by my grandfather, he would not allow a penny to be wasted. They rented offices at 50 Broad Street, and the four new partners would acquire a staff of twelve, but they first shopped for secondhand furniture, bookkeeping machines and carpet from a firm going out of business.

In the early days of Carl M. Loeb and Company, floor brokering was a physically challenging occupation that literally took place on the floor of the Stock Exchange. My father was not well liked and—despite being a football player in his youth—was not equal to the rough treatment he got. He was likely singled out because of his ferocious temper and arrogant reputation. Father aggravated other brokers, who retaliated by obstructing his passage to the specialists who executed the orders. Though today everyone sits in front of their computers, in those days getting your orders placed was a push-and-shove

This portrait of Father was taken by celebrated photographer Yousuf Karsh.

Portraits by Salvador Dali are rare, and I am glad to have inherited this one of Father. Looking almost wistful here, Father must have had something heavy on his mind at the time this was painted, because Dali included dark clouds over his head.

operation. And my father was usually at the receiving end of both.

Father sent an SOS to a friend from Harvard, Steve Koshland, who replaced him on the floor. My father was left to tend other aspects of the fledgling firm—much more successfully. The well-known economist Hans A. Widenmann, a person of considerable insight in the firm's early days, noted in a short history of Loeb, Rhoades in 1945 that there was no guarantee of success at the outset, starting as it did in the depth of the Great Depression.

Rhoades & Co. was a white shoe firm in the old mold of Wall Street. Mr. John Rhoades, an elderly man in his eighties, and his stepson, a visionary named Everett Cady, sensed that Rhoades needed new blood. Rhoades & Co. still had a great deal of business, but it was beginning to lose money. On a Manhattan

Here my usually stern-looking Grandfather Loeb looks relaxed and genial. He is holding the family dachshund—not too surprisingly, a German breed.

street one day, Cady walked up to my father and introduced himself. He then made an offer: "We're an old-line Christian firm with a lot of business losing a lot of money," he said. "You're a highly thought of Jewish firm with a great deal of capital but not a lot of business." Cady proposed a merger; my grandfather and father agreed. Though the names were a merger, Loeb essentially took over Rhoades & Co. Cady's great breakthrough was that he went all over the country and found smaller firms to connect through correspondence. Loeb, Rhoades would share its research department and loan capital to these firms—and take a substantial commission. As the country grew after the war, this arrangement allowed Loeb, Rhoades to grow enormously as the commissions came pouring in. After the war, up to a hundred firms in New York City "cleared" through Loeb, Rhoades, and so our name and our company became known everywhere.*

Widenmann's comment about my self-confident grandfather is quite amusing: "He warned us to be humble when things were going well. . . . [He said] 'The only time you can afford to be cocky is when you're down and out—then you may turn out to be right.'"[51]

---

* At some point, Everett Cady and C.M. had a falling out and my grandfather let Cady go.

On the brisk day of March 12, 1954, the vision and generosity of Adeline and Carl M. Loeb were celebrated at a grand opening of the newly named Loeb Boathouse, attended by city officials and well-wishers. This view shows boats for rent, the new building, and a chilly crowd, looking east. (New York City Department of Parks and Recreation)

Manhattan Borough President Hulan Jack (far left) and Parks Commissioner Robert Moses (far right) seem to be enjoying a boat ride, with Mayor Robert Wagner manning the oars. The two small girls in the center are Nancy Roosevelt (left), six-year-old daughter of Mr. and Mrs. Emlen Roosevelt of Oyster Bay, Long Island, and seven-year-old Nancy Olds, Mayor Wagner's granddaughter. A short while later the mayor picked up another customer, Deborah Loeb, the eight-year-old granddaughter of the Loebs. (New York City Department of Parks and Recreation)

No matter how that turned out, I am forever indebted to the legacies of my influential ancestors, and I could not tell my own story without sharing their stories of determination, grace and generosity.

There are two stories about how the Loeb Boathouse came into being. One is that my grandparents were at a dinner party with the famous Robert Moses of New York, who developed many of the most well-known features of New York City. The subject of the boathouse came up, whereupon my grandfather decided he would make a gift to the city to restore it.

Another adorable story is that it might have been my grandmother who influenced my grandfather to restore the boathouse. It's a story told by James Poll of the famous William Poll Gourmet Foods on Lexington

THE LAKE in Central Park and THE LOEB BOATHOUSE

The Loeb Boathouse quickly became such an essential part of New York City that *The New Yorker* magazine put it on the cover just two years after it opened. This framed copy hangs in my Manhattan townhouse.

Avenue. James is the father of Dean Poll, the current concessionaire of the Loeb Boathouse. The story comes from James's father, William Poll, a friend and colleague of Peter Pappas, who provided rental boats for rowing on the lake, as well as snacks from a little food stand.

According to Peter, "This woman used to come walking by in the snow in the wintertime, early in the morning—an elderly lady. Practically no one else was out that early in the morning. I'd always call out and say, 'Hello, Mama. Come over here. Let me buy you some hot coffee.'" One day she replied, "You know, this boathouse looks terrible. We'll have to do something about it." He didn't give it any thought.

About two weeks later, architects came in and started to take measurements and ask him questions. Peter said, "What are you people doing here? Who are you?" They said, "Well, we're going to build a new boathouse." Peter harrumphed, "That's strange. The parks commissioner didn't tell me about it. I would be the first one to know. I don't believe it." And the men said, "The parks department isn't building it. Mrs. Carl Loeb is building it." That was how he found out who the lady he'd been giving coffee to was.

HARALD SLOTT-MØLLER 1864–1937
Summer Day (1888)
(Ambassador John L. Loeb Jr. Danish Art Collection)

OTTO BACHE 1839–1927

Flag Day in Copenhagen on a Summer Day in Vimmelskaftet (after 1892)
(Ambassador John L. Loeb Jr. Danish Art Collection)

L. A. RING 1854–1933
Harvest (1885)
(Ambassador John L. Loeb Jr. Danish Art Collection)

BERTHA WEGMANN 1847–1926
A Young Woman, Marie Triepcke, Sitting in a Boat
(later Mrs. P. S. Kroyer in Tivoli Garden, Denmark – 1884)
(Ambassador John L. Loeb Jr. Danish Art Collection)

I loved books from very early on.
Mother read to me a lot but taught
me to read early. I could read by
myself long before I started school.

PART TWO

Starting Out

If our family wasn't Jewish, you would think that Arthur, Ann and I were dressed up for Easter. Here we are in spring 1937, ready to go someplace special.

CHAPTER ONE

≡

The Happy Years, 1930–1940

Judging from the romantic letters they exchanged during their engagement, my parents were very much in love when they married on November 18, 1926. The wedding was held in the Fifth Avenue mansion of my great-grandfather Adolph Lewisohn, a giant of mining, real estate and philanthropy. It was a social occasion attended by several hundred guests who enjoyed a lavish reception, which included dancing to lighthearted 1920s tunes provided by a band of twenty musicians. Their wedding was covered by *The New York Times*, and it received first mention in the "Milestones" section of *Time* magazine, outranking even the death of Hollywood legend Rudolph Valentino.

The young couple could look forward to a financially comfortable life. Besides Lehman and Loeb money, a Lewisohn fortune also awaited the newlyweds—or so everyone believed at the time. My mother's father, Arthur Lehman, was one of the two managing partners at Lehman Brothers, one of New York's most successful investment banking firms. Grandpa Lehman was not entirely pleased by the prospect of his new son-in-law, convinced that my father—not yet independently wealthy—was "marrying up." This was somewhat ironic, for twenty-five years earlier Grandpa Lehman's own in-laws, Emma and Adolph Lewisohn, had objected to him as a future son-in-law. Indeed, when Adolph Lewisohn rose to toast the couple, he leaned over to someone at his table to ask the name of the groom. It is unclear whether it was lapse of memory or an indication of disapproval—likely a little bit of both.

Even more than wealth, social standing in America is frequently determined by how far back one can trace one's ancestry in our country. *Mayflower* descendants have traditionally claimed a certain cachet. By that yardstick, it was my mother who was

The November 18, 1926, marriage of John L. Loeb and Frances Lehman merited the notice of both *The New York Times* and *Time* magazine's popular "Milestones" section.

marrying up. The ancestors of my father's mother, Adeline Moses Loeb, arrived on these shores in 1697, only forty-three years after the "Jewish *Mayflower*" arrived in New Amsterdam in 1654.

As for money, the Loebs weren't exactly paupers in 1926, no matter what Grandpa Lehman thought. As noted in the previous chapter, my grandfather C.M. Loeb was CEO of the very profitable American Metal Company, the largest nonferrous metals company in the United States, where my father also worked. Though some could debate who was marrying "up," it's sufficient to say neither newlywed was taking too big a risk.

My mother, Frances Lehman, also known as "Peter," was a brilliant, beautiful girl with aspirations of being a writer. She studied for two years at Vassar College, where she enjoyed both the intellectual challenge and the friendship of her classmates. In her sophomore year, blessed with good looks and a slender form, she was elected by the senior class to the prestigious "Daisy Chain"—the school's prettiest girls as voted by their respective classes. However, by spring of that year, she was more than ready to abandon books and the social scene for my father's arms.

Mother had seen John Loeb at a few college parties, but it was a Christmas party co-hosted by my father and Louis Gimbel (of the department store family) that would change the course of their lives. Mother sat between the two young men, who both eagerly vied for her attention. It was Father who escorted her home. Not much later, her mother and sister Dorothy asked if she was in love with him. Mother said she wasn't the least bit sure what being in love felt like; the only thing she knew for certain was that John Loeb was the man she intended to marry.

My father started his college education at Dartmouth, and anti-Semitism likely contributed to his unhappiness there. My parents write in their memoir, *All in a Lifetime*, that he was invited to join a fraternity, but when told to say he was a Unitarian—or *anything* but Jewish—he refused.[53] He happily finished his last three years at Harvard, majoring in history and English. At the age of twenty-four, sure of himself and gainfully employed at American Metal Company, he felt ready for marriage to Frances—rich and beautiful and quite the prize.

Mother's pre-wedding letters were more romantic and imaginative than Father's more prosaic declarations. Though Mother wrote with more passion, she came to the marriage woefully uninformed about sex. Their wedding night got off to an abysmal start—"a disaster!" she wrote in her memoir.[54]

The day after the wedding, she left my father to visit her parents in Paris. She complained that John Loeb was not at all what she expected. She already wanted a divorce! Her father's response was that she had made her bed, and now she must lie in it. Frances returned to John's arms, and they stayed married for the next seventy years. "John, of course, has been the fulcrum of my life," she wrote, adding that "the years have added to his stature, to his wisdom and to his innate gentleness."[55]

My older sister Judy was born on September 11, 1927. My arrival as their first boy, on May 2, 1930, was especially welcome, as men were traditionally considered to be business-partners-in-waiting in our world.

My mother and father had a very short courtship, but they had time to write wonderful love letters, copies of which I still have. Mother's letters were more romantic; his expressed an eagerness to marry soon.

They named me John Langeloth Loeb *Junior*, not a very Jewish thing to do; traditionally, Ashkenazi Jews do not name their offspring after the living. My naming could have been due to the fact that my parents were not religiously observant, though it's possible that they were more influenced by Grandmother Loeb's Sephardic ancestry in this regard.*

By the theory of prenatal influence, it's possible that my passion for politics began in the womb. While pregnant with me, Mother worked in the 1930 campaign to re-elect Franklin D. Roosevelt as New York governor alongside her uncle, Herbert Lehman, as lieutenant governor. Prenatal influence may have also had a hand in my lifelong anxiety about money, since I was conceived at the brink of the Great Depression. By then, my father had left American Metal to become a novice stockbroker at Wertheim & Co., where he was not having an easy time of it.

Grandfather Loeb's frequently voiced philosophy on the subject of money was direct: "Happiness is fine, but it won't get you any money." Always hovering at the edge of my consciousness has been a concern about preserving the value of "my two silver spoons." We

---

* There were no Ashkenazi synagogues in America until 1825—even German Jews worshipped at Sephardic temples.

Left: On a chilly day in 1932, Judy and I stood still for a picture somewhere on the Ridgeleigh estate. I was about two and she about five.

Below: These early photos of me were retrieved from the complete archives of my parents, which they left entirely to me. I then gave those archives to the American Jewish Historical Society, which has categorized their contents and made them available for viewing.

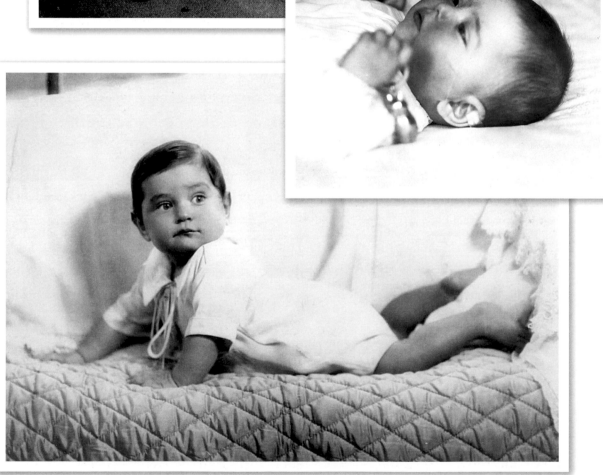

are all products of our anxieties—however unprovoked—and I must admit that I have, at times, been consumed by mine.

My clearest childhood memories are a wonderful mélange of woodsy smells, lush lawns, rock gardens, inquisitive chipmunks, lazy ducks and a series of attentive governesses. This Eden was Ridgeleigh, my Lehman grandparents' Westchester estate in Purchase, New York. In 1928, Arthur and Adele Lehman gave a twelve-acre portion of their estate to my parents, on which my mother and father built a sprawling washed-brick colonial house.

In the days before air-conditioning, Judy and I both slept on the porch as children. I used to tell her stories that I just made up out of whole cloth, though all of those have been lost to age and history. I remember my parents getting enraged once at Judy after a particularly bad injury I suffered under her watch. She was showing me how to jump into the swimming pool backwards, and I stupidly held on to the concrete and put my face forward. I just about knocked out my teeth. My parents were so angry with Judy, and I got all kinds of presents. We bonded a great deal in those early years as the only children. Even when we were both sent off to boarding schools, we stayed particularly close. She would tell me about her boyfriends, like our distant cousin Arthur Ochs "Punch" Sulzberger, whose family ran *The New York Times*. She would show me his humorous letters, about which we would roll on the floor laughing. I also remember a funny story she told me when she was going out for the first time with a very good-looking boy named Jimmy Ludwig—she was so excited that when he kissed her, she threw up.

It was only a two-minute walk across a beautifully landscaped garden to see my Lehman grandparents, so visits were easy and frequent. The Arthur Lehmans had purchased sixty-three acres in 1923 from a previous owner. Before that it was owned by Oliver Harriman Jr., who was part of a prestigious family and a cousin of the future governor and diplomat W. Averell Harriman, whom I would one day get to know well.

I have always loved Ridgeleigh, evidenced by a wistfully nostalgic college essay of mine. "I love it for its peace, so apart from reality," I wrote as a freshman at Harvard. "I love the land, moist in spring, caked hard under a fringe of grass by the first frosts of winter, and I love it best when I am alone."[56] Ridgeleigh has been my home since the day of my birth. Though I'm an avid traveler, a card-carrying Anglophile and the owner of a flat in London and a townhouse in Manhattan, that bucolic home holds so much of my memories and family history. To this day, it remains where I am the happiest.

My grandfather Arthur Lehman bought Ridgeleigh around the same time the Century Country Club moved from the Bronx to its new site right across the road in Purchase.

Whether Grandfather bought it because he wanted to live near the club or it was a happy coincidence, I do not know, but it has been a favorite social arena for both sides of the family ever since I can remember.

The Century is one of the oldest men's country clubs in America and, certainly, the oldest Jewish one. It was founded in May 1898 with 136 members, among them Great-Grandfather Adolph Lewisohn, Grandfather Arthur Lehman, his brothers Irving and Sigmund and his cousin Philip. By the 1930s, women and children were welcome at the club, although not as members. When my grandmother Adele Lehman died in 1965, the flag at the Century was lowered to half-mast. At that time, she was the only female member of the club.

Ours was an athletic family. My uncle Carl's athletic ability was legion: he was captain of the Princeton basketball team and golf champion in Montana, where he worked for American Metal. His athletic success and popularity made him Grandfather Loeb's favorite when we were children.

I wish I had the golf talent of my Grandma Lehman or the riding grace of my father, but I was only modestly athletic. I did some running, but the one thing I truly loved was swimming. I had the fortune of being coached by Steve Forsythe, who taught a couple of Olympic protégés at the Century Club. Since athletics were valued in the family, and I was always looking to please my mother, those two things are intertwined in my memory. Success in one seemed to bring approval from the other.

I distinctly remember a Fourth of July race I competed in at a young age. As I turned my head in the pool, I caught a blurry image of Mother, whom I had never seen so animated. "Keep going, Johnny!" I heard her yell amid the clamor and the splashing. When I emerged victorious out of the pool, she was as excited as I had ever seen her. It was something of a feedback loop: Mother seemed to offer more attention and affection for my athletic successes, so I valued them as a path to her love.

My earliest schooling was at the nearby Rye Country Day School. The most vivid kindergarten memory I have is of losing my heart to a pretty girl, a pattern that would repeat itself over the course of my life. Her name, incredibly, was Jane Eyre. She had long red ringlets and a beatific smile. In an example of how times have changed, there were periods each day when we were told to "just lie down on the floor and be quiet." Perhaps we were allowed to read, but I spent the time gazing at Jane. I don't remember if my adoration was returned, only that I felt enormous waves of affection for this little girl with the adorable curls and Victorian name. At our fiftieth class reunion in 1996, while discussing my sixth birthday party, I asked if anyone remembered her. Perhaps

The original Ridgeleigh estate. This aerial photo shows the house and a portion of the Ridgeleigh estate in Purchase, New York, which my Lehman grandparents bought in 1923. Located at 194 Anderson Hill Road, it is directly across the street from the Century Country Club. After they died, my widowed aunt Dorothy Bernhard had the original house razed and built in its place a lovely ranch-style house, where I now live.

Original view of house on the left and indoor squash court on the right at 194 Anderson Hill Road. When we were growing up, we swam in my grandparents' swimming pool. Father didn't build us a pool until I was seventeen.

My grandparents had generously given my mother and father the acreage needed to build their own home, just a two-minute walk away, at 170 Anderson Hill Road. My parents' home had everything a growing family could possibly want: plenty of bedrooms with some to spare, a cozy den, a large kitchen and a dining room. I have recently named the house "Lions Gate" to keep it distinct from the home in which I now live.

Posing in our cozy den are my beautiful mother, grumpy me, the recently born twins, Ann and Arthur, and Judy—who already knew you should smile for the camera.

Father was a champion polo player, so of course riding classes were on his "must take" list for me. Here I am comfortably and happily astride a horse at the polo club to which he belonged and where I learned to ride—though I never became interested in the sport.

I had invented out of thin air this angelic child. But it turns out she was real. The lady sitting next to me smiled and laughed. "*I* was that little girl with the red hair," she said, introducing herself as Mrs. Jane Repp.

Mother's dedication to public service kept her thoroughly occupied, even through the pregnancy and the birth of my younger twin siblings, Arthur and Ann, on September 19, 1932. My youngest sister, Debby, wasn't born until February 19, 1946; with such a substantial age gap, Debby did most of her growing up after we had all left home. It didn't bother me that my mother was always busy. Nor was I lonely, for I was always surrounded by siblings, cousins, hovering nannies and governesses, tennis pros and swimming teachers. As we grew older, there were instructors for riding, piano and French, none of which really took. It was a tightly structured life, which no doubt contributed to my early sense of security.

However busy she was, Mother still made a point of doing certain tasks herself, such as teaching me to read before I started school. I remember our sitting together to read my favorite book, *Dumbo*, the Disney classic about a strange-looking elephant and its mother's love. Mother also took on the responsibility of teaching me how to ride a bicycle. I can still feel her firm hand on the back of my new two-wheeler, steadying me as I wobbled down an unpaved road on Ridgeleigh's grounds.

Vivacious and ambitious, Mother wanted to be involved in meaningful things outside of her role as wife and mother. When I commented once that she wasn't like the warm Jewish mothers I'd heard about, she tartly replied, "Well, I'm not a *typical* Jewish mother." This was true, though I'm not sure I would've wanted her to be. She may not have cuddled us, but she certainly inspired us to live life to the fullest—a gift that has sustained me all these decades later.

I remember being upset on some evenings when my parents were getting ready to leave for a dinner in Manhattan with other glamorous couples. Usually they went dancing afterward, which was what their set did in those prewar days. They would depart after our nightly hugs, trailing scents of expensive cologne and cigarettes in their wake. The rustle of Mother's taffeta gown, or a swish of silk, was the last thing we heard before they left.

It always seemed perfectly natural to me that my parents led separate lives from us. We never ate with them, our bedrooms were a comfortable distance from theirs and our daily discipline came from the staff. Most of our time was spent with each other and with governesses and instructors. Mother read to us when we were sick, and, occasionally, she'd play board and card games with us. Father never did anything with me until I was in my late teens, when we'd play the occasional tennis game.

My beautiful mother was twenty-eight when this portrait of her was painted in 1934.

For the Loeb children, birthdays were special occasions. It was the one time each year we were allowed to join Father for breakfast, which he ate in his room before leaving for work in Manhattan. We didn't exactly know what he did in the city, except that it was "business," a subject never discussed in front of us. These birthday breakfasts were brought up on trays and placed on little tables from which we solemnly downed the contents of our egg cups. We learned that the art of decapitating the shells was "all in the wrist." After cautiously removing the top, we dipped silver spoons into the yolks.

Father was a giant in my eyes, so I tried hard during my yearly treat to act with proper decorum. He was a stickler for order and neatness, and I tried to convey both during my one-on-one time with him. If physiognomy is destiny, as I have read, then my father was born to be a leader. Perhaps it was the way his eyebrows grew: thick and black, nearly meeting at the center of his formidable brow. At home and at the office, a gaze from him was universally perceived as a command.

Father was obsessed with rules, which were never to be disobeyed. Being thin was the most important on his list, so it became the family obsession as well. Judy and Ann, prone to a slight youthful plumpness, suffered more than the boys ever did. During my sisters' teenage years, Father ordered the kitchen refrigerator locked to prevent late-night noshing. Neatness, to the point of minimalism, was another of his requirements. At his office, staff were required to have their desktops uncluttered to such a degree that it was a great mystery how any work could be done. Neatness seemed to be an offshoot of Father's penchant for secrecy; people couldn't know—or talk about—what they couldn't see.

Holidays remain vivid in my memory of childhood, because of both the joy they brought and their comfortable routine. As children, it never occurred to us that celebrating Christmas was not what Jewish people did. What we celebrated was centered around Santa Claus, and in no way religious. Christmas traditionally began with a November trip with Mother to the FAO Schwarz toy store in Manhattan, where she noted our hopes for what Santa would bring.

On Christmas Eve at my great-grandfather Adolph's house, all of Adolph's living relatives convened in his huge ballroom—a crowd that seemed like hundreds. A gigantic, handsomely decorated tree stood at one end of the room, with stacks and stacks of packages underneath. Great-Grandpa Lewisohn's chief steward, Mr. Meyer, would choose a present, call the name of the recipient, and then slide the gift across the polished ballroom floor. My siblings and I would await the sound of our name; at the first syllable we would dash out, grab the package and dash back to our staked-out place amid the crowd. We would add each gift to our piles, all of which became obscenely high by the evening's end.

Picking posies was always fun and easy for Ann, Arthur and me because there were so many flowers in every area of the Ridgeleigh estate. All my life, I have felt that being surrounded by flowers is almost as necessary as oxygen.

unpleasant or personal. Father wouldn't discuss what he did during work hours, and Mother didn't discuss that he might die. When Father finally returned to health, he took up yoga. That was something the family could share, and we all became somewhat adept at standing on our heads—in more ways than one. He continued practicing yoga for the rest of his long life.

On a summer day in 1938, when I was eight, Great-Aunt Edith, Governor Herbert Lehman's wife, called Mother. "Shirley Temple is coming to visit us," she said. "Would Johnny like to drop over?" *Would* I!

In a flash, I joined my cousins Billy and Bobby Bernhard and Dick Rossbach.* When I arrived, Hollywood's youngest star was standing by Herbert Lehman's swimming pool, her famous curls wrapped in a protective scarf. Very much in command, ten-year-old Shirley

---

* The Rossbach cousins were descended from Clara Lehman, and thus we shared great-grandparents, Mayer Lehman and Babette Lehman, and Great-Uncle Herbert Lehman. Richard Rossbach became a much-decorated hero during WWII and was an older brother of the writer June Rossbach Bingham Birge.

had taken a pair of handcuffs from one of Uncle Herbert's state troopers. She had locked up poor Dick, the oldest and tallest of us, who stood there looking sheepish. I took it upon myself to confront Shirley, boldly demanding that "The Little Colonel" return the key.

"Who do you think you are," she countered, "the law?"

My bravado vanished, and I backed down. Eventually Dick was unlocked, and we all played together for a while, but Shirley wasn't overly friendly. I suppose she was tired of being charming, always expected to provide Hollywood stardust.*

As a teenager, I came home one summer day to the house after repeatedly beating Grandfather Loeb in gin rummy. Mother decided the time had come to teach me bridge, a major part of my parents' social life and a skill she valued. It was a fruitless attempt—I had absolutely no interest in it—and she finally gave up. She stomped away from the table, shaking her head and muttering that I had "absolutely no bridge sense." She was absolutely right. My brother, Arthur, would go on to play as passionately and as skillfully as my parents. I wanted to please Mother, of course, but I couldn't fake an interest in something for which I had no natural affinity. I've never been able to.

Of all my siblings, I had the closest relationship with my brother. Arthur was born with a mild case of cerebral palsy; he could walk, play tennis, even ride horses—and even once stood on his head, with the rest of us—but he was never able to excel in athletics in a way that my parents seemed to demand. I would characterize Father and Mother's focus on athletic success, as well as thinness and dress, as bordering on obsessive. Of course, Arthur was never able to satisfy the athletic demands of my parents. Despite this inability to please, Arthur always maintained a great loyalty and communion with our parents' belief system. In their memoir, he is quoted as saying, "I shared completely my parents' values; that it is important to be rich, to be civic-minded, to be highly educated, to be ambitious and to work hard . . . we enjoyed the feeling that we were royalty."[57] It saddens me that even though my parents could not embrace everything that Arthur was and is, he never wavered from believing in them.

Because of Arthur's lack of athletic prowess, I never felt any competitive tension with my only brother, so we bonded much more easily and naturally. Unfortunately for Arthur, my parents' attempt to push this world on him, and his failure to live up to it, would have a dramatic effect on him in later years. Arthur was a brilliant, well-read and articulate young man; I have fond memories of our discussing books and newspapers from a relatively early age.

---

* Forty years later, Shirley and I would meet under different circumstances when, as a new ambassador, I was trained by none other than the former ambassador to Ghana, Shirley Temple Black.

A POOL PARTY FOR SHIRLEY TEMPLE

Top: Shirley Temple looks very pleased with herself, having locked up my nearly submerged and handcuffed cousin, Dick Rossbach. The occasion was a pool party in the summer of 1938 given for the youthful film star by my great-uncle Governor Herbert Lehman and his wife, Edith. Having just arrived, I can be seen in the background appraising the situation.

Bottom: I challenged the saucy Shirley and told her to unlock my cousin but looked for support from Uncle Herbert's policemen standing guard close by. (It was their handcuffs Shirley had "borrowed" for her little charade.)

Right page: Shirley showed no interest in one of the treats of the day—an ice cream bar—but when I asked if I could have it, she responded by starting to eat it. Despite her naughtiness, I think I fell a little in love with her that day. We would meet again many years later under very different circumstances, when she was perfectly charming.

Arthur's twin, Ann, was a beautiful little blond child with blue eyes. Everybody always made a big fuss over her, and my earliest memories of her are from Christmas time, when she always got the most presents. Ann was always there when Arthur was there, and vice versa—they were two sides of the same coin and, early on, a single entity in my mind. Ann was a wonderful swimmer and an attractive young woman. Over the years, when I brought male schoolmates home, quite a number were drawn magnetically to my sister's beauty and developed a crush on her. Although she was often the center of attention, Ann always carried a slight melancholy that I never quite understood. Perhaps that kind of attention simply merited some balance in her self-image.

She went to Rosemary Hall for boarding school, and because Mother and Judy had both gone to Vassar, Ann was expected to attend as well. (In our family, the tradition was that girls went to Vassar and boys went to Harvard. Also, our aunt Margaret Seligman Lewisohn was a trustee of Vassar.) At her interview, Ann made sure that didn't happen.

"Why do you want go to Vassar?" the admissions officer asked.

"*I* don't want to go to Vassar!" Ann replied. "*My mother* wants me to go to Vassar." That was the end of that.

As an undergraduate, she attended Bennington College, a private liberal-arts school in Vermont that Father and Mother didn't approve of. While she was there, she met a boy from Yale whom nobody in our family seemed to care much for. I remember this upsetting her very much, a rejection by her family that cut her deeply. It seemed all of us siblings were constantly trying—and not always succeeding—to gain our parents' stubborn approval.

My cousins Robert (Bobby) and William (Billy) Bernhard, the sons of Mother's sister and brother-in-law, Dorothy and Richard Bernhard, were like brothers to me. They spent every summer and school holiday at my grandparents' home next door. During the war, the Buttenwiesers stayed with Grandma Lehman: Uncle Benjamin,* Aunt Helen and their four children, Larry, Carol, Paul and Peter. Having bonded as children in the Ridgeleigh sandbox, we cousins have stayed close all of our lives.†

The move to the New York apartment in 1936 represented a shift for the family, marking the beginning of our time away from Ridgeleigh. For the next three years, we still

---

* Both my Uncle Benjamin and my Uncle Richard were on active duty in the Navy during WWII. Ben served on a carrier in the Pacific, and Dick served in Naval Intelligence both in the U.S. and London.

† Once a year, the four Loeb children, the two Bernhards and one Buttenwieser have lunch in Manhattan to celebrate Billy Bernhard's birthday.

spent weekends and holidays there during the school year. In July and August,* however, we headed north to Prospect Point, my Great-Grandfather Adolph Lewisohn's enormous camp on Upper Saranac Lake, an annual highlight of my childhood. There were fish to be caught, an enormous lake to swim in, endless woods to hike and exotic camp food to eat. We took the night train to Saranac Lake, excited to join our extended family, which sometimes numbered up to fifty cousins. We were "roughing it" at the camp, eating outdoor meals cooked by the guides, sitting alongside governesses at sturdy pine tables.

On Sunday mornings, we roared off in a motorboat, heading to the general store near the famed Saranac Inn via the back bay to buy the funny papers. Years later, I told my mother that I didn't have any memory of the Saranac Inn and wondered why.

"You were never there," she said. "It was restricted. The reason we used the back bay was because Jews weren't allowed in the front of the inn."

Many of "*Our Crowd*," all of whom had places on the lake—the Lewisohns, the Hellmans, the Loebs—never saw the inside of the inn. Of course, we kids knew nothing about restrictions. Living in paradise as we did, we likely wouldn't have cared.

In 1937, my parents bought a much more modest camp called Gull Bay, just across the lake from Prospect Point. Mother paid $11,000 for thirty acres of property (about fifteen of which were on the waterfront) and five buildings: the main house, a children's cottage, a guest cottage, the caretaker's house and a boathouse with two speedboats and two cars. From that point on until I was nineteen, I would spend every summer at Gull Bay, and at least part of every summer from the time I was twenty onward.

It was at Gull Bay in September 1939 that we heard on the radio that the Germans had invaded Poland, and also where we heard Hitler's speech about the invasion. The adults were extremely worried, but I remember that Hitler sounded squeaky to me and seemed funny to us kids. We children were as oblivious of the Nazis as we were of Jewish restrictions at the Saranac Inn, but our parents were not. They actively followed the news about the Nazi movements. After Kristallnacht—a destructive Nazi rampage through Jewish communities, businesses and homes in Germany and Austria—my father persuaded a reluctant C.M. to disband the Loeb, Rhoades offices in Germany and France for the safety of its employees.[58] It was a wise move that likely saved a lot of lives.

Off and on during World War II, there were as many as seventeen youngsters romping around the Ridgeleigh estate at one time. They included immediate family and the daughter

---

* From 1933 to 1936 our family went to the Adirondacks at Prospect Point, Great-Grandfather Lewisohn's camp. From 1937, we went to Gull Bay after Mother's purchase of that camp.

BLISSFUL DAYS
AT UPPER SARANAC LAKE

From 1938, a wonderful man named Ed Trimn managed our Gull Bay property for eighteen years, until he and his wife, Valda—our cook—retired in 1956.

Standing here outside the main cottage at Gull Bay are (left to right) my brother, Arthur, sister Judy and Mother. Seated are my sister Ann and me. We had dressed up for a western-style party with friends at Saranac sometime in the 1940s.

A boat ride in "Peter," the Loeb family Chris-Craft, was one of the summer joys for me and my siblings, Ann and Arthur. Our pilot, Oscar Ackerstrom, was not only the family chauffeur, he was also a member of the New York State National Guard and came out of the Second World War as a colonel. Here we are in 1937.

Here I am with Father in a convivial moment at the Gull Bay boathouse.

This aerial photo shows much of "Prospect Point," my Great-Grandfather Lewisohn's huge Saranac Lake property. Sheltered by well-weathered pine trees, the boathouse is seen in the foreground. The main house is partially visible, though not its many guest cottages.

The youthful hearts of my siblings and cousins raced with anticipation as we approached the boathouse of Prospect Point, looking forward to all the summer joys of Adolph Lewisohn's "camp."

My mother bought Gull Bay, our Loeb family camp on Upper Saranac Lake in 1937, for about $11,000. This included around thirty acres of property, much of it on the waterfront, a fully furnished main cottage, several smaller ones, a boathouse, a barn and an ice house.

of Jimmy Garbett, Grandma Lehman's chauffeur, as well as the children of family friends. The Bernhards brought two children of close British friends over from London to keep them safe while their parents went about their war duties. The family of our young English pals, Dennis and Stella Courage, owned the Courage Brewery, a company that owned pubs and sold ales and beers all over England. (The country was plastered with ads that advised people to "Take Courage.") I enjoyed "high tea" with the Courages and regularly shared their traditional British sandwiches before dashing off for a hearty American dinner at home.

Other wartime visitors who stayed at Ridgeleigh were Baron Antonio d'Almeida and his stunningly beautiful wife, Barbara, who were on their way to Buenos Aires. Their three sons would stay with us at 820 Park Avenue through the war. The baron, who had been in charge of the Paris office of Loeb, Rhoades, came to New York after the Paris office was closed. The war dislocated so many people, and many visitors made their way through Ridgeleigh, a safe place in a chaotic world.

Some summers during the war, the Bernhards and the Buttenwiesers took up the whole of the third floor of my grandparents' home. Billy Bernhard and I were particularly close and spent magical days together. Billy felt the same way I did about Ridgeleigh. "We kids knew every hiding place, every stump, every fallen tree and thicket on the estate," I wrote years later in an essay titled, "I Remember." I continued,

> *Summer was best, but we loved [Ridgeleigh] even in the winter. When the snow was too crisp to use our sleds, and the runners would stick, we brought pans and trays from the kitchen and spun crazily down the snow-covered hills. . . . On the truly hot, heavy days, half naked we roamed like bandits on our bicycles over the back roads and forest paths, or played fox and hounds for hours in the pool.*[*][59]

My distinguished grandparents loom as giants in my memory. I will always associate the smell of toast and honey with my Grandfather Lehman. On Sunday mornings, either by myself or with the family, I crossed the Ridgeleigh estate for a visit with Grandpa, who would be having breakfast on the back porch. With a warm greeting, he always offered to share his buttered toast slathered with golden honey. Some found him formal and austere with his silver hair, white moustache and brown eyes that seemed to observe everything in his view. But to me, Grandfather Lehman could not have been a kinder, gentler man.

My visits with him were even better if his lifetime friend, Mr. Strauss, happened to be

---

[*] The entire essay is included in the appendix.

there, Mr. Strauss was a tall, elegant man who was in the toy business. He always carried small toys in his pockets for any stray grandchild who came to call.* I was only six when Grandpa Lehman died, so I didn't know him well, but my mother wrote that he was "very jolly, he loved parties, he loved to go out, he adored the ladies and he never drank."[60]

Grandpa Lehman lived up to the family tradition of philanthropy in many arenas. He was one of the founders of the Federation of Jewish Philanthropies in New York, of which my grandmother Adele Lewisohn Lehman became honorary chair. He was a major contributor to the Mayer Lehman Charity Fund, which was able to rescue seventy-five to eighty Lehman distant cousins from the Holocaust. Like my father and me, he went to Harvard, and for the 30th anniversary of his graduation he gave his alma mater a new administration building, Lehman Hall.†

Grandmother Lehman, whom I was never close to, lived much longer than Grandpa. Mother wrote that a great deal of Grandma Lehman's time was taken up with charitable work, especially with an organization she founded in the 1920s called the "Purple Box,"[61] which sold the handiwork of crippled women.[62] Grandma was also an early suffrage activist. She loved flowers and gardening, and later in life she started to paint, producing simple but charming still lifes and florals, a few of which I still have.

Grandma Lehman was sweet, gentle, refined and somewhat remote to me. Since they lived under her roof, she was closer to the Bernhards than to the Loebs. The Buttenwiesers were also closer to the Lehmans. Both Buttenwieser parents worked, so Grandma Lehman took care of their four children a great deal. The Lehmans were not a demonstrative family, which is not to say they were without affection. They simply weren't huggers and kissers, except at public parties, where everyone offered cheeks to be pecked.

Grandfather Loeb was more austere than Grandfather Lehman. C.M.—never Carl—stood so straight, it seemed like he had a ramrod up his back. Though he was not especially tall, his carriage gave the illusion that he was at least six feet. I don't think Father was afraid of C.M., but he certainly was in awe of his father and treated him with enormous deference. However, I have been told they argued vigorously in the years of their working

---

* Years later, Anthony Ittleson, Strauss's grandson, married Marianne Sundby, my first wife's sister. Anthony's other grandfather, Mr. Ittleson, came to St. Louis from Germany at the turn of the century and subsequently founded the CIT corporation, the first company that allowed customers to finance automobiles.

† Lehman Hall became the gathering house for students at Harvard who didn't live on campus. It was subsequently named "Dudley House at Lehman Hall," after the second governor of Massachusetts. I was quite distressed at this change, as well as at the numerous stark portraits of Governor Dudley's family that hung all over the building. I insisted they move the Dudley pictures to the back and commissioned portraits of my Lehman ancestors to be placed up front.

together at Loeb, Rhoades. C.M. crossed every "t" and dotted every "i"—while also keeping his eye on the big picture. Father left the accounting to others, never being one to worry about every penny. This might have been a wise way to minimize anxiety, but it would become a fatal flaw in Loeb, Rhoades's final years in the 1970s.

Granny Adeline Moses Loeb was the sweetest and warmest of all my grandparents. ("*My* Grandma Moses," I called her.) There was nothing more comforting than to be pressed to Adeline's ample bosom and assured with wonderful predictions about my future, such as that one day I would become an ambassador. Though I didn't really believe her, I still loved hearing it.

Granny had a reputation as a "Mrs. Malaprop," famously mixing up names and words, but who cared when you could bask in such unconditional approval? Though we didn't always believe her stories about the Old South in Montgomery, Alabama, we loved to hear them, especially in her charming southern accent. Most of all, we loved how she loved us. Her interest in us was genuine, and it turned out many of her stories were true. They say that people don't remember what you do; they remember how you made them feel. Granny Adeline made me feel loved, and it is that which remains fixed in my memory of her.[63]

Besides the war raging in Europe, there were other things to fear in the outside world. Few people today remember the epidemic that inspired terror in 1940s America: poliomyelitis, known generally as "infantile paralysis." The disease mainly attacked children, but adults were vulnerable as well. All parents were in a state of panic, fearing that their children would be exposed and paralyzed, as President Roosevelt had tragically been. I recall being in movie theaters as a child where ushers would walk through the audience rattling and passing cans down the aisle for Roosevelt's "March of Dimes" program to combat the disease. The Salk vaccine was still eleven years away.

The epidemic led to the Loeb children's quarantine. During the summers, we were forbidden to venture to any public place. On one particularly hot day, Arthur and I, usually obedient to parental strictures, decided to ignore the rules. We snuck off the estate and hiked the two and a half miles from Purchase to White Plains to see a new movie, *Mr. Skeffington*, starring Bette Davis and Claude Raines. Apparently, our transgression wasn't discovered, because I have no memory of any punishment. What I do remember is that we dared to disobey—and it was a thrill.

My cousin Dr. Paul Buttenwieser, who has practiced and taught psychiatry and psycho-analysis at Harvard Medical School for many years, is also a writer. In 1987 he wrote a novel called *Their Pride and Joy*. Ostensibly fiction, the prologue describes a family and an estate quite identifiable as the Ridgeleigh inhabited by the Lehmans, Loebs, Bernhards, Buttenwiesers and all their wartime visitors. It is clear that we children were mostly free of the anxieties our elders felt during the war, yet we could still feel the underlying sadness in the air:

> *Even the idyllic landscape of Rosefield was now and then bloodied by a telegram or a call bringing news of death: a distant cousin, a friend's son, an acquaintance, lost in action. Amid all that beauty tears were shed in private, and no one spoke of the terrible anxiety hidden away just under the surface. Still, it was an exhilarating time, and Rosefield was a wonderful place to be, especially for the children. The war summers were a long house party for them.*[64]

It is fitting that Ridgeleigh has been fictionalized in this way, for it was somewhat of an idyllic place—a storybook home. We were young and insensible to adult concerns, and nothing seriously disturbed our carefree days as children at Ridgeleigh and Saranac Lake in the 1930s and 1940s. There was indeed a dangerous world outside, especially for Jews, but it was one from which we were insulated—at least for the time being.

This is how I looked at age eleven while I was attending the Harvey School. This was the year Pearl Harbor was bombed, on December 7, 1941.

≡

CHAPTER TWO

Learning to Be a WASP: Collegiate and Harvey Schools, 1936–1944

Our family move from Ridgeleigh to New York City in 1936 had been full of pleasant new experiences: I was still with my parents and siblings, Ridgeleigh was part of our lives in the summer and on weekends, and because the changes were gradual, I took them in stride.

It never occurred to me that there was a special reason why our new apartment at 820 Park Avenue had visiting squad cars and its own policeman. Didn't everyone's? Uncle Herbert Lehman had an apartment in our building, and, as New York's governor, he was entitled to special protection. Also, ever since the Lindbergh baby's kidnapping in 1932, there was concern for the safety of children of the rich and famous. After the Lindbergh baby's murder, Grandfather Loeb received a note threatening his grandchildren, so police cars checking on us in Purchase and in Manhattan became the norm.

Something that was *not* the norm occurred the night of October 30, 1938. Our Norwegian nanny, Agard Olson, became greatly agitated and woke my siblings and me around midnight. "Get up! Get up!" she ordered in a panicked voice. "We must leave right away!" We scurried about, dressing as fast as we could, with no idea why we had been catapulted out of our beds. Fortunately, my parents returned just then, stopping our headlong dash to God-knows-where. Agard had been listening to Orson Welles's eerily realistic production of *The War of the Worlds*, which was presented as a radio newscast of Martians landing in New Jersey and heading to Manhattan. Like many Americans, she was convinced it was real and was determined to take her young wards to safety. Parental sense prevailed, how-

In this 1936 photo of my class at the Collegiate School for Boys, I am the last boy in the back row. I was fond of Ms. Farnum, my first grade teacher, who is seen seated at the far right. My three years at Collegiate were happy, and I discovered there that studying hard was something I liked to do.

ever, and we went back to bed, still mystified by the whole event. The hoax would become part of American lore. It seems we had participated in one of our country's more bizarre pieces of history.

Until I went to kindergarten at Rye Country Day at the age of four, I had only played with my brothers, sisters and cousins at home and at the Century Country Club. Mother thought it would be too much for me to go to kindergarten every day, so I went every other day. I started first grade in the fall of 1936 at the Collegiate School for Boys. Founded by Dutch colonists in 1628 under the auspices of the Reformed Protestant Dutch Church, Collegiate eventually became nondenominational. The oldest independent school in the United States, it had moved to West 78th Street in 1892. For a young East Sider, traveling to the Upper West Side seemed like going to another planet. I was chauffeured in our new Lincoln, its elegance inspiring awe among my less wealthy classmates. Collegiate was not a school exclusively for the elite, and I admit that I was guilty of boasting about that Lincoln to my classmates.

The strongest memory I have of Collegiate is the study hall. By third grade I discovered that I actually enjoyed studying hard. In due course, I became aware that not only

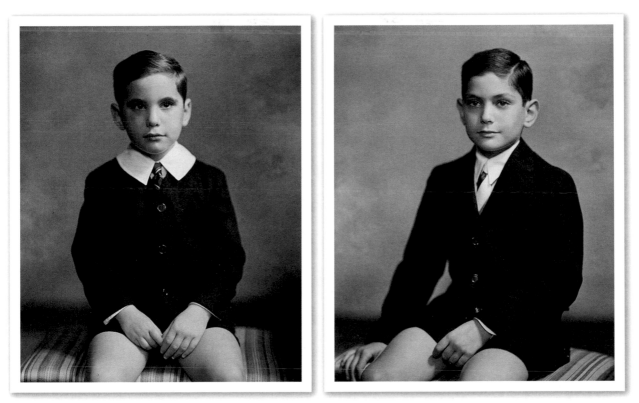

All dressed up, Arthur and I posed for a professional photographer when he was about four years old and I was about six.

did I have to go, but I also *wanted* to go to Grandfather Loeb and Father's alma mater, a magical place called Harvard. Good grades were the only way to get there, so I got them. I participated in athletic events as well, winning a medal for the hundred-yard dash at one of the gymkhana games held near Baker Field at Columbia University, and a woodworking award in a shop class. (A picture I painted at the school still hangs in my bathroom.) My memories of Collegiate are warm and full. It was a place where I was openly accepted and where I discovered a lifelong love of learning, which would send me in all kinds of directions later in life.

My first kiss came from our pretty Swedish maid, Adele. Striking a match one evening, the charming young Adele held it up to me. "If you can blow this out," she said to me with a smile, "that means I can give you a kiss." I blew it out quite easily, gazed into her blue Scandinavian eyes and awaited my reward, which I got smack on the lips. Thus began my attraction to Swedish misses and kisses. Oscar Ackerstrom, our Swedish chauffeur, was also in love with Adele. Much to my disappointment, they never married. Oscar was a member of the U.S. National Guard and went into active duty after World War II broke out. The army became his lifetime career, so it was Colonel Ackerstrom who wrote my parents during the Korean War, just as I was being called up to active duty myself, to let them know that, as he was now a colonel, he could possibly be helpful to me.

During the period that I was at Collegiate, I had my first exposure to Judaism, thanks to my aunts Dorothy Bernhard and Helen Buttenwieser. Though my family belonged to Temple Emanu-El, I had never gone as a child, not even to High Holiday services, and there was no expectation of my having a bar mitzvah. My parents had no interest in religion, but my aunts thought my cousins and I should meet with a rabbi once a month to learn about Judaism. At both the Bernhard and Buttenwieser homes, the rabbi would come and tell us stories from the Old Testament. We learned about David killing a fearsome giant with a slingshot, and about Samson overcoming the Philistines. Stories from the Bible struck me as fairy tales, in no way connected to how one's life should be led.

The Loeb family was once invited to a Seder at the Buttenwieser home, along with their observant friends. To my secular eyes, they dressed oddly: the men wore funny little beanies fastened with bobby pins to keep them from slipping off their heads. And the food was awful. I had not been accustomed to kosher food, much less kosher for Passover food, which was made without any bread or leaven whatsoever. I knew I was Jewish, but this hadn't really mattered much up to that point. I was too sheltered to realize that this meant that some people would not only consider me different, but a pariah.

In the summer of 1939, before I started fourth grade, I received the greatest blow of my childhood, the crux on which everything in my childhood turned. Without discussion, Father told me I was going to be transferred to the Harvey School, an ostensibly nondenominational (but in reality, Christian) boarding school for boys in Hawthorne, New York.

My parents' decision left me believing that I was being punished for loving my mother too much. This initiated a feeling I would have for the rest of my life—that if I loved someone too much, I'd be punished. At the time, I had no idea what I'd done wrong; I was a goody-two-shoes, eager to please and a good student to boot. When I was first told, I burst into tears. I howled, raged, argued and staged tantrums. But the decision was final, and my father intractable.

I was an obedient child,* so I internalized the hurt, leaving scars that never totally healed. The reasons for my banishment were multiple: I was too spoiled; all the house-

---

* Bob Hutzler was the son of Piddington Hutzler, my father's nurse throughout his eight-month recovery from cancer surgery in 1936. In 2006, Bob met my son, Nicholas, and humorously complained that his mother used to admonish him when he was small: "Why can't you be a good little boy like Johnny Loeb?"

hold staff made too much fuss over me; I was too much the "king of the mountain" among my siblings and cousins; I was too dependent on my mother, an unmanly trait that would leave me unfit to face the real world; I had too many colds and it would be healthier for me to be in the country. Lastly, Father was sure there was going to be a war and that I would be safer out of Manhattan. Even at the age of nine, the logic of that argument completely escaped me. How could I be safe if the rest of my family had been killed in Manhattan?

I've come to believe there was another reason girding the decision to send me to boarding school. At that time my parents' marriage was having one of its periodic hiccups. My mother and I were close, and Father surmised that he would get more of her attention with me out of the house. In due course, all four of my siblings were sent to boarding school, but none as early as I was. I was absolutely devastated. Though Harvey was only a fifteen-minute car ride away from Ridgeleigh, I felt as though I were being sent to another country. I might as well have been, since there would be no returning home for weekends, and visits from my parents would be rare. I was nine years old and forced into exile.

My first roommates at Harvey were Plato Skouras, whose father, Spyros Skouras, was a movie mogul with 20th Century Fox, and Charlie Smithers, who actually liked it at Harvey, and seemed to like me as well.* In the spring of 1940, Peter Dixon, whose father was a partner at Loeb, Rhoades, became my roommate. We didn't get along at all and had ferocious fights. During one of our tangles over a comic book, I broke a finger on Peter's head and had to wear a cast for several weeks. Many years hence, Peter himself joined Loeb, Rhoades as a senior analyst, and we became good friends.

When my mother came for her first and only visit to Harvey, I cried so hard that she likely would have taken me home if Father wouldn't have made her bring me back. My only visits home were for Thanksgiving, Christmas and Easter. Somehow I muddled through the first year, studying hard. If I was being punished, I thought, perhaps I could win back my parents' approval with good grades. Maybe then I could come home.

At Harvey I was always homesick and unable to sleep. One night, at 3 a.m., I was in acute emotional pain. I decided to call my mother from the phone system in the school office. I had to creep down three flights of stairs to reach the unlocked office. The phone system was controlled by an operator who sat in front of a board full of holes and plugged

---

* Charlie's family owned the F.S. Smithers Company, which provided the original funds to underwrite a firm that ultimately became IBM. At first, investors were not interested in an unknown company, so the Smithers Company found itself stuck with unmarketable stock. What was once a financial albatross eventually turned into a huge fortune for the family, which they have shared generously over the years with many philanthropies.

a metal prong into the proper hole to get the desired number. As a top student, I was sometimes commissioned to be the telephone operator in the absence of the regular attendant. My parents were living in Washington, D.C., at the time, and Mother was visiting my grandmother in Manhattan. It was Katie, one of Grandmother's maids, whom I awoke from a sound sleep. Katie leapt out of bed in the dark to answer the insistent ring. On her way, she crashed into something and fell hard, breaking her arm. My shame and guilt about that were hard to shed.

Shortly after my arrival on the Harvey campus, I experienced my first encounter with anti-Semitism. A group of us were playing touch football, a distraction that had begun to take the edge off my unhappiness. During a timeout, a burly fourteen-year-old named Burke sauntered menacingly toward me and loomed over my head. I was only nine and he seemed like a giant. I was so thin and feeble that I once ordered and devoured every Charles Atlas exercise book in print, but they didn't help much.

"Loeb," Burke sneered, "You're a Jew, aren't you?" The giant said the word with disdain—something I had yet to experience.

"Yes," I responded innocently. To me it was like being asked if my first name was John. It hadn't dawned on me that in most WASPs' eyes at that time, it was a terrible thing to be Jewish. Everyone around stopped dead still and stared at me. *A Jew?* They acted as though they'd never seen one before, though there were a few others in the school. I might as well have been the devil incarnate, personally responsible for killing their lord and savior. Jesus

This is the Harvey baseball fourth team in 1940, when I was ten. I am the boy on the far left of the second row, wearing a cap and a solemn face. Not terribly athletic, I nevertheless earned letters both in baseball and football at Harvey. From the looks on the faces of some of my teammates, I was not the only unhappy boy there, but I believed I was the *most* unhappy.

was a man about whom I would soon learn a great deal. I didn't know much then, though I knew Jews didn't believe Jesus was God. But I certainly didn't want to be held responsible for killing him.

My religious confusion worsened at the Protestant prayer services and evening vespers, where someone always gave a short talk about the Bible, usually the Old Testament. We were being taught "truth" from the Old Testament, a book written by Jews, yet all around me Jews were being demonized. The logic of all this was difficult to fathom.

I later learned that the other Jews at Harvey—mostly upperclassmen—experienced the same kind of confrontations I had. I made friends with another Jewish boy in my own class named Bobby Abraham, and we made plans to room together the following year, if I was forced to return. In the meantime, I bore down on the books. I was so focused on good grades and how they could redeem me that I studied after lights out with a flashlight under the blankets.

Every month our rankings in the school were posted on yellow cards on the hall bulletin board for all to see. We were ranked in each subject against everyone in our class. Our total grade, to the first decimal point, was then compared to that of every other student in the school. The pressure to perform was tremendous, and I rose to the challenge, always landing first in my class, which of course did nothing to make me better liked. It couldn't erase the inescapable fact that I was a Jew.

I managed a smile for a photo with the third team. I am in the last row on the far left.

Father visited me once while I was at Harvey for a father-son baseball game. Pictured here, I am in the top row, third from the left.

Though I liked some of my teachers, they rarely offered words of praise and encouragement. There was no one I could approach to discuss my problems, and no teacher ever reached out to me. I don't know if any of them even noticed my sadness. I suppose the staff was inured to homesick boys who didn't want to be there, and so my unhappiness was not unique.

I had never met a child from a divorced family before, but most of the boys at Harvey came from broken homes. Some of them came from other countries, displaced by World War II: George and James Patiño from Bolivia and Europe, Folke Bernadotte Jr. from Sweden, Thomas Fred Olssen from Norway. Some came from families who sent their children to boarding school in the hopes that they would turn into versions of their well-educated selves. The most amazing thing to me was that some of these kids were actually glad to be there.

My unhappy first year finally came to an end. I reveled in my summer at Ridgeleigh, Gull Bay and Prospect Point. As fall drew near, my pleas not to return to Harvey for a second year grew louder. I even staged a last-ditch tantrum with Mother on the train from Grand Central up to Hawthorne, a ruckus that likely was heard all over the car. It was a useless campaign. Finally recognizing defeat, I subsided. "Well, at least I'll be rooming with Bobby Abraham," I said.

"No, you're not," my mother replied.

I couldn't believe my ears. "Why not?"

"We don't want you to know only Jews," she said. "You have to make friends with Christians, too."

Though I didn't know it at the time, this was one of the reasons my parents had sent me to Harvey in the first place: they wanted me to assimilate. But on that train, I didn't have a clue. Because I was Jewish I shouldn't have a Jewish roommate? Bobby wasn't even terribly Jewish, certainly not religiously observant. It was 1940, and I suppose my parents were increasingly sensitive to the Jewish question now that Hitler had come into power. The national hero, Charles Lindbergh, by now a known anti-Semite,

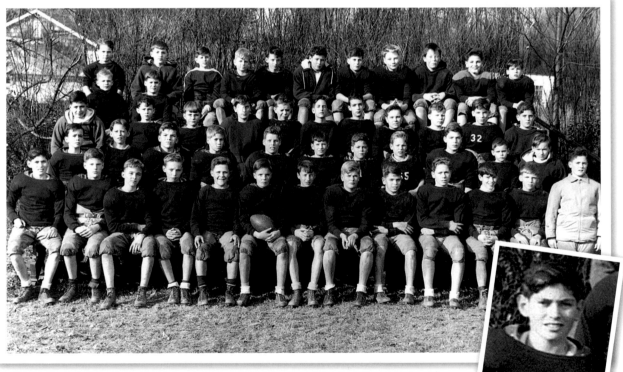

I am pictured here in the first row at the far left. I had made it to the Number One football team by the last of my five years at Harvey. Earlier, I had one brief moment of football glory when I made a touchdown in an intramural game that even got written up in the school paper, *The Harvey Rambler*. The touchdown for the "Pocanticos" was a fluke, and it happened partly because the one thing I could do was run fast. The score was tied at zero. It was raining hard that day, and the field was terribly muddy and slick. At the kick-off, the fellow on the opposite team kicked the ball to the side where I was standing. I grabbed it, started to run one way, then surprised everyone and reversed field. Everyone behind me was slipping and sliding in the mud as they tried to catch me. Miraculously I stayed on my feet, was able to make the touchdown, and we won the game. It was a heady moment, but moments like that were few and far between.

had embraced Hitler as "good for Germany and America as well." The years of peaceful acceptance of Jews in this country, indeed respect for their place in its history, were rapidly being erased.

During my five years at Harvey, Father visited but once, during my second year, for a father-son baseball game. It seems fitting that it would be sports that would draw him to my school, since he and Mother always put enormous value in athletic pursuits. I think that he was happy to have me away from home, that he was aware of my unhappiness and simply didn't want to face it, especially since he knew my anger was directed at him.

Little by little, I made a few friends at Harvey. Memorably, Bob Doherty invited me for a weekend at his home, where I was flabbergasted to see his mother do the cooking herself! I'd never visited a home in my entire life where the mother did the cooking, and she was fantastic at it. Also, to my astonishment, the parents slept in the same king-size bed; no one's parents I knew stayed in the same bed at that time. Bob was captain of the football team, the "most popular" and "most admirable," so it was no small thing to have him as a friend, especially for a Jewish boy who first struggled to find friends.

Bob and I were both cast in a school play, Maxwell Anderson's *Key Largo*. The school's play was only the prologue of the play. It takes place on a mountaintop during the Spanish Civil War (1936–1939). I had the lead role and can still recite some of the lines today. Another member of our cast was John Kerr, who in 1954 won a Tony Award for his role as a sensitive prep school teenager in Robert Anderson's *Tea and Sympathy*. At the opening of

This photo was taken in 1942, when Judy was fifteen and I was twelve and both of us were home from our respective boarding schools for the summer. Playland, a mini version of Coney Island located in Rye, New York, is only a few miles from our home in Purchase. Even during the gas-rationed war years, we Loeb kids managed to get to Playland at least once every summer. Shown in Playland costumes are my sister Judy (left), me in the middle, and at the right, one of Judy's friends.

Vacations from Harvey were all too short. Here, in 1942, I made use of my time at home making a warship.

Key Largo, the actress June Walker, Kerr's mother, told my Aunt Dorothy Bernhard—who attended the play in the stead of my parents—that I might become a professional actor someday. It never happened. But at the time, I thought so, too, the glow and attention having gone to my head.

The night of December 7, 1941, we were told during vespers about the bombing at Pearl Harbor. The next day, students and teachers gathered around a radio on the porch of the main building to hear the broadcast of Roosevelt's short but dramatic speech about "a date which will live in infamy." He urged Congress to declare war on Japan, which it did later that day, December 8, 1941, with only one vote against. Hitler declared war on the United States the day after that.

We began to pay attention to the newspapers, following the maps that showed black wherever the Axis powers had taken over. We were told that America was not only the best country in the world, but also the strongest and most powerful. In his speech to Congress, FDR maintained, "No matter how long it may take us to overcome this premeditated invasion, the American people . . . will win through to absolute victory." But everyone wondered how we'd do it; day after day we seemed to be losing. The black areas on the map were increasing, giving cause for alarm and anxiety.

By the eighth grade and nearing graduation from Harvey in 1944, I had cheered up considerably, thanks in part to serving on the editorial board of *The Rambler*, and to having the friendship of a wonderful humanities teacher.

My father bought a farm in upstate New York, where he planned to take us if the Germans invaded the United States. A great many people thought we might be either invaded or bombed by the Nazis, but I don't remember being frightened. There were practical changes in our civilian lives: at home we had an apple orchard, housed chickens for our eggs and began a garden for most of our vegetables. Gas rationing made going anywhere in the car a big event. I was so overjoyed to return to Ridgeleigh that summer that I didn't care if we traveled or not. I would've been happy if we had been locked in all summer.

Father, however, was not so happy being stuck at home. Like many men during World War II, he wanted to be part of the action, and he ached to join the other enlisted men from Loeb, Rhoades. My father had studied navigation in the year before the country got into the war, and he had hoped to get into the Navy, where some of his ancestors had served in earlier American wars. Then he tried the Army, and again was rejected. Not only was he already forty years old, but he was also a cancer survivor, a fact that he didn't even know. (Mother hadn't told him of the doctor's diagnosis until he was turned down by the military. He was told instead that he had a serious stomach problem, and the word "cancer" never crossed anyone's lips.) With typical perseverance, he found a way to "do his duty" for the country, wrangling a job through the influence of Mother's cousin-in-law Henry Morgenthau, then secretary of the treasury.

Father didn't enjoy his job as assistant director in procurement, which involved operational tasks rather than policymaking. He was not suited to being subservient to anyone, much less bureaucratic supervisors. Once, when essential matériel was needed for the Lend-Lease program, and Father was told the delay was due to a mandatory Civil Defense blackout, he risked the equivalent of a court-martial by giving permission for his men to work through the night.[65] He also demanded a higher civil service rating for his file clerks, because, as he put it, he needed clerks who could "not only file the documents but find them as well."

In 1942, the family rented a house on Woodland Drive in the northwest part of Washington, D.C., where they lived until the end of the war. Arriving by train in Washington one snowy night before Christmas, I enraged Father after he and Mother picked me up at Union Station. In the Treasury Department, Father had been working very closely with some Russians—of whom he had become very fond—on the Lend-Lease program. At the time, he was also passionately pro–Soviet Union, which was then our ally in the war against the Nazis.

My French teacher at Harvey was Mr. Berkeley W. Hotchkiss, who had strong political opinions that he openly shared with my class. Among them was his conviction that within ten years America would be at war with Russia. One day, prattling away in the backseat, I innocently mentioned this remark to my parents. My father stopped the car.

"Get out!" he roared. "You can walk home."

Mystified, I got out, even as my mother protested, "John, he was just quoting his teacher!" But there was no swaying him, and I started walking.

I trudged along the road disconsolately, feeling that I had once again displeased Father beyond redemption. After I slogged through the snow for a few blocks, the car stopped and waited for me to catch up. Mother had convinced Father to let me back in, but the heavy silence on the ride home hung portentously on the upcoming holiday. I was devastated by the amount of rage I had unleashed in my father.

Oddly enough, my father could be more understanding about things that seemed like a bigger deal, including my first experience with smoking. In Washington during the war, we lived on Woodland Drive next door to T.V. (Tse-ven) Soong (brother of Mme. Chiang Kai-shek), a prominent statesman and businessman from the Republic of China. The Harvard-educated T.V. held assorted high-level financial

When I graduated from Harvey in June 1944, *The Rambler* noted that I had been chosen Most Likely to Succeed, Best Student, Hardest Worker, and that I had won the Baoth Wiborg prize in Latin. I'd also won the Almirall Scholarship Cup and graduated as a "decemvir"—among the top ten in the class.

A History of The Harvey School
Celebrating 100 Years

Fifth Form Choices

Most Likely to Succeed	Loeb	Favorite Cartoon	Blondie
Most Popular	Doherty	Favorite Song	Love, Love, Love
Handsomest	Doherty	Favorite Football Team	Yale
Biggest Eater	Nagle	Favorite Baseball Team	Yankees
Most Modest	Dodge and Knox	Favorite Sport	Baseball
Best Student	Loeb	Favorite Stage Actor	Boris Karloff
Best Athlete	MacArthur	Favorite Stage Actress	
Hardest Worker	Loeb		Mary Martin—Helen Hayes
Done Most for School	Work	Favorite Entertainment	Movies
Wittiest	Shirk	Favorite Vesper Speaker	Father Chalmers
Best Dressed	Foord	Favorite Movie Actor	Humphrey Bogart
Boy with Best Excuses	Mueller, P.	Favorite Movie Actress	Hedy Lamarr
Hardest Subject	Latin	Favorite Orchestra	Tommy Dorsey
Easiest Subject	Algebra	Most Perfect Gentleman	Dodge
Favorite Subject	Algebra	Most Admirable Boy	Doherty
Favorite Master in Class	Mr. Howes	Most Original Boy	Shirk
Favorite Master out of Class	Mr. Humason	Most Energetic Boy	Work
Favorite Prep School	Exeter	Most Admirable Public Figure	Churchill
Favorite College	Yale and Dartmouth	Most Overworked Expression in School	
Favorite Magazine	Life		"Tough to Chew"
Favorite Newspaper	N. Y. Times	Political Party	Republican
Favorite Author	Forester		

FROM THE HARVEY CENTENNIAL YEARBOOK

An Alumnus You Should Know

JOHN L. LOEB JR. '44

Diplomat, Businessman, Art Collector, Philanthropist

Long before he became an adult who distinguished himself in many arenas, John L. Loeb Jr. was a leader at Harvey. The young Mr. Loeb came to Harvey at age nine, determined to succeed. His name consistently appeared on the Headmaster's List, and he received the 1943 Almirall Award for Scholarship for what teachers described as "showing the most interest in class discussions, keeping the best notes and, as far as could be determined, getting the most out of the course."

Fellow students also recognized Mr. Loeb's initiative, voting him Most Likely to Succeed, Best Student, Hardest Worker, and Favorite Public Figure, among his class. A class prophecy printed in *The Rambler* said, "I know Loeb got voted into the Senate last week."

Although Mr. Loeb never ran for office, he was appointed by President Ronald Reagan to serve as the U.S. ambassador to the Kingdom of Denmark from 1981 to 1983, and as a delegate to the United Nations in 1984. Mr. Loeb's contributions as ambassador were later recognized by Queen Margrethe II of Denmark with the Grand Cross of the Order of Dannebrog, an honor at the same level as knighthood.

The competitive spirit at Harvey, Mr. Loeb said, provided early inspiration to always do his best. Although he fondly recalls once scoring a touchdown for the Pocanticos, Mr. Loeb admitted that he wasn't a natural athlete. Instead, he strived to excel in the classroom.

In 2009, Mr. Loeb founded the George Washington Institute for Religious Freedom, which highlights a letter written by the founding father to promote a greater awareness of the historic roots of religious freedom, the separation of church and state, and tolerance in our country. The foundation has brought international exposure for George Washington's writing on this topic, resulting in thousands of students nationwide writing essays about this important value of U.S. society and government.

Mr. Loeb spoke at Harvey's second Upper School commencement in 1983, and was recognized with the title "Distinguished Alumnus."

and political posts in China, including being the head of the Bank of China and the Chinese minister of finance.[*] He evidently still had political sway in China, because sometimes when I'd go into the house, there would be military officers carefully studying maps. Whatever was going on, I found the atmosphere there mysterious, exciting and exotic.

T.V.'s daughter, Catherine, became my very first girlfriend, and she liked to smoke. She seemed to like me even better when she discovered that I had access to cigarettes at our house. We took long walks in the nearby wooded area, where we would sneak cigarettes. One day, just as I was secretly returning the remains of a pack, Father caught me in the act.

"Do you like to smoke?" he began mildly.

"Yes," I said cautiously. "Sort of." There was a heavy pause, so I added, "I guess I like it because Catherine does."

"Well," he said. "I'll make a deal with you."

A deal? With my father? I listened cautiously. Father didn't usually make deals with me. He issued edicts, which I obeyed.

"If you promise not to smoke until you're twenty-one," he said, "I will give you either $1,000 or a car—your choice."

My interest in both Catherine and smoking took a sudden nosedive. I immediately agreed. I kept my promise, as did my father. When I was twenty-one, I chose a Pontiac convertible over the money. (By that time, the cost of a car far exceeded $1,000.) Thanks to my father and that Pontiac, I have not smoked since.

In Washington, my younger sister Ann, a student at the Potomac School, became great friends with Diana Hopkins, the daughter of Secretary of Commerce Harry Hopkins, one

As a teenager, I was so skinny that I ordered a copy of a Charles Atlas transformational book where he said, "I was a 97-pound weakling" and told how he overcame his problem. Not surprisingly, the book didn't help much!

---

[*] T.V. had three sisters (including Mme. Chiang Kai-shek), who all married well: his brothers-in-law were Sun Yat-sen, Generalissimo Chiang Kai-shek and the financier H.H. Kung.

of President Roosevelt's most trusted advisor and a prime architect of the New Deal. A widower, Hopkins and his daughter lived at the White House for two years during WWII because FDR valued Hopkins's company and sage advice. Diana frequently invited Ann to play at the White House, and several times the president asked the two girls to lunch with him in the Oval Office. FDR sat at his desk while the girls ate from trays. When Ann told us these stories, I was wild with jealousy.

When our whole family was invited to the White House to meet both the president and Harry Hopkins, I was elated. Though we did meet Mr. Hopkins, to my great disappointment, President Roosevelt's schedule was changed at the last minute. I consoled myself that we had been asked to the White House as invited guests, not tourists, which provided a modicum of bragging rights.

Gradually, over my five years at Harvey, the taunts subsided, and I found pleasure in a few activities. Besides my interest in drama, I loved writing for the school paper, *The Rambler*. By the eighth grade, I had become fond of one teacher, Mr. John Humason, whose humanities class included lectures on philosophy, literature and art—all taught from the historical perspective. He also took us to see Leonard Bernstein's *On the Town* when I was thirteen or fourteen. When I left Harvey in 1944, I gave Mr. Humason a present and called him "my Mister Chips," a reference to the 1939 movie *Goodbye, Mr. Chips.*

Though I was rarely happy, I did exceedingly well academically at Harvey. From the fourth through the eighth grade, I had always been first in my class, winning, among other accolades, the Almirall Scholarship Cup for the best grades in the school, the Latin prize and the honor of graduating as a decemvir (among the top ten in the class). My class voted me Most Likely to Succeed, Best Student, Hardest Worker and Favorite Public Figure. I also earned the nickname "Ear Loeb," since my head hadn't caught up with the size of my ears. But no one ever believed how deeply unhappy I was during my "prison sentence" at Harvey. I believe it was during those years that I was embedded with a lifelong distrust of happiness.

My subconscious became convinced that if I became too happy again, I would be punished. "Ways will be found to destroy happiness," a voice would whisper subliminally. It is a habit that I wanted to shun, and a voice I wanted to silence, but we are all products of what we experience at these formative ages—and I am no exception.

A studio portrait of me taken about the time I began my four years at Hotchkiss.

≡

CHAPTER THREE

Coping with Anti-Semitism: Hotchkiss, 1944–1948

"He is Jewish, but of the right sort."

So wrote Theodore Blair about me to the admissions director of the Hotchkiss School for boys in 1943. My father had asked Ted Blair—a senior figure at the esteemed law firm Hughes, Hubbard, Blair & Reed, and a WASP with good connections—to write a letter of recommendation for me. Ted meant that as established merchants and bankers, my Jewish ancestry was satisfactory enough for my admittance into the picturesque WASP prep school. Because of the letter, my good grades at Harvey and being the "right sort of Jewish," I was accepted.

I suppose my parents felt comfortable about sending me to Hotchkiss, which at the time was for boys only, because two male relatives who preceded me there spoke of no untoward incidents. A second cousin of my mother's, Robert (Bobbie) Lehman, was a Hotchkiss alumnus. A grandson of one of the original three Lehman Brothers, Bobbie, who died in 1969, was the last family member to head the firm. Arthur Lehman Goodhart, Mother's first cousin (and son of the quotable Aunt Hattie), also attended the school before graduating from Yale and Cambridge Law School.*

---

* Arthur Goodhart was part of the Judge Advocate's Office and played a minor role in the Treaty of Versailles before becoming a teacher at Cambridge. After Cambridge, he became a professor at Oxford in political theory and philosophy, and master of University College (he was the first American and Jew to be a master of an Oxford college). Arthur was eventually knighted by Queen Elizabeth. One of his three sons, Philip, also attended Hotchkiss and later became a Conservative member of Parliament. He too was knighted. Philip Goodhart had two other brothers: William wrote the constitution for the Liberal Party and became a member of the House of Lords. Charles became a professor at the London School of Economics and served on the Interest Committee of the Bank of England. He recently wrote a Morgan Stanley Research report, covered in *Barron's*, disputing Thomas Piketty's well-received theory about the increasing gap between the rich and the working class.

Other relatives who attended Hotchkiss (distantly related to me through my Grandmother Loeb) were all four Cullman brothers of the Philip Morris family; Edgar Cullman at one point was even chairman of the Hotchkiss board of directors. Nevertheless, this lineage didn't spare me the anxiety-ridden struggle of making my way through a WASP high school as a Jew. When I complained to my parents that there were no other Jewish students at Hotchkiss, they countered with, "What about Peter Sharp?" The next time I saw Peter, I asked him if he was Jewish. Aghast at my inquiry, he blurted, "I can't tell you." He then quickly changed the subject, and I got the message.

I was the victim of not infrequent anti-Semitic behavior at Hotchkiss, which Stephen Birmingham (in *Our Crowd*) called a "popular sport" there. One of the incidents was captured in his book:

> *At the Hotchkiss School, not too many years ago, the son of one of New York's most prominent Jewish families, a bright, active, and well-liked boy, was considered a promising sculptor and was given a one-man show. . . .*
>
> *One morning it was discovered that someone, in the night, had defaced each of the heads by giving it a large Semitic nose. The desecration outraged Headmaster George Van Santvoord, who made it the basis of a stirring chapel sermon. Most interesting was the attitude of the young sculptor himself, who had begged that the matter be forgotten and was so embarrassed at being the subject of a sermon that he became sick to his stomach.*[66]

This story is indeed about me, though some of the facts are off. George Van Santvoord never gave a speech about it, and I never got sick to my stomach, though I was upset about it for years. Another time they rolled one of my pieces down the corridor, though it was soft clay that didn't harden and so was undamaged.

Though I enjoyed my time on the school newspaper and escaped to sculpting, my experience at Hotchkiss was checkered, punctuated with periodic fistfights during my first two years. The pipe-puffing headmaster, George Van Santvoord—dubbed "the Duke"—would later write me a flattering recommendation to Harvard.* His letter noted the following:

---

* Abraham Isaacks, my earliest ancestor, who arrived in 1697, and Cornelius Van Santvoord, the Duke's earliest ancestor, who arrived twenty years later, were both naturalized by act of the General Assembly of the Colony of New York approved by Governor William Burnet on July 6, 1723.

Hotchkiss prep school is tucked snugly amid the rolling hills of Lakeville, Connecticut, about a two-hour drive from Manhattan.

> *John is chairman of the editorial board of the school newspaper. He is not a popular boy and his election as chairman is evidence of the respect he has won for integrity of character, honesty and intelligence. He has largely overcome the traits of sensitiveness and quick temper, which brought him many difficulties during his early years here. He now handles himself very well, and with a start in a new environment should win popularity as well as respect.*

The Duke failed to mention *why* I had a quick temper during my first two years at Hotchkiss. He had more than an inkling that anti-Semitism was the match that lit my short fuse. In my sophomore year, after a particularly public skirmish, I had been summoned to his office, where I told him about the anti-Semitic harassment by my classmates. Perhaps he willfully forgot about it, or maybe he didn't want to spread the word on to Harvard about what was going on under his watch.

Still painfully intact is a memory from 1945, during the second half of my freshman year. In fact, it arguably set me on the course for what I think of as my life's work. World War II was mercifully coming to an end. The concentration camp in Auschwitz had been liberated that January. On a Saturday night we all gathered in the old auditorium where we were treated to weekly movies. As we settled in, the Movietone newsreel began. A basso profundo voice narrated as the first pictures of the Holocaust death camps flickered across the screen. The horrors of what had been going on in the camps washed over me with harrowing reality. It also occurred to me that some of those tortured, emaciated bodies could be my relatives. At the end of these devastating scenes—and to my utter shock—a cheer went up and obnoxious comments rippled through the audience.

Afterward, a group of classmates approached me. "We don't like Hitler," one of them sneered, "but at least he's killing the Jews."

The anti-Semitic cloud that surrounded me that night was a prelude of the torment to come. I pretended not to hear the snickered insults, but of course they pierced me

Summer holidays frequently included a trip to Playland, an amusement park in Rye, not far from Purchase. The park offered an opportunity for Ann, Arthur and me to forget about school, get into Dutch costumes and have a picture taken, as we did here in 1946.

to my core. I said nothing; I simply walked away with anger churning inside of me. I focused on my studies, and at the end of the year I wound up being second in the class, winning honors and the English prize. But being a "grind" only added to my unpopularity.

I had persistently complained to my parents about the anti-Semitic atmosphere at Hotchkiss. At first they thought I was exaggerating, but they eventually believed me, as did my beloved Granny Adeline Loeb. Granny offered me a way to cope with the insults and occasional physical assaults. In her Alabama drawl, dripping with elongated vowels, she told me one of her family stories.

"Darling Johnny," she said, "when your great-granddaddy went off to the Civil War as a captain in the Confederacy"—she never failed to mention his rank—"he met someone who called him a 'dirty Jew.' So your

Home movies taken in 1945, when I was fifteen. Eddie Galorie is teaching me to box to help protect me against anti-Semitic assaults at school.

great-granddaddy just knocked that man down. Afterwards, they became best friends. What you must do the next time anybody insults you, just sock him!"

I wasn't sure I would ever become best friends with any of my tormentors, but I certainly liked the "sock 'em" part of Granny's advice. So much for the turn-the-other-cheek business we heard about at weekly chapel. If Granny Adeline thought it was okay to hit back, that's what I would do. There was just one problem: I wasn't very athletic, and I really didn't know how to fight. So I went to Father, a fighter in his youth, who came to my aid in his typically practical way.*

In the summer between my first and second years at Hotchkiss, Father hired one of the older "runners"— company messengers—from Loeb, Rhoades to teach me how to fight. Eddie Galorie had at one time been a moderately successful featherweight boxer. Galorie, who had two cauliflower ears from doing so much fighting in his youth, showed me how to strengthen muscles I didn't even know I had. I acquired quickness on my feet, learned how to duck and weave, and emerged from the summer with a good bit of confidence, which might have been more important than any skill. When it was time to return to school for my sophomore year, I was spoiling for a fight.

On the way out of chapel on my first day back, I felt a deliberate shove from behind. As one of my tormentors started to pass me, I heard him hiss close to my ear: "Dirty Jew." Without missing a beat, I turned around and slugged him. In a second we were going at it, and, just as quickly, we were escorted to the Duke's office. A beneficent soul, the headmaster was "surprised" to hear that there was anti-Semitism on the campus. He was very pro-Jewish, he said, as he puffed on his pipe from behind

---

* Father's sister, my aunt Margaret, told me that he had been a somewhat bellicose young man, given to resolving conflicts with his fists. She wrote about the night he and David Sulzberger (of *The New York Times* Sulzbergers) got in an altercation at a Century Club dance, and my father knocked David down. Aunt Margaret reports, "Mother [Granny Adeline] heard about it and was not at all pleased. She said, 'John, how could a son of mine, a southern gentleman, do that?' John replied, 'But Mother, I had to! He called me a son of a bitch.' Mother answered, 'How could he? He doesn't even know me!'" Granny Adeline had a not totally unwarranted reputation for being a bit literal-minded.

My senior year I became chairman of the *Hotchkiss Record* editorial board. I am pictured in the front row, center. Also in the front row, second boy from the right (apparently yawning), is my good friend Peter Sharp. Another very good friend, Dan Lufkin, stands in the second row, third boy in from the right.

his desk. He rambled on about my wonderful family, especially my great-uncle Senator Herbert Lehman. Our reprimand turned into a monologue from the headmaster, which had nothing to do with why we'd been called there in the first place. I received no dressing down for starting the fight, but neither was my opponent rebuked for lighting the fuse.

There were so many fights as the year progressed that finally some of the teachers decided on an unorthodox solution. In the fall of 1946, they proposed that the hecklers' ringleader and I don boxing gloves for a supervised fight in the gymnasium. He was a fellow from Montana named George Nelson. What made the faculty think this would stop the anti-Jewish sentiment in the school, I haven't the slightest idea. Nevertheless, I was delighted to accept the challenge.

The fight was attended only by Peter Beaumont (the boxing coach and a French teacher), who acted as referee, George, myself and two classmates, who acted as seconds. There were three one-minute rounds, and we were evenly matched. As we fought, members of the Lower Mid-Class banged on the doors, trying to get in. By the third round, it was a draw. By some miracle I landed a blow right under George's eye. When my tormentor emerged sporting the bruise that developed into a black eye, word got around that I had won. As it turned out, the fight succeeded in curtailing the most overt bullying. It was the beginning of the end of the taunts; my opponent and I did not become best friends, but the next year and a half was relatively fight-free.

Members of the student council posed for a portrait in 1948. I am standing in the second row, second from the left. My nemesis, George Nelson, president of the student council, evidently well recovered from the black eye I gave him, sits at the center of the desk.

A half-century later I learned that the incident left an indelible memory with my fellow student Al Silberman, who was the Jewish "second" at the fight. "At that time, anti-Semitism was quite open and prevalent and unfortunately not particularly discouraged by the headmaster," he wrote. "Although I have not seen John Loeb since graduation, I have always carried admiration for him for standing up for himself . . . in a rather hostile environment."[67]

The boxing match provided me with some breathing room—if not the respect of most of my peers—and I was able to focus on things I enjoyed, especially working on the *Hotchkiss Record*. By senior year I had become chairman of the editorial board, as well as a member of the student council. When I was made editor in chief, all my competitors in the class for that position refused to work for me and resigned en masse. The grade beneath us stepped up to the challenge, and we all worked well together.

Seemingly a magnet for controversy, I found myself embroiled in another one. My problem began when the *Record*'s editorial writer, Peter Sharp, with whom I had a great rapport, wrote a piece that was critical of the headmaster and the faculty. After publication of the controversial editorial, the *Record*'s faculty advisor demanded that the student council reprimand Peter. Nettled, I announced that, as chairman of the editorial board, *I* should be the one to accept any punishment, but I also asserted that the editorial required no apology. The advisor, Mr. Bodell, and I had a heated debate in front of the student council, during which he called me a "word weasler" (I later looked it up in the dictionary and found that it means a type of slander using words in an ambiguous or misleading way). In the end, Peter and I were both dressed down by the council in what I viewed as a blatant infringement of freedom of the press. This was one of my earliest forays into defending the First Amendment, a track I would find myself quite comfortable on in the years ahead.

At the next student council meeting, a motion for impeachment was brought against me for "conduct unbecoming a member of the student council"—specifically for being a "word weasler"—which upset me enormously. I left that meeting, found a place on campus where no one could see me, and burst into tears. I then walked to Mr. Bodell's house and knocked on his door.

"What's wrong?" he asked me.

"This is all your fault," I announced, "you called me a word weasler!"

The impeachment never happened, and two positive after-effects came out of that dispute: my further bonding with Peter Sharp, and my lifelong commitment to public vigilance regarding freedom of the press.

During my senior year, I became convinced that I wanted to become a journalist. While working on the *Record*, I had the opportunity to interview one of my idols, the journalist John Hersey. Hersey covered the war in Europe and Asia for *Time, Life* and

I was thrilled to have a role in *A Bell for Adano*, adapted as a play from the novel written by Hotchkiss alum John Hersey, class of '32. Pictured here, I am at the left, with my good friend Dan Lufkin. He became a founder of a famous investment firm, Donaldson, Lufkin and Jenrette.

The New Yorker. A member of the Hotchkiss class of '32, Hersey wrote many books; the most famous, *A Bell for Adano,* won the Pulitzer Prize in 1945. His powerful *New Yorker* short story "Hiroshima" caused a worldwide sensation in 1946, not only for its content but also for its technique. Hersey's form of "New Journalism" combined "the momentum of fiction" with the voices of witnesses and facts, as in a documentary.[68] His story about six victims of the atomic bomb dropped on that Japanese city by the United States on August 6, 1945, was powerful and deeply affecting.

With a bit of detective work, I learned when Hersey would be coming to New York City. The Duke made an introduction for me, and Hersey agreed to an interview at the University Club in Manhattan. Over lunch in January 1947, he went far beyond just letting me interview him. While I was writing the story, he was my mentor, providing encouragement and editorial advice. The experience fired up my youthful aspirations. My future was clear. I would not be an actor, as I'd dreamed at Harvey. I would be a journalist who traveled the world—and perhaps helped change it.

I never did become well liked at Hotchkiss. I was a nerd without much of a sense of humor or

Here I am in a Hotchkiss school play. I once thought seriously about becoming a professional actor but wisely abandoned that plan.

athleticism who was destined never to become "one of the boys." I felt so unpopular that I never invited a girl to one of the school dances.

When I was fifteen, I wistfully noticed that many of my classmates received letters from young ladies with whom they were "going steady."* My mailbox was empty, so I asked my resourceful mother to "please find me a girlfriend." She suggested Mary Rodgers, a neighbor who lived upstairs from my parents at their Park Avenue apart-

---

* That year at Grandmother Lehman's New Year's Eve Party, I mentioned to her about "going steady." She instantly replied, "Don't worry, Johnny, only the help go steady."

Mary Rodgers, who wrote songs and children's books and by virtue of genetics and serendipity as well as talent, lived at the red-hot center of American musical theater until she died in 2014.

ment. I didn't know who Mary was until Mother commented that "now you'll have a personal entrée to all those wonderful Rodgers and Hammerstein musicals." Mother, who loved the theater, no doubt had enlightened self-interest in promoting Mary as a potential girlfriend. She was the daughter of the famous Broadway composer Richard Rodgers.

When I came home for the Christmas holidays, Mary and I were introduced, so I had a date to my Grandmother Lehman's traditional New Year's Eve party. When the clock struck midnight, I gave her a chaste peck on the cheek. After I returned to school we started our correspondence, which went smoothly until I summoned the courage to ask if she would be my girlfriend. Her answer was a definite and resounding "No."

"Okay, but I'm not going to write you anymore," I countered.

Fortunately, she changed her mind, agreed to be my girlfriend, and our letters flowed for some time. Mary ended up marrying my future brother-in-law's brother, Julian Beaty, and we managed to stay in touch through the years, exchanging letters from time to time. I followed her successful career in the musical world (she wrote the music for *Once Upon a Mattress*) until she died in 2014.

A couple of years before she died, Mary wrote me the most adorable letter. I have included part of it here:

I was home in Purchase the summer of 1946 when this family photo was taken. Ann, seated on the lawn, holds one of our many family dachshunds. Mother holds our youngest sister, Debby, who had been born in February of that year. Father looks on very lovingly, as Arthur, Judy and I smile for the camera.

So here's what I remember about us: My first kiss at your grandmother's party. Our letters back and forth and how much I looked forward to them. One, in particular, in which you allowed how you were kind of lonely. Two peas in a pod we were — I was the daughter of a famous Broadway composer, but you had never heard of him. You were the scion of one of the most distinguished German Jewish families in America, and I'd never heard of you!

Despite the prevalent anti-Semitism, I began to emerge in the eyes of old-guard WASPs as someone desirable to have around. On my rare weekends and holidays at home in New York, I was busy attending dancing classes and parties for budding socialites. I went to a Jewish dancing class on Park Avenue, where the girls wore short white gloves and the boys wore jackets and ties. It was run by a memorable lady named Viola Wolff, who was captured by the author Anne Roiphe in her memoir, *1185 Park Avenue.* "Viola Wolff was a large woman with a heaving breast," Roiphe wrote, "long purple satin gowns and gold and silver rings on her fingers and lavender powder on her upswept hair."[69] As the nucleus of the Manhattan Jewish social scene for teenagers, Viola Wolff had an impact on the futures of a few of my relations.

At Viola Wolff's I met a girl named Joan Mack, whom I dated for about six months. I liked her so much I invited her to come to one of Grandma Lehman's New Year's Eve

My siblings Ann, Arthur and Judy as teenagers at the time my baby sister Deborah was born.

parties. After the New Year rang in, Joan and I accompanied Bobby Bernhard[*] and his date, Nancy Bookman, to Nancy's apartment. All I remember is that in the early morning hours, Bobby ended up with Joan and I ended up with Nancy. Bobby and Joan stayed together for a number of years until he met Franny Wells, heiress to a vast fortune.[†] Joan ended up going out with Tom Kempner, my cousin on the Loeb side; he would marry Nan Schlesinger, and she would marry Barrie Sommerfield. Years later, after Joan and Bobby each divorced, they reunited and got married.

It was also at a Viola Wolff party that my sister Ann met her future husband, Edgar Bronfman. Edgar was from a family that was considered "not appropriate" at the time. During Prohibition, before Edgar was born, his family made their huge fortune bringing liquor into the U.S. from Canada. Father was hesitant about the union, particularly because the Bronfmans were Russian Jews. I remember Father asking me once what I thought of Edgar, and I said, "You know, I have one poor WASP brother-in-law, I would really like a rich Jewish one." According to Stephen Birmingham, my grandfather C.M. was overheard to say at Ann's wedding, "Now I know what it feels like to be a poor relation." In the five decades since, due to the Bronfmans' accomplishments and philanthropy, they became one of the leading families of New York.

---

* Bobby Bernhard, my older first cousin on the Lehman side.

† Her father, George Wells, ran the American Optical Company, and her family had built Old Sturbridge Village, a re-creation of a postcolonial New England town.

No matter what their impact would be on my future family tree, I wasn't satisfied with Ms. Wolff's classes and dances. I'd heard how much more "relaxed" and "freer" the girls were at the Christian dance parties. Hotchkiss boys went to these dances over the holidays, and though I wasn't friendly with most of my classmates, I nevertheless wanted to be invited. I found out that one's parents orchestrated invitations to these parties, so I told my mother that I wanted her to phone the lady in charge of the invitee list. Mrs. Brown* controlled the social list not just for these dances, but for other socialite gatherings as well. Because Mrs. Brown had social standing, Mother was less accommodating.

"You can't go to the parties," she said flatly.

"Why not?"

"Because you're Jewish," she said, as if it were the most obvious fact in the world.

I could not accept this so easily. "Have you ever asked?" I inquired.

"No."

"Well ask!" I demanded.

"No," my mother said. "I won't put myself in that position."

I was so persistent that Mother finally gave in. She sat in our library as she called the arbiter of my future social life. I noticed tiny little beads of wetness on her forehead and heard her voice acquire a phony quasi-English accent. Was my formidable mother actually *sweating* over a phone call?

"Mrs. Brown? Oh good! This is Mrs. John Loeb. I understand you have a guest list for parties organized for young people here in New York . . . and some of my son John's classmates at Hotchkiss come to them . . . and it would be very nice. . . ." (Pause.) "Yes, he would like to go to. . . ." (Pause.) "Now, how would we go about this?" (Another pause. I was on tenterhooks.) "Yes! Oh, thank you," Mother said, "we'll see you then."

Mother hung up gently, as though in shock, and turned to me. "We're invited for tea with Mrs. Brown next Tuesday."

Victory!

The following week, both of us anxious, we visited Mrs. Brown's modest apartment. She looked like the wives of Hotchkiss teachers or a younger version of TV's Miss Marple. She peppered me with questions about school: Did I like it? What were my interests? What did I like to read? It was all polite and formal. Finally, she thanked

---

* This is not her real name.

MY SCULPTURES

At Hotchkiss, I discovered a latent talent in a private sculpture class, and I became quite serious about sculpting for the next ten years.

The private class in my teens was an idea that grew out of my goal of getting nothing but good grades. Having a tin ear, I knew I'd do poorly in the required music appreciation class. I suggested to the faculty that I study sculpture instead, since at the time I was seriously interested in becoming a doctor. Happily, there was a teacher willing to give me a private sculpture class: Tom Blagden, the head of the art department. I not only loved sculpting, but I was considered to be a rare talent by both my teacher and my classmates, and received the coveted highest grade.

I'm not sure why I chose biblical themes, but I was very aware of being Jewish. Perhaps Old Testament stories heard at chapel were on my mind.

Moses breaking the first tablets of the Ten Commandments.
(Deuteronomy 9)

126

Angel saving Abraham's beloved son Isaac from sacrifice.
(Genesis 22)

Among other pieces, I produced these two clay sculptures at Hotchkiss. But the clay molds couldn't be finished because the school didn't have casting facilities.

I continued sculpting in my twenties in New York City at a place called the Sculpture Center. This is the only piece that I still have.

Some of my anti-Semitic experience at Hotchkiss was included in a book about the school by Ernest Kolowrat, published in 1992. It was only as an adult that I came to appreciate my education there.

name. Their marriage and her lapse into a twenty-eight-year coma would become infamous, covered by the newspapers and turned into a book by Alan Dershowitz, as well as a film—both titled *Reversal of Fortune*. Subsequently, Claus worked for Mark Millard at Loeb, Rhoades, and we occasionally run into each other at the Brooks Club in London, where we are both members.

Though girls weren't a big part of my life at Hotchkiss, I was still interested in sex. To that end, I was fortunate enough to have Carlos Delgado as my roommate. Carlos was half French and half Brazilian and, in my eyes, supremely sophisticated. I was delighted when Carlos took it upon himself to oversee my sex education. During one school holiday, while both at our respective homes in New York City, Carlos phoned with an adventurous idea. We would visit the Copacabana night club, where we'd get a first-class education in . . . well, everything. The Copa, which was only a few years old at the time, was a mysterious and exciting place, rumored to be bankrolled by the Mob. This made the idea of visiting it all the more titillating. In its heyday the Copa featured big-name entertainers, but Carlos promised that there would also be girls, wearing not much if anything at all. It sounded wonderfully decadent, and I said yes to Carlos's plans with enthusiasm.

On the evening of the planned caper, I told my parents I was retiring early to read. I left pillows tucked under the covers and snuck out of our Park Avenue apartment. I was supposed to meet Carlos at the Copa, nearby on East 60th Street. We had difficulty getting in. When we finally did, we couldn't get a seat close enough to see what we were there for. On top of which, the girls were neither nude nor very attractive. Their dance costumes were skimpy but not all that revealing. The entire evening was a huge disappointment and not worth the worry about being caught, which we were.

When Carlos's mother discovered that he wasn't at home, she phoned my mother. Mother checked my room, discovered the pillows and reported that neither of us were there. When I came home around midnight, Mother was waiting up. She was very upset with me, and as I slunk off to bed she said, more important than anything, if I ever went off like that again, I must leave word.

Father's reaction was notably different. The next morning, Father phoned me from the office and asked whether I'd had a good time.

I braced for a serious lecture. "No, not really," I mumbled inaudibly.

"Well," he said cheerfully, "I suppose you're old enough to go to nightclubs," and hung up. No wages of sin were paid that time. Like the incident with the cigarettes, Father didn't lay into me when I thought he would. Father could be a cold man, but he was surprisingly forgiving. He was a mystery in that regard. I left Hotchkiss well prepared for college, with a *cum laude* attached to my diploma. I graduated ready to cope with the real world, especially because of my brushes with anti-Semitism, which were downright personal. Although those experiences were painful and isolating at times, that period would end up shaping so much of my adult life. Ironically, in doing their best to turn me into a WASP, my parents pushed me the other way. My experiences at both Harvey and Hotchkiss and the anti-Semitism I faced during those years gave me a strong sense of Jewish identity, which has only deepened over the years.

A roving photographer with a sense of humor shot this picture of the Loeb family on our way to a royal tea at Buckingham Palace. My mother and father led the way, followed by me and my sister Ann, while an unimpressed British moppet kept on jumping rope. This photo appeared on the front page of the *Liverpool Daily Post* on July 22, 1949. Cousins of mine named Stern still in the cotton business, who live outside of Liverpool, saw the article and sent it to us.

CHAPTER FOUR

≡

Harvard Is Heaven,
1948–1952

It never entered my mind that I would go to any college but Harvard. My grandfather Arthur Lehman had gone there, as had my father. It was the only school I even applied to, confident that my legacy, grades and extracurricular activities would get me accepted. Nevertheless, I still felt anxious, given my anti-Semitic experience at Hotchkiss. Even Harvard, which had been relatively open to Jewish students, was influenced by the swell of anti-Semitism in the United States after World War I. In 1922, after Harvard's president A. Lawrence Lowell prescribed a 15 percent limit for the admission of Jews, Harvard's overseers organized a committee to discuss Harvard's "Jewish problem." President Lowell thought that Harvard's student body needed to reflect the kind of people who lived in the United States, and he did not want Jews—who regularly had the highest test scores—to disproportionately represent his institution.

Traditionally chosen from New England prep schools such as Groton, St. Mark's and St. Paul's, Harvard applicants also included top students from public schools all over the country. The influx of public school students was largely due to the development of the SAT test in the 1920s, which was born from educators' desire to democratically reach out to the whole country. With so much competition, my nervousness was not unwarranted.

My acceptance letter arrived the same week as my sister Judy's wedding to Richard Beaty. Richard was a handsome World War II hero who had been shot down three times overseas and was one of only two survivors of his thirty-man unit. He was a member of the Eagle Squadron, made up of American and Canadian pilots who wanted to participate in the war before America got involved. After the war, Richard had been getting his law degree at Columbia when one summer he got a job looking after

My brother-in-law's Eagle Squadron helped win the Battle of Britain. Afterward,
Churchill said, "Never in the field of human conflict was so much owed by so many to so few."
On Dick's right is Harry Hopkins, FDR's closest friend. His daughter was at the Potomac School with
my sister Ann. Late in the war years Hopkins was secretary of commerce.

our Buttenwieser cousins. We all went together to hear an orchestra play Gershwin
at Lewisohn Stadium, which is where Judy
and Dick met. Judy* was a virgin when they
got married. Since Judy and I were great
friends I couldn't resist asking her about her
wedding night. "Oh, it went just great," she
remarked. Dick would become a partner at
Loeb, Rhoades, and he and Judy would go
on to become a glamorous couple in investment banking circles.

I look pretty frisky in this shot of my sister
Judy (center) and her bridesmaids. My sister
Ann (second from the right) was one of her
attendants.

I had never set foot in Cambridge, Mas-
sachusetts, prior to enrolling that fall, but once there I knew I was home. "Harvard is
heaven, Hotchkiss hell," I wrote my father. After nine years of being harassed, shunned

---

* Judy was always full of life and had many boyfriends, including a distant blood cousin of ours, "Punch" Sulzberger.
  The Sulzbergers have owned *The New York Times* since 1896.

My unit of the ROTC stood on the steps of Widener Hall for this picture, taken in the spring of 1952. Left: This close-up of me was enlarged from the group ROTC picture. I graduated with the ROTC citation "Distinguished Military Graduate." Right: This headshot of my dear, dear friend and fellow cadet George W. Miller III is also an enlargement from our ROTC portrait. He was leader of our ROTC unit and became my roommate at the Harvard Business School.

Widener Hall, which houses one of the world's most comprehensive libraries, is a thing of glory to see, especially in the early fall, which is when I first glimpsed it.

and attacked at boarding schools for being Jewish, I was immediately embraced into the Harvard mainstream. Admittedly, there was another reason Harvard seemed divine. Radcliffe College, Wellesley College and a half dozen other schools were nearby, teeming with fascinating girls who were allowed in our dorm rooms—as long as doors were kept open and the couple kept "three feet on the floor."[70]

Brenton Creelman, a classmate from Hotchkiss, and I were compatible roommates that first year in a spacious suite at Thayer North, a large men's dorm located in Harvard Yard. By the end of my first year, I had become good friends with Roy Goodman, who took excellent notes. I was sure his were better than mine, so I asked to read his before our final history exam. Always a good sport, Roy didn't complain when I got an A and he a B plus.*

From the beginning, I loved Harvard's intellectual atmosphere and the feeling that every student was accepted; everyone from the captain of the football team to the president of the butterfly association was welcomed on that campus. I found my courses interesting and inspiring, especially history—a fascination that would last my whole life. For my major, I chose government (often referred to today as political science) with a focus on political philosophy and comparative institutions.

When I arrived at Harvard in the fall of 1948 as a freshman, I had actually never seen a Harvard building or campus. My father had graduated in 1924. Mother's father, my grandfather Arthur Lehman, graduated in 1896. Because I was a very good student and had these two legacies, I guess my parents thought I was a shoo-in. They never got anyone to write a letter on my behalf. They'd never spoken to anyone at Harvard, and they had never bothered to take me to see the place.

Much to my surprise, I found a building there named Lehman Hall, given by my grandfather Arthur Lehman on his 30th graduation reunion. Coincidentally, it was given in 1924, the year my father graduated from Harvard College.

However, the name Lehman was not on the building when I arrived. During the next six years, at Harvard College and Harvard Business School, I made significant efforts to have my grandfather's name put on the building. Whether by oversight or not, this wasn't done until 1954, the year I graduated from HBS.

Years later, my sister Judy and other members of the family were at Loeb House for an event in honor of my late parents. Lawrence Summers, then the president of Harvard, and a former U.S. secretary of the treasury, hosted us in a very casual lunch,

---

* Roy later became a powerful Republican, serving in the New York State Senate from 1969 to 2002.

one not given in a very gracious or warm manner. After the event, Judy and I walked to see the Lehman building. Much to our surprise, underneath the name Lehman Hall was the name Dudley House. A Dudley had been the second governor in Massachusetts in 1630. A half dozen of the dreariest portraits of his family had been hung in the building. It was to be a home at Harvard College for students who were day students, not boarders. Adding insult to injury, the Lehman name had been covered over altogether.

Again, I complained strongly to Harvard's administration, asking that the name Dudley be removed. I was turned down. I did, however, have large portraits of Grandmother and Grandfather painted, which are now in the front hall of Lehman Hall/ Dudley House.

Early in my freshman year, I joined the Reserve Officers Training Corps (ROTC). By 1951 the Cold War tensions predicted by my Hotchkiss French teacher were coming to fruition, so it seemed wise to get some military training. We had to march up and down the football field and do simple maneuvers, but I can't say any of these activities equipped me to face a war zone. In ROTC, I met George W. Miller III, who re-

A recent photo of Lehman Hall, given by my grandfather, Arthur Lehman, Class of 1896. Now known as Lehman Hall/Dudley House.

mained a close friend of mine for his entire life. (Sadly, he died in 2015.) George made the rank of major general before he retired from the Air Force. He worked with me at Loeb, Rhoades in the 1950s, and later at the Pentagon.

Having been successful at the Harvey School as editor of *The Rambler* and as chairman of the *Hotchkiss Record*, I yearned for a place on the staff of the *Harvard Crimson,* Harvard's legendary daily newspaper. The competition for these positions was fierce, and even if I were accepted, the *Crimson* would take too much time away from my studies. I instead tried for the *Harvard Lampoon,* a publication that touted itself as "the world's oldest continuously published humor magazine." The *Lampoon,* modeled after Britain's *Punch,* was considered a social club as well as a literary magazine, so exclusivity might apply. "Either you will get in or you won't," my father advised, "but stick it out." I did and was accepted, to my great relief and delight. A few

I can identify only some of the members of the *Lampoon* in this staff portrait: In the first row, second from the left, is Charlie Flood, who wrote his first novel at the age of twenty-three. In the center is our chairman, Fred Gwynne; next is Peter Dixon, my Harvey School roommate. Last in the first row is Dick Storey, who carried me back to my dorm after a wild *Lampoon* initiation party; In the second row is Michael Arlen, my roommate while living at Apley Court. I appear in the top row, fifth from the left.

William
Randolph
Hearst

The appropriately whimsical-looking home of the *Harvard Lampoon* was designed by one of the satirical publication's founders, Edmund Wheelwright. The building opened in 1909. This building was a gift of William Randolph Hearst. Hearst was a member of the *Lampoon*.

months after going to work at the *Lampoon*, I found out that I was the first Jew ever admitted to the staff.

At the *Lampoon*'s initiation party, I got sloshed, for the first and almost last time in my life. The initiates had to chug an unidentified mix while standing on a bench until we could no longer stay on it. Fellow initiate Dick Storey carried me back to Thayer North that night. I don't know how he was able to navigate that trip, since he was quite drunk as well.

Another *Lampoon* initiation tradition was "Fool's Week," when outrageous stunts had to be carried out by the initiates—the "Fools." Inspired by the World Federalism[*] movement sweeping the campus, our group decided that the *Lampoon* building, situated on a little triangular island in mid-campus, should secede not only from Harvard

---

* World Federalists did not (and still do not) approve of the UN, thinking it too much like the League of Nations. Therefore, they formed their own, more ambitious organization, backed by such well-known figures as Alan Cranston and Norman Cousins.

Kitty Carlisle Hart was the emcee for the Lehman College Leadership award given to me in 1997. A nationally known writer, actress and arts advocate, Kitty was also a close Loeb family friend.

Author George Plimpton brought down the house with his roast of me at the Lehman College award dinner.

mouth and graduated from Harvard in 1924 and had not gone back all of those years. Nor had he given a penny to Harvard University. He got on a train and went up to Harvard to see what this business of social probation was, and he went in to see the dean—a man called Bill Bender, a man of immense charm.

Nobody knows quite what happened between Mr. Loeb and Mr. Bender, but subsequently, over the years, Mr. Loeb gave Harvard University $150,000,000. All of that, of course, is John's money!

So you can see that John rues the day that he became a Lampooner.

George Plimpton neglected to add that Father's contributions to Harvard did not get me off probation, though George was right that a good chunk of money that might have come my way went to Harvard.*

Social probation notwithstanding, being elected to the *Lampoon* gave me a status

---

* At my parents' respective funerals, former Harvard president Neil Rudenstine mentioned that their gifts had been the largest in Harvard's history.

boost at Harvard, and I was no longer perceived as a square. After years of being considered a Goody Two-shoes and a nerd, I enjoyed all the benefits of my new image.

The summer after my first year at Harvard, Mother, Father, Arthur and Ann (the twins) and I took a mini "grand tour." On the day of my last exam in May 1949, we were to sail for Europe on the *Queen Mary* and planned to visit France, England, Belgium and Holland. I had permission from Harvard to take the test that morning at my Lehman grandparents' townhouse at 45 East 70th Street, with a monitor keeping an eye on me. Rumors flew that I had taken the exam on board the *Queen Mary* itself.

This trip was one of the best experiences of my life. It was the first and only time I traveled with both of my parents, as well as with Arthur and Ann. Life in first class was one big party, during which I competed for the attention of a glamorous twenty-nine-year-old actress named Ella Raines. I had been hearing about Europe all of my life because of my parents' vivid descriptions of their trips before World War II. I would finally see it all for myself. We landed in Cherbourg, France, and then boarded the train to Paris, where we stayed at the historic Hôtel de Crillon. Each of us children had our own room. Arthur and I, with our voracious teenage appetites, were so taken by the hotel's savory cuisine that we ordered two lunches one day, an extravagance that really upset Father, who rarely fussed about expense.

On our second day in Paris, Guy, Alain and Élie de Rothschild all showed up in my parents' suite. Alain and Élie's father, Robert, had recently died, and they had come to ask Father for professional help liquidating Robert's estate. My parents were particularly close to Guy, who had been my parents' guest in Washington, D.C., during the war. Alain later

Baron Élie de Rothschild

Baron Guy de Rothschild

Baron Alain de Rothschild

Two friends, Jack Rosenthal and Veronique Honoree, joined me (at the left), Arthur and Ann (in the center) outside the Hôtel de Crillon for a sightseeing trip around Paris.

introduced me to his daughter, Beatrice, a tall, attractive and extremely bright girl. She and I would go out together a few times while I was in Paris, but it didn't turn into a romance.[*†]

My first taste of England made me an Anglophile permanently. In 1949, England was nearing the end of King George VI's sixteen-year reign. I remember a cocktail party at the embassy where Paul "Piggy" Warburg jokingly pulled Princess Margaret down on his lap for a moment. It was at this cocktail party that I first met the Duke of Marlborough, then called the Marquess of Blandford (also known as "Sunny"). He was flirting with Susan Mary Hornby, who became his first wife. Princess Margaret caused quite a stir by dancing the cancan with "Charmin' Sharmin" Douglas, who was the daughter of the U.S. ambassador to England. There was another party where everyone came dressed as fictional characters; Mother, Father and I all dressed as characters out of Dickens. I met Princess Elizabeth (the soon-to-be queen) and the Duke of Edinburgh, who came dressed as a maid and a butler, which caused a serious outcry in England among the actual maids and butlers.

It was a time of recovery, with the war over, its aftermath fading and the rationing of

---

*Alain's son, Eric, brought a bottle of 1902 Lafite-Rothschild wine from Europe in 1992 for Father's ninetieth birthday and would play a role in advising me on my own wines.

† Élie helped Alain and Guy rebuild the Rothschild Frères investment bank and its Companie des Chemins de Fer du Nord (on whose board I served for a number of years). In 1946, Élie took charge of Chateau Lafite-Rothschild, the premier Cru Pauillac vineyard in the Médoc. Élie's nephew by marriage (his mother's sister was Élie's wife), Felipe Propper, was the son of Eduardo Propper de Callejon, a Spanish diplomat to France. Eduardo used his immunity to save valuable art and provide Jews fleeing the Holocaust transit visas through Spain to Portugal. Ambassador Propper received the "Righteous Among Nations" award from Israel, and he was honored by the Wallenberg Foundation as well. Loeb, Rhoades did quite a bit of business with the Rothschilds through Felipe, who later became a partner at the firm.

things like clothing and chocolate phased out. We were welcomed in England by old friends who had stayed at Ridgeleigh with the Bernhards during World War II, the Courage family and Barbara D'Almeida, the widow of Baron Antonio D'Almeida (who had once been head of the Loeb, Rhoades office in Paris). After the baron's death, Barbara had married Father's close friend Paul Warburg. The couple was living in London at the time we were there. Paul was then the right-hand man to Lewis Douglas, U.S. ambassador to the United Kingdom. Barbara and Paul arranged an invitation for us to a royal tea party at Buckingham Palace.

Lewis Douglas

Thanks to a lovely "older woman" (all of twenty-eight), I left the British Isles no longer a virgin. Jean Dawnay was a top Dior model on the British scene.* Ours was a short romance, but neither of us has ever forgotten it.

Shortly after Father's death in 1996, I ran into Jean (now Princess Galitzine) in London. We shared a cab to Claridge's, where she told me that before he died, Father had promised a substantial contribution for the Prince George Galitzine Memorial Library in St. Petersburg. She asked if I would honor his pledge? I answered that, of course, I would give her "something."

Jean Dawnay

Princess Galitzine with me and my son, Nicholas, at Lord William Dartmouth's cocktail party for me at the House of Lords in 1999.

---

* In 1956, Jean Dawnay published *Model Girl*, a popular book about her successful modeling career in the early 1950s. Friend and muse to Sir Terrence Rattigan, Jean inspired the role of Sibyl Railton-Bell in his play *Separate Tables*.

Then I turned to Jean and said, "I'm very upset with you." "Why," she asked, with open eyes. "Because you had a fling with my own father," I answered. She grabbed my hand, overcome with emotion, burst into tears and said, "I loved you both!"

My family was scheduled to return to New York, but I wanted more time in France. My parents were reluctant to let me stay in Europe by myself, but their good friend Nancy Mitford* (one of the six celebrated Mitford sisters and a successful author) persuaded them to let me enroll in the French language school at the university in Grenoble. Nancy also put me in touch with her nephew, the Honorable Desmond Guinness, who lived in Grenoble. I wrote him, asking for help to find an affordable flat, since Father had given me a limited budget. Desmond wrote back immediately and said he'd found one, so I went to Grenoble and found the address: 19 Avenue Conte.

Baggage in hand, I rode up in the rickety elevator and knocked at the door. When it opened, there stood a small, gorgeous blond boy with dramatic blue eyes. It was the Hon. Desmond Guinness, whom I judged to be about seventeen and all of five foot six. Though I was only nineteen, I nevertheless felt as though I were meeting a young child. I'd barely crossed the threshold when he informed me that he loved the flat so much and that he wanted to keep it for himself. He promised to find me another and did. Desmond and I became great friends; he was likely the most popular young man in Grenoble at the time. Grenoble social climbers were clamoring to meet the aristocrat. He was the *Honorable* Desmond Guinness,† a title whose importance I didn't quite recognize at the time.

Desmond's mother was Diana Mitford, the former wife of Bryan Guinness of the brewery Guinness family. At the time I met Desmond she was married to Oswald Mosley, who had been a leading fascist in prewar England.‡ Desmond was planning to visit his mother and stepfather, so he'd gone shopping and returned with a dozen long-sleeved black shirts. When I asked why so many shirts, he explained that the pro-Hitlerites in England were called "Black Shirts," and he thought the shirts would please his pro-Hitler stepfather. My

---

* Nancy Mitford and Gaston Palewski were lovers. Palewski was a colonel in the Free French Army under President Charles de Gaulle, and later his director of the Cabinet—he was de Gaulle's right-hand man.

† Desmond Guinness, a lifelong friend, founded the Irish Georgian Society. Coincidentally, sixty-seven years later, I attended an Irish Georgian Society dinner at the Metropolitan Club in New York City. It was 2016, and Sir David Davies, my former brother-in-law, had become chairman of the society.

‡ Oswald Mosley, once a member of Parliament, organized a group called the "New Party," which later merged with the British Union of Fascists (BUF), whose members wore black shirts—hence they were called "Black Shirts." Considered a British Nazi, Mosley was interned in 1940 but released in 1943, remaining under house arrest for some time. Eventually, he moved abroad and lived in France until his death in 1980.

Nancy Mitford   Charles de Gaulle   Desmond Guinness

European tour was providing a much more liberal education than I'd bargained for.

I stayed on in Grenoble at another flat for about a month, working on my French at the university. I was pleased with my progress until I said to my teacher, "Madame, maintenant, je parle français."

"Monsieur Loeb," she responded, "vous parlez, mais vous ne parlez pas français" (Mr. Loeb, you speak, but you do not speak French).

I received a letter from Veronique Honoree, a French girl I had met at the break after "Long"–Longchamp Racecourse—earlier in my visit. "I hope you will come and visit me," she wrote, words that I took to mean, "and of course you'll stay with me." I bid au revoir to Grenoble, taking a bus from the mountains to the Mediterranean.

I arrived at Veronique's place, luggage in hand, a smile on my face. When she opened the door, I was stunned. A somewhat older, handsome man towered possessively behind her, his arm on her shoulder. I realized that though she'd invited me to visit, she had not said "as a houseguest." Veronique persuaded a friend of hers to rent me a room for a few days in picturesque Menton. Veronique joined me for lunch a couple of times and showed me around the Riviera. At the American Express office in Nice, I sent an urgent telegram to Father: "Visiting Veronique South of France. Not staying there. Send money to come home." Father must have realized I was down to my last sou, because the money arrived without delay. I paid for my room and flew home, greatly relieved. My "grand tour" had been a more intense, but very interesting, learning experience than I had expected.

Back at Harvard, sophomores move from rooms in the Harvard Yard to one of many "Houses." I didn't make it into my first choice, the prestigious Eliot House, which was likely the only real repercussion from my Fool's prank the previous semester.

Nancy Mitford's sister Deborah, Duchess of Devonshire, with the Duke, Andrew Cavendish. His brother Billy married Joseph Kennedy's daughter Kathleen (known as "Kick") in 1944. Billy died in the war just four months later, and Kick died in a plane crash in 1948.

I ended up at Apley Court, an elegant building erected in 1897. Once home to T.S. Eliot, it boasted high ceilings and a handsome marble staircase. My roommate was an Armenian boy named Michael Arlen, who would go on to become a writer, serving as a television critic for *The New Yorker*, as well as the author of many books, including the Vietnam book *Living-Room War*. At the time I knew him, he was living in the reflected glory of his father, Michael Arlen Sr., whose book *The Green Hat* had been made into both a successful stage play, starring Tallulah Bankhead, and a movie, *A Woman of Affairs*, starring Greta Garbo.

John Rosenwald's family, like mine, were members of the Century Country Club and part of "Our Crowd.* We bonded at Harvard when he came down from Dartmouth for the Harvard-Dartmouth games. We really connected one evening when we tried to get into a girl's dorm at Wellesley College. We both had a crush on the same girl.

John has had an outstanding career on Wall Street at Bear Stearns. A few weeks after Bear Stearns collapsed in 2008, the firm was taken over by JPMorgan Chase, and John became a vice chairman of that firm. By this time Loeb Partners, which succeeded Loeb, Rhoades, had begun to clear trades through Bear Stearns, and then through JPMorgan Chase. As a result of my work with that firm, John and I began to see each other more frequently. In addition to a great career on Wall Street, John Rosenwald is a famous philanthropist and sits on many boards. He is also a very talented and amusing toastmaster.

I also reconnected with Jamie Dimon, who by this time had become chairman of the board and CEO at JPMorgan Chase. I first became friendly with Jamie when he and Sandy Weill, for a few months in 1985, moved into my father's and my office in the Seagram Building. A number of years ago, Jamie found a memo about investing written by my father, which, to my delight, he distributed to everyone at his firm to read.

---

* Steven Birmingham's best-selling book, written in the 1960s, refers to "Our Crowd" not only as the book's title, but also the elite German Jewish New York City world of the nineteenth and early twentieth centuries.

Jamie Dimon   Sandy Weill   John Rosenwald

After about six months at Apley Court, I accepted an invitation to join Kirkland House, located near the Charles River and named for John Thornton Kirkland, Harvard's president from 1810 to 1828.* I had been asked to room at Kirkland by John McDonald, a charming, attractive boy who had been to St. Paul's, a prestigious New Hampshire prep school. In fact, all four of my new roommates were from St. Paul's: Randy Harris (a descendant of the Randolphs of Virginia), Tim Fales and Bill McCagg.† At the time I joined them, Randy Harris had taken a year off. When he came back, conveniently, Tim Fales left Harvard.‡

Randy graduated with me. He subsequently married Susan Carter, whom I had known since I was nine and she was three at the Harvey School, which her family had founded. Randy and I stayed very close over the years. He recently died. He was at every important event, from my fiftieth reunion at Harvard to my birthday party at Blenheim.

When I arrived at Harvard in the fall of 1948, I almost immediately began to get invitations to debutante parties. My aunt Dorothy, my mother's sister, whom over the years I had become increasingly close to, had many great friends in Boston. I happily went to a

---

* Harvard sophomore Mark Zuckerberg invented what became Facebook from his room at Kirkland House in 2004.

† Bill was an odd duck from a very well-known family. He was hearing impaired and a bit awkward. Even with these issues, he had a wonderful career. He graduated from Harvard and received a PhD from Columbia in history. He had a professorship for over thirty years at Michigan State University. Bill wrote several books, including a few on Eastern European Jews, titled *Jewish Nobles and Geniuses in Modern Hungary* and *A History of Habsburg Jews, 1670–1918*. He married Louise Heublein, an heiress to the Heublein liquor fortune, and they had two daughters. Sadly, he died very young.

‡ Tim was a fascinating character and extremely good-looking. He came from an old New England family. His father was commodore of the New York Yacht Club. Tim's first wife was a beautiful model whom he divorced to marry Josephine Premice, a famous black comedienne. When they married, there was an outpouring of letters protesting the marriage. Tim and Josephine's daughter, Susan Fales-Hill, became a friend of my daughter, Alexandra, at Harvard. Susan and her husband have since become very good friends of Sharon and me.

Abraham Rodrigues Brandon
(1766–1831). (Portrait by John
Wesley Jarvis)

number of these coming-out parties. One evening, I found myself dancing with a very beautiful young woman. She began asking me very pointed questions and soon discovered that I was neither a member of a "Final Club" at Harvard nor in the Social Register. After this conversation, she excused herself and said she had to go to the ladies' room. She never came back. My grandmother was in the Social Register, which I had seen on her desk, but none of her daughters were, including my mother.

I finally got up the courage to ask Randy Harris (who I knew was in the Social Register), "How does one get into the Social Register?" He wasn't sure, but his mother knew a woman at the Social Register who explained that you just apply. I submitted my application, with references such as Lansing Lamont, Rodman Rockefeller (Nelson Rockefeller's son) and others. My application was accepted, and I became a member of the Social Register.

Interestingly, several decades later, it turned out that one of Randy's ancestors, Abraham Rodrigues Brandon, who was born in Barbados, was Jewish and featured in the Museum of the City of New York, one of my favorite philanthropies and on whose board I sat for thirty years. He was a great-grandfather of Randy's. He also had ancestors who were members of Shearith Israel, the oldest synagogue in America. Randy was excited and fascinated that he was partly Jewish and, furthermore, had quite a number of ancestors who had been members of Shearith Israel.

Not long after I moved into Kirkland House, I was inducted into the Hasty Pudding Institute, the oldest collegiate social club in America. I never made a Final Club. The number one club at Harvard was the Porcellian, sometimes compared with Yale's Skull and Bones. The second in prestige was the A.D., which told me that they wanted me as a member, but because I was Jewish there was no point in "punching" me (inviting me to be interviewed at a cocktail party). I was interviewed by several clubs, but, as far as I know, no Jews were chosen by any of them at that time (unless they slipped through because of opaque last names).[*]

There was one more *Lampoon* escapade worthy of note. In fact, George Frazier, a

---

[*] Of course, this has changed dramatically today. I've heard that Andrew Farkas became a member of A.D.—Andrew was in my daughter Alexandra's class at Harvard. John Hess, whose father founded the Hess Oil Company, was a member of Porcellian.

Harvard grad and well-known journalist, made it a centerpiece of "Yale's Secret Societies," a nationally read exposé he wrote for *Esquire*. Frazier drew his information from an article George Plimpton had written five years earlier for the November 1949 issue of the *Lampoon*.

Skull and Bones is Yale's number one secret society.* When Plimpton's *Lampoon* article came out, revealing unknown information about the secret societies, the issue became an instant hot ticket. At the time, I was serving as the *Lampoon*'s business and circulation manager, so I gathered a team of two others from the business board to discuss an idea. The three of us (Baker, Monrad and myself) would head to New Haven the day before the football game, taking five thousand copies of the issue to sell. Arrangements were made, extra copies and posters about the story printed, and off we went.

The night before the game, word got out that Monrad and I were out nailing up posters all around New Haven and the Yale campus that read "Exposé—The Yale Secret Societies." When a group of Yalies heard what we were up to, some of them attacked us. Others were busy tearing down our posters all around town. Meanwhile, Baker was guarding the precious copies in our room at the Taft Hotel. Seven or eight big Yalies burst into the hotel room and roughed up poor Baker. They bound and gagged him and confiscated the five thousand copies.

Fortunately, Baker had gotten a good look at the face of the ringleader. After Baker was released, we located a yearbook, found his picture and name, and dashed to the police station. Ultimately, Baker's tormentor was identified in a lineup. The villain confessed and, under pressure, revealed that the magazines had been stashed in the Skull and Bones campus "temple," awaiting destruction. Under police escort, we retrieved our magazines and sold them out completely by dawn the next morning. Alas, Yale won the ball game the next day, 29–6, but the *Lampoon*'s trio returned to Harvard as heroes.

I remember with equal pleasure some of the Lampooners (better known as "Pooners") of my time. George Plimpton became a literary legend, making his mark through his own extraordinary output (fifteen books and countless articles and essays) and by championing other talents through the *Paris Review*. Our era included Fred Gwynne, who was the magazine's cartoonist. Gwynne would become famous as a character actor, best known for appearances in TV sitcoms of the 1960s, such as *Car 54, Where Are You?* and *The Munsters*, and later in films like *My Cousin Vinny*.

---

* Both President George H.W. Bush and President George W. Bush, among many other politically prominent Americans, have been members of Skull and Bones. I've known the elder Bush most of my life and met George W. Bush from time to time over the years, including since he was president of the United States.

Prince Sadruddin Aga Khan

Our *Lampoon* president, John P.C. Train, went on to found a money management firm, Train Smith Advisors. Charlie Flood, author of *Love Is a Bridge*, became an especially good friend. The author John Updike joined the *Lampoon* while I was there, but he arrived at the end of my tenure. Though we shared some meals at the *Lampoon* house, I didn't get to know him as well as some of the others I remember so fondly, such as Prince Sadruddin "Sammy" Aga Khan (Aly Khan's brother), whom we often pelted with food on Saturday nights. He was our house cook and would someday become UN High Commissioner for Refugees.

In the summer of 1950, before my junior year, I opted to gain some experience in the business world. With my Loeb, Rhoades connections, I was able to get a job with the Rome Cable Company, one of the most important companies in upstate New York. Rome Cable was founded by Herbert Dyett, a business associate of C.M., my grandfather. While head of American Metal, C.M. had sold copper to Dyett, then head of General Cable. When Mr. Dyett left that company to start his own firm, he turned to C.M. and Father as his bankers. This was one of the first investment underwritings that Carl M. Loeb & Co. took on. They brought Rome Cable Company public. Later, the firm became part of Alcoa.

Rome was a charming little town. Everybody at the cable company made quite a fuss over me, and I enjoyed life there. I was exposed to all the company's departments, and so I had a much clearer sense of how things were organized, produced and distributed. At night, I wrote reports to Father. Rome Cable's management team comprised the town's elite. There was a lot of intrigue among the company families, and I was privy to some of the gossip. Mr. Dyett was extremely likable. An elderly widower, he seemed to be enjoying his retirement, especially after marrying the company's telephone operator. I also liked his son, Jack, number two in the company, who was married with two children. By the end of my several weeks at Rome Cable, I almost felt like one of the family.

Before the summer ended, I set off on another European trip, going from Rome, New York, to the more famous one in Italy. For several years, my grandfather Loeb had vacationed annually in Europe without Granny Adeline. Father wanted C.M., who was about seventy-five then, to have a traveling companion. He urged me to accept Grandfather Loeb's invitation to travel with him. C.M. always revisited his favorite restaurants in southern France, so I knew I could look forward to grand meals. C.M. made me a proposition. He half-joked that he would foot all the travel bills for me and a girlfriend, provided I "bring the [girlfriend's] mother along." I wasn't seeing anyone special, so there was no girlfriend, but he paid my bills anyway.

I was in a studious mode at the time, and my nose was in a book during the Pan Am direct flight from New York to the cobbled roads of ancient Rome. Every moment I could find, even when traveling around Italy, was spent reading and re-reading *War and Peace.*

Father told me to be sure to look up the brother of a Loeb, Rhoades partner, Hugo Gerlardin, a scion of a well-to-do Egyptian Jewish family. He invited us to lunch at a beautiful estate owned, I suspected, by a war profiteer. I then took a train to Venice to rejoin C.M., my head still buried in *War and Peace.* When I arrived, I found my grandfather at the Grand Excelsior Lido-Venice chatting with the Loeb, Rhoades partner and his frequent traveling companions, Hubert Simon and his wife, Vivian. I got to know Hubert and would someday work in London under his guidance. I also got to know Vivian, who came from one of England's leading Jewish families, the Baers. Hubert had run the only Loeb, Rhoades office that remained open in Europe during World War II. A brilliant man, he developed a transactional vehicle called "Investment Dollars." Because of the currency controls after the war, British institutions had to purchase these financial vehicles in order to buy American stocks. As a result, Hubert Simon became a critical and famous figure in the world of London finance.

In Venice, there was a lot of time between breakfast and dinner to visit, muse and philosophize. Instead of chasing girls, I stayed on the beach with *War and Peace.* I was so engrossed that I got sunstroke, having lain out there for most of the day. By sunset I retreated to my room to collapse in pain. When I didn't show up for dinner, C.M. came to my room to check on me. He was appalled, not by my appearance, but by my messy room. Like my father, C.M. was an obsessive "neatnik." He was so horrified he fled. From then on, he resorted to leaving me phone messages, never again entering my room!

To paraphrase Robert Burns, "There's a child among ye, takin' notes and faith, he'll print it."[71] I wasn't taking notes during this trip, but traveling with C.M. gave me indelible impressions of him. I gained confidences that I never would have back in Purchase. (As the poet predicts, the child now finds himself printing some of them.) It was in a private moment during our trip that C.M. confided he'd made a serious mistake by marrying at twenty-one. He revealed that he'd been terribly homesick for Germany when he first came to America and was lonely in St. Louis, so when he met my grandmother, the beautiful southern charmer Adeline Moses, he fell in love. He entered marriage too quickly, and he had come to regret it. Because I adored Granny Adeline, this was not a happy revelation. In fact, C.M. once told me that the only mistake he made in life was getting married at all. Frankly, I thought he was kidding at the time.

I also learned that C.M. was more conscious of being Jewish than I was. On the beach, he would point out children, saying, "I'm sure that little girl is Jewish," or "That boy over there is certainly Jewish." He was quick to comment if he thought he had been snubbed, or if a Gentile waiter had been less than properly deferential. "It's because we're Jewish, of course," he'd say.

I was impressed by how meticulous he was, not only with his dress, but also with money. At the end of any meal, C.M. would study the bill minutely, adding the numbers in his head. (He was once triumphant when he found a fifteen-dollar overcharge.) He was a better role model than Father on that score.*

We then traveled to southern France and stayed at the Hotel de Paris in Monte Carlo. In St. Tropez, we visited my father's very good friend Dan Silberberg, who invited us to several lavish parties. At one such event we found ourselves in a group that included Baron Erich von Goldschmidt-Rothschild, one of Greta Garbo's lovers. Greta was with the baron, chatting in a group we had joined. I heard a woman invite Garbo to a party she was giving, either ignoring or forgetting the star's much publicized preference for seclusion.

"Oh, dear," the woman said. "I just realized you'd probably rather not come."

Garbo laughed, "You want to know the truth? I *don't* want to be alone." The party was a marvelous capstone to a wonderful trip, but it was soon time to get back to the books.

I had memorable mentors during my undergraduate years, especially Herbert Spiro, a brilliant educator and political scientist. Spiro was a German Jew who became an ardent American citizen, winning both a Purple Heart and a Bronze Star for his service in the U.S. Army. He graduated summa cum laude from Harvard College and also received his PhD from Harvard. He was my Honors tutor. Spiro taught at Amherst College, the University of Pennsylvania and the Free University of Berlin, and he served as ambassa-

---

* When I was home from the Air Force, I went to see my grandfather, who was to have a very serious operation the next day at Mount Sinai Hospital. I remember, that before I said good-bye, he turned to my father and said, "Did you get the night rate?" "Oh C.M.," Father said, "don't be ridiculous. It's only a hundred dollars!" C.M. turned to me and in a low voice said, "He'll never learn." Sadly, my grandfather had been living with a colostomy bag, which was attached to the outside of his body. This was because a surgeon, years before, had left a sponge in his body when he had taken out my grandfather's appendix. The sponge grew dramatically but was not infected. Nonetheless, it was necessary to remove it—hence the colostomy. C.M. could not live with this contraption, so he asked for it to be taken out and everything put back to normal. He was advised against it and told that he might die in the process. He didn't care and, sadly, that is what happened.

dor to Cameroon and Equatorial Guinea during the Ford administration.

Henry Kissinger also occasionally taught a section in Government 1-A, headed by his mentor, the politically savvy professor William Yandell Elliott, whose lectures drew 400 to 500 students.[*] I remember Kissinger as fairly pedantic in these classes. Sadly, I did not get to see the wit and political brilliance for which he became famous. More significant to me were such noted Harvard professors as Louis Hartz, Samuel H. Beer and Carl Joachim Friedrich.

Beer had been a speechwriter for President Roosevelt in the 1930s and won a Bronze Star for his actions during the Normandy landing. He became one of Harvard's most popular professors. For more than three decades, he taught a class called "Western Thought and Institutions." Louis Hartz was a charismatic teacher whose classic book *The Liberal Tradition in America* attributed the triumph of the liberal worldview in America to its lack of a feudal past.

Carl Joachim Friedrich was German-born and educated. His writings on law and constitutionalism made him one of the world's leading political scientists after World War II, when he served as the constitutional and governmental affairs advisor to the military governor of Germany for de-Nazifying Allied-occupied Germany.[†]

The influence of these gentlemen has played a major role in many areas of my professional life. Almost all my teachers at Harvard were what I considered politically left of center. That is not to imply that they were socialists, but I can't remember anyone on the faculty admitting to being a Republican. Having grown up in a capitalist environment, I first found these professors' views totally alien. But I kept this to myself, believing that arguing for conservatism would not be academically beneficial. Family background notwithstanding, I became fascinated

Herbert Spiro, a brilliant educator and political scientist. My mentor.

Henry Kissinger—we all know who he is. My section man in Gov 1-A, at Harvard.

---

[*] Professor Elliott was a friend, mentor and speechwriter for both Republican and Democratic presidents; I believe Kissinger's career went into the stratosphere because of his close relationship with his influential mentor.

[†] Friedrich helped prepare the draft for West German Basic Law. In later years, he did some work on the constitutions of Puerto Rico, the Virgin Islands and Israel, among others.

with the British socialist Harold Laski, who had died just two years before I arrived at Harvard.

Laski had been a lecturer in Harvard's government classes prior to 1920, but he became persona non grata with the school's administration after his support of a controversial Boston police strike. Though the Harvard administration didn't dismiss him, Laski resigned his post and returned to England, where he became chairman of the Labour Party, leading Clement Atlee to a landslide victory over Churchill's Conservatives in 1945.

Laski was a brilliant scholar and lecturer at the London School of Economics. He wrote fifty books, including a series in which he elaborated his theory of why America would someday become a Communist country. Always a controversial figure, Laski nevertheless commanded a good deal of international respect and was considered one of the giants of twentieth-century British socialism. Although influenced more by John Stuart Mill than Marx, he was the only Communist theoretician who had ever predicted that the United States would become Communist, using American statistics and a study of the American political environment for support. My undergraduate thesis was entitled "Harold Laski: The Development of His American Political Thought." Although I disagreed with his theories and philosophy, the intellectual wrestling required to produce the paper was a mental exercise I relished.

There is "education" in terms of what one learns in school. Then there is education in the European sense: what one learns in the classroom *combined* with one's life experiences. The summer following my junior year, I persuaded my parents that my "education" would not be complete unless I spent another summer in Europe learning Spanish the "right way," by living among the Spanish.

Through a Venezuelan friend of mine, I contacted a dentist in Madrid and made arrangements to live with him, his wife, his two daughters and his three sons. Room and board would be an affordable ten dollars a week. There was no swimming pool, not even air conditioning in the dentist's home. These were both rare in Franco-era Spain, which was in terrible economic straits.

Even in the heat, my Spanish lessons came right along, coached by the dentist's fourteen-year-old daughter, who started me out with comic books as her texts. Although Superman was not likely to be a major topic of conversation, my tutor's strategy proved surprisingly successful.

In the evening, my attention was diverted to my tutor's three older brothers, all in medical school and engaged to be married. The brothers were charming, intelligent and ambitious. Their intended brides came from good families, significantly more prosperous than their father. In the evening after class, these young men strolled around with their respectable fiancées—with a chaperone following at a discreet distance. After their obligatory walks, they would drop off their fiancées and go out for drinks and dinner, inviting me to join them.

By 11:30 p.m., we would visit an outdoor nightclub for a nightcap. The nightclub was full of beautiful young girls, all professional ladies of the evening. Each night the brothers would choose a different girl for themselves, and one for me—costing us each a dollar or two. My liberal education was turning out to be more liberal than my parents dreamed. And my Spanish proved ample enough.

Before I'd left home, my father, who believed in "good contacts," made a list of people he thought I should meet. I had avoided it up to that point, but, frantic from the heat, I *had* to find a swimming pool. I flipped through Father's list of princes, dukes and other notables. After a series of fruitless calls, I realized that nobody of sound mind and bank account would be in Madrid in mid-July. Then I found one marquis still in town who said he would be "happy indeed" to see John Loeb's son.

The Marquis de Santo Domingo had a house the size of a city block, guarded by a formidable butler who looked askance at my attire when I appeared with neither coat nor tie. It was an old-fashioned home, its walls laden with priceless but gloomy tapestries. The marquis led me first to his library, chatting amiably as he guided me through the rest of the house. We ended the tour in his bedroom, where he proudly displayed pictures of his country home. While showing me the pictures, he asked casually if I would like to join him in an orgy.

"Um, let me think about it." I said.

Then I offered, "Perhaps, um, maybe, I could just watch?"

"No, that won't do," he replied. "Why not take part? I'm sure you will find it very pleasurable." He brought out his collection of orgy pictures.

I gulped and stammered, "My, aren't these interesting? Well, dear me, yes terribly interesting. But let me give it some thought."

Harold Laski

His actions during the Boston police strike brought Calvin Coolidge, then governor of Massachusetts, to national prominence and to the presidency.

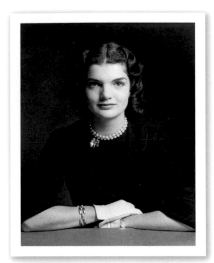

Jackie Bouvier

I was totally unnerved. With less than sophisticated aplomb I blurted out, "Mmm. Yes. Well, I'm afraid I have to go now." I bolted, totally forgetting about my swim. I was no babe-in-the-woods, especially after frolicking with Madrid's ladies of the night, but what he was suggesting was well beyond my idea of good fun.

About a week later, the dentist's household phone rang. It was the marquis, calling for me.

"You know, Johnny, two friends of mine are coming to see me—daughters of a great American friend of mine, a Mrs. Auchincloss. Why don't you come for dinner this Friday evening? They'll be here."

Before I could answer, he went on: "Oh! One other thing, if you don't mind. We're going to pretend you're a toreador. They're dying to meet a bullfighter, and I don't want to disappoint them."

The idea of meeting two young American girls sounded more my speed. I'd also had thoughts of becoming an actor, and here was my chance, presented on a silver platter. Still, I was hesitant. "I'll try," I told the marquis, "but I don't know if this idea will work."

"Don't worry," said the Marquis. "You look the part!" I didn't, but perhaps my swimmer's muscles would help carry off the charade. I told my Spanish tutors what was afoot; the whole family pitched in for three days to coach me, teaching me phrases they thought would help me fake my way through the evening as a genuine Spanish matador.

Friday night I arrived again at the home of the Marquis de Santo Domingo. This time the butler approved of me, all dressed up in suit and tie. I was led to the library, where sat a quite drunk Jackie and Lee Bouvier. (I knew the Bouvier sisters, of course, but I had never heard of Mrs. Auchincloss.) They couldn't have been happier to see me, which I found hilarious; I did not have the courage to even approach them back at the teenage dance parties in New York. The sisters greeted me with open arms and trills of pleasure at meeting "Miguel Domingo Ramirez somebody or other."

The more we drank, the better they liked me. I played the strong silent type and said little, nodding my head now and again, raising my eyebrows quizzically if they spoke in English, and giving them admiring glances, which did not go unnoticed. The marquis happily carried the conversation, obviously pleased.

At dinner the marquis touted my bullfighting prowess to the ladies. They could not have been more adoring, occasionally pressing my arm and looking into my eyes. As the evening wound down, they insisted on taking me home in their taxi. The marquis explained that they would find my living quarters a little shabby. "He is not yet rich," he explained, "but he is so talented a bullfighter, one day soon he will be wealthy."

The sisters were staying at the Ritz, which was very expensive (in those days it cost $5 dollars a day!). As they dropped me off, I kissed their well-manicured hands and cast soulful looks into their eyes. They reluctantly parted, saying, "You *must* come and have lunch with us tomorrow." I bravely showed up the next day, and again they were all over me. I pointed at the menu to indicate my

John F. Kennedy

choice, not wanting to tax my limited vocabulary. But without the marquis to orchestrate our conversation, I couldn't keep up the deception for very long. I soon caved, explaining in English, "Look, I'm really not a bullfighter. I'm John Loeb, and we used to run into each other at teenage dance parties in New York."

They were furious! I didn't stay through lunch because they were so terribly upset and didn't hesitate to let me know it. Years later, I heard from Jackie's social secretary, Letitia Baldrige, that Jackie had told her the bullfighter story as if she'd thought it terribly funny. But she certainly didn't think it was funny at the time.

Several years later, I saw Jackie again in a receiving line at the White House. She and President Kennedy were giving a dinner for the International Council of the Museum of Modern Art during the week of the Cuban Missile Crisis in 1962. As the line was hurried through, I quickly said to Jackie, "I haven't seen you since Spain." She didn't even blink; she just gave me her signature wide-eyed look and offered her white-gloved hand to the next in line.

Though my toreador career was short-lived, more adventures lay ahead that same summer. The dentist's three sons planned a trip to San Sebastián, where they were to join their fiancées. I gladly accepted the brothers' invitation to tag along. In San Sebastián, I ran into my Yale friend Ted Bensinger. He and his two brothers, each accompanied by a girlfriend, had rented an apartment together there for a month. Ted was with an absolutely stunning English girl. She was so beautiful that a perfect stranger, who had seen me with the group, asked if I would introduce him. I demurred, adding that I'd only just met her myself, and wasn't even sure of her name. It turned out the beauty was Fiona Campbell-Walter, the daughter of a British rear admiral.

The next morning I dropped by Teddy's apartment. The three girlfriends were running around in their lingerie, not quite dressed to leave for the trip to Bilbao. "Look, we're headed to the bullfights," Teddy said. "Why don't you come along?"

"Teddy, you don't need or want me," I said. "You three guys have three girls." I would obviously be a fifth (or seventh) wheel.

"No, no, no," Teddy protested. "Fiona and I are finished. *Kaput.* For good. I'm having nothing more to do with her, ever. We're all furious with her."

"You broke up with that beauty? You must be crazy."

"She tried to seduce my brothers," Teddy said. "It got all of us in an uproar, even the other girls. Your presence will ease things a bit." He added that if I took Fiona off their hands he would be grateful. So the nine of us set off to Bilbao for a bullfight featuring an actual toreador star, Luis Miguel Dominguín.* Miguel even invited us to dinner after the fight, his eyes on Fiona, of course.

The Bensinger boys reserved three rooms in a Bilbao hotel and offered me one of them if I would share it with Fiona. I barely knew Fiona, and we hadn't talked alone at all. The one time I tried to put my arm around her in the car she brushed it off.

As Fiona and I were about to head up to our room, I hesitated. While still in the lobby, I said tentatively, "Fiona, would you rather not stay here with me? We don't really know each other."

"Don't worry," she quickly replied. "Staying together here is fine!"

When she started undressing I *really* didn't know how to proceed, because so far we'd barely even held hands. I darted to the bathroom to shed my clothes. Dithering, I stayed in the bathroom so long she called out, "Johnny, are you all right?" I emerged finally, turning out the lights quickly, feeling terribly embarrassed, and crept into bed with her. But soon we were making love.

The next day, our group all returned to San Sebastián, where Ted Bensinger announced that they were heading to Paris and then going home to New York. "Johnny," he said, "why don't you stay and enjoy our apartment, it's paid up for another week. You and Fiona might as well take advantage of it." As if the Bilbao hotel room hadn't been generous enough, they left me and Fiona their apartment in San Sebastián.

After another glorious week, Fiona and I traveled by train to Paris, where we stayed in the Hotel Florida for the last weeks of summer. She had done a bit of modeling in London

---

* Ernest Hemingway is said to have written about Dominguín in his book *The Dangerous Summer.* The toreador star's smoldering affair with the American actress Ava Gardner was widely publicized.

and thought she would try her luck in Paris. I didn't have much cash left, but she now had an inflow of cash and shared the hotel bill so we could spend the last of my money going to nightclubs. Inevitably, the end of summer came, when Fiona went back to England and I returned to Harvard.

The one serious romance I had during my years at Harvard began on the day I graduated from Harvard College in 1952. I dented a fender in my brand-new Pontiac convertible, the same car Father had promised me ten years earlier for not smoking. Proud and protective of its elegant beauty, I headed straight to the garage for repair.

Driving over the Larz Anderson Bridge to get the car repaired, I spotted a gorgeous girl walking along the street, carrying a tennis racket. For some reason, I decided she must be the daughter of an alumnus attending his twenty-fifth Harvard reunion. Captivated with the sight of her, I nearly missed my exit. At the garage, they told me it would take at least an hour to repair the damage. "Wonderful!" I yelped to the astonished attendant; I dashed off to find the beauty before she disappeared.

She was walking leisurely along the same street where I'd first seen her, and when I raced up to her, she stopped, looking amused. Where I found the courage to approach her I don't know, because I'd never been able to pick up girls, even at bars. The words came tumbling out: "I've just graduated with honors, and now I've got a dent on my new convertible, but I'm in a great mood. Why don't you come and celebrate with me at Cronin's while it's being repaired?"

"A likely story," she said, smiling.

"It's absolutely true! I'm going to Cronin's to celebrate graduating and to wait for my car. Won't you please, please keep me company?"

"Well, okay. That's either the truth or one of the best lines I've ever heard."

"I'm John Loeb," I said, offering my hand; she extended her tennis racket for me to shake, putting me on notice that I was to be kept at more than arm's length. Her name was Leslie Wehrheim. She was not a student at Harvard nor the daughter of an alumnus. She was an art student from upstate New York, recently graduated from Syracuse University. Leslie was now living in Cambridge and employed as a commercial artist at Filene's department store. We had that drink, or maybe two or three. As we parted that day, I asked for her address and phone number, even though I would be gone from Cambridge until the fall. It would be almost another year before I would see her again.

Little did I know, when I had this portrait taken shortly before entering Harvard Business School in the fall of 1952, just how difficult the next two years were going to be.

CHAPTER FIVE

≡

HBS Not So Heavenly, *1952–1954*

In the summer of 1951, the Korean War was entering its second year. If I hadn't moved from the Army ROTC into the Air Force ROTC, I might have been on my way to the front lines. But the Air Force needed officers with business school backgrounds for its procurement offices, as well as for its research and development divisions, and so they allowed me to postpone my active duty for two additional years. So instead of Korea, I was headed back to Cambridge, Massachusetts—to Harvard Business School for my MBA. Though the Korean War was ostensibly about defending the West, I wanted nothing to do with the fighting. Father advised me both to join the ROTC and to attend Harvard Business School (HBS), so I did both.

As an undergraduate, I had pondered my options for a future career. Dreams of heading Loeb, Rhoades always hovered in my mind, but I sometimes thought of a medical career, and I warmed to the idea of teaching history.* Joining my family's firm, the financially attractive option that everyone expected, had its drawbacks. Most glaringly, I was all too aware of the pitfalls of working for my father. He would say, half-heartedly, "Well, if there is anything else you really, *really* want to do . . ." and his voice would trail off. It was clear where he stood. He would follow this up with a more energetic, "If there *isn't* anything you really, really want to do, you'll have a wonderful future at Loeb, Rhoades."

---

* This may have been in my DNA. "When I graduated from Harvard," my father wrote in his own memoir, "I wasn't quite sure of what I wanted to do. . . . I thought I might teach for a year or go to the Harvard Business School."

This is the Baker Library at Harvard Business School in Cambridge, Massachusetts.

Obviously, if I were to join the family firm, I should follow Father's advice and get an MBA. I'd find out years later that Father's motives were not entirely paternal—he wanted access to my own money and trusts in order to bundle it into Loeb, Rhoades, as he wanted to do with all of his children's money and trusts. But he couched it all in familial duty, and I was none the wiser.

Most of the buildings at the Harvard Business School were named after treasury secretaries. (For example, I lived in Mellon Hall, named after Andrew Mellon, who was secretary of the treasury from 1921 to 1932. At that time, Mellon was the richest man in America. He was frequently lonely and began buying great European art through Joseph Duveen, who was one of the world's greatest salesmen. The result, upon Mellon's death, was that he left most of his collection to establish what is today the National Gallery of Art in Washington, D.C.)

At some point in Loeb, Rhoades's history, a great American, Robert Anderson, who had been secretary of the treasury under Eisenhower, became a partner at Loeb, Rhoades. He was a wonderful man, beloved by everybody. Unfortunately, in his later years, he got into some very serious trouble, which besmirched his great reputation. As a result, unbeknownst to him and my father, the building at the Harvard Business School that had been named in honor of Anderson became the Loeb House in honor of my father, whose sterling reputation was known worldwide.

Part of what tilted me toward Loeb, Rhoades was my strong sense of familial obliga-

Loeb House, named after my father, John L. Loeb, previously known as Anderson House, for the former secretary of the treasury Robert Anderson.

tion. In my eyes, the firm could be like the Rothschild family business, with its great traditions and heritage carried on by generations of family members.

In 1952, there was no admissions test for Harvard Business School, nor was past work experience required (though I would soon find out that I was the only one without any). However, in order to get in you had to pass one or two very far-ranging interviews, as well as a close examination of your history, transcript and recommendations. George W. Miller III, my best friend from our first days at ROTC, who was at Harvard College on full scholarship, gave me practical and moral support at HBS. Unlike me, he'd had summer jobs all through high school and college, had taken accounting classes in high school, and was able to guide me through more than a few perilous HBS shoals.

The first year in graduate school brought me to earth with a thud. Despite working around the clock, I was put on academic probation. It seemed that everyone else in my class had some personal experience in business or the professional world. Many had already worked for several years and had graduated from colleges with a business or engineering focus. The average age of my classmates was twenty-eight (some were even in their late thirties), while I was a totally green and naïve twenty-two.

Another disadvantage I had was that, unlike in most of my classmates' families, my father refused to discuss business with me at all. He bristled even at basic questions like "What is a stock?" or "What is a bond?" The professors just assumed that anyone accepted to HBS would know these things, but I was in the dark. Fortunately, I was aware of the gaps in my education and had taken a summer course in accounting at Baruch College before entering HBS in the fall.

Though I flunked that Baruch course, those six weeks saved me. I emerged from the class with an understanding of how a debit could be an asset and a credit a liability, as well an acquaintance with double-entry bookkeeping. The course set me up for my first year at HBS, where instructors covered material at warp speed, assuming we could grasp things like accounting in a week.

The first year was devoted to mandatory courses, and we studied and worked practically nonstop from dawn to midnight seven days a week. There were daily classes, meetings, group papers to write, an exam every Saturday and an individual paper due every Saturday night. If I drew a breath at all, it was on Sunday mornings to read the newspaper.

As a student, I'd been accustomed to working by myself and to studying and analyzing on my own. HBS forced us to work in groups and prepare papers as part of a team. The methodology there was based in part on "case study research." Whether following a product from inception into the marketplace or understanding the operation of a particular company, we were trained to analyze and evaluate every aspect to find ways to improve its performance. We also were taught to keep an eye out for new products and new kinds of businesses. I remember one of our professors holding up something called a transistor and saying it was "going to change the world." I didn't know what he was talking about at the time, but when I got to Loeb, Rhoades, the first thing I invested in was a private placement of General Transistor.

Those students with direct experience in companies or businesses were at a clear advantage at HBS. I had had only limited exposure to the "real world." I remember being lost once during a class discussion of discount stores. Our professors talked about consumers' buying habits and how they comparison-shopped. One teacher asked the class, "How many of your family members shop at discount stores?" I assumed my parents didn't shop at discount stores, so I didn't raise my hand. I checked with Mother and was surprised to learn the Loebs "of course" shopped at discount stores. In all my sheltered life, I'd never thought about shopping any more than I'd thought about ways to make money. Money was just always there. If I needed any, Father just asked, "How much?" We didn't discuss where it came from or how he got it.

I was also at a disadvantage socially. Over half of my classmates were already married, and if they weren't married they had steady girlfriends who were terribly obliging about typing papers. There was precious little time for me to go a-courting, but somehow I did manage a few flirtations with some women from other campuses (females weren't admitted to HBS until 1965). One night, sick of studying and in a mood of gloom and doom, I thought of the lively, winsome Leslie Wehrheim and called her. At just the sound of her voice, the dark clouds over my head began to lift.

That call resulted in my first great romance. The next few months with Leslie were some of the happiest in my life. My problems as a student smoothed out—though Leslie did *not* type my papers—and my fear of academic failure faded away. Leslie and I knew that our romance was probably not going to lead to marriage. I would be serving in the Air Force for the next two years, and I had no idea where I might be stationed. Father had said that I could "go ahead and marry Leslie, but it would ruin my life." In his eyes, since she was not to the manor born, she would be a hindrance in my business and personal life. In retrospect, this was nonsense, and only due to Father's ambitions that I "marry well."

In a course called "Management of New Enterprises," I got a D for Distinction, the highest grade you could get at HBS. Among my assorted career fantasies, I'd thought of owning a farm or a plantation, so I wrote a paper on starting a dairy farm. Classmates were amused by the rumor that I'd been spotted heading out to inspect dairy cows dressed in a homburg hat and Chesterfield coat. Those dairy farm explorations turned into a lifelong interest in land investments.[*]

During the second year at HBS, each student could take an elective curriculum. In the summer, students could undertake a field study or a research project, but a majority of my classmates took jobs. I proposed to my mentors that an HBS teammate, John F. Walker, and I take a research trip to Yugoslavia the summer before our second year. Yugoslavia had just broken with Russia and therefore was one of the first Communist countries one could visit.

In my proposal to HBS, I wrote that I'd already gained the consent and approval of "my father, my future employer." I argued that the trip would further my study of business and its relation to government, citing Harold Laski's statement that the political and economic structure of a nation is not something to be considered in the abstract. It must be experienced firsthand; I intended to do just that—and see the world in the process.

John and I chose Yugoslavia because its president, Marshal Tito, maintained independence for his country. Though he was Communist, he was determined not to be domi-

---

[*] I would later own land that was once a former dairy farm. It also led to the most satisfying purchase of my life: in 1971, I bought Riverbend Vineyards.

Among my most unusual meetings was one with Churchill. This classic photo is one of my all-time favorites of the great man.

Fiona Campbell-Walter, daughter of a British admiral and one of the great UK models in the 1950s, was introduced to me by Teddy Bensinger in San Sebastián, Spain, during summer vacation after my junior year at Harvard.

nated by Moscow. We thought Yugoslavia's economy would be a fertile field for our study.

After Yugoslavia, my intention was to visit Israel by myself. Israel had been founded only five years earlier, with the UN's recognition. Previously, it had not existed as a state since 70 CE, when the Romans had sacked it and closed off Jerusalem to all the Jews. My parents were not thrilled with the prospect of my visiting Israel; they were afraid it would only increase my interest in my Jewish identity, and perhaps I'd even stay.

Before meeting John in Vienna, I began my 1953 summer with a trip to London, arriving in time for Queen Elizabeth II's coronation on June 2. I was not invited to the coronation itself, but there were many parties surrounding the main event. The coronation was part of a "season," which meant several dinners a night for coming-out debutantes. Unlike at American debutante parties—which I had attended—English ones featured the parents, friends and children of all ages. At one party at Number 1 London, the ancestral home of the Duke of Wellington, I had one of the greatest encounters of my life.

At the party, I saw a chubby little man standing no more than five foot five. I turned to someone and asked if it could really be who it appeared to be: Prime Minister Winston Churchill himself. The war had ended eight years before, and Churchill had been re-elected about two years before. I went over, introduced myself and shook his hand. He smiled, said nothing, but continued to stand in front of me. Just to say something I referenced a letter that my brother, Arthur, had written him, to which Churchill had replied. Then I said how much our family admired him and how shocked we were that he was not re-elected

My HBS classmate John Walker and I found an agreeable young lady to have dinner with us in Trieste, Italy. On the next day we would be on a dilapidated steamer for the last leg of our trip to Yugoslavia.

in 1945. On behalf of my family, I again thanked him for his letter, which was on the House of Commons stationery and in his own handwriting. Churchill didn't say a word to me and just kept smiling. Though he said nothing, it was still an awe-inspiring moment: meeting Mr. Churchill was like shaking hands with history itself.

In London, I stayed with the head of Hill Samuel, a prominent investment bank and a client of Loeb, Rhoades. The Samuels were founders of Royal Dutch Shell, whose business life began in the early nineteenth century, importing shells from the Dutch East Indies.[*] With warm memories of the year before, I phoned Fiona Campbell-Walter and left a message. She called back and left a message with my host, who greeted me with incredulity when I returned.

"You really know Fiona Campbell-Walter?" he asked.

"Yes. *Quite* well, actually," I replied.

"You certainly travel in enviable circles!"

"Why do you say that?" I asked.

"She's the number one model here and the talk of London," he said. "I've heard she is Cecil Beaton's favorite model. Everyone wants to know her."

I smiled smugly, but the irony was that Fiona's success meant I wasn't going to be a star in her life anymore. My experience only the year before with the unknown nineteen-year-

---

[*] Sir David Davies ran the Hill Samuel office in New York for a time after he had married my sister Debby.

old beauty was etched in my memory. It left me able to say, "I knew her when."*

Going from the glamour of Fiona and the coronation summer to Yugoslavia was quite a sea change. John Walker and I traveled from Vienna to Trieste on the Paris Orient Express, which was old, dilapidated and uncomfortable. We then took a steamer down the Adriatic Sea to Dubrovnik, which was even more uncomfortable. Our first-class room lacked plumbing, and the boat had only two other passengers. It was so hot and airless that we slept on deck.

When we arrived in Yugoslavia, we were struck by its drab contrast to the West. There were no neon signs, no billboards and practically no public transportation. The ubiquitous motorcycles and bicycles of Italy and France were completely missing. In an article after the trip, I wrote,

> *In Belgrade on an evening, there is an almost frightening quiet to the city. One of the first sounds I had heard was a song from a barge on the Blue Danube, which, by the way, was not blue but a dirty brown. The song was one from WWII that begins "Kiss me once and kiss me twice and kiss me once again." I was struck by the fact that the first song I heard was an American pop song. There is little noise, little gaiety or laughter. The sound you hear most audibly is the click-clack of heels on hard pavement.*

The article was less a discourse on Yugoslavian politics and economics and more of "a kaleidoscope of incidents, conversations, people [and] impressions," organized around two main issues: material welfare and freedom. I continued,

> *Two great forces shaped the history of Yugoslavia in the 20th century: the desire for independence, and the desire for peace and security at any price. The War to End All Wars brought the first. The Second World War and the Communist movement under Tito brought Yugoslavia the second.*

Before the war, foreign capitalists and a small minority of Yugoslavs dominated the economy. All of its lead, bauxite, copper and half of its soft coal were then owned by foreigners. "Now everybody is guaranteed a job over here," I wrote.

---

* Fiona would marry Baron Heinrich Thyssen ("Heini") and have two children: Francesca, an art collector, and Baron Lorne Thyssen-Bornemisza de Kászon, a film producer. Fiona later had a long affair with Alexander Onassis, the only son of Aristotle. She was Alexander's senior by sixteen years, and Onassis did his utmost to break them up. Alexander tragically died in a plane crash in 1973. Photographs show that Fiona remains a beautiful woman to this day.

"Of course, we don't make as much money as you do," one man told us, "but we try not to let anybody starve. Here we have only one employer and one employment agency: the State."

A woman asked me if it was true that in America most women have refrigerators, washing machines, radios and televisions, and that the men all have cars. The question was asked without a trace of envy; she couldn't be jealous of that which she never expected to have. To her, they were like part of another world.

A young man who had studied in Paris dared to criticize the status quo. "These people do not know what freedom is like," he told us. "They have never lived outside of Yugoslavia. It is impossible ever to live without fear in this country. It's all right for the common laborer or the unimportant white collar worker, but as soon as you rise to some position of responsibility, your life is in danger."

Two things had happened prior to our arrival that influenced our experiences there. Stalin had died the previous March, and his would-be successor, Lavrenty Beria, and his henchman had been deposed by the end of June. The young dissident we interviewed worried about what would happen if Tito died and there was a struggle for succession. He was right to be worried, considering the ethnic tensions that then arose, eventually leading to the wars in the 1990s that resulted in the breakup of Yugoslavia.

The other event that influenced our experience had occurred a few months before our arrival. In April 1953, Roy Cohn and G. David Schine, two chief aides of the notorious Communist hunter Senator Joseph McCarthy, had visited Yugoslavia on their book-sanitizing tour of the United States Information Services libraries. It was one of seven countries where they removed thirty thousand books they considered too "pro-Communist" from USIS libraries, including the work of Melville, Thoreau and Steinbeck. McCarthy and his witch-hunting tactics had been bravely opposed on the floor of the Senate by my great-uncle Herbert Lehman early in the McCarthy era. However, Uncle Herbert's fellow senators were slow to identify the dangers of McCarthyism. McCarthy would not be censured by the Senate until December 1954, after years of causing irreparable damage.

Arriving so soon after the book raid, John and I were treated by some of our Communist hosts with great caution and accorded the kind of respect that's bred from fear. For all they knew, we were not graduate students on summer vacation but part of McCarthy's second wave.

Surprisingly, it turned out that the Loeb name was actually known in Yugoslavia. At one factory we visited, I was startled when the manager asked if I was in any way connected to Loeb, Rhoades. "Yes," I said, "That's my family's firm," astonished to learn that we were doing business with a factory that made rubber, one of C.M.'s earliest investments.

After three weeks, John and I parted, and I headed to Israel via Athens. The flight was uneventful until I heard the click of the loudspeaker and our pilot said, "We have just entered Israeli airspace." I glanced at my fellow passengers, Jewish senior citizens with a scattering of blond, blue-eyed farmers, perhaps making a first visit to the Holy Land. They were all visibly moved, tears in their eyes. Sudden tears welled up in mine as well. It was a powerful and poignant moment—solitary, but shared with strangers.

I was surprised by my own elation and wonder in Israel. Exiting the plane into the warm, dry air of Tel Aviv's airport, surrounded by palm trees, I was struck by a realization—everyone there was a Jew: the baggage handlers, the taxi drivers, the policemen, the soldiers, everyone on the street. After nine years at two boarding schools of being taunted for being a Jew, it was incredible to me that such a country existed.

My emotional reaction was unexpected; I didn't visit Israel because of any Zionist passion. I came because I'd been invited by Cleveland "Buttons" Fuller, a fellow Harvard alum who had become the U.S. vice consul in Jerusalem. I had known Buttons for most of my life. Our fathers had been at Harvard together, and his father became my father's first lawyer and estate planner. Buttons's sister, known simply as "O," was also a very good friend of my sister Judy's.

When I reached Jerusalem, then divided between the Arab section and the Jewish section, I found that Buttons, a practicing Episcopalian, was madly in love with a "sabra" (an Israeli-born woman) who had fought in the country's War of Independence. My friend was also in love with everything about Israel; he learned Hebrew and had become extremely knowledgeable about everything in this new country. When he volunteered to be my tutor for Judaism and Israel's history, I couldn't have been more pleased or in better hands.

With Buttons's support, I visited many of Israel's historic sites. I went to the Sea of Galilee and to Masada and took a swim in the Dead Sea, where the salt content is so high that you easily float. I visited the beaches in Tel Aviv, where I met an assortment of people from all nationalities and religious persuasions. I was awed by all of it.

At the time of my visit, the focus was on absorbing and integrating the recent influx of immigrants into the country. In my conversations with people, there wasn't much talk about the tragedies that brought them to their new homeland. The main issue was one of survival in their adopted country. A lot of people still lived in what looked like tin shacks, housing developments that were far from Israel's booming construction of today. Though it was more built up than I expected, parts were still primitive. People were also curious to find out just how Jewish I really was. How could any *real* Jew feel at home in America? Didn't I realize that Israel was my actual homeland? I responded that it was an enormously emotional experience to come to Israel but that America was my true home.

Israelis then were predominantly secular, and I felt a kinship with them. However, I felt no pull to leave my American life and move to Israel. But something in my soul recognized a common ancestry, a connection that came from somewhere deep inside of me. I had no idea how far back my connection went, but I was sure my ancestry originated in Israel. I returned home feeling for the first time a deep gratitude for having been born Jewish.

In the fall when I returned to HBS, I took the time to expand my report on the trip to Yugoslavia, which turned into an article I hoped to publish. When I sent a copy to Father, he found nothing to praise. He thought I had too many positive things to say about the Communists, while somehow simultaneously framing them in a bad light. "If you publish this," he wrote, "you risk being considered a fellow traveler here [in America] and persona non grata in Yugoslavia. Besides, it's not interesting or new. . . . You have everything to lose and nothing to gain." Father's response upset me. I never touched the article again nor made any effort to publish it.

Following graduation from HBS in June 1954 (my brother, Arthur, graduated from Harvard College that same month), the U.S. Air Force claimed their right to the fruits of Second Lieutenant John L. Loeb Jr.'s hard-won business degree. Soon I would be fighting the waning Korean War—in sunny Southern California.

I really liked my blue-gray Air Force uniform and was proud to wear it. However, the actress and Westinghouse spokesperson Betty Furness, whom I occasionally escorted to Hollywood events, didn't like it. She said it made me look like a Greyhound bus driver.

CHAPTER SIX

≡

The Air Force, Hollywood and Paris, 1954–1956

Incredibly, the Korean War has still never been declared officially over.* A cease-fire was called in July 1953, but it was not formally recognized until November 1954, when the last prisoner exchanges took place. Despite the truce, in the summer of 1954, the U.S. Air Force expected the immediate services of Second Lieutenant John L. Loeb Jr., proudly bearing the ROTC citation of "Distinguished Military Graduate." My Harvard best friend and HBS roommate, George W. Miller III, was called up as well. George and I were to report in June 1954 for two months of training in procurement at Wright-Patterson Air Force Base in Dayton, Ohio. Though I would never fire a gun in practice, I was technically on active duty, and a war was still in progress.

The Wright-Patterson base was, and still is, in charge of air matériel for the entire Air Force. Its main mission is to keep U.S. weapons systems ready for war. At the time, the four-star general Edwin W. Rawlings was commander of the Air Materiel Command.† Rawlings was in ROTC in college, a pilot during World War II and a graduate of the Harvard Business School. The relationship between HBS and the Air Force had grown over the years, since there was a new mindset that the branches of the military should be run "more like a business." In fact, Harvard Business School professors mentored Air Force leaders when the Air Force was first created as a separate branch from the Army and the Navy after World War II. With active duty experience and an advanced degree,

---

* Technically, since Congress never declared war on North Korea, the war was a United Nations "police action."

† This included a great many personnel besides the actual system (the business side, which included the purchase of all needed supplies). "Weapons systems" doesn't just include the weapons.

Rawlings rose through the ranks to become the chief business general for the Air Force. Using new management methods, he brought his corner of the Air Force into the jet, missile and space era.*

Being under the command of such a powerful officer proved fortuitous for me. I enjoyed the frequent get-togethers with other HBS alumni, a group treated as an elite corps by the general and other officers. Life did not seem very military, although a fair amount of snappy saluting was exchanged regularly, and our barracks were well-furnished officers' quarters.

After eight weeks of training, we were deemed ready to be of service in the Rawlings command. The graduates of HBS were given the option of serving anywhere we wanted under the purview of General Rawlings. George opted for Air Research and Development Command (ARDC), then located at Andrews Air Force Base, so he headed east to Maryland. I had signed up for Air Materiel Command (AMC) and had my eye on the West Coast. Father's good friend Dan Silberberg, who had known Rawlings during the war, asked the general to look after me. As he did with all the other HBS alumni, General Rawlings asked me what area I would like for my next assignment. He also cordially said that I should call him if I ever needed any help.

With an open door to so many possibilities, I might have asked to be posted as an aide- de-camp to some general in Spain, Germany or England. But I wanted to know more about business, so I requested a post on the West Coast, where the great aircraft factories were located. I also had a hidden agenda: the glamour of Hollywood was a major draw, and I knew that I could room with two good friends planning to move to Los Angeles.

With the wind of General Rawlings at my back, I was on my way to fight what friends have teased me about ever since: the war in the jungles of the Hollywood Hills.

In August, I showed up at the office of the Douglas Aircraft Company, which I would share with about a hundred others. Close to twenty thousand people worked at the adjacent factory that made the airplanes and repair parts purchased by the Air Force. I became part of a team approving the cost of those purchases. Of those in the Air Force Plant Representative Office, only seven or eight of us were Air Force officers; the rest were civilian employees. Of the Air Force personnel, I was the only non-pilot. But, as far as I knew, none of the Air Force pilots or civilians had prior experience in business, nor were any armed with a business degree.

---

* After retiring from the military several years later, General Rawlings again proved his leadership skills as the chief executive officer of General Mills.

Fighter planes played a central role in the Korean War. Douglas Aircraft produced the jet-propulsion systems of the Skyknight and the Skyray. However, most of the Air Force purchases from Douglas were for B-66s and huge C-124 heavy-lift cargo planes and repair parts, bought on a cost-plus-fixed-fee basis. The C-124 had been used extensively during the conflict to transport tanks, guns, trucks and heavy equipment vast distances across the Pacific and to bring home the wounded.

Douglas Aircraft's C-124 cargo plane was nicknamed "Old Shaky."

With the war now over, a primary concern became reducing the costs of these airplanes. We reviewed the Douglas figures, making sure the costs were "reasonable" and the fixed fee added was correct. We were essentially monitors charged with keeping Douglas on the straight and narrow.

Because of my business training, I was originally named a procurement officer to approve any special equipment that Douglas claimed that the C-124 needed. The government had been purchasing millions of dollars' worth of equipment beyond the usual requirements in the past; it was my job to be sure that the new equipment was actually warranted. In 1954, President Eisenhower was making an enormous push to cut back defense spending. I had heard rumors that the special equipment purchases I was to review might not be necessary because the contracts for the C-124 were being phased out, to be replaced by new DC-9s or DC-10s. I was conscience-bound to investigate the new orders thoroughly.

Being a young "eager beaver," I soon learned that alertness to errors was not going to win me any approval, much less applause, from anyone. Some of my older team members hoped for employment with Douglas Aircraft when they retired from the military. It obviously did not behoove them to bear down on cost-cutting. Nevertheless, I was determined to inspect the costs closely, which eventually slowed down payment. The company's data simply proved worthy of close inspection; the U.S. Air Force clearly didn't need everything it ordered.

President Eisenhower and the Defense Department began to phase out overtime pay for all government contracts. I zealously studied the unnecessarily complex overtime report and gained input from each department of Douglas Aircraft about what kind of overtime they actually needed. I got approval from my superiors at the San Bernardino Air

Command for every step of this overtime report. According to regulations, I added my own evaluation about necessary or unnecessary overtime, concluding that Douglas had more overtime than any other defense plant in America. The result of the overtime report stunned the top brass of Douglas Aircraft. Some of the top officers at the Air Materiel Command were delighted but the general reviews of my overtime report were mixed. To some, I was a whistle-blower.

Everyone at Douglas was sure I must have been doing something wrong: how could everyone be out of step but Johnny Loeb? Because I had meticulously documented my work according to the Defense Department's guidelines, I stood my ground.

After that, all hell broke loose. The officers at Wright-Patterson decided that overtime reports of the entire defense industry, all over the country, had to be redone so that the figures were more transparent. The entire defense industry was furious; after all, they had been making a great deal of money on overtime, and now it was going to disappear to the tune of millions of dollars.

None of my superiors liked looking bad for not having caught this earlier, and none of my colleagues appreciated a whistle-blower. Douglas Aircraft officials tried to put a good face on what had happened. I was wined and dined by top officials and complimented by the top management (including Donald Douglas himself), though the praise came with starchy smiles. I was even flown to Edwards Air Force Base to review a flight test of the country's most advanced methods of aerial warfare. As I wrote home to my aunt Dorothy, "The 'contraptions' (one could hardly call them airplanes) looked like something out of a Buck Rogers comic book!"[72] I enjoyed the attention but refused to succumb to the not-too-subtle pressure to cease and desist my scrupulous monitoring.

In February, about a month later, I received unexpected orders: I was to be transferred to Cheyenne, Wyoming, for retraining as a procurement officer—that very Friday! My colleagues were amused and not at all unhappy: the hotshot lieutenant with his Harvard MBA who had been causing so much trouble was to be exiled to the snowdrifts of Wyoming.

Wyoming? In the dead of winter? For *retraining*? Incredulous, I raced to Colonel Wright to ask for an explanation.* Colonel Wright agreed that I didn't need further procurement training, but he knew no more than I did about the new orders, though he may have suspected what lay behind them. But because they had come from higher up in the chain of command, he could do nothing to reverse them.

---

* Colonel Wright was the leader of our unit.

I had been in the Air Force long enough to know that second lieutenants don't easily become four-star generals from a phone booth. But I remembered General Rawlings's offer to help if I needed it, so I collected a large pocketful of change and dashed for the nearest phone booth. General Rawlings was on the line almost immediately. After apologizing for taking up his time, I blurted out my entire story. "This is not logical," I argued, "nor a rational decision on somebody's part!"

The general was not thrilled. He thanked me rather dismissively, saying he would "look into it," and hung up quickly. It did not sound promising. I was despondent, my only hope of rescue gone.

Friday morning, I came into the office early to clean out my desk, as I had to be out by noon. My colleagues watched me pack up, amused by my unfortunate detour. But at 11:30 a.m. a reprieve arrived. New orders came in, reversing my transfer to Wyoming and keeping me at my current post at Douglas. I practically wept with relief.

During my next nearly two years of service at Douglas, everyone treated me with caution and respect. How I had miraculously managed to get those Wyoming orders reversed, no one had a clue. Shortly thereafter, an order came down from another general, reminding junior officers that in *all cases*, you must "go through the chain of command." I was the only one who realized the directive was likely precipitated by my mysterious reprieve. I had come out the victor in a fight that was financially significant to the country at the time. To this day, I admire and have felt a kinship with whistle-blowers. I not only think they should be protected, but also that we must provide incentives for those who are willing to stick their necks out on behalf of the common good.

When I arrived in California, my first concern, even before reporting for duty, had been to find a good place to live. The Douglas factory and offices were located just off the Santa Ana Freeway, an inch away from Hollywood on my map. My intent was to reach Los Angeles and find an apartment in Hollywood, but that inch turned out to be a significant commute. I didn't want to live near work, a small bump in the road that was home to not much more than a shopping center and the Douglas factory—and boasted no Hollywood starlets whatsoever.

When I graduated from HBS, Leslie and I discussed the possibility of her moving out to California with me. But I didn't insist, and she didn't ask; our relationship wound down in the way that youthful romances tend to do. Leslie moved on from being a commercial artist, married twice and had two children. She has become a well-known painter in upstate New York, now known as Leslie Heen.

Here I am, all ready to report for duty in the United States Air Force, where I would serve for the next two years.

In California, I settled for a bachelor's pad on a stretch of sea and sand in Long Beach, which would do until my friends joined me to find something else. I then ventured into the new world of grocery stores, along with a self-taught class in mastering hamburgers and scrambled eggs.

Long Beach proved boring, and I frequently went into Hollywood in search of friends and entertainment. I traded my old Pontiac for a temperamental, two-seat green Jaguar that cost a small fortune in gas, repairs and parking fees. By day, I continued to take my work seriously; I was proud to wear my gray-blue Air Force uniform and kept it on for dates as well. Betty Furness, an actress whom I often escorted to Hollywood affairs, liked me better in civilian clothes. She told me I looked like a Greyhound bus driver or a postman in my Air Force uniform. I humored her by almost always showing up for our dates in civvies.[*]

My housemates showed up in February 1955: Yale roommates Richard Feigen and B.E. "Teddy" Bensinger III. Feigen was also a fellow HBS classmate of mine. Teddy arrived with his souped-up Oldsmobile, and a week later Dick came in his new black and yellow Ford convertible. I remember that his Ford was loaded down with $150,000 worth of Old Masters' paintings from New York galleries that Dick was commissioned to sell. One was a Delacroix my great-grandfather Lewisohn had owned. Dick tried selling it back to me, but I wasn't interested in Old Masters.[73] Dick's passion was collecting art, something he had started at the unbelievably young age of eleven. Dick planned to work with a Feigen family member's insurance firm in Los Angeles to make the money necessary to fund his real love—collecting (and selling) art.

Dick would eventually establish the now internationally famous Richard L. Feigen and

---

[*] Betty was a regular panelist on a popular TV show called *What's My Line,* but she was more famous for her Westinghouse appliance commercials, similar to Ronald Reagan's job at the same time for General Electric.

Co., with art galleries in New York, Chicago and London. His book *Tales from the Art Crypt* capped a lifetime devoted to an enormously successful career, which had the advantages of a Harvard Business School training and an impeccable artistic eye. I have often called him a poster child for Joseph Campbell's advice to "follow your bliss" if you want to succeed in life.

I like to think of myself as a godfather of sorts to Dick's galleries, which started in the house we shared. He fell in love with German Expressionism well before the art world embraced it. Dick was a fantastic salesman, and he persuaded me to buy one of George Grosz's paintings, *The Lovesick Man*; I thought it quite ugly, but I bought it as an investment for $3,000 (half a year's salary at that time), with Dick's assurance that it would increase greatly in value. In 1975, when German Expressionism was beginning to come into its own, I sold it back to him for $200,000. It is now owned by a museum and is probably worth $45 million. Selling that painting was one of the worst financial decisions of my life.*

My friendship with Teddy Bensinger went

My very close friend, the world-famous art dealer Dick Feigen, had a passion for art before he was eleven years old. I watched that passion turn into a business while we shared a house in Hollywood.

Here I am at a beach near Hollywood with Kim Kendall and Ted Bensinger. (The story of Ted's incredible generosity during my summer vacation in Spain is told in the Harvard chapter.)

back a long way. My father had once dated his mother, and our families were friends. Teddy's family owned the successful Brunswick Corporation, the marine/boating company known for years for its bowling alley supply business, which his Jewish grandfather had founded. Teddy planned to work at their branch in Los Angeles. Teddy had flair and pizzazz. He was enormously lively, told wacky stories and was marvelously fun to be with.

I happily gave up my apartment in Long Beach for the more glamorous life I had

---

* Years later, on a German museum tour with the International Committee for the Museum of Modern Art, I saw the painting on display in an exhibit in a Dusseldorf museum.

Perhaps it was while posing under hot lights for a Hollywood photographer that wisdom prevailed and I quickly dropped the short-lived idea of becoming a film actor.

envisioned. We all moved into the Garden of Allah Hotel in Hollywood, once home to F. Scott Fitzgerald, but now long past its prime. It was a "Brave New World" kind of place, with colored lights playing on the walls, swaying palm trees, a heated swimming pool and a view looking down the last slope of Hollywood Hills.

As soon as Teddy learned there was no phone and that it would take three weeks to get one, he immediately moved to the Beverly Wilshire Hotel, well beyond the reach of Dick's and my wallets. But the charm of the low rent at the Garden of Allah soon wore off, and Dick and I began the search for better quarters.

People were pouring into Los Angeles County at an astounding rate, and it was not easy to find an acceptable place to live. After several false starts and disappointments, I found a wonderful little bungalow high up in the Hollywood Hills. I crowed to Dick that the place on Sunset Plaza Drive would be real "girl-bait." It had two bedrooms, two baths, a kitchen and an enclosed terrace next to a swimming pool overlooking a panoramic view of Hollywood that would be wonderful at sunset when the valley below twinkled and glittered. A congenial bachelor who lived on the other side of a shared swimming pool had built the house as a rental. Fully furnished and decorated, it was ours for $500 a month. What more could we want?

Early in the evening of the first day we moved in, we heard a car pull up and a door slam, followed by the tantalizing click-clack of high heels. I answered the door and came back to Dick, wide-eyed. In an amazed whisper I said, "The house's charm is working already!"

"*What's* working?"

"Anita Ekberg's here!" Dick's disbelieving retort was, "Sure and I'm Superman."

In 1955, Universal Studio's lusty, busty Swedish import, Anita Ekberg, was a rising star. She would be best remembered for her 1960 role as the "unattainable dream woman" in Fellini's classic movie *La Dolce Vita*. I announced that this dream woman was at our door. Dick responded that he was too tired from the move for any jokes.

"No, no, Dick! I'm not kidding. Anita Ekberg is here! I tell you—this house is already working!"

We sprinted into the living room and there she was, a voluptuous mountain of beauty and sex standing in the doorway. She smiled. I smiled. Dick smiled. "Is this place for rent?" she purred.

"No, but come in, and maybe we can discuss it," I said. She did, and we learned that she had lived there the year before with a lover. She liked it so well that she wanted to come back and live there by herself. Would we sublet it to her? We demurred. We would not consider giving up our new home, even to Anita Ekberg. We considered her appearance on our first day in our new nest a good omen for our Hollywood future.

The next morning while Dick was still upstairs in bed, I came into his room, almost shouting, "It's working! It's working again! There are *twelve* girls in our swimming pool! Come and see!"

Sure enough, there were. Our landlord was a friend of an American Airlines pilot who invited stewardesses to visit our shared pool on weekends. Though the stewardesses were delightful, I really wanted to meet people in the movie business. There were two actresses I was especially yearning to meet: Grace Kelly and Leslie Caron. I ended up dating Leslie for a short while. She had an adorable face, a perky little dancer's body and a lively personality, but we never had a fiery romance. To my everlasting regret, I never got to meet Grace Kelly.

Among my parents' Hollywood connections was a brilliant older couple, Dr. Jules and Doris Stein. Jules was an eye doctor with a passion for music. This led to his founding of the Music Corporation of America, better known as MCA. At the time, it was primarily a talent agency, but in a few short years it would take over Universal Studios.

Doris and Jules opened all kinds of Hollywood doors to me: dinners, dances, cast parties and film openings. One indelible memory I have is a party attended by both Marlon Brando (the same year he won an Oscar for *On the Waterfront*) and the producer-director

Joe Mankiewicz, who made *All About Eve*. At one point Marlon took a piece of chewed gum out of his mouth and handed it to Joe, who chewed it and then gave it back to Marlon, who popped it back in his mouth. I didn't know whether to be amazed or appalled.

The idea of becoming an actor, which I had flirted with after my theatrical debut at the Harvey School, occasionally flickered through my mind. I could see how women adored film greats such as Clark Gable, Errol Flynn and Cary Grant. I even went so far as to pose for some Hollywood glamour shots, but I was never serious enough to take acting classes or learn how to audition for movie roles.

Though my movie star dreams faded before they really started, they didn't prevent me from socializing with those who fulfilled theirs. In a letter to a friend, I wrote,

> *[Our] young set spent a rather quiet weekend . . . dinner at La Rue—Gene Kelly's afterwards. Met Jerry Paris, the married brother-in-law in* Marty; *Joan Collins, last week's cover of* LIFE; *and Lena Horne, who is very beautiful indeed.*[74]

Though the girls in Hollywood were tempting, I found myself thinking more and more about someone else: Kim Kendall, an English girl I had met in 1955 when I returned to New York on furlough for Christmas. Kim was tall, lissome and incredibly beautiful. We had caught each other's eyes at a debutante party and hit it off from there, until I returned to the West Coast to move to Los Angeles. Now that I was settled in, she was on my mind.

I was thrilled when the beautiful and talented Kim Kendall came for a visit—and then stayed for the rest of my tour of duty.

People tell me that picking up the phone on impulse is one of my trademarks. I called Kim in New York and asked her to come see me in Los Angeles, and she miraculously accepted. Our erstwhile bachelor pad was soon home to the three of us—Dick, Kim and me. Like her sister, Kay Kendall, the famous madcap comedy actress married to Rex Harrison, Kim was a professional dancer and actress. She was also a marvelous hostess for our parties and enormously fun. Kim was a fantastic

Kim was frequently asked to model for various charitable women's organizations during her time in Hollywood.

Kim Kendall and I are in the center of this picture. We were joined by two friends at a Hollywood swimming pool—not the much smaller one adjoining the cottage where we lived.

woman who loved to keep house, and I adored her.

Both Kim and Dick were talented chefs, and they loved to perform, with me as their enthusiastic audience, my fork ever at the ready. There were more than a few turf wars. One day, Dick came to me to complain about Kim's use of our small kitchen.

"John, either Kim goes or I go," Dick said.

I asked if he was kidding. He said he wasn't.

"Well, Dick," I said, "from my point of view, there's only one way to solve this: you move out." Dick agreed. Ostensibly, it was over our kitchen disputes, but Dick told me it was because he felt like a third wheel. There is probably some truth to both.

The rest of my time in the Air Force went smoothly. Kim and I lived like an old married couple—me going to the Air Force Plant Representative Office and Kim taking care of our home. I would soon leave the Air Force in good standing.

During this time, Father began to press for me to come join him at Loeb, Rhoades. With my grandfather's death the year before, Father had total command of Loeb, Rhoades and had become the proverbial wolf at my door. My last few weeks in Los Angeles in 1956 were peppered with heated exchanges with Father about my future, a subject he barely found worthy of his time and attention. Father had reluctantly agreed to give me a few months' hiatus between the Air Force and my future career. I wanted that time not only to unwind, but also to think things through, both about Kim and my concern about working with Father at Loeb, Rhoades.

My two-year stint in the Air Force ended in early July. The big question at the time was whether Kim and I should go on as a couple or go our separate ways. Kim was five years older than I was and not yet divorced from her previous husband. Also, in those days, actresses and models were not considered appropriate wives for leaders in the conservative banking world, which is where I appeared to be heading. While the issue of marriage came up, it was not going to be easily resolved. I also didn't get out of Los Angeles so easily. In fact, I almost ended up in jail.

I had amassed quite a large amount of tickets driving my Jaguar around town. I had never heard anything about these tickets until I distractedly put my Los Angeles address on one of them rather than my New York address during my final weeks in Los Angeles. I was summarily called down to the courthouse and told that I owed close to $300 in fines. I told the judge I only had $100 on me. He happily offered to give me a free night in jail. Assuming there was a Bank of America nearby, I asked the judge to allow me to get money from my account there, which I didn't actually have. I got there just as the bank was closing and told the bank manager who I was and who my father was. The manager had not heard of Father or me or Loeb, Rhoades. However, they had heard of Sutro and Co., a major California firm that cleared through Loeb, Rhoades, and the manager loaned me $200 in cash. I then went back to the courthouse to pay the fines and avoid a night in jail.

Kim and I returned together to New York City, where we continued to see each other for a month or so, until I departed for Paris, where I would sort out my future. After sailing on the *France*, I arrived in the City of Lights and rented an apartment at 19 Avenue Hoche, just off the Étoile metro line. I had to sign a year's lease, which would later prove to be a problem. And there was one other small glitch. A few Rothschild family members lived at 19 Avenue Foch; more than once friends would mistake the address and confuse "Hoche" with "Foch," so the Rothschilds would occasionally have unexpected visitors. I met the family occasionally during this period, including Eric and Bettina Rothschild (whom I had dated briefly when she was single during an earlier trip to France).

While I wanted to do some serious thinking in France, I also wanted to have some fun. I didn't intend to spend long hours in existential debates, but making new friends went slowly. I didn't speak French, and there was no central place to meet visiting Americans like myself. The American colony was mainly composed of GIs, bohemian types, expatriates, intellectuals and students—groups I didn't fit into.

For a brief time I became a *bon viveur* (one who lives well), rather than a *flaneur* (an aimless idler), although *boulevardier* (a social man who frequents fashionable places) might be a more apt description. Some mornings I'd get up with no set plan on how I would spend my day — the one and only period in my life when this was the case. Some days I had French lessons, but I didn't know enough French to have real conversations with anyone who didn't also speak English. Nevertheless, in spite of my fractured French, my social life began to bloom.

Through my then brother-in-law, Edgar Bronfman, I met Edgar's brother-in-law Baron Alain de Gunzberg. He told us a story about his famous father-in-law Samuel Bronfman. Apparently, Sam asked Alain, "Why did you marry my daughter, Minda?" "Oh," the Baron replied, "it was very simple. She married me for my title, and I married her for her money."

One of the interesting evenings I had with Alain and his wife, Minda (Edgar's sister), and Valery Giscard d'Estaing and his wife, Ann-Aymone, was shortly after Giscard became president of France. Also joining us was Baron Edmond de Rothschild, the wealthiest of all the Rothschilds. We were celebrating a winery, Chateau Clarke, which he had just bought. He founded Compagnie Financière Edmond de Rothschild in Geneva, which his son Benjamin now controls.

Thanks to the influence of Dick Feigen, I'd developed a serious interest in art—both for itself and as an investment. With the help of Mrs. John Lithiby, an art aficionado, whose British husband represented Loeb, Rhoades in Paris, I began my own eclectic art collection. I bought a Rodin lithograph from Rodin's mistress, who was still alive. This was only eleven years after the war, and everything was incredibly inexpensive; the dollar was strong and the French were enthusiastic about their Allied liberators. As an American from a banking family, it was assumed that I was wildly rich and therefore extremely eligible; some French acquaintances were eager to meet me or introduce me to their daughters or sisters. I was written up for the first time in a gossip column in the *International Herald Tribune* for being seen in Maxim's with Aly, Prince Aga Khan, Rita Hayworth's third husband.*

For a time, I dated Linda Christian, the actress who played Mara in the early *Tarzan* films and the first ever "Bond Girl," in the 1954 TV version of *Casino Royale*. Linda was either just divorced from Tyrone Power or about to be.

At one point I took off for the Riviera. While sunning on the beach, a handsome woman in her late forties started chatting with me. She seemed to think I was a poor beach boy. She offered to take me to lunch, and I accepted. After lunch, she took me shopping because, in her opinion, I didn't dress very well. "You really have to have better clothes,"

---

* Known as a playboy, Prince Aga Khan would be named Pakistan's representative to the UN a year or so after this. He died in a car accident in 1960.

Merle Oberon

she clucked as she propelled me into a men's store and insisted on making some purchases. Some days later I confessed that I hadn't really needed her financial help. My short-term patroness was Merle Oberon, the screen beauty who played Anne Boleyn in Charles Laughton's *Henry the Eighth*, and also starred in *The Scarlet Pimpernel* and *Wuthering Heights*.

For all the glamour I found during those months in Paris, there was no *grand amour*. Kim and I continued on as a couple, on and off, but in spite of our mutual attraction, our relationship remained ambiguous. In the end, Kim would go on to marry George Baker Jr., a grandson of the founder of Citicorp. Kim would also head an organization called the Lighthouse Foundation, set up in memory of her sister, Kay, who died tragically young at thirty-two. Kim and I have stayed in touch after all these years. I still have in my home today the only piece of sculpture, of Kim, I ever did from memory.

After a beautiful Parisian autumn, November was dreary. I began to contemplate an extended side trip to the Orient, but I was having a tough time finding anyone to sublet my apartment. Before leaving Paris, I spent an evening at the famous Crazy Horse Saloon, the sexiest, most tasteful and well-respected nightclub in the world. In those days, America was a puritanical place, with little nudity in magazines or establishments.

I was surprised to see someone I knew back in New York dancing in the show, a beautiful black girl. I went backstage afterward to say hello; as fate would have it, she was looking for a love nest to entertain her English boyfriend when he came to town. She even offered to pay the remaining eight months' rent on my apartment in advance. It turned out her boyfriend was none other than Jimmy Hansen, or rather *Lord* Hansen, who ran one of the largest corporations in England. I had met Jimmy through Kim, as they both came from the same part of England. He was now considered such a reprobate that Mr. Bates, of Bates & Co., a major advertising agency, refused to let him marry his daughter; nevertheless, I assumed finances would not be a problem, so I sublet the apartment to her. I thought I was freed of any further responsibility and began my journey home via the Orient.

Upon my return to New York, I would receive a letter from a French law firm on behalf of my Avenue Hoche landlord, a Colombian by the name of Mr. Valenzuela. He was upset that I had sublet the apartment to a black woman—and without his permission. At the same time, the rental agency was protesting unpaid phone bills: $3,000, which I ended up having to pay.

In Paris, I'd met a young man named Steven Tse, whose family had been associated with C.V. Starr, the founder of the American International Group (AIG). Because of the Communist takeover, AIG had moved its corporate headquarters from mainland China to Hong Kong. Loeb, Rhoades already had a connection to AIG through Palmer Dixon, an important partner who was serving on the AIG board, and eventually Loeb, Rhoades would invest in the company. Thus it was that I was welcomed by both the Tse family and Mr. Starr himself in Hong Kong. The highlights of my trip to Hong Kong were staying at Mr. Starr's house, touring the town with Steven Tse and his family and learning to write my name in Chinese.

Soon I was in the air again, this time on my way to Japan, where I made contacts at Yamaichi Securities, a Loeb, Rhoades Japanese correspondent. I became friendly with a number of young men my age working at the firm. One night over dinner, I felt comfortable enough to ask, "Why did Japan start the war? Why did you bomb Pearl Harbor?"

One of them answered quietly, "We didn't start the war."

"What do you mean?" I asked, incredulous. "You think America started it?"

"Yes. You cut off our strategic matériel supply when we were in the midst of a war with China."

I could see he wasn't just trying to be argumentative. I remembered postcards with photographs of the Chinese-Japanese war, including one of the "Rape of Nanking," which I had studied at Collegiate. I knew that conservative members of Congress had lodged serious objections to American shipments of scrap iron to Japan. Senator Gerald Nye of North Dakota told FDR as far back as 1937, "Stop sending scrap metal to Japan. Can't you see they are getting ready to go to war with us?" When the U.S. stopped sending supplies, the Japanese leadership saw it as grounds for retaliation. The conversation that night was an extraordinary lesson to me on how differently people can see the same event.

During my Paris interlude, I'd weighed the many pros and cons of starting a career at Loeb, Rhoades, the chief downside being the risk of working for my father. Even with all the perils, if and when I entered the world of Loeb, Rhoades, I would do it with zest and hope and hard work.

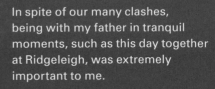

In spite of our many clashes, being with my father in tranquil moments, such as this day together at Ridgeleigh, was extremely important to me.

CHAPTER SEVEN

===

Father, Mother and Me

At some point during my "salad days," Father handed me a copy of a novel by the nineteenth-century British author George Meredith titled *The Ordeal of Richard Feverel*. "I think you should read this," Father announced without explanation.

Not much later, we sat together at Ridgeleigh, both of us in a relaxed mood, idly chatting. I loved these moments; despite our differences, being alone with my father was always special to me, beginning with those birthday breakfasts during my childhood.

"Johnny, you are at an age when what you do now will affect your entire life," he said. "You're a very bright boy. What do you want out of life? Have you thought about it?"

Had I thought about it? It was constantly on my mind, so it was a question I could answer without hesitation. "I want to work hard, travel a lot, have a lot of friends," I told him. "Most of all, I want to be happily married to a woman I'm in love with and is in love with me, and I want children. I know I may never be as wealthy as you, but I want to be financially very comfortable and live close to the way I've grown up."

A silence fell over us. He stood up and started to leave. "Marry well, Johnny," he added with a wry little smile. "Marry well. Have you read the book I gave you yet?"

After that nudge, I read it, and immediately understood why he had given it to me. Its plot follows a father-son relationship (not unlike our own), and the protagonist's marriage to a neighboring farm girl ends disastrously. I got the point: scions of the upper class should not fall in love with, much less marry, anyone from a lower class. I give Father credit for recommending the book, because the aristocratic, controlling father does not come off very well. In any case, I tried for a long time to "marry well."

One day at Gull Bay when I was in my teens, Mother and I raced as a team in a canoe to the opposite side of the lake, competing with other family members and some visitors. We won handily. Panting as we waited for the rest of the racers to catch up, she laughed about how intense I'd been about winning. (She was, too.) "I guess you've inherited the family competitive gene—and that's okay. In fact, it's good. Just don't turn into a Sammy Glick." Mother's reference came from the best-selling 1941 novel *What Makes Sammy Run?* Author Budd Schulberg wrote about an ambitious Jewish boy (Sammy), who makes it big in Hollywood through double-crossing and ruthless backstabbing. "Sammy Glick" became a metaphor in the 1940s for anyone overly competitive. Mother was right that I am competitive, but I've never become a Sammy. And I've never forgotten that day in the canoe with my mother.

Back then, families understandably wanted their offspring to marry "up" or at least to choose mates close to their own social and financial level. Business interests were (and still are) frequently a major influence in upscale marriages. Father's marriage to a Lehman in the 1920s was a step up the social ladder for him. Father and Grandfather's success with Loeb, Rhoades moved our family upward in the 1930s and 1940s, though in some eyes, we were still "nouveau"—despite the fact that one of my grandmothers was a Daughter of the American Revolution, and her family dated back to 1697. Even so, my aunt Dorothy Bernhard (a Lehman and my mother's sister) observed with sly amusement, "Your money got 'old' very quickly." She was right; by the time I was eligible, marrying a Loeb was a very large step up for most.

Being a bona fide romantic, I wanted it all—a monogamous marriage that included companionship, common interests and a strong, lasting physical bond. If my wife were wealthy, that would be wonderful; but if I had to choose, I would choose love over a business partnership. My parents did everything they could to see that I married according to their definition of "well." But the girls who met their criteria never met mine. Their candidates came from "good" families (preferably not *too* Jewish, unless they were Warburgs or Rothschilds). I did my best to fall in love with every girl my parents suggested, but there was never any sizzle to these pairings.

When my parents died within months of each other in 1996—after almost seventy

Lunch with my parents when I was twenty-two.

years of marriage—a new chapter began for me, at the age of sixty-six. My mother always had told me that I'd be much happier once they both had died. Though it's hard to admit, she was right. In different degrees, all of my siblings felt the same way.

The vacuum left by their absence was dramatically different for me than it was for my siblings, not only because of my long tenure at Loeb, Rhoades, but also because we were such close neighbors on the Ridgeleigh estate. I was the only one with a 24/7 connection to them. Our lives were intertwined in a way that my siblings didn't experience. Though I felt the same deep loss, I also felt a certain relief. Their absence was a release from my lifelong effort to please them, especially Father—a Sisyphean effort if ever there was one.

The complicated relationship I had with my parents illuminates the struggle I had in first deciding to join Loeb, Rhoades after leaving the Air Force. After some contentious phone calls and letters with my father just prior to my leaving California, he finally agreed to grant me a few months' rest before going to work for him. My life was going to permanently shift. I would no longer be working for "God and Country" but for God, Father and Loeb, Rhoades.

Mother and Father had such an extraordinary presence that, despite the fact that I was financially independent, I felt somehow controlled by them, constantly worried about their judgment. Admittedly, sometimes I miss that need for their approval. As a couple, their combined strength could be overwhelming. For so many years,

Mother was just delighted when Nina Sundby and I married in April 1960. Here Mother and I are dancing at the reception of the wedding, which took place in Sweden.

I'd endured heartbreak when—courage in hand—I disagreed with them, often incurring their disapproval and sometimes their wrath. My mother would almost always try to defend me, but, in the end, she would invariably concede to Father. In family and business, Father wielded his power not with a sledgehammer, but with a steely presence that brooked no question or dispute from anyone. I can never remember my father ever raising his voice at the office or at home.

Father and I engaged in countless classic battles over the years, but, in the end, like Mother, I usually capitulated as well. Looking back on the confrontations I had with Father prior to my joining Loeb, Rhoades, I have pondered the early problems that set the recurring pattern of our relationship. The one that left the most scar tissue was Father's insistence on sending me to boarding school at the age of nine. Despite offering all the usual reasons rich Jewish parents had for sending their sons to WASP schools, it became clear to me that Father wanted more of Mother to himself. In fact, I don't think he ever stopped being jealous of her affection for me.

Having pushed me out of the house as a child, he was now pulling me with both hands to join him at Loeb, Rhoades. I believe his reasons were not just familial, but also financial. Hindsight has allowed me to frame the conflict quite clearly: Father wanted to keep all the family money together—invested in Loeb, Rhoades—and I was too intimidated to say no to him.

Other than occasional jobs during the summer, my years in the Air Force represented my first real job. As my military service was coming to a close, I was thinking about the value of working for another firm before going to work for Father. I had tried many times to discuss my future with him, but he always managed to avoid the conversation. In fact, his favorite word when I tried to talk about it with him was that it was "boring."

On furlough for Christmas 1955, I tried to raise the subject with him at Grandma Lehman's annual New Year's Eve party. Father walked away, stopping long enough to say, "You are the most boring person I have ever known." In the spring, when he announced he was coming to the West Coast, I once again asked to take up the subject with him. His response was, "I certainly don't intend to spend my whole time in California having a boring discussion about your future." Not too surprisingly, I instead confided my thoughts and plans to my brother, Arthur. It was clear that Father was either not interested in or not happy with what he thought I was going to say.

On a phone call in June 1956, Father's voice like God's, but quiet, said "Leave Eden and Eve and get thee hence to Loeb, Rhoades!" Father was determined that as soon as my tour of duty ended, I was to immediately join the family firm. He said he "needed help" since Grandfather Loeb had died the prior January. Father may truly have needed help, but his argument about my replacing C.M. was disingenuous at best and deceptive at worst. What help, after all, could I provide compared to C.M.? Father was in sole charge now, and I would be a green apprentice, not even worthy of being his personal assistant.

I hadn't known the true impetus for Father's insistence. My brother, Arthur, had unintentionally spilled the beans that I was considering working for another financial firm. Father was furious, reacting as if my plans were set in cement and deliberately kept secret from him. The fact was, of course, that he hadn't *wanted* to hear about them. After all, he made it clear that I was "too boring" for him to listen to on the subject.

What Father saw as rebellion at the end of my California sojourn was actually a continuation of a long-fought battle. This time Father's "wrath" and quiet insults made me both acutely stressed and literally sick. I was so horrified by his attacks—and their negative impact on a critical phase of my work at Douglas—that I stood my ground. We had been communicating solely through letters by this point, and in my most intemperate letter to him yet, I confronted him:

> *Not only do you disapprove of my plans, but you now threaten me as*
> *well . . . with not only closing the opportunity to take over from you, but*
> *from ever working there; with disinheritance; with never having anything to*
> *do with me in a business way if I don't work for you; and most terrible and*
> *monstrous of all, you threaten to hinder me if I should work on my own or*
> *for somebody else.*

Perhaps I felt braver not having to face him in the flesh. I continued in this vein, using the opportunity to lay it all on the table for him:

> *I want to say here and now, because you have used somewhat similar, although less harsh, threats in the past and might again in the future, that I cannot and will not be intimidated. I discount all your horrible threats, not because I don't think you would carry them out, but because I do not intend to go through my whole life guided by fear and with a sword of Damocles hanging over my head. . . . No man with any self-respect—unless he was starving—would work or could work under such tyranny.*[75]

The advantages of working at Loeb, Rhoades may have seemed obvious to Father and others in the financial world, but I had reservations about joining the family business. I thought it wrong for Father to bludgeon me at a time when I had no real business experience, didn't know the inside politics of Loeb, Rhoades and, perhaps most significantly, had never had a working relationship with him.[76]

I cited sons in similar situations who had gone to work for others before entering the family business: Robert Woodruff, for example, had great success at Mack Trucks before his father called him back to head Coca-Cola. But my father warned me that I would never get a job *anywhere* on Wall Street if I didn't join Loeb, Rhoades. And, if I didn't come immediately upon leaving the Air Force, he added, "Then don't come at all."

After thirteen years in school and workplaces learning how to reason, to look at a situation as a whole and to carefully work out the steps toward achieving defined goals, I came to one conclusion. Only trouble would come from my joining Loeb, Rhoades:

> *I cannot emphasize enough the psychological importance to me . . . of working at another firm first in a related field and in a city I like and not dominated by my family. This all may seem very intangible to you, but often the most intangible factors are, in reality, the most tangible.*[77]

Father may have viewed my decision as a mutiny, one that might have a ripple effect and influence other family members to put their money somewhere other than the family firm. It appeared that he had to put a stop to that before it even began. His ultimate accusation in a letter sent in both my parents' names (letting me know

Both of my parents held honorary degrees. One of Father's came from Harvard. Here they both are receiving honorary degrees from New York University.

my mother concurred in his assessment) was my, somewhat redundant, "self-centered selfishness."

"You have been given everything we could give you all your life—love, money, backing—and generously," they wrote. "You have been made financially independent without strings."[*] While this was true, he did not take into account that I had been exiled to boarding schools, separated physically and emotionally from the family since the age of nine. Nor did he mention that I was financially independent because of grandfathers' trusts, not him.

That summer, when I refused to take part in any more upsetting communications, Father—with an ice pack on his head—penned me a handwritten letter from his chair next to the Ridgeleigh swimming pool. He spelled out not only my duties as he saw them, but also the role he had long envisioned for me:

> *Loeb, Rhoades, even though controlled by me, is a big business and . . . a public trust with responsibilities to many, including its partners, employees, customers, correspondents, associated businesses & the public in general. It needs additional help at the top, and for special jobs too. . . . Whoever is loyal to me and over a*

---

[*] I was twenty-six at this point and had not really been at "home" for seventeen years. Eight to nine months of every year I was at school. The last years in the Air Force, I was away for almost all of the two years.

period relieves me of responsibilities* I have been carrying for years, whoever is a builder and leader will be rewarded out of all proportion. If this turns out to be someone other than you, my boy . . . so be it . . .

I have been keeping the position open [in fact, I was never given a position] for you and hoping you would want to follow in your grandfather's and my footsteps. If you don't want it, I will do my best to find a substitute. What causes you to want to do similar work elsewhere when you have a high tradition to carry on, a responsibility to your family . . . is more than I can understand and does you no credit. If you want to be a history teacher (although I question this or your competence), go ahead. Whatever you do, you have my love always but not necessarily my respect and approval.

In the end, Father reluctantly agreed to grant me four untethered months before coming to Loeb, Rhoades. Even though I'd flirted with other careers, what Father didn't know was that heading Loeb, Rhoades had been my real goal since childhood. If I'm honest about it all these decades later, I probably made a mistake. I should have spent

Though my mother usually tried her best to defend me, and though my father wrote an accusative letter to me by himself, she signed it, too.

two or three years getting my feet wet somewhere else. What would Father have done? Despite his threats, he still would have accepted me when I returned, and our relationship would have been better for it.

On the last leg of my journey back from Paris and the Orient, with fond memories of holiday family gatherings and tinsel on the tree, I was glad to be getting home in time for our annual Christmas celebrations. Exactly one year earlier, I had first tried to introduce the subject of my career with Father. This time, he and I shared a conversation over drinks at Grandma's party. By then I had surrendered. I took advantage of the moment to make a soft entry into the subject of my new career, having no idea what

---

* Until my grandfather died, all final decisions were made by him personally. He had died about a year earlier.

I would be faced with when I walked into the Loeb, Rhoades offices. I asked what I thought was a noncontroversial three-part question, something I asked about every business we studied at HBS—especially since I'd really never been exposed to any of our firm's operations: "Father, what do you feel Loeb, Rhoades has accomplished in the past, how is it doing now, and where do you see it heading?"

He looked at me. "That is without doubt the stupidest question I have ever heard in my life," he replied. He would, in the years to come, ask the same questions of others, perhaps forgetting where he'd first heard it, as well as his dismissive reaction.

With his words echoing in my ears, I entered the doors of Loeb, Rhoades the following week. A canny card player, Father had counted on my deep sense of family responsibility and my presumption of a financially secure life. My two most powerful motivations had, in the end, given him the winning hand.

VILHELM HAMMERSHØI 1864–1916
Interior, Strandgade 30 (1899)
(Ambassador John L. Loeb Jr. Danish Art Collection)

J.L. JENSEN 1800–1856
Still Life of Fruits with Pineapple (1833)
(Ambassador John L. Loeb Jr. Danish Art Collection)

PEDER MØNSTED 1859–1941
Woodland Scene with Pond Near Vejle (1920)
(Ambassador John L. Loeb Jr. Danish Art Collection)

PART THREE

Business and

Politics

Though I tried to appear confident and assured, I knew I had a lot to learn when I joined Wall Street and the world of Loeb, Rhoades.

≡

CHAPTER EIGHT

Loeb, Rhoades (Not So) Heir Apparent, 1957–1969

When I joined Loeb, Rhoades in January 1957, I was about one year older than the firm founded by my grandfather and father in 1931. Twenty years had elapsed since their original company, Carl M. Loeb & Co., had merged with the "white shoe" brokerage firm of Rhoades & Company. Loeb, Rhoades was moving quickly toward the peak of its glory. For the next fifteen years, it would be the darling of the Wall Street press. The banner headline of a *Fortune* magazine article in April 1963 summed it up: "Wherever You Look, There's Loeb, Rhoades." In the article, T.A. Wise praised the company's impact in the financial world, noting "Wall Street's curiosity about the house that appears to be in the middle of everything."[78]*

When I arrived, we had twenty-one general partners and extensive correspondent relationships with firms throughout the country, many of them in New York City. Although our London office remained open throughout the war, the offices in Paris, Frankfurt and Berlin were closed when Hitler's rise threatened our Jewish employees. The youngest major Wall Street firm at the time, Loeb, Rhoades nonetheless occupied a strong position in the securities business, including brokerage, investment banking and underwriting.[79]

---

* In the *Fortune* article, Wise wrote, "Few men claim to know [John Loeb Sr.] well. Those who do discern a prevailing warmth, charm, and quiet good humor. From even a slight distance, however, he appears to be the 'aristocrat of autocrats', courteous, quiet-spoken, attentive in one mood, yet glacial, enigmatic, acid in the next—with the moods subject to change sharply and swiftly."

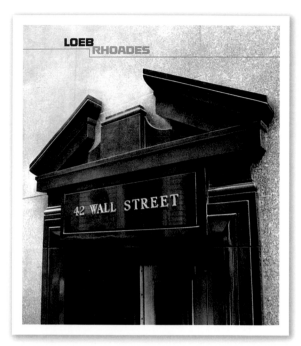

42 Wall Street private entrance and elevator to Loeb, Rhoades. When I started there, Loeb, Rhoades enjoyed extremely warm approval of the financial world's media.

The greatest percentage of our company business was brokerage, most of which came from our twenty-two correspondents in different cities, including: J.C. Bradford in Nashville, Piper Jaffray in Minneapolis, Prescott in Pittsburgh, A. G. Edwards in St. Louis, William Blair in Chicago, Wainwright in Boston, Boettcher in Denver, and Sutro in California, among others, as well as a growing number of New York City correspondents (more than forty).[80] Foreign correspondents included Greenshields in Canada, Roldos and Mercantil de Inversiones in Argentina and Yamaichi Securities in Tokyo (a firm I had visited on my way home from Paris via a trip through the Orient).

As a broker's broker, we were the firm that cleared its buying and selling with the New York Stock Exchange and the American Stock Exchange. Increasingly over the years, many small firms began to clear their business with us as well. Even though we were clearing business for many firms, their business (as well as ours) was still 90 percent individuals. There were no big institutions such as insurance companies or mutual, pension or hedge funds that owned stocks. These gigantic institutions did not yet exist or were still in their infancy.*

Father had repeatedly assured me, both in person and in letters, that I would someday head this great company. Very recently, he had told me he had a position open for me now. In fact, he implied it was to report directly to him. However, at this time there was no position, no office, not even a desk. In due course, I would even have to threaten to leave in order to get a job. But for now, I was well aware that I was low man on the totem pole. I knew that my father was not likely to hand over the reins while he was alive. His own father never really retired, staying in control until the day he died.

Although Father insisted that he needed me at the company, I had no actual role, title or specific job awaiting me. In short, all his talk about needing me immediately was just that—talk. My first six months were spent learning how the company functioned. Even

---

* Today everything is reversed—nearly 90 percent of business on the exchanges is from institutions.

with my Harvard MBA and Air Force experience, I'd never been exposed to the inner sanctum of Loeb, Rhoades and knew little of how it functioned. My father had a close business relationship with C.M. from the beginning, but Father had made a point of never involving me in any aspect of his business affairs. I knew I had a lot to learn and that my "ascension" within the firm would depend on hard work and, more important, mastering the complex politics of the firm and family. In the meantime, while learning the ropes, I longed for just a desk to call my own.

Father was considered an autocrat, not only in the family but also in the business world. The *Bawl Street Journal*, a parody

The *Bawl Street Journal* cartoon reads, "No, I didn't have a hard time at the office. But everybody else at Loeb, Rhoades did!"

publication, frequently lampooned Loeb, Rhoades management. One jibe printed in the 1960s shows my father asking for the time from a quivering employee. "Whatever time you want it to be, Mr. Loeb," he responds. According to *Our Crowd* author Stephen Birmingham, Father was "held in almost dreadful awe in Wall Street."[81]

Though Father rarely fired anyone, everyone at Loeb, Rhoades was amused by this cartoon: "FIRED? I always thought slaves were sold."

In terms of management style, Father played everything close to his chest, dealing one-on-one with the "stars" of the firm and sometimes playing one off another. My Harvard Business School training emphasized team effort: a more open atmosphere in which stars worked together as a constellation. But Loeb, Rhoades was a patchwork of little fiefdoms, with each partner ferociously protecting his turf. All vied for my father's favor, and each wanted to be the contact point for the best clients and juiciest deals. The chances of anyone helping me—the boss's son—were nonexistent. My peers, I've been told, perceived me as arrogant. The truth was the opposite; I was just plain scared. My efforts to appear confident must have come across as imperious.

Richard Feigen, my friend from college, Harvard Business School and Hollywood, was working at another firm. He and I would compare notes. Although Loeb, Rhoades was composed of the "best and the brightest," he observed, "it was also a pool of piranhas." In his opinion, Father never offered me "so much as a life jacket." Father's attempts to remain impartial toward me tilted too far in the opposite direction. His support was instead focused on my cousin Tommy Kempner, who considered himself my rival.

In 1955, Tommy believed we were competitors for the top job at Loeb, Rhoades. We had both visited our Grandfather Loeb at the hospital shortly before he died. As we left C.M.'s room, Tommy quietly noted, "Now you and I will be rivals for the throne." I was startled; I thought it was clear to everyone that just as my father would succeed his father as head of the company, in due time, I would succeed mine. I never dreamed anyone else would even be in the running. I had known that Tommy, the son of Father's only sister, Margaret Loeb Kempner, was brilliant, good with numbers and very hardworking, but not always good with people. Quiet, soft-spoken and observant, Tommy was also a devoted grandson of C.M.'s

Other members of the family worked at Loeb, Rhoades, but no one else seemed to aspire to head the company. They included my father's youngest brother, Uncle Henry Loeb. Uncle Henry had gone to Princeton and Harvard Law School and was one of the great heroes of our family. He volunteered as a private in World War II, despite the fact he was overage and married with two children. He landed on Utah Beach on D-Day and participated in an artillery unit in every major battle in the war. Luckily, he came out with only deafness in one ear. John Levin (married to Uncle Henry's daughter Betty), my brother-in-law Richard Beaty (my sister Judy's husband) and my cousin Peter Loeb (son of Carl Loeb Jr., Father's middle brother) also worked at the firm. Peter was also brilliant and an extremely hard worker, and he was an outstanding graduate of the Columbia University Business School. Carl Jr., a graduate of MIT, a metallurgist and a senior officer at the American Metal Climax Company, was a limited partner, but he never worked for the firm. Only Tommy viewed himself as my true rival.

One of the reasons Father never really trained me in the business, or anyone else, for that matter, is he never planned for the future at all. In my opinion, Father saw planning as a threat to his control and leadership. Understanding Father's insecurities, I can see why he let things develop as they did. He remembered that his father, CEO of American Metal Company, had been removed from the company (if not fired), and there was no way he was going to let that happen to him. He wouldn't plan for the future because it inevitably involved his sharing power.

So when I joined Loeb, Rhoades, there was no training program at all at the firm, and none was instituted throughout Loeb, Rhoades's existence, although I endlessly brought up the subject and pushed for it. Father never put in place any plans for a successor—neither for himself nor for any other members of the management committee. He operated in a perpetuate state of denial; even as many of the heads of the great correspondent firms turned over their jobs to the next generation, Father held fast. He never thought about the company's future beyond his time, much less did anything about it.

In spite of the less than friendly atmosphere, I was soon writing enthusiastic letters to friends, not revealing my underlying angst. Three days after starting at Loeb, Rhoades, I described to George Miller (who subsequently became an Air Force general) the mechanics of the back office:

> *At the moment I am in the order room at the "turret," the word given to the order desk, the fulcrum between the customer and the floor of the Stock Exchange where the actual execution of the order takes place. . . . It is a most hectic and exciting place. . . . I must admit that . . . I am very impressed by the firm and there are two men here who border on being geniuses.*

One of these "geniuses" was Mark Millard, who would become a friend over the years. When he first started at Loeb, Rhoades, my grandfather told him to change his name from the Russian "Minitsky," and Mark chose "Millard" from the New York telephone directory. Mark ran the new business department and was the most outstanding investment banker in the field of energy on Wall Street. He would play a major role in the 1968 merger that formed the Amerada Hess Corporation.

Armand Erpf was director of the research department and one of the savviest, most respected men on Wall Street. He was a brilliant investor and a proponent of the Graham and Dodd theory of "value investing." Armand was an enthusiastic early backer and financial advisor to *New York Magazine*'s founder, Clay Felker, so my family and I were among early major investors in what since 1968 has been a road map to New York culture. I was especially close to Armand and loved visiting him in his handsome home in the Catskills. When he had a heart attack in 1971, I rode beside him in the ambulance, where he died en route to the hospital. It was not only a great loss to the firm, but also a great shock and personal loss to me.

Among other lowly tasks, I spent time as a "runner" or "gofer," delivering messages all over Wall Street, just as my father had done in his early days after leaving the American Metal Company. By March of my first year, I wrote a friend in England that I had been exposed to the order room, the purchase and sales department, the cage, the dividend department, the IBM and the margin department. I also reported with awe that the company's treasurer, Jacob Brown, knew "more about money as a commodity than any professor of economics at dear old Harvard."

One of the first investments I made that year was in a private placement for General Transistor, a recommendation of a Harvard classmate, Carl Knobloch. I had also remembered one of my HBS professors holding up a transistor in our classroom, assuring us that "these things" would change the world. At that time, I didn't know much about transistors, but I decided to make an investment without the advice of anyone at Loeb, Rhoades. One partner, Sam Stedman, acted quickly on my recommendation before promoting it to others.

At first I only listened during the meetings and took advantage of driving home with Father to privately bring up my suggestions. He frequently acted on them, which is how I was able to bring on board many financial talents who contributed to the company's success. Years later, in my parents' memoir, Father gave me credit for bringing able people to the firm: Sidney Knafel, Bill Spears, Francis Fraenkel, Felipe Propper, Francois Bohn and Paul Mejean. In due course, I brought in about twenty-five important individuals to our firm.[82]

Alas, there was one very significant piece of my advice Father never took. I strongly felt we should change the company from a partnership to a corporation. The primary reason was that Loeb, Rhoades partnership agreements were renewed annually. This meant that if a partner decided to leave, his invested money could—and usually did—go with him.* This meant we couldn't count on a reliable amount of capital from one year to the next—except for family money. Having more consistent capital would enable us to expand into profitable new arenas. Father, however, was more interested in having a vehicle in which to invest his and the family's money than to grow the firm. In fact, as related in Leon Levy's book *The Mind of Wall Street*, Father was shocked that some firms had begun to go public in the early 1970s. When Levy, an established financier, asked him what he did if his firm needed outside capital, Father replied, "Why, we simply call one of our aunts."[83]

Not incidentally, Father was a brilliant investor. He had an unerring sense of what to

---

* I recently learned an unbelievable story from Richard Harriton, a back-office official at Loeb, Rhoades. Among Richard's responsibilities, per Father's edict, was getting each partner to add his signature to the annual partnership agreement without being allowed to read it! Nevertheless, they always signed.

buy, when to buy and when to sell. His worst threat to any of us in the family was that if we didn't "shape up," he might stop managing our investments. My two persistent pleas, to expand the company and for Loeb, Rhoades to become a corporation, were a constant source of irritation to him. I could never press too far, lest he follow through on his threat. After all, he was the best investment manager I ever had.

After the six-month training period, I was placed in the research department, reporting to my cousin Tommy, who had preceded me at Loeb, Rhoades by seven years and had recently become a general partner. Tommy turned me over for training to Paul Zeisler Jr., a brilliant and aloof man who was a miserable teacher. Extremely unhappy, I urged Father to send me to London to work under Hubert Simon, whom I liked and admired, from my summer visit to Europe with C.M. Fortunately, Father was in a good mood right then, because of a business coup in Cuba, and he agreed.

Early in their marriage, Father had told my mother that he "didn't want to get stuck in a rut with one [social] group"[84] and that they should branch out and find new experiences. After he left American Metal in 1928, they were discussing where to go on vacation. At first they contacted a hotel in Bermuda—where Father had gone as a boy—to set up a reservation. On the call, the hotel manager noted, "and you'll be glad to know that we don't cater to any Jews."[85]

They opted to vacation in Cuba, a place that accepted them openly and where they would go on to spend part of every winter. Father said it was the only place they went where they were "active with . . . the top of the social class."[86] They entirely embraced Havana and its culture and were welcomed into all kinds of high-society clubs. As was typical, Father would get bored while down there, and over the years he began to invest in sugar deals in Cuba. By the 1950s, Cuba was the world's biggest sugar exporter. He became friendly with two powerful sugar families, the Fallas and the Sueros. But it was Julio Lobo, the "Sugar King," who was head of the Cuban-Atlantic Sugar Company and the big dog in the industry. An admirer of Napoleon, Lobo filled his office with statuettes and other memorabilia of the French general and emperor.

In 1956, Lobo had been forced to sell the Cuban-Atlantic Sugar Company. Fulgencio Batista, Cuba's dictator, told Julio that he couldn't be the largest sugar trader in Cuba while also controlling the largest sugar company in the country. Father was friendly with Julio and owned shares in his company. Julio went to Father and suggested he put a group together to take over Julio's controlling position in Cuban-Atlantic. Father organized a few investors, and, as a group, they did just that. Father then restructured the company and quickly made Cuban-Atlantic much more profitable.

By 1957 Lobo, who had been very unhappy about being forced to sell, was told by Batista that he could buy back the Hershey refineries, which had been part of Cuban-Atlantic, but not the six great mills, which produced almost 10 percent of the sugar refined in Cuba.

While Cuban-Atlantic's sale of the Hershey refineries was underway, there were troubling signs of political unrest in Cuba. Lobo began to drag his feet about completing the purchase, but Father told Julio that if he didn't act by midnight, December 31, 1957, he couldn't buy it at all. Lobo dallied until the last moment, but I remember Father leaving the New Year's Eve party at Grandma Lehman's house (45 East 70th Street) early to go back home and close the deal.

Lobo's $25 million purchase of the Hershey refineries covered most of what Father's investment group had initially paid for a controlling interest in Cuban-Atlantic. Father had put me on the board of Cuban-Atlantic almost immediately after he took control. I kept telling Father that Fidel Castro, who was causing the political unrest, was a Communist and that we were in danger of losing everything. He told me I didn't know what I was talking about—again accusing me of being a Chicken Little. There was no way the U.S. government would let anything like that happen on an island just ninety miles off its coast, he confidently assured me. A year later, the Cuban Revolution began, Batista fled Havana, and Castro took over. There was no way of dealing with him. Soon, Father would come to the same conclusions I did.

But that day in his office, with the Lobo deal closed, Father was in benevolent spirits. He knew how much I loved England, so he sent me across the Atlantic. Hubert Simon's branch had held on to its earlier name, "Carl M. Loeb, Rhoades & Co." I was glad to learn that my grandfather's name was still well known and highly thought of in Europe, a place where family names in business meant even more than they did in America. Hubert had started working for C.M. at our Berlin office in 1932, and then wisely transferred to London before the war, where he grew into a major figure in the company. He proved an admirable mentor for me, and, under his guidance, I became more valuable to Loeb, Rhoades.

I loved calling on customers with Hubert, who not only knew all of our current and prospective clients, but also much of the personal history of their fathers, grandfathers and great-grandfathers. He was an endless fountain of information about which families in British society were important, who was intelligent, who was a contender, whose son was a drug addict, which son would inherit the family firm, and so on. I soaked up his stories and still remember many of them.

Hubert was a stickler for proper dress. Upon my arrival, he took one look and hastily dispatched me to Father's Savile Row tailor. I wasn't let out of the office until properly outfitted and equipped with a black "brolly" to protect my new wardrobe from London's unpredictable daily showers. Kim Kendall's sister Kay was married to the British actor Rex Harrison, and while Kim and I were still flirting with marriage, Rex had been like a brother-in-law to me. Though the relationship with Kim was dwindling, my friendship with Rex flourished, and the impeccably dressed star of *My Fair Lady* suggested I try his tailor, Kilgour. Father was quite upset that I didn't go to his tailor, Huntsman, apparently considering this an act of disloyalty.

Rex Harrison

I found a flat to live in at Bryanston Mews East, near Marble Arch. Not the upscale address it is now, the Mews had first been a stable and then a garage. Upon my arrival, it was ready for human habitation, and with the dollar strong against the pound, it was more than affordable.

It took a bit more time to get used to the social and sexual mores of the British. I had my eyes opened at a weekend in the country arranged by my friend Bobby Buxton, whom I'd met in Paris two years earlier. By my second weekend in England, he had gotten us an invitation to visit the Duke and Duchess of Bedford in their castle, Woburn Abbey, a historic estate a little over an hour's drive from London. England was in poor straits, recovering slowly from the financial and physical scars of World War II. The Duke of Bedford was forced to keep the wolf from his castle door through a number of eyebrow-raising commercial enterprises. His estate was home to a nudist colony, a small zoo and a circus!

Bobby and I arrived on a Friday and spent a convivial evening with the royal Bedfords. On Saturday morning, I was awoken by a knock on my guest room door. Without waiting for a response, in walked the duchess herself, carrying a breakfast tray.

"Johnny, are you up?"

"Yes. Well, I'm getting up," I said, while trying to untangle myself from the bedclothes. The beautiful older woman had already laid the tray on a nearby table and sat down on the edge of my bed. Naïvely, I thought it was wonderful of her to be so thoughtful a hostess, and we wound up having nothing more than a lovely chat. A few months later I ran into her at a cocktail party, arm in arm with a man even younger than I was.

Baron Jacob de Rothschild

Sir Evelyn de Rothschild

Baron David de Rothschild

This was my introduction to the accepted attitudes of upper-class British society toward marital sidelines.

An assortment of attractive London girls perceived me as richer than I was and therefore worthy of their attention. As Bobby Buxton* once joked with me, "Just pronounce your words properly and don't frighten the horses." It was an enormous edge to be thought a rich American in postwar England, and I was delighted to find that there was no social stigma in being Jewish. However, I discovered that most of these attractive young ladies had boyfriends, leaving me more than a little confused and bemused by their "inspections."

As I was considered at that time to be the heir to the Lehman/Loeb fortune and the future head of Loeb, Rhoades, I was treated to lunch and dinner by most of the great investment firms. Evelyn de Rothschild had me to dinner a few times, once with Lady Carolyn Townshend, who subsequently became my brother-in-law Edgar Bronfman's second wife. A number of years later, Evelyn invited me and Nina, on our honeymoon, to stay at Ascott House, a country estate owned by the National Trust in Buckinghamshire, outside of London.

There were no romances in England such as I'd had with Jill Spaulding. Jill was a brilliant, beautiful Radcliffe student, and my romance with her was one that my parents vigorously opposed, as did her parents. I have no idea why, but Jill and I are still great friends.

Evelyn emerged in London as one of the two great Rothschilds of my generation. He inherited N M Rothschild & Sons. He did a great job and then retired and turned it over to his French cousin David de Rothschild, who ended up managing both French and English busi-

---

* Bobby Buxton and Sir Tobias Clarke made me a member of Whites Club. I had already been a member of the Brooks and Buck's Clubs.

nesses. Jacob Rothschild inherited the English title of Lord from his father, Victor Rothschild. He personally founded a great financial conglomerate called Rothschild Investment Trust (now RIT Capital Partners).

I joined several men's clubs, including St. James's (now merged with Brooks), one of the oldest in London. On one memorable occasion, I was invited to lunch by a Buck's Club member. Sitting at the bar waiting for my host, I ordered a Virgin Mary, not being much of a drinker. When my tardy host still had not arrived, I pushed my empty glass toward the bartender and asked, "Could I have another one please?"

The man standing next to me touched my arm gently and said earnestly, "No, no, never say, 'I'll have another one.' Just say, 'I'll have one.'"

To my shock, this was none other than Harold Macmillan, the prime minister of England. We got to talking, and I was very sorry when my host arrived, for the prime minister had proved quite engaging.

Although it did not turn into a romance, I became a good friend of Mary Fitzalan-Howard, the daughter of Bernard Fitzalan-Howard, 16th Duke of Norfolk. We saw each other from time to time, and she invited me on a number of weekends down to her home, Arundel Castle, the home of the Duke of Norfolk.

The duke was frustrated. He had no sons, only four daughters, and he looked like he came right out of central casting. His wife, Lavinia, Duchess of Norfolk, along with John Dunlop, ran a successful racing stable called Castle Stables. Whenever I came down to Arundel, Lavinia would always chide me and say, "All rich Americans should own horses."

Finally, I surrendered and said I would buy three horses, but only if Mary agreed to be my full partner. Wonderfully, Mary agreed. We competed in quite a lot of local races, including the one in the picture, showing me, Mary, and Rising Falcon. One year we even had a horse running at Ascot with both our racing colors. Of course, it didn't hurt that Mary's father was Her Majesty's representative to Ascot. Frankly, I didn't get deeply involved in racing, but to quote a Texan friend of mine, "Aw shure don't know much about racing, but I do like the people who go with it."

The most exciting day in London with

Me and Lady Mary Fitzalan-Howard, with "Rising Falcon" after taking Second Place, Watneys Special Handicap at Sandown, Thursday, July 21, 1977.

Grandmother Lehman and my parents were more than eager to own this wonderful Manet self-portrait.
They asked Hubert Simon to bid anonymously on their behalf at the 1958 Sotheby's auction in London.
I was with Hubert at the sale.

Hubert was spent not on behalf of Loeb, Rhoades, but for my family. It took place at a price-shattering Sotheby's auction on October 15, 1958. My parents and grandmother assigned Hubert to bid for them on the Manet self-portrait of 1879, one of only two that he ever painted. Hubert invited me to come along.

The Manet portrait was among the seven famous Impressionist paintings that the wealthy art collector Jakob Goldschmidt had been able to remove from Germany just before World War II. Two years after the collector died in 1956, Goldschmidt's son, Erwin, chose Sotheby's London to auction his father's three Manets, two Cezannes, a Van Gogh and a Renoir. The Manet self-portrait was described by Charles Moffett, Sotheby's executive vice president, as "not only the greatest Manet portrait in private hands, but also one of the very greatest self-portraits in the entire canon of art history."[87]

Sotheby's decided to hold an elegant evening auction solely for the seven Goldschmidt masterpieces. An incredible amount of media fanfare, with press releases going to twenty-three countries, touted the event as the "sale of the century." And indeed it was. Two hours before the sale, a queue of 1,500 buyers, media reps and the curious vied to squeeze inside when the doors first opened. Only a chosen few made it into the main salesroom; the rest of the crowd had to sit in adjacent rooms or the corridor where television sets relayed the auction.

We ended up front row center after Hubert told the Sotheby's chairman, Peter Wilson, that he would be a serious bidder. All necks were swiveling to see famous bidders such as

The *Illustrated London News* ran this photo the day after the Sotheby's auction of the seven Goldschmidt paintings in Ocotber 1958. I can be seen directly under the auctioneer's podium in the second row center, with my head slightly turned.

Lady Churchill, the writer Somerset Maugham, ballet diva Dame Margot Fonteyn, Tate Gallery director Sir John Rothenstein and actors Kirk Douglas and Anthony Quinn.

The Manet portrait was the first to come up for sale.[88] As the bidding began, my heart was in my mouth until Peter Wilson, acting as auctioneer, called out "going, going, GONE!" His ivory gavel came down in just sixty-five seconds on Hubert's bid of £65,000,[89] the approximate equivalent then of $182,000.[90] All seven of the French Impressionist masterpieces were sold in twenty-one minutes for a record-breaking £781,000.* Though the Manet portrait was a joint purchase made by my parents and my grandmother Adele Lewisohn Lehman, my memory is that it stayed permanently with my parents. It was sold for $18.7 million at the May 12, 1997, Christie's auction of their complete collection, following their deaths in 1996.

For close to a year, I worked happily in London, building relations with clients, creating new business and believing that I'd found the right niche for myself at Loeb, Rhoades. I'd initiated a major deal with Diebold Europe that closed triumphantly. I was beginning to think that I should plant my roots and stay in England for good. After all, I had friends who made permanent careers in London and had done very well.

However, a phone call from Father scuttled those nascent plans. "Johnny," he began, "I understand that you'd like to stay in England." He didn't say how he knew that, but it was true.

I said cautiously, "Yes, Father, that's true."

"Well, that's too bad. It's all right if you stay in England." He paused. "Of course, if you were to come back to New York, I had been planning to make you a partner, but . . ."

A partner! Wouldn't that mean a meaningful position for me back in New York? I was practically on the first flight home.

With much fanfare in the press, Father kept his promise and made me a general partner on January 2, 1959. *The New York Times* covered the promotion under the headline, "Continuity of Old Street Names Assured by New Partnerships." Even though Father hadn't said anything about my role, it certainly sounded as though there was a meaningful job in the offing.

As partner, I would also now share in any profit the company made. But it also meant that I'd be financially liable for any major debts the firm might incur, along with all the oth-

---

* Hubert registered under a fictitious name, Martin Summers. As it happened, there really was a young up-and-coming London art dealer of that name, who was more than startled to be congratulated on making so successful a bid at the prestigious Sotheby's event.

er general partners. The question of incorporation rose in my mind again, but I let the matter drop, satisfied to finally be given a position with Father's firm. Or so I thought.

My status as a general partner did not, as I'd hoped, include a higher rung on the company ladder. I found myself at the beginning of my third year at Loeb, Rhoades stuck in neutral, with no permanent office and no position that would groom me for a managerial post. I'd had a sense of real purpose and accomplishment in England, but back in New York, I was on the ground floor again. Whatever small missions I was assigned were scattered all over many different offices.

Sam Stedman

When Father pronounced me "floundering," I heatedly responded that I needed continuity. I proposed that I should either be his assistant or work under a senior analyst in our research department. I needed one specific mission and an assigned place to work in a specific area of our business. Father finally offered that I work part-time with a research analyst, Sam Stedman or Tommy Kempner, and part-time for him. Neither working with Tommy—who viewed himself as my rival—or as my father's assistant seemed like wise ideas.

I opted to work with Sam, believing he could help improve my analytic skills. Sam gave me credit for finding the General Transistor stock, which meant a great deal to me. We started out on an excellent footing, and that good relationship never changed. Sam was also living proof that you shouldn't judge a book by its cover; sartorially speaking, he would not have been Hubert Simon's cup of tea. The gregarious, craggy-faced Missouri native usually looked like an "unmade bed." One of our most important correspondents once confided to me that Sam's attire and general mien were so non–Wall Street that Father wouldn't have kept him—or allowed him to travel on behalf of the firm—if he weren't so brilliant in assessing stocks. A *Fortune* magazine article in 1960 titled "Powerful Men Downtown" included a picture of Sam and noted, "His reputation today is such that floor traders will buy heavily into a stock as soon as they hear that Stedman is due to discuss it in a luncheon speech." Perhaps more than any other one man on the Street, Stedman is responsible for the public acceptance of high price-earnings ratios of growth stocks, notably of stocks like Polaroid. In another article, *Fortune* dubbed him "The Wiz-

Loeb, Rhoades management committee in the 1960s. Seated, left to right: John L. Loeb Jr., John L. Loeb and Carl M. Mueller. Standing, left to right: Walter H. Walz, Thomas L. Kempner, Mark J. Millard, Henry A. Loeb and Gene M. Woodlin. Father, Walter Walz and I were involved with the brokerage end of our business. The other members of the committee were involved with investment banking deals. Brokerage was approximately 90 percent of the firm's revenues.

Because Father kept his promise to make me a Loeb, Rhoades general partner, I was included in this group portrait of the firm's partners in 1960. Seated, left to right: Mark Millard, Clifford Michel, John L. Loeb (Sr.), Armand Erpf, Palmer Dixon and Henry Loeb. Standing, left to right: Kenrick Gillespie, Herbert Higgins, Richard Beaty, Hans Widenmann, Carl Mueller, Stanley Grant, John L. Loeb Jr., Stephen Koshland, Samuel Stedman, Thomas L. Kempner Sr., Howard Carlson, Raymond McKernan, Henry Parish II, Hunter Goodrich Jr. and Gordon Hensley.

ard of Wall Street." Sam had the unorthodox strategy of evaluating companies on their potential rather than their current asset value. His "growth stocks" were, in a way, the opposite of Armand Erpf's "value investments."

When I came to work at Loeb, Rhoades, every brokerage house received exactly the same commission percentage. Very often, it was the research departments that made the difference to potential clients. Sam's uncanny ability to predict a growth stock made Loeb, Rhoades a star. Sam's foresight gave Loeb, Rhoades a big edge and made us the go-to company for many new institutional firms. I couldn't have found a better mentor and role model for my future as Loeb, Rhoades heir apparent than Sam Stedman.

In November 1959, I took a skiing holiday in Switzerland. Father tracked me down by phone in St. Moritz, saying that one of our clients, Murphy Oil, wanted to buy a group of gas stations in Scandinavia, starting in Sweden. "I know you like Sweden," he said. "Why don't you go there before coming back to New York and help Murphy Oil any way you can."

I immediately called my well-connected Swedish friend Rolf Af Sandberg, whom I'd met through Bobby Buxton in Paris. "I'm coming to Stockholm on business," I said. "Why don't you throw me a party?"

Rolf, who came from a distinguished family, knew everyone I'd like to know, including the most beautiful women. He was an ideal host and orchestrated a wonderful event, where I was taken with a blonde beauty named Marianne Sundby. At the time, Marianne was in love with a Swedish baron, so I asked Rolf, "Can you find me someone *like* Marianne?"

"Well," said Rolf, "she has a sister just as beautiful, but she's not a blonde." He then persuaded Marianne's sister to meet me on a blind date. Nina Sundby turned out to be more beautiful than her sister, and clearly to the manor born. Even my parents would approve.

Ours was not a whirlwind courtship; it was a tornado. Nina and I connected instantly and were never out of each other's sight from the day we met. With my departure from Switzerland looming, Nina wanted me to meet her family before I left. We drove to Krontorps, her parents' estate about four and a half hours outside of Stockholm. I was anxious not to lose this magnificent woman, and I wanted Nina to know I was seriously in love with her.

I turned to her in the car and blurted, "Marry me!"

Without a beat, she said, "Yes!" We entered her family's home as a happily committed couple.

I'd assumed the Sundby family was Swedish, but it turned out that they were actually Norwegian. Nina's father was a successful timber entrepreneur who owned and operated a large lumber mill in Norway. He had bought the Swedish estate in Kristinehamn primarily because of its five thousand acres of pristine timberland. Once owned by a Swedish king, the property had been in the hands of a Swedish bank for some time, and the large home was in need of repair. Johannes and Alfild Sundby had moved from Norway to Sweden several years earlier with their five children and restored Krontorps to some of its former glory. As we drove onto the restored estate, I was instantly reminded of the Tara plantation from *Gone with the Wind.*

On cloud nine and with her parents' blessing, we returned to Stockholm with marriage in our future, and then flew on to New York. As I knew they would, my parents completely approved of Nina, but things were not entirely smooth. I'd assumed, as had Nina's parents, that we'd live as an engaged couple for a few years before marrying, especially since we had just met. Nina had been a secretary in the Foreign Service and wanted to get a job at the United Nations in New York, possibly as a guide. My mother was aghast; how could her future daughter-in-law have to work? Mother was having none of it. She insisted that Nina go back to Sweden—like a number of women her age, Mother resented the very idea of "free love." She made such a to-do about it, threatening to call Nina's mother and making life more difficult for us. I gave in—as I often did to my parents—and set forth with wedding plans.

We were married on April 9, 1960, in a storybook wedding. A Lutheran bishop performed the service in a small church in Kristinehamn. There were so many American friends and relatives who took the almost six-hour train ride from Stockholm that they took up one entire coach and spilled into a second.

Shortly after our arrival back in New York, Father officially named me Sam Stedman's deputy. Sam had become head of the institutional department in 1959, which gave me an actual position with a title, office space and a chance to work in one consistent area. Most of our VIP partners were now focused on corporate finance and "doing deals." While not as glamorous, brokerage was still the firm's bread and butter, and Sam and I were happy to focus on the less dramatic but more profitable business.

Institutions were just beginning to take hold in the financial world, but they had a lot of money to invest and were always looking for potentially profitable stocks. Institutions or mutual funds had tremendous business to offer, but Wall Street VIPs didn't pay them much attention. Sam, however, saw them as a potential gold mine, and we began to court them.

When Sam found strong investment possibilities, he spoke to a few select institutions about them. If he found one or two investor institutions warming to his choices, he would see that his suggestions were written up at Loeb, Rhoades. Our team then pitched these write-ups to more institutions and also gave them to our current clients. Sam was a riveting speaker and pitched so well that if he liked a stock, it was bound to soar.

In some ways, Sam was flying too close to the sun. Sam had a practice of buying both "puts" and "calls" on a stock he favored to increase his own gains. It was a way to hedge his bets, and at the time it was still a legal practice. A "call" lets you buy, and a "put" lets you sell. If Sam liked Polaroid, he would buy a call to be able to buy Polaroid at a set price. He would—at the same time—sell a "put" for half that amount, which would significantly reduce the cost of the call. It was akin to putting a hundred dollars on one team to win but then putting fifty on the other. Overall, he would be taking less risk.

But Sam was not blindly gambling; he could influence the outcome. He was confident that the stock he was buying calls for was going to go up; he would ensure this by promoting it. Also, when he bought a call and sold a put through a broker, the brokers had to buy one hundred shares of the stock to hedge themselves. Sam was also promoting the stock to the institutions and all our correspondents. Seeing how well this worked, all of us working with Sam decided to do the same thing. If the stock didn't go up, we were able to get out with little or no loss. If it all worked, we made a lot of money, having risked very little. Contributing to Stedman's influence was the broad selling power of Loeb, Rhoades.

This went on beautifully for about two years until I woke up in the middle of the night with a worrisome thought. When you sell a put, somebody has to buy it. I began to wonder: *Who do they have the put against? Was it against me, Sam Stedman, or somehow against Loeb, Rhoades? Who has to buy it? Does Loeb, Rhoades have the liability?* A flashing red light went off in my head. It must be our firm!

The next morning, I immediately went to the back office. "Where is the record of our puts kept?" I asked. "There must be a list."

"What record? What list are you talking about?" Richard Harriton replied.

"The list of *puts.*"

"Why? What do you need it for?"

"Never mind why, I just want to look at it *right now,*" I demanded.

"Oh, it's around here somewhere," Richard blithely noted. "Somebody will find it for you in a day or two. Don't worry about it."

I ransacked the back office until I found the records tucked in an unmarked drawer. Reading quickly, I was aghast. There was somewhere between $150 to $200 million worth of puts against the firm. I went to Father immediately, explaining that while Sam's system was wonderfully profitable for a few of us, it had the potential of becoming a disas-

A STORYBOOK WEDDING IN SWEDEN, APRIL 9, 1960

After the reception and dinner-dance held at Krontorps, the wedding party emerged for a group photo in front of the handsome family home. My ushers included my friend Marc Wallenberg Jr. My brother, Arthur, was my best man, and Nina's sister, Marianne, was her maid of honor. Marianne married my friend Tony Ittleson, whose family founded CIT. Tony and Marianne had three children. Sadly, Marianne died in 2001.

An enormous crowd of Kristinehamn townspeople lined up to watch the wedding guests arrive. Here we see Nina's father, Johannes Sundby, escort her into the Lutheran church where we were married. My aunt Margaret Kempner later wrote, "Nina looked like an exquisite fairy princess."

Shortly after my marriage to Nina in 1960, the Loeb family posed for this portrait. On the far left of the first row, my sister Ann sits with four of her five children with Edgar Bronfman—Sam, Edgar Jr., Matthew and Holly (Adam was not born until 1963). Edgar stands directly behind Ann.

My parents, John and "Peter" Loeb, sit in the middle of the first row, with my fourteen-year-old sister Debby sitting on the floor in front of them.

Next to my parents in the first row, my sister Judy holds the youngest of her six children with husband Richard Beaty, who stands behind her. Three of their six children are on the floor by her knees. Behind Judy are her two oldest children. In a later marriage, Judy would have two more children.

I am standing in the middle of the top row with my new bride, Nina Sundby Loeb, and my brother, Arthur (Ann's twin). Next to Arthur is Richard Beaty, with his daughter by a former marriage standing beside him.

Nina stayed home and kept house in our first home, a small house in Riverview Terrace, located in a charming little enclave close to New York's East River. This oil painting was one of our favorite wedding gifts.

227

The late George Miller and I were close friends ever since our days in the ROTC. Here he is at the dinner Lehman College gave me in April 1997, some forty-plus years after helping me at Loeb, Rhoades.

ter for the whole firm. Father agreed that something must be done. I drafted a memo: without permission from the management committee, no one could buy calls and sell puts at the same time for the same stock. The announcement was met with groans and did not improve my standing with my close colleagues. (As I knew from the Air Force, nobody likes a whistle-blower.) The practice is illegal today, but at the time it was legal, just incredibly risky. Fortunately, I was able to halt the practice before disaster struck.

In the beginning of the 1960s, I enjoyed the most positive experiences of my seventeen years at Loeb, Rhoades. Under Sam's guidance, I finally felt comfortable making investments myself. I was an eager student who learned quickly and was a devoted deputy to Sam. When Sam died of inoperable cancer at the age of forty-five in 1961, I was devastated.

Having worked with Sam so closely and effectively, I expected to follow in his footsteps as head of the institutional department. Instead, Father gave the post to Tommy Kempner, leaving me as Tommy's deputy. It was a triple blow: losing Sam, not inheriting his mantle and having to endure the oversight of my rival cousin. The pressures of the next year and a half were tremendous. Father gave me no support, and there was no one in the office I trusted.

In 1962, I wrote to Mark Millard about the office issues I had discussed with Mother for over ten years, but only recently with Father. I told him that it was my sense of filial duty that had cemented my decision to come to Loeb, Rhoades. I had hopes that our company could become structured like that of the Rothschilds, with each member having a specific and meaningful role to play. I'd found this was "patently not the case" at our firm:

> *Father and Mother have made it absolutely clear to me in many, many repeated statements that they do not recognize this sense of duty, that they are not appreciative of what I have done, that everything I have done in my life has been totally selfish and only to my interest.*

At the time, Father had become hypercritical of me, calling me too "academic" and saying that I "irritated people." My letter to Millard continued,

In other words, what is important to him are my manners, my outward appearance and not the work I do. . . . However I cannot live in a world where form, not substance, is expected from me.

I also described my attempt to bring in some minimal cost accounting so that we would have an understanding of which departments—and therefore, which individuals—were making money for the firm and which were not. I also brought in my old HBS roommate and ROTC friend George Miller to study the back office. I told Father that I was worried about the lack of connection between the back office and the stars in the front office. In short, the left hand didn't know what the right hand was doing. Therefore, there was no clear understanding of the *costs* of any part of the firm. This was not a problem as a small firm, but because we had grown rapidly, this was an increasing threat to our survival. Miller was greeted reluctantly, treated as something of a spy and given little assistance in making sense of the back office. As for long-range planning, the joke was: "What do we do after lunch?"

I hired Cresap, McCormick & Paget, specialists in studying data management, to make a presentation to the key partners of the firm. Among the presentations they made was one that showed what the net income of the firm would look like if "fixed" commissions ended and "negotiated" rates were instituted due to new Security and Exchange Commission regulations. The projections showed that Loeb, Rhoades might become marginally profitable and, depending on how things went, might possibly even lose money. Father persisted in calling my approach "academic," but I was pragmatically looking to protect and advance our firm.

By the late 1960s, powerful institutions began to challenge the fixed-rate commission. My pessimism on the subject did not help my relationship with Father. Like an ostrich with its head in the sand, Father refused to believe that the "fixed rate" system would ever end. This willful denial would become the company's downfall.

My emotional distress throughout this period had a negative impact on my health and on my marriage to Nina. I never shared my career woes with her, and my frequent bouts of unexplained ill humor and depression were destroying our life together. She never really knew how tormented I was by Father's lack of support and my parents' constant meddling in my personal life. Father, to his credit, even urged me to leave Loeb, Rhoades if it would save my marriage. For once in my life, I didn't take his advice. I only intended on leaving if he continued his accusations and insults. I also ignored his advice about my marriage, since the flame that burned between Nina and me was still flickering. But he was right.

Father told me I was the "heir apparent" at Loeb, Rhoades, and this formal portrait of us together makes it look as though that was going to be true.

≡

CHAPTER NINE

Loeb, Rhoades: The Roller Coaster and Its Death Knell, 1969–1979

On August 26, 1961, beautiful Alexandra was born. Of course, everybody loved my daughter—here in the States and when she visited Sweden. I was thrilled with being a father, but the role also added to my increasing sense of responsibility. I felt trapped not only at Loeb, Rhoades, but also by the necessity of earning a substantial living for my new family. In addition, I began having severe abdominal pains that couldn't be medically explained.

I should have told Nina how upset I was at work, but I was never able to talk to her about business. Perhaps this was a genetic disposition, as my father was famously tight-lipped about business with his own family. Not even my brother, Arthur, to whom I was extremely close, knew of my troubles at the company. Nina and I simply were not each other's confidantes, so she had been suffering my moodiness and short temper—which I never explained. And my marriage was in distress because of it.

In 1963, Nina and I had to face the facts, and we decided the best thing to do was divorce. I'm sure it was no coincidence that my stomach pains soon disappeared. Apparently they had been triggered by emotional conflict. Feeling better physically, and with a clearer head, I came to a hard decision: I would not continue working at Loeb, Rhoades unless given a position with managerial responsibility. I asked for a meeting with Father, letter of resignation in hand. I told him that after six years at the firm my assignments had not trained me sufficiently to follow in his footsteps, and he clearly did not consider me his heir. Unless I was wrong about this conclusion, I was leaving. He could see that I meant it.

"Well, what job do you want?" he asked from behind his huge oak desk. He acted as though I had never before mentioned my discontent. I had a ready answer: "I'd like to head the international department." I didn't expect he'd give it to me. He thought for a moment, and then offered an alternative: "How would you like to head the *brokerage division* of the international department?"

I took the offer. Though not as large a promotion as I'd wanted, the new position would give me management experience. Derek Grewcock was head of the brokerage division of the international department. He was someone I liked and respected, and he was supportive of Father's decision, unlike some of the other people in the firm. Derek deferred to me, even though he was nominally my superior, and I enjoyed working with him. I would send weekly activity reports to my erstwhile London boss, Hubert Simon, and Hubert would need to be aware of all my initiatives regarding our European clients. With my hope for a meaningful future at Loeb, Rhoades resurrected, I decided to stay.

I was bursting with ideas on how to build up our overseas operations and capitalize on the Loeb name, which still commanded the respect it had enjoyed on the European continent under C.M. before the war. An early plan that I immediately set in motion was to expand foreign over-the-counter stock trades. I'd watched the success of Joe Gordon, our wonderful commodities trader, who was in charge of foreign over-the-counter stock trades. At the time, most foreign stocks were traded over-the-counter, not on an exchange. My plan was for us to sell and trade stocks with foreign companies, using an innovative strategy. This relationship would motivate them to give us their brokerage business.

When I called on a potential client, such as Credit Suisse or Union Bank of Switzerland, I would first suggest that we do some trading with each other to open a relationship. I'd say, "Loeb, Rhoades would like to buy 10,000 shares of your Nestlé stock." Only after that would I bring up the subject and ask for some of their brokerage business. I assumed we would lose money in the short run, but Joe Gordon was so adept that we actually *made* money from the outset. I got Joe additional company funds to use in his foreign trading, and it proved to be a major profit center for Loeb, Rhoades.

In the course of building up the international brokerage, I traveled constantly. Sometimes Father went with me to countries where he was well known and respected, such as Switzerland. He also had strong business connections with Cubans who had moved to Mexico and Europe after the Castro revolution. I met and hired Eduardo Orlansky, who

Eduardo Orlansky with his wife, Jane, and myself on a trip to meet with officials of a number of Mexican banks.

Felipe Propper became a partner of Loeb, Rhoades and one of my very best friends.

had wonderful foreign connections, thanks to his brother's ties to the Banco Espirito Santo of Portugal. He and I had memorable trips together to Mexico and Argentina, building up our Latin American business significantly.*

I placed Felipe Propper in charge of France and Spain. Felipe was actually related to the Rothschilds—a serendipitous connection for us—and he had ties in Europe that opened profitable doors. (Felipe is related to Élie de Rothschild, whose wife is Felipe's aunt. Élie was in a Nazi prison camp when he married his wife. Both Élie and his cousin Alain were captured by the Nazis, but they survived the prison camp.) I placed Francois Bohn in charge of Switzerland† and Frank Shields and Gianni Uzielli in charge of Italy. (Gianni was married to Henry Ford II's daughter Anne, another helpful family connection.) Under my leadership, our international brokerage was really humming. However, there was a fly in the ointment.

One of the ways Loeb, Rhoades made money was in trade debt, known today as emerging market debt. Jacob Brown, the genius of the cashier department, had by now developed a fiefdom of his own by making a market in different kinds of Latin American debt. As a

---

* Eduardo became a very close friend of mine, and I was very unhappy when he left the firm. He and his brother Hector—in conjunction with Banco Espirito Santo—set up a company called Bankest, which began successfully but eventually became involved in a terrible situation. His key employee essentially embezzled money, and when the authorities closed in, he put the blame on the Orlanskys. Eduardo and Hector were sentenced to prison.

† I wooed Francois Bohn away from Goldman Sachs by guaranteeing him a partnership in three years at Loeb, Rhoades if he did well. I cemented this by bringing him to meet Father at 730 Park Avenue.

result of Brown's success, Father had set up a separate company, Loeb, Rhoades International, Inc., to handle emerging market debt based in Nassau, Bahamas. The new company needed someone to man their office in the Caribbean. Enter Roger Coe, a man Father knew from previous business dealings.

Roger had been a savvy trader for Cuban-Atlantic Sugar. In 1964, Father hired Coe as an employee of Loeb, Rhoades International. Father's plan was for Roger to buy foreign company debt and resell it at a profit to international and American banks. At the time, this new offshoot company was an innovative vehicle, though today many firms engage in emerging markets and emerging market debt.

As far as Father was concerned, Roger Coe walked on water. All of the partners, especially those in corporate finance, agreed: Coe was a magician who made a great deal of money with a small investment. Because Roger's geographic range often overlapped with mine, he was supposed to coordinate with me. Unfortunately, there was not a shred of cooperation on his part, only roadblocks and lies to my father about me.

I complained frequently to Father about Coe's fictions and fabrications, along with his lack of communication with me and his deliberately misleading communications with important clients. Father refused to believe that these were more than just petty annoyances to me. But I recognized them for what they were: red flags. However, the underlying *reason* for Coe's behavior remained a mystery for almost four years.

Everyone at Loeb, Rhoades knew that Coe and I were at odds, and they all sided with Roger. The day Father called me a liar to my face regarding Coe, I again drafted a letter of resignation. Eduardo Orlansky, my dear friend, persuaded me not to send it, so I soldiered on, though things with Coe went from bad to worse.

Then, in 1968, the day of revelation arrived. Mark Millard walked into my office, his face ashen. He tossed some papers on my desk, saying bleakly, "Well, you were right all along, Johnny." The papers revealed a potential disaster for Loeb, Rhoades: Coe had been putting the entire firm at major risk. We headed to Father's office, first hurriedly calling Carl Mueller, one of Roger's strongest allies, to join us there. When briefed, Father and Carl were even more stunned and shaken than Mark Millard had been. I was the only one who did not find it hard to believe.

Coe had, indeed, purchased foreign debt on behalf of Loeb, Rhoades International and then quickly resold it at a profit. Because Coe had managed to keep his system completely obscured, no one in the firm knew that when he resold the debt, he had contractually promised the buyers that they could sell it back to Loeb, Rhoades International if the debt proved bad.

Incredibly, Roger Coe had never once made a true sale. His volume of "sales" rose steadily only because the buyers took no risk whatsoever. We found out that our company was obligated to buy back any "bad paper," making the Nassau-based arm of Loeb, Rhoades International potentially liable for more than $100 million. While our companies were technically separate entities, Loeb, Rhoades itself wouldn't survive if the parent firm didn't pay off the liability Coe had incurred for us.

Fortunately, most of the foreign debt proved to be good, and our company wound up only having to pay $10 million on a bad Argentinian debt. Coe stayed around long enough to untangle the mess he'd made, after which he became a pariah and then disappeared. Even Father admitted ruefully, as had Mark Millard, that I was "right all along about Roger." Father was furious with the management committee—Carl Mueller in particular—all of whom had had a warm relationship with Roger. For a change, they were in the doghouse, and I was a hero.

Though divorced, Nina and I never really fell out of love. Though we began to see other people, Nina and I kept seeing each other—for five years after the divorce—and returning to the idea of remarrying.

Nina and I finally settled our often-discussed possibility of remarriage, and in a quiet ceremony at New York's Municipal Building, we became Mr. and Mrs. Loeb once more. It seemed like the right decision at the time—but only for a short while. Before the year was out, we realized it was best that we part as a couple for good. This time it was Nina who felt closed in and wanted the divorce. She was really in love with another man, Julio Noyes. We divorced for a second time a little over one year later, and she married Julio very shortly thereafter. I became single again. During that period, I enjoyed being a father to Alexandra, though not as frequently as I would have liked. Nina and I continued as good friends. It took a while for me to recognize the divorce was the best thing for the both of us.

In the late 1960s, Loeb, Rhoades was on the rise and I was also getting noticed. A very favorable *Forbes* article about me appeared on May 15, 1968, headlined "John L. Loeb Jr., A Name of His Own." I had been asked by the reporter what it was like to work under my father, and I was candid: "I have to work four times as hard to prove that I have a personal contribution to make."[91] The article described how profits from our international operations had quadrupled under my leadership and that I was making a name for myself in structuring corporate deals. After years of frustration, it was gratifying that the financial press was noting my progress. I have to admit that the public recognition felt good.

It is considered quite a plum to be invited to serve on boards, especially those of prestigious firms and institutions. Invitations or inquiries from other companies crossed my father's desk with more and more frequency as our public image grew. Father would dole out these invitations to the partners he most respected or to those who were due some perk or reward. But my invitation from Father to serve on boards never came. So I found my own. And when Father did intervene, it was to hinder me.

W. Palmer Dixon, a former senior partner at Rhoades & Co., served on the board of the powerful insurance firm AIG, run by C.V. Starr. As a senior partner of Loeb, Rhoades, Palmer convinced Father to make a significant personal investment in AIG on behalf of Loeb, Rhoades, or our family, with the understanding that Starr would ensure that the firm would receive a set amount of brokerage commissions annually. Father knew almost nothing about the insurance business, but with Palmer's encouragement, he invested $500,000 from one of Mother's Lehman trust funds. Loeb, Rhoades received considerable brokerage business from the company, and the investment for a long time was a tremendous success.[*]

When Palmer died in July 1968, Father was looking to remove Mother's investment. But I looked into Palmer's connections, many of which were international. When C.V. Starr died the following December, I told Father we should take the time to look into AIG. "A man named Hank Greenberg is now running the company," I reported. "We should get to know him."

"Hank Greenberg? That's impossible," Father scoffed. "You've got him confused with the baseball player."

Maurice (Hank) Greenberg

"No, this is a different Hank Greenberg."

"You don't know what you're talking about," Father maintained. "AIG is a very Waspish firm. Nobody named Greenberg is running that company."

I persisted, backed up by Derek Grewcock, who happened to be living in the same building as Greenberg. I asked Derek to arrange a luncheon with Hank. At the lunch, Hank Greenberg said candidly that he had liked Palmer Dixon, but Palmer really hadn't known much about the insurance business. He would like to have a Loeb, Rhoades representative on board, but it would have to be "someone who really under-

---

[*] In 2008, AIG collapsed, precipitating the larger financial collapse all over the world. Mother's investment, which had done well for forty years, nearly disappeared.

stands our business." I reported all this to Father, who had been thinking of selling Mother's interest in AIG. I recommended that we have our own best insurance analyst, Peter Gilbert, study the company—which had just recently gone public—before making a decision.

Hank Greenberg opened up the AIG books to Peter. "Mr. Loeb, this company is fantastic," Peter reported back to Father: "Don't sell your shares. In fact, buy more." In due course, AIG become a major recommendation of Loeb, Rhoades. Then he added, "Also, Greenberg is impressed with John Jr. and would like him to represent Loeb, Rhoades on the board."

Father nodded noncommittally and said he would like to meet Hank Greenberg. After the meeting, Father called me into his office. "Johnny, you were right about AIG," he said. My feelings of gratification, however, were soon waylaid. "But I want Carl Mueller to go on the board, not you," he added. Father would do this all the time—give with one hand while taking with the other. Disheartened hardly describes what I felt at that moment. Loeb, Rhoades

Edgar Bronfman, heir to the Seagram empire, was once my brother-in-law. We remained good friends even after he and my sister Ann divorced. After retirement he became deeply involved in philanthropy and Jewish concerns. He was leader of the World Jewish Congress, and he persuaded Switzerland to return Jewish money in their bank vaults to the heirs. He was awarded the Medal of Freedom by President Clinton.

continued to realize large brokerage profits from AIG, and there was talk of our two companies merging. Eventually, C.V. Starr, the corporation that controls AIG, became a limited partner of Loeb, Rhoades.*

One of my board memberships was more colorful than the others. I was invited in late 1968 to join the board of the famed film studio Metro Goldwyn Mayer by Edgar Bronfman, a scion of the Seagram founding family and my sister Ann's husband at the time. Edgar was trying to take over the board leadership at MGM, which was in deep financial trouble. Because he had a 16 percent interest in MGM, he was motivated to try to take over and get the lion's roar back.

Edgar was considering Louis "Bo" Polk, a former General Mills executive, as CEO, but some, like Louis Nizer, the highest-paid lawyer in America, were vehemently opposed. I

---

* Today, C.V. Starr is a 15 percent shareholder of Loeb Partners. Although AIG was a major factor in the financial collapse of 2008, it is still alive, though pared down and minus Greenberg. Once considered a giant in the business world, Greenberg is now battling to save his reputation.

knew that Bo had a flamboyant, even bizarre, personal life not unnoticed by the tabloids, but I urged Edgar to back him anyhow. I argued that his sex life had nothing to do with his business prowess. Louis Nizer had detectives investigate Polk's personal life and presented the board with a major study on it. I took a different tack, suggesting we get a top business analyst to give us a report on his *business* successes, and those won out in the end. Polk was appointed CEO of MGM in January 1969.

My directorship on the Holly Sugar board, where I served as chairman, provided a "what-if" choice that might have changed my life. At a social event I'd met Billy White, an empire-building investor who had bought Great Western Sugar, the number one beet sugar company in the country, in 1967. Billy was aware that Holly Sugar, billed as the "world's largest independent beet sugar processor," was facing a hostile takeover. Although Billy's Great Western Sugar and Holly Sugar were in the same business, he introduced me to John Bunker, who had just been named president of Holly Sugar. With the initial mission of stopping a takeover of Holly Sugar*, Billy thought I and Loeb, Rhoades could help. Holly Sugar was cash rich, but management wasn't using its cash to expand. The sixty-four-year-old company had become too set in its ways, too content to operate as it always had.

"Why don't you try an aggressive approach?" I suggested to John Bunker. "Fight fire with fire. Identify yourself with a major investment firm"—such as Loeb, Rhoades, I didn't add—"and invest in fields other than sugar. Go out and make acquisitions. Dilute Holly's stock that way." John, a scrappy fellow, immediately warmed to my ideas. I mapped out a plan of action for him and Holly put me on its board.

Word about my involvement in Holly Sugar reached Father, and he invited me to lunch, the first and last time he ever did this. He listened well and agreed with my approach. With his support, Loeb, Rhoades provided the funds to buy enough Holly stock to put my ideas into action. The would-be raiders were soon routed. They sold their stock back to Holly that same year, and the company remained free. Even my fellow partners at Loeb, Rhoades were impressed, while the Holly board members were just this side of ecstatic.

John Evans was my most ardent fan on the Holly board. His family had founded Evanston, Illinois, and he was chairman of the biggest bank in Colorado; in fact, he was thought of as "Mr. Colorado." Through the Evanses, word got around Colorado that I was a rising star in the financial world. John Evans had put me on the board of the Denver & Rio Grande Western Railroad, which in Colorado was like being knighted. He want-

---

* John was the son of Ellsworth Bunker, U.S. ambassador to Vietnam during the Vietnam War (1967–1973).

ed Loeb, Rhoades to protect the Denver & Rio Grande Western Railroad if raiders ever came to its door. During my years on Holly's board, I researched ways to invest their funds wisely, and Holly Sugar continued to do very well, with management in a strong position. The company spent some of its cash updating its buildings and facilities and buying other companies, but it still had enough liquidity to make outsiders salivate. The Pritzker Group, run by a prestigious family from Chicago, suggested that I help them get on the inside track to run the company. The financiers Jimmy Goldsmith and Jay Pritzker both offered to buy Holly Sugar. I resisted their overtures, fearing they would run roughshod not only over the current management, but also over me as well.

Here with Barbara Walters and me is my daughter, Alexandra, at a party given by Louis "Bo" Polk in the late 1970s. I had been supportive of Bo during his tenure as president of MGM when I was serving on its board ten years earlier. We remained friends even after we had both left our posts at MGM.

At one point I had even thought about leaving Loeb, Rhoades to become the activist partner at Holly that the Pritzker Group wanted me to be. But it was not to be—part of it was that I never found the right partner to complement my skills, and part of it was timing. When Father invited me to become a co-managing partner at Loeb, Rhoades, I accepted. I had to resign my roles as chair of the Holly Sugar board and as head of the brokerage division of the Loeb, Rhoades international department, both of which I did with great regret. But the offer to become one of the two managing partners of the "family firm," a place where I had begun with no title or office, was too good to pass up.

I believe that the day Father admitted I'd been right about Roger Coe all along was when he again began to think of me as the future head of the firm. I admit that I enjoyed the sunshine of his approval. In that one morning I had gone from liar and troublemaker to heir apparent.

Starting in the 1950s, I had noticed that many young men I had met were going into real estate. What was most intriguing was that these young men were able to borrow—through nonrecourse loans—almost as much money as the property they were buying was worth! I realized it would be possible—and wise—for Loeb, Rhoades to handle such transactions. The firm was generating large amounts of ordinary income on which we had to pay enormous taxes. One day, out of the blue, John J. Mortimer urged me to hire a smart young gentleman named William P. Carey. William Polk Carey was a descendent of President James K. Polk, and he was very well connected in both Philadelphia and Baltimore. One thing that impressed me was that he had repaid his stepfather for his college expenses by working at his stepfather's auto dealership. While working there, he learned a great deal about sale-leaseback financing, knowledge that would serve him well at Loeb, Rhoades, where his successful deals involved this complex type of financing. Unfortunately, Carl Mueller, one of the top people in the new business side of the firm, did not get along with Bill. Carl and Tom Kempner were more focused on how real estate could be a major profit center than on what Carey was doing. Using a sale-leaseback technique, income before taxes, but no cash, Bill built a unique and very successful investment in a short time.

As part of this new focus, Mueller and Kempner brought in a brilliant man named Joe Lesser, who had been dealing in second mortgages at Kirkeby-Natus in California. A few months after Joe Lesser arrived, regrettably, Bill Carey left. In 1973, he started his own firm, W.P. Carey, Ltd. and built the largest sale-leaseback company in the world. The company became one of the world's largest publicly traded limited liability companies and owns more than 90 million square feet throughout the United States, Europe and Asia. Bill became a billionaire and a major philanthropist. Sadly, Bill passed away in 2012.

From the 1960s into the 1970s, I gained new confidence and stature but remained seriously worried about some areas of Loeb, Rhoades. Though I proposed a series of corrective measures to the management committee, such as a cost-accounting system, Cliff Michel, Father's deputy, was unresponsive. In June 1971, I wrote to Father: "All of us . . . would welcome Cliff Michel's leadership and help. But he gives none."

Another issue was incorporation. The only means to protect the company from dependency on outside capital was to incorporate. This was necessary not only for the firm, but also for the family members' capital. I understand now that the reason Father wouldn't incorporate was because it meant that he might lose control of Loeb, Rhoades.

On August 9, 1971, I wrote to Father:

The longer we delay, the more equity the family and the firm will have to give up to outsiders to get the new money which could have been generated in the corporation. And more importantly still, the less you and the family will have to say about the shape incorporation will take.[92]

It was becoming clear to everyone that the end of fixed-rate commissions was on the horizon, with stories appearing in every financial publication. But Father thought that fixed rate commissions were set in cement. As far as he was concerned, I was simply an irritating pessimist, a "Chicken Little" who always thought the sky was falling. He complained to my Uncle Henry Loeb, who would then urge me to "be more positive."

I was a product of the Harvard Business School, trained to look for downward trends, quagmires, pitfalls and ebbing tides, as well as the positive. It didn't help to be proven right when the end came. As with all empires, the seeds of destruction were sown at the height of success. Triumph frequently breeds an unwillingness to change one's habits.

Other partners, including my cousin Peter Loeb, who had done brilliantly at the Columbia Business School, and Richard Pollock of HBS, frequently fretted about our problems, but I was the only one pounding the table. "John Loeb Jr. understood better than anyone," Peter once wrote, "but because of who he was could not get his points across."

I became less worried when Father wrote a memo to the partners claiming that it was his plan that "John Jr. would eventually be the senior partner succeeding me. Carl Mueller will be the managing partner." My elation lasted about a second. The appointment ended abruptly with howls of protest from some of the general partners. Father capitulated to their objections and instead announced that Carl Mueller and I would become *joint* managing partners. I took the change of plans with as much grace as I could. Working constructively with Carl could bring Loeb, Rhoades to new heights. The new managerial plans were discussed with Cliff Michel at a luncheon hosted by Father. Cliff was delighted with giving up his role as managing partner—and Father's deputy—and seemed very happy that Carl and I would take over his job. We all toasted a "new era."

The story broke on November 28, 1971, in *The New York Times*. Carl and I would become joint managing partners, with Father's deputy, Cliff Michel, having been unceremoniously dropped. He and Father were at odds. Apparently, there had been a growing rift between Cliff and Father that had been brewing for a few years and had absolutely nothing to do with me. The final break between Father and Cliff came when Father refused to meet directly with Cliff to discuss the new Partnership Agreement—a discussion they had every year. Instead, Father sent his new attorney, Abe Fortas, to meet with Cliff. This infuriated Cliff.* Cliff immediately called John Schiff, the senior and controlling partner of Kuhn, Loeb (no relation to Loeb, Rhoades) and at the end of the day, Cliff resigned from Loeb, Rhoades and became a partner at Kuhn, Loeb.

According to news reports and gossip, which had "the Wall Street talk factories

---

* Abe Fortas, an associate Supreme Court justice, resigned from the Court on May 15, 1968, to return to private law practice. He was the first Supreme Court justice to resign under threat of impeachment. After Fortas was dropped from the Supreme Court, and then by his own firm, Father made him his chief counsel.

working overtime,"[93] Cliff was leaving because of me, which was flat out untrue. Besides the conflict with Father, Cliff's other reason for leaving might have been that negotiated rates were coming soon. Loeb, Rhoades was essentially a brokerage firm, while Kuhn, Loeb was one of the great investment banking firms and did a minimal amount of brokerage. The firm was heavily capitalized; practically all of its money was in the hands of the Schiff family.*

Father was quoted in the *Times* as saying that he was still in command and was to be thought of as the chief executive, while Carl and I would be the chief operating officers. I suggested to Carl that he oversee all the investment banking and new deal activity, while I would oversee brokerage, by far the largest part of the firm. About three thousand people worked for Loeb, Rhoades, and 95 percent were either directly involved in brokerage or in various entities that supported brokerage, such as research, over-the-counter departments (domestic and foreign) and many more accounting/financial activities in the so-called back office.

Knowing that my strength was in sales and general strategy (not in day-to-day administration), I wanted a strong administrator as my deputy. I promoted our head of research, Richard Pollock, known for his intellectual ability and particularly his administrative skills. John Levin wanted to succeed Richard Pollock as head of the research department. John was a graduate of Yale and Yale Law School and was married to my cousin, Betty Loeb. He had come to see me several times to persuade me to persuade Father to make him head of that department. I pointed out that John was an excellent analyst and lawyer and would make a good head of research.

I also pointed out to Father that John had excellent judgment and furthermore, he was family, being married to Betty. As for Betty, I was very devoted to her. She had a brilliant intellect and was very ambitious for John and the firm. Father agreed.†

One of the research department's stars, Mario Gabelli, left to start his own highly successful asset management firm just a few years later.‡ I also wanted to find someone

---

* In 1977, Kuhn, Loeb merged with Lehman Brothers. In 1984, Lehman Brothers Kuhn Loeb was acquired by the American Express Company.

† As I got to know John over the years, he and I saw the firm in the same way. He left Loeb, Rhoades and became a partner of Steinhardt Partners. Michael Steinhardt had been an analyst at Loeb, Rhoades. He went on to found one of the most successful hedge fund companies of all time. John Levin left Steinhardt to form his own company, Levin Capital Strategies. Before he died, Father handed a significant amount of the family investments over to John Levin to manage.

‡ While Mario was still in Loeb, Rhoades's research department, Father gave him a significant amount of money from our family trust to manage. He did an excellent job and today is still managing some family monies.

who could initiate cost accounting, so we could see *where* we were actually making money. Was the international department doing well? How about the institutional department? What areas of brokerage were doing well—correspondents out of town, in-town brokerage firms, individual brokers, foreign brokerage, institutional brokerage, etc.?

In my new role, I quickly instituted regular group meetings of all key people under my purview. For the first time, the left hand of Loeb, Rhoades knew what the right hand was doing. My greatest concern was the back office, which was in disarray. Walter Walz, head of that division, was a key figure at these group meetings. Like other bureaucrats, Walter believed that the more people you have working for you, the higher your pay grade. I also began to understand how big a job running the firm was, and I came to the conclusion that neither Carl nor I were capable of running it. I began looking for someone who really understood, and could run, an investment bank and brokerage firm. Carl knew from his time at Bankers Trust that when a commercial bank is closed for the weekend, the bank is still making money. An investment bank and brokerage firm only makes money when someone picks up the telephone. Carl never really understood this.

Management had been unaware of the severity of the problems in the back office because the slide had been so gradual. They had taken for granted the meticulous work of a group of German-Jewish exiles who had come to Loeb, Rhoades during and after the war. For more than thirty years, those men had kept scrupulous records. But, one by one, they had retired or died, and no one noticed that their replacements were nowhere near the same caliber.

As the next few months unfolded, I thought we were making real progress toward a back office turnaround. On a fateful night more than a year into our co-managing partnership, Carl and I had dinner together to discuss business matters. Afterward, we adjourned to his apartment to continue our talk. It all seemed quite amicable—I didn't notice any red flags. The next morning, I discovered that Carl and Father had, without my knowledge, behind my back, fired Walter Walz and brought in a man named Andy McLaughlin to replace him.

Father's decision not to consult me on such a major firing and hiring implied he had lost faith in my leadership. Carl and I had spent a warm and collegial evening together going over everything important at the firm that we were working on together. Carl's failure to discuss with me something as crucially important as bringing in a new man to run a key part of the firm shocked me. Hiding this information from me (with Father) stunned me. Naturally, I was very upset and angry and, understandably, let it be known to Carl forcefully. He did not apologize or explain.

A few hours later, Carl went into Father's office and issued an ultimatum. My understandably strong criticism of Mueller's duplicity provided what I believe Carl had been looking for all along: an excuse to say to Father, "Either Johnny goes or I go." Father was in a difficult position. Cliff had recently left, and now Carl was threatening to leave. Like Cliff, Carl was scared. He knew the firm was in trouble. If he was going to stay, he wanted to be the boss. But Father had created this situation by himself. He must have known that his going behind my back (and with Mueller) might seriously damage my relationship with him.

Later in the week, during a reception in my home honoring a visiting dignitary, I learned of Father's decision. Father took me into my bedroom and broke the news: he was making Carl Mueller sole managing partner, and I was out. I was devastated. I'd come so close to fulfilling my dream, and to have it disappear—in the middle of a Loeb, Rhoades event in my own home—broke my heart. In that bleak moment, I wept for myself, for Father and for Loeb, Rhoades, its partners and employees. I realized that Loeb, Rhoades would now barrel full speed into disaster. And that is what happened.

When I first became co-managing partner, Father's lawyer, Abe Fortas, gave me some good advice. "Concentrate on your partners," he told me. "Spend a lot of time with them. Tell them what you're doing. Listen to what they say." He was absolutely right. I should have been more generous with my attention to other partners. In my eagerness to make things happen after I had become the co-managing partner, I realized I had done little to reach out to the partners and the management committee. However, over the years I had tried to explain to the management committee, comprised overwhelmingly of investment bankers and deal makers, that what made everything possible was the extraordinarily large brokerage business we had—foreign, domestic, individuals, institutions, correspondence—worldwide.

We were about to be faced with a major change after two hundred years of what was known as "fixed commissions." Fixed commissions meant that every single firm that was a member of the New York Stock Exchange had to charge exactly the same commission. By 1972 it was clear that fixed commissions were going to be replaced by negotiated rates. Three years later, negotiated rates were ordered by the Securities and Exchange Commission. Subsequently, five hundred firms went out of business, including Loeb, Rhoades. I had tried to explain over and over again (including bringing in a management consulting firm) what would happen when negotiated rates came into effect. But it had fallen on deaf ears, including Father's. As it was "late in the day" and we had made no effort to prepare for negotiated rates, I suggested, in order to survive, that we had to merge or shrink. I repeated this so often that Father got fed up hearing it. Mueller sided with him, at least to begin with. Mueller became the sole managing partner, but two years later he came to agree with me about everything I had been saying, including that we must merge or shrink. Three years into Mueller's management, Father removed him. On the day in 1975 when negotiated rates came into effect, Father refused to let anyone negotiate. The result was that everything came to a halt. Every phone stopped ringing. By early afternoon, Father surrendered and allowed the firm to negotiate.

Francis "Shorty" Fraenkel, a Loeb, Rhoades partner, told me that my greatest contribution to the firm was my vision, an ability to see the big picture. I like to believe he was right. With powerful opposition from major partners and Father's unwillingness to challenge them, I was left in an untenable position. There was no hope for my ideas or for my future at Loeb, Rhoades. It was time to go. Exactly where, or what I should do next, was not clear.

I kept my investment in Loeb, Rhoades for several months. I was still a general partner and sat on the management committee; but it was a precarious perch. Carl had insisted that Father give him the right to fire me at any time, a stipulation that was granted but never exercised. Ultimately, with no confidence in the firm's management, I realized I had to lessen my financial liability in the company.

In 1973, still owning 10 percent of the partnership, I told Father I was going to withdraw the majority of my capital from the firm and become a limited partner. Though Loeb, Rhoades was still making money, I could tell that we would soon see major losses from our commission business, which would no longer be based on fixed fees. If the firm wasn't incorporated, I didn't want to be responsible for 10 percent of the potential losses, especially since I no longer had any managerial input.

The June 30, 1973, issue of *The Economist* noted that "[John L. Loeb Jr. will] stop being a general partner and will change his status to limited liability. He will then devote more of his time to the environment."[94] Father was furious, feeling that my exit was a huge embarrassment to himself and to the firm. Abe Fortas quietly took me aside and told me I should see a psychiatrist. To Abe, 10 percent of Loeb, Rhoades was a goldmine. But Abe did not understand the brokerage business nor what negotiated rates would mean.

Money certainly had played a role in keeping me there, but my greatest motivation had been the promise of someday heading our family firm. With a heavy heart, I had no choice but to accept that now this would never happen.

Soon after, Abe Fortas called me about an ominous development that was slowly unraveling. He told me that former governor David Hall of Oklahoma had been indicted for racketeering and extortion. His trial loomed as a possible nightmare for Loeb, Rhoades's partners. The Feds thought a $25,000 contribution made four years earlier

FROM *THE ECONOMIST*

THE ECONOMIST JUNE 30, 1973 91

BUSINESS *Investment*

Wall Street's environment's upsetting the animals

New York

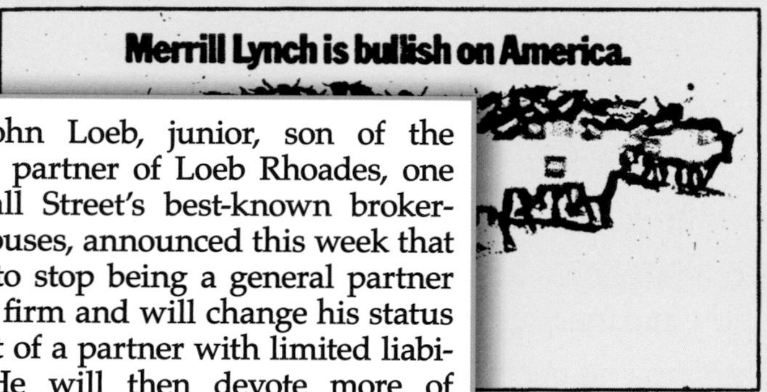

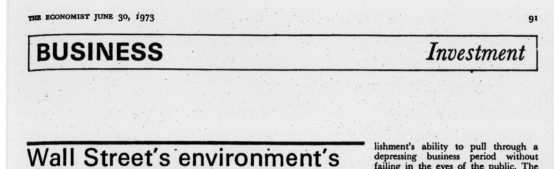

Mr John Loeb, junior, son of the senior partner of Loeb Rhoades, one of Wall Street's best-known brokerage houses, announced this week that he is to stop being a general partner in the firm and will change his status to that of a partner with limited liability. He will then devote more of his time to the environment. The environment in New York's financial area suggests there may be as much shrewdness as vocation behind this.

in the firm and will change his status to that of a partner with limited liability. He will then devote more of his time to the environment. The environment in New York's financial area suggests there may be as much shrewdness as vocation behind this.

The American stockbroking business looks pretty sick at the moment. Two firms have been involved in a public slanging match that had a particularly vulture-like sound to it. Hornblower and Weekes, Hemphill, Noyes accused Edwards and Hanly of spreading false rumours about Hornblower's financial position, ostensibly with the aim of scaring investor account from one firm to the other. Over the weekend it was revealed that the New York Stock Exchange had 68, or over 12%, of its member firms on a surveillance list because losses had vitiated their capital positions to the point at which the exchange felt

monitor their progress. Nine firms were said to be parti-ckety.

esday it transpired that two ne firms were F. S. Smithers and Hale and Stieglitz. Smithers is a well-known and respected brokerage house dealing mainly with institutional clients. It is to put the bulk of its business into the hands of Paine Webber Jackson and Curtis, including its London operation.

The Independent Investor Protective League, an investor group, has now sued the NYSE in a bid to make the exchange board reveal the names of the 68 firms on which it is keeping tabs. This suit puts the big board in a tricky position because the object of the early warning system is to keep firms solvent or, in the last extreme, to merge them with other firms before they declare bankruptcy. To tell the public which firms are in danger would produce an instant emigration of accounts from just those houses that can least afford to lose them.

The situation is adding up to a crucial test of the Wall Street establishment's ability to pull through a depressing business period without failing in the eyes of the public. The small investor is already disillusioned with the equity market—although the Street is counting on his return. He will certainly not return if he sees his next door neighbour's shirt lost in the brokerage laundry.

June is shaping up as a lousy month for trading volume, with the daily turnover so far averaging a meagre 12.9m shares, compared with 14.3m last year. On the American stock exchange the cutback has been much more severe, with May's average daily volume falling from 5.3m last year to 3.2m. The effect on commission income has, of course, been greatly amplified by the fall in stock prices. According to the NYSE the business of brokerage turned in a loss of $115m over the first four months of this year, compared with a pre-tax profit of $485m in the equivalent stretch of 1972.

The fact is that the stockbroking business desperately needs a rise in rates—an unpalatable decision in a weak market but definitely the lesser of two evils. The necessary pruning of the industry now seems to be well under way and it is vital to prevent this process turning into a rout. Last week the New York Stock Exchange dropped plans for a rather specialised price increase—on orders worth more

Continued on page 95

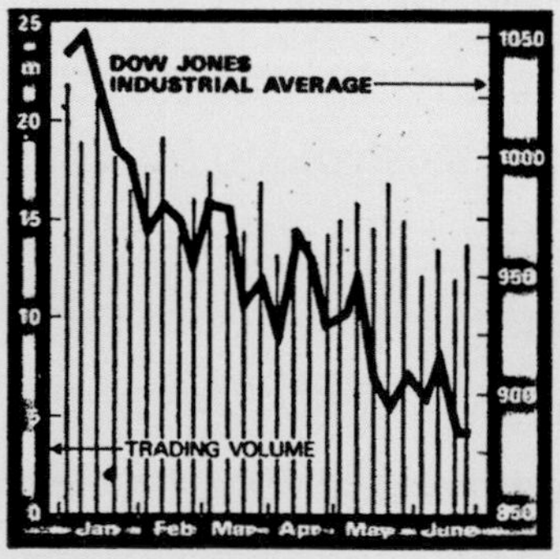

me from overseas.
eady has enough
what's good for
cessarily good for
shares have fallen
ement; its share-
otically peruse the
n it arrives.
kers' shop, share-
itton have already
m a fight. Ward
values them at
he offer is in 8%
ck not convertible
ash alternative of
tractive, but if all
s accepted it, this
oup highly geared,
½m to the £2¼m
outstanding. Since
Britton share in the
ets in their 4 main
shops are worth
re, Britton share-
Britton. If Britton
00,000 for the cur-
ember, this would
er share of about
ares on a prospec-
9 at the current
/e in the past has

City and Grace-
Trust should ask
ffer a 10% dilution
of their shares in
981,000 privately-
t. The City and
say they need to
f their company's
sented by the hold-
s of Australia; an
sk disqualification
trust if it holds
any one company
SL Trust was set
hairman of the
roup of investment
iters, and the 31%
group has in City
will no doubt be
SSL takeover. All
under the F&C
ella. If the deal is
ld Estates will still
City and Grace-
well above 1975's
tal net assets will
he current 61p to
ue that the hold-
(which the board
ally valuable) will have been maintained, and by buying SSL at market value no old friends will have been hurt. But in the absence of fuller explanations, this looks too like a cosy in-house deal.

covered the Equity Funding scandal? However, the SEC has struck another chill into brokers' spines. Just to rub in the point that some means of earning a living remain foul, the SEC also

compound growth rate in pre-tax profits over the past five years has come in lumps. It is not clear where future, uncyclical growth will come from. Hanson hopes that, as part of

Highlighted above, an excerpt from the June 30, 1973, issue of the world-famous magazine, *The Economist*.

by individual partners in our firm was legally questionable and might be fodder at Hall's upcoming trial.

The story began two years earlier, in 1971, when I'd been standing in line at the cashier's counter at a Walgreens on Manhattan's Upper East Side. While in line, Maurice Sonneberg, a business acquaintance of mine, and I started a casual conversation about municipal bonds, an area Loeb, Rhoades wanted to explore and expand into. Maurice said that the recently elected governor of Oklahoma, David Hall, was looking for an investment bank to help underwrite the state's road building. When he offered to make arrangements for me to meet Governor Hall, I took him up on it. In the recent election, the democratic governor of Oklahoma had received little support from most investment banks in New York.

I flew out to Oklahoma, where the governor and I hit it off immediately, even warbling "Oklahoma" together in a convivial duet in the governor's mansion. He was warm, outgoing and—I thought—as squeaky clean as a Boy Scout. By the end of the visit, he had assured me that Oklahoma would be working with our firm to secure funds they needed for major highway construction. I returned to Loeb, Rhoades an instant hero.

I was soon approached by the governor's best friend and chief fundraiser, who "suggested" that it would be very nice if Loeb, Rhoades made a contribution to help the governor retire his campaign debt. The fundraiser recommended a gift of $100,000. I quickly replied that the company itself couldn't do this, but I would see if our partners as individuals could come up with a more modest sum of $25,000. I asked a senior partner, Gene Woodfin, to check the legality of such a contribution. Woodfin's former firm, the prestigious Vinson & Elkins, gave the contribution a resounding clearance. But I began to have second thoughts.

"I think we should pass on this deal," I told the management committee, "and forget about making any contributions."

I was rebuffed. "Vinson & Elkins has cleared its legality," everyone said. "What are you worried about?"

In the minority, I reluctantly turned over the partners' money to Gene Woodfin, who went personally to Oklahoma to deliver it. To celebrate our deal and new relationship, Loeb, Rhoades hosted a big dinner at the 21 Club. Carl Albert, an Oklahoma congressman and Speaker of the U.S. House of Representatives at the time, came to the dinner and paid a call at our offices.

In 1973, representatives of the SEC and the FBI came to query Father, who sat with Abe Fortas right beside him. I was soon summoned to the meeting. Father said he had little memory of the details of the Oklahoma deal. He then called in the other partners,

Carl Albert

many of whom said the same. The few who did claim to remember it all said they had contributed money because of "Johnny's deal." It was obvious they were looking for an easy scapegoat, and I was their choice.

Abe Fortas took me aside. "This is very serious, Johnny," he warned. "You must get a criminal lawyer here in New York and also one in Oklahoma." Then he added, "When the Feds interview you, say that *you* contributed all of the money because Hall was a Harvard classmate of yours." This would have been perjury of course—Hall happened to be at Harvard Law School for a year or two while I was at Harvard, though I never met him or knew him. Perhaps this was not unexpected advice from a former justice who had left the U.S. Supreme Court under a deep shadow.

I did hire one of the country's finest defense lawyers: James P. Linn, head of the Oklahoma firm of Linn & Kirk. Jim, who looked like a sheriff from a western movie, was exactly what I needed. When I challenged Father's repeated claim that the situation was my fault, he had calmly said, "If this goes to court, who are they going to believe—you or me?"

When I shared this with Jim Linn, he said, "Let *me* talk to Daddy."

"Listen," Jim said to Father, "either you hang together or you hang separately—that's up to you. But Johnny here is not going to jail for the rest of you. The deal was done and the contributions made with the approval of the management committee—and *you*, Mr. Loeb, are head of the firm." Father heard him loud and clear.

In regard to the courts in Oklahoma, Jim pointed out to Bill Burkett, then the U.S. attorney in Oklahoma, that if they seriously intended to indict Loeb, Rhoades, "You're going to have to pay to fly every last one of the 60 partners down to Oklahoma to testify." By then, we had more than sixty partners. In the end, not one of us was summoned to Oklahoma. After David Hall's conviction, a letter was sent to me from the U.S. attorney in Oklahoma City, William R. Burkett, advising me, "You are not and never have been the subject of the investigation." I still have that letter in my safe deposit box.

Sometime in 1973, when for all intents and purposes I was no longer at Loeb, Rhoades, Sandy Weill took me to lunch. The Brooklyn-born, self-made entrepreneur picked me up in a smoke-filled stretch limousine, brandishing his ever-present Te-Amo black cigar. Sandy and his firm at that time, Cogan, Berlind, Weill and Levitt, knew the brokerage business inside and out. They had become the "go-to" company when firms had trouble tracking expenses. Sandy had long been interested in being part of the circle epitomized by Loeb, Rhoades.

Sandy thought it was an auspicious time to buy into Loeb, Rhoades and wanted me to pave the way with Father. I was delighted by his offer, having realized for a long time that the only option for Loeb, Rhoades was to shrink or merge. I reported Sandy's proposal to Father and urged him to accept. "This is the answer to our prayers," I said. "Sandy Weill and his team know the cost of each order. And we don't."

Father's response was both emphatic and dismissive. "The last person I would ever merge with is Sandy Weill," he said. No matter his brilliance, Weill came from a lower socioeconomic status, and Father didn't want to be identified with him. After I pressed him further, Father said, "Do you think Sandy Weill can run this firm better than I can?"

A former associate justice of the U.S. Supreme Court, Abe Fortas became my father's attorney. Some of his advice to me about the David Hall incident would have been perjury, had I taken it, which I had no intention of doing.

Emphatically, I said, "Yes." But I added, "Not because you couldn't. You could probably run it better than Sandy if you ran the firm full-time. But you're spending a great deal of time on individual deals and raising money for Harvard." Then I asked if he would at least meet with Sandy, and Father said, strongly, "No."*

Father could not or would not see a future that didn't involve him as the boss of an increasingly expanding Loeb, Rhoades. In the end, his blindness in this regard would be the company's death knell. Like many entrepreneurs, he couldn't envision a future that didn't include him. Perhaps Father was haunted by what had happened to his father, who had been pushed out of the American Metal Company in 1929.

I had repeatedly suggested to Father that we reduce our size or merge, due to the fact that negotiated rates would go into effect in the middle of 1975. There had been discussions concerning this change for more than a decade, but Father continually ignored the warning signs until it was too late. As a broker's broker, Loeb, Rhoades was more vulnerable than most to negotiated rates. Father's aversion to them was so pro-

---

* I had urged Father to meet Sandy Weill in 1973, shortly after I left the firm. He finally met Sandy Weill in 1978.

"What have you done with Loeb and Rhoades?"

nounced that the day they began, he refused to negotiate for half the day. All business at the company came to a halt.

For the four years after I left, Loeb, Rhoades struggled under Carl Mueller's management. Still under Father's thumb, he had to deal with many of the same problems I had anticipated. When Carl came to the same conclusion that I had about Loeb, Rhoades needing to merge or shrink, Father removed him as managing partner. Shortly thereafter, in what I would call "upward failure," Carl went back to Bankers Trust, where he was appointed vice chairman. Subsequently, Bankers Trust ran into serious trouble and was forced to merge with Deutsche Bank.

After Carl Mueller's departure in 1977, when Father removed him from his position as managing partner, I urged Father to rehire me or find a top CEO who was familiar not only with investment banking, but also with retail brokerage and branch management. Instead, Father went right ahead and appointed my cousin Tommy Kempner as managing partner of Loeb, Rhoades.

Despite my warnings about Loeb, Rhoades's future and my continuing push to shrink or merge, the opposite happened. Tommy understood Father's entrepreneurial personality and found a way to expand the firm. Loeb, Rhoades had already expanded beyond what they could handle in the back office. Tommy chose to expand further by acquiring another firm, Hornblower & Weeks, which had as many if not more problems than Loeb, Rhoades. (The company would be renamed Loeb, Rhoades, Hornblower.) Once one of the great old firms on Wall Street, by 1977, Hornblower was a sinking ship. However, it had one great advantage for Father: it could be bought and controlled. Perhaps Father and Tom saw it as similar to the merger years earlier of Rhoades and Company with Carl M. Loeb & Co. In any case, it turned out to be a disaster.

Hornblower had recently worked out what it thought was a brilliant new data processing system for the back office. The only problem was that it didn't fit with Loeb, Rhoades's, which no one in either camp knew. I had been warning Father for many years about the complexity of the back office. In fact, years ago I had brought in my classmate George Miller (later Major General George Miller), expressly for this purpose. Charles Geisst, in his book *The Last Partnerships*, reported that Loeb, Rhoades had a breakdown in backroom activities and that management "did not pay attention to such mundane matters."[95] The fact remained: we never learned what our costs were.

By the end of 1977, the newly merged firm was hemorrhaging money and looking for outside capital. Father now found himself in the uncomfortable position of needing Sandy Weill's help. I had told Father five years earlier that this was "the answer to our prayers." At last he was listening. Since making his first offer to buy Loeb, Rhoades, Sandy had continued to acquire and manage a cluster of several brokerage firms. As the red ink was flowing and Loeb, Rhoades was dangerously approaching bankruptcy, Father did something he had never done before: he asked me for money.

He called and said, "John, we need money for the firm, which, as you know, is in trouble. I'd like to borrow some money from your mother's trust." His tone was friendly, but I was shocked. And I said, "I don't think it's wise, but of course you can." He borrowed a significant amount of money, and, in due course, it was all returned.

In his book *The Real Deal*, Sandy details the merger with Loeb, Rhoades in the spring of 1978 and his dealings with Tommy Kempner. Finally taking my suggestion of five years before, in 1973, Father called Sandy Weill. He invited Sandy to meet with him at his midtown office for a more formal discussion; he then asked Tommy to follow up.[96]

The initial meeting with my father went splendidly. Weill wrote that their meeting "turned out to be a lovefest, or at least the closest thing one could have with someone of a patrician stature."[97] Father handed Weill a letter that essentially explained, "'I've put my trust in you and I have confidence that you'll keep things moving ahead while I'm gone.' . . . Loeb indirectly was addressing Kempner."[98]*

Sandy rarely left anything on the table, but he decided not to take over Loeb, Rhoades's enormous correspondence system, which went to Bear Stearns for one dollar. Luckily, Sandy did not take over Loeb Partners Realty, which has been a very successful real estate operation and is now an independent company.†

On a cold, gray afternoon in December 1979, after having watched his beloved Loeb, Rhoades empire come to an end, my proud father endured a final exercise in humility. At the age of seventy-seven, he slowly entered the door of the Harmonie Club in Manhattan, the leading Jewish social club in the country, to attend a reception and board meeting celebrating the newly merged firm. Father had come to congratulate Sandy Weill, which he did, and then quietly slipped away.

The first chapter of *The New Crowd* sets the scene for this poignant moment in time. It also includes a memorable observation about Father and Loeb, Rhoades: "He and his crowd had been overtaken as Wall Street leaders. Afterward, and to this day, no member of an *Our Crowd* family has been in a position of great power or prominence on the Street. An era had come to an end."[99] It had, indeed.

As I sift through old memories of Loeb, Rhoades, I feel more sadness than anger. Perhaps the company's decline was inevitable. Nevertheless, it is still hard not to feel regret. Dr. Lydia Bronte, who interviewed Father for her book *The Longevity Factor* (he lived to ninety-four in almost perfect shape), told me that Father said he deeply regretted his decision to remove me as co-managing director. Apparently, he expressed the same regret to others. *The New Crowd* notes that Father "told several people in the firm that he never should have given in to the partners who had insisted that he select Mueller over his son."[100]

The sad thing is Father never said it to me. Thinking about Father and Loeb, Rhoades, I wonder if he wanted anyone to succeed him. I wonder if he really wanted Loeb, Rhoades to go on without him—and it didn't.

Those of you who worked for Loeb, Rhoades will be interested in the following: My fa-

---

* Sandy's firm was Shearson Hayden Stone. Upon completion of the merger, the new company was named Shearson Loeb Rhoades.

† The Loebs continue in the financial world under Loeb Partners, a holding company for family funds, which Tommy Kempner has headed since 1981. A few years ago, I read in the newspaper about individuals who were buying up famous old names that had recently been dropped. It turned out that Sandy Weill had just let the Loeb, Rhoades name go. My lawyer told me that the name was in limbo, and no one controlled it. I got it back, happy to have it again under family control.

ther's true feelings about Loeb, Rhoades surfaced in a memoir he wrote with Mother titled *All in a Lifetime* (p. 198). In that book, he said he regretted letting me go as co-managing partner; he regretted keeping Carl Mueller as the sole managing partner; and he regretted not having shrunk the firm, as I had suggested to him many times, before negotiated rates came in. In retrospect, he said, "I wish I had said to Carl, 'You'll just have to live with the Loebs.' But I didn't. Instead Johnny eventually resigned."

Father also wrote:

> *Carl's management style was bureaucratic. He treated everyone with the same job title the same way, irrespective of their contributions. One day I said, "Carl, we really have a hell of an overhead, and you're also letting people who are not that experienced handle business." "The only way they can learn," he replied, "is to let them make mistakes." "But we're not a bank with unlimited capital from bank depositors," I said. "We only have our own capital and we can't afford many mistakes."*

> *Because Carl insisted that everything be channeled through him, he put himself between me and the other members of the firm. As a result, I wasn't kept fully informed. The main problems, whatever they were, were not always discussed with me. There was a conspiracy of silence. Otherwise, I would have shrunk the firm and we could have changed direction and emphasis. We should have continued doing our own thing. We were unique; we did quite well in certain areas, in particular in oil and gas and savings and loan associations. Instead, Carl tried keeping up with the Joneses by expanding into the government bond business, an area in which we had no expertise. We did not do well. By then, advances in communications had made the correspondent business less attractive.*

Carl left shortly after Father had removed him as managing partner.

Alex always drew admiring attention, but especially at the races we attended when she went with me to England.

CHAPTER TEN

≡

My Children and the Trials of Single Parenting

Throughout my lifelong quest for professional success, I have tried to balance the exigencies of my career with single parenting. I cannot claim the results were always triumphant, however. As a young man contemplating my future, I dreamed of a happy, monogamous marriage and several beautiful, well-behaved children. When youthful fantasy became stark reality, I found myself a single parent. Nevertheless, I vowed I would never use this handicap as an excuse for any parental shortcomings. I certainly read enough "how-to" books. By the time both of my children were out of kindergarten, my copy of *Dr. Spock* was in shreds. I was confident that as a parent, I would be very different from my own father and mother. On that score, I like to think I had some success. Today, my two children should know this above all else: I love them dearly and did the best I could.

ALEXANDRA

Alexandra was born beautiful and has remained beautiful all of her life. She is statuesque, with a natural elegance and aristocratic poise—whenever she walks into a room, heads turn. She has always displayed the best qualities of Virgos: a bright mind and abundant charm. However, our father-daughter relationship has had its share of ups and downs, especially because her mother, Nina, and I divorced when Alex was only three, and she went to live with her mother. Consequently, that important early bond with my daughter did not have a chance to develop the way it should have. Because her mother was awarded custody of Alex, my daughter and I were together only

Alex always enjoyed swimming in my Purchase pool.

Alex seems here to be very pleased with the sounds she plunked out at the piano in the sitting room of my New York City home.

My dearest darling Alexandra on the beach at age four.

on weekends and holidays. Sadly, driven by my professional ambitions as a young man on Wall Street, I did not make the most of our earliest time together   one of the great regrets of my life. My love for her has been and always will be unconditional.

Alex's early schooling was at the Spence Day School for Girls, located on 91st Street in Manhattan. Perhaps because of my own academic focus and drive, I might have pushed her too early and too hard regarding school. As a student, I had felt the pressure of competition, and when Alex was growing up, school seemed even more competitive. A complete novice with young children, I just did not know how to relate to my daughter. All I could think of was to ask questions such as, "Alexandra, can you say the alphabet?" Before long I was called in for a meeting at her nursery school because she was not doing well on tests.

"Are you teaching Alex at home?" the teacher asked.

"I guess I am," I said hesitantly.

"You shouldn't," the teacher said. "When you're with her, don't teach. Just play with her. Ask to see her toys. Don't ask her to perform."

The next time Alexandra stayed with me, she tried to please me by reciting the alphabet, but this time I knew better. "Wonderful," I said, "but wouldn't it be fun to play with Piglet for a while?" She squealed with delight and ran for Piglet, and before long I was taught all about the House of Pooh.

At the age of thirteen, Alexandra wanted to get out from under her parents' supervision and see what life was like away from her family. Many of her Spence friends had enrolled in boarding schools, so she applied to Hotchkiss and St. Paul's. She was accepted at both, but because of my own painful experiences at Hotchkiss, I urged her to choose St. Paul's. Fortunately, she did not take my advice. She chose Hotchkiss, which turned out to be a very good fit for her. To this day, she still maintains some of the strong friendships she made there. Alex encountered no signs of the anti-Semitism that plagued my time there, a sign of how things had changed in thirty years.

Alex and her Grandmother Loeb in the walkway between our two homes.

Alexandra did well in classwork at Hotchkiss, and she was also a standout in several school plays. I made a point of attending any performance I was invited to, remembering all too well that my own parents never attended mine, always sending surrogates instead. In fact, Alexandra was so talented an actress that when she started college at Harvard, I encouraged her to look into its theater program. She opted, however, to stay focused on her real passion, art studies. Her impeccable aesthetic eye had been evident even as a young teenager, and it would carry on into adulthood.

When she turned sixteen, I started taking Alex with me on trips to Europe. She was a delightful traveling companion from the outset, and we visited England together many times in those years. I beamed when someone I did not know well would come up to me at the Royal Ascot races to remark on her beauty. I like to think those European trips were among some of our strongest bonding experiences. It also gave Alexandra a taste of Europe that would blossom into another passion of hers as she got older.

Though pleased with her work at Hotchkiss and Harvard, I had trouble handling her bouts of occasional rebellion. One incident is all too memorable to both of us. Alcohol was never my temptation, so it did not occur to me that Alexandra would be doing any drinking. On the day before her Hotchkiss graduation, she and a group of friends held a picnic off campus. They were caught with some beer, and the administration seriously considered not letting them graduate. When I learned of this threat, I went into high gear, waging a fierce battle on her behalf. It got pretty heated, but I prevailed, and she and her friends were allowed to graduate. Perhaps the scene I made was a bit over the top, but there was no way my daughter was not going to graduate over one small incident.

Alex sailed on to Harvard College, where she got good grades, with straight A's in all her art classes. After taking a year off from her studies while living in Paris (during the same time I was an ambassador in Denmark), she returned to graduate from Harvard.

Shortly after Harvard, Alexandra was accepted to INSEAD, France's prestigious business school (comparable to America's Harvard Business School), but she opted not to go for a master's degree. Though she loved Paris, she realized the business world neither utilized her talents nor made her happy. I was relieved when she decided enough was enough and came back to the art world in New York.

When Alex moved to New York City, she first worked for Christie's and then went on to work for the prestigious art dealer John Good while he operated his own art

Alexandra and I hosting her graduation party from Hotchkiss in 1979.

Alex and Baron Otto Reedtz-Thott, who lives in southern Zealand.

gallery in Manhattan. (Subsequently, he went on to work at the Gagosian Gallery and then Christie's.) While with John, Alex gained a greater interest and expertise in contemporary art, and for the first time had some exposure to the business side of the art world. In conversation with her, I complimented her on her quick rise and told her she was sitting on an auspicious opportunity.

"Someday," I told her, "you'll look back and wish you had bought these artists early—before they became so expensive." Then an idea popped into my mind. I said to her, "Why don't you pick some art out, and we'll buy some together now?"

She was enthusiastic about the idea, and I offered to provide two-thirds of the investment and to share the profits fifty-fifty. She put up her third by using some of the funds inherited from her grandparents. I also offered to be a silent partner and promised that she could make all the decisions. All twenty-three of the paintings she finally selected have increased in value over the years, particularly two German standouts. One is by Sigmar Polke, and the other is by Germany's most famous living artist, Gerhard Richter. (The Richter is currently worth over $3 million and still climbing.) Just a few years ago, while I was visiting Alex's beautiful home in Chestnut Hill, outside Philadelphia, she said, "Dad, come take a look at our picture." Although I was pleased to see it, what pleased me most was that she made a point of identifying it as "ours"—a project we had done together.

When it came to Alex's love life, I had an annoying habit (in my daughter's eyes) of

Alexandra and her
husband, Joe Driscoll.

introducing her to young men I considered "eligible" for her—and in whom she inevitably had absolutely no interest. One such courter was the son of Lord James Hansen, one of England's richest nobles. The young count arrived in a stretch limousine laden with flowers and champagne, which had the exact opposite effect on my egalitarian daughter. In fact, it was the worst possible approach with her. Despite that failure, I persisted with my good intentions in making these introductions. Though she did not seem to appreciate my efforts, Alex's girlfriends marveled at my attempts at matchmaking.

Eventually, of course, fate stepped in. An avid skier, Alexandra traveled frequently to Aspen. In 1991, she met her future husband there, a charming and handsome Harvard College and Harvard MBA graduate named Joe Driscoll. They married three years later. Warm-hearted and good-natured, Joe is one of those people so easy to like immediately. He is from an Irish-Catholic family. His father was a prominent lawyer in Boston, a partner at the former law firm of Louis Brandeis. Joe made his own tracks in the world of business and politics. He and Alex were in London when he proposed. With Joe standing beside her, Alex telephoned me, weeping happily. The fact that she

The newly engaged Alexandra and Joe were more interested in each other than the camera when this picture was taken at the prenuptial party I held for them in my Manhattan home.

Alex and Joe at the prenuptial party I gave for them.

Alexandra paid me some lovely compliments at my 80th birthday party, which she and Nicholas gave in the Loeb Boathouse.

called me immediately to share her joy meant the world to me.

Alexandra and Joe have provided me with two glorious, adorable grandchildren—Aidan, born September 9, 1998, and Allegra, born October 5, 2000. Both of them have the handsome goods looks and the intelligence of their parents. Each is unique as an individual, and, best of all, they love each other very much—as well as loving me, too.

Aidan is a serious student who earns stellar grades and is focused and motivated. Like his father, Aidan gets along with everyone. Allegra is athletic, excelling in tennis and squash, and musically she is incredibly talented. She is blessed with a beautiful singing voice; she plays the piano, the guitar and the ukulele skillfully; and she has the confidence to perform in public.

My wife, Sharon, and I have taken the grandchildren on trips over the years to places like Lyford Cay in the Bahamas, Gstaad in Switzerland and Aspen in Colorado. "Land and sea, and sun and ski"—all filled with many wonderful memories. Over the years, the two of them have come to visit Sharon and me at Ridgeleigh, which brings the greatest joy to both of us. As they grow older and their free time diminishes, we hope they will continue the tradition of coming to visit.

MY GRANDCHILDREN

The long gown Alex wore at her christening had an encore appearance at Aidan's.

Here are Alex and Joe Driscoll rejoicing over the safe arrival of baby Aidan, born September 9, 1998.

Aidan's high school senior picture.

Alex and Aidan sharing a good laugh.

Nina, Alex and Allegra.

This picture captures Allegra's spirit.

This is one of my favorite pictures of Allegra.

My grandchildren, Aidan and Allegra Driscoll.

Friends say that Nicholas's eyes
have the same luminous quality
that Paul Newman's had.

NICHOLAS

There was no lack of drama in my life during the period immediately following my exit from the family firm in 1973. I was still licking my wounds from Loeb, Rhoades when Meta Harrsen entered my life. At first, she was a welcome breath of fresh air. She would soon become much more than that.

When I met Meta, I found her lovely, enigmatic and intriguing. Like an elusive will-o'-the-wisp, she was sometimes present, sometimes not, receding if one came too near. The memory of the painful last months at Loeb, Rhoades was making me feel rebellious—something normally not part of my makeup. Meta had possessed that emotion most of her life, and I found it contagious. I embraced it as elating and inspiring.

I'd been trying to find a bright college student as an occasional tutor and companion for Alexandra, who was a teenager and continued to visit me on weekends and holidays. When I posted an ad on a local college bulletin board, Meta was among those who responded. During our preliminary interview, I found her bright and articulate—and distractingly beautiful. She loved poetry and even wrote some herself. She was also interested in politics and world affairs, big pluses in my eyes. At the end of our interview, I confessed that she was much too attractive to be an employee of mine. Instead of hiring her, I asked her to dinner.

I found another young woman to look after Alexandra, and Meta and I began to date. In due time, Meta became a frequent visitor at Ridgeleigh, in Purchase, so she and Alex did end up spending time together. I was smitten with Meta. She was like a rushing wave, turning from winsome to tantalizing to extremely restless.

By 1974 I had no meaningful role in the family firm except as a minor limited partner. My relationship with Meta had become the primary positive relationship in my life, and, because of this, it started to turn serious. When I invited her to take a long romantic trip with me to the Middle East, she accepted without hesitation. The Middle East seemed to be the right place to recover and dream new dreams. My previous visit to the region had only been to Israel, and the area seemed enticing because it was so wonderfully removed from my current life. It also struck me as exotic place.

Meta and I were having a wonderful time together, sightseeing in the daytime and staying out late in the evening. I had left my inhibitions in New York, and the angst about my future magically disappeared. She helped me feel open and relaxed. One night in Beirut, she startled me with an out-of-the-blue proposal: "Johnny darling," she

Nicholas was a heavy armful for his slender mother, Meta.

said, "let's start a baby right now! I don't even have to get married," she added. "I don't even need to be engaged. I just want to have a baby with you!"

In the delightful suspension of time and the real world, totally detached from my usual cautious self, I gave in. By the time we returned to New York, Meta was pregnant, and I was once again a delighted prospective father.

After we got back to New York, Meta moved into my home in Purchase. We were happy, excited about the baby on the way. But I was back in the real world, and it wasn't long before my conventional self reemerged. I increasingly thought about marriage and began to press her about it. She finally capitulated to my request—for our baby's sake—and we married in a private ceremony in Williamsburg, Virginia, followed by a short trip to Charleston, South Carolina, where my favorite grandmother's family came from.

Our son was born on August 2, 1975. We chose his name, Nicholas, which echoed a piece of Russian history (as did my daughter's name, Alexandra). Nicholas was perfect and beautiful, and my love for him knew no bounds. Presents and congratulations poured in from all circles, including from John Lindsay, the former mayor of New York. Lindsay had become close to our family after appointing my mother as New York City Commissioner for the United Nations and the Consular Corps.

From the beginning, Nicholas was a charmer who captured everyone's heart. He was a happy, outgoing infant who welcomed attention, and I was a proud, doting dad. However, my relationship with Meta fared less well. As it happened, I did not know that, sadly, Meta was afflicted with what today is called bipolar disorder. For the sake of the child she was carrying, she had stopped taking her medications during pregnancy. But I wasn't aware of this information. In those days, Meta's condition carried a stigma that has hopefully lessened, but she understandably felt a need to keep it from me at the time. Gradually, the variations in her mood and my reactions to them led to our estrangement and finally, divorce. Although Meta clearly loved Nicholas, her condition made it preferable for me to have full custody, which I was granted by the court.

On April 29, 1977, at the age of forty-seven, feeling enormous sadness and relief paired with great anxiety, I faced the challenges of rearing two-year-old Nicholas as a single parent. As he grew up, even with my determination to be a different kind of a father than my own had been, neither Nicholas nor I had an easy time of it. During his "terrible twos," when he would really misbehave, I would put him in his room and close the door. He would go banging around the room, and then there would be total silence. Certain that something bad must have happened, I would open the door slightly to see him sitting in the corner growling. When I would let him out, every-

This is a picture of the late Julie Wong with Nicholas, probably not even a year old. Julie and her husband, Jimmy, were a wonderful couple, refugees from Communist China, who looked after our family for quite a number of years. Originally, I hired Jimmy, then one day Julie showed up. A few months later, five children showed up.

Meta at Nicholas's first birthday party.

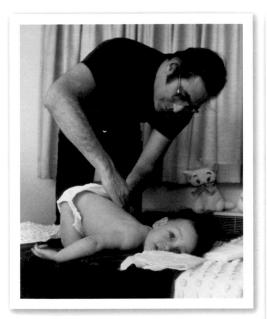

Believe it or not, I was a masterful diaper changer.

I almost got my face washed at one of Nicholas's baths.

A father-son chat on the sun porch of Rydhave in Copenhagen, Denmark.

I kept this photo of Nicholas and me in my 50 Broad Street office.

Nicholas is a natural athlete, and
he seemed delighted when I tried
to show him what I knew about
boxing when he was about six.
However, wrestling and baseball
interested him more, so his boxing
lessons were of short duration.

I tried vainly to interest
Nicholas in the portrait of
a distant family connection,
Grace Mears Levy.

NICHOLAS SALUTES CREDENTIALS DAY

On the day I was to present my credentials, Ambassador Albert Kønigsfeldt from the Danish Foreign Ministry came to Rydhave in full regalia to escort me to Amalienborg Palace in Copenhagen. There Her Majesty, Queen Margrethe II, would receive me, and that would mean that I had arrived in Denmark officially.

I'm not sure why Nicholas was saluting. Perhaps it was because he knew I was going to see the queen and it was a big event, and he thought a salute to the camera would show proper respect for the importance of the occasion.

A snapshot of Nicholas and Renee Doolan, who would become his nanny, in the kitchen of my Purchase home.

Nicholas and Renee together at East 61st Street.

thing would go back to normal. Eventually, all I had to say was, "If you don't stop, I'm putting you in your room," and he would straighten right out.

We were both blessed with good fortune when Renee Doolan came into our lives and took charge of my two-year-old "handful." My mother had heard that the Irish-born Renee had just ended a commitment to a New York family whose children had gone off to boarding school. A tall, handsome woman with an erect carriage, Renee emanated good breeding. A little reticent, she had an aura of serenity and calm. She would need those qualities, since my household has always been a little like the happily chaotic home in the Kaufman and Hart play *You Can't Take It with You*—a hundred things going on at once.

I was impressed with Renee's aristocratic manner of speaking—more British than Irish—and later realized that her reticence stemmed from an enormous sense of discretion, a necessary quality for someone intimately involved in the day-to-day affairs of someone else's home. Renee was our savior, often playing diplomatic intermediary during our father-son bouts. She would become more than a second mother to Nicholas for more than thirty years. When he finally went off to boarding school, she stayed on, continuing to help manage both my household and me.*

Nicholas's rebelliousness was something of a mystery to me. After all, pleasing my own father had been one of the central tenets of my life. As a student, I committed

---

* When Renee died in 2015, Nicholas and I felt so close to her that we laid her to rest at our home at Ridgeleigh, on land that looks out over Long Island Sound.

myself to studying and getting good grades, partly because I knew it was necessary, but mostly because it was what Father expected. Nicholas had some trouble academically (which, in fact, was due to dyslexia, but this was not discovered until later in his academic career), and he was more of a rebel at heart than I ever was.

Nicholas, born in August, is a true Leo—a natural-born leader, full of exuberance and strong opinions. As a child, he was always gregarious and popular, a leader among his young classmates. Renee told me that when she took him to the Century Country Club across the street from our home in Purchase, he was "like a pied piper," organizing the other children into baseball teams. He first attended a Montessori school close to my East 61st Street home, then a kindergarten called the Episcopal School, which was totally nondenominational. Nick lived with me during the week, and on the weekend, we would sprint up to Purchase. Just as I do, he has always felt that Ridgeleigh is his real home.

When I was stationed in Denmark as the U.S. ambassador, six-year-old Nicholas came along with Renee. He was a huge success there and sat quietly at many of the meetings I held at Rydhave (the U.S. ambassadorial home). We both warmly remember the birthday party I held for him when he turned seven, in 1982. The fifty-five invited guests were his classmates plus the children and grandchildren of my fellow diplomats in Copenhagen, including those of the Communist envoys—an event that landed us on the front page of a Copenhagen newspaper.

When we returned to New York in the latter part of September 1983, most private schools were already in session or too full. However, the Collegiate School accepted Nich-

Nicholas was thrilled when his mother came to Canaan, New Hampshire, for his graduation from Cardigan Mountain School in 1990. Pictured here, left to right are his mother, Meta Harrsen Bauer, Nicholas and me.

A wonderful picture of Nicholas with me.

olas anyway. It helped that Mother was on the board and that my brother, Arthur, and I were alumni. Collegiate proved very difficult for Nicholas, given his learning challenges. I felt terrible when I finally discovered that, instead of shirking his studies, he was actually struggling with a learning disability. Unfortunately, not knowing this at the time, and over Renee's many protests, I pushed Nick hard on his studies, which to this day I greatly regret.

After his year of struggle at Collegiate, his teachers suggested Cardigan Mountain summer school in New Hampshire (near Dartmouth University). There he could receive some remedial help. Early in the summer, he called home. "Dad, I love it here," he crowed. "I want to come back here in the fall instead of Collegiate. I want to stay here." I agreed to the change in plans, reassured by the fact that one of my favorite nephews, Matthew Bronfman, also went to Cardigan.

Cardigan wisely tracked its students, teaming them with their academic equals. It gave Nicholas tremendous confidence. After graduation from Cardigan's middle school, Nicholas went to high school at the prestigious Loomis Chaffee in Windsor, Connecticut. Only when he was fifteen did the school finally diagnose his dyslexia. The discovery boosted his confidence enormously. Finding out that his difficulties had a real source was a big relief to both of us. The school provided the extra assistance he needed, and he flourished.

When it came time for college, Nicholas chose to attend Tulane University in New Orleans. It was located in a warm climate, had an excellent faculty and, yes, a good party reputation. He called me during that first semester to let me know: "Dad," he

Alex, Nicholas and their half-sister, Lacey Mehran.

said, "it may be tough here, so I may not get through in four years. A lot of students are here for five or six years." "Well, Nick," I said, "I'll pay for four, but that's it."

I also clucked with disapproval upon learning he had been working as a bouncer at a local club. Though I offered to increase his allowance, he demurred. "It's not the money, Dad," he said. "I just like the job." Nicholas has always been his own man.

I always encouraged Meta to stay in touch with Nicholas, and she wrote to him regularly from Iran, where she lived for several years with her second husband until their divorce.

Sadly, 1996 was the year in which Meta, as well as both of my parents, died. After his mother's death, Nicholas retreated inward, and our relationship became very strained. In fact, he stopped speaking to me altogether for nearly two years while at Tulane. Fortunately, we shared a mutual friend, Eduardo Orlansky—a man who cared deeply for family. It was difficult not to notice that Nicholas was ignoring me. One night, the three of us found ourselves together at a dinner given by common friends in a New Orleans restaurant. At some point Eduardo took Nicholas aside, and, although I do not know what he said to him, Nicholas came back to the table nearly transformed. We began speaking again, and (having been invited by him) I proudly saw Nicholas graduate in 1998, with a BS degree in management and finance—and he did it in four years.

After graduation, Nicholas had an eye toward making it in Hollywood. During one of his summer breaks from college, he worked on the set of Mike Nichols's film *Primary Colors*, produced by Universal, which was owned by Nicholas's first cousin Edgar Bronfman Jr., the CEO of Seagram's. Impressed by Edgar and his world, Nicholas even got him to speak at his Tulane commencement the year he graduated.

As a smart and gregarious young man, Nicholas made friends quickly after his move to Hollywood. Encouraged by a friend, the producer-musician Quincy Jones, he self-financed, produced, directed and played a leading role in a film, *The Smokers*, about rebellious teenagers at a boarding school. He even gave me a cameo role, but only after I passed muster trying out for the part. I played the father of a very rebellious daughter.

When financing for a second film fell through, Nicholas decided to turn his attention to a very different endeavor. After the horror of 9/11, he told me he was thinking of enlisting in the military. I said, "That's commendable, as I know how patriotic you are." (Despite the fact that I had served in the Air Force, as a father I was quite upset that he would consider such a dangerous thing. But I treaded lightly.) "But that would be a great mistake at this time. I'm sure there are other things you could do." After some consideration, he agreed, but he still felt the call of service to his country and community. Consequently, he applied and was accepted for training at a police academy in Southern California, where he became a volunteer deputy. He also became a "Big Brother" through an inner-city program.

While out in Los Angeles, Nicholas's entrepreneurial spirit also led him to invest in real estate. In addition, he started his own environmental company, Carbon Solutions America. He put together a first-class team to go into towns and analyze their environmental issues and carbon footprints in the hopes of monetizing the environmental credits that they might be generating. If legislation mandating the capping and trading of carbon emissions went through, Nicholas and his team would be in a position to make a great deal of money. Unfortunately, this legislation is still on hold, but Nicholas did do a first-rate job running the company. He became so proficient and knowledgeable in this field that he went on to lecture to lawyers who specialize in the environment. Thereafter, he went on to work for Lehman Brothers in Palm Beach.* Unfortunately, this was not auspicious timing, as within two years, and much to everyone's surprise, the firm would sink into bankruptcy, precipitating the global financial crisis.

---

* Not the real Lehman Brothers. The real Lehman Brothers had merged, in 1977, with Kuhn Loeb and then into the American Express Company. American Express held the Lehman Brothers name, which they gave to Richard Fuld's company in 1994. Fifteen years later that company went into bankruptcy.

Alexandra, along with her brother, Nicholas, organized my 80th birthday party at the Loeb Boat House in 2010.

Nicholas always had a taste for politics. When Lehman collapsed, he turned his focus to these ambitions. He believed politics, especially running for office, would make good use of his people skills and his intense interest in public service. Nicholas then moved to Delray Beach, Florida, a place more in line with his conservative views than Los Angeles. He also continued his real estate ventures while eyeing opportunities to run for office.

As for Nicholas's heart, while on vacation in Sweden, he fell in love with a beautiful Scandinavian girl, Anna Petterssen, whom he would eventually marry. After spending time with her in Sweden, he invited her to visit him in Florida. She came, but without a long-term visa. When it was time for Anna to return to Sweden, not wanting to part, they quietly married in the Office of the County Clerk.

Soon afterwards, Nicholas began his first political campaign, running for the Delray City Council. He came within a handful of votes of winning—a very good experience for his first try.

In the summer of 2007, Nicholas and Anna were formally married in Sweden, in a beautiful wedding for friends and family. He bowled everyone over, especially his stunning bride, when he surprised us all by giving his wedding vows to his bride in impeccable Swedish. Returning to the States, they lived happily for a while. Nick then decided to throw his hat into the political ring again, this time running for the Florida State Senate. However, between his real estate career and the political race, he had little time to focus on his marriage, which he did not realize was unraveling. In the middle of the campaign, Anna left. Heartsick and unable to focus on his Senate race, Nicholas reluctantly bowed out. Admirably, he returned to his donors all of the campaign money he had raised—including the money he had already spent for the race. This astounded everybody. Nicholas showed that he is a man of integrity; and if ever he wants to return to politics, I know donors will remember him warmly and with respect.

After his divorce from Anna in 2009, Nicholas went to Hollywood to recuperate and see friends. One evening in a restaurant he was introduced to a beautiful Colombian model and soap opera actress named Sofia Vergara. There was instant chemistry between the two, and Nicholas and Sofia soon became a couple. A number of months after they started dating, Sofia was chosen for a new television comedy show, *Modern Family*. The show became an instant hit, and with each passing week, Sofia gradually became more famous. Soon news and gossip items would be covering Sofia's and Nicholas's every move.

In August 2010, while house hunting for the two of them, Nicholas was driving down a dirt road above Beverly Hills when the road suddenly narrowed and ended. As he started to try and back up in the tight space, the wheels slipped, and the car began to tip over the edge of the cliff. As the car began to fall, Nick jumped out, but as he hit the ground the car landed on top of him, breaking his leg and shattering his pelvis. The accident was frightening and dangerous. By the time Sofia called us in London to tell us the news (calling from the lobby of the hospital), we were almost simultaneously being called by friends in New York. Amazingly they had heard the news from their Spanish-speaking maids, who in turn had heard the Spanish radio news of the terrible car accident Sofia's man was in. When Nicholas was well enough to leave the hospital, he went to live with Sofia, who helped him through the long and painful recovery. The two soon became engaged. Hollywood life is not easy, however, and in 2014 Sofia and Nicholas broke off their engagement. Sadly, subsequent fallout would become more fodder for the gossip columns, which unfairly delved into their private lives.

In 2011, Nicholas had started a company called the Crunchy Condiment Company,

Renee lived with us for thirty-four years from when Nicholas was two years old until he was 36. She moved in 2011 to a wonderful home at Carnegie House which was not that far from our house in New York. Sadly, Renee died four years later.

which to this day has taken the bulk of his time and attention. Its main product, Onion Crunch, is a crispy, fried onion topping for hamburgers and hot dogs that Nicholas encountered as a child in Scandinavia. Thanks to his vision and promotional savvy, the product has taken off, making it to Nathan's, Wal-Mart, high-end grocery stores in Manhattan and athletic stadiums around the country. The company attracted some high-powered investors. *The Wall Street Journal*, *amNewYork* and *The New York Times* all wrote flattering profiles of Nicholas, with the *Times* calling him "Mr. Condiment" and *amNewYork* labeling him a "modern-day Renaissance man." Nick kindly told the interviewer that from his father he learned "etiquette, right from wrong, respect and to be a gentleman."[101] I hope I actually had something to do with this, but either way, I see these virtues in my son, and hearing him say that fills my heart with pride.

In fact, I am proud of both of my children. Most importantly, they are both generous and kind souls whom I love very much.

Lt. Governor Malcolm Wilson was pleased to swear me in as chair of the Council of Environmental Advisers in 1970, but by 1973, he saw me as a threat to his run for governor.

CHAPTER ELEVEN

On My Own: The Siren Song of Politics, 1973–1974

At a bleak moment in my life, my Harvard classmate Jerry Goodman wrote me a letter of encouragement saying that I was really good at "making lemonade out of lemons." I like to believe that, but in 1973, with my dream of heading Loeb, Rhoades a lost cause, it seemed as though I'd accumulated enough lemons to start a lemonade business.

Should I stay in the business world? I wrestled with uncertainty for a long while. I'd had seventeen profitable years at Loeb, Rhoades, and having seen the handwriting on the wall, I had withdrawn most of my capital from the firm to avoid any major liability. I still had a secretary and an office at Loeb, Rhoades, and I attended management committee meetings. Happily, I could also still bring in "deals" for the firm and receive compensation. One popped up quickly.

At a social occasion in London in 1972, I hit it off with Adnan Khashoggi, a Saudi Arabian reputed to be, at that time, one of the richest men in the world. (Adnan's father had been the family physician of the Saudi royals.) Adnan wanted to introduce me to Deputy Prime Minister Fahd bin Abdulaziz Al Saud, who was soon to be crown prince and the future king of Saudi Arabia. Fahd was planning to sell a special kind of oil to utilities in the United States.[*] Adnan wanted to be the liaison who worked out

---

[*] The Saudi royals live on an allowance, which is never enough for their exorbitant lifestyle. Thus they all engage in side business dealings.

Adnan Khashoggi introduced me to Prince Sultan bin Fahd bin Abdulaziz Al Saud. He was charming, and we hit it off perfectly. The Yom Kippur War in 1973 ended our brilliant oil deal.

the details of bringing the oil to America and thought Loeb, Rhoades was the right company to handle it.

When I mentioned the possibility of a Saudi oil deal to Father and others at Loeb, Rhoades, they didn't believe me. But there I was, meeting with the future king of Saudi Arabia. The meeting with Fahd was quite a process. Adnan and I flew on his private plane from London—during a European "grounding" of all planes on the continent—with ten to fifteen female "gifts" to Fahd,* who met us in Cannes, France. After our session on the Riviera, the oil minister of Saudi Arabia, Ahmed Zaki Yamani, was advised of our plans, as was Loeb, Rhoades senior partner Mark Millard, an expert in energy finance. During our meeting, Fahd said something very touching to me. "Mr. Loeb," he said, "As you know, it'd be difficult for you to come to Saudi Arabia [since I was Jewish], but I do wish to have someone from your firm equal to your status to come to be my special guest."

The deal moved forward with speed, putting real wind in the Loeb, Rhoades's sails. My parents were so pleased they gave Adnan and his wife a huge dinner party in their honor. However, on October 6, 1973, just as we were ready to sign the deal, the Yom Kippur War broke out when Egypt and Syria launched a surprise attack on Israel. The Americans sent arms and supplies to Israel, and, in retaliation, OPEC set an embargo on the export of oil, which lasted until April 1974. Oil prices rose an astronomical 70 percent, and a recession followed. The whole oil economy was in upheaval, and our deal fell through. I was hugely disappointed, but also philosophical. I'd long ago realized that when something seems too good to be true, it usually is. The experience also made me

---

* Adnan Khashoggi had become one of the world's greatest brokers. He lived as well as, if not better than, his clients, the Saudi princes. He owned a gigantic jetliner, a DC-8, and a yacht. He named the yacht *Nabila*, after his daughter. I learned this from his major domo. He kept 25 to 30 girls in individual apartments along the Riviera—most were "gifts," and a few were for himself.

realize that bringing in deals could only be a career sideline, never my main focus.

I took a career aptitude test in the 1970s, looking for some insight. I learned that I would do well in genealogy, which I saw as a hobby, not a potential career. The test shone no spotlights on anything except my verbal skills. Where could that talent best be served? Politics, which I'd had in the back of my mind for a long time, seemed obvious. I'd been active in party politics and environmental protection well before unlocking the golden handcuffs of Loeb, Rhoades. But for quite a long time after I left, I still wasn't sure politics was the wise way to go. Though I yearned to run for office, I knew I needed political visibility to do so, and I didn't have much.

As a younger man, I'd been drawn to "the hustings," meetings where potential candidates spoke to potential voters. As a member of the Young Republicans Club, I stumped for John Lindsay when he ran for mayor of New York City.* We were a group of half a dozen volunteers who went out into the five New York City boroughs equipped with a little soapbox, small American flags and Lindsay leaflets. We'd try to get a small crowd to gather and then take turns speaking about Lindsay and his plans for the city.

In that group of volunteers, I became friendly with James Zirin, who once served under my cousin Robert Morgenthau as the assistant U.S. attorney for the Southern District of New York. Currently host of *Digital Age*, a talk show in New York City, Jim recently refreshed my memories of those campaign days. He tells a funny story about my first day as a soapbox orator:

> *One cold October Saturday in 1965 a group of us assembled at the Roosevelt Hotel and decided we would campaign for Lindsay out on Coney Island. It was the first time that John Loeb had joined us, wearing a long cashmere coat, I remember.*
>
> *We got to Coney Island's boardwalk, and we set up our soapbox, a small speaker's stand. We got a pretty good crowd together, including some elderly ladies who sat on the boardwalk benches with blankets covering their knees.*
>
> *The original group ad-libbed standard stump speeches, but John, as a newcomer, came prepared with notes and a copy of a full page ad he'd paid to run in* The New York Times, *and which he now read to the crowd. The headline asked, "Why Does* The New York Times *Support John Lindsay?" The body of the ad went on to say that the*

---

* John Lindsay was the first Republican to win the New York City mayor's seat after a long series of Democrats. More liberal than his fellow Republicans would have liked, Lindsay switched parties and became a Democrat in 1971, in the middle of his second term as mayor.

Times traditionally supported Democratic candidates but then listed the reasons they were this time supporting (then Republican) John Lindsay.

Suddenly, one of the little old ladies on a park bench yelled out, "Why do you think they're supporting Lindsay? For MONEY of course!"

John turned to me and said, "Jim, do the people out here think money will buy everything? I wish it were true." And then he went on reading from the ad he'd bought!

A bit later, while he was reading reasons to vote for Lindsay from his notes typed on 4 x 5 index cards, another little old lady under a blanket yelled out, "Sonny boy, I have a question for you!" He paused politely and let her continue:

Is John Lindsay Jewish?

No, ma'am.

Is Abe Beame Jewish? *

No, ma'am.

Are YOU Jewish?

Yes, ma'am.

You should be ASHAMED of yourself!

Undaunted, John Loeb continued going with us to the other boroughs, honing his presentation and becoming a really good street corner speaker.

My approach to public speaking still includes those little white index cards. The fact remains that I can only be spontaneous if I'm well prepared. I've found that I don't misspeak that way—as politicians frequently do—and thus I never have to explain what I *really* meant.

My exit from Loeb, Rhoades did not go unnoticed. An article in *The Economist* in June 1973 had trumpeted my exit, which had angered Father considerably. Some of the media noted that my plans for the future would include environmental programs, as I had been instrumental in formulating the first legislation that established New York State's Department of Environmental Conservation. I was active in the movement to preserve our natural resources, sounding the alarm about air and water pollution long before it became a mainstream issue. I am proud to say that I was in the vanguard of America's early environmental movement as far back as 1967.

At Loeb, Rhoades in the mid-1960s, I had become a very good friend of Julian Gin-

---

* Abraham Beame, who indeed was Jewish, was one of three contenders for the mayoral office that year. The third was the writer William F. Buckley Jr.

gold's, fascinated by what I thought to be his extreme right-wing views. Julian seemed to be politically to the right of Attila the Hun, but I loved our spirited political sparring. Gradually, I began to see that, in some areas, he wasn't all that off base. (In fact, compared with today's GOP, he stands almost in the middle.) He wanted to get me involved in politics, even though I was considered a "Rockefeller Republican," meaning a liberal Republican. He urged me to run in a possible Republican primary for state comptroller, since Governor Nelson Rockefeller had not yet picked anyone to run (and lose)

Julian Gingold and I have been close friends ever since the mid-1960s. Here we are in my brother's bookshop at the 2001 book signing of *The Levy Family and Monticello, 1834–1923: Saving Thomas Jefferson's House.*

against the governor's friend, the Democrat Arthur Levitt. It got considerable publicity at the time that someone would even dare to interfere with Rockefeller's plans.

In 1967, Governor Rockefeller invited me to come and see him. My parents knew the governor well, but our relationship began when word reached his office about my political plans. I'd been visibly active in GOP circles for quite a while, raising money and speaking and holding events on behalf of candidates.

I was overwhelmed by the governor's cordiality and warmth. Not a tall man, he wrapped me in a huge bear hug, his head barely reaching my chest. We chatted briefly, and I told him I was being urged to run for a statewide office, specifically for New York State comptroller.

"Johnny, don't do that," he said. "You're going to be governor someday like your uncle Herbert. You're going to be sitting where I am now." I was surprised, and I didn't comment.

"First of all," Rockefeller continued, "you're not going to win the comptroller's seat, even if you get the nomination. I want you to be governor, but running for comptroller now is not the way to do it."

He pulled out a large book from behind his desk, which listed all the government jobs in New York State. "Johnny, take this home with you and see where you'd like to be involved," he said. "Then come back, and we'll talk."

I left the office amazed that Governor Rockefeller was thinking of me as gubernatorial material. I returned to his office a couple of weeks later, having realized

Once during my environmental treks around New York State, I had to don a shiny yellow plastic suit and helmet before seeing the inside of the company I was visiting.

three things in the interim. For one, the governor was willing to give me exactly the kind of public exposure that I'd been looking for. Second, in 1967, I wasn't ready to leave Loeb, Rhoades just yet. Third, there was a growing public concern about air pollution, but not much was being done about it.

I discussed the Rockefeller offer with some of my knowledgeable Republican pals, and they agreed that pollution was going to be an increasingly important issue. So far, no one in the Rockefeller administration was focused on it. "Go for it," they all said.

At our next meeting, I told Rockefeller, "Governor, the job I want isn't listed in your book. I would like to be your first assistant on air pollution."

"Great," he replied. He said he would immediately create the new post, and I would report directly to him. The title would be Special Advisor on Air Pollution.* Just before I left, he took my arm, pointed to his desk and said, "Someday you will sit over there." I left his office elated.

In 1970, the year of the first Earth Day, Governor Rockefeller named me chairman of the New York State Council of Environmental Advisors. The executive director, Austin Heller, and I went to all sixty-two counties in New York State and listened to the issues the public was having with some new regulations. We then reported back to the governor and to Henry Diamond, the first commissioner of the New York State Department of Environmental Conservation. The position also gave me visibility, which I needed for my political goals.

I organized the first workshop for the New York State Council of Environmental Advisors at Tarrytown House in November 1971. We were a gathering of business leaders, government officials and representatives of leading environmental groups.

---

* In due course, I became a special advisor on air and water pollution. After Earth Day, I became special environmental advisor instead of air and water advisor.

Governor Nelson Rockefeller leaving a workshop of the Council of Environmental Advisors with the Council's chairman, me, and also with leading environmentalist, Laurance Rockefeller (Nelson's brother).

Governor Rockefeller was on hand to give his warm approval when I announced the environmental committee's ambitious statewide anti-litter campaign in the spring of 1973.

I introduced Arthur Godfrey, a passionate environmentalist, who was invited to speak at a local radio station in Tarrytown, New York, following his appearance at my council's workshop.

A very popular radio star, Arthur Godfrey was our guest speaker at the Friday night dinner of the first workshop held by the Council of Environmental Advisors in 1971.

Our keynote speaker was Russell Train, the first chair of Nixon's fledgling Council on Environmental Quality, initiated one year earlier. The radio star Arthur Godfrey, an ardent environmentalist, was our Friday night dinner speaker. He had recently edited an anthology, *The Arthur Godfrey Environmental Reader*, focusing on Earth's survival.

Governor Rockefeller spoke of the leadership his administration was providing and emphasized the themes reflected in his book *Our Environment Can Be Saved*. The Tarrytown event was a real stem-winder, infusing the whole group with zest for the daunting task ahead. We were chomping at the bit to get started.

Godfrey, who became a friend of mine, introduced me to Ayn Rand, the famous Russian-American novelist, philosopher, playwright and screenwriter. She is best known for her two best-selling novels, *The Fountainhead* and *Atlas Shrugged*, as well as for developing a philosophical system called Objectivism. Both my brother, Arthur, and I were riveted by *The Fountainhead*—not only a fascinating novel, but it also subtly preached a philosophy of reason and selfishness.

I met Ayn shortly after Earth Day at her home in Lower Manhattan, where she lived with her husband. The apartment was sparsely furnished and monastic in feeling. The light was quite low, and there were no paintings or pictures on the walls. She was short, maybe five foot four, with cold black hair and bangs falling down near her eyes. Her voice was clear and steady but did not sound particularly enthusiastic even about her philosophy. I told her I was an investment banker and special advisor to Governor Rockefeller on environmental matters. Ayn told me that she believed that the environmental movement was a communist plot to destroy capitalism. Whether or not this was true, Ayn believed that the environmental movement would cripple the advancement of capitalism and put many people out of work. She liked the fact that I worked on Wall Street—the center of capitalism. She supported laissez-faire capitalism, which she believed was a system based on recognizing individual rights. She told me she supported rational and ethical egotism and rejected altruism. The whole atmosphere was quite depressing, and I did not stay long.

The next few years were a never-ending public relations campaign for the environment. Our team of seven council members and executive director covered the state trying to win the hearts, minds and commitment of New York's citizens and businesses. Our main targets were mandatory beverage can and bottle deposit legislation; waste-lubricating oil conservation and recovery; a total resource recovery system for urban areas; development of long-term energy and environment policy; the visual environment; transportation and air policies in urban communities; and a review of controls on sulfur dioxide and sulfur emissions in urban communities. We also initiated a statewide anti-litter program—"Keep New York State Clean"—and secured support from the academic and business communities for our long-range studies. I even helped to write the state's first environmental bill. I was chairman of the Council of Environmental Advisors until the new governor, the Democrat Hugh Carey, defunded the modest needs of our program in 1975. It was our council's death knell. Carey's budget statement shockingly implied that our council was "redundant."

"If we were redundant," our executive director, Austin Heller, responded, "then one might ask: 'Why haven't all of these items that we've put on the table now been achieved?'" Environmental issues continued to be critically urgent, but they were underfunded and controversial. The entire experience was rewarding and illuminating.*

I learned almost as much about politics from the challenges of environmentalism as I ever did at Loeb, Rhoades. Working on behalf of the environment readied me for a turn of events in New York's Twenty-Fourth Congressional District in 1973. I started my voting life as a Democrat. My father and his father were both ardent Republicans, but I had been much more influenced politically by my mother's side of the family. Mother had been a working Democrat as far back as 1928, when she campaigned for Franklin Roosevelt, first during his run for governor (and for her Uncle Herbert, for lieutenant governor), and later for president.

Mother jumped the Democrat ship when she supported Eisenhower, working for "I Like Ike" and "Citizens for Eisenhower" in 1951 and 1952. Over the years, my parents supported members of *both* parties, often siding with philosophy over political affiliation. I was still a Democrat until well after graduation from Harvard, where I had been all for Adlai Stevenson II, whose son, Adlai III, was a friend, classmate and later a U.S. senator.

While still a Democrat, I enjoyed a short but memorable connection with Jack Kennedy. I first crossed paths with him in 1957 or 1958 at one of Bobby Friedman's famous singles parties. Bobby was a Yale grad and captain of the tennis team. He also threw fantastic parties, inviting the richest guys in town, thereby luring the prettiest girls. I was riveted the day Jack Kennedy dropped by—though he hadn't been a bachelor since 1953. He was as charismatic as the media claimed, and I liked him enor-

---

* In June 1972, I served as a representative to the UN Conference on the Environment in Stockholm. The historic meeting led to the "Stockholm Declaration," a landmark proclamation regarding the world's responsibility to the environment. Its focus was "stimulating and providing guidelines for action by national governments and international organizations."

mously, even though it was clear he would rather charm the pretty girls than chat with me. Somehow he managed to do both. At the same party, I met Chuck Spalding, one of Kennedy's wedding ushers and a major political supporter of Jack's campaigns.

Enormously impressed with Senator Kennedy, I decided that he merited an invitation to one of the formal Loeb, Rhoades luncheons. Partners got "points" from Father if we brought in what he deemed "interesting guests," even if they weren't potential clients. The suggestion to bring Kennedy brought a vehement veto from my father, who pronounced Jack "nothing but a playboy," whose father was "a crook."

Fast forward to 1960. By then I was married to Nina and still struggling to find a meaningful role at Loeb, Rhoades. On January 2, Jack Kennedy officially announced his run for the presidency.

Peter Flanigan, a great friend and next-door neighbor, graduated Princeton summa cum laude and was a Navy pilot in World War II, an economic aide to President Richard Nixon, and a senior partner at Dillon Road; he helped implement major developments in public education.

Chuck Spalding contacted me and said Jack would like me to come aboard a new Kennedy committee composed of both Democrats and Republicans. Bobby Friedman also urged me to become involved with the new Independent Citizens Committee for Kennedy. I suspect that because of the well-documented anti-Semitism of Jack's father, they were especially interested in my being visible early in the campaign. An additional enticement was that if I made a $1,000 contribution to the committee, I could hand the check to Jack in person, a photo op I relished. I looked forward to being active in a historic campaign, but Father and fate intervened.

Horace "Hap" Flanigan, a good friend and close neighbor of my parents in Purchase, heard about my potential alliance with Kennedy. Hap was also chairman of Manufacturers Hanover Trust and a major figure in the New York financial world. Even though they were Irish Catholics themselves, Hap and all the Flanigans, including his son Peter, were Nixon supporters, vigorously opposed to the Kennedys. Hap's revelation to Father about my potential commitment to Kennedy set off a family scene. My parents were backing Nixon, which is why I hadn't told Father about the Kennedy committee in the first place. The call from Father was mostly a one-way conversation. It went something like this:

"Well, it just shows what you don't know. There's no way a Catholic can be elected president," Father railed. "Even Hap Flanigan wouldn't let a Kennedy in his house. Of course, it's up to you. You can do what you want, but if you support Kennedy, you can't stay a general partner at Loeb, Rhoades."

I had no idea Father would be quite so draconian in his position. I couldn't afford to lose my partnership, so I had no choice but to cave and not join the Kennedy committee. Looking back, I can see that decision might have been a major crossroads, and I wonder ruefully about the "what ifs." If I had held my ground, Father might well have been the one to cave.

The irony is that two years later my parents attended a much-publicized Kennedy White House dinner honoring André Malraux, France's first minister of culture.

"What do you think of Kennedy now?" I asked Father soon after.

"He's learned a lot," my father replied.

The invitation came about like this. Harry Parish, who was a Loeb, Rhoades partner, was married to Dorothy Kinnicutt, whom everyone called "Sister Parish." She was my parents' decorator and would become one of the top interior decorators in the world. Jackie Kennedy asked Sister Parish to help her redecorate the White House. Through Sister Parish, Mother and Father donated a considerable sum to the project. As a result of this contribution, Jackie saw to it that Mother and Father were invited to the White House. As time would reveal, Jackie seemed to like dark, older men and developed a close relationship with Father.

I had my own intimate relationship with the White House, though it was decidedly of a different kind. After Kennedy's death in 1963, Vice President Lyndon Johnson became president. He immediately began to plan his 1964 presidential campaign. A proud man, LBJ found it imperative to prove that he could be elected on his own. He called up Robert B. Anderson, a Texas friend and former cabinet member under President Eisenhower, who had become a limited partner of Loeb, Rhoades. Anderson said he'd love to help, but he didn't want to spend time on politics. However, he suggested his senior partner, my father, for the role. Father and LBJ hit it off, and Father was made head of the National Independent Committee for Johnson and Humphrey. This surprised a lot of people who considered Father to be a right-wing Republican. Father put together a tremendous team of investment bankers and corporate types to run the committee.

In 1967, the White House announced that Lynda Bird Johnson, the twenty-three year-old daughter of the president, was giving a party for her closest friends. The party

Miss Lynda Bird Johnson
requests the pleasure of the company of
Mr. Loeb
The White House
on Friday, February 17, 1967
at eight o'clock

Dinner-dance   Black Tie

This is the photo of Lynda Bird Johnson and me that caused a huge flurry of gossip. I was amused by all the publicity the picture generated. Lynda Bird was not.

was to be a state dinner in honor of the princess of Greece. The White House released a guest list of the invitees, and, incredibly, my name was on it! I was tremendously excited to be invited to a White House state dinner, especially since I had never even met Lynda Bird. Those invited included children of LBJ's friends and supporters, such as Father.

I went to Washington for the party in February and was seated at Lynda Bird's table, which included the actor Warren Beatty and the honoree, Princess Irene. At

Charity Ball

Lynda Bird Johnson's escort at the New York City ball to raise funds for closed-circuit radio for patients in Veterans Administration hospitals Friday night was John Loeb, Jr., a broker.—A. P. wirephotos.

People from all over the country sent me copies of clippings like this one about my dating Lynda Bird Johnson. This was a charity ball for patients at VA hospitals.

the time, Lynda Bird was dating the actor George Hamilton, who was away filming. He sent 365 roses to Lynda Bird for Valentine's Day, which were placed at all the tables. The Johnson White House decidedly did not approve of Hamilton, who had avoided the draft and never served in the military.[*]

At that party, all the men got a chance to dance with Lynda Bird. When it was my turn, I stood up and was surprised that, with high heels on, the First Daughter was nearly my height. She was an impressive dancer, very intelligent, and her southern accent was not nearly as heavy as it was reputed to be. She told me she was working for the *Ladies Home Journal*, based in New York, and came to the city nearly every month.

"Well, next time you come to New York," I said, "maybe you and I could get together." She said she would love to.

About two months later I got a call at the office from the White House; everyone crowded around me, ears leaned in. It was Lynda Bird. "Hi John," I heard in that familiar southern accent. "I'm coming to New York next week and staying with friends of my family, Mr. and Mrs. Krim.[†] I've got tickets to the theater. Would you like to take me?"

"I'd love to," I replied.

The evening I picked up Lynda Bird, as

---

[*] The word was that Hamilton taught Lynda Bird a lot about makeup.

[†] Coincidentally, they were also friends of my parents. Mr. Arthur B. Krim was an advisor to Lyndon Johnson and chairman of United Artists and Orion Pictures. His wife is Dr. Mathilde Krim, who founded the American Foundation for AIDS Research (AMFAR).

we drove to the theater, I noticed we were being followed by the Secret Service, who trailed us the whole way. (Lynda Bird was the first child of a president to get protection wherever she went.) As we entered the theater, I spotted a single cameraman waiting by the door. Right on cue, he snapped a bunch of pictures of Lynda Bird and me. The next day, in at least a thousand publications around the world, I was introduced as her new boyfriend. Every single article mentioned that I had served two years in the U.S. Air Force. Clearly, the Johnson inner circle had set me up, but I got a kick out of it. My mother was over the moon. Not only was Lynda Bird the president's daughter, but also the Lady Bird side of the family was quite wealthy, owners of a radio and television company in Dallas. President Johnson instructed the FCC not to grant any other licenses in the area, so Lady Bird's family essentially had a monopoly there.

Lynda Bird and I dated for six months or so. I was her frequent escort to charity balls. She would come visit me in New York, and I'd go down to Washington. It was a long trip and, based on plane schedules, I'd frequently be late. Sometimes President Johnson was there when I arrived, waiting for me to pick her up. The president would be sitting in the living room like a used car salesman in his suspenders with his legs spread out, watching four television sets at once.

"You know, John," he said to me once, "there are not many people in the world who keep the president of the United States waiting."

I wanted to fall in love with Lynda Bird, but we lacked the chemistry. One day she called me up and invited me down to play bridge with her—a game she loved but one for which I had no skill going back to when my mother briefly tried to teach me. I made up a reason why I couldn't come. She ended up finding a young marine stationed in the White House, Charles "Chuck" Robb, to play with her. As fate would have it, the two ended up marrying. In the end, it was not meant to be between Lynda Bird and me. Perhaps if Mother had taken more time teaching me bridge, I might have married the wealthy daughter of a president.

On December 9, 1967, I was in the reception line congratulating Lynda Bird on her marriage to a young marine, Charles (Chuck) Robb. Her new husband would become both a Virginia governor and a United States senator.

Lyndon Johnson was the last Democrat I ever supported for national office. Over the years my core political philosophy and values have been consistent. I am, and al-

SINCE I HAVE BEEN OLD ENOUGH TO VOTE, I HAVE KNOWN ALL THE PRESIDENTS FROM EISENHOWER THROUGH TRUMP, EXCEPT BARACK OBAMA. FOLLOWING ARE FIVE OF THEM, AS WELL AS HILLARY CLINTON, WHO, IN 2016, WON THE POPULAR VOTE BUT LOST THE KEY ELECTORAL VOTES TO TRUMP.

I sometimes saw President Johnson (1963–1969) in unusually informal circumstances in the White House private quarters. Here the back of my head is seen with him in the reception line at Lynda Bird's wedding in 1967.

President Ford (1974–1977) and I had something in common. We both were Sons of the American Revolution. During this meeting I "introduced" President Ford to my Grandmother Loeb's portrait after he spoke at the opening of the exhibit called *The Jewish Community in Early America*, held in 1980 at the DAR museum in Washington, D.C.

President Reagan (1981–1989) seemed quite glad to see me again at a White House reception in January 1985. Standing next to him is his longtime chief of protocol, Selwa "Lucky" Roosevelt, wife of Archibald B. Roosevelt Jr., a grandson of President Teddy Roosevelt.

President Clinton (1993–2001) stopped to chat with me before delivering his speech at American University in the fall of 2000. A former Rhodes scholar, he spoke warmly of my cousin Arthur Lehman Goodhart, who had been a "master" (the equivalent of president) in one of Oxford's thirty-eight colleges while Clinton was a student there.

Sharon and I were glad to be with President George W. Bush (2001–2009), who spoke at the opening dinner celebrating the yearlong celebration of the 350th anniversary of "The Jewish Arrival in America." More than a thousand people attended the event, held in the National Building Museum in Washington, D.C.

I found Hillary Clinton charming when I met her at an event held in the White House when she was First Lady. She later became a U.S. senator from New York and subsequently secretary of state.

I worked together closely with Andrew P. O'Rourke, longtime county executive and tireless chair of the Republican Party in Westchester County. The GOP candidates running for office were grateful for our support.

ways have been, a fiscal conservative but a social liberal. I will always be a supporter of Planned Parenthood and the right to choose. I could see by the mid-1960s that the Republicans were closer to my own values than the Democrats, rightly tagged today as the "Tax and Spend Party."

I became active with the Young Republicans in Westchester County. The Twenty-Fourth District's GOP was laced with warm-hearted Italians. I liked them, and they seemed to like me, not seeming to mind a bit that I was Jewish. It was wonderful to be so enthusiastically welcomed, especially after the turf wars I experienced at Loeb, Rhoades.

I soon began to support GOP candidates all over the district, not only with money but also with speeches and events on their behalf, some of them at my home. I worked closely with the party chair, Andrew P. O'Rourke, a popular and respected eye surgeon in our community and father of thirteen children. He only had to mention that a fellow Republican needed support and I was "Johnny-on-the-spot."

In March of 1972, Ogden "Brownie" Reid, the Republican congressman from my district, who had held his seat for ten years, made a major announcement. The newly liberal congressman said he would run again in November, but as a Democrat. He won the election handily but later announced that he would not be running for his House seat in 1974. It would be wide open to both Democrats and Republicans at the next election.* The time had come to throw my own hat in the ring, though several other Republican hats would also be tossed. However, by the time I formally announced my candidacy, they had dropped out, primarily because the GOP district leadership was backing me.

I didn't make an official announcement until early 1974, but it had been an open secret that I intended to run. I'd already organized a campaign team, produced ads,

---

* Reid was planning to run for the New York State governorship in 1974, but he dropped out before the election. Instead, he served the next governor, the Democrat Hugh Carey, as commissioner of environmental conservation.

scheduled events and was gaining visibility in the district, though I was attacked for being too rich. Potential donors didn't realize that neither my family nor I could legally contribute more than $25,000 to my campaign (a minuscule amount, considering the cost of a congressional run). As I began to lay the groundwork for a vigorous campaign, I was grateful for the immediate contribution from one special friend and potential constituent, the inimitable Brooke Astor, whose Holly Hill estate was in my district in Westchester County.

Two incidents during my campaign, both centered in a portion of Yonkers in the Twenty-Fourth Congressional District, are amusing only in hindsight. After a meeting of the Yonkers City Council, a few council members and I were heading out for dinner. A drunk woman, who had been at the council meeting, lurched toward our group and announced loudly that she was going to accompany us. She was told politely but firmly that she was *not* coming with us, and she melted back into a small group milling around City Hall.

When I picked up my office phone the next morning, a cold voice asked, "Are you John Loeb?"

I cautiously admitted that I was and said, "Who's calling, please?"

The steely and terrifying voice said, "I'M GOING TO KILL YOU."

I was thoroughly shaken; mystified, I assumed the call had been precipitated by some incident in Yonkers, a city with a reputation for tough customers. Knowing that any death threat had to be taken seriously, I phoned the Yonkers mayor. He promised to investigate and called back shortly. It turned out the inebriated woman was the wife of a Yonkers council member. She was having an affair with "Mr. Steely Voice," and, intending to make her lover jealous, she told him she was sleeping with me. I never knew how the mayor handled it, but I didn't hear another peep from either Mr. Steely Voice or the council member's wife.

Our GOP officials were Italian, and our Italian district was rumored to include a sprinkling of Mafia-connected individuals. A local schoolteacher, a charming and funny young Italian man, showed up at almost every Loeb political event. The GOP leaders, who had begun to keep a protective watch over me, warned that this young fan had "connections" and that I should avoid him at all costs. Most important, I should *never* have my picture taken with him. This proved to be a problem; the young teacher was a glue pot, and I seemed stuck with him. Wherever I was, he rushed up to speak to me.

Things got dicey. A recently fired Westchester cop started showing up regularly

He'll level with you.

LOEB
FOR CONGRESS

I had small campaign cards printed well before I even announced my intention to run for Congress in 1974.

wherever I appeared, taking pictures of this teacher talking to me. The ex-cop blamed someone in the GOP leadership for his dismissal and wanted revenge. He dropped a packet of his photographs at a local newspaper, along with a story he'd made up about how I was in bed with the Mafia. He then phoned the head of the GOP in Yonkers to brag about what he'd done. The GOP leader called an emergency meeting in the middle of the night of the other Twenty-Fourth District GOP leaders, during which they threatened the ex-cop with "very severe problems" if he didn't retrieve the story before it was in print. Sufficiently cowed, the ex-cop broke into the newspaper office and retrieved the packet before dawn.

I had some disappointments along the way, one of which was the reluctance of Aunt Edith Lehman (Herbert Lehman's widow) to endorse me. She had a political friendship with Democratic congressman Richard Ottinger, who was about to move into to my district to run for Ogden Reid's seat. I knew he would make a tough opponent in my famously dubbed "limousine liberal" district—a moniker that mocked those rich enough to afford the luxury of being liberal.

Nelson Rockefeller offered to help me in any way he could. I asked him to persuade Aunt Edith to support me instead of Ottinger. Nelson promised to try but pointed out the obvious—a request from a Republican governor to the widow of a powerful Democrat would not likely have much impact. In the end, Aunt Edith agreed not to make her preference for Ottinger public immediately. This was helpful, but far less than her support would have been. The loving memory of Herbert Lehman was still fresh in voters' minds, so she could have been a potent ally in my quest for a U.S. House seat.

I had a political knack for using media coverage to my advantage. One example of this came in December 1973, when the British government invited me to visit for an exchange of information and ideas about environmental issues. The visit was capped

Although this picture of me hiking was taken for use in a prospective 1974 congressional campaign, it could well have been a snapshot of me in my everyday life, because serious walking is something I really love.

Fresh snap peas went for 49 cents a pound when I visited a small grocery store during my campaign for a U.S. House seat in 1974. I've learned that today, they would run anywhere from $3.50 to $4.99 a pound!

by a media conference where an enterprising young correspondent for *The New York Times* named Terry Robards interviewed me.

When I mentioned that I was in the midst of a congressional GOP primary campaign in my district, Terry urged me to run for governor instead, and he wanted to write a story about the possibility. I had been told, though it was not yet widely known at the time, that Nelson Rockefeller was not going to run for governor again the next year. I admitted to Terry that his idea sounded tempting and then listed the reasons I had a chance, "provided Governor Rockefeller doesn't run."

I didn't mention to Terry that a trial balloon via a *New York Times* article might well enhance my standing with the leaders in GOP circles as a candidate for the House. Though I was visible and popular with many Republicans in the Twenty-Fourth District, I was a thorn in the side of some, specifically Lieutenant Governor Malcolm Wilson. I was no fan of his, either. He had been grumbling about my running for the Reid House seat and was becoming more and more vocal about his disapproval. Although I had lived on and off in Purchase all my life, he told me that I had "just put down the rugs," implying that I spent my time in New York City. Wilson was in line to run for governor himself, and any flurry of publicity about my interest in the governorship was sure to draw his ire. Why not provoke Wilson into endorsing me? In retrospect, I might have had a shot for the governorship myself at that time.

The *Times* article—a full spread with a large picture—appeared on December 8,

1973, and for a little over a week there was a flurry of speculative publicity. I fanned the flames by not disputing the possibility of a gubernatorial run. One newspaper even floated the theory that Governor Rockefeller was behind the story, which was patently untrue. Like magic, Malcolm Wilson's objection to my running for the House seat miraculously disappeared! "Oh, hell, let Loeb run," he apparently told the GOP leaders. A little over a week later, I announced that I was *not* going to run for governor. Machiavelli would have approved.*

When I first announced my candidacy for the House of Representatives, in March 1974, things looked very positive for my run. By June, however, they had gone precipitously south. The candidacy of Democrat Richard Ottinger was taking off like an "Arizona wildfire." The Watergate backlash against all Republicans had become more ferocious, tarring any Republican up for public office. At the same time, my campaign funds had become increasingly short. Even people who wanted me to win didn't understand the legal limitations of funding one's own campaign. Some found it hard to believe that the son of a man as rich as my father was scraping the bottom of the campaign barrel. Taking a hard look at my prospects, I knew I had to bow out. I reluctantly made the announcement in early June, citing personal and business reasons, but primarily blaming the Watergate spillover. Richard Ottinger easily won the seat, as expected. Political ambition dies hard, and the House primary campaign not only didn't kill my appetite for national office, it whetted it. I was nowhere near done.

---

* In December 1974, Rockefeller was chosen by President Ford to be the new vice president of the United States.

I tried my best to emulate California's hugely successful Howard Jarvis helping to pass Proposition 13. Jarvis stabilized everybody's property tax in California. When campaigning for VOTE, I imitated his vigorous fist-bump.

≡

CHAPTER TWELVE

On My Own:
The Siren Song of Politics,
1974–1981

For people like me, politics is addictive, much like the smell of greasepaint and the roar of the crowd are to an actor. I worked like the proverbial beaver for the GOP during the next few years, but I also made time in late 1978 to found a nonpartisan movement called Voice of the Electorate, or VOTE. Part of my motivation was that I knew VOTE would be an enormous boost for my political visibility across the state.

I was appalled that an astonishing 37 percent of registered voters in New York had not voted in the previous election. VOTE was based on the idea that disenchanted New York voters would become more engaged if it were possible to repeal unpopular legislation and add their own propositions to election ballots. That kind of referendum existed in twenty-three states, and citizens were free to put an issue on the ballot if they got enough signatures. VOTE's most important mission was lobbying for an enabling amendment to New York's constitution. An amendment would require passage through two successive legislatures and subsequent voter approval in a referendum. Over the months, we met the opposition of powerful vested interests, as well as that of Governor Carey and Senate Republican Majority Leader Warren M. Anderson. But we also gained warm and fervent support from the influential United Taxpayers of New York, the League of Women Voters and the Conservative Party.

We drew wide media support, most notably from *The New York Times*. Radio and TV stations were particularly receptive to running public service announcements for us. I

A future ambassador, Robin Chandler Duke (Mrs. Angier Biddle Duke) signed the first VOTE petition for our referendum at the front entrance of Grand Central Station in January 1979. In less than two hours, we garnered more than 2,000 signatures that day.

made a point to personally deliver our scripts and tapes to the stations, often to the same woman in a tiny office who decided what would air. Usually organizations just mail in their PSA requests, but there's nothing like in-person visits to pave the way. I also made personal appearances on talk shows such as *Straight Talk*, the syndicated *David Susskind Show* and *Midday Live.*

When I started VOTE, voter turnout in states that had these options was double that of New York. Connecticut and New Jersey joined our program to educate the public about the potential power within reach of the voting public. I was hailed in the Adirondack region's newspaper, the *Post-Star,* as "New York's Howard Jarvis," which couldn't have pleased me more. Howard was my hero for recently spearheading the successful passage of California's tax revolt against property taxes, known as Proposition 13.

Late in 1979, Jarvis came to New York for a kick-off rally for VOTE and to accompany us on our appearances in the state. He was a galvanizing speaker at the Senate hearings on initiative and referendum, in Albany, as well as at the press conferences afterward. I reminded the Senate members about a few historical milestones brought about by voter initiatives in other states, such as shorter work weeks, compulsory education and workers' compensation laws.

I caused a well-publicized scene in the summer of 1979 in an argument with New York mayor Ed Koch. Koch was about to sign a bill giving himself and the City Council signifi-

Shedding coat and tie, I sat on the floor with members of the Young Republican Club at Fordham University and explained the goals of VOTE.

cant payroll raises, even though everyone was worried about the city's stark financial state. The public was outraged, and VOTE's members thought it unconscionable—New York City was a hair away from bankruptcy! The public backlash forced Koch to hold a hearing about the raises. He scheduled it for a late Friday afternoon, thinking the turnout and media coverage would be minimal. It didn't work; the hearing had huge coverage—and one very vocal attendee.

Koch had allotted three minutes for each of the twenty-six people slated to speak. I was first and had finished most of my written speech when Koch interrupted loudly, "Time's up!" Undeterred, I got in three more sentences as a cop tugged at my belt and Koch shouted, "I want him out of here!"

"You can't throw me out!" I shouted back, almost daring them to cause such a scene.

"I want him removed now!" Koch yelled again. Two more policemen grabbed me by the elbows and shoved me out. Others called out, "Give him my three minutes! He can have my three minutes!" The crowd was enraged, and there were shouts of "Police brutality!" and "Let the man finish!" as I was dragged to the door. Once outside, I was slammed unnecessarily against the wall and told to spread my arms and legs as the cops roughed me up. Who was I to speak to the mayor like that? The incident was captured by the press and caused quite the outrage. Just before the hearing was over, I was readmitted, though I was not allowed to finish my speech.

Despite the protests, Mayor Koch signed the bill that shot his salary from $60,000 to $80,000, making him the highest paid mayor in the country at that time. Subsequently, Ed Koch and I became good friends. Over four decades later, despite VOTE's earlier persistent efforts, the New York State legislature has yet to pass the necessary constitutional amendment to allow for initiatives and referendums on the ballot. I haven't given up hope that someday it will, though I'm far past the age where I can ignite a scene to air my disapproval.

My close friend Julian Gingold, whom I'd met during my early years at Loeb, Rhoades, was at the time an independent broker affiliated with our company. In 1975, Julian confided in me that Ronald Reagan planned to challenge President Ford at the Republican National Convention the next year and had scheduled a visit to Manhattan to woo voters. My ears perked up. Reagan was originally a Democrat but became a Republican just a few years before I made the same move, for basically the same reasons. I saw in him a kindred spirit who had a real chance at the White House. Ford was never that popular, and crowds seemed to really respond to the energetic Reagan.

Katherine Gurley, a friend of mine in the late 1970s, is pictured with my son, Nicholas. Her son, George, and Nicholas were playmates. I still see George and his wife, Hilly.

In 1978, Perry Duryea, the speaker of the New York State Assembly and an old friend of mine, asked me to raise money for his governorship campaign. I had met with Ronald Reagan at a dinner Nelson Rockefeller gave (in the 1960s), and again when I asked him to come to New York in 1975. I asked him to come again for Duryea, and he agreed.

Originally, I went to a number of the great corporations in Westchester but wasn't able to raise any money—not even a dime—offering a $250 ticket to meet Reagan. When I opened the event to the general public for $100 a couple, more than a hundred men, women and young adults

My friend Julian Gingold with his wife, Irene, who is an author. Julian was an early Reagan supporter, a strong conservative Republican and a brilliant political strategist.

From left to right: myself; then Governor Reagan; Dr. Kilbourn, New York State Republican Party chairman; Helene von Damm (Governor Reagan's secretary) and Marion Granowitz, Ryetown Republican Party chairwoman. Reagan was there to support Perry Duryea, Speaker of the New York Assembly, who was running for governor.

came to hear Governor Ronald Reagan. When he started to speak, you could literally hear a pin drop. It was like a new messiah had arrived.

Clearly, Governor Reagan was in touch with the average middle-class American. At the time, he was ignored by the so-called upper class and certain corporate executives. That was going to change.

I had been inclined toward Reagan ever since meeting him at the dinner Rockefeller gave for his fellow governors a few years earlier. The affable Reagan laughed when I told him his face was quite familiar, since my teenage sister Judy had hung a Hollywood photo of him in one of our bathrooms. Though I was not as taken with his charisma as I had been with Jack Kennedy's, I still liked him a great deal. When Julian suggested that I join a group he was forming in New York City to meet the would-be presidential candidate, I agreed to come. Most New York Republicans thought he was a joke, still pigeonholing him as a B-grade actor and ignoring his successful years as California's governor.

The University Club lunch on November 25, 1975, was small: Reagan, his California aide Mike Deaver, Julian and me. Though Julian had done his best to gather a crowd, not one other Republican came! They missed a wonderful opportunity to hear the persuasive former governor's positions on taxes (too high); inflation (rising); a sound dollar (in much peril); monetary policy (keep prices stable); strong support of Israel (much weakened under Carter); and foreign policy. The dynamic Reagan won me over, and I would shortly become an active supporter.

Reagan then invited Julian and me to be his special guests at the Republican National Convention in Kansas City, sending us blue chip tickets for every night of the convention. Reagan didn't get the nomination, but it was a squeaker of a win for the incumbent Ford. Julian and I were confident our candidate would make it the next time around. In the meantime, there was much work to be done.

After I told Nelson Rockefeller of my decision to support Reagan, I never heard from him again. It wasn't that I thought Nelson wasn't a good vice president; it was that I simply could not support President Ford. As it turned out, Ford never let Nelson into his inner circle. Nelson never got to be president, something that still makes me sad. I think he would've been a strong candidate and a terrific president.

My friend and one of my advisors, Mordecai Hacohen, arranged for me to meet Richard V. Allen, then Reagan's foreign policy advisor. In 1979, Dick was setting up an advisory committee for the run-up to the presidential campaign and appointed me to the committee. Dick had become a good friend and would play a key role in furthering my ambition to be included in a Reagan administration, hopefully as a diplomat.

Dick introduced me to William Middendorf. Bill had not originally supported Reagan, but eventually he came aboard. Bill had been an investment banker, ambassador to the Netherlands and the secretary of the Navy. Dick turned several key economic issues over to Bill, including the U.S. dollar. Bill, in turn, turned over a study of the dollar to me.

Under Carter, who was then president, the dollar was in free fall. This was due to

Curious bystanders as well as invited guests milled around the front entrance of my decorated house well before the arrival of Nancy Reagan. She was expected there to lead a fundraiser for her husband, Ronald Reagan, who two weeks later would be nominated for president by the Republican Party in Detroit.

Carter's policy of "benign neglect." After getting my hands on everything that had been written about the dollar in the previous few years, I came to the conclusion that our policy should be a strong dollar. I wrote a memo supporting this point of view. As I remember, I gave a copy to Bill Middendorf and to Dick Allen. This fit in with Reagan's ideas and supported his views. All through Reagan's campaign for the White House, I became the go-to person for the dollar. During the Reagan administration, the dollar would become robust, not reaching that peak again for thirty-five years.

One morning during the campaign I happened to be in Dick Allen's office. He'd just been speaking with Max Fisher, undoubtedly the leading and most prestigious Jewish Republican. Based in Detroit, he had been a brilliant success in many business areas. Fisher was a strong supporter of Israel and was continually in touch with Dick Allen to be sure Reagan was strongly in support of Israel and not the so-called "balanced" or "even-handed" position Carter was taking. Dick told me Reagan was strongly in support of Israel, but Dick was exhausted by so many Jewish leaders pressing him on the subject.

Offhand, Dick said something like, "Why aren't you one of these Jewish leaders?" He was implying, I believe, that I would not be as irritating or press him as hard as some of the Jewish leaders had been doing. I jokingly said to Dick, "Well, you can make me a Jewish leader." Dick replied, "How can I do that?" I said, "You can give me an important job in the administration once we've won." Dick asked, "What area were you thinking about?" I said, "I'd like to be in the diplomatic service." Jokingly,

My parents joined me outside the house to await the arrival of Nancy Reagan. George H.W. Bush's mother, who came unexpectedly to meet Nancy Reagan, stands just behind my mother, talking to Harry Parish, a Loeb, Rhoades partner and husband of famed decorator "Sister" Parish.

After helping Nancy Reagan from her limousine, I drew her attention to the banner proclaiming "New York Loves Nancy."

he replied, "You really want to go to work? You really want a job?" I said, "Yes!" "Well then," he said, "I have just the job for you in the diplomatic corps—ambassador to Upper Volta." I said, "I'll take it."

Frankly, I had no idea what he was talking about, whether it was Africa or Russia. Upper Volta is a West African country now called Burkina Faso, and the capital is Ouagadougou. From then on during the campaign, Dick would introduce me as our next ambassador to Upper Volta. This would always get a laugh or a chuckle, because most people had no idea what he was talking about.

This turned into our ongoing joke about how he would make sure I got to be the ambassador to Upper Volta. At that time, I wasn't even sure the country had an ambassador. I was pretty confident, despite all the joking, that Dick would support me strongly after Reagan won. In the meantime, we had to get our guy elected.

Of course, the moment the campaign ended, Dick became so important and so busy that he was generally impossible to reach. He did tell me, however, that I mustn't just ask for an ambassadorship in general, but I must ask for a specific country. I then asked Dick to be ambassador to Belgium. He informed me that position had already been taken. Finally,

Peeking from behind me is Mrs. Maxwell Rabb, one of my four hostesses. The lady who seems to be assessing Nancy's handsome white jacket is Mrs. Hilson. Behind Nancy's right shoulder is Mercedes Bass, and to her right in the forefront is Mercedes's first husband, Ambassador Francis Kellogg.

I remember, he asked whether I might be interested in Denmark. I said that would be a dream, and I would be thrilled to be ambassador to Denmark.

In the spring of 1980, with the upcoming presidential election only a few months away, I worked long and hard for Reagan, including an event I organized and hosted to both raise money and bring in the Jewish vote. On June 19, 1980, a little less than a month before the GOP national convention in Detroit, I was asked to hold an event for the Republican Party at my house in New York City in honor of Nancy Reagan. The excitement about candidate Reagan was running high, and the crowd was thrilled to meet the woman whom everyone thought would surely be our next First Lady. Without even being invited, Reagan's vice-presidential candidate George Bush's mother showed up to meet her. I had the pleasure of introducing them.

My mother was one of my four hostesses, a group that included Ruth Rabb, whose husband Maxwell Rabb launched Reagan's campaign in New York City. The other two hostesses were Mercedes Kellogg, the wife of Ambassador Francis Kellogg (who later became Mrs. Sid Bass), and Norma Dana, whose husband was heir to the Dana Corporation.

I found the Nancy Reagan party to be the most enjoyable part of the whole campaign. I went out whole hog, hiring Park Avenue decorators Renny & Reed, who festooned my five-story house with red and blue bunting. Huge white balloons were suspended from the windows, with smaller red and blue balloons hanging beneath. Red and blue flowering plants stood at the entrance, and a banner running across the front of the house read "Nancy Loves New York and New York Loves Nancy." Another banner read "Lehmans,

Nancy Reagan spoke engagingly about the kind of president her husband would be, and was roundly applauded by the three hundred guests.

Loebs Love Nancy." More than three hundred people came. Some waited outside for Nancy to arrive, and neighborhood bystanders were delighted when they recognized other celebrities: the actress Gloria Swanson, jazz musician Lionel Hampton, fashion icon C.Z. Guest and fashion designer Oscar de la Renta.

I told Mother to just be a hostess and avoid being the center of attention. But, of course, she couldn't help herself. When she felt people were not paying enough attention to her, she went upstairs and retrieved four-year-old Nicholas, dressed him up and brought him down to the party. Attention quickly veered from Nancy to the two of them, and—to my great annoyance—Mother and Nicholas occupied center stage for a short time.

Besides taking the spotlight away from Nancy, Mother also brought some unwanted attention onto both of them. Outside after the party, Mother, always one to share her opinions, had a flare-up with Nancy within earshot of the press on the street. Mother was strongly in the pro-choice camp, while Nancy was vigorously in the right-to-life camp. When Nancy left the party, police cars, well-wishers and press all pulled up. Mother worked her way into the crowd to say good-bye. "You know, Nancy," Mother said, "we love your husband. But you have to change his mind about this," and she brazenly pointed to Nancy's stomach.

Nancy was taken aback. "Well," she replied. "That's something we deeply believe in."

The ensuing argument was covered in the next day's press. The *New York Post* printed a photo of Mother wagging her finger close to the face of an implacable Nancy Reagan. *Women's Wear Daily* ran a story about Mother pointing at Nancy's stomach. One columnist reported that Mother was heard to pass through the crowd saying, "I'm not sure I'm for the Reagans. They're against pro-choice and the Equal Rights Amendment."

The press also reported that I was a Reagan supporter who had given a party for the candidate, but my mother, a niece of Herbert Lehman, did not support him. Father became very irritated with Mother and made her write an apology letter to the future First Lady. An exchange of mutual apologies was later reported, but no one knows exactly what was said or settled between those two strong-minded ladies. Every time I saw Nancy after this, she asked me, "How is your mother?" I doubt she ever forgot her.

Jimmy Carter had swept up the majority (75 percent) of the New York Jewish vote in the 1976 election. Four year later, Republicans were determined to win the state back for Reagan. Plans for a GOP event in my Purchase home were hatched sometime during the

Republican convention week in July of 1980, Detroit multi-millionaire and power broker Max Fisher, who was chairman of the Jewish Agency for Israel and known as "Mr. Jewish Republican," held a Jewish strategy meeting at his home. Max was the son of an immigrant Jewish peddler whose anti-Semitic experiences as a teenager mirrored mine. We hit it off immediately, and I was elated when he agreed to be the star at the Purchase event.

Easy as an old shoe, the very tall, understated Max proved a major draw at the October 23rd reception at Ridgeleigh. We had expected a turnout of about three hundred to meet him, but five hundred came. A rapt crowd stood outside the house to hear Fisher's speech on Israel relations:

> *If President Carter is re-elected, Israel will be under intense pressure. . . . Israel has only one ally, and that is the United States. . . . Arab countries have exerted such pressure that Israel is virtually isolated. . . . Reagan is a man of integrity who will stand up for his friends and will not abandon them.*

The audience clapped their hands red, and Fisher's extemporaneous remarks, which we recorded, were widely distributed soon after the event.

Even while I was working for Reagan's campaign, I still harbored a hope of running for national office myself. It appeared that the long-held U.S. Senate seat of the liberal Jacob Javits would be vulnerable in 1980. Many in the Republican Party thought Javits was too liberal. Also, he was physically fragile. "Jake" Javits had succeeded Great-Uncle Herbert Lehman in 1957 and had held the seat ever since. In 1979, he was taking his time to announce whether or not he would run for a fifth term in the Senate. Speculation was high among the pundits that he would not.

I focused on the idea of running for the Javits seat. At the outset, there were only two other men I knew who wanted to make the primary run: young Congressman Bruce Caputo from the Twenty-Third District, who would have to resign his House seat; and Alfonse D'Amato, the town supervisor of Hempstead, Long Island. I saw the results of a poll that showed an unknown Italian and an unknown Irishman both beating Javits in a Republican primary. I was within shouting distance of all three. If Javits were forced into a Republican primary, I might be able to win. I thought I had a good chance of beating both Caputo and D'Amato and set about what had to be done in advance of announcing my candidacy.

Mordecai Hacohen, a top officer at New York's Bank Leumi and originally from Austria, took me under his wing and served as my volunteer Jewish advisor. Morde-

Banker Mordecai Hacohen, a passionate supporter of Israel, became my enthusiastic mentor when he heard I might make a run for the Senate.

cai persuaded me that anyone running for the U.S. Senate had to pay a visit to Israel to meet with officials there. Wisdom once held that when you ran for office in New York State you had to go to the three I's: Israel, Ireland and Italy. Mordecai orchestrated a trip wherein I would meet "all the proper people." It was on the way to Israel that I stopped in Italy and met Pope John Paul II briefly, though not at a private audience.

In Israel, I met Prime Minister Menachem Begin for the second time in my life, having been introduced to him briefly while on summer break from Harvard in 1953. The Russian-born Begin was schooled in Poland, joined a World War II Polish army group and served in Palestine. Begin had been a passionate disciple of the fiery Russian-born visionary and writer Ze'ev Jabotinsky, considered to be the father of the Zionist movement.

When Jabotinsky died in 1940, Begin became the leader of the Zionist militants

Left to right are Pope John Paul II (declared a saint in 2014), Joseph DioGuardi (a GOP stalwart who became a congressman in 1985), a priest active in youth work; and me, a potential senatorial candidate.

known as Irgun Zvai Leumi, a pre-independence Israeli underground group founded by Jabotinsky. Irgun, an organization controversial even in Jewish circles for its terrorist tactics, targeted the British in Palestine. Nevertheless, Prime Minister Begin would go on to win the Nobel Peace Prize in 1978 for signing a peace treaty with Egypt's Anwar Sadat. I was quite impressed with Begin during my visit with him on that pre-campaign trip. We would meet again—much sooner than I expected.

Senator Javits did indeed take his time, but he surprised the pundits when he decided to run again for the Senate. After returning from Israel, I began to rethink my original plan to challenge him. There were encouraging hints coming from Reagan insiders that

Menachem Begin, Israel's sixth prime minister, seemed more than pleased when a crowd of 3,000 broke into spontaneous applause at the Jabotinksy dinner. In my introduction, I had just called him "Israel's George Washington." This photo of us together was taken on my visit to Israel in 1980.

there might be a diplomatic role for me in the new administration. Also feeding my reluctance was my parents' increasing hope that I would not run against Javits, who had been their friend for many years. I began to feel uncomfortable with what might have been a cold-hearted campaign against an elderly family friend. In the end, though frail, Javits ran, and I did not.

Javits ended up losing the primary to Al D'Amato, but, energized by the defeat, he ran in the fall election as an Independent endorsed by the Liberal Party. This move split the November vote of liberal Democrats, handing D'Amato a slim victory over the Democratic congresswoman Elizabeth Holtzman. Even though I might have won, I never regretted my decision not to challenge Javits. After all, I was optimistic about my chances for a diplomatic appointment. I had worked hard to get the Jewish vote for Reagan (he received 40 percent of the New York Jewish vote), and I received a flattering letter from the chairman of the Republican National Finance Committee informing me that I was their best fundraiser.

Election night was historic—both on a personal and a national level. Even today, I can relive the powerful emotions that welled up in me the night of November 4, 1980, when Ronald Reagan was elected the fortieth president of the United States in a landslide over

President Jimmy Carter. Having played even a small part in his victory still gives me a sense of satisfaction like few other things in my life.

Several weeks earlier, when the Reagan campaign was headed into its final sprint, I had been making a hard push for a national "Prelude to Victory" dinner to be held in cities all across the country. I also agreed to be dinner chairman for a major event observing the centennial of Jabotinsky's birthday at the Waldorf Astoria, to be held soon after the November election. Menachem Begin would be the keynote speaker, and I was to introduce him. When the news of my Jabotinsky dinner chairmanship was released, I caught holy hell from some key Jewish figures:[*]

"Are you *crazy*?

"Do you know who Jabotinksy is??

"Do you *really* know who Begin is??

"You don't know what you're doing."

"You'll be supporting terrorists!"

"You know, of course, that absolutely *no one* will come to the Jabotinsky dinner."

No one? Only about three thousand! The enthusiastic crowd, composed of nearly every major Jewish and Israel-related organization in the country, plus non-Jewish well-wishers, entertainers and politicians, spilled into three Waldorf ballrooms. The event was held a week after Reagan's landslide victory, so two of our new president's national supporters were invited to represent him on the dais alongside Menachem Begin: Reagan's campaign manager and soon-to-be CIA director, William Casey, and my dear friend Richard Allen, Reagan's soon-to-be national security advisor. My introduction of Begin as the "George Washington of Israel" was applauded and covered by the press. It was an electrifying evening.

On January 20, 1981, I was in Washington, D.C., taking part in all the wonderful inauguration celebrations: the swearing-in ceremony on the west front of the U.S. Capitol building, the luncheons, the receptions, the multiple balls and the untold number of private parties. Reagan gave a magnificent inaugural address, where he announced, "We have every right to dream heroic dreams. Those who say that we're in a time when there are no heroes, they just don't know where to look." At the luncheon for congressional leaders afterward, Reagan announced that the fifty-two American hostages in Iran had

---

[*] Historically, my parents had not been Zionists and had even been identified with the anti-Zionist Council for American Judaism. But they became great friends with Abba Eban (Israeli ambassador to the U.S. and to the UN) and Jerusalem mayor Teddy Kollek. While Mother was New York City Commissioner for the UN and the Consular Corps, she met Eban through his brother-in-law, Chaim Herzog, Israeli's ambassador to the UN.

finally been released after 444 days in captivity, and planes carrying the hostages had just left Iranian airspace. As *The New York Times* reported, "The news seemed to turn the inauguration celebration, normally a highly festive occasion, into an event of unbridled joy for Mr. Reagan and his supporters."[102] It was truly a day for the history books.

As the days turned into weeks, word was coming from people in a position to know that I was among those who would be offered an ambassadorship. I am not a nail-biter, but if I were, my nails would have been down to the quick.

Although one must never *appear* to be campaigning for these posts, I had been told you must do it—but covertly. I was advised to start subtly lining up supporters, particularly U.S. senators, who would write letters to the White House administration suggesting I be considered for an ambassadorship—anywhere but Upper Volta. Over a dozen friendly senators wrote enthusiastic letters to the president on my behalf.

Even though Watergate had proved to be a Waterloo for many Republican candidates six years earlier, the good opinion of President Nixon still had considerable clout. Richard Allen suggested that, with my parents' strong connection to Nixon and the fact that I'd met him several times myself, I should make a courtesy call on the former president, though I should not mention my diplomatic hopes.* When I phoned Nixon's office, a secretary called back to say, "President and Mrs. Nixon would like you to come to dinner at their New Jersey home in Park Ridge."

The Nixons were cordial and relaxed on the appointed night, as we sipped martinis the president had mixed himself. John Davis Lodge, a former actor, governor of Connecticut and ambassador to Spain, was also at the dinner. He was a tall, charming man, part of one of America's most famous families, with a lovely Italian wife, Francesca Braggiotti. He was hoping to become ambassador to Switzerland and was irritated that he hadn't yet been appointed.†

At the door as I left that night, President Nixon put his hand on my shoulder and said quietly, "John, I think you're going to make it."

---

* My parents had known Nixon for a long time, likely starting when he was a lawyer for 20th Century Fox and Father was the film company's board chairman. Many years later, my parents became significant financial supporters of Nixon's presidential campaigns.

† Lodge was appointed ambassador to Switzerland, but after a year he was recalled to make room for Faith Whittlesey, a former ambassador to Switzerland who had been working at the White House. Whittlesey had rubbed a lot of people the wrong way and was moved to Lodge's post, a move that upset Lodge a great deal. Shortly after Lodge's return, the Women's National Republican Club threw a large party in his honor. In the middle of a speech, thanking all of his friends, Lodge had a heart attack. He was pronounced dead an hour later.

Newly retired as California's governor, Ronald Reagan came to speak at my 1978 GOP fundraiser for New York gubernatorial candidate Perry Duryea. Arriving with Reagan was his secretary, Helene von Damm, pictured here between us. I should have paid more attention to her, because she would become my ambassadorial adversary when he was elected president in 1981.

Even so, I was right to be anxious. Everyone knew that few posts would go to noncareer diplomats, and of those few, even fewer were being chosen from New York, a region filled with Rockefeller liberals. I also knew that long-time Reagan aide and respected confidante Helene von Damm had been made the administration's patronage contact. Word was that Helene did not look favorably upon me as an appointee because she thought I hadn't contributed enough money to the campaign. I may not have given a great deal of money, but I had worked tirelessly and raised a considerable amount of money from others. People are always curious about how much in the way of contributions is needed to merit coveted appointments. I have always loved what a later political appointee to Denmark, Ambassador Edward Elson, had to say to a rude lady at a Copenhagen dinner party.

"Of course," she sniped, "you only got to be ambassador to Denmark because you paid for it."

"My only regret, Madame," he reportedly responded, "is that I didn't contribute $5 million more. Then I would be ambassador to England and not have to sit next to you."

I continued to keep the worry beads busy but took comfort from a number of news reports that trickled in over the next five months. In *The Washington Post* on February 18, 1981, Betty Beale mentioned in her column that John Loeb Jr. was "rumored to be headed to Brussels." The same column mentioned that my friend Lee (Leonore) Annenberg would be the thirty-third chief of protocol, the first to have a private plane at her disposal.

On March 19, the Danish paper *Berlingske Tidende* ran a long article, including my photo, saying I was a "possible candidate" for ambassador to Denmark, but Danish diplomats said they didn't expect any appointment in the near future. The article went on, "The U.S. Ministry of Foreign Affairs claimed this was the first they'd heard about Loeb's appointment" and that "the White House had no comment."

My parents received a letter containing a copy of the story from a Danish friend, Mrs. Harald Hallberg (whose nickname was "Pook"), whose husband was a Swedish diplomat. She had attended a political event the same night the *Berlingske Tidende* article came out and was besieged with queries about my marital status. Pook commented that if the story about my post was true, I would find being the Danish ambassador a tough job. "Many of the younger generation here are very anti-American," she wrote. "It will be hard work in the office, and even more so socially."

But all of this had to be on hold. Sixty-nine days into his presidency, the unthinkable happened. On March 30, 1981, an attempt was made on the life of President Reagan when he was shot by an unhinged young man named John Hinckley Jr. Reagan recovered, even joking with aides soon after the incident, but the country was rightly worried. Within a few weeks, the horror of the shooting had begun to recede, and work at the White House seemed to be back to normal. Only a few insiders knew how close the president had come to dying, especially since he made light of his recovery and was soon back at nearly full steam.

I took heart in April when the National Committee on American Foreign Policy, Inc. wrote in its newsletter, "It is reliably reported that Mr. John Loeb Jr. will be invited to become the next United States ambassador to Denmark." Soon after, a thoughtful friend, Marne Obernauer, sent me a clipping from the *Jewish Chronicle of Pittsburgh*:

> *There had been complaints from America's Jewry of the absence of Jews from high posts in the Reagan administration, but apparently the voices were heard because the signs are beginning to look more promising. . . . The President has sent to Capitol Hill for approval of the names of Theodore Cummings of California to be Ambassador to Austria, and John Loeb, Jr. of New York to be our envoy to Denmark. Both have been bastions of Jewish philanthropy in their respective communities as well as longtime supporters of the President.*

In June, Eugenia Sheppard announced confidently in a *New York Post* column, "Around the Town," that "John Loeb Jr. has been appointed Ambassador to Denmark. John, twice married but now a bachelor," she continued, "has a wide circle of acquain-

Richard Allen and I have remained extremely close friends ever since our days of campaigning for Ronald Reagan— well over thirty-five years ago. We are pictured here in May 2014 at a George Washington Institute for Religious Freedom seminar held in Harvard's Tsai Auditorium.

tances and a Wall Street background that should make him a success in the post." The press was encouraging, but I still hadn't heard one word from President Reagan himself. Desperately in need of distraction, I took a spur-of-the-moment trip to Paris, where I stayed at the luxurious Hotel Bristol. I was quickly running up a sizable tab when a call came from Father. "Johnny, you've just received a letter from the State Department addressed to 'Ambassador Loeb.' Should I open it and read it to you?"

I shouted loudly to be sure I was heard across the great ocean: "OF COURSE!"

I must admit that it was doubly gratifying having my father be the one to bring me the news. The presence of "Ambassador Loeb" was required in Washington for briefings on his new post. Never have bags been packed so quickly. Coattails flapping, I dashed from the Bristol, hailed a taxi and raced to the airport. Just as I was about to put my foot onto the Concorde, two gendarmes grabbed my arms, none too gently, and marched me back to the terminal. I was dumbfounded. It turned out that in my rush I'd neglected to pay my hefty hotel bill. I was terrified that this mistake would show up as a big black blot on my record, large enough to kill the ambassadorial appointment. It took almost a day of filling out forms to settle the whole matter, but I made it back home the next day in time for the briefings. I never heard one more word about the brouhaha.

The State Department letter contained details of a two-day seminar for thirteen soon-to-be ambassadors to be held in one of the Federal Reserve buildings. There would be classified briefings and an opportunity to learn various aspects of our responsibilities and challenges in an informal atmosphere. When I walked into the appointed room, I found my seat with a card that said simply, "Ambassador Loeb." I sank into my chair and almost wept.

I was happy to see that one of my fellow ambassadors-to-be was my long-time friend Maxwell Rabb, who had been a major figure in Reagan's run from the get-go. Rabb was a delegate at the Republican convention, and he was in charge of all the events for Reagan's campaign in his kick-off state of New York. I was also delighted to find that Shirley Temple Black—who had exchanged Hollywood stardom for a leading role in the Republican Party in the late 1960s—would be one of the instructors. Over the years, she had earned several plum political assignments, including a Nixon appointment to represent the United States at the twenty-fourth UN General Assembly and as ambassador to Ghana under President Ford. In her role as the first woman chief of protocol in 1976, she had written a small booklet called "How to Be an Ambassador," which I would now be studying. I couldn't help but remember our day by the pool as children when she had handcuffed one of my cousins. Now she was teaching ambassadors around the world how to greet heads of state. I marveled at the dissonance and the way time had swept us all away.

The future ambassadors were briefed by both political appointees and career diplomats on a broad range of subjects, from international protocol to where we should turn if a critical situation arose. The one briefing that worried me was on security. I was told that my host country would officially be responsible for my safety, although in reality the United States would be involved to some extent. The whole briefing felt too cursory to me. I was distressed to hear that America would supply me with only a bulletproof raincoat and a car. I was particularly interested in the car.

"I assume the car is armored," I said.

"Yes, Ambassador," an advisor responded. "Well—half-armored."

"Yes, well, *which* half?

"The bottom half, Ambassador."

That did not sit well at all. I had a sudden vision of myself in formal attire (top hat and all) stretched out on the floor of the car on the way to present my credentials to the queen of Denmark.*

---

* I was disappointed to learn that the charming custom I'd read about—how new ambassadors were traditionally transported to the palace to present their credentials to the queen in her own eight-horse coach, had by now vanished into history.

I continued to press the advisor about security, particularly since he'd made a point that ambassadors are more vulnerable to terrorists than generals are.

"Shouldn't we all be supplied with a *fully* armored car?" I inquired.

"Ambassador, we'd like to give everyone that kind of protection, but it's simply not in our budget."

"Given the current terrorist threats and bomb scares," I said, "shouldn't I have full protection? If need be, I will rent one at my own expense."

They didn't outright reject my idea, but their tone was unmistakable: *We'd rather you didn't.*

I let it drop at that point, not wanting to rock the boat too much and so early. But it was far from a dead issue in my own mind. I did, indeed, rent a fully armored car shortly after arriving in Denmark, something with which the State Department did not seem happy. As I had correctly sensed, security would be an ongoing problem in my new role.

But, I had not yet received a call from the president inviting me to serve. As we neared the end of our briefings, I pointed this out to Ambassador Kennedy, who was the administrator in charge. He grinned. "Well, then what are you doing here?" he kidded. He then asked me, "Where will you be for the rest of the day?"

"Well, where do you want me to be? I'll be at my hotel by 4 p.m."

I stayed awake at my hotel all night. By 3 a.m., I still had not received a call.

The next day, July 6, I returned to the State Department. I asked Ambassador Kennedy's secretary, "Do you remember if Ambassador Kennedy sent my name over to the White House for President Reagan's call?"

She sent me to a gentleman down the hall. I asked him the same question. The man looked embarrassed and asked where I would be over the next few hours. I was being briefed again at the State Department by a number of career diplomats who specialized in the Middle East. During our briefing, the secretary came in and said, "The president is on the line for Ambassador Loeb." Everyone rose and left the room. I picked up the telephone with great relief and excitement.

"John, I apologize for not being in touch with you sooner," President Reagan said, "but I was hoping you wouldn't mind spending a few years representing the United States in Copenhagen."

"Mr. President, I would be honored and delighted to represent you and the United States in Denmark."

The appointment was officially announced in the media four days later, and I immediately wrote my friend and greatest supporter, Richard Allen. "This would not have happened without you," I wrote, "and I only wish there was some adequate way to express my thanks and gratitude. I just wanted you to know that you are forever in my heart and mind. . . . I am on cloud nine, ten, eleven and twelve—up to the stratosphere."

And that's exactly where I was—for a short time. But the floating had to be brief. I had been knee-deep in homework about Denmark for weeks leading up to that call. Now it was time for total immersion.

Lee Annenberg, chief of protocol, looked on as I signed the official documents that said I was now the U.S. ambassador to Denmark.

≡

CHAPTER THIRTEEN

Denmark! Part I: Mr. Ambassador, 1981–1982

No doctoral candidate ever crammed more intensely than I did for the "advise and consent" hearing of the Senate Foreign Relations Committee. I focused on the governmental structure of Denmark's constitutional monarchy, and even more on Denmark's cautious relationship with NATO (the North Atlantic Treaty Organization). I would be arriving in Copenhagen when the Cold War with the Soviet Union was in full force. This was a constant source of fear on both sides of the ocean, a threat that was very real to any American living through it. The USSR posed a frightening nuclear threat. Softening the negative Danish attitude toward NATO's war-preventive measures would be my most important assignment as ambassador.

The Danish, however, were not convinced of the threat. In 1977, when the USSR aimed intermediate-range nuclear missiles at the leading capitals of Europe, including Copenhagen, the Danish media all but ignored the crisis. NATO's primary purpose was to keep peace in Europe and deter the use of nuclear weapons. Even though NATO clearly served the Danish national interest, translating American and NATO policy to the Danes would be more than a challenging task. Denmark had an ambivalent relationship with NATO, an alliance of countries in Europe and North America formed in April 1949. All members were committed to assist any member country attacked, with armed forces if necessary.

Denmark was one of the first of twelve countries to join, although it did so with stipulations and caveats because the Danes wanted to maintain their position of strict neutrality. That seemed more important to them than their safety. A foreign military presence in their kingdom was anathema to the Danes, and they reacted with suspicion to all NATO and U.S. interventions in their defense.

Denmark was firmly opposed to NATO's plan to counterbalance the Soviet arms buildup of nuclear missiles aimed at major Western European cities.* They insisted that no nuclear weapons be placed on their soil and that allied troops not be stationed there during peacetime. The Danes also wanted assurance that none of the money they contributed to NATO would be used to place nuclear weapons in other NATO countries. It was baffling to me that they took this stance even though Russian missiles were aimed at Denmark.

NATO's "two-track" policy was intended to keep the world from catastrophic nuclear war. (It was also known as "MAD," an apt acronym for "Mutually Assured Destruction.") The first "track" was to match strength with strength, missile for missile. The only way to deter the Soviets from using their missiles was by affirming that they would be destroyed in equal measure if they dared to use them. The second track, more appealing to the Danes, was for NATO to negotiate the gradual removal of nuclear weapons equally on both sides.†

When I arrived in Copenhagen, NATO and the USSR were engaged in a game of chicken with the highest stakes imaginable. The Reagan Doctrine, as it became known, was focused on "peace through strength": NATO should have weapons equal in power to those of the USSR, so that it was in a position to retaliate if any NATO country was attacked. Persuading the Danish public to accept that position would draw on every last arrow in my diplomatic quiver.

The Danes also had personal complaints about our new president. Another one of my ambassadorial tasks would be to neutralize the anti-Reagan bias in Denmark. I needed to "sell" Reagan and his policies to a skeptical public and press. The Danish media framed him as a warmonger who was more dangerous than the Russians. They also thought of Reagan as a B-grade Hollywood actor playing a role he couldn't possibly handle.‡ The Danes were also agitated by his support of the military-led junta against the FMLN (a coalition of left-wing groups) in El Salvador's civil war. American support

---

* Soviet short-range missiles couldn't cross the Atlantic, but they could easily reach such major cities as Paris, London and Copenhagen.

† There was also a small but serious "peacenik" movement in Denmark. A joke in the cocktail rounds in Copenhagen was that their idea of a foreign policy was that if attacked, they would march en masse to the nearest pay phone to surrender.

‡ President Reagan frequently responded to this particular criticism with some version of the quip, "You can't be a good president without being a good actor."

In May 1980, well before knowing for sure that I would become an ambassador, I received an honorary Doctor of Laws degree from Georgetown University. Pictured here is Father Timothy S. Healy, the 46th president of the much respected Catholic school, presenting the degree. It is an honor I cherish.

for the El Salvador government began during the Carter administration, and President Reagan continued it. The Danes, however, favored the insurgents and even supplied them with an office in Copenhagen. They also disapproved of Reagan's handling of the Nicaraguan conflict going on at the same time. Reagan wanted to support the Contras' effort to oust the Nicaraguan government, the Cuban-backed, left-wing Sandinistas. Reagan's position in both instances was that any anti-Communist government would serve U.S. interests better than any Communist regime. That stated intent was part of the "Reagan Doctrine."* I had to be well prepared to discuss all of these controversial issues at the hearing with the Senate Committee on Foreign Relations. I believed I was ready, but as the fateful day drew close, I had more than a few butterflies.

My appearance before the Senate committee was held in the Dirksen Senate Office Building on July 21, 1981, with Indiana senator Richard Lugar presiding. I joined two others also up for ambassadorial approval during the afternoon session: William J. Dyess of Alabama, who would be the U.S. ambassador to the Netherlands, and Keith F. Nyborg of Idaho, headed to Finland. Speaking on my behalf were two New York senators, the inimitable Daniel Patrick Moynihan and the newly elected Alfonse D'Amato, as well as a New York congressman (and my Harvard schoolmate), Hamilton Fish IV.

---

* It was the support for the Contras that precipitated the infamous "Iran-Contra" scandal that would flare up in 1986.

MY SECOND AMBASSADORIAL SWEARING IN, SEPTEMBER 14, 1981

William P. Clark Jr., then U.S. deputy secretary of state, swore me in officially. Here, looking on in the background, are my father and daughter, as well as the chief of protocol, Lee Annenberg.

I'm sure Lee Annenberg must have been chuckling to herself as she congratulated me as the new ambassador, knowing that I was already an ambassador because she had sworn me in several weeks earlier!

Pictured here, left to right, sharing my happy day are my mother, father, daughter Alexandra, and dear friend Patricia Walton Shelby, a former national president of the DAR.

Though It was serious business, the hearing was not without a bit of humor. Referring to my honorary degree from Georgetown University, Senator Moynihan said, "He received one of the most cheerful encomiums that gloomy Jesuit institution ever bestowed upon a nongraduate." Congressman Fish also drew a laugh when he said, "If confirmed as ambassador, John Loeb will blend into the landscape, as he is six-feet-four inches tall and about the size of most great Danes."

Senator Charles Percy of Illinois, chair of the Foreign Relations Committee, mentioned that former senator Jacob Javits had approved of my appointment. Senator Larry Pressler of South Dakota, chair of both the European Subcommittee and the Arms Control Subcommittee, questioned me on Denmark's rocky NATO membership. Following Senator Pressler, Senator Lugar invited each of the appointees to provide insights regarding what our host countries thought about the United States. I took this opportunity to bring up some remarks of Denmark's outspoken Socialist prime minister. Anker Jørgensen had made disparaging comments about the new Republican president and his administration, calling Reagan's election "a death knell for liberals in America." He had also been extremely critical of U.S. policy in El Salvador.

The hearing took only about two hours. Senator Lugar closed with gratifying words to ours ears: "I am certain that we will be acting favorably on your nominations at our next business meeting." In just a few weeks, I would be America's newest ambassador to the Kingdom of Denmark. There was a lot of hard work ahead, but it was the kind of work I loved.

I admit to being one who errs on the side of caution, and it's true that I am a prudent soul who might well wear a belt and suspenders at the same time. The almost fatal attempt on President Reagan's life had unnerved the country. I was concerned that if anything more should threaten his presidency before I was sworn in, I might wind up having the shortest ambassadorship on record.

I certainly didn't want the lifetime title of "Ambassador" to slip through my fingers. The truth is that I had genuine reason for concern. For one thing, I was well aware that some advisors in the administration—specifically Helene von Damm and Mike Deaver—were not thrilled with my appointment.* Also, if the new vice president, George H.W. Bush, were to become president, I was afraid that some of my detractors

---

* Helene von Damm, who had been President Reagan's assistant, rose in the ranks when Reagan won the election. She was charged with seeing that Reagan's supporters got government posts if they wanted them and was outspoken in her disapproval of my appointment. Mike Deaver also felt I hadn't contributed enough money to the campaign to be appointed. I wrote to both of them, but neither would meet with me.

might have his ear, and my name would be withdrawn.

In the name of caution, and perhaps a touch of paranoia, I asked my friend Lee (Leonore) Annenberg, the newly appointed U.S. chief of protocol, if she would swear me in prior to the scheduled official event. With the help of my good friend Tim Towell, then deputy protocol chief, she agreed, and in a small ceremony several weeks earlier than my official swearing-in, I took the oath.

Deputy Secretary of State William P. Clark Jr. performed the second ceremony on September 14, 1981, in the beautiful Benjamin Franklin Room of the State Department. It was followed by a large reception with about three hundred well-wishers attending, including family, good friends and political allies. It was a joyous and proud day, and because of my excessive caution, I was able to fully enjoy it.

Shortly after my swearing-in, President Reagan invited my parents, my son, Nicholas, and me to visit him in the Oval Office. Offering me his warmest congratulations, he then gave Nicholas a large glass jar full of his trademark jellybeans, which Nicholas offered us all while we chatted. (My son still has the historic jar bearing the seal of the United States.) President Reagan told the famous story of how the Danish king had worn a yellow star to show his personal support of the Jews during the Nazi occupation of Denmark during World War II. I mentioned the story to Queen Margrethe the day I presented my credentials and learned from her that the lovely tale is actually a myth.

A portrait of George Washington looked down on us as Mother, Father, Nicholas and I posed with President Reagan in the Oval Office.

Secretary of Defense Caspar Weinberger was happy to discuss the work I would be doing in Denmark on behalf of NATO, but unwilling to share my Grandmother Lehman's painting of Benjamin Franklin.

Here I am with Portuguese Ambassador and Mrs. Vasco Futscher Pereira, who hosted one of the parties held for me just prior to leaving for Denmark in late September 1981. It was the lead "item" that week in Betty Beale's syndicated column.

Before leaving for Denmark, I asked for an appointment with Secretary of Defense Caspar Weinberger to discuss the work I would do regarding NATO—but I also had a personal favor to ask. In 1961, my grandmother Adele Lehman gave her famous oil-on-canvas portrait of Benjamin Franklin, painted by Jean-Baptiste Greuze, to the White House.[*]

It was transferred in 1971 to the National Gallery in Washington, D.C., where Weinberger saw it and arranged to have it hung in his office. I thought he might be willing to release it to me for my Denmark office. Alas, he refused—he liked it too much to part with it.

I couldn't take up my new post until early October, and so planned to leave for Copenhagen in late September. My arrival in Denmark had been delayed for two reasons. First, the assassination attempt on President Reagan's life in March delayed some of his ambassadorial appointments. Second, the queen had requested that I not arrive in Denmark until early October, when she would be home from her annual vacation and could receive my credentials. Ambassadors are not allowed to officially take up their roles until their credentials are properly presented to the head of state.

---

[*] While the portrait is often attributed to Jean-Baptiste Greuze, the National Gallery attributes it to an anonymous artist "after Jean-Baptiste Greuze." See http://www.nga.gov/content/ngaweb/Collection/art-object-page.53104.html.

PRESENTING CREDENTIALS, OCTOBER 13, 1981

Arthur Hughes, my DCM (deputy chief of mission) came to my office to wish me well for my visit to the queen.

Ambassador Albert W. Kønigsfeldt, Denmark's chief of protocol, came to Rydhave to escort me to Amalienborg Palace, where Her Majesty, Queen Margrethe II, would receive my credentials. I suppose Nicholas saluted to show respect for the importance of the occasion.

Hurray! I was now officially (and warmly) recognized as the U.S. ambassador. The queen had been more than gracious, and we established a wonderful rapport. We met privately, so I bowed—ever so slightly. My bow, according to David d'Ambrumenil, was what kept Denmark in NATO.

Mindful of the power of first impressions and wanting Denmark to know that I was a family man, I'd strategized our arrival very carefully. Six-year-old Nicholas and Renee Doolan, his beloved governess, were visiting Renee's family in Ireland at the time and would fly from there to London to meet me. My twenty-year-old daughter Alexandra would fly in from Paris, where she was taking a one-year break from her Harvard studies. We would all meet at the Savoy Hotel, spend two days in London and then all fly together to Denmark.

Vice President George Bush, whom I'd known for a long while, offered warm support and good advice when I visited him in his office before leaving for Denmark.

An old family friend, David d'Ambrumenil, who happened to be in the seat across from me on the Concorde, joined us for dinner one night during our London stay. In the news at the time was the deep curtsy that Lee Annenberg had given in greeting Prince Charles, which had caused a storm of controversy among Americans. In the discussion at the table that night, the question came up if I should bow to the Danish queen when we met. I felt strongly that I should not. David—half-joking—insisted that my bowing was absolutely essential to maintaining Denmark's membership in NATO. I laughed, but the issue was something I weighed. I decided on a compromise. If the queen and I met in public, I would not bow; if we met in private, I would.

My family landed at Kastrup, Copenhagen's airport, on October 2. Bearing a fat briefcase, an umbrella and a newspaper, I was greeted by a battery of photographers, reporters, Danish officials and the American embassy staff. Among them were Ambassador Albert W. Kønigsfeldt from the Danish Foreign Ministry; Matthew Lorimer, the chargé d'affaires; and Wes Stewart, the embassy staff member who dealt with the press and public relations. There was much hand shaking, warm expressions of welcome and repeated bursts of flash bulbs.

Alexandra, Nicholas and Renee joined us after disembarking, and the whole group trooped off for a press conference. Ambassador Kønigsfeldt and Matt Lorimer said diplomatic things about how happy they were that I'd arrived, and I said diplomatic things about how happy I was to be there. When pressed, I ducked questions about political issues and official positions. It was far too early to rock any boats in my new guest coun-

This is just one of many pictures of Alexandra, Nicholas and me taken by the Danish press just after our arrival in Denmark.

Alexandra and Nicholas came with me for a short press conference after we arrived in Copenhagen.

try. I let the reporters know that they would have to wait until I had my official meeting with the queen. We then zoomed off in a black limousine to our new home.

The Danes are known to be broad-minded, but this doesn't mean they don't love gossip.* The first chatter on the gossip circuit about our arrival reached my ears quickly, relayed by the longtime U.S. embassy's chief of protocol, Jørgen Werner. Werner reported that there was a rumor that the new bachelor ambassador had brought his beautiful mistress with him! Alexandra had tried to downplay her good looks, arriving with her long hair pulled into a Marian-the-librarian nonstyle, perfect with her simple dress and low-heeled pumps. These attempts to appear understated made her look older than her twenty years, but she couldn't overcome her innate chic. My attempt to let Denmark know I was a family man had backfired.

America's home for its Danish ambassador, which is located in a Copenhagen suburb, is on an estate called Rydhave. Only a cemetery separated the embassies of the United States and the Soviet Union—a perfect metaphor for the tensions of the time. During the Nazi occupation of Denmark during World War II, Rydhave had housed

---

* Hans Christian Andersen, Denmark's master storyteller, knew this well. He makes the point about the dangers of rumor in his story "There Is No Doubt About It," about a group of silly chickens spreading gossip that results in problems for the entire flock "when one little feather easily [grows] into five hens."

Dr. Werner Best, the Nazi supervisor of civilian affairs, his staff and his armed guards. It became the U.S. ambassador's residence in 1945, soon after the exodus of Best, who had constructed a new wing and a basement bomb shelter.

Rydhave sits high on a hill in the neighborhood of Skovshoved, a few miles north of Copenhagen. It overlooks the Øresund Strait, the waterway that separates Denmark and Sweden. As we drove slowly onto the almost four-acre estate, I was stunned by the beauty of the mansion, its magnificent gardens and welcoming pool. The formerly red bricks of the residence had been painted a picturesque white. Rydhave reminded me of homes you might find in a well-to-do suburb in Westchester County—like one I had grown up in—so I felt at home immediately.

Almost as soon as we walked in the door, the four of us fanned out to explore the forty-room mansion like excited kids. Our voices echoed across the large, elegant reception rooms as we called out to one another about each new discovery. The house was tastefully, though sparsely, furnished; the previous ambassador owned much of Rydhave's furniture and had taken it with him when he left.

Each new ambassador is allowed to make alterations to the home—a boon for new ambassadors but expensive for American taxpayers. One of the previous ambassadors, Guilford Dudley Jr., was an avid horseman and had decorated the grounds in his style, which was at odds with mine. He had not

Ready for a party at Rydhave.

No one really knows when or why the forty-room mansion that houses U.S. ambassadors was named "Rydhave." Translated literally, it means "Clear the lot," so one theory is that long ago its surrounding acreage was overrun with vegetation!

RYDHAVE INTERIOR

Alexandra, Nicholas and I sat in the library for a photographer from *Architectural Digest* sometime in 1983.

The high ceilings of Rydhave accommodated the very large American paintings I wanted to hang.

The formal dining room, just off the front hallway, seats fourteen guests comfortably.

A long carpeted hallway at the front of the mansion leads on the right into the dining room, and on the left to the private family rooms.

I brought one of my Roy Lichtenstein paintings from home for Rydhave's master bedroom.

only added the swimming pool, but also altered the look of the Germans' dreary fortified cellar. Guilford turned the Nazi's air raid shelter into a nightclub decorated as a horse barn with private, stall-like cubicles. I would eventually learn from my protocol officer that the Copenhagen rumor was that I had installed the horse-themed nightclub for my wild parties. We never had a single party in that basement. In fact, I turned it into a gallery for contemporary Danish art.

I conferred regularly with these well-decorated members of the military, whom I dubbed "my colonels." The Danes did not believe that Russia might invade Denmark at any time, but the "colonels" and I knew it was a grave possibility.

In redecorating the main house with help from an American decorator, Anika Gaal, I installed only American art.* Later, I would invite an assortment of groups to visit once a week. Rydhave turned into a popular mini-gallery where visitors received a small catalogue about the work of established American painters. Several pieces came from my own collection, such as a Roy Lichtenstein and one by James Rosenquist, a lesser-known painter from North Dakota. My goal was to create a culturally rich atmosphere that encouraged discussion and appreciation of American art. I also had a vision for giving American artists the opportunity to display their works abroad. Somewhere between four thousand and five thousand guests visited the Rydhave "gallery" during the time I lived there. Guests came from all over, including art associations, high schools and commercial enterprises such as Scandinavian Airlines and IBM.

In ambassador "school," we learned repeatedly about the necessity for an ambassador to never travel along the same route; in fact, they warned us to never do anything on a regulated schedule. This wasn't a problem for me, since my life usually followed a varied schedule. Six months into my appointment, I got a thick package of classified documents to give to my driver on precautions, routes and security information. But since my driver was a Dane, I was not legally allowed to give it to him! (Of course, I ignored this backward rule.) A significant percentage of the embassy—more than half—was run by the Danes. And only about 40 percent of the

---

* Word spread about the new décor of Rydhave, and in 1983 a team from *Architectural Digest* arrived to take photographs.

339

I'm pictured here with Peter Dyvig (left), Denmark's ambassador to the U.S. from 1989 to 1995, and Maxwell Rabb (right), America's ambassador to Italy from 1981 to 1989. Both ambassadors played important roles in my life.

Ambassador Dyvig had become a friend while I was ambassador to Denmark, and at my request, was invited to be the main speaker at the opening of Harvard's Busch-Reisinger 1994 exhibit of my Danish art. Some years earlier, he had asked me to represent Denmark at the Smithsonian Institution, where I discussed Danish art.

Ambassador Rabb played many roles in the Republican Party all of his professional life, and he was a political mentor to me for many years. We worked together closely on President Reagan's campaigns and both became ambassadors in 1981.

Americans at the embassy were even connected to the State Department; the rest were from Commerce, Agriculture, the Drug Enforcement Administration and the military. There was a whole team of military personnel around the embassy that I jokingly called my "colonels."

I inherited a splendid staff, both at the embassy and at Rydhave. There were about 150 staff members at the embassy, and Rydhave's staff numbered about 10, including a groundskeeper. Though the State Department highlighted the "high morale of the embassy staff" at Rydhave, there was the occasional clash, frequently with my protocol officer, Jørgen Werner, about Rydhave guest lists. Jørgen was the extremely efficient and long-entrenched chief of social protocol. I was so in awe of this seemingly permanent embassy fixture that I couldn't summon the courage to fire him. Jørgen found my American ways too egalitarian. He operated from the Orwellian standpoint that while all people may be equal, "some are more equal than others." He believed only those who were "more equal" merited a place on any guest list; more than once, I had to pull rank about who was to be invited. During my briefing at State, I'd been told that I not only could, but probably *should,* replace senior staff members with my own people. I belatedly realized this was sound advice. Jørgen Werner had given me the strong impression that he came with the territory; in any case, he was extremely knowledgeable, efficient and intimidating, so I kept him on.

Arthur Hughes, the embassy deputy chief of mission (DCM), was one of the State Department's best. He had been holding the fort alone at the embassy, running things by himself for more than half a year before my arrival. Before leaving for Denmark, I phoned both him and Mary Rossignoli, who would become my personal secretary. Because everything about the embassy and Foreign Service was new to me, it seemed wise to keep these two knowledgeable professionals on board to keep things running smoothly. Though I didn't intend to be a hands-on administrator of office minutiae, I had to be involved in all policy decisions, implementing any positions and directives sent from the State Department. I would also be responsible for communicating with all levels of the Danish government, the Danish community at large and the country's sometimes very difficult media.

But Arthur Hughes was accustomed to being totally in charge of running the embassy, and he assumed that things would continue in much the same way. The new ambassador was a political appointee, good for parties and glad-handing, but Arthur assumed he'd be in charge of all the administrative work. I agreed to an extent, seeing myself as the "outside man" to his "inside man." However, even with the division of labor, there were a few turf wars, and feathers were ruffled on both sides. For instance, an enormous number of cablegrams and other communications poured in daily to the embassy; it was impossible to read them all. While happy for Arthur to do the screening, I began to suspect there were important messages that never crossed my desk. Once I mentioned this to him, the floodgates opened, and I began to see many more Washington cables. We also clashed on the subject of security, which was a legitimate concern on my part—and seemingly a low priority for everyone else.

Arthur and I put up with each other for quite a while, until he surprised me one day, asking to leave. I wrote him a glowing recommendation letter, and he thought winning a top position in the Foreign Service should be easy. But it wasn't; there were too many qualified people vying for the few available posts. Even before I'd had time to replace him, he asked to return.

"Arthur," I said, "I'll take you back on two conditions: One, you must keep me completely updated on all the 'inside' cable correspondence, with nothing held back from me. Second, you must promise never to leave again." He promised, though he did end up leaving again, becoming Paul Bremer's DCM when Bremer was appointed ambassador to the Netherlands.* I chose my next DCM myself, a State Department professional named Theodore Russell, who worked with me beautifully.†

During the State Department briefings for new ambassadors, two full days were spent on terrorism and security measures. We were warned that we would be under threat as long as we served. It was made crystal clear that our safety lay in the goodwill and protection of the countries where we served—only their vigilance would keep us safe. I held frequent security meetings with staffs at Rydhave, convinced that my fears were warranted.

In the fall of 1981, soon after arriving at Rydhave, I'd received alarmed phone calls from American friends. Libya's despotic ruler, Muammar al-Qaddafi, had been making death threats against three recently named American ambassadors, all of whom were Jewish—me, Theodore Cummings in Vienna and Maxwell Rabb in Italy. Somewhat alarmed, I advised the Danish security officers about the threat. To call their response lax would not do justice to how casual everyone seemed to be about my security.‡

"Ambassador, don't worry. Your room in Rydhave is like a safe house," one of them assured me. "Your bedroom door is reinforced with steel. If anything happens, just go into your room, lock the door, pick up the red phone and call for the police."

But I couldn't shake my uneasiness. One day I decided to test the red phone myself. After about five minutes someone picked up the line and said "Hej" (hello in Danish), which sounded to my ears like, "Hey you!"

"Is this the police?" I asked.

"Yes," he said in excellent English. "You have reached the police. How can I help you?"

I explained that I was Ambassador Loeb from the United States and was just testing my emergency phone.

---

* Arthur went on to become ambassador to Yemen. Bremer is best known for his appointment by President George W. Bush as the first administrator of the Coalition Provisional Authority in Iraq following the 2003 U.S. invasion. Unfortunately, his decisions and leadership were heavily criticized, especially his choice to disband the Iraqi army.

† Ted ultimately went on to become the first ambassador to Slovakia. An expert in international security affairs, he capped his career with the title of Minister Counselor.

‡ Just after the threat, Max was summoned from Italy to go immediately to Washington. When he arrived, he learned the Italians had uncovered a plot to assassinate him. The Italians found and arrested six Libyans in a hotel near the embassy in Rome, but they were extradited to Libya and never prosecuted. (Italy had financial and political ties to that country.) Not one word about the plot appeared in either the Italian or American press.

"Oh," he said, "you won't have any kind of trouble here. Nothing ever happens in Copenhagen."

This breezy assurance did little to ease my mind. "Now, let's just see what happens when I push the panic button you've installed." I'd been told both the Danish police and military personnel would come within fifteen minutes of a call for help. Instead, a good half hour passed before the police showed up.

On the phone, I pushed on to another concern. "I've been told my bedroom door is reinforced with steel but wonder if the bedroom doors of my son and his governess could be reinforced the same way. Can you arrange that?"

"Oh yes, yes," he said. "Someone will see to it right away."

When the men came to do the reinforcing, I hovered close. "I'd like you to do a test," I said. "Let's just see what happens if you shoot at the door."

They looked at each other, surprised, then back at me. I assured them I would pay for the damage and replacement. Reluctantly, they took out their guns and fired. And their bullets went right through the door! The door had *not* been fitted with steel, as I was assured, but with reinforced wood.

There was also supposed to be a guard from a private security firm patrolling the residence twenty-four hours a day. Because I'd never seen one, I called the security service. "I never see any of your guards," I remarked. "Are they really here twenty-four hours a day? Is there any way of checking?"

"Oh yes, we keep tapes from when they sign in," they told me.

Once the tapes were reviewed, they confirmed that half the time no guard ever showed up at all, an issue that I eventually got settled.

I went to the Danish government security office and told an official there that I wasn't getting proper protection. The official gave an exaggerated sigh, like *I* was the problem, not my wood-enforced door and the absent guards.

"Ambassador," he said, "if we give you any more protection than you have, then we have to give it to the British embassy, which is threatened by the Irish terrorists. Then we'd have to protect the Turkish embassy being threatened by the Armenians, and then the Israelis being threatened by the Palestinians, all wanting more protection. It's simply not in our budget."*

"Yes," I countered, "but I am the American ambassador, and my country is responsible for Denmark's security. Shouldn't that justify special consideration?" Eventually,

---

* While I was in Denmark, the deputy ambassador of Turkey to Denmark was attacked and nearly killed by an Armenian.

Rydhave's security was shored up considerably, but it ended up costing both the Danish Security Department and our State Department. My persistence really irritated U.S. officials, but I honestly didn't care.[*]

We had frequent bomb scares during my tenure, and I always ordered complete evacuations of the embassy, over the protests of Arthur Hughes. Hughes claimed this "cowardice" might get in the papers; apparently, my fear would look very un-American. Well, I *was* scared, and I also felt responsible for the safety of everyone in the building.

One day I decided to see just how secure the embassy's front entrance was. ("Trust but verify," as President Reagan put it when talking about Russia's nuclear capabilities.) The embassy foyer was equipped with metal detectors, but not much furniture, except for a couch close to the front door. Just past the metal detectors a guard stood behind a glass-enclosed area where the U.S. visa processer worked at a desk. On this particular day, the foyer was crowded with people waiting for visas. Before I went through the metal detectors myself, I deliberately left my briefcase on the couch, got in line and passed through the metal detectors. Shortly, I came back out, as if planning to leave. Sure enough, the briefcase was still there, unobserved and unexamined by the guard, the visa official and the metal detection officer. I picked up the briefcase and approached those on duty, brandishing the package.

"Listen, guys," I said loudly, "anyone can enter, leave something on the couch, pass through the metal detector, go into the embassy, come back out and exit the premises—with a potential bomb still sitting on the couch!"

The attending staff looked appropriately mortified. Word must have gotten around that the new ambassador meant business about security. At any rate, I never stopped my vigilance to be safe rather than sorry.[†]

During my tenure in Denmark, I was an eligible bachelor, and, to my great chagrin, the public seemed to think I was much wealthier than I actually was. This made for more marketable grist for the press than my ambassadorial activities. Creative fiction beats facts every time, especially as far as tabloids are concerned. Father had been listed in *Fortune* magazine that year as one of the richest men in the world, and everyone assumed I would one day inherit an enormous fortune.

---

[*] When Terence Todman succeeded me, State ordered him to immediately dismantle the new security. But Todman balked. "The security stays," he told them flatly—and then he promptly increased it.

[†] My American office staff loved these Danish security stories, which cheered up the group during practice sessions for the protective gear in the wake of the World Trade Center attacks in 2001. We had gas masks and chemical protection suits, which everyone thought might be needed in the event of an al-Qaeda chemical attack.

In the early weeks of my life in Copenhagen, after Alexandra had returned to Paris, I roamed the high-ceilinged halls of Rydhave at dusk feeling very alone. In the evening the staff either went home, to their quarters or made themselves invisible. I was invited to formal events and hosted many, but in the beginning, I had very few friends. I was ever mindful of the warning from Ambassador James "Jimmy" Lowenstein, who'd served in Luxembourg under Jimmy Carter. "Never date the locals," he advised.

This didn't seem to be an option. The only locals who seemed the least bit interested were the staid dowagers who flirted with me at diplomatic parties. It was a total myth that all Scandinavian girls are blonde, beautiful and immediately ready to jump into bed. I had to laugh when American visitors thought I could fix them up with such fantasy girls. I honestly told them that I didn't know any.

My observation was that Danes are quite reserved and did not often invite people to their homes, opting to entertain at restaurants or other public places. However, an outgoing and extremely successful Danish businessman took a liking to me, and I was invited to some of his parties at home. At one of his events, I met a Grace Kelly look-alike, a divorced lawyer with a son about Nicholas's age. Our sons were a point of common interest, and we became good friends for a while; unfortunately, she would become a source of endless problems and rumors later during my tenure ("Hell hath no fury like a woman scorned," as William Congreve wrote.) I also met a lovely young ballerina at a Fourth of July event at the embassy. We became friends, but, for the most part, I remained the lonely eligible bachelor. The fact was that my ambassador duties kept me from any serious courting.

Fortunately, invitations to art galleries began to reach my desk, and I attended events at the Jacob Asbæk Gallery, which specializes in contemporary art. Wine and Danish hors d'oeuvres were served at these events, where I met and conversed with friendly Danes, many of them young artists. Under the tutelage and friendship of Jacob Asbæk, my education in contemporary art

This study of his son, Jonas, by Kurt Trampedach, was my first purchase of Danish art, in 1981. In 1983, the Royal Danish Academy of Fine Arts awarded him the coveted Eckersberg Medal.

began. His gallery opened a new world to me. I'd grown up in a family whose collections were mostly of Impressionist paintings (although some were avant-garde back when they bought them).

My first contemporary purchase was from a Kurt Trampedach exhibition, a charming portrait of his son, Jonas. Trampedach became one of Denmark's most successful contemporary artists, and his work has appeared at the Allen Stone Gallery in New York. His paintings today are now too abstract to appeal to me, but I still treasure my lovely Jonas. When word spread that the new ambassador was interested in Danish art, I started to receive beautifully produced catalogues from Bruun Rasmussen, the leading auction house in Copenhagen, filled with the work of some of the greatest nineteenth-century Danish artists. These appealed to me more than the contemporary paintings I'd been seeing. The auction house owners, Jesper and Bertha Rasmussen, became close friends. They suggested visiting the Hirschsprung Collection, which I found to be an absolute gem.

Heinrich Hirschsprung was a famously successful tobacco merchant who collected the contemporary artists of his day, the late nineteenth century. His wife gave his collection to the Danish state, which housed it in a small museum. He was partial to the artists from a town called Skagen, as am I, which is like the St. Tropez of the north. I so admired Hirschsprung's taste that I decided he would be my Danish art "mentor," though he had been dead for seventy-five years. I planned to collect only work by artists represented in his museum, and today the vast majority of my current collection of 147 works of Danish art was based on my mentor's guidance. My collection, now the largest in the world outside of Denmark's museums, all came about simply because I'd grown lonely. Though I didn't realize it at the time, I started something that would become a major part of my life when I returned to New York—and for decades to come.

Anker Jørgensen was Denmark's prime minister when I arrived, and he would hold that post for about another year thereafter. As prime minister, he had led five coalition governments, and he had headed the Social Democratic Party for over thirty years. He was a down-to-earth politician who spoke his mind; no one was ever in doubt about where Jørgensen stood on any issue. He never forgot his working-class roots, and he and his wife, Ingrid, never lived in the official prime minister's residence, Marienborg. They preferred the apartment they had shared all their married life in a working-class area of Copenhagen.

I already knew that one of the first things I had to do in Copenhagen was address the "Anker Jørgensen problem," a delicate undertaking at best. Jørgensen was not a fan of the United States or of President Reagan. Even so, I was taken aback by Washington's first directive to me: *Issue him a stern warning.* Unless he stopped verbally attacking President Reagan, he would not be invited to the White House dinner given in honor of the new European Economic Community (EEC) presidency. Joining the European Union had been controversial in Denmark, and even though his party was against it, Anker Jørgensen had opted for Denmark to join. It was to be the Danish leader's turn to hold the presidency of the EEC in mid-1982, and it would be an embarrassment to him—and to his country—if he were not invited. It was a dilemma for me. I couldn't just go up to Anker Jørgensen and say, "Guess who's *not* coming to dinner at the White House unless he stops saying nasty things about my president." Diplomacy requires substantially more subtlety.

No one on my staff had any strategy for how to handle the situation. I had recently met Hemming Gottlieb, Jørgensen's key foreign relations advisor, and invited him for a private lunch at Rydhave. While chatting about nonthreatening issues, I wordlessly passed him a copy of Washington's directive to me. He read it quickly and then looked up. Our eyes met, he smiled slightly and gave a brief nod as if to say, "I get it," and he handed the note back. Our conversation proceeded without a word about it. I do not know how Hemming handled it with the prime minister, but for several months thereafter, Anker Jørgensen made no more personal digs about President Reagan.

One of my early missions was disabusing the Danes of their perception that President Reagan was a lightweight. A little more than a month after taking up my post, he showed it to the world. On November 18, 1981, he delivered what came to be known as his "Zero Option" speech at the National Press Club in Washington. I was able to persuade Lauritz Bindsløv, the CEO of the state-owned Danish TV, to air Reagan's entire speech in prime time, the first and last time they allowed President Reagan to appear on Denmark's only television station. As it turned out, Denmark was the only Nordic country to air the entire speech.

Against the advice of some of his advisors (including Henry Kissinger), President Reagan proposed that both sides eliminate an entire class of nuclear arms. He called his proposal the "Zero Nuclear Option," which would effectively end the nuclear arms race. He spoke brilliantly and persuasively, with his trademark geniality and sincerity shining through. Many Danes were absolutely bowled over by his address, not knowing about teleprompters. It seemed incredible to them that he was not only so knowledgeable, but also capable of speaking for almost a half hour about a very complicated issue—without any notes!

The day after his speech, *Politiken*, the leftist and most prestigious Danish newspaper, ran a long story headlined in boldface type: "From Cowboy to Statesman." The Danes had never before seen Reagan on TV, and the coverage was a turning point in how they viewed him. Though I can't say the Danes ever truly warmed to Reagan, their opinions of him shot up significantly. They gave increasing, if grudging, recognition to the effectiveness of his economic policies.

In discussions with some of the high-ranking members of the Danish government, I was pleased when they reported that the Soviet response to Reagan's speech was "confused and uncertain." Another good sign for my NATO mission was that the fervor of the Danish peace movement was slightly dampened after a Soviet nuclear submarine was found stranded on Swedish shores in October 1981; another sub was found there a month later, this one suspected of carrying nuclear weapons. The positive results of my early diplomatic efforts gave me assurance that I was on the right track. I moved ahead with confidence into what would be the busiest and most satisfying work I'd ever done in my life. Both discoveries and headaches lay ahead.

Besides traveling around my host country, there were also several occasions when it was necessary for me to make trips home. I gave an important address about NATO to the Danish-American Chamber of Commerce at the Waldorf Astoria in New York City on March 26, 1982. The next day, my speech was covered by *The New York Times*.[103]

THE NEW YORK TIMES, SATURDAY, MARCH 27, 1982

Notes on People

Ambassador Loeb Addresses the Nuclear Question

"I do not believe that Western Europe's instinct for survival in freedom has become so atrophied that its people are unwilling or unable to confront the hard challenges before them," said John L. Loeb Jr., the United States Ambassador to Denmark.

Mr. Loeb, in remarks prepared for a dinner last night of the Danish American Chamber of Commerce at the Waldorf-Astoria Hotel, said: "It is an illusion to think that any of us, on a national basis, can avoid the risks of this dangerous world.

Nuclear weapons will not go away simply because we are horrified to deal with them."

Mr. Loeb, a New York financier who assumed his duties in Copenhagen six months ago, made particular mention in his speech to the possible dangerous effects that "today's young peace marchers" such as the "No to Nuclear Weapons" groups in Denmark, might have on the North Atlantic Treaty Organization.

"The question of nuclear weapons is an issue which torments us all," he said. "It is a topic of public controversy in all our countries, and the Soviet Union shamelessly attempts to exploit it. The so-called peace

marchers are in fact endangering the peace when they call for unilaterally dismantling the strategy of deterrence which has made it possible for their generation to grow up in conditions of peace and security."

—*By Albin Krebs and Robert McG. Thomas Jr.*

I never had enough time at my desk, needing 48-hour days to be able to read all the State Department telexes, memos from my DCM, background on Danish officials whom I would be meeting, dictating letters and writing talks about NATO.

CHAPTER FOURTEEN

Denmark! Part II: Life as an Ambassador, 1982–1983

The daily life of an ambassador is not what many people imagine: glamorous luncheons, delicious teas in magnificent gardens on huge estates and gourmet dinners every night. There *are* many dinners, but not every night and not always gourmet.

The minute the queen accepted my credentials, I began lining up appointments with Danish leaders. I'd heard that Danes would be a little aloof, but I found them to be warm and receptive. The chief topics we covered ranged from NATO, to Denmark's financial problems, to President Reagan's economic and foreign policies, to the environment, to America's race relations. I had especially productive meetings with the minister of finance, Knud Heinesen, the second most powerful person in the Social Democratic Party after the prime minister.

I first met with Prime Minister Anker Jørgensen a couple of months after my arrival, on November 23, 1981. Though our political views were poles apart, I liked him personally from the outset. He was in political trouble because of the public's anger and frustration over Denmark's economic problems, which had begun in the early 1970s. By the time of my arrival, public fury had risen to a boil. Just ten days before we met, the Danish Parliament had rejected the program Jørgensen considered vital to reviving the nation's economy. As a result, Jørgensen was bracing for the possibility that he would be removed from office.

Jørgensen began by telling me how pleased he'd been by President Reagan's Zero Option speech, broadcast a few days earlier. Because Jørgensen was so opposed to

NATO, I asked what specific strategies he suggested to induce the Soviet Union to reduce their missile deployment other than NATO's two-track strategy. He had none, but he deftly changed the subject to complain about NATO member countries, especially the United States. He took particular umbrage at the fact that the U.S. had missiles throughout Europe, whereas Soviet missiles were based only on their own soil. My response was an oblique warning. "There is a rising movement in the United States, Mr. Prime Minister," I said, "which is opposed to the heavy commitment we have in Europe." I wanted him to know that our protective presence should not be taken for granted. Despite our differences, which we both made clear at the outset, we ended on a congenial note.

One of the things that helped in my relationship with Jørgensen was my extensive knowledge of the work of his hero—the famous socialist Harold Laski. Having written my Harvard College thesis on Laski's theories, I was able to discuss Laski in depth, which surprised and pleased the prime minister. Also, because Jørgensen once attended a six-week Harvard conference for labor leaders and because there was a large contingent of Harvard alumni in Denmark, I held an alumni dinner at Rydhave in Anker's honor. Everyone in Copenhagen with a bond to Harvard was invited, and more than two hundred alumni attended. In retrospect, I find it remarkable that this passionate socialist, who was orphaned early in life, who rose in the ranks of labor, was honored by two hundred alumni from Harvard, of all places.

As he feared, Jørgensen's party suffered a major setback in December 1981. Jørgensen resigned as prime minister, but he took on the role of "caretaker" until a new government could be formed, which didn't happen until September 1982. By February 1982, undaunted by his diminished position, in response to the U.S. reaction against martial law in Poland, he said on Danish prime-time television that he thought U.S. foreign policy had an "unacceptable double standard," supporting the junta in El Salvador while opposing Soviet occupation on the Eastern front. The United States was "wearing a patch over one eye," he said. The Danish press did not make too much of the speech, but it was picked up by *The New York Times*, which reported that Jørgensen had attacked not only our foreign policy, but also Secretary of State Alexander Haig and President Reagan. The prime minister had refrained from these kinds of attacks immediately after Reagan was elected, but apparently the need to court favor with his own party outweighed the prospect of dinner at the White House.

In March 1982, when Jørgensen openly praised the Soviet leader Leonid Brezhnev's recent speech on the reduction of nuclear armaments, I wrote to Washington:

The Danish prime minister's latest statement is clearly unhelpful in terms of both US and NATO interests. . . . Jørgensen's openness to Brezhnev's proposal will no doubt receive positive response from the left wing of the Social Democratic Party and serve Jørgensen's domestic political interests, but can only complicate efforts to develop public understanding and support for the Western position on this sensitive and complex issue.

I had properly hedged my diplomatic bets regarding Jørgensen's successor. Right after arriving in Copenhagen, I'd sought out the opposition leaders I thought likely to follow Jørgensen's Social Democratic government. Most of my top staff at the embassy believed the Social Democrats would return to office if the current government resigned. But I'd watched signs of a swing to the right in other parts of Europe, as well as in America, and believed that Denmark would soon follow. In preparation, I began a series of luncheons for all the leaders of the center-right parties. I believed that the leader of the Conservative Party, Poul Schlüter, was most likely to be the next prime minister and included him on the A-list for a June dinner I planned for the queen.

After Jørgensen's official resignation as caretaker in September 1982, he turned the government over to Schlüter, without an election ever being held. Instead, the Danish Parliament, the Folketing, had held a "Queen's Round," wherein all parties express their preferences for a new government, or *formateur*. Schlüter would lead a "clover leaf," a four-party coalition. Particularly on economic issues, Schlüter was much more in line with U.S. policy than Jørgensen had been. Though politically I greeted Jørgensen's departure with relief, on a personal level, I was sorry to see him go. I would miss his warm personality and his feisty straightforwardness, even though his resignation made my job easier.

I visited Schlüter shortly after he took office to offer congratulations and to pay sincere compliments on his initial speech to the Folketing. He had spoken candidly about the world financial markets and seemed pleased when I assured him that the banking community would embrace his speech. Besides discussing the world economy, I took the opportunity to report on a recent five-day visit I'd taken to Greenland's military bases. It opened up a way for me to talk about NATO and, specifically, to make the case for Denmark's support.

Right after Schlüter took office, I arranged an appointment for the new prime minister to meet with President Reagan. Accompanying him to Washington, I had a chance to get better acquainted with him on our trip. Our relationship was always more buttoned up because Schlüter was much more formal than Jørgensen had been. Reagan told Schlüter that he was pleased that the new prime minister was in full support of Reagan's positions. Privately, Reagan was jovial with me before I left the White House. "You must be doing a

Dame Anne Warburton, in the middle, Britain's first female ambassador, represented Britain all over the world in multiple diplomatic positions. I was more than lucky she was still serving as ambassador to Denmark while I was there.

great job in Denmark, John," Reagan said. "In just a few months you've produced the first Conservative Danish prime minister of this century!" While in America, I'd arranged for the New York Council on Foreign Relations to hold a dinner in the prime minister's honor. At the last minute, the council was unable to host it, so I held it at my New York home.

One of the roles of an ambassador and his staff is to act as a greeting party for distinguished foreign visitors. Whenever Washington dignitaries came to Denmark, my staff or I arranged large luncheons for them. Two notable ones were for Ambassador Jack R. Binns, director of Northern European Affairs, and my immediate superior, Assistant Secretary of State for Europe Richard Burt. Burt came to address the Copenhagen Regional Seminar on Trends and Developments in Western Security—the Complications for Atlantic Security. Danish journalists, professors, labor leaders and members of professional business organizations such as Rotary, as well as members of the Danish Parliament, would attend these luncheons and meet with the visiting dignitaries.

The goal was to provide our guests with insights into American positions that would reach the ears of at least some of the Danish public. NATO and the Intermediate-Range Nuclear Treaty (INF) were always a top priority in our discussions. Other concerns came up, such as the American position on free trade, a troublesome subject to the Danes. The Danish Agricultural Council, a powerful farm organization, was supportive of the heavy Danish agricultural subsidies that made equal trade difficult for the United States. I felt comfortable in addressing the vociferous criticisms voiced by a particularly prickly member of the Agricultural Council. I leaned on my experience as the former chairman of Holly Sugar Corporation to deflect his complaints, as well as other issues that came up about international trade.

Another of my ambassadorial duties was meeting with important foreign leaders, such as the French president François Mitterrand, when they visited Denmark. I was actually able to communicate in French with Mitterrand about my year in Paris.

A diplomatic move I made that turned out particularly well involved the British ambassador. I wanted to see more coordinated ambassadorial presentations regarding NATO with the Danish government, so I invited other ambassadors to join me for a series of dinners, especially if their home countries were NATO members. I asked Dame Anne Warburton, the British ambassador, to take the lead in orchestrating our collaboration.* I thought it would be politic if a country other than the United States led our united approach in NATO matters. She performed the role beautifully, and our fellow ambassadors spoke with a more unified voice than ever before.

I was frequently called on to provide speakers for various occasions in Copenhagen and often brought appropriate experts over from the United States. When the keynote speaker for a Western security conference couldn't make it at the last minute, I sent an SOS to my former honors tutor, Harvard professor Samuel Huntington. He came to the rescue on very short notice. He had just cowritten a book titled *Living with Nuclear Weapons*, and his talk was supportive of my diplomatic mission, adding an in-depth perspective on the American point of view. Even though he was a liberal Democrat and a member of President Carter's National Security Council, he was in total sync with our position on NATO. I was delighted when his talk resulted in a positive interview in *Politiken*.

My Harvard First Honors tutor, Professor Samuel Huntington, is pictured here, on the right, shortly after his brilliant address to a conference in Denmark, given on short notice as a favor to me. When he died in late 2008 at the age of 81, the *Harvard Gazette* called him "one of the most influential political scientists of the last 50 years."

I also spent significant time visiting all seven European NATO bases, where I would meet with State Department officials, who sometimes flew in from Washington to take

---

* Dame Warburton served in Denmark from 1976 to 1983 and was Britain's first female ambassador.

Just a few weeks after arriving in Denmark, I made my first ambassadorial visit to a NATO base. Called the "Allied Forces Baltic Approaches," it was located in Jutland, Denmark's northern peninsula. Pictured here with me is the base commander, Marine Lieutenant Colonel H.M. Hoffman, who received a special commendation.

part in meetings, discussions and updates on our negotiations with the Soviets. One of the bases was in Casteau, Belgium, which had become the headquarters of the Supreme Headquarters Allied Powers Europe (SHAPE) for a short period in 1963. The other bases were in La Spezia, Italy; Thule, Greenland; Ramstadt, Germany; Geilenkirchen, Germany; Brunssum, the Netherlands; and Stavanger, Norway. Besides holding meetings with Copenhagen leaders and outlying community officials, I took and made every opportunity to give short talks to convince reluctant Danes that they had "a dog in this fight."

I put on a full-court press to find and woo every public relations avenue possible. One of the most significant actions I took, which would be of lasting help to my successors, was to update and increase mailing lists of more than six hundred groups and individuals considered to be Denmark's top opinion makers. I wrote to them frequently, sometimes sending a personally signed cover letter with copies of important news clippings, such as Ambassador Arthur Hartman's bylined article, "A Visit to Pravda," which was reprinted in papers all over Denmark.

In the 1980s, most of the reporting in Denmark was still done by newspapers and magazines. When I made personal calls on media sources, I sought the goodwill not only of publishers and editors, but also of top executives and producers at the state-run TV and radio station. A former ambassador to Denmark, William Blair, advised me to visit each of the fourteen cities and villages outside Copenhagen that had a newspaper, because the papers' editors could help in my mission of making NATO palatable to the Danes. It was good advice, and I took it.

Paying calls on the media in the more rural areas was one of the best uses of my time. In my travels outside Copenhagen, I was always met with warmth and sometimes with amazement that an American ambassador would actually venture outside the embassy and come to see them personally. I made at least twenty-five short talks on these trips; my theme was always America's constant press for peace through negotiations with the Soviets after World War II. My talks mostly went across well, but any explanation I gave regarding NATO's need to mount missiles equal to the number the USSR had aimed at European cities was often met with skepticism.

Lauritz Bindsløv was CEO of the state-operated radio—Radio Denmark—as well as Denmark's sole TV station, which had begun operating in 1951. I was shocked to find that Lauritz had never been invited to Rydhave prior to my arrival. During my tenure, he became a popular regular at many of our functions, and he was one of the best guest speakers to address our programs for the senior staff.

Even with my personal media campaign, the United States was still being treated rather insultingly in the press—exactly what new ambassadors were warned to expect. One example involved not just anti-American sentiment, but also just plain bad journalism: an anti-American, anti-capitalist TV program with the scabrous title *The Eagle Shits*. Written and produced by an angry American journalist, the show painted America as though it were Louis XVI's and Marie Antoinette's France. In a typical segment, the host stood in front of the Statue of Liberty talking about America's abuse of (and dependence on) the poor. "Poverty is the fuel," the host bellowed. "Without poverty, nothing would go 'round. Poor people are the route, and prosperity is the blossom." The show harped on the idea that leaders in America wanted poverty to continue so they could hire cheap labor, control the masses and remain in power. It framed those who worked in social services as "poverty professionals," meant to keep the lower class where they are. The show was pure yellow journalism, but, as in the case of tabloid newspapers, it was ac-

Among the fourteen newspapers I visited was the one in Randers, a city in the center of the Jutland peninsula. Here I am being told by their technical manager about the "modern editorial screens" (computers) that would be replacing their journalists' typewriters in two months. Looking on are members of the paper's administration.

cepted without question by an audience skeptical of capitalism. Much as I thought the content dreadful, I did not, as reported by one tabloid, try to strong-arm my way into equal airtime to refute its inaccuracies. Maybe I should have.

My sense of what should be reported and what the Danish press thought worthy of bringing to public attention didn't always coincide. Contrary to what the Danish security people assured me, dangerous things did indeed happen in Denmark. In September 1982, the CIA alerted me to a situation: the Saudi embassy in Copenhagen had been invaded by Palestinians living in Denmark, who were holding the Saudi staff hostage. The Israeli military, under Defense Minister Ariel Sharon, had recently invaded Lebanon, trying to root out the PLO. It turned out to be a terrible massacre in which mostly Palestinians and Lebanese Shiites in Beirut refugee camps were killed. Sharon took the majority of the blame.* The Palestinians living in Denmark were outraged that not one country in the Middle East had come to the aid of the Lebanese Palestinians. The Danish Palestinians blamed Saudi Arabia for ignoring the situation. In retaliation, they held everyone in the Saudi embassy hostage for a day and a half. I was shocked to find nothing about this in any Danish news outlet. I contacted several media outlets about the story, to no avail. I believe that the story may have been scuttled because the Danish government never wanted Denmark to appear in a bad light to the international community, and the population tended to go along with that charade. The response that I got when checking with security officials—nothing dangerous ever happens in Denmark—seemed to be a bit more complex. Perhaps such things did happen, it's just that they were never reported.

One particular thorny issue was brought up everywhere I went: an intractable mindset against the "evils" of American capitalism, which was especially entrenched among younger Danes. I discovered that the source of this strong opinion was a book called *American Pictures: A Personal Journey through the American Underclass*, published in 1977, and still a bestseller in Denmark in 1981. The sensationalist tabloid *Ekstra Bladet* wrote that it had "sold more copies than any Danish publisher can dream about during his most euphoric moments." The youthful author and photographer was Jacob Holdt, who had become a latter-day folk hero, especially to younger Danes. The rebellious son of a Copenhagen minister, Jacob started a four-year hitchhike across America at the age of twenty-three. He lived mostly as the guest of America's severely impoverished, mostly black families. Perpetually lacking money, he often sold his blood to buy food and film for his cheap pocket

---

* An Israeli commission determined that Sharon had "personal responsibility" for the massacre, and he was forced to resign a year later. Nonetheless, he would be a member of various Israeli cabinets throughout the 1980s and 1990s, before becoming prime minister in 2001.

camera. He recorded 350 family lives on that tiny camera, and his bestseller was based on the pictures from his sojourn.

Holdt's book compared the disparity between his American hosts' lifestyles and those of the rich and famous, singling out the Rockefellers, with whom Holdt had once stayed. He flogged the idea that America had to keep the poor in their lower caste status for the high and mighty to stay rich. At every single school I visited, Holdt's version of America's ill treatment of its black population was raised either by the teachers or the students themselves.* I found out only later that it was used as a textbook in Danish secondary schools! I also learned that the Denmark Radio and Film Institute had even subsidized a movie based on the book. No wonder its theme had poisoned the well of Danish public opinion.†

Not too incidentally, when PBS came to sell some of its programs to the Danish TV station, the Danes chose documentaries about the United States' social and economic problems. I felt strongly that without proper information to show what our country was doing about the problems, the airing of these programs would do nothing to improve our relationship with Denmark. I contacted the TV programmers to offer U.S. embassy representatives as interview subjects, if and when these documentaries were to be aired. I thought a balancing out would only be fair.

The power of pictures versus words was never clearer to me than when I began my effort to educate the skeptical Danes about the benefits of capitalism to *all* Americans. The pen may be mightier than the sword, but the camera is mightier yet. Words pale when provocative—and, I might argue, manipulative—photographs are etched in memory. No matter how passionately I spoke about how successfully the U.S. system works for everyone, it was daunting to praise capitalism when Holdt's book was so firmly entrenched in the consciousness of Danish youths. Nevertheless, I remained persistent, pointing out the skewed reportage like that in Holdt's book. What seemed to surprise students most was that we have Civil Rights Commission offices throughout our country, as well as affirmative action programs that give hiring preference to minorities and women. I believe my contact with these young students gave them new insights, but it was a tough slog. Holdt's book had totally omitted any recognition of a black middle class in America, and there was no inclusion whatsoever of the many American people

---

* I think it was a good thing that Ambassador Terence Todman, who was appointed to Denmark after me, was not only a career diplomat but was also black. Just his presence made a very strong case that America was not the terminally prejudiced culture portrayed in Holdt's book.

† When Holdt heard in 1977 that the KGB intended to use his book to frame President Carter as egregious on human rights as the USSR was purported to be, Holdt sued to have his book not printed in any new countries. He won, and it was not reprinted anywhere new until the end of the Cold War.

of color who were not living in poverty. In short, it was a popular form of propaganda, and the Danes swallowed it whole.

Deputy Secretary of State Kenneth W. Dam and his wife, Marcia, were my guests at Rydhave for a few days in March 1983. Ken was on a trip through Europe to partake in disarmament discussions. He joined my constant pressure on the Danish government to be more supportive of NATO's positions. Knowing of the close personal relationship that Mrs. Dam had developed with Prime Minister Schlüter's wife during the leader's visit to our nation's capital, I suggested Marcia accompany her husband on the trip, and Washington agreed.

I'd learned that Ken had Danish roots on the beautiful island of Bornholm, so I arranged a memorable side trip there. There they visited the hometown of Ken's paternal great-grandfather (Peder Dam) and grandfather (Hans Christian Dam). Our tour of the island, located east of Denmark, included the Østerlars Church to see his family records. Our day was capped with a reception given by the lord mayor of Røenne, the largest town on the island. The icing on the cake for me came years later when I was able to buy *A Street in Bornholm, Mother Walking with Her Children*, a painting by one of Denmark's most famous women painters, Anna Ancher. It will always be a reminder of the walk with the Dam entourage through Bornholm streets.

When I visited the areas of Denmark outside Copenhagen, I was almost always asked to give a talk. Sometimes I spoke off the cuff, or maybe glanced at a few notes,

Standing for a photo op at the Copenhagen airport, left to right, are a Danish official, me, Deputy Secretary of State Kenneth W. Dam, his wife, Marcia, his aide, Christy Valentine, and Danish Foreign Minister Uffe Ellemann-Jensen.

My State Department guests, accompanied by a few Danish officials and me, are seen here after visiting Østerlars Church on the island of Bornholm. The church, which contains records of Ken Dam's ancestors, is one of the famed four round churches in Denmark.

but I rarely gave a formal speech on these trips. However, in Copenhagen I was called on frequently for more formal presentations, which I usually wrote myself. Almost without exception, I spoke in English. Once, after intensive immersion in a Berlitz course, I gave a fifteen-minute tribute without notes to the Danish foreign minister, Kjeld Olesen, at a dinner I held for him. I believe he was touched by my effort. It has been said that no American in the twentieth century ever mastered Danish, and, alas, I was not the first to do so.

My relationship with Kjeld Olesen got off to a good start because I'd personally made special arrangements for him to meet in Washington with Secretary of State George Shultz, National Security Advisor William Clark and Vice President George Bush. Foreign Minister Olesen reported to me they were the "best and most productive meetings I have ever had with American leaders." We had a close relationship throughout my tenure.

When I gave a speech titled "The American Dream" to the Denmark-Amerika Fond-

My Anna Ancher painting, *A Street in Bornholm*, always reminds me of a wonderful visit to that picturesque city.

Protocol chief Jørgen Werner and I are seen here in 1982 as uncharacteristically amicable. This was no doubt because I wasn't showing him a guest list— always a source of contention—but instead the notes of what I planned to say at the Fourth of July party at Rydhave.

My Fourth of July party at Rydhave in 1982 offered a perfect opportunity to talk briefly to three hundred Danish guests about American idealism. Nicholas is here with me, having again escaped his governess.

et (Danish-American Foundation) in April 1982, I was mindful of the power of pictures over words, and I showed a film before speaking. Originally produced for the American bicentennial, the movie gave a broad view of American history and set the stage for my talk about American idealism. Having heard all too often from more than a few Danes about American "hypocrisy" vis-à-vis our treatment of the poor and minorities, I wove in examples of the progress, if not perfection, that America has made in achieving our forefathers' dreams of equality:

> *Our laws in support of full civil rights for all of our citizens are strong and in place. . . . There are more than 4,600 black elected officials in the United States. The mayors of Los Angeles, Detroit, Atlanta and New Orleans are black. Even the mayor of our nation's capital, Washington, D.C., is now a black man. . . . More than 40 percent of the federal budget goes to transfer payments to needy individuals—approximately the same as in Denmark. But the American Dream is, after all, an ideal. No country is perfect . . . but freedom and opportunity remain the pillars of the American Dream, and both remain strong in the United States today.*

There are 226 million Americans today. We are a mix of the world's races, religions and cultures. We struggle and argue constantly among ourselves—in the open—as we did in formulating the Declaration of Independence. The whole world sees and hears our causes and opinions.

In the continuing course of human events, we are making progress toward full equality, greater compassion, deeper fulfillment of the human potential and the final realization of the American Dream.

In the summer of 1982, though focused on very serious matters, I was able to plan a pair of major parties at Rydhave. The British doyenne Betty Kenward wrote a column called "Jennifer's Diary" for *Harpers & Queen.* She flew from Paris to cover my two parties, head-lining her stories "Super Parties." Two pages of text and pictures appeared in the paper, shot by my favorite Copenhagen photographer, Jan van Steenwijk.

The first party was a dinner dance held at the Royal Shooting Club, an organization dating back to the fourteenth century, located in a historic building on the Sølyst estate in the northern outskirts of Copenhagen. The club boasts an elite membership, including Danish kings, queens and other royalty. I'd planned the dinner to honor Jack and Bunny Wrather, my good friends of many years, both of whom had been members of Reagan's "Kitchen Cabinet."[*] Bunny (the 1940s actress Bonita Granville) and Jack, a successful film producer, would have provided Hollywood luster to the party, but unfortunately, it had to be held without them.[†] Bunny had a last-minute medical emergency, and it was too late for me to cancel; many of the guests were already on flights to Copenhagen. Along with the U.S. visitors were five former U.S. ambassadors to Denmark, some with their spouses: Robert Coe, Katherine White, Angier Biddle Duke, Guilford Dudley and Fred Russell. Ambassador Evan Galbraith came from France, and Ambas-

Here Nicholas and I are seen escorting the queen to the huge tent where dinner was about to be served.

---

[*] The Kitchen Cabinet group of his California friends and supporters who helped with both advice and money in the early days of his candidacy and continued advising even after his election.

[†] Jack was a petroleum billionaire before becoming a major film and TV producer (*Lassie* and *The Lone Ranger*). Bunny was remembered for roles in Mickey Rooney movies and her *Nancy Drew* movie series.

A REPRISE OF A STORY ABOUT MY DINNER-DANCE HONORING HER MAJESTY, QUEEN MARGRETHE II, AND HRH PRINCE HENRIK SUMMARIZES THE EVENING PERFECTLY:

It was written by the British social columnist Betty Kenward for "Jennifer's Diary" in *Harpers & Queen* magazine:

The young queen arrived looking radiant in a long dress of silk tartan taffeta. Accompanied by the ambassador, she very sweetly went round meeting many of the guests. . . . It was a warm evening so guests were assembled on the terrace, the swimming pool, and on the lawn where a band played, as well as one in the house. . . . Dinner was served in a large prettily decorated marquee across the lawn. . . . At the end of dinner we listened to a few songs by the Mormon Tabernacle Choir, who were giving concerts in Copenhagen that week. . . . dancing went on until around 1 a.m. . . . In true American fashion, there was cutting in, and I noticed Queen Margrethe frequently dancing happily with different partners. . . . They were two most gracious and enjoyable evenings, which I shall always remember.

The Duke and Duchess of Rutland are seen here conversing with Veronica Gabel-Jørgensen, wife of Chamberlain Ulf Gabel-Jørgensen, the queen's Master of Ceremonies.

Left to right in this picture are Baron Otto Reedtz-Thott, young owner of the Gavnø castle; my daughter, Alexandra; Robert Goldsamt of New York; and Baroness Caroline Reedtz-Thott, Baron Otto's sister.

Queen Margrethe and I are chatting with Joanne King Herring, who, despite a broken leg, traveled from her home in Texas for my party. Famous as a diplomat, philanthropist and former TV host, she is perhaps best remembered for inspiring the book and movie *Charlie Wilson's War*.

Ambassador Vernon Walters, a well-known U.S. State Department troubleshooter, is pictured here dancing with Molise Lillelund (Mrs. Christian Lillelund).

sador Maxwell Rabb and his wife were on their way from Italy.

The following evening, I hosted a dinner dance at Rydhave primarily to honor Queen Margrethe and Prince Henrik. That dinner was truly worthy of the red carpet rolled out for the event. One incident during that dinner, however, is funny only in hindsight. Mother and Father flew over for the party and had seats of honor; Mother sat next to Prince Henrik, who absolutely charmed her. Knowing her penchant for making little impromptu speeches at dinner parties, I had cautioned her ahead of time. "Mother," I warned, "the Danes are very strict about protocol in the presence of royalty. You mustn't give one of your unplanned toasts. They go over well in America, but it's different here."

Late in the meal, she stood up, tapping a wine glass with her customary authority. My heart sank. She quickly quieted the crowd, while I squirmed, fearing the worst. She waxed eloquent, going on and on about how wonderful Prince Henrik was—how intelligent, how good looking, how simply delightful. She was "so glad to see what a nice girl Margrethe is"

Left to right are Baron Hans Heinrich Thyssen-Bornemisza, whose art collection in Lugano, Switzerland, is world famous; Viscountess Jacqueline de Ribes, of Paris, dubbed "the muse of haute couture fashion designers"; HRH Prince Henrik; my mother; and Count Flemming of Rosenborg, a relative of Queen Margrethe's.

Though Mother's toast to the royals mortified me, Prince Henrik's sense of humor brought relieved laughs to the shocked guests, who hadn't quite known how to react.

and referred to the queen several times as "such a pretty girl." She congratulated them both about what a great job "Margrethe" was doing for her country, and what a superb, wonderful couple they were. She never once referred to either of them as "His Royal Highness" or "Her Majesty." Everyone was stunned. Motionless as wax dolls, the royals sat gamely through it all. As for me, I would have welcomed a black hole to swallow me up on the spot. I was mortified, and after the event ended, I had words with my disobedient parent. "Mother, how *could* you!"

Mother did not care that Copenhagen tongues would be wagging nonstop about the disrespect Americans had for their royalty. "Well," she said. "I'm at an age when I can say anything I want to." And that was the end of that as far as she was concerned. Nobody who was there will ever forget Mother's egalitarian disregard for royal protocol, least of all her son.

One trip I made back home had nothing to do with politics. It was with Prince Henrik to promote a major exhibit called *Scandinavia Today*—an international cultural exhibit and joint undertaking of all five Scandinavian countries. We had just officially launched the Danish section at a red-carpet dinner at Rydhave. The eighteen-month-long exhibit was to travel all across the U.S., and Prince Henrik and I were to attend opening ceremonies in three American cities: New York, Washington and Minneapolis. Funded by the U.S. National Endowment for the Humanities and the National Endowment for the Arts, it was cosponsored by the American-Scandinavian Foundation and the Smithsonian Institution.* *Scandinavia Today* also included an exhibit of the Royal Museum's impressive Judaica collection and a photographic story of how the Danes saved the country's Jews at the end of World War II.

As part of *Scandinavia Today*, the late Kirk Varnedoe, then senior professor of art at New York University, was asked to put on an exhibition of all the great Scandinavian painters—from Iceland, Finland, Demark, Sweden and Norway. This exhibition, known as *Northern Light: Realism and Symbolism in Scandinavian Painting, 1880–1910*, was widely hailed and traveled from the Brooklyn Museum to the Corcoran in Washington, D.C. The exhibition convinced me that Danish art would ultimately be recognized in a major way in both America and Europe. It also gave me the courage to continue collecting. *Northern Light* gave Scandinavian art a coming-out forum, reminiscent of the famous 1976 competition in France where American wines held their own against the French.

While in New York City, I took Niels-Jørgen Kaiser, the director of the Tivoli Gardens and a major figure in Denmark's cultural affairs, to meet the chairman and director of the Jewish Museum. We were to discuss the launch of the final major Danish event of *Scandinavia Today*.† His section was a three-part exhibit called *Kings and Citizens: The Jewish Community in Denmark from 1662 to 1983*. It showed paintings and portraits of Danish Jews throughout that period, including one of my ancestor Joseph Hambro, part of the illustrious Hambro banking family (his portrait hangs in

---

* Originally, the NEA featured a new region every year and promoted its history, culture, art and music. Unfortunately, with Reagan's cuts to the NEA, the program was deemed too expensive; *Scandinavia Today* was its last promotion of foreign culture.

† Niels-Jørgen Kaiser became chairman of the Royal Theatre's board of directors in 1992.

Here I am at a White House reception, shaking hands with President Reagan just before I met his guest of honor, Iceland's president, Miss Vigdis Finnbogadóttir. She was in Washington to help kick off the *Scandinavia Today* exhibit, as was I. Nancy Reagan (back to the camera) stands next to President Finnbogadóttir. At the left of President Reagan is his chief of protocol, Selwa Roosevelt.

the Copenhagen "Bourse," Denmark's stock exchange). Therein lies the story of one of my favorite coincidences.

Joseph Hambro was distantly related to my great-grandfather Adolph Lewisohn. Because of my lifelong interest in our family genealogy, I had clipped an article and photo of the Bourse painting of Joseph Hambro from a Danish magazine, which identified the portrait as one of two very similar paintings of him by the foremost Danish artist, C.A. Jensen. Back home in New York, I had the picture framed and placed prominently in the living room. One day, flipping through a Danish art auction catalogue, I stopped at a painting listed simply as *An Unidentified Man*. I was sure it was Joseph Hambro and realized that the painting for sale must be the second of the two known Jensen portraits of him. I bid on it, my bid prevailed, and I turned out to be correct. It was indeed the Jensen portrait of Hambro, who helped turn Denmark's finances around after its losses to the English in the Napoleonic Wars. Had the general public known the painting was of Hambro, the bidding would have been much more robust.

Starting my very first week in Denmark, and continuing until the day I left, visitors and houseguests arrived, almost in droves. Some were official, some invited and some self-invited, but I loved having them all. Playing host is one of my greatest pleasures. My very first Rydhave party was given for the flamboyant composer Leonard

Luck and a good bit of serendipity brought me this portrait of a distant ancestor, Danish financier Joseph Hambro. One of only two painted by C.A. Jensen, the other hangs in the "Bourse," Copenhagen's stock exchange.

Bernstein, held only twenty-four hours after presenting my credentials to the queen. Lenny was in Copenhagen to conduct the 100-piece Vienna Orchestra at the city's Falkoner Theater that night. The party was in full swing at 11:00 p.m. when he and several of his musical entourage arrived. He must have had a good time, since he stayed until 2:00 a.m. A fellow Harvard alum, he learned only that night that I was the brother of two of his good friends, my twin siblings Arthur Loeb and Ann Loeb Bronfman. In another small-world coincidence, we found we had other mutual friends—the Tony D'Almeida family, who had lived with the Loeb family for a period during World War II. A compulsive flirt, Lenny didn't save all his charm for the concert hall and actually tried to flirt with me, before quickly moving on to more viable prospects.

When former President and Mrs. Carter came to Copenhagen on an unofficial visit in May 1982, I met them at the airport and accompanied them to all their planned events. When I was asked to speak at a dinner in his honor, I mentioned my southern "connections," citing my great-grandfather Moses, who had been a captain in the Confederacy. Unfortunately, the way I phrased it made the audience think I was claiming to be a direct descendant of the biblical Moses, which brought a round of hearty laughter, gleefully reported in the press.

Secretary of State Alexander Haig stayed with me at Rydhave for three days when he came to speak to the Danish equivalent of the U.S. Council on Foreign Relations. I thoroughly enjoyed every minute of his visit. It helped that Haig approved of politically ap-

Leonard Bernstein arrived for his party accompanied by Mrs. Hanne Wilhelm Hansen, who had arranged for him to conduct the Vienna Philharmonic Orchestra in Copenhagen. Here I am welcoming them at the front door of Rydhave.

A RIDGELEIGH LAWN PARTY
HONORING PRINCE HENRIK

In honour of His Royal Highness,
Prince Henrik of Denmark
Mr. and Mrs. John L. Loeb
request the pleasure of your company
at a reception
Sunday, the twelfth of September
5:30 - 7:30
Anderson Hill Road
Purchase, New York

The prince and I never ran out of things to discuss, quite apart from our mutual interest in promoting Denmark. We especially liked to talk about our wine vineyards (each of us owned one).

Mother led Prince Henrik to our guests— Loeb family friends, neighbors, and my political allies. Everyone was eager to meet him, and he charmed them all.

Prince Henrik and I are seen here strolling through the handsome grounds of my parents' Ridgeleigh home.

Conversation with Prince Henrik is easy partly because he is a completely engaged and attentive listener. Our trip together in 1982 was the foundation of my warm friendship with Prince Henrik. His portrait has a place of honor in my home.

Translated, this newspaper picture caption reads, "Hold it John, I'll just borrow your fork!", which Bernstein said to the party's host, Ambassador John Langeloth Loeb Jr., at Rydhave. (In the middle: Lenny's best friend in Denmark, the music critic and editor Robert Naur.)

pointed, noncareer diplomats (like me), whereas his successor—George Shultz—did not.* Haig had served as NATO's Supreme Commander in the 1970s, and he shared insights to help me gain more enthusiastic Danish support of NATO. Always a candid man, Haig had more than a few problems during his White House days, no doubt exacerbated by his bluntness and candor. He found me a rapt audience for his behind-the-scenes stories of the contretemps he'd had there. He also explained the flurry of bad press he received when President Reagan was shot in March 1981, and he'd taken the podium and stated that he was "in control here." As Haig tried vainly to explain at the time, the president was alive, so the line of succession was not the question; the issue was that Vice President Bush had not yet returned from Texas, which is where he was when the president was shot. Haig had meant that he was in charge *until Bush returned*, so there would be no chaos and panic at the White House. As Nixon's chief of staff during Watergate, Haig had been the glue that kept the White House together in those last grim days. In March 1981, he had again simply been trying to keep order and maintain calm.

In July 1983, Chief Justice Warren Burger called me on the phone at the embassy. He wanted to visit Denmark and see its prisons. He mentioned that he generally tried to see prisons on his vacation. Would he be able to stay with me? Of course, I said. So in August, Chief Justice Burger was my guest at Rydhave, accompanied by his wife, Elvera, Senator Mark Hatfield, Representative Robert Kastenmeier and Utah state senator Karl Snow. Also with him were Norman Carlson, director of the U.S. Federal Bureau of Prisons, and J. Albert Woll, general counsel of the AFL-CIO. Denmark's minister of justice, Erik Ninn-Hansen, was one of the country's leaders who took part in hosting their prison visit.

---

* Shultz felt only career diplomats should serve in ambassadorial posts. Not too surprisingly, I would find Shultz to be quite prickly.

Secretary of State Alexander Haig and I were in the dining room of Rydhave when this photo of us was shot.

When George P. Shultz became secretary of state in July 1982, I immediately flew to meet with him in Washington. We are pictured together in his office there.

On a tour of the state prison at Vridsløselille, Justice Burger was shocked that conjugal visits were allowed and that relationships between male and female prisoners were not discouraged.

"Well, I certainly wouldn't allow that in my prisons," the chief justice said.

Some unidentified brave soul spoke up and said, "Well, they're *not* your prisons, Mr. Justice."

My guest list for a party to honor Justice Burger's visit caused one of my many confrontations with Jørgen Werner, my chief of protocol, who was not happy that mere lawyers were to be invited. "Lawyers have never been invited to a social occasion at Rydhave," he sniffed. Nevertheless, they were invited; of course they were the perfect guests to discuss Denmark's legal system with Burger and his entourage.

One of my best friends and my Harvard classmate, former state senator Roy Goodman, came to Copenhagen to visit me as well. Roy represented the Twenty-Sixth District of our state for thirty-three years, one of the longest tenures in New York's history. Our political roots went deep: he had been the leader of the liberal Rockefeller wing of the

Chief Justice Warren Burger came to Denmark in 1983 for a tour of Denmark's prisons. Quite a few members of his large entourage stayed with me at Rydhave. He sent me this photo after his visit.

Republican Party at the same time I became chairman of Rockefeller's Council of Environmental Advisors. Roy served as the GOP chair of New York County for twenty years and was a key figure in New York Republican politics his entire life.

Another warm visit was from Mr. and Mrs. Frank Carlucci. Frank was Reagan's deputy secretary of defense. Besides being Reagan stalwarts, Frank and I were Harvard Business School alumni. I was also delighted to host a celebratory dinner at Rydhave for my friend Samuel J. LeFrak, who made his name and fortune with development projects such as Battery Park City in Manhattan and LeFrak City in Queens. He was on his way back to the United States after receiving the Order of the Lion from Finland.* A few years later, Sam was also recognized by the UN for his global contributions through Habitat International.

The visit to Rydhave of a fellow environmentalist, Russell Train, was particularly meaningful to me. Russell had been President Nixon's first chair of the White House Council on Environmental Quality. Under President Ford, he served as head of the Environmental Protection Agency from 1973 to 1977. He was my go-to person in Washington in the early 1970s, when I chaired Governor Rockefeller's State Council of Environmental Advisors, and the keynote speaker at our council's first environmental workshop in 1971. He had been invited to speak in Copenhagen by a major environmental group, and he was impressed by how environmentally conscious the Danes were. Denmark was a pioneer in developing commercial wind power as far back as the 1970s, and today, wind power furnishes over 30 percent of Denmark's electricity.

Much to my delight, a close friend of many years, the international banker and New York philanthropist Ezra Zilkha brought his easygoing charm to the U.S. embassy in Denmark on one of his countless business trips. Ezra can trace his ancestry back to Baghdad

---

* Sam was so excited about the award that he compared it to a knighthood, though Finland has no monarchy.

and the Jewish community of Nebuchadnezzar's day. In 1998, he wrote a compelling memoir, *From Baghdad to Boardrooms: My Family's Odyssey.*

My Danish cousin Oscar Lewisohn remembers Rydhave visits warmly, as well. He and his wife, Margaret, attended functions at Rydhave while I was ambassador and wrote that I am "clearly a gentleman with a zest for life and a sense of humor." I'd met Oscar in the 1970s in New York City, where, as executive director of the London-based investment bank S.G. Warburg, he had occasional business. Not long after my arrival in Copenhagen, a coincidence helped us reunite.

A Danish businessman named Torben Lenzberg was at the embassy quite frequently. He had three little girls who would run around the house and play with Nicholas, and I remember my son was always embarrassed because the girls always took their clothes off to go swimming. Torben needed help with some trade issues with the United States about his meat importing business. (One of my ambassadorial responsibilities was liaising between Danish businessmen and appropriate officials in the U.S., usually in the Commerce Department.) Mr. Lenzberg and I became friendly over the course of these frequent meetings, and, at some point, I must have mentioned that I had Danish relatives named Lewisohn. Torben came to discuss a business problem one day and announced that he'd just had dinner with some of my relatives, which is how I learned that Oscar Lewisohn's mother and three sisters lived in Copenhagen. I invited them to Ryd-have, and the fine piece of Flora Danica they brought me was the beginning of my collection of Denmark's famous bone china. Oscar and I have been friends ever since.

There was nonstop entertaining at Rydhave. There were meetings, large and small, relating to matters in Denmark, and then a steady stream of friends who wanted to see Denmark and see me as an ambassador.

The Falklands War in 1982 created an enormous amount of discussion, debate and dissension in Danish political circles. It was extremely controversial—the Great English Empire had, in effect, declared war against the tiny Falkland Islands. This created a great deal of anti-English feelings.

State Senator Roy Goodman, one of my dearest friends, was a particularly welcome guest at Rydhave. He is pictured with me here at a Republican event sometime in the 1990s.

Winston Spencer Churchill with his wife, Minnie d'Erlanger, meeting with the British ambassador to Denmark, Dame Anne Warburton, at my residence. My son, Nicholas, is looking up at the British ambassador, and I believe I am unseen on the side of the British ambassador.

"Young" Winston Churchill and I had become great friends over the years. He was, for many years, one of the trustees of the Winston Churchill Foundation in the United States, of which I was president. Because of all the debates about the Falklands War, I wrote and suggested to Winston that he and Minnie, his wife, come for a weekend. I also suggested that there were a number of venues in Copenhagen where he could speak about the war. He said he wanted to come but couldn't afford it. I said I would love him to come, and I would pay for it, but he refused that.

At that time, there was a unique news program on English television every week that dealt not only with political news, but also with unusual stories at times. Winston dreamt up the extraordinary plan that he would come to Denmark and debate the Argentinian ambassador to Denmark. Incredibly, he sold this idea to the news program, and they paid for his trip to Copenhagen, which included a team of photographers. By some miracle, I persuaded the very distinguished Argentinian ambassador to participate in such a debate.

I arranged for the debate to be held in a large auditorium in Copenhagen on a Saturday night. The place was full to the brim, with many people outside wanting to get in, and, of course, an endless number of photographers and press.

It was an unfair debate, because the Argentinian ambassador was not used to debating, and this was one of Winston's fortes. Needless to say, Winston overwhelmingly won the debate, after which there were endless questions from the floor to both Winston and the ambassador.

I must mention two other memorable Rydhave visitors whom I was delighted to host. The opera star Beverly Sills lived up to her reputation as a real charmer; I quickly realized why she was known to her friends as "Bubbles." Equally charming, if less ebullient, was the "most trusted man in America," the legendary news anchor Walter Cronkite. Cronkite had recently retired, and he was a relaxed and congenial guest at Rydhave.*

The ever affable Walter Cronkite was the 1967 honored speaker at the annual Rebild celebration, which is when he first fell in love with Denmark. He is pictured here on a 1983 return visit when he was my guest at Rydhave.

June 1983 was an unusually busy month. For one thing, I'd been playing catch-up after a quick trip to the States. Upon my return, I had to focus on preparations for my next visitor. Vice President Bush was scheduled for some major events in Denmark in July, so the embassy staff and I were up to our ears in a flurry of cables between us and the State Department, planning and arranging all the details attendant to his visit. I'd known George from when he was a congressman in the late 1960s and early 1970s, and we'd been friendly ever since; I was really looking forward to being with him and Barbara for several days. Obviously, the next few weeks were going to be even busier than usual. Little did I know that the days ahead would be more difficult than I could possibly have imagined. The course of my life was about to be changed by an unexpected phone call from Air Force One.

---

* Cronkite had been the honored guest speaker at the 1967 Independence Day celebration at Rebild and had fallen in love with Denmark.

My pipe was reassuring during a somewhat tense meeting held during the Bush visit to discuss Denmark's reluctant membership in NATO.

CHAPTER FIFTEEN

Farvel Danmark, 1983

"Vice President Bush is on the line, Mr. Ambassador," my secretary sang out. I picked up immediately, certain George had something on his mind about his upcoming visit. It was June 9, 1983. I was expecting him and his entourage in Denmark in less than a month.

"John," he began, "President Reagan wants you to come home in about three months. I will explain this to you." Before I could ask why, the vice president continued, "You've been doing a very good job, John, and he really appreciates all you've done and are doing, but he has to move Ambassador Todman from Spain to Denmark. He'd like to find you another diplomatic post, but in the meantime he'd like you to serve as a public delegate to the thirty-eighth session of the UN General Assembly convening in September."

To say the least, I was shocked and enormously disappointed. Why was this happening? I tried to control myself. If Dick Allen, my dear friend, were still Reagan's national security advisor, this would not be happening. I was a political appointee, and shifts of appointments like mine frequently became necessary. My last State Department report had been stellar, so I tried not to take it personally; I knew this must be a case of "ambassadorial musical chairs." A president sometimes needs the post for another person important to the administration for one reason or another. To make room, someone—in most cases a political appointee—gets removed.

I asked George if I might be offered another ambassadorial post, and when that might happen. He said that the current change wouldn't take place for several months; and although a new post for me might be in the offing, he urged me to take the UN appointment. With great self-control, I, of course, told George I would accept, though I hoped for anoth-

After Vice President Bush's arrival in Denmark, I reviewed details of his schedule with him in Rydhave's sunroom. Seated next to the vice president is one of his aides taking notes, with my son, Nicholas, quietly looking on.

er diplomatic appointment. I told him how glad I was that I would be in Copenhagen for his and Barbara's visit. We began to discuss plans for him, Barbara and some of their group to stay with me at Rydhave.

After the call I sat quietly, absorbing the import of the vice president's call and how it affected me personally. I was also thinking ahead to all that had to be done before I was to leave in the fall.

On July 3, a few weeks after the Bush phone call, Prime Minister Schlüter and I greeted George and Barbara Bush at the airport. For the good of NATO and Denmark, it was vitally important that our vice president and Schlüter spend time together.

The financially pressed Danes had already indicated their intention of suspending their payments to NATO. Ever since I arrived in Copenhagen almost two years ago, I had been forceful in pressing upon Prime Minister Anker Jørgensen and now Prime Minister Schlüter that all that stood between them and Soviet missiles was NATO. George Bush could be of great help in my diplomatic efforts to persuade the Danish government to pay its fair share to NATO, because the Danes needed a strong NATO for their protection.

The avalanche of press releases my staff and I generated for the Bush visit paid off handsomely. It was front page news that our vice president would make the keynote address at the country's annual outdoor celebration of America's Independence Day at Rebild, a 190-acre park in northern Denmark. Every Fourth of July, the Danes celebrate America's

Air Force II flew the Bushes and me to Aalborg, the northern city closest to Rebild park. We were accompanied by three Danish officials and two of their wives. Pictured here, third from the left, is Foreign Minister Eigil Jørgensen, who would soon be named Danish ambassador to the U.S. I can be seen behind George Bush.

independence at Rebild; this has become a huge public event at which prestigious Americans are honored and asked to make an address. Dr. Max Henius, a Dane who became wealthy in the United States, began the annual event back in 1912. Along with other grateful Danish Americans, Henius had bought the acreage for Denmark as a gift. It became the locale for an annual gathering of Danish Americans and Danes of all stripes.

The vice president's participation at the Rebild festival turned into a diplomatic challenge. Once again the issue of security was raised. The State Department's advance team made a fuss about Vice President Bush's giving a speech to a huge crowd in a vast open-air location. They weren't confident he could be adequately protected outdoors. When I suggested to Prime Minister Schlüter that the address be given somewhere indoors, he was adamant.

"No," he said. "Vice President Bush must speak outdoors at Rebild, and he must not cancel. There will be no risk *whatsoever.* This isn't Woodstock, you know," he added huffily. (I was surprised Schlüter had even heard of the 1960s music festival.)

Eigil Jørgensen, director of the Danish Foreign Ministry, was even more obstinate. He added that it would be "most unfortunate for Danish-American relations and the grass-roots view of Denmark's place in the Atlantic Alliance if your vice president doesn't speak outdoors at the Rebild festival." Danish opinion about intermediate-range nuclear forces (INFs) was a grave concern to the U.S., and discussing it with Danish officials was one of the key reasons for Bush's visit.

**REBILD PARK
ON JULY 4, 1983**

Here I am wearing my bulletproof raincoat as I introduce the Rebild guest of honor, Vice President Bush.

I convinced Washington that the Danes would supply the heavy security they proposed for Rebild, and the U.S. advance team finally capitulated. I also reminded them that Vice President Hubert Humphrey had been a Rebild speaker some years earlier, and there had been no problems. In the end, Bush's speech was warmly received without incident by an enormous crowd in the fresh air at Rebild.

During his visit, George and I only briefly discussed the president's need to replace me as Denmark's ambassador. I told him it was a comfort that my successor would be Terence Todman, a brilliant career diplomat and the most outstanding black ambassador in our history.* I held no hard feelings toward Todman, the vice president or the president, but I did feel like the greatest opportunity of my diplomatic career was being pulled right out from under me. There was nothing I could do about it, but I had given it my all.

During my remaining months as ambassador, one important task was to prepare for an upcoming September visit from Max Kampelman. I wouldn't be there for Kampelman's visit, but it was my job to ensure that everything was put in place for it. A powerful advocate of human rights, Kampelman was a State Department emissary who served as a leading negotiator with the Communists under both Presidents Carter and Reagan. He is

---

* Terence and I would become good friends; years later, when he was serving as ambassador to Argentina, I stayed with him in the official residence in Buenos Aires, where we traded stories about our respective times in Copenhagen.

Vice President of the United States George Bush, the 1983 honoree at Rebild, speaking to a crowd of over 600,000 people.

credited with the evolution of Reagan's Zero Option speech.[x] As ambassador to the Conference on Security and Cooperation in Europe (CSCE), he advanced global awareness of the Soviets' human rights abuses; he was to speak about them in Copenhagen. Known for "naming names" and citing specific cases of human rights abuses in the Soviet bloc countries, he was always a compelling speaker.

Our embassy sent out six hundred copies of one of Kampelman's best-known human rights speeches to other chiefs of mission in Denmark, enclosed with invitations to the event. We received two hundred acceptances, and the leading newspapers published the speeches in its entirety. Kampelman's persuasiveness on these issues would be much needed in Denmark, a country that didn't adequately perceive the Soviet threat.

Ironically, one of my last challenges was a resurrection of the "Jørgensen problem." Though out of power, Anker Jørgensen was still the leader of the Social Democratic Party, and he was busy vehemently criticizing U.S. policies concerning Central America and NATO. Though I liked Anker, I was not sorry to leave his complaints to my successor.

During events held in my honor throughout the last days of my tenure, I was warmed by the kind remarks of both my embassy and Rydhave staffs. They also assured me that I

---

* The "Zero Option speech," given by President Reagan on November 18, 1981, was the first time a world leader had suggested that every country dismantle its nuclear weapons. I was able to get Reagan's entire speech on Denmark's sole TV station, which was controlled by the Socialist government. This was quite a coup. Denmark's leading newspaper ran the headline "From Cowboy to Statesman."

My staffs at the embassy and Rydhave gathered to honor me shortly before I left Copenhagen. At the gathering, Deputy Chief of Mission Theodore Russell presented me with a framed copy of the group photo taken just a few weeks earlier.

A few weeks before I returned to the United States, my ambassadorial staff and I posed for a picture on the steps of the American embassy in Copenhagen.

had lived up to the "Boy Scout Rule" of leaving the campgrounds better than I had found them. The embassy grounds were certainly *safer*, something Terry Todman appreciated when he arrived. I was particularly moved by the remarks made at a farewell luncheon at the Danish Foreign Ministry. Among those attending the event were Foreign Minister Ellemann-Jensen; Deputy Prime Minister and Finance Minister Henning Christophersen; Niels Norland, editor of the conservative newspaper; my friends Maersk Mc-Kinney Moller of A.P. Møller–Maersk; and Niels-Jørgen Kaiser, CEO of Tivoli Gardens. I appreciated their recognition of the initiatives I valued most myself. The foreign minister cited the stronger connections between our two nations and the increased trade between the United States and Denmark. He also noted my activity in promoting Danish culture, saying,

> *During my visit to Rebild with the vice president, he and I had the opportunity to point to the historic and strong ties between Denmark and the United States based upon a close community of outlook and ideals. . . . Your mission here has served that purpose, John, and we are grateful for your contribution.*

The final events during my last few weeks and days brought me almost to tears. At my last meeting with Her Majesty Queen Margrethe and Prince Henrik, the queen said that during my tenure in Denmark, popular support for NATO had reached unprecedented

Designed especially for me, this Danish coat of arms may be used in perpetuity by my family as well.

Here is my Grand Cross of the Order of Dannebrog. This award is likened to a knighthood, and I was told by a Danish official that, before me, no American ambassador had ever received one.

I treasure this portrait of the Danish royal family, and am grateful that our friendship has held strong all through the years. Left to right are Prince Joachim, Queen Margrethe II, Prince Henrik and Crown Prince Frederik.

levels. She added that she had great respect for and confidence in me, both personally and officially, before presenting me with the Grand Cross of the Order of Dannebrog. It is the highest-ranking decoration in the Dannebrog Order, awarded outside the royal family, one of the most important and prestigious awards Denmark gives, and is considered equivalent to a knighthood.* The queen also presented me with a Danish coat of arms to be used by my family in perpetuity. The Danish authorities and I would work out the exact design of the coat of arms later, in order to differentiate it from all others. After my return to the States, at a lunch with Denmark's ambassador to the United States, Eigil Jørgensen, I learned that not all ambassadors to Denmark receive the Dannebrog Grand Cross. In fact, Jørgensen told me that no American ambassador before me had ever received it and that it was usually given only to Danish citizens for extraordinary meritorious service.

I was enormously pleased by a gracious letter from Alexander Haig, who had been secretary of state during the early part of my tenure. I cannot resist including it here:

> *John,*
>
> *Just in case I never put it in writing, let me tell you how much I admired your distinguished service in Copenhagen. Your effectiveness in representing American interests and views, your success in winning the good will and understanding of the Danish government and people—indeed, your professional and personal conduct as a whole—earned the respect and admiration of the government and people of Denmark, the colleagues with whom you served in the U.S. State Department and others such as myself who served in the Administration of President Reagan. Thank you for the great contribution you made.*
>
> *Al Haig*

My last two weeks were focused on leaving things in good shape for Ambassador Todman, as well as gathering and packing all the things I'd managed to accumulate over the past two years. The cable that went out from my DCM right after I left read,

> *Ambassador departed post September 17 upon termination of duty. I am in charge. Signed: [Theodore] Russell.*

---

* There are four categories in the Order of the Dannebrog. The first is called the "Special Class," given only to royalty, and the only category higher than the Grand Cross.

The two years I spent in Copenhagen as America's ambassador to the Kingdom of Denmark were two of the most important years of my life, if not *the* most important. I never worked so hard, nor have I ever had a more meaningful and fascinating experience. According to the glowing evaluation of my work, the White House and the State Department were pleased with what I accomplished.

In my last performance evaluation of April 14, 1983, Richard Burt, the assistant secretary of state for European affairs and subsequently ambassador to Germany, to whom I reported, highlighted my success in improving relationships with U.S. businesses in Denmark, noting praise from senior executives at Honeywell, Ford and Manpower, Inc. He also underscored the increase of commercial activity between our countries, especially agricultural trade, and praised my "grasp of the substantive issues and the interplay of politics and personalities in Denmark," adding that I was "alert and adaptive in dealing with all aspects of Danish culture."

Given the Burt Report, the positive feedback via the State Department and my remarks reported in *The New York Times*, I was initially fairly confident that I would receive another post after serving as a UN delegate. Unfortunately, it was not to be.

Naïvely, I hadn't factored in the influence of my friend and ally Richard Allen, who had nurtured my appointment to Denmark. Allen had since left the Reagan administration, and there was now no one close to the president who had my back. In fact, two people who had initially strongly opposed my appointment were currently in Reagan's favor. Helene von Damm and Mike Deaver had vigorously opposed my original appointment because they thought I hadn't contributed enough money to the Reagan campaign for the position. As Reagan's personal assistant, Helene no doubt also remembered a phone call I had with Reagan early in the 1980 campaign.

"John," he had said, "I'd like to announce you as one of the first hundred supporters to endorse me." At the time, I had been thinking about running against Al D'Amato for the Javits Senate seat and countered his request.

"Well, Governor," I said, "would you consider supporting me for the Senate?"

He gave his famous little chuckle—"heh heh heh"—and said, "Well, you know, John, I believe in the eleventh commandment." This was his well-known policy of never speaking ill of another Republican or backing one Republican over another. (Perhaps it didn't occur to him that he was asking me to do the same thing!) Because of his unwillingness to support my candidacy, I didn't become one of his "First Hundred." Though Reagan forgave me, I don't think Helene von Damm ever did.

Helene's disapproval of my appointment had become public a year after I arrived in

Copenhagen. The journalist Elizabeth Drew mentioned it in the December 13, 1982, issue of *The New Yorker*, in the second part of her in-depth article titled "Politics and Money." Drew wrote,

> *John Loeb, Jr., who is now ambassador to Denmark, was also helpful to the Reagan campaign. He gave a thousand dollars to Reagan and twenty-five hundred to one of the "independent committees" that were formed on Reagan's behalf, and, more important, he helped raise money for Reagan in New York. Yet the major reason for Loeb's getting the ambassadorship, according to Reagan sources, was that he had curried favor with such people as [Justin] Dart and [Holmes] Tuttle. Helene von Damm, Reagan's executive assistant, had the role of seeing that the Reagan supporters got government jobs. (Miss von Damm was later made head of the personnel office.) Miss von Damm is said to have been indignant over Loeb's appointment; she felt that he had not raised enough money to earn it, in comparison with, say, [Labor leader Ray] Donovan.[104]**

Helene was never willing to acknowledge that my personal financial contribution was not what brought me the ambassadorial post. It was my early and effective support of the Reagan candidacy in New York, a reliably Democratic state. Despite Reagan's successful years as California's governor, most New Yorkers at the time still thought of him as a B-movie actor, but I recognized and publicly touted his potential. I was among his most vigorous supporters in his bid for the Republican nomination in 1976 and again in 1980. I buttonholed both Republican and Democratic friends, persuading even liberal Jewish Democrats to back Reagan and help me campaign for him. Reagan ended up with an impressive 40 percent of the New York Jewish vote in 1980 and again in 1984. Von Damm apparently didn't recognize the value in all this.

In *The New Yorker* article, Helene gives credit for my appointment to the influence of Reagan's California Kitchen Cabinet members Justin Dart and Holmes Tuttle. It was Richard Allen who deserved *all* the credit for having the White House's ear regarding my appointment. Allen also ensured that the early and effective support I helped coalesce, especially among the Jewish community, was never forgotten by the Reagans.

Time has healed some of the wounds from my removal, but at the time I was hurt

---

* Many people believed I had given substantial sums of money to receive my ambassadorship. In fact, as Elizabeth Drew said in her article in *The New Yorker*, I only gave $3,500. As to the Kitchen Cabinet, I was friendly with Justin Dart and Holmes Tuttle, but they were not important at all in regard to my ambassadorship.

about the choice to take me out of Denmark.* I knew I was doing a very good job, and to have something so important taken from me for political reasons just seemed unjust; the anger took some time to subside. If I were to make a list of "should haves" that might have landed me another ambassadorial post, the first thing on the list would be that I "should have" made a more enthusiastic effort to win Helene's approval. When I first met her, supporting Perry Duryea, she was Reagan's secretary, but after the 1980 election she rose in the ranks and became a key figure in Reagan's White House. My crystal ball had been foggy, and I hadn't focused on the depth of her influence. I did take her to lunch early in my quest to be an ambassador, but only once. Not trying harder to win her favor was a big mistake on my part. It no doubt hindered—in fact, likely ended—my diplomatic career.

I learned that a series of shifts in other ambassadorial posts were what triggered Terence Todman's taking my place in Denmark, much of it tied to the Iran-Contra scandal. Reagan had a deep concern for the inroads Communism was making in Central America. In November 1981, President Reagan authorized money (some sources say as much as one million dollars a day) for CIA military aid to guerrilla groups cumulatively known as the "Contras," an umbrella group fighting Nicaragua's Communist Sandinista government. The Sandinistas were a group of revolutionaries who, in 1979, had ousted the dictator Anastasio "Tachito" Somoza DeBayle, whose family had been in power since 1936. At the outset, the U.S. had supported the Sandinistas; however, when they set up a Communist-type government, Reagan began supporting the Contras. Unfortunately, the Contras were so brutal that Congress didn't care that they were anti-Communist and passed legislation to end U.S. support. When Reagan circumvented the congressional roadblocks by selling arms to Iran and using the profit to help the Contras, a scandal was born, forever known as "Iran-Contra."

In 1982, Ambassador Thomas O. Enders was the assistant secretary of state for inter-American affairs, and he was very well respected throughout the diplomatic community. However, he had publicly denounced the Contras' brutality and thus could not approve

---

* I don't know if one believes in Karma Kickback. Helene von Damm, who came from a very modest Austrian family, personally appointed herself to be ambassador of Austria when she was head of personnel. Then she divorced her American husband and married one of Austria's most eligible men. Jealousy by the Austrians was so great that Helene had to be recalled. Subsequently, her husband committed suicide. As for Mr. Deaver (whom I also couldn't reach during my two years as ambassador or before), he appeared on the cover of *Time* magazine with a telephone in his hand calling someone. The implication was he was speaking to the president of the United States. Immediately thereafter, he tried to start a public relations firm. However, Walter Annenberg, a great friend of Ronald Reagan and formerly ambassador to United Kingdom under Nixon, was furious with the way Deaver treated his wife, who was Reagan's chief of protocol at the time. He let all his friends and colleagues know not to have anything to do with Deaver. Mike never got his PR firm established. During this time he fell into a period of heavy drinking and almost died.

of U.S. aid to them. Reagan fired Enders because of his opposition to the Contras, but the president did not tell Secretary of State Shultz beforehand. This left Shultz with an unwelcome fait accompli, and he pressed the president unusually hard to find a comparably prestigious post for Enders.* Enders wanted to be ambassador to Spain, but the current ambassador, Terence Todman, was also an especially valued statesman. If Enders went to Spain, he would displace the most important black diplomat in the Foreign Service.

Born on St. Thomas in the U.S. Virgin Islands, Todman was on a fast upward track in U.S. diplomacy. Given how strongly the Danes believed that America did not treat its black citizens well, Todman's appointment was a smart diplomatic move. In fact, I had invited Todman to Denmark for a short visit, hoping that the presence of this highly ranked diplomat could help neutralize the hold that Jacob Holdt's book had on Danish opinion. Todman's appointment would be a strong statement to Denmark that U.S. race relations were not as problematic as they had been portrayed by Holdt. So to whose post would it be best to move Todman? Apparently, mine. It was ironic that I was being ousted because of a political concern that I had championed in my role as ambassador.

I also remembered my mother's Cassandra-like warning just before I took office. "You know, Johnny," she said, "you really shouldn't be an ambassador without a wife." I had given my work all the passion I could give. Perhaps marriage would have rounded me out more. But my minimal romantic life did not seem a credible cause for withdrawing an effective ambassador, which some critics believed. I felt I was an eligible, divorced man living a fairly isolated life in the sprawling expanse of the American embassy. Apparently any appearance I made with a woman on my arm was grist for the rumor mill. I had never given it much thought, because most Scandinavians appeared to be more open-minded about bachelor lifestyles than many Americans. Times have changed in our country. Thirty years later, New York City's popular mayor Michael Bloomberg and New York State's popular governor Andrew Cuomo would both live openly with women to whom they were not married, with little or no public disapproval. Several people in Copenhagen also told me that there had been another bachelor U.S. ambassador to Denmark, Robert Coe of Wyoming, who had been a career diplomat and "Mr. Perfect." Well, Mr. Perfect ended up falling in love and leaving with the Rydhave butler! In another notice of how times have changed, the most recent ambassador to Denmark, Rufus Gifford, is gay and brought his lover to live with him at Rydhave.

---

* I became good friends both with Tom and his talented wife, Gaetana, who made her own mark in world affairs during Tom's extensive diplomatic career. Sadly, both have recently died.

On the other hand, maybe Mother was right—back in 1981 perhaps I should have been a married man. The bachelor issue and the Danish press's misleading coverage of my private life could have been a factor in my removal. Also, I probably hadn't endeared myself to State Department insiders with my fussing about security in Denmark. I've finally concluded that all of these issues combined to kill any hope of being offered another post. Nevertheless, my friendship with the Reagans never wavered.

Mother in front of the United States Mission to the United Nations.

CHAPTER SIXTEEN

≡

United Nations, 1983–1984

On September 17, 1983, I left Copenhagen to take up my new post as a representative of the United States delegation to the thirty-eighth session of the United Nations General Assembly. It would convene in just five days, so off I flew to a new challenge and a new, though a brief, life chapter. I was sworn in as one of our country's five delegates, along with five alternates, all appointed by President Reagan. We were given the requisite approval from the U.S. Senate (though this time I was not questioned by the Foreign Relations Committee), and we were all duly fingerprinted, sworn in as a group and awarded security clearance.

Now officially representing the United States, I joined our formidable ambassador to the UN, Jeane F. Kirkpatrick, who had been appointed to the cabinet-level post by President Reagan in 1981. In her position, Kirkpatrick dealt with foreign ministers of other countries, but it was no secret that she had more than a few heated skirmishes with Secretary of State Haig about who was in charge of American foreign policy. He would have been delighted to have had her removed from the UN, but she had Reagan's admiration and support. Jeane held her own in this battle of large egos and survived a controversial tenure at the UN from 1981 to 1985. Under her leadership, our team would speak about the United States' positions on a host of issues to the representatives of all of the UN's member nations. We spoke not only at committee meetings, but also frequently to the entire General Assembly, many of whose members were not fans of the United States.

Mother's work as the New York City Commissioner for the United Nations and the Consular Corps from 1966 to 1978 paved the way for many warm welcomes when I first set foot in those busy halls. "Oh, are you by any chance related to Frances Loeb? I knew her when she was here—a wonderful woman," was a not infrequent greeting from various long-term UN staff members. I was happy to say I was, indeed, the proud son of the lady who had spent twelve years at her full-time but unsalaried job, which was to welcome, help, advise and entertain New York City's thirty thousand members of the diplomatic and consular corps. Appointed by both Mayors John Lindsay and Abraham Beame, she was, to the great dismay of all diplomats, unceremoniously removed in 1978 by Mayor Koch when he took office. What Mother managed to do with a small staff and a miniscule budget (she spent a lot of time fundraising for her UN commission) is today handled by the Mayor's Office for International Affairs. The *Herald Tribune* had once written a wonderful editorial about her, and the headline of her *New York Times* obituary read "Lifesaver to Foreign Diplomats."

As I tried to fold my six-foot four-inch frame into what was essentially a cubicle, I had to come to terms with no longer being the "big cheese." Among other ego-shrinkers, a personal assistant would not be at my beck and call. In Copenhagen, I had gotten used to two full staffs, one at the residence and another at the embassy. On a more important level, my pride in American power and leadership was affronted by the fact that though the United States bears the largest burden of the costs of the UN, we get only one vote. Smaller countries constantly swap votes, acting as a bloc to support each other's positions, which are often contrary to America's. It was a UN fact of life that I had trouble swallowing.

Nevertheless, I dug in and began to do some homework about the "not so united" United Nations. Learning UN acronyms was only one of my first challenges. Surely, I thought, mastering the unique language of the United Nations couldn't be any more difficult than learning Danish. But it nearly was. Fortunately, multipage lists for the acronyms and a glossary of uniquely UN terms were provided. My copies of both publications were soon worn at the edges. Acronyms such as UNGA (United Nations General Assembly) were obvious, but ones like ABLOS (Advisory Board on the Law of the Sea) and ACABQ (Advisory Committee on Administrative and Budgetary Questions) were much less decipherable.

I found Ambassador Kirkpatrick business-like, efficient and—contrary to some opinions—easy to work with, possibly because we saw eye-to-eye on most key issues. She quickly assessed my background and appointed me to two committees, one on arms control, because of my work with NATO, and the other involving Cuba. I was well informed on America's ongoing friction with "our neighbor" because of my family's large investment in a Cuban sugar company just prior to the country's turning

Communist.* I was quite familiar with the machinations of Cuba's government under Castro, and on October 7, 1983, I made my first speech to the General Assembly. It was a rebuttal to an outrageous and tedious address given two days earlier by the Cuban representative. Among other inflammatory assertions, he had denounced U.S. policies as a threat to peace. It was clear that the Soviet lackey had timed his remarks to coincide with American-Russian negotiations taking place right then in Geneva. (Our proposals were being received coldly by the Soviets.) I made my speech pointedly short, zeroing in on the ongoing Russian resistance to serious negotiations to stem the arms race.†

I noted Cuba's subservience to its Soviet master and mentioned that Cuba's own government had come about through brutal, repressive tactics. "In the interest of time and respect for the limits of this body's endurance," I ended with, "let me conclude by paraphrasing the Danish philosopher Kierkegaard, that it was strange that when Cuban representatives look at the world around them, they only perceive projections of their own attitudes and practices."

On September 19, just three days prior to my joining the UN delegation, there had been a much-publicized skirmish about our country's permanent hosting of the United Nations. It began with the events of September 1, 1983, when Soviet fighter jets shot down, in the Sea of Japan, a Korean airliner on its way from Anchorage, Alaska, to Seoul. All 269 people aboard, including Larry McDonald, a U.S. congressman from Georgia, were killed. The Soviets claimed their airspace had been deliberately invaded, and they had been forced to take defensive action. Incensed by this Soviet overreaction, the New York and New Jersey state legislatures immediately passed laws banning Soviet aircraft from landing in their states—effectively preventing Soviet leaders from attending the UN session.

President Reagan, however, thought the legislation ill advised and offered the Soviets landing rights at a U.S. military base, making it possible for the Soviet minister of foreign affairs, Andrei Gromyko, to fly in for the General Assembly meeting. Despite this olive branch, the Soviets boycotted the meeting.

In an urgent meeting called by the UN Host Country Relations Committee, the Soviet delegate, Igor Yakovlev, suggested that with the ban on Soviet planes landing in New York and New Jersey, the UN should perhaps move out of the United States altogether. Incensed, U.S. delegate Charles Mark Lichenstein retorted that the Russians should consider remov-

---

* After Castro's takeover in 1959, our property was summarily confiscated by the new regime. I have tried in recent years to get in touch with his government, including through my acquaintance with Gabriel García Márquez, but to no avail. Perhaps with the lifted embargo, things may change.

† Although the 1979 SALT II agreement went through, it only addressed a specific limitation on certain arms.

ing themselves from the United States, and that "the members of the U.S. Mission to the UN will be down at the dockside waving you a fond farewell as you sail off into the sunset."

This less than diplomatic pronouncement was not endorsed by the Reagan administration, which quickly and forcefully denied that the United States wanted the Soviets out of the UN. This was the diplomatic tightrope our delegation was walking just as I arrived on the scene. Calmer heads prevailed, and the UN stayed put, although the issue still comes up with regularity.*

There were various reasons for me to make public statements to the General Assembly over the next few months. Occasionally, remarks made by other members called for vigorous statements or rebuttals, and sometimes I spoke to explain and amplify the reasons for a vote made by the American Mission. One time I addressed the General Assembly at length regarding an assortment of proposals on the nuclear freeze, which were attracting a lot of press and public attention. The Soviets wanted to "freeze" the nuclear armaments we each currently had, but it was at a point where U.S. arms were of a significantly lower grade than theirs. Ours were fifteen years old, while theirs were only five years old. Obviously, we objected. Most of my public statements concerned NATO and the prevention of nuclear war.

When I was ambassador to Denmark, I had always made room on my calendar for any Americans who asked to see me. One day during my tenure, when I returned to my office after speaking to a group of young Danes, I found a family from North Dakota waiting to see me. My guests were Dr. Larry R. Peterson, a North Dakota University professor, and his two young sons, Geoff, 14, and Erik, 12. When I mentioned the talk I'd just made to young Danish students, Geoff asked if I would come and speak to one of his classes in Fargo when I returned to the United States. Erik, his brother, echoed the invitation. I promised to come "someday."

Feeling a need for a short break from UN duties, I decided to make good on my promise to the Peterson family, and so, in December 1983, I visited North Dakota. I phoned young Geoff, who was thrilled to hear why I was calling. He said he would "arrange things." I was pleasantly surprised to be met at the Fargo airport not only by the Peterson family, but also by Governor Allen Olson's representative, who had driven down from Bismarck to greet me.

It was a whirlwind forty-eight hours. The Peterson brothers had lined up more appearances and talks than I thought could possibly be squeezed into one day. In my

---

* In my address to the General Assembly on October 7, 1983, I referenced Cuba's puppet-like support of the Soviet shoot-down of the Korean commercial airliner, which was a wholly unnecessary flexing of air power muscle.

speech to Geoff's social studies class, I was candid regarding my reservations about the UN. I spoke of my dismay at discovering the UN's funding of terrorist groups such as the Palestine Liberation Army and the Southwest Africa People's Organization (SWA-PO). I mentioned the Soviet downing of Korean Airline Flight 007 and the difficulty the United States had in squeezing out nine of fifteen votes in the Security Council to condemn the obviously heinous action.

Besides the speech to the social studies class, I answered questions in a geography class, a journalism class and a German language class. All of the students were delighted to meet a "real ambassador" for the first time. At a student press conference, I was peppered with questions from young budding journalists, who asked discerning and informed questions about NATO and U.S. missiles in Europe.

At the end of the school day, Principal Warren Gullickson thanked me profusely and pointed out that the "great thing is that these boys have arranged it all themselves." I was then bustled off to the state university audience to speak about the UN. From Fargo, I was driven to Bismarck, where I met Governor Olson and Secretary of State Ben Meier, along with various other political figures. Their offices were housed in the towering state capitol building, an anomaly in the midst of the city's one- and two-story structures, which were all surrounded by prairie. It was an exhilarating two days, and I've had a special place in my heart for North Dakota ever since.

After I left the UN, I decided to make my voice heard about the United States' role in this organization. On December 12, 1983, when President Reagan formally withdrew the United States from UNESCO (the United Nations Educational, Scientific and Cultural Organization), it seemed like the perfect time to write an op-ed piece I'd been thinking about for a long time. UNESCO was a hotbed of controversy. As a special agency and an expensive arm of the United Nations, its broad mission statement is "to contribute to the building of peace, the eradication of poverty, sustainable development and intercultural dialogue through education, the sciences, culture, communication and information." Reagan's stated reasons for withdrawing were that UNESCO was too highly politicized and was fraught with financial mismanagement.[*]

---

[*] The United States stayed out of UNESCO for eighteen years, until 2003. At that time, President George W. Bush thought the organization had been reformed, and we rejoined. In 2011, we stopped paying our dues because of the UNESCO vote to admit Palestine as a full member. According to UNESCO rules, any member not paying its dues for two years loses its voting rights, and we lost ours in late 2013. As of 2015, we have still not paid our dues and still have no voting rights.

THE NEW YORK TIMES, FRIDAY, FEBRUARY 10, 1984

Quit the U.N.?

By Ambassador John L. Loeb, Jr.

President Reagan's decision to withdraw the United States from Unesco raises a question in the public's mind: Is our national interest served by our remaining in the United Nations? Such an issue, publicly debated, would serve as a timely warning about how the United Nations has alienated its friends.

I do not call for withdrawal – at least not at the present time. I still hope that the United Nations will become, as envisioned, the arena in which the world's conflicts can be discussed and resolved with understanding, humanity and fairness. It is true, however, that the organization has proved ineffectual as a peacemaker and protector of human rights.

At worst, it has become a patron of terrorists. It has encouraged, even supported, such terrorist groups as the Palestine Liberation Organization and the South West African People's Organization – both dignified with the status of "permanent observer" – and not only with resolutions and public displays of honor but also with funds. Between 1975 and 1981, the United Nations spent tens of millions of dollars on the P.L.O., Swapo and similar outfits – not counting funds made available in camouflaged items in various agency budgets. (The Heritage Foundation, in Washington, estimates the figure at $116 million. The American tax-payer pays 25 percent of this bill.)

For decades, the United Nations has practiced a double standard. It justifies support of such terrorist organizations on the grounds that it seeks to encourage liberation movements struggling against colonialist regimes. But it does not back pro-Western national liberation movements such as the one in Angola, which is struggling against a Soviet- and Cuban-backed Marxist regime. Further, it sees no struggle for national liberation in Solidarity's efforts to reclaim Poland for the Poles. It has adopted the infamous resolution equating Zionism with racism and is swift to condemn Israel for retaliating against terrorists. But it remains silent in the face of terrorism inspired and executed by Arab extremists against American and French peace-keeping forces in Lebanon.

This double standard is nowhere more evident than in the area of human rights. Alleged infringements by Western or pro-Western governments are promptly denounced, but documented outrages by socialist and third world countries evoke no comparable outrage. The United Nations blatantly ignored Indonesia's genocidal massacre of much of its Chinese population in the 1960's. It proposed no intervention and issued no condemnation while three million Cambodians died under Pol Pot. When America proposed a resolution to condemn Idi Amin's slaughter of 250,000 Ugandans, the African bloc prevented a vote.

Bloc voting, more than anything else, accounts for the often bizarre behavior. The United Nations was conceived as a forum of independent peace-loving nations bound by a common com-mitment to prevent aggression and foster the freedom and well-being of all peoples. That assumption proved wrong and soon the United Nations became compartmentalized into blocs: geographical, ideological, economic. These blocs, formed into alliances on specific issues, largely determine what happens in the 158-nation General Assembly. Since the Assembly's membership, swollen by inclusion of the tiniest states, is mostly hostile or at least unsympathetic to American interests, America is largely impotent in its councils.

Clearly, the United Nations has not fulfilled – even remotely – its founders' hopes. Nations have not acted in accordance with Charter expectations. The world would be better served if we all acknowledged the real nature of the United Nations and gave up many expectations. However, despite its in-effectuality in dealing with major conflicts, the United Nations has recorded important accomplishments in assisting the development of emerging countries. It serves a crucial purpose by bringing together world leaders so they can get to know one another personally and officially, and share ideas and information outside the public debate. These are legitimate reasons for continuing our membership.

Specific steps can improve the United States' effectiveness. Our representatives should serve in office longer. They tend to serve far fewer years than foreign colleagues and have far less opportunity to master the organization's complex workings. American embassies abroad, where our country's case is too often misunderstood and mispresented, should put a higher priority on public diplomacy to explain our positions on United Nations issues.

Washington should take a harder line on funding the United Nations activities that are clearly inconsistent with the Charter, and should, in keeping with a Congress-ional amendment enacted in 1983, take into account the conduct of nations toward us in the United Nations in our negotiations and agreements with them.

John L. Loeb, Jr., Ambassador to Denmark from October 1981 to October 1983, was a delegate to the 38th General Assembly session, which ended in December.

Our withdrawal brought up the question, yet again, of whether it was in our best national interest to be in the UN at all. On February 10, 1984, my op-ed appeared in *The New York Times* under the headline, "Quit the U.N.?"

Though I made the point that terms should be longer, I had no regrets when my tenure was over. In large part, this was because of the frustration I had with the UN's flaws, which many Americans shared. I cited its inconsistencies, its double standards in the area of human rights, its quiescence in the face of terrorism[*] and the fact that U.S. tax-

Here I am with Senator Al D'Amato at a Republican event in the early 1990s, several years after he asked me to run for a seat in the House of Representatives. Though flattered by his respect for me, I declined. With us are Karen McGowan and Governor George Pataki.

payers foot the lion's share of UN bills. However, even with its many drawbacks, the UN nevertheless provides a worldwide forum for debate. I therefore came down on the side of staying in, at least for the time being. Landing on the side of optimism and hope just seemed like the right place to be.

My time at the UN sped by quickly, and when my term ended, I was ready to focus on new agendas. Senator Alfonse D'Amato urged me to run for Congress when my UN assignment was finished. Indeed, it would have been an auspicious time to do so if I wanted to stay active in politics. Reagan's popularity was soaring, and his coattails would have been lengthy and helpful, but the fire to sit in Congress no longer burned in me. I thanked Senator D'Amato but declined his suggestion.

Following the example of my ancestors, I'd thus far devoted a portion of my life to business and a portion to politics and public affairs. Now it seemed the time was right to focus on philanthropy. I didn't want to just sign checks and attend groundbreakings. I wanted to be personally involved, to get my hands dirty, as it were. Those endeavors would take me to places familiar and foreign—and bring great joy to my life.

---

[*] As one former UN delegate, Dr. Cheryl Saban, once wrote, "One man's terrorist is another man's freedom fighter, which is why it can take years for the UN to adopt agreed-upon resolutions on the definition of a terrorist." She also wrote, "The U.S. must have a seat at this table and a voice in the decision-making room—even if the room gets rowdy and the table is messy, and yes—even if we usually have to pay for the lunch that is served."

Mother and Father on the beach in Cuba in 1935.

CHAPTER SEVENTEEN

Cuba and the Cuban-Atlantic Sugar Company

My time on the UN Cuban committee was thanks to the experiences in Cuba that my family and I had there.

Our family's Cuba story begins with my father, who loved Cuba. Before he married Mother, he and two of his friends, Henry Ittleson (whose father had founded the CIT financial company) and Andrew Goodman (whose family controlled Bergdorf Goodman), would vacation frequently in Cuba rather than Palm Beach. After Father and Mother married, they continued to go to Cuba for winter vacations. The following is what my father wrote in his and my mother's memoir, *All in a Lifetime*, about the Cuban-Atlantic Sugar Company. I am including this story of my family in Cuba because the country has become so important to all of us today.

ALL IN A LIFETIME: CUBAN-ATLANTIC SUGAR

In the course of time, I became interested in the sugar business. Cuba then was by far the biggest exporter of sugar in the world. When we first went to Cuba, we became friendly with members of the Falla and Suero families. The Fallas, who owned several sugar mills, were very successful. The firm under which they operated, called Sucesión Falla Gutiérrez, was founded by Alejandro (Alin) Suero Falla's grandfather, Laureano. In addition to sugar mills and related interests, the family owned a considerable amount of real estate.

Alin and I became great friends. He was running his family's mills. I learned a lot from him, and by studying the financial aspects of the sugar business, I concluded that the shares of some publicly owned companies were selling well below their true value. Before long, I was ready to make a commitment.

The first company looked at was Central Violeta. I formed a syndicate that tried to gain control of the company. When Eddie Hilson, then a partner of Wertheim and Company, heard about this, he persuaded Julio Lobo, a major actor in the Cuban sugar industry, to compete with us, and we lost out. Having failed to gain control of Central Violeta, I became interested in the Cuban-Atlantic Sugar Company, the largest sugar enterprise in Cuba. Cuban-Atlantic accounted for 10 percent of the country's raw sugar output as well as substantial quantities of blackstrap molasses, a by-product of the milling operations.

In addition to controlling 450,000 acres of land and six mills, which produced roughly a billion pounds of raw sugar a year, Cuban-Atlantic owned the Hershey refinery and two small mills that supplied raw sugar to it. Based on its assets, Cuban-Atlantic shares looked cheap. Cuban-Atlantic was not particularly well run, and I saw an opportunity to buy control of the company in the open market. I was joined by the Fallas and the family of my then son-in-law, Edgar Bronfman.

Julio Lobo also wanted to assert control. However, Lawrence Crosby, Cuban-Atlantic's chairman of the board, backed by the Batista government, let it be known that any takeover attempt of Cuban-Atlantic by Lobo would be blocked. A realist if anything, Lobo sold us his interest in Cuban-Atlantic in April 1956—more than 300,000 shares out of roughly 2,000,000—raising our total to 40 percent.

I decided at this point to go to Cuba and see what I could do on the ground to work out a deal with Crosby and the government. Wanting a strong, well-known personality with me as my counselor, I asked Tom Dewey to come along. We met with Crosby but made little headway. Tom assumed Batista would receive us, but he had left town. We met instead with the equivalent of the head of the Federal Reserve Bank. Tom was put out that a former governor of New York and former presidential candidate was getting the brush-off from Batista. But that didn't slow him down. I never knew anyone who was more supportive or worked harder than Tom. He was a great partner. On the plane back to New York, Tom was already planning the rest of our campaign when I said to him, "Tom, Relax. The next time we come down, we will own over 50 percent,

This photo shows a Cuban sugar factory in operation circa 1960, after the revolution. Prior to that time, the United States had a financial interest in half of the Cuban sugar refineries.

and there will be no argument." And that is exactly what happened. We bought additional shares on the open market. In December 1956, we took control, and I became chairman and chief executive.

A few months later, Herbert Matthews of *The New York Times* visited Castro up in the hills and wrote a series of articles glorifying him as "the rebel leader of Cuba's youth." U.S. Ambassador Arthur Gardner, who was anti-Castro, was furious at Matthews. There was a general feeling that Batista was crooked and cruel. But that applied to most Latin American politicians at the time. Based on his experience in Mexico when he was president of American Metal, Father used to say, "South of the Rio Grande, being elected to office is a license to steal."

When Tom and I returned to Cuba, we shared the bridal suite at the Hotel Nacional. Arthur Gardner and his wife, Susie, asked us to dinner one night at the ambassador's residence. They had a local piano player to entertain their guests. One of the guests, who had heard that Tom had a fine voice, asked if he would like to sing something. He said he would and chose "Onward Christian Soldiers," which was a bit different from the cabaret songs we had been singing before. But everyone joined in.

A giant rusty wheel that once squeezed the juice from sugarcane, in Camilo Cienfuegos, about thirty miles east of Havana.

What we did with Cuban-Atlantic is now called "restructuring." We installed a completely Cuban management from the Falla organization, who'd been running sugar mills successfully for years. As chairman, I took responsibility for the overall financing and the marketing of sugar, which I had studied before the takeover. During the Cutting season, through the *colonos*, 10,000 cane cutters were employed. The Fallas were progressive and went along with our desire to provide better living conditions for our workers.

ALL IN A LIFETIME: SELLING THE HERSHEY INTERESTS

We controlled Cuban-Atlantic for a relatively short time—from December 1956 until Castro took over in early 1959—but during that period we turned the company into a profitable one. In 1957, we sold the Hershey refinery, the largest in Cuba, and its two raw sugar mills to Julio Lobo. Hershey was another jewel for Julio's crown. Long active in the raw sugar market, Julio was taking a bold step by entering the refinery business.

Julio was a rather unusual man, whose most memorable quality for me was his Napoleon complex. His office was filled with bronze statuettes of Napoleon and all kinds of other Napoleonic memorabilia. In addition to owning Napoleon's death mask, he kept a bed of Josephine's in one of his many *fincas*.

I was eager to sell Hershey for three reasons: First, I was worried about Castro's activities in the hills; second, the Falla organization was expert in growing cane and running raw sugar mills but had no experience in refining sugar or marketing it; and third, in 1956 and 1957, the combination of the Hungarian uprising, the Suez crisis, a poor European beet harvest and drought conditions in the Caribbean touched off a speculative boom that doubled the world price of sugar. Conditions could not have been better for selling. Julio was willing to pay a premium, and as the refinery was not only very expensive to run but also needed new equipment, it all fit together.

We negotiated with Julio and finally agreed on a price, which netted $25 million in cash, covering the Loeb investment in Cuban-Atlantic Sugar. Julio was not the easiest man to deal with. He kept dragging his feet until I had to say, "Julio, either you buy it before the end of the year, or you're not going to get it." I hoped this would get him off dead center. Finally, Julio agreed to have his representatives come to our apartment on the night of December 31, 1957. I came home from my mother-in-law's New Year's Eve party just around the block, and Julio's lawyers were waiting for me. We closed the deal before midnight. One year later, almost to the day, Batista fled Havana and Castro took over.

ALL IN A LIFETIME: THE HOLLAND-LOEB PLAN

In February 1959, Peter [Frances] and I decided to spend six weeks in Cuba to see for ourselves what the situation was under Castro. I gradually came to the conclusion that there was no way of dealing with him. This was not the view of the United States government or of many Cubans at the time. They thought they could deal with Castro the way they had with Batista. Before returning to the United States, I went to see the recently appointed American ambassador, Philip Bonsal, and expressed my opinion that Castro was an out-and-out Communist and that there was no way of doing business with him. Mr. Bonsal, following the State Department line, did not agree with me, and in fact was antagonistic. Later in the year, he came to my office in New York and apologized. That was decent of him, but it did not help.

The day Peter and I were leaving Havana, I was stripped and examined to see if I was taking anything out of Cuba, which I wasn't. I came out furious. Peter said, "You always blow your top. Relax." Then they examined her and she changed her tune. We never knew what they were looking for.

Castro indicated initially that he would pay something for all the American properties he was taking over. He mentioned 2 or 3 percent long-term bonds. Actually, nothing happed at all until one day his militia walked into our office and kicked our management out. Unlike Batista, who only stole 15 to 20 million dollars a year, Castro stole the whole country.

Around this time, I wrote a letter to the State Department saying that I thought if we did not get rid of Castro, we would have a Russian missile base ninety miles off the coast of the United States before long. This was prophetic, as it turned out. However, my fears were not taken seriously.

I then approached Henry Holland of the law firm of Roberts and Holland. In 1958, Henry represented Loeb, Rhoades in successfully negotiating a contract with the Argentine government of President Arturo Frondizi for the investment of $100 million in the finding and production of oil in the westernmost province of Mendoza. Henry, who had been assistant secretary of state for Latin American affairs under Eisenhower, played a major role in the expulsion of Communists from Guatemala. "Henry, is there any we can get rid of Mr. Castro?" I asked. "I will be glad to underwrite whatever expenses you have in preparing a plan." Henry, who shared my views completely, was enthusiastic about doing something to try to get rid of Castro.

About two weeks later, Henry came to me with the following plan: "Many of the best of the young Cubans are coming out of Cuba these days," he said. "We should train these boys in military matters. When we have a large enough group, we should gradually infiltrate them back into Cuba in very small units over a period of months. They would meet on an appointed date somewhere in Pinar del Rio, the westernmost province of Cuba, and declare a government in opposition to Castro's. At that point, the United States would recognize the group as the legitimate government of Cuba and give them full military and diplomatic support."

"That's a great idea," I said. "Where do we go from here?" Henry replied, "Bob Anderson, my former partner, who is now secretary of the treasury, has to sell the plan to Dick Nixon and then to President Eisenhower." Some weeks later, Henry told me the United States would adopt the plan. "Obviously," he added, "we cannot be a part of it from now on." Nonetheless, I was contacted by the CIA. My secretary, Daphne Chalk, and I were given clearance. We were provided a telephone number and told to contact "Colonel King" with any information from friends of mine who were still coming out of Cuba.

I was still in contact with Colonel King in the fall of 1960, some weeks before the presidential election, when I received a call from CIA director Allen Dulles, whom I had never met before. He said that he and a few of his "operatives" would like to come by and thank me for my assistance. I invited them to dinner at our home at 730 Park Avenue. They came, and they were rather critical of the Cubans. The only words I remember Dulles uttering that can possibly explain what happened subsequently were, "I think time is running against us."

After Jack Kennedy was elected, I did not hear from the CIA again. Apparently, they had given up the Holland-Loeb Plan. Instead of being willing to wait and infiltrate over a period of time with no military or diplomatic support from the United States, a half-baked frontal assault was made at the Bay of Pigs, which turned out to be a disaster.

Author's note: Since the Bay of Pigs fiasco in 1961, a great deal has subsequently happened. Without going into all the details, under the Kennedy administration, our family was allowed to put in claims against the Cuban government for our lost property. I think it is highly unlikely we will be able to receive anything from these claims, but I am making every effort to make it happen.

This picture was taken while taping a TV commercial for Sonoma-Loeb. Although my wines were in the hands of professional wine producers, I was personally involved with marketing, and served as Sonoma-Loeb spokesman.

CHAPTER EIGHTEEN

Sonoma-Loeb: Forrest Gump of the Wine World, Since 1971

Sometimes it's better to be lucky than smart. It also helps to be blessed with a good helping of serendipity and, particularly in the case of the wine business, a willingness to do a lot of hard work—even if it's a true labor of love.

On the chance that, someday in the future, a reader should be puzzled about why I have dubbed myself the "Forrest Gump of Wine," it's because of the classic 1994 film *Forrest Gump*. The fictional Forrest, played beautifully by Tom Hanks, was perhaps the luckiest man the world has ever produced. Though not the sharpest knife in the drawer, Forrest never failed to land on his feet, with no real understanding of how circumstances always seemed to wind up to his advantage. That has certainly been the case in my experience in the wine business. Although my feet never stomped the grapes, I did just about everything else to bring my wine to fruition.

My wine story begins in 1971, the heyday of tax shelters, while I was still a partner at Loeb, Rhoades. Since Loeb, Rhoades was a partnership, all the taxes were paid individually by the partners. At the time, city, state and federal taxes were unfairly high; not too surprisingly, tax shelters were keenly sought. When they were found, people jumped on them without a great deal of due diligence.

Toward the end of 1971, Tom Kempner, my cousin and Loeb, Rhoades fellow partner, popped his head into my office with a fortuitous question. "I'm planning to invest in land in Sonoma County that is going to be turned into grapes to be sold to different wineries," he said. "Are you interested?"

This particular opportunity was intriguing because it was being promoted by Mar-

I oversaw every bit of the design, color and copy for all Sonoma-Loeb labels. My Danish coat of arms bestowed by Her Majesty, Queen Margrethe II, in 1983 appears on every label.

vin Shanken, who subsequently built the magazine, *Wine Spectator* from newsletters he was writing at the time. Shanken was also in the tax shelter business, selling plots of land in Sonoma County, which at the time were growing prunes. They tore up the prunes and began planting different kinds of grapes, some chardonnay and some cabernet.

Never wanting to jump in blindly with both feet, I told Tom that we'd have to study it. Tom replied, "You wouldn't know one piece of land from another, and I wouldn't, either." I laughed, because he was right. Once I was assured he was going in, I decided that I would invest as well. While I had always enjoyed a convivial glass of wine or two at dinner, the only thing I really knew about wine was whether I liked it or not. I had to make up my mind quickly, because it was the end of the 1971 tax year.

Uncharacteristically, I committed to the deal without ever seeing the land or getting answers to a number of significant questions. Doing this without any investigation was in itself not particularly surprising. In those days, at the end of each year, investors went into one tax shelter or another, almost without studying them at all. It turned out that the land I had bought was a plot of land that came to be known as the Russian Riverbend Vineyard, 150 acres of prime grape-growing property in Sonoma County in northern California.

The property was in two lots, one of which was next to the Robert Young Vineyard in the Alexander Valley, regarded as some of the best grape farmland in California. Young's grapes sold at a premium of 50–100 percent over normal cabernet grapes, a fact I didn't know at the time. The second parcel was on the Russian River, next to the Davis Bynum Winery, an area not far from the famous Bohemian Grove. It was planted with chardonnay and pinot noir grapes. Subsequently, my friend John Dyson bought Williams Selyem,[*]

---

[*] Wine aficionados will recognize the name Williams Selyem, which is famous for its pinot noir, chardonnay and zinfandel.

whose property is also next to Davis Bynum. Recently, John told me he is interested in buying the former Davis Bynum property on the Russian River as well as my property.

Many of the great wine-growing regions of the world are found along a river: France's Bordeaux, Burgundy and Loire; and Germany's Rhine and Mosel. Like those famous regions, the broad valley floor of the Russian River in Sonoma County provides exactly the right soil, drainage and climate to grow some of the most sought-after premium grapes in Sonoma County.

At the beginning, I had no intention of producing wine myself. California wine was just beginning to come into its own and had not yet approached the prestige of French wines. Indeed, California wine was thought to be too sweet and uninteresting—pedestrian, even—by the wine-drinking elite. My plan was to sell the Riverbend Vineyard grapes to leading wineries in California, such as Robert Mondavi, Clos du Bois and the Franciscan Vineyards, and let them turn it into good wine. I had no idea at the time that this last-minute tax shelter would eventually turn into one of the great passions of my life. I would one day learn the language and feel the passion of true wine connoisseurs. Now I can bandy about such phrases as "smoky," "toasty," "new oak," "ripe," "earthy," "tapered finish" and "decadent spicy aftertaste" right along with the most dedicated wine aficionados.

It did not begin auspiciously for me. Within weeks of my purchase, grape prices began to fall precipitously. The Prudential Life Insurance Company had loaned a great deal of money to these tax shelters, large, nonrecourse loans with an interest rate close to 15 percent or

Sight unseen, in 1971 I bought Riverbend Vineyards, 150 acres of magnificent grape-growing farmland located in northern California. It proved to be more than a wise decision.

409

ANOTHER VINTAGE WORK OF ART

The Cezanne

The Manet

The Picasso

The Toulouse-Lautrec

The Pissarro

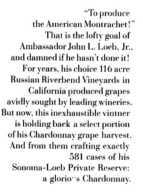
The Van Gogh

"To produce the American Montrachet!" That is the lofty goal of Ambassador John L. Loeb, Jr., and damned if he hasn't done it! For years, his choice 116 acre Russian Riverbend Vineyards in California produced grapes avidly sought by leading wineries. But now, this inexhaustible vintner is holding back a select portion of his Chardonnay grape harvest. And from them crafting exactly 581 cases of his Sonoma-Loeb Private Reserve: a glorious Chardonnay.

Oenophilic reaction?

The Wine Spectator declares: "Smooth and spicy with a silky texture...elegant and smoky... impressive texture and length."

Peter Morrell raves: "...extremely complex, intensely rich, with generous, persistent flavors and a lingering aftertaste."

Now it's your turn.

Available at the finest restaurants. In short supply at your wine merchant.

Some of my family's French Impressionists were used to promote Sonoma-Loeb wine. (From the Loeb Collection.)

410

higher. Intentionally or not, the company had become the largest owner of vineyards in the United States for a period of time. This was a result of the fact that many buyers found their tax losses growing so large that they felt they couldn't hold on to the property. They "dropped the property," which then became the property of Prudential Life. Other buyers had dropped out by the dozens, but maybe because I'm stubborn, or maybe just because I'd fallen in love with the idea of owning a vineyard, I decided to hold on to mine. It was a fortuitous decision. In due course, I was able to persuade both Marvin Shanken and a team of farmers who were working on the property in Sonoma County to give up their interests. I pointed out that their projections were unrealistic, and I didn't even have to mention the possibility of a lawsuit about misrepresentation. The 150 acres were now mine.

Then I made a phone call to the now largest of my fellow vineyard owners—Prudential Life. I've always believed that picking up the phone and finding good advisors who know more than you do is one of the keys to success. Since Prudential was also now neck-deep in the business of viticulture, I went to them for advice about vineyard farmers. I'd quickly found out that good ones are hard to find unless you know somebody who knows somebody. A Prudential advisor led me to a family named Ledbetter—a father and two sons—who were major California vineyard contract farmers and owners. This began a turnaround for my Sonoma investment. My relationship with the Ledbetters proved to be ideal. It has not only been good business but it has also turned into a long-distance friendship spanning the many miles between California and New York. It began in 1972 and is still going today—forty-five years later.

By the early 1980s, under the green thumbs of the Ledbetters, my vineyard was producing magnificent grapes—six hundred tons of them annually—from which my client wineries could make wonderful chardonnay. I was actually beginning to make a profit—sometimes a considerable one. Along the way, I was also being educated on the finer points of wine. I learned many new words, but most important was what the French call *terroir*. *Terroir* doesn't have a one-word English translation, even though "the climate" might be an approximation. It actually means *all* of the unique physical aspects of the vineyard site that combine to make really great wines: the soil composition, the lay of the land, the microclimate (the prevailing weather conditions of discrete plant communities), the hours of sunshine each day, the amount of rainfall and the length of the growing season. I was told that my property had a perfect *terroir* for chardonnay and cabernet grapes.

My brilliant, wine-savvy nephew Samuel Bronfman II—one of four sons of my sister Ann Loeb Bronfman and her former husband, Edgar Bronfman Sr.—encouraged me to start making my own wine. Young Samuel is one of the heirs of the original Seagram liquor firm founded in Canada by Joseph Seagram in 1919, which was ultimately taken over by the Bronfman family. Formerly headquartered at 375 Park Avenue in New York City, Sam Bronfman, the patriarch of the Bronfman family, personally oversaw the building of the now famous Seagram Building with the advice and encouragement of his daughter Phillis, an architect. The key architects were Mies van der Rohe and Philip Johnson. The Seagram Company was once the largest distiller of alcoholic beverages in the world. Living in California, young Sam, grandson of the patriarch and my nephew, knew exactly where my parcels were located and about the quality of the grapes produced there. "Uncle John, you have a great chance to produce a superb wine," he told me. "*Do it!*"

By now it was 1981, ten years after I'd first invested in Riverbend Vineyards. I had just been named the American ambassador to Denmark and become friendly there with Prince Henrik, Queen Margrethe II's husband, who also owned a winery. When he heard about the quality of grapes grown in my vineyard—and that I had taken the next step of producing my own brand—the prince enthusiastically applauded my decision. This added fuel to my enthusiasm for undertaking the many, many preparations that making my own wine would entail. I knew that a Sonoma-Loeb wine must be worthy of the Loeb name, which was entrenched in the public mind by my father and grandfather because of the Wall Street prestige of Loeb, Rhoades.

When I returned from Denmark, young Sam Bronfman introduced me to a very successful winemaking couple, Donn and Molly Chappellet of Napa. Donn Chappel-

Workers handled the grapes quickly but gently, checking their ripeness daily when it came close to harvest time. The wine would be "boring" if bottled too early, Phillip Corralo-Titus told me.

let founded Chappellet Winery in 1967[*] and built it into one of Napa's acclaimed brands. Guided by the pioneer winemaker André Tchelistcheff of Beaulieu Vineyards, he bought 320 acres of tough terrain on Prichard Hill at the eastern edge of Napa Valley. However, at the time I was introduced to Donn Chappellet, the industry was in a major downturn, and Donn asked me if I'd be interested in buying his whole company and land for $30 million. Because of his difficulties, he was happy to start doing private label work for a boutique winery like mine.

No one can tell by looking at the picture of these golden casks holding my wine just how much time, thought and money went into the selection of the right wood to store Sonoma-Loeb.

Also at that time, he had just hired a new winemaker named Phillip Corralo-Titus.

If I had to pick only one thing that led to Sonoma-Loeb's success besides the quality of my grapes, it would be having Phillip Corralo-Titus as my winemaker. Phillip held this post for more than twenty-one years, achieving a product that went beyond my fondest dreams. After meeting young Phillip, my wine education really began. Phillip had worked in the wine business from the time he was twelve years old and had absorbed enough esoteric wine knowledge to be worthy of a PhD in both viticulture (grape farming) and oenology (winemaking). He gave me a crash course in wine, explaining what it would take to achieve my goal. I think if I had truly grasped how time-consuming and complicated it would be— all the steps to be taken from the picking of the grapes to marketing them—I might have backed out. Fortunately, in Gump-like fashion, ignorance was my saving grace.

Phillip explained that the grapes must be treated gently from the moment they are plucked from the vine throughout the entire process of turning them into wine. He persuaded me that we should use the same technique the French traditionally used for centuries in producing their white Burgundy. I agreed when he insisted that no compromises should be made along the line, from the types of barrels we used for fermentation and aging, to the length of the corks used, to the shape and color of the bottles chosen.

Then, Phillip explained, there was the matter of the grape ripeness. The majority of the "boring" chardonnays produced in California at the time were made from fruit harvested too early. He wanted to harvest at 23.5 Brix (the level of sugar) and would send workers in

---

[*] Donn's father was a pilot who, with six partners, bought Lockheed Aircraft and turned it into an aviation giant.

to monitor Brix levels on a daily basis as the critical point approached. This would occasionally lower the alcohol level to a still-robust 14 percent, and he promised I would like the results. There would also be the matter of a complicated process called "malolactic fermentation," known as "malo" in the industry. This would add to the complexity of the already tricky winemaking process and would take many months to accomplish.

His tutorials included the fact that we would have to experiment. The first efforts might not be marketable—or at least not as good as I wanted them to be. He wanted barrel fermentation, a labor-intensive aspect with which many winemakers do not bother. We experimented with wooden barrels made from four different French forests and three different cooperages (the places wine barrels are made), and favored barrels of medium toast levels from the Allier region. To avoid too much oak in the flavor, we processed our grapes in no more than 50 percent new oak barrels and stirred the lees manually while they were in the barrels, about seven months before bottling. Finally, after nine years, in 1990, we knew we had achieved the magical goal. This magical goal was symbolized by the fact that the first fifty cases of Sonoma-Loeb Private Reserve Chardonnay that went on the market received, much to my astonishment, a rating of 90 from the *Wine Spectator*.

By this time, Marvin Shanken, who had sold me my 150 acres of prunes in 1972, was the owner of the world famous magazine *Wine Spectator*. Only two names mattered in judging wine: Shanken's *Wine Spectator* and Robert Parker's *Wine Advocate*. Once the making of the wine was in Phillip's able hands, I could turn my attention to distribution and marketing—areas I was more familiar with, though still on a considerable learning curve.

In the years to come, Sonoma-Loeb wines, especially the chardonnay, became my favorite calling card. I proudly sent cases as special gifts to friends who said they treasured them, and I made sure that my favorite restaurants carried it—from the Four Seasons and Café Boulud in New York City to Harry's Bar in London to the Hotel D'Angleterre in Copenhagen, to name but four of the hundreds. After we were sure of an A-1 product, I wanted to celebrate with a major event. Taking a hint from Great-Grandfather Adolph Lewisohn's lifestyle, I always gave myself lavish birthday parties that I could share with my friends. Sonoma-Loeb was to be the star attraction at my sixty-fifth birthday party at the Loeb Boathouse in Central Park in 1995. I was as anxiety-ridden as a Broadway director on opening night. I knew my wine was excellent, but would the wine world agree?

They did!

Among my most treasured letters about Sonoma-Loeb is a handwritten note from Barbara Bush written on a Sunday evening in 1992. She and the president had just finished a quiet Sunday supper. "We drank the most wonderful wine," she wrote. "I looked at the bot-

Sonoma-Loeb's chardonnay and restaurateur Daniel Boulud's cookbook drew a lot of attention in the front window of my brother, Arthur's Madison Avenue Bookshop.

tle and . . . it was Ambassador John L. Loeb Jr.'s Sonoma-Loeb 1990 Chardonnay. John, it was truly a lovely wine." Barbara Bush must have spread the word to the immediate family, because her granddaughter Jenna Bush ordered it for her wedding reception in 2008. It was such a satisfying arc for my wine: evolving from nothing but a tax shelter for a wine novice to being served—and enjoyed—at the White House. Like the inimitable Forrest Gump, I had fallen backward into something wonderful.

In the 2000s, after a particularly exasperating experience with Sonoma-Loeb's most recent wine representative, I was culling applications for someone to replace him. My remarkable office manager, Debbee Jones, turned to me with her signature self-confidence and asked, "Why not me?"

Debbee could have a chapter in this book all to herself. A truly handsome woman, she had arrived at my office in the Seagram Building on Park Avenue in 1996. Almost as tall as I am, she had come in as a temp to take care of some accounting issues. Debbee's comfortable but commanding presence, along with her accounting skills, were immediately apparent. She was exactly what I needed, at exactly the right time, and I wanted to hire her full time. Renata Propper, a friend of mine and a professional handwriting analyst, had been encouraging me to screen candidates for full-time positions by having their writing analyzed. It would be a way to make sure they would fit in my sometimes tumultuous office. Debbee agreed to submit her handwriting, warning that she was a free spirit who really preferred working as a temp. She was not at all sure she wanted to be hired, even if Renata's report proved positive. Renata's several-page analysis was effusive. Her accuracy in assessing Debbee's strengths has made me a lifetime believer in the art of graphology.* I overcame Debbee's reluctance to sign on permanently. It was the beginning of a twelve-year business relationship that for me has never been equaled.

Debbee quickly moved into the role of my office manager. Whatever the office problem was, Debbee would say, "Not a problem," and I immediately relaxed, knowing she could, and would, handle it. Her fellow staff members adored her, and she managed them with all the political skills of a Lyndon Johnson, sometimes artfully persuading, sometimes firmly insisting, sometimes leading by example. When I went into the winemaking business, she took on many of the financial aspects, interacting with the winemaker, the distributor, my wine representative and the media. She not only helped edit my television and radio ads for Sonoma-Loeb, but also—being something of an actress herself—coached my delivery. She was intrigued by the whole subject of wine and went to night school to learn about it in depth. When she suggested that she could run my office *and* be Sonoma-Loeb's marketing director, I decided that if she thought she could handle it, she could. Her business card soon had dual titles: "Marketing Director" and "Chief Operating Officer." It was an inspired move, and Sonoma-Loeb continued down the road of success. Debbee lit up a room just by walking into it. She loved to meet people, loved to travel and was a born saleswoman. Her powerful presentations made her a well-known and beloved figure in the highly competitive wine world, not only in this country but all the way over in Denmark as well.

In late May 2008, Debbee became terminally ill with a rare and untreatable disease called amyloidosis. On July 1 of that year, my beautiful and vibrant friend passed at the unjust age of forty-five. Perhaps no one is irreplaceable, but if anyone was, it was surely Debbee.

I went on with my wine business for three more years, but the fun was gone. Ecclesiastes, that wise sage of the Old Testament, says there is a time for everything. I realized in 2011 that the time had come for me to pass my beloved Sonoma-Loeb wine business to younger

---

* An earlier experience with Renata's handwriting analysis should have already sold me on graphology. A seemingly impeccable young man who interviewed for a job clerking for me had handwriting that set off Renata's alert system. She warned me that he would be a disaster, but his résumé and appearance were impressive, so I hired him. A year later I discovered he had done not one iota of work but had been trading on his own during his time working for me.

My big smile in this picture of Debbee Jones and me at a wine promotion event gives only a hint at how pleased I was with her work at John L. Loeb Jr. Associates. She was not only my firm's office manager, but a brilliant and unique Sonoma-Loeb marketing director at the same time.

Phillip Corralo-Titus began his wine career at twelve, tending his father's fifty-acre vineyard in California. Today he is hailed across the industry for his storied expertise in winemaking.

hands. I could see I had two choices: expand the line to accommodate the ever-increasing demand and expend all the time, money and energy that such an undertaking would entail; or let the winemaking and distribution business go and keep my grapes—Riverbend Vineyards. At the age of eighty-one, I decided the latter option seemed the wiser. But to whose hands should my labor of love be entrusted?

On May 24, 2016, sadly, Donn Chappellet died. Donn and Molly had six children, and young Cyril and Clarissa have taken over running the winery. The last paragraph of Donn's obit reads, "With the help of his family and wisely chosen staff—a few of whom have now been with the winery for 47 years—the Chappellet winery thrived, in quality and business alike." The last sentence of the obit reads, "Today it produces 30,000 cases of wine, and now an additional 15,000 cases under the Sonoma-Loeb label, whose wines had long been made at the Chappellet facility." The family licensed my brand in 2011.

Because my "Forrest Gump luck" was still hanging around, Sonoma-Loeb is now in the hands of the Chappellet group for almost the next hundred years, since I licensed the name to them. If I have a descendant who is alive around ninety-five years from now, he or she can then claim the name back from Chappellet. Although it is not required, labels on the bottles read "Founder John L. Loeb Jr." The talented Phillip Corralo-Titus is still the Sonoma-Loeb winemaker.

L.A. SMITH 1820–1906 (Student of C. W. Eckersberg)
Female Model Before a Mirror (1841)
(Ambassador John L. Loeb Jr. Danish Art Collection)

EGILL JACOBSEN 1910–1998
Green Mask (1977)
(Ambassador John L. Loeb Jr. Danish Art Collection)

JENS JUEL 1745–1803
Seated Chinese Man in Mandarin Dress (c. 1780)
(Ambassador John L. Loeb Jr. Danish Art Collection)

P.S. KRØYER 1851–1909
Portrait of the Artist's Wife Marie (presumably 1889)
(Ambassador John L. Loeb Jr. Danish Art Collection)

An American Experience
Adeline Moses Loeb
(1876–1953)
and Her Early American Jewish Ancestors

With an introduction by
ELI N. EVANS

PART FOUR

Philanthropy, Family and Endeavors

I have admired Prime Minister Winston Churchill all my life, and was fortunate enough to meet him once. My philanthropic work on behalf of the Winston Churchill Foundation of the United States supports Churchill's vision of advancing science and technology on both sides of the Atlantic through public awareness, fundraising and the awarding of academic scholarships.

CHAPTER NINETEEN

Family Foundations: Churchill, Langeloth and Loeb

I had once been told, perhaps by my father, that a full life contains three parts, each with equal weight. The first is your education, where you build up who you are, what you know and what you want to become. The second is your career, where you establish yourself in the world, make your money and support your family. The third, which can cover a wide variety of areas, can be placed under the banner of "philanthropy."

Upon returning from Denmark and completing my UN assignment in the mid-1980s, I began to make inroads into this third phase, which has carried on for the past thirty years. Philanthropy has become the most gratifying part of my life, and I have done my best to use my time, money and knowledge to further the causes that matter most to me.

Whether we recognize it or not, almost everybody, even if only subconsciously, wants to make a difference in this world. That motivation has certainly been true in my life, perhaps because the ancestors I most admire made ours a better world through their foundations and personal philanthropy. If I am remembered in the years to come, I hope it will be for the work I've done in this regard.

Ken Libo was right. The true religion of my Lehman, Lewisohn and Moses-Loeb ancestors was philanthropy, a Greek term that means "love of humankind." Philanthropy is the practice of giving money, time and service to help make life better for other people and to advance causes that benefit humanity for the public good. That practice has been a strong thread that has linked my family together and has wound its way down through the generations. I hope that this thread will continue to wind through generations to come.

The Winston Churchill Foundation and the Langeloth Foundation were legacies from my father. I have enjoyed very much being chairman of both of these foundations. In addition, I have also gained a great deal of satisfaction from the causes with which I have been involved through my John L. Loeb Jr. Foundation.

THE WINSTON CHURCHILL FOUNDATION

Like many of the Loeb connections that span several generations, our involvement with the Winston Churchill Foundation (WCF) began with my father—specifically his friendship with Lew Douglas, a former ambassador of the United States to the Court of St. James (the formal name given to the U.S. ambassador to the United Kingdom). Douglas had been an Arizona congressman and then director of the budget under President Franklin D. Roosevelt. Like that of my grandfather C.M. Loeb, Douglas's family had been involved in mining nonferrous metals; his father, Lewis Stuart Douglas, was a multi-millionaire in the copper industry.[105] In 1949, when our family visited England, Father met Lew through his good friend Paul Warburg, Douglas's special assistant at that time, and they, too, became close.

For all of his illustrious achievements, Lew Douglas had another highly distinctive claim to fame. He was an enthusiastic fisherman and in his later years wore a black patch

Pictured here is Gerald Grosvenor, the sixth Duke of Westminster, listening as I introduced him in May 1989 as the recipient of an honorary degree from Westminster College. The college chaplain, Dr. William Young, stands behind us. Because of my work with the Winston Churchill Foundation, I had been invited to make this introduction at the Fulton, Missouri, school where Winston Churchill made his "Iron Curtain" speech in 1946.

over one eye after losing it to a wayward fish-hook. When the Madison Avenue advertising mogul David Ogilvy saw a picture of Douglas, he was so struck by Lew's arresting image that he created an entire ad campaign for Hathaway Shirts around his commanding appearance. Even today, people remember Lew as the "Hathaway Man," though it was someone else who appeared in the ads. "When the ads ran in *The New Yorker*," *Advertising Age* magazine noted, "Hathaway's entire stock sold out."[106] Lew Douglas became more fa-

This magnificent portrait of Winston Churchill includes his ever-present cigar.

miliar to the man on the street than he ever was as ambassador. Such is the power and reach of advertising to the American psyche.

In 1959, Churchill College of Cambridge University was completed as a tribute to Britain's indomitable World War II prime minister. It was envisioned as the United Kingdom's answer to MIT. Recognizing that science and technology had significantly shaped the Allied victory, Churchill was looking to promote further advances in those fields. He hoped for a cooperative program that would, at Churchill College's invitation, bring top Americans in engineering, math and science to do postgraduate work at the college.

A year later, in 1960, the Winston Churchill Foundation of the United States was created largely through the efforts of Dr. James R. Killian of MIT and Sir John "Jock" Colville. Colville, Churchill's private secretary, was a banker and formidable figure in his own right.[107] Lew Douglas, though no longer ambassador to the UK, took an active interest in this initiative. The foundation's first step was to establish a small fellowship fund to defray expenses for distinguished American scientists who had been invited by Churchill College to pursue their academic interests. Seven of these scientists became Nobel laureates—five received their prizes subsequent to their appointments as fellows. Among the first recipients was James Watson, who, along with Francis Crick and Maurice Wilkins, won the Nobel Prize in 1962 for discovering the structure of DNA.

Lew Douglas and Carl Gilbert, chairman of Gillette Industries and the first to chair the foundation, were two heavy hitters who got the scholarship program running stateside. Board members included such academic luminaries as James Rhyne Killian, the tenth president of MIT as well as President Eisenhower's science advisor, and Lee Alvin DuBridge, the president of Caltech, who helped develop radar during World War II. By

With me here are my good friend Winston Spencer Churchill and Karen McGowan at a reception in London.

1963, the scholarship program was in place. Three scholars won the first grants, which provided full tuition and living expenses for one year of study.

When Carl Gilbert stepped down as chair of the foundation in 1971, Lew Douglas took his place. Lew invited Father to join the board. Father, knowing how much I loved England, nominated me to the board in 1975. Neither Father nor I were what you would call "Churchillians" like my brother, Arthur, who wrote to the prime minister after Churchill's party lost the 1946 election. Arthur was a huge fan and the whole family was thrilled when he got an answer back from Churchill on House of Commons stationery.

Father and I were, however, serious Anglophiles. Social anti-Semitism in the UK began diminishing in the middle of the nineteenth century when Jewish-born Benjamin Disraeli became prime minister. All of the best friends of Queen Victoria's son were Jews—children of bankers like the Rothschilds and Sassoons. When we went to England, in 1949, we got the red-carpet treatment not only because America saved England from the Nazis, but also because the Loeb, Rhoades office chose to stay open during the war. We met families who were Jewish, including some who were hereditary lords sitting in Parliament. I was mesmerized by the thought that Jews weren't separated from the leaders of WASP society in England. This sense of inclusiveness added to my lifelong love of the country.

I stayed with my parents and Arthur and Ann at the home of Mr. and Mrs. Peter Samuels. I remember how the butler unpacked and laid out all my clothes to change for

The talented and charming Lady Mary Soames served with zest and enthusiasm on the WCF board until her death in 2014. The youngest of Winston and Clementine Churchill's five children, she wrote several bestsellers about her historic family, and my brother, Arthur, hosted a book-signing for her *Biography of a Marriage* at his Madison Avenue Bookshop. Lady Soames is pictured with Harold Epstein, our great executive director, and his wife, Lillian.

dinner. Peter's family founded Royal Dutch Shell. His family were originally importers of shells from the Dutch East Indies. It was common for people in the early nineteenth century to put shells on their fireplace mantels. When the Samuels and their employees were gathering shells for importing, they discovered oil on the beaches. Thus the name Royal Dutch Shell.

Lord and Lady Melchett (Julian and Sonia) were also guests that weekend at the Samuelses. Julian was a charming and fascinating young man who founded a farming company. Subsequently, he received a hereditary title from his grandfather, who started Brunner Mond, which later became Imperial Chemical Industries, the largest chemical company in the world at that time. This was quite unusual for a Jew. Sadly, Julian died very young, and suddenly, of a heart attack after swimming at his summer home in Majorca. I was devoted to Julian and his wife, Sonia, who is still my friend.

When Lew died in 1979, Father became chairman, and I was elected president of the WCF. By then I had been on the board for four years, along with Lew's daughter, Sharman Douglas, and her husband, Andrew Hay (a cousin of my closest English friend, Bobby Buxton); W. Averell Harriman and, later, his new wife, Pamela Harriman (formerly married to Churchill's son Randolph); and Winston Spencer Churchill, a member of Parliament (Pamela's son and Sir Winston's grandson). Young Winston and his beautiful second wife, Luce, also became close personal friends, and his death in 2010 was a great loss to me.

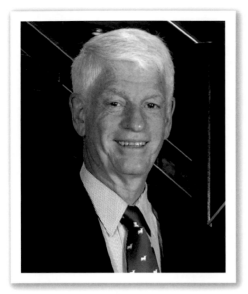

My friend Mario Gabelli, an extremely strong and steady supporter of the Winston Churchill Foundation. He is the founder and CEO of Gabelli Asset Management Company Investors, based in Rye, New York. Mario's $30 billion global investment firm makes him, without a doubt, the most financially successful of the Loeb, Rhoades alumni.

Following in the footsteps of his grandfather, Winston Spencer Churchill was a journalist early in his career, and he later authored a number of books. In my favorite book of his, *His Father's Son*, Winston explores the relationship between Sir Winston and Randolph, his own father. Through my interest in family genealogy, Winston Spencer and I discovered that we were distantly connected through Moses Levy, an early American ancestor of my grandmother Adeline Moses Loeb.

At a dinner I hosted for the young Churchills in 2003, Winston repeated a story Sir Winston himself loved to tell. When young Winston Spencer was born, a friend of the prime minister clucked and said "Winston, how wonderful! Your new grandson resembles you!"

"All babies look like me," the prime minister retorted. "But then again, I look like all babies."

Randolph Spencer, Winston Spencer's son and a great-grandson of Winston Churchill, is now a leading figure among the English board members of the WCF of the U.S. Sir Winston Churchill's youngest daughter, Lady Mary Soames, was an important member of the foundation's board and a good friend of my family until her death, in 2014. Arthur hosted her U.S. book launch at his Madison Avenue bookstore, in 2003. There she signed copies of her well-received and uniquely insightful book, *Clementine Churchill: The Biography of a Marriage.* Mary was also an extremely popular guest at my seventy-fifth birthday party at Blenheim Palace, in 2005.

Mario Gabelli has been among the longest-serving board members and the most consistently generous contributors to the Winston Churchill Foundation. Mario began his career at Loeb, Rhoades, but the brilliant financial analyst branched out on his own in 1977, forming a hugely successful money management firm. He is regularly listed among the richest Americans and is featured prominently in such publications as *The Wall Street Journal* and *Barron's.* During my years as president of the foundation, I frequently sought Mario's advice.

Unfortunately, by the time I became head of the foundation, the fundraising had waned. While the board members initially gave generously to the Churchill Foundation, those that remained were not strong fundraisers. With the exception of a five-year grant from AIG, even Father hadn't been able to solicit large gifts. Once the situation became dire in the late 1970s, Father said he needed my help. He knew how much I cared about the foundation's success and longevity, and he made it clear that it would be my job to raise money and save the foundation from being merged with the English Speaking Union or the Institute of International Education.

I was to employ my skills in public relations to help the Churchill Foundation recover from its financial woes. I accepted the challenge with the understanding that Harold Epstein, the foundation's executive director since 1971, would work closely with me.

By the time I joined the board, in 1975, Harold was already the heart and soul of the foundation. Harold first became well known through Herbert Agar, the Pulitzer Prize–winning author of *The People's Choice, from Washington to Harding: A Study in Democracy.* Harold's research for Agar led to his position as personal secretary to Bernard Baruch, the illustrious financier, philanthropist and advisor to Presidents Wilson and Roosevelt. He later joined the Institute of International Education, where he oversaw the distribution of Fulbright fellowships as well as other international student exchanges. An enormously talented writer, Harold could have done well in a more profitable career, such as a biographer or full-time historian. In fact, he was primarily responsible for Baruch's best-selling two-volume autobiography. Baruch's view of philanthropy may well have guided Harold into a life of nonprofit work.

For thirty-four years until his retirement, in 2006, Harold ran the foundation out of his Manhattan home, while also holding other executive positions in development work. He did "everything from ordering paper clips to making major decisions, with which, fortunately, the board agreed." Everyone had complete confidence in what Harold was doing and planned to do. With Father presiding, the board only met once a year. Father ran a tight ship at these meetings, tapping his ivory cigarette holder impatiently and forcibly moving the agenda along. Father was never one to spend time unnecessarily, so the meetings remained short during his time in charge.

Harold Epstein was the executive director of the Winston Churchill Foundation, cofounder, and a key builder of the foundation as we know it today. Without him, it would not have survived.

In the early days there weren't many applications for scholarships. Few in the American academic world had even heard of the Winston Churchill Foundation. Harold deserves credit for changing all that. He visited colleges and universities all over the country and mined them for their best and brightest, "chosen in a very rigorous competition."[108] Harold also took charge of the screening and selection process of the young scholars, whose applications were reviewed by former Churchill Scholars. To this day—years after his retirement—Harold remains in touch with many of the recipients.

Since the selection of the first three Churchill Scholars in 1963, more than five hundred men and women, chosen in a rigorous competition from among the most promising students in science and technology at the nation's leading colleges and universities, have gone off to Churchill College with the foundation's support. They comprise a legion of talent.

Today, Churchill Scholars hold professorships at major institutions of higher education, such as Harvard, Caltech, MIT and Stanford, instructing and inspiring a younger generation in the wonders of science and technology.

They are conducting research in such areas as atomic energy, space exploration and environmental pollution at NASA and NIH, and at other laboratories such as Argonne, Sandia and Los Alamos. Still others have made their careers in management or research at such high-tech corporations as IBM, Intel, DuPont, Google and Cisco.

Reviewing the history of the Churchill Scholarships, it is no exaggeration to say that they have enriched America.

When it came to the task of fundraising, the partnership between Harold and me was a perfect fit: I had the contacts and Harold had the administrative skills. He did the lion's share of the work and deserved a large portion of the accolades. After Father asked me to take on the job of raising money for the foundation, I gave it a great deal of thought, concluding that an effective way to raise money would be to give out an award with special meaning to the recipient.

Harold gave me all the credit for the idea of a Winston Churchill Foundation Award. Young Winston and Mary Soames gave the concept enthusiastic stamps of approval and agreed to issue the award in Churchill's name. Our criteria: the winners were to be leaders who (1) were interested in education; (2) were focused on matters of science; (3) were interested in international relations, particularly Anglo-American relations; and (4) exhibited some of the character of Sir Winston himself.

Our first choice, in 1981, for the inaugural recipient was W. Averell Harriman. A distinguished and handsome man, Averell was one of the richest and most highly re-

Averell Harriman listened attentively while I read his citation from the Winston Churchill Foundation.

In his late eighties and without notes, Averell Harriman, upon receiving his award, spoke eloquently for about thirty minutes at the WCF luncheon.

garded individuals in America. The son of railroad tycoon E.H. Harriman, Averell was vice president of Union Pacific Railroad. He helped to create Brown Brothers Harriman, to this day one of the most distinguished investment firms in the world. He also founded the Sun Valley resort in Idaho. During World War II, Averell had an active role in the Lend-Lease program and had been FDR's special representative to Churchill prior to becoming our ambassador to the Soviet Union. He was ambassador when the USSR was considered our ally and Stalin a "friend" in a united front against Hitler. Harriman, however, was all the while aware of "Stalin's ultimate designs."[109]

After the war, Averell would become the U.S. ambassador to the Court of St. James's. His many years of service also included his roles as secretary of commerce under Truman and governor of New York from 1955 to 1958. Harriman ran as a Democratic candidate for the presidency in both 1952 and 1956, and he later became one of JFK's prominent advisors, a member of the so-called Wise Men. The Harrimans lived not too far from Ridgeleigh, in Westchester County, and Harriman had become a friend of my father.

For some time I'd known Harriman's wife, Pamela, who was Randolph Churchill's ex-wife and young Winston's mother. I discussed with her offering the award to Averell. She thought it was a wonderful idea and urged me to ask him. I met with Averell in his living room, where I proposed the idea. He was so moved by the offer that tears came to his eyes at the thought of being honored in Winston Churchill's name. He had over-

Prime Minister Margaret Thatcher loved my introduction of her at the WCF Award Dinner in 1983. She spoke gloriously of the Winston Churchill Foundation of the United States.

seen—or participated in—many of the major conferences among Churchill, FDR and Stalin that would determine the strategies for military victory and postwar reconstruction. He graciously accepted.

Instead of trying to raise money through this event, we opted to elevate the Winston Churchill Foundation's profile in a way that would encourage major contributors. Father underwrote the luncheon, which was given at the River Club in New York City in the summer of 1981, just before Harriman's ninetieth birthday. The event was cohosted by Marietta Tree, another member of the board and a contemporary of Pamela Harriman. The beautiful Marietta was famous for her international political and diplomatic skills, as well as for the men in her life, such as the one-time presidential hopeful Adlai Stevenson and the legendary film director John Huston. The luncheon was a huge success with an unbelievable turnout. Some of the illustrious guests included the Master of Churchill College, Sir William Hawthorne; the Nobel Peace Prize laureate Henry

Kissinger, who played so important a role in diplomacy in the Nixon years; Sol Linowitz, who helped negotiate the return of the Panama Canal to Panama and was the winner of the Presidential Medal of Freedom; and C. Douglas Dillon, a Republican who served as the fifty-seventh secretary of the treasury under Presidents Kennedy and Johnson. The Danish diplomats Ambassador Borch to the United States and Ambassador Ulrichsen to the United Nations also attended.

Harriman's presentation was memorable in every way. I was amazed that he could speak so eloquently for thirty minutes without notes about his impressive career and life. In giving him the award, I honored this aspect as well: "How can a man of these years look so well, display such vigor, retain so many interests, and pursue so many activities? The answer no doubt lies in some inner strength."[110] My last vision of him was seeing him walk out of the River Club with no cane and Pamela on his arm.

In London in 1982, after participating in a NATO conference, I began talking with Sir William Hawthorne about whom to honor next. It was toward the end of the Falklands War and the Conservative Party's popularity was soaring. "What about the prime minister?" I suggested. Margaret Thatcher, Britain's "Iron Lady" and the first woman prime minister, was perfect for the Churchill Award. However, persuading her to accept it might prove problematic, given the number of awards she was already being offered.

We reached Mrs. Thatcher through Jock Colville, who made contact with her private secretary. Even with Jock's help, it was quite a while before we received a response from the prime minister's office. She would be delighted to accept the award, but they would have to let us know when it could be worked into her schedule. The prime minister proposed a date in September 1983, but she chose to host the evening herself in Washington. (Mrs. Thatcher was always careful about "other people's money" and is reputed to have paid for her own ironing board during her residency at 10 Downing Street.) The Winston Churchill Foundation would not have to pay for the dinner, but we were also not allowed to sell tables at the British embassy. Again, the award dinner was not a moneymaker, but rather an occasion to build prestige and public awareness about the Winston Churchill Foundation.

Although President Reagan was absent that night, most of his cabinet attended the dinner. I was honored to be standing in the receiving line at the British embassy with the prime minister and her husband. A column in the *Washington Post* enumerated some of the 120 American and British luminaries attending and their remarks about the prime minister: Secretary of State George Shultz called Mrs. Thatcher "steadfast." UN

Ambassador Jeane Kirkpatrick called her "indomitable." Federal Reserve Board chair Paul Volcker said that Thatcher had "backbone." Other high-profile names who attended included Senator Claiborne Pell from Rhode Island, Senator John Tower from Texas, presidential assistant Michael Deaver and Treasury Secretary Donald Regan. Anne Armstrong, the first woman U.S. ambassador to the United Kingdom, attended, along with the previous recipient, Averell Harriman.

Mrs. Thatcher responded warmly to my introduction, especially when I said that, like Churchill, she thrived in adversity. The *New York Post* reporter commented that feminists would have approved of my speech because I did not mention Mrs. Thatcher's gender as setting her apart from her predecessors. Instead, listing the long line of leading prime ministers from Walpole to Churchill, I said, "Mrs. Thatcher stands alone as the only one to reach 10 Downing Street from the rank of . . ."—I paused for effect—"science." Indeed, one of the reasons the foundation chose to honor Margaret Thatcher was that she had originally been a scientist, majoring in chemistry at Cambridge.

In the Iron Lady's own speech, by way of thanks, she frequently made reference to "the president." The Cabinet members thought at first she meant President Reagan, but it soon became clear that she was referring to me—president of the Winston Churchill Foundation. After my speech, Treasury Secretary Don Regan, who sat to my left at the prime minister's table, turned to me.

"Who wrote that for you?" he asked. Implicit in his tone was that he was impressed and would like to hire this person as a speechwriter.

"Donald," I responded, "you may have people who write speeches for you—but I don't."

I would see Lady Thatcher several times over the years, including once at Cambridge University when I attended the ceremony at which she turned over her archives to Churchill College. After the Thatcher event, I was in a state of bliss—for a brief moment. Soon after, Father presented me with a challenge. "You've had two successful events for the Churchill Foundation, Johnny," he said. "I paid for one and the British government paid for the other. So when are *you* going to start raising money?"

First, I made an enormous effort to give the next award to Lee Iacocca, the former head of the Ford Motor Company and the CEO of Chrysler, but he turned it down. I even went so far as to buy a table at an event honoring him in order to get close to him, but he was unresponsive. In 1985, well before H. Ross Perot became known to the general public during his presidential campaigns in 1992 and 1996, the Churchill Foundation chose to honor the bold Texan. In 1979, the businessman had launched the private rescue of two executives of his company, Electronic Data Systems (EDS), who were being held hostage in Iran. The employees were freed, along with ten thousand political prisoners seized prior to the Iranian Revolution. Americans were enthralled with the story, immortalized in Ken Follett's best-selling novel *On Wings of Eagles*, which was made into a television miniseries with Richard Crenna playing Perot.

I was as much impressed with Perot's courage and determination as his business acumen; a year earlier, he had sold EDS to General Motors. I have to confess that, in selecting him, it certainly didn't hurt that Perot was a wealthy man (the second richest in America, behind Sam Walton) with many significant friends. Perot was also an Anglophile who owned an early copy of Britain's Magna Carta, one of the few copies to leave Britain. But how to reach him? People like Perot have an army of gatekeepers, and neither Harold nor I knew him personally. So I did what I do best. I picked up the phone and made a few calls. Miraculously, through Michael Kempner's father, my first cousin Carl, I soon got Perot himself on the line.

"Hello," he answered in his thick Texas twang.

"I'm John Loeb," I said. Realizing that time was scarce, I launched into it. "I'm head of the Winston Churchill Foundation, and I'd like to honor you with the Winston Churchill Award. Would you accept?"

"Absolutely," he said. He then invited me to visit him in Dallas. Harold Epstein and I traveled to Texas. The copy of the Magna Carta was hanging on the wall of Perot's office. Perot could not have been more admiring of Churchill, nor more grateful and modest about being considered for the award.

"Tell me about your people," Perot said.

"Uh," I stumbled, "My father is John Loeb and my mother is . . ." I went into my ancestry, the Loebs and Lehmans and Lewisohns.

We talked about Churchill and the Magna Carta, and I asked where he would like to receive the award. "Anywhere you like," he said. Obviously, if we were going to invite Perot's friends and associates, the event should be held in Dallas.

"What about right here in Dallas?" I proposed.

"Great," he said. Everything was fitting into place. But then he added, "But you know, I can't help you in any way."

Unfortunately, I didn't have any connections in Dallas. Though he said he could not be part of the planning, he did mention a friend of his, a major figure in the advertising business named Liener Temerlin. He added that were I to contact him, I should not use Perot's name.

I got Temerlin's number from Perot's receptionist and dashed to the nearest Wendy's to place the call. Harold didn't know where I got the chutzpah to do such a thing. But one thing I had learned was that when I call someone for the first time and say, "This is John Loeb," they take the call. I have always felt so honored that the name of Loeb, Rhoades was known everywhere. I could call any corporate executive and use this approach, and it would work like a charm.

Temerlin said he was tied up and couldn't possibly see me that day; but time was of the essence, since I was planning to go back to New York the next day. I had no choice but to break confidence and tell him that Perot had given me his name. That changed his mind, and he invited me to come over to his house later that day. Talking to Temerlin at his house, we learned that Perot had never once been honored in his hometown. When I boldly asked Temerlin to help us give Perot the honor he deserved, he agreed. He was a senior executive at one of the biggest advertising agencies in Texas, which had never had Perot or his businesses as a client. The dinner became an opportunity for Temerlin to connect with the richest man in Texas. We decided to go all out for the event, which would require a tremendous amount of coordination among Temerlin, Harold and myself. Landing Perot as our honoree was like firing one shot and hitting a bull's eye. There were events, editorials and free press all over town. We went to the newspapers, who declared a "Churchill Week" and offered an essay contest for high school students in Dallas, with the three winners landing an invitation to the dinner with their parents.

As luck would have it, Texas was about to celebrate the 150th anniversary of its independence as a nation before it became a state. (It was Texas's "sesquicentennial," a word that was tossed around a lot that week.) During its brief independence, Texas had maintained diplomatic relations directly with England, so Prince Charles was arriving that week to participate in the commemoration. Through Oliver Wright, the UK ambassador to the U.S., I contacted Prince Charles, who agreed to make the presentation to Perot on behalf of the Winston Churchill Foundation. Harold and I designed a medal with a ribbon in silver with Churchill's profile on it in honor of the occasion.

Temerlin took over the dinner and organized the whole thing, selling an incredible $2.5 million worth of tickets (the foundation ended up netting about $1.5 million). The event was held at the biggest hotel in Dallas in a ballroom that seated eighteen hundred guests. The dinner was one of the most lavish, elaborate parties I had ever seen. Everybody who was anybody in Dallas came out of respect for Ross Perot. Even First Lady Nancy Reagan, recognizing the import of the event, invited herself. There was a story, probably apocryphal, that the local Neiman Marcus sold out of evening gowns. The Navy's

PRESENTING THE WINSTON CHURCHILL AWARD TO H. ROSS PEROT

Prince Charles awards the Winston Churchill Foundation medallion to billionaire H. Ross Perot. The award had been given only twice previously.

Here are Prince Charles and Nancy Reagan after the WCF award to Ross Perot.

Ross Perot was enormously pleased with his specially designed medal of honor from the Winston Churchill Foundation.

glee club marched in and sang, a Marine Corps band marched in and played, and the famous soprano Leontyne Price sang a solo.

The enormous attendance reflected the words with which I began my introduction that night: "Mr. Perot, like Churchill, is one of the remarkable men of his time." Prince Charles made a wonderful and moving speech, with the winner of the essay contest standing nearby on the platform.

After Prince Charles presented the award and we finished a dinner that was a feast, everyone moved into a huge ballroom to mingle over coffee and dessert. On the balcony above, there were five or six pianos with superb artists playing *en concert*. This was Texas, which does everything big, and they certainly didn't disappoint; I've never experienced anything like that dinner before or since.

The next morning there was a meeting of those members of the Churchill board of directors who were in Dallas, including my father, Harold and me. Father, who completely dominated these meetings, went through a few managerial items and then said, "I guess that's it," and got up to leave. Before Father could go, Harold interjected. "Don't you think we should talk first about our tremendous success?" he asked.

Father clearly couldn't find it in himself to congratulate Harold or me on what was not only a great success, but also one that surpassed Father's goals. Over the years, Harold's carefully balanced diplomacy and editing of my contentious letters muted our frequent father-son skirmishes. If Harold hadn't brought it up at the meeting, no mention

I am pictured here in 1985 with Walter Annenberg and Prince Charles at Lee and Walter Annenberg's magnificent estate in La Mirage, California. Walter Annenberg, a fellow Anglophile, was our ambassador to the Court of St. James's during the Nixon years. The occasion was the Annenberg fund-raising event on behalf of The Prince's Trust, which Prince Charles established in 1976 for disadvantaged young people in the UK; it is an organization I have supported for many years.

The last time I saw Reagan was in 1989, when, on behalf of the Winston Churchill Foundation of the United States (of which I was the chairman), the Duke of Edinburgh presented him with the Winston Churchill Award. That award has been given only four other times in the fifty-eight-year history of the foundation: in 1981 to Averell Harriman, in 1983 to Margaret Thatcher, in 1985 to Ross Perot (presented by Prince Charles), and in 1991 to President George H.W. Bush (presented by the Queen of England).

would have been made that we had just netted $1.5 million dollars, $500,000 more than the campaign goal Father had set for me.

From the beginning, it was my intention that the Churchill Foundation Awards should be made selectively and not necessarily every year. This was both practical—as the honoree had to be someone truly special—and strategic. The rarity of the award raised its value. In 1989, three years after the Perot event, I proposed to Harold that the foundation next recognize President Reagan. The president had just finished his second term, and the Reagans had returned to their home in California, where presumably he would have fewer demands on his time. Because the president and I always had such a warm and positive relationship, the task of persuading him to accept the award didn't daunt me. He graciously accepted.

For help organizing the event I went to Leonore Annenberg. A philanthropist in her own right, Leonore had been chief of protocol under President Reagan and had sworn me in as the U.S. ambassador to Denmark in 1981. Leonore's husband, Walter Annenberg, a multi-millionaire publishing magnate, had also been a U.S. ambassador to the UK. I asked Leonore to chair the gala, but she demurred. Instead, she recommended Robert Wycoff, president of the Atlantic Richfield Oil Company, who would be very helpful with the California community. When Wycoff accepted, Leonore agreed to co-chair. Wycoff chose the posh Beverly Hilton for the party's setting. He had a whole team at Atlantic Richfield preparing the event, set for May 19, 1989. Like Temerlin had for Perot, Wycoff gathered all the right people to attend. With Nancy Reagan present, the event was announced at the L.A. Country Club, where Leonore had been one of the first Jewish members.

A breakthrough for the foundation came over the weekend. Lady Mary Soames and I were invited to the Annenbergs. We strategized as we drove there together. At that point, Robert Maxwell, the Eastern European-born British media mogul and a controversial member of Parliament, was the top donor to the dinner. Mary volunteered to say that, "Maxwell is giving $100,000, so we are planning on giving him the right to toast to the queen." Our hope was that somebody else would compete for that privilege. Perhaps Walter would rise to the occasion, since Maxwell was quite a contentious figure.

When Mary told Leonore about the toast, she got the hint. She replied: "It's up to Walter." I then went off to play, and later appeared for drinks before dinner in the library, where Walter, Lee and Mary were sitting. Leonore must have spoken to Walter, because as I walked in he got up immediately and said, "John, I have to talk to you." He took me privately out to the porch, where I thought I was going to receive a scolding. "Do you *know* who this fellow Robert Maxwell is?" he said.

"Well, I really don't, but he's been tremendously generous," I answered.

"He's a crook," Walter said, "and he has a terrible reputation. And I understand you want him to give a toast to the queen."

I replied, "I don't want him to toast the queen, but this is the only way we could get $100,000."

The hook was in, and Walter bit. "I'll give you $100,000," Walter offered, "plus another $100,000 for a table." Walter received the honor of toasting the queen, and the foundation received $200,000.

Once again, British royalty was a big draw. Prince Philip graciously presented President Reagan with the award, and a good chunk of the 1980s Hollywood A-list showed up, including the actor Tom Selleck and comedienne Phyllis Diller. The Los Angeles Chamber Orchestra performed, Bob Hope headlined the entertainment and Rosemary Clooney belted out all-time favorites for the audience. The next day, the *Los Angeles Examiner* gave the party extensive coverage, with a caption noting, "Any socialite who wasn't in intensive care was there." The *Los Angeles Times* also gave the party a six-column write-up, claiming that the president and Mrs. Reagan were "politely mobbed."[111] "It all seems to have come off rather well, hasn't it?" Lady Mary Soames modestly remarked. This was an understatement. The event netted $800,000 for the Churchill Foundation. Between the Perot and Reagan events, we had now raised $2.2 million, and, with our previous $400,000 and the market going up, we now had a nest egg to

It was historically significant when Queen Elizabeth II presented the Winston Churchill Foundation Award to President George H.W. Bush in the Rose Garden outside the White House on May 14, 1991. No British monarch had ever before presented an award outside of England, much less in public, until Queen Elizabeth II broke that tradition.

In this picture Queen Elizabeth and I look on approvingly as the president reads the text of his WCF award, both of us grateful that his acceptance speech was short because of the 100 degree heat.

help our scholars for the coming years. Those two events saved the Winston Churchill Foundation.

The *Los Angeles Examiner* had also interviewed me for its May 20th edition. I talked about the state of education in America, noting that our students in math and science ranked low in the fields that the Winston Churchill Foundation sponsors. "Commercialization of school sports is sabotaging American education," I said, pointing out how sports figures at many American universities have more prestige than their top students. I also pushed for minorities to be allowed to share more fully in academic opportunities. The *Examiner* headline read, "Sabotaging American Education: Loeb Contends System under Siege." The paper sensationalized what seemed to be a common-sense issue at the time—and one that, indeed, still is.

In 1991, we decided again to give the award to the sitting U.S. president—George H.W. Bush—but it came with a few significant hurdles. We also didn't know it was to be our last hurrah. I had known George Bush for years in different circumstances, and our

Ambassador Patricia Gates Lynch admiring my newly acquired C.B.E. medal.

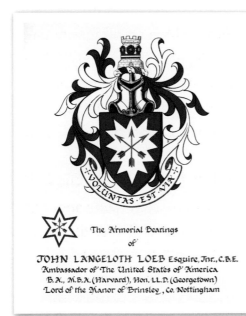

The Armorial Bearings
of
JOHN LANGELOTH LOEB Esquire, Jnr., C.B.E.
Ambassador of The United States of America
B.A., M.B.A. (Harvard), Hon. LL.D. (Georgetown)
Lord of the Manor of Brinsley, Co. Nottingham

This coat of arms came with my C.B.E. award, and a framed replica hangs in my New York home.

fathers knew each other when Prescott Bush was at Brown Brothers Harriman and my father was at Loeb, Rhoades.*

I attended an event at the White House where President Bush was being honored by former prime minister Margaret Thatcher. I happened to be standing at the bar next to White House chief of staff John Sununu. When I brought up the prospect of giving Bush the award, his eyes glazed over. Fortunately, he said, "Send me something in writing."

A few weeks later, while in Budapest, I got a call from Sununu at the White House. He said that the president would be delighted to receive the award—but it must be given to him by the Queen of England! Needless to say, we both knew this was a "highly unusual" request. Undaunted, I told him that we would work it out.

Antony Acland, the British ambassador to the U.S., had been an aide to Margaret Thatcher when we gave her the WCF award. I phoned him to intercede on our behalf. When I mentioned the prospect of the queen giving the president the award, I could hear the phone freeze over. There was a long pause before he said, "The queen *never* gives awards in public. And this is a foreign award—on top of which you are raising money."

"I know," I lamented, "but this is really, really important to the president." Antony said he would see what he could do, but I was not at all optimistic.

Miraculously, the queen agreed. As it happened, she was coming to the United States for, among other events, the planting of a linden tree

* In 1969, when Bush was a U.S. congressman and I was managing partner of Loeb, Rhoades, I went to see him in Washington. At lunch, I raised the issue that the staff for the Joint Committee on Taxation was planning to urge its members to raise the capital gains tax. I felt it was important that this not happen, and I said so. Bush hadn't even known about it and had to call the committee to confirm that I was right. He was not much help; what he really had on his mind that day was joining President Nixon at the Arkansas-Texas football game.

at the White House to replace one planted in 1937 in honor of her father's ascension to the throne. The ceremonial tree had been knocked down in a storm the previous year. It would be her first official visit to the United States since the Bicentennial in 1976. Her only conditions were that there be no gala and no fundraising at all. The event was to take place in the Rose Garden before a small audience: the queen and the president, along with their families and entourages and Churchill Foundation trustees and their invited guests. No matter the size of the event, the historical significance was huge. No British monarch had ever personally made an award presentation to a non-British honoree.

I had a serious discussion with Joseph Verner Reed, the White House chief of protocol. We deliberated and carefully planned every detail of what would occur in the Rose Garden, from who would say what to who would hand the award to the queen. It was planned that I was to have no role in the event. The queen was to pick the award up off a table and say, "I am delighted to present . . ."

On the day of the event, it was 100 degrees outside and climbing. I was standing in the Rose Garden, waiting for the president and the queen to come from a luncheon in the White House. There were microphones on the podium, which stood just outside the door in the assembly grounds where presidents often speak. But despite all the detailed prearrangements, nothing happened as planned. Instead, President Bush and the queen walked straight over to me, and he said, "I think you know Her Majesty." The queen, who looked quite lovely in a lilac suit with the proverbial brooch, was wearing a purple and white hat.

I made a few remarks regarding the Winston Churchill Foundation and "the spirit of the Anglo-American relationship," Churchill himself, and some comments about the scholars who had benefitted from the foundation. The queen handed President Bush the award and remarked that it was being given "in recognition of the leadership you've shared with the world in recent months."

When it was President Bush's turn to speak, he was overwhelmed by the heat. "I have prepared about a 45-minute speech," Bush said, to laughter, "but if I gave it, we would all melt."[112] Bush graciously thanked both the queen and me and spoke very briefly about Churchill's influence on both sides of the Atlantic. The event was covered for thirty seconds on CNN, which oddly showed me doing most of the talking. The president wrote me a letter soon after, thanking me and noting how he was "impressed with the foundation's objectives, which they seem to be meeting with flying colors."

One day after the event, Winston Churchill joked about how I had gotten Prince Charles, Prince Philip and now Queen Elizabeth II to present the Churchill Foundation

Awards. At a luncheon afterward, Pamela Harriman toasted me for this achievement, in particular for "landing" the queen. Three years later, in 1994, Her Majesty the Queen appointed me an honorary Commander of the British Empire in recognition of my "contribution to strengthening Anglo-American relations in the field of science and technology"—an honor I hold dear to my heart to this day.

While the two major fundraising events—the award dinners for Ross Perot and President Reagan—helped solidify the foundation's finances, to date no further Winston Churchill Foundation Award has been given. Father continued to chair the board until his death in 1996. In 2003, I asked Patrick Gerschel, who had been on the board for some time, to replace me as president while I became chairman. Harold had been executive director since 1961; he retired in 2006 after completing the Directory of Scholars. At that time, the foundation moved to the Fifth Avenue office of Gerschel & Co., and Peter Patrikis came in as the new executive director. (Patrikis recently retired, and Michael Morse has replaced him.)

Patrick Gerschel and Peter Patrikis together did an admirable job in carrying on what Carl Gilbert, Lew Douglas, Father, I and particularly Harold began. All have helped to make the Winston Churchill Foundation a successful reality. We started with $400,000 when I took over in 1979. When I stepped down from my fundraising role after twenty-four years as president, we had $13 million in the bank, largely from monies invested from the proceeds of our award dinners, enabling us to promote more annual postgraduate scholars.

The purpose of the foundation lives on, and it now awards fifteen scholarships a year to Churchill College. As someone who believes firmly and passionately in the necessity of supporting education—especially the sciences—I am gratified about all the work that has been done through this foundation.

THE JACOB AND VALERIA LANGELOTH FOUNDATION

The seats that my father and I held on the Langeloth Foundation board were truly legacies. We inherited both the honor and the responsibility because of the close business and personal relationship Jacob Langeloth had with my grandfather Carl M. (C.M.) Loeb in the 1900s. C.M. was Langeloth's protégé at the American Metal Company (AMCO). Langeloth died in 1914, and C.M., at the age of forty, eventually succeeded him as president. My Loeb grandparents named my father (and, by extension, me) for Langeloth out of admiration, gratitude and friendship. Father became chairman of the Langeloth board in 1963 and brought me on as a trustee in 1968.

Jacob Langeloth
(1852–1914)

This is the man for whom my father was named, and in turn, I too was so named.

Short in stature but large in vision, in 1887 Langeloth was one of two men who founded the American Metal Company (AMCO) as a subsidiary of a major German firm, Metallgesellschaft. The other founder was Berthold Hochschild, grandfather of the author Adam Hochschild. Langeloth served as president of the new company and Hochschild was treasurer. Subsequently, AMCO merged with Climax Molybdenum.

My grandfather Loeb was Jacob's star protégé, and when Langeloth died unexpectedly soon after the start of World War I, he succeeded him as head of American Metal. Grandfather was barely forty.

Our namesake came from a comfortable merchant family in Mannheim, Germany. Jacob Langeloth had studied French and English and was schooled at a *Handelsschule*, a trade school. He was a whiz at double-entry bookkeeping by 1873, when he was hired by the London branch of a very successful German company in Frankfurt called Metallgesellschaft, which dealt in nonferrous metals.[113] The young Jacob, both ambitious and smart, kept track of the company's figures by day and studied metallurgy into the wee hours of the night. His grasp of the subject catapulted him in just a few years from bookkeeping into management at Metallgesellschaft.

Because of the increasing importance of copper mining in America, Jacob Langeloth and Berthold Hochschild, both prominent figures in the parent firm, were dispatched from Frankfurt in 1885 to establish and manage a branch of the company in New York City. Jacob was named chairman of the newly formed American Metal Company, and Berthold Hochschild became the president and treasurer. The branch became successful, and the two men were allotted a good chunk of stock in the company. In 1913, before the Sixteenth Amendment would institute a personal federal income tax, both men quickly became wealthy.

Langeloth didn't marry until he was fifty-one, when he met thirty-two-year-old

THE AMCO FOUNDERS
In May 1912, the two founders of the American Metal Company (AMCO) posed for a picture with five of their managerial associates. Seated are Berthold Hochschild, founder and treasurer, and Jacob Langeloth, founder and president. Standing left to right are Theodore Stanfield, S. Adler, C.M. Loeb (my grandfather, looking very young), M. Roos and M. Schott.

According to a handwritten note on the photo, it was taken in the "old board room at 61 Broad," only two years before Jacob Langeloth died. My grandfather then succeeded him as company president at the age of forty and served in that post until 1929.

Valeria Knapp, the daughter of a talented itinerant portrait artist and the youngest child of a farm girl from Ossining, New York. In her memoir, *Utopia in the Hills*, Valeria wrote that she and her widowed mother wound up living in New York City, where she enjoyed an enviable sociable life.[114] She attended tea dances at the old Waldorf Astoria and stately dinners at Delmonico's, where women wore "gowns of heavy satins, and brocades and long white kid gloves."[115] She and a friend were managing a booth at an Actors Benefit bazaar when her friend's father dropped by, accompanied by his client, Langeloth. "He seemed to stand apart from every other person there," she wrote. "Our eyes met and my world stood still. Something told me I had met my future husband."[116]

As a young man, Jacob Langeloth had been too busy for courtship, but now he pursued Valeria as single-mindedly as he'd pursued success in industry. Impeccably groomed, the cherub-faced man, five feet tall with a chin dimple like Kirk Douglas's, was instantly smitten with the almost equally short Valeria. He took to wooing her with red roses and passion. In 1903, Langeloth took two big steps: he became an American citizen and then promptly married Valeria, despite their almost twenty-year age difference and the vigorous objections of her mother.

The Langeloths enjoyed eleven happy years together until August 2, 1914. In big block letters, Jacob wrote only one word in his diary that day: "WAR." Twelve days later, on August 14, he succumbed to a fatal heart attack. "His friends believe his death was hastened by worry over the European war,"[117] one newspaper wrote. Langeloth's will included a special assignment for Valeria: establish and maintain a facility to be known in perpetuity as "the Valeria Home." It was to be a recreation and convalescent home. It would serve a particular clientele:

> *People of education and refinement who cannot afford independent homes or to pay the charges exacted at health resorts or sanitaria. The home shall be open to all creeds, entirely non-sectarian and absolutely free from all religious tendencies whatsoever.* Such Home shall, so far as may be feasible, be self-supporting, and it is my preference that inmates pay weekly charges to be determined by the Directors, though in special cases, inmates may be accepted without any payment.*

Langeloth also explained his rationale for this unique legacy:

> *I have observed that homes of this character have been organized for the benefit of the very poor, who are not able to pay anything for their support during their convalescence or during the period of rest necessitated by ill health, while no provisions seem to have been made for people of education and refinement belonging to the middle classes, who would not be justified in asking for or accepting charity, but who are, nevertheless, not able to pay the prices exacted for a sojourn in the usual health resorts or sanitaria. It is for this reason that I do not desire the Home to be organized as a charitable institution but, in so far as the directors may deem it advisable, that it be upon a self-supporting basis.*

He added that "in no event shall the general character of the institution as herein outlined, be changed; nor shall the Home at any time be known by any other name than Valeria Home." He did give the trustees and directors some leeway, explaining that they should not consider themselves obligated to "slavishly follow any of the details in connection with the organization and management of the corporation." He added that he had "full confidence that they

---

* Though born into a Lutheran family, John Jacob Langeloth was an agnostic (Julian Aronson, *Valeria: The Story of Jacob Langeloth and His Legacy*, 1963).

LAYING THE VALERIA HOME CORNERSTONE

Jacob Langeloth's widow, the always elegant Valeria, stands here on a platform surrounded by the men responsible for the construction of the facility which she planned and supervised from start to finish. Presumably the group of men included the architect, John H. Duncan, who was also the designer of Grant's tomb.

Invited guests stood just below the platform, built for the occasion, which took place sometime in the early 1920s.

VALERIA HOME

The magnificent Valeria Home stood on over 800 wooded acres in the highest part of Westchester County, about three miles east of the Hudson River outside the town of Cortlandt, New York. The recreation and convalescent facility offered its guests many outdoor activities, including boating, swimming, tennis and hiking. Besides a handsome dining room, the central building held a well-stocked library. The home opened in 1924 to a grateful clientele, but because of an IRS ruling it had to be closed, and the property was sold in 1979.

CENTRAL BUILDING OF VALERIA HOME

It took more than 300 workmen and almost ten years to construct Valeria Home, whose central building is pictured here. Valeria Langeloth herself supervised the undertaking every step of the way, from the selection of a site to its completion. She then assumed management of the facility thereafter. Guests were charged only a nominal fee for their stay, for which Valeria received literally hundreds of letters of gratitude until she died at the age of eighty in 1952.

will carry out the general idea, wishes and purposes that actuate me in making this bequest."

Valeria personally oversaw every step of the construction of the Valeria Home, which took almost ten years to complete. Opened in 1924 outside the town of Cortlandt in Westchester County, Valeria Home included eight hundred acres with mountain trails, boating, an outdoor swimming pool, tennis courts, a library and a field house. Valeria not only guided her husband's dream facility into reality, she oversaw its operations thereafter, with stunning attention to detail, until her own death in 1952.

As a latter-day trustee of the Langeloth Foundation, joining the board in 1968, I knew the story of Jacob Langeloth and his remarkable wife. I also felt a strong connection to this man who had meant so much to my grandfather, and whose name my father and I shared. Consequently, I felt strongly that the terms of his will should be carried out in perpetuity. I believe that those entrusted with a foundation are obligated to follow not only the spirit, but also the *letter*, of its founder's will; consequently, I was sometimes a thorn in the sides of my fellow board members.

A major step had to be taken after the IRS ruled against its 501c3 (tax-exempt) status in April 1975. That IRS decision was precipitated because of Langeloth's stipulation that Valeria Home's middle-income guests should not be treated as "poor." They instead should be charged modest fees for their visits to the resort, even though these nominal fees did not cover Valeria Home's expenses. (It had been running in the red well before the IRS clamped down.) The IRS position was that by charging fees, the home was not eligible for tax-exempt status. The Valeria Home itself was therefore sold in August 1979. No longer paying the Valeria Home's expenses, the board now needed other ways to distribute the substantial foundation funds that became available after the sale.

The board majority leaned heavily on Langeloth's words about not expecting the trustees to "slavishly" follow his outlined desires. On the other hand, I frequently pointed out that Langeloth also wrote that he had confidence that the trustees would carry out his "general idea, wishes and purposes." Both sides passionately defended their positions, and there were more than a few heated exchanges at board meetings over the years. I was opposed to grants that, while going to worthy causes and people in need, did not qualify for what Jacob Langeloth intended—to help members of the middle class. I was almost always outvoted. Even my daughter Alexandra, who was then on the board, wouldn't side with me. While my father was still the board chairman, grants had been made only to hospitals as a way to defray the expenses of people who couldn't pay their medical bills. This frequently included the middle class as well as the poor and thus came under the umbrella of Langeloth's stipulations.

For many years, through service on the Langeloth Foundation board, Adam Hochschild (pictured above) and I shared a tradition treasured by both families, the Hochschilds and the Loebs. For almost all of the over 100-year existence of the foundation, the board was made up of only Hochschild and Loeb family descendants. In recent years, with a big push from Adam and me, non-family members have been invited to join the board. Their presence ensures the health and enduring existence of a foundation that means a great deal to both of us.

Harold Epstein, my right arm at the Winston Churchill Foundation, came on the Langeloth board a few years after I did. He remembers Father's short meetings, which sometimes ran only a half-hour or less. Because grants were made without formal applications being required, the board knew little about the grantees. As Harold has said, "Nobody dared to disagree with your father." When I became chairman, the meetings became longer and everyone spoke freely. Harold was experienced in working with foundations, and he agreed with me: grants should be awarded only when applications were complete and then reviewed by competent professionals. We also believed that grants should go to those proposals that could produce long-term positive results.

We managed to get a motion passed that made applications for grants mandatory, but even that was a squeaker of a vote. From then on, professionally prescreened applications were examined, discussed and voted on at board meetings, not just rubber-stamped. While I was still chairman, it was distressing to me that the board continued to rationalize grants that clearly did not help the middle class. I couldn't argue that the money wasn't going to worthy causes, only that the causes didn't fit the Langeloth intent, which was our mandate.

Because I was almost always on the other side of the board majority, Adam Hochschild, Berthold's very very left-wing grandson, came up with the idea that we split the foundation: Harold Epstein and I would run one half, where we could award applications for grants that addressed middle-income convalescence. Adam would run the other half, so he and the others could support liberal causes without my howls of protest.* However, the foundation was never split. In 2001, I resigned as board chair and Adam succeeded

---

* As a young man, Adam Hochschild co-founded *Mother Jones*, a politically left-wing magazine. He went on to become an author of seven nationally acclaimed books.

me. I did remain on the board, still advocating for Langeloth's wish to provide middle-class assistance.

Father Time eventually caught up with both Harold Epstein and me. Retirement from the board became mandatory at the age of eighty—a resolution that had been added to the board rules over both of our objections. In 2010, I submitted my formal resignation, wishing my fellow board members Godspeed. Knowing of my long battle with peripheral neuropathy, they made a generous grant in my honor to the Neuropathy Association, a national organization based in Manhattan. The current and open-ended scope of the foundation awards can be found, succinctly worded, on its website, www.langeloth.org. The top of the list of recent grants reads:

> *THE JACOB AND VALERIA LANGELOTH FOUNDATION:*
> *Supporting innovation in physical and emotional healing*
> *for underserved populations.*

Alas, no mention is made of the underserved middle class.

In 2011, Adam Hochschild wrote to my editor, Kathy Plotkin: "It is extremely rare to see a foundation or other nonprofit whose portfolio, after deducting investment advisory fees, has consistently outperformed the market over a long term. But Langeloth's did, and that's due to him [John Loeb Jr.]."[118] I am grateful to Adam for his warm words of approval of my management, and am proud to have been a part of such a prestigious organization that shares a connection to my family's legacy.

THE JOHN L. LOEB JR. FOUNDATION

While service on the boards of the two foundations—Langeloth and Churchill—were important familial legacies, another legacy from my family was the imperative of philanthropy.

Over the last twenty years, my major philanthropic interest has been in the field of religious freedom. Chapters 24 and 25 will tell that story. Besides my focus on religious freedom, I have contributed to over 650 organizations, covering a wide range of interests. Some have been relatively small, but I have deemed their need to be critical. I am grateful, indeed, that I have had the opportunity to help in sustaining so many worthy organizations.

I am only focusing on a few of the very important philanthropies I have been dedicated to over the years before my parents' gift in 1997.

HEALTH

National Meningitis Association

The philanthropy that has touched me the deepest deals with the childhood illness meningococcal meningitis. This disease directly and direly affected my friend Gary Springer, his wife Nancy and family, and especially his son, Nick.

In the spring of 1999, I was at Gary's Broadway office. Gary's father had, for many years, been the leading public relations person in Hollywood, and Gary had continued the business. He helped me promote my wine, Sonoma-Loeb, in a number of ways, although this was not in his usual business expertise. That day in his office, his son, who was just graduating from the eighth grade, had come to say good-bye to his father before he went off to summer hockey camp. Nicholas was a delightful, engaging and very athletic young man who loved hockey so much that he was going to spend the following summer improving his hockey skills so he could make the team at the high school he was heading to in the fall. He was hoping to be the team's goalie.

Two weeks into his summer at Camp Beckett in the Berkshires, Nick and his cab-

Pictured, left to right: Susan Calise, Victor Calise, me, Nick, Billy Hannigan and Sharon. I had donated money to support the New York Islanders sled hockey team, and Nick and two other team members came to my home to present me with a team jersey signed by all the members of the team.

in mates went for a three-day hike on the Appalachian Trail. At some point over the next few days he felt sick and started throwing up. He then went into a coma.

Nick had contracted meningococcal meningitis. He was picked up and taken by helicopter to a hospital. The doctors didn't expect him to live through the night. His family watched Nick's fingertips, toes, ears and all his limbs slowly turn black, while the doctors fought frantically to get his circulation flowing. The following week, still alive, his temperature soared to 108 degrees. He was moved to another hospital in New York City, where he underwent more than nineteen operations to amputate his legs above the knees and both arms to mid-forearm.

The family was devastated. But the miracle was that when young Nick Springer finally woke up, he incredibly accepted the situation without collapsing and actually with some good humor.

Nick has gone on to star on the United States Paralympic Wheelchair Rugby ("Murderball") Team, winning medals at the Paralympic Games in Beijing and London. His first year on the U.S. team, they won a Gold Medal at the International Wheelchair games in Rio de Janeiro.

Nicholas Springer

Nick finished high school and chose to play for the Sarasota, Florida, team, and he attended Eckerd College, from which he graduated with a degree in communications.

Nick is now thirty years old. He does a lot of work promoting the National Meningitis Association, which his mother, Nancy, and three other mothers had founded after Nick survived the illness.* He has the most wonderful outlook on life. I have never seen him sad. When I myself get upset, I think of Nick, and that helps me to put everything in my life into perspective.

---

* This fast-moving illness takes the lives of children from six months old to those in their twenties. It is usually contracted in facilities in which children gather: schools, camps, clubs, etc. A simple vaccine can protect a child from this horrific disease. But even for those who survive, the disease maims them, taking their arms or legs or both.

I became involved with Nick's life a few days after he contracted this terrible disease. Like many of his friends and neighbors, I gave money immediately to his church to help his family, who were facing a crushing financial burden. Over time, I supported a number of teams on which Nick played. Sharon and I have chaired the National Meningitis Association dinner every year. Sadly, Nick's mother died from liver cancer while Nick was winning his gold medal at the 2008 Paralympics in Beijing.

I have seen Nick at least a few times every year and, of course, at the annual gala. Not long ago, I was delighted to know that he was still seeing a lovely Chinese woman whom he really loves and who loves him. He contacted me very recently to learn how he could keep his Chinese girlfriend in America longer. Unfortunately, I told him there is only one solution—"you have to get married"—which has not happened yet.

Everything else I have done philanthropically pales in comparison to the Nick Springer story.

POVERTY

The Food Pantry in Harrison

I have often heard it said that 30 million Americans go to bed hungry. Whether that is an accurate figure or not, I wanted to be sure that no one in the Town of Harrison (Purchase is a district of Harrison), where I have lived since I was born eighty-seven years ago, goes to bed hungry. I contacted a former mayor of Harrison, Steve Malfitano, to ask his advice. He told me there was a food pantry in Harrison that was supported partially by the town and partially by individual contributions.

I began contributing annually to the Harrison Food Pantry, which, I have heard, more than a hundred families, at times, make use of. It is filled with food one can buy at a grocery store. Any individual can, without any questions being asked, go there and take what they need. I also discovered that the County of Westchester has a very large centralized food pantry that provides food, if needed, to residents of other towns and villages in the county. I don't know if it has always been this way, but upon investigation I have learned that not only is no one going to bed hungry in the town of Harrison, but also that no one goes to bed hungry in Westchester County.

AMERICAN DIPLOMACY

Council of American Ambassadors

For many years, I have been the vice chair of the Council of American Ambassadors. The Council of American Ambassadors is a relatively new organization promoting ambassadors who were political appointees—not Foreign Service Officers. I am also one of the key members of their Endowment Committee.

The Council is a very interesting organization because the political appointees are men and women, coming from all over the country, who have accomplished important, exciting things in their lives. It may come as a surprise to people that some of these non-career appointees have paid no money to become ambassadors. Instead, they have contributed to the country in other important, impactful ways.

The U.S. Diplomacy Center Foundation

I have become a friend of several of the ambassadors to Denmark over the years, both non-career and Foreign Service. Ambassador Stuart Bernstein, who lives in Washington, D.C., Palm Beach and Aspen, is a particularly good friend. He encouraged me to become one of the first hundred people to support the Diplomacy Center. The Diplomacy Center will be a museum to tell the story of our Foreign Service. It will be attached to our State Department.

VISUAL ARTS

International Council of The Museum of Modern Art (ICMOMA)

The International Council of MOMA was founded in the late 1950s. I believe I am one of the two or three longest-serving members of the International Council who are still alive today. I was there in 1962 when the International Council met at the White House. This happened to be in the middle of the Cuban Missile Crisis. Ironically, Jack Kennedy ended up spending half an hour with the council that day because Jackie had not arrived back from riding in Virginia.

The council was organized by Blanchette Rockefeller (Mrs. John D. Rockefeller III) and Eliza Parkinson. The original purpose of the International Council was to support new American artists. These artists, as well as MOMA itself, wanted to have their paintings shown at major exhibitions around the world. Most countries finance their artists so that they can show their works across the globe. Our government does not.

Another original purpose of ICMOMA was to help American ambassadors by providing paintings to show in their ambassadorial residences. I brought twenty-five paintings of new American artists to my residence in Denmark. I created a catalogue for these paintings, and every few weeks I had groups of Danish citizens come to my residence to see and learn about these paintings and American artists.

ICMOMA has grown from being a strictly American organization to an international one. Most of the greatest collectors in the world today from both the U.S. and around the world are members of ICMOMA. There is now another organization that was primarily established to help ambassadors bring American art to their residences, the Foundation for Art & Preservation in Embassies (FAPE).

American-Scandinavian Foundation and Danish Art

When I went to Denmark, I fell in love . . . with Danish art. Today, I have the largest private collection of Danish art in the world outside of Denmark's museums.

As a trustee of the American-Scandinavian Foundation, I have promoted Scandinavian art in general, and focused on Danish art in particular. I have supported a number of exhibitions at the American-Scandinavian Foundation as well as a number of lectures by professors and leading collectors of Scandinavian art.

Recently, the American-Scandinavian Foundation mounted an exhibition of thirty-seven of my most important Danish paintings. The show was a tremendous success. It gained a lot of recognition, and, for the first time, *The New York Times* reviewed an exhibition of Danish paintings owned by an individual. There is also increasing interest in Scandinavian art in general. Edvard Munch was the Norwegian painter of *The Scream* that sold a few years ago at auction for $120 million. Vilhelm Hammershøi, who lived in Denmark at the same time that Munch lived in Norway, is increasingly being recognized internationally as a very important artist.

EDUCATION

Educational Testing Service (ETS)

I had the opportunity to serve for six years on the board of the Educational Testing Service (ETS), founded in 1947. The service develops, administers and scores more than fifty million tests annually. A nonprofit organization, ETS advances quality and equity in education for people worldwide by creating assessments based on rigorous research. ETS serves individuals, educational institutions and government agencies by providing customized solutions for teacher certification, English-language learning, and elementary, secondary and postsecondary education, as well as conducting education research, analysis and policy studies.

All U.S. parents who have children who have gone to college or applied to college know they have taken a test called the "SAT." The Scholastic Aptitude Tests are written by the Educational Testing Service. The ETS and the SATs were set up in order to reach out to men and women applicants across the country because American colleges no longer wanted just wealthy private school students entering schools of higher education. They wanted the best and the brightest from wherever they were in America. The result was the development of these standardized tests, and of ETS to write them.

In 1986, I joined the board of ETS, based in Princeton, New Jersey. The ETS had been operating since the 1940s. It had done a good job of reaching out to pupils across the country, but at that time it was being severely criticized because women and minorities thought that the tests were oriented to white males born in America. There was tremendous pressure on the ETS and the SATs to see that the tests did not in any way discriminate against women or minorities of any kind.

It is interesting to note that in the average liberal arts college in this country, although not the Ivy League, the majority of students are women. Most of these liberal arts colleges currently have approximately 55–60 percent female and 40–45 percent male students. In fact, many educators are now concerned that men are dropping out of the educational system and are not even willing to take the SATs.

Harvard Divinity School and Loeb Fellowships

I also supported the Religious Literacy Project, a program within the Harvard Divinity School. This program coordinates well with fellowships provided by the Ambassador John L. Loeb Jr. Initiative on Religious Freedom at Harvard. These fellowships were created with income generated from a Loeb, Rhoades donation in 1967 to the Harvard Business School.

Prince of Wales Foundation

My love of England has involved me in two educational projects. First is the Winston Churchill Foundation of the United States (WCF), discussed earlier. The WCF sends approximately fifteen college science students each year to Churchill College at Cambridge University for a year of graduate study in the scientific field.

The second involvement I have with English charities involves contributions made to a variety of causes either supported by Prince Charles personally or by the Prince of Wales Foundation. The foundation was founded in 1997, and I became a member in 2003. The contributions are decided on by the Prince of Wales himself, such as the Prince's Foundation for Building Community, the Royal Drawing School and the Rose Town project in Jamaica. Some contributions have even been given to special projects in the United States, such as Phoenix House. He has also supported a number of projects to preserve English architectural masterpieces.

For Sharon and myself, the Prince of Wales Foundation, besides its serious work, has provided us with very enjoyable social occasions. In addition to increasing my knowledge of English history, the prince is extremely intelligent and knowledgeable on almost every subject, charming, totally down to earth and very easy to talk to. We have also had the opportunity to share time with him at a number of venues, including his private home, Clarence House, and almost every year at a dinner at Buckingham Palace. Before I joined the Prince of Wales Foundation, I had met the prince a number of times, including once with Princess Diana, when I had a dance with her.

RELIGION

Although I do not consider myself to be a particularly religious being in terms of ritual and observance, I do have great respect for religion, for various religions and for the healing and spiritual comfort that they bring to many.

My love for Judaism, including Israel and, more specifically, American Judaism and its history, has become a more and more salient aspect of my life over the years—perhaps because I was raised with no Jewish education. In fact, I grew up celebrating Christmas and Easter. My parents told me these were national holidays. I actually was never inside a synagogue until I was nineteen years old, when my Uncle Herbert Lehman, a former senator and governor of New York, died. I was never bar mitzvahed; my father was never bar mitzvahed. Only one of my many first cousins, Larry Buttenwieser, was bar mitzvahed.

To my great surprise, I found that many Americans had no knowledge that Jews were living in our country as early as before the Civil War. So, in conjunction with the American Jewish Historical Society, I developed and supported the creation of the Loeb Jewish Portrait Database, which is available on the Internet and contains portraits of approximately four hundred noted American Jews who lived here before 1865. I felt that this was an important part of history to be shared, as it signifies the longevity and early contributions of Jews in our nation. (You can read more about the database in chapter 24.)

I have also contributed to various Jewish museums and archival repositories, a range of synagogues and temples, and organizations supporting human rights. Regarding Israel, I have been taken with it ever since I first visited as a young man, and have supported universities and museums there.

I have many friends who are not of the Jewish persuasion and have donated to their religious institutions as well.

While I am well aware that countless wars have been fought over religion throughout the ages, I heartily endorse the statement of the Appeal of Conscience Foundation, founded in 1965 by my dear friend Rabbi Arthur Schneier: "A crime committed in the name of religion is the greatest crime against religion."

RELIGIOUS FREEDOM

In addition to my personal foundation funding the above-mentioned organizations, I thought long and hard about how I could have a significant impact in a particular arena that had not been a popular recipient of philanthropy: religious freedom. This was due to the anti-Semitism I experienced as a schoolboy. More specifically, I felt it very important to promote the very moving historic letter that George Washington wrote to the Hebrew Congregation of Newport, Rhode Island, in 1790. That letter proclaimed religious freedom for all in our newly formed nation—the first time any head of state had said such a statement.

As a subset of religious freedom, I organized three exhibits to tell the story of American Jews who had arrived in this country as early as 1654. I gave one exhibition in connection with the Fraunces Tavern, home of the Sons of the Revolution; one in connection with the Daughters of the American Revolution* in Washington, D.C.; and one at the Museum of the City of New York. I am happy to know that just recently there was an exhibition of a similar concept produced by the New York Historical Society.

My most ambitious project in the area of religious freedom was made possible by the sale, upon my parents' death, of their brilliantly reviewed $85 million art collection. Although they left no money directly to us (my four siblings and me), the sale's proceeds were used to establish a family foundation. Originally, I was the chairman. My sister Debby had a good idea of dividing the foundation into five foundations. Each of us received approximately $17 million.

It was this money that provided the wherewithal to buy two buildings on the campus of Touro Synagogue in Newport, Rhode Island, and build a visitors center there. In chapter 24, you will read the story of the Loeb Visitors Center. This Center tells the story of how religious freedom for all thirteen states began in Rhode Island in the 1600s under the leadership of Roger Williams, a minister from Boston and England.

I have been told that a full-fledged freestanding visitors center with an educational mission like the Loeb Visitors Center for a church, mosque, or synagogue is unique. There is no visitors center for Westminster Abbey, St. Patrick's Cathedral, the Taj Mahal, or the Great Am-

---

* I discovered in my youth that my grandmother was a Daughter of the American Revolution. This surprised me; I was not aware that the Daughters of the American Revolution and the Sons of the American Revolution are genealogical organizations, and that if you are a descendant of someone who fought in the American Revolution, you become a member of the Daughters of the American Revolution regardless of whether you are Christian, Jewish, Muslim, black or Hispanic. This discovery propelled my interest not only in my genealogy, but also in genealogy in general. (See Appendix F: Genealogy, including Sons of the Revolution and Lord of the Manor.)

sterdam synagogue, as far as I know. Dr. Michael Feldberg has researched this issue for me.

Once I opened the Loeb Visitors Center (LVC) in August 2009, I felt that the information therein should be exported to the world at large. To do this, I created the George Washington Institute for Religious Freedom (GWIRF).

With a very substantial gift in 2016, seven years after I created GWIRF, I founded the Loeb Institute for Religious Freedom at the George Washington University. You will read more about GWIRF and the Loeb Institute at George Washington University in chapter 25.

I am extremely pleased that, as a result of these various endeavors, the George Washington Letter has become increasingly embedded in the public conscience.

MY SIBLINGS AND THEIR PHILANTHROPY

My siblings all have the same Lehman/Loeb philosophical attitude about philanthropy. Like me it was, in a way, their *religion*.

Judy, my late beloved older sister, contributed to many charities and causes. Her favorite charity was Exponents. Exponents provides individualized strategies that respond to the personal needs of men and women with histories of substance abuse and incarceration, regardless of their stage of addiction or recovery. Many are at risk because of HIV or hepatitis C. Exponents has assisted individuals to stabilize their lives through health and wellness training. Its vision is to create an equal playing field for all and help them to live in a world without AIDS and where addiction is a disease and not a criminal act.

My sister Judy

My sister Ann

My lovely sister Ann, whom I was very close to growing up, was married to Edgar Bronfman Sr., with whom she had five children and twenty-five grandchildren. Ann contributed to charities all over the world, but particularly in New York and Washington. Indeed, she did so many things it is impossible to list them all. Her favorite charity was the Jewish Community Center of Washington, D.C. (the DCJCC). There is a gallery named in her honor at the DCJCC. More important is what was said about her shortly after her death in 2011: "The Washington Community has lost a great person who made the life of so many around her better in so many ways. She did so quietly and with little fanfare."

Arthur, Ann's twin, is my only brother. I have developed a deep, caring bond with him, especially in these later years, that gives me great happiness. Everyone who knows Arthur is aware he is a great philanthropist. However, due to his reserved, quiet nature, most of his contributions, although generous, have been anonymous.

My youngest sister, Debby, has lived most of her adult life overseas in London. She says, "I've always been interested in giving to causes, places and institutions that I feel could benefit from my foundation. I started by giving small amounts to many places, and then decided that I would rather give more money to small institutions where I could really make a difference. The places that I am most interested in are Villa I Tatti, the Harvard school for Italian renaissance studies; Sir John Soane's Museum; the Watts Gallery; and the Courtauld Institute. I am also a great supporter of the National Gallery, the National Portrait Gallery, the National Theatre, Sadler's Wells, the Royal Opera House—all institutions that benefit the minds and hearts of my adopted country, Great Britain."

My sister Debby

My brother, Arthur

My aunt Dorothy and Richard Bernhard were in London when this picture was taken. Among the countless causes Dorothy served was the administration of the Lehman fund that helped German relatives escape the Holocaust.

CHAPTER TWENTY

Family Roots:
Reunions at the Lehman Wing of the Metropolitan Museum of Art (1989) and Rimpar, Germany (1996)

Growing up, I was led to believe by my parents that there was really no difference between Jews and Protestants and Catholics. The only notable difference was that Jews did not believe that Jesus was God. We thought he was a wise and generous man and a great teacher, who also happened to be Jewish. Until I was nine years old and went away to boarding school, I'd never had any experience that led me to believe that my mother and father's views were incorrect. Neither identified too strongly with being Jewish—Mother attended temple on the High Holidays, but Father didn't even do that. He was not interested in being Jewish. He was an American and a Son of the American Revolution (descended from Jacob Phillips, who was in the South Carolina Militia). He once wrote a letter to a friend, Frank Wyman, who was from one of the most famous and wealthiest families in Czechoslovakia and had come to America in the 1930s. Father wrote that he was different from Frank in that he was a "real American," since his grandmother's family went back to 1697 in the United States. Frank, although a great friend, bristled at what felt like an unnecessary declaration and division between the two men.

Abe Foxman of the Anti-Defamation League told me that during the Hitler years, anti-Semitism grew tremendously in the United States. It was only after World War II that it began dropping to where it is today, to a more modest level. Over the years, I have tried to understand anti-Semitism, precipitated by the callousness of my classmates that Saturday night so many years ago. In 2011, Phyllis Goldstein wrote an enlightening book called

A Convenient Hatred: The History of Antisemitism. Goldstein follows the history of this peculiar prejudice—which actually began six hundred years before Christ. The book traces stories of Jews all over the world in their constant search for a safe place to call home.

One of the things that confused me about the harassment I received as a child was that I'd always thought of myself as an American. I didn't understand the nuances of history and heritage that caused my classmates to view me as a "Jew," separate and different. As I learned more and thought more, my sense of identity was formed—born from a prejudice that had ambushed me as a child.

Sometime in the late 1940s or early 1950s, I discovered a hardcover brochure put out by Lehman Brothers. It referred to the fact that the original three Lehman brothers had come from a town in Germany called Rimpar. They were called "itinerant merchants" because Henry had been a peddler, but the brochure ignored the fact that his parents were well-to-do cattle brokers. It turned out that the first Lehman arrived in America in 1844 and, indeed, had peddled his way from Mobile to Montgomery, Alabama, where he set up a little store named H. Lehman. When Emanuel arrived, the name became H. Lehman and Bro. When my great-grandfather Mayer arrived in 1850, the name became Lehman Brothers.

In 1979, I was in Frankfurt on a business trip at the same time that a good friend, Bob Marston, and his new bride, Carol, were honeymooning there. I called the Marstons and asked if they would be up for a weekend trip to go ancestor hunting in Rimpar. Despite the fact that it was their honeymoon, they were good sports and said they would come. At the front desk of my hotel, we inquired about the location of Rimpar. The concierge got out a large map and a huge directory, listing all the towns of Germany and pointing out that Rimpar was in a region known as Lower Franconia. Showing us the route to travel, he indicated that the town was near Würzburg, less than two hours away.

We arrived, with high spirits and high hopes, in Würzburg, a beautiful university town in the heart of vineyard country. By now, my companions were thoroughly caught up with the search. At first, we found no one who spoke a word of English. Accosting several natives with inventive sign language, we managed to learn the way to Rimpar.

Upon reaching the Lehman hometown, we found a priest who spoke English. I told him that my family originally came from Rimpar in the early 1800s and that I was trying to trace those German roots. We had certainly found the right man, as he was in charge of keeping all the town's family records. He couldn't have been more cordial, and after tea at his home, he showed us a huge book of records. The Marstons helped me pore over them, but there were no Lehmans (or Lehmanns, the original spelling) in the books. Not one. It was then that our new friend asked carefully, "By the way, was your family Jewish?"

"Yes," I answered.

"Oh dear." He paused, and then with evident reluctance added, "Unfortunately, the records of all the Jews were destroyed." A dead silence fell on our little group as the import of that sentence washed over us. I thanked him warmly. He'd done all he could.

The Nazis had not only killed many of my relatives, but they had destroyed all traces of their presence. There was nothing to show that they had ever been there. Our dispirited little group left Rimpar. "Well, that's that," I said to the Marstons. "So much for tracing the Mayer Lehman family."

But this was only the beginning of what would become a long quest. As is so often the case, the world had to change before new revelations would surface. In November 1979, the first gathering of the Children of Holocaust Survivors took place in New York, and by 1981, the first international gathering of twenty thousand survivors and their children was held in Israel, attended by Elie Wiesel and many others. The suppression of their trauma would finally come to an end. Survivors told their stories, and therapists developed new techniques for healing. Even before documentation actually began to surface from police and secret military archives, recordings of survivors' memories opened the way to a whole new body of research.

The Lehman family held its first family reunion in the Robert Lehman Wing of the Metropolitan Museum on June 15, 1989. I did much of the public relations work along with my cousin Billy Bernhard. Father helped plan the event while Mother secured the museum. But Wendy Lehman Lash, Herbert's granddaughter and a civic leader in her own right, was its prime mover. The year before, Wendy had updated the family tree originally compiled by Herbert and Edith Lehman. Wendy had realized there was a "whole generation I knew nothing about" [119] and thought it was long past time for us all to meet and learn about each other.

For the opening night at the Met, Wendy created a beautiful Lehman family tree with every member of four Lehman generations represented. She even color-coded the name tags so that a member could know to which of the ten branches he or she belonged. And she distributed a directory. *The New York Times* wrote about it:

> *The huge and colorful family tree, displayed on an easel, was much admired but still unframed. "That's because I'm waiting for all the relatives to tell me I spelled their names wrong," Mrs. Lash said with a wink. . . . Everybody, especially the children, seemed intrigued by the tree. Pointing to a branch near the top, Sandra Friedman told her 6-year-old son, Daniel, "See, that's you up there." "That twig?" asked Daniel.*

Four generations of Lehmans attended the family's first reunion, held in the Lehman Wing at the Metropolitan Museum in June 1989.

> *Also on display were family photographs, taken at the turn of the century, on loan from the Lehman Suite of Columbia University's School of International Affairs. The sign under a photo of a little Lehman in a frilly Victorian dress asked, "Do you know who this baby is?"*
>
> *Nobody seemed to know. Nor did they seem to know why the family had never held a reunion before. But 83-year-old Helen Lehman Buttenwieser, a lawyer and the first woman to head the Legal Aid Society, had an idea. "Perhaps we never thought about it," she mused.*[120]

That night, 170 members of the Lehman family line discovered connections they never knew existed. Georgia Dullea in *The New York Times* cited all the illustrious figures present, from the original families extolled in *Our Crowd* to others related through marriage. Mother was quoted in the article as noting what outstanding citizens we all were, even in the youngest generation.[121]

That event lit a fire within me. All the marvelous exchanges and discoveries, along with the wonderful sense of personal identity that came from being together in this remarkable setting, whetted my appetite to do it again, this time as a pilgrimage into the past.

A few weeks after the Lehman reunion, in the spring of 1989, fate intervened regarding my more than twenty-year-old search for the original Lehmans of Rimpar. It all began because of a beautiful woman I was seeing during my bachelor years. While visiting London, I was much taken with Baroness Nadia von Seckendorff of Hamburg. The Seckendorffs are a very illustrious German noble family going back for centuries. Their diverse name-bearers include Veit Ludwig von Seckendorff, the famed statesman and economist who helped unite Germany after the Thirty Years' War. Their family tree of many branches—only three of which remain—includes poets, writers and journalists in more contemporary times. The family had lost much of its money because of World War II. While the baroness lived modestly, she retained the beauty, culture and grace of her noble family's values. Uncle Herbert had quoted Great-Grandfather Mayer as saying that he left Germany because he couldn't abide the aristocrats and their ways. I think he would have made an exception for the baroness.

I later flew to her home in Germany for a visit, during which we prowled a bookstore together. While waiting for the lovely baroness to make her purchases, I wasn't even trying to read the books, since I didn't speak or read German. However, my eye fell on one title that drew me: *Würzburg Juden*. Even with my limited German vocabulary, I recognized those two words: Würzburg and Jews. I picked up the book and began leafing through it. I remembered the town's name from my trip to Rimpar with the Marstons. I had also just seen the Lehman brochure a few weeks earlier at the Lehman family reunion that mentioned the family was from a small town called Rimpar near Würzburg. And I knew the word "Juden"—Jew—an expletive scrawled across stores and synagogues during the mounting anti-Semitism that led to the Holocaust. I picked up the volume and quickly

My son, Nicholas, is shown here meeting Wendy Lehman Lash and her husband, Stephen, at the Lehman reunion held in the Robert Lehman Wing of the Metropolitan Museum.

turned the pages, then glanced through the index. There was not a single mention of the Lehmans.

As I stood in the German bookstore with the Baroness Nadia, my memory whirled back to my trip to Rimpar and those missing Jewish records. Upon returning to my hotel, I immediately picked up the telephone. I tracked down the phone number of the author of *Würzburg Juden*, Dr. Roland Flade, who was also the editor of the *Würzburg Main Post*. Flade, who had done graduate work in the UK and received his PhD from SUNY Oswego, spoke very good English. Introducing myself, I asked him if he was familiar with the name "Lehman." He was not.

"Well, then, perhaps you've heard of Lehman Brothers?" He answered that he had; the well-known investment firm had recently established a large office in Frankfurt. Explaining to Dr. Flade that Lehman Brothers was no longer my family's firm, I gave him an outline of our family history, including Herbert Lehman's work as governor of New York and later as head of the United Nations Relief and Rehabilitation Administration. He was indeed familiar with my great-uncle's postwar refugee work. I mentioned that in looking through his book, I had found no mention of any Lehmans.

"Where were they from?" he asked.

"Rimpar," I said.

"Well, that's why they're not there," he replied. "They came from Rimpar, not Würzburg." There was a well-defined regionalism in that part of the world, and such differences were not taken lightly. I told Flade about the recent Lehman family reunion in New York and that the Lehman story in America is well documented, going back to 1844; but virtually nothing is known about their German roots.

Roland Flade had a deep interest in the Holocaust. To write *Würzburg Juden*, he had received a grant from the Obermayer Foundation, as had many other German scholars.[*]

An increasing number of non-Jewish scholars had been encouraged to write the history of their local German-Jewish communities. Studies had shown that in Germany, education about the Holocaust was having the opposite of its intended effect. It was actually *fueling* anti-Semitism. One of the reasons was that the constant framing of Jews as victims brought out guilt and victim fatigue in the younger German population, which manifested as anti-Semitism. The grant's purpose was not to elicit guilt but rather to show how the Jewish presence over the centuries—now erased from history—had enhanced German

---

[*] The Obermayer German Jewish History Awards are given annually by the German government to non-Jewish Germans seeking to restore remembrance of Jewish culture in their regions (see Dan Fleshler, "Does Education Fuel Anti-Semitism?" *Jewish Daily Forward*, February 17, 2012).

civilization. In the words of Anton Kutt, the mayor of Rimpar, "Under the Nazis, this cultural heritage—just like the Jews and the documents proving their presence—had been destroyed and all but disappeared."

When I asked Dr. Flade if he would consider writing something about the Lehmans of Rimpar, he indicated that he had very little free time, but he would "think about it." I interpreted this to mean that he was going to look into it. Flade set about trying to find documents where we'd been told there were none. A year and a half later, I got a letter from Roland. His first success had come late in 1989 with the discovery of a single document in the Rimpar town hall bearing Abraham Lehman's name. "Success came so late that I almost gave up," he wrote. "But . . . now I could start to dig further into the history of [Loeb's] forebears."[122]

But the real bonanza came when Dr. Flade found an enormous archive on microfilm in the basement of the palace of the prince-bishop in Würzburg.* The palace itself had been turned into a museum, with paintings on the wall from the Italian master Giovanni Tiepolo, who worked extensively in Germany. The basement was being used to store part of the Bavarian State Archives. Since Munich didn't have room for them, they had sent the records back to the region from which they originated. Dr. Flade was excited, having not only found traces of our family, but also extensive material *directly* mentioning the Lehmans. He also had unearthed one of the largest troves of Gestapo records in Germany. Although the original documents had been destroyed, the materials on microfilm enabled Flade to begin matching up various names and attempting to retrace the Lehman family history. Only a truly dedicated and skilled researcher like Roland could have achieved what initially seemed a "mission impossible." Roland acknowledged that the experience of "chips starting to fall into place" had happened to him before in historical research—he calls them "magic moments"—but it happened "most often in connection with my work for and about the Lehman family."[123]

This is how we learned that Abraham Lehmann (originally Løw) had been a successful cattle merchant, judging from the high property tax he paid. The family house,

---

* In 1576, the prince-bishop of Würzburg used the money from a vineyard to build a new hospital. He decided the best location for this would be the Jewish cemetery and then used the stones from the cemetery for other buildings in Würzburg. In the 1980s, when one of these buildings was being rebuilt, a developer came across Jewish writing on the stone and all construction stopped. On our visit we met with the professor at the University of Würzburg who had helped to recover most of the stones from the Jewish cemetery. All the stones were re-created and laid out inside an enormous barn-like structure—on two levels. The professor then became so fascinated with everything Jewish that he planned to create a traveling exhibit of the stones to show the world. Most of the 1,435 headstones are now in the Shalom Europa Jewish Museum, "constituting the world's single largest collection of medieval Jewish tombstones" ("Letter from Würzburg," *Canadian Jewish News*, April 24, 2013).

In 1994, Roland Flade and I discovered this moss-covered gravestone of Eva Lehmann in a Jewish cemetery near Würzburg. She was my great-great-grandmother (Mayer Lehman's mother).

which is now a pharmacy, had originally belonged to the prince-bishop of Würzburg. The prince sold it, along with the town hall, around the late 1700s or early 1800s, and it was then broken up into apartments. Roland brought to light not only whole sections of our earlier family history, but an integral missing piece that had been lost. In fact, Flade's book, *The Lehmans: From Rimpar to the New World: A Family History*, begins with the story.

With the Nuremberg Laws of 1935, Jews in Germany were disenfranchised and forbidden from marrying or having sexual relations with non-Jews. The Nazis set out to systematically impoverish the Jewish population, forcing most of them to live off their savings or charity. Hundreds of Jews appealed to influential Jewish people in the United States—especially New York Governor Herbert Lehman—for help. In 1938, the American Lehmans set up the Mayer Lehman Charity Fund, managed by my aunt Dorothy Bernhard, to help family members. The open immigration policy to America from Mayer's time had ended. The United States had quotas, which made the situation for Jews in Germany quite desperate. For a while, the Lehman Fund offered affidavits promising to support not only family members but anyone with the name of Lehmann, until the demand became too great. Emigration to the United States ceased in 1941. In many cases, it took additional help from overseas organizations like the Joint Distribution Committee to ensure as many Jews as possible got out of Germany in time.

Under my great-uncle's considerable influence, a hundred affidavits of support were issued to bring the remaining Lehmanns from Germany to America. Of those, only sixty-five emigrated. With the destruction of the Rimpar and Rieneck synagogues on Kristallnacht, November 9–10, 1938, my cousin Berthold Neugass was arrested and sent to Dachau. Since all documents for his emigration were soon in order, he was released, although it took another year for the family to leave Germany. This was alarming because of the Germans' cut-off date of 1941. In the meantime, all the remaining Jews of Rieneck had moved to Frankfurt am Main. By 1941, Berthold and his family were settled in Newark, New Jersey. Berthold's sister Lina wrote to Governor Lehman asking for an affidavit, as she was now "all alone." The Lehman Fund tried to help her, but she was shipped to an unnamed camp in Eastern Europe and left no further trace. Another family the fund was unable to rescue entirely were the Thalheimers. Eva Lehman, the daughter of Seligman and Mathilde, married into the Thalheimer family of Würzburg. The Thalheimers had helped build the city's synagogue, which was also destroyed on Kristallnacht. Eva's grandson Leo was arrested that night but released. By that time, Eva was a widow, as was her daughter, Lina, whose husband had died in "protective custody." Eva stayed behind in Germany to care for Lina, who by now was terminally ill. When the roundup of Jews began, Leo fled Germany with his wife, Selma, and daughter, Ruth, thanks to the affidavits and support offered by the American side of the family. Upon their arrival, they received $125 a month. Herbert took a personal interest in them, inviting them to his house for Thanksgiving and inquiring after Ruth's education.

Back in Germany, Eva and her daughter had already been reduced to living in one room of their house. In December 1940, the Gestapo came to confiscate their linens and other values but left empty-handed. Eva was deaf, and Lina had locked all the closets and cabinets before she went into the hospital. In September 1941, Lina died in the Jewish old age home to which they had all been moved in February. She likely had cancer. Eva was sent away a year later with her caretaker, Minna Ausbacher, and Minna's fifteen-year-old daughter. All three women died in Treblinka. Sadly, they could not be rescued.

But at least their *stories* have been, thanks to the work and efforts of Dr. Flade. With Roland Flade's book heading for publication, I began to press for a Lehman reunion—this time where we all began, in Rimpar. With Roland's help and yet more from fate, doors began to open. In 1996, my cousin Arthur Altschul went to Würzburg to lend five Tiepolo paintings to the Würzburg *Residenz* for a show called *Der Himmel auf Erden: Tiepolo in Würzburg* (*Heaven on Earth: Tiepolo in Würzburg*). Arthur made a trip to Rimpar, where he had animated discussions with the mayor, Anton Kutt, and Christian Will, a Bavarian parliamentarian who had witnessed Nazi atrocities firsthand. A year later, I returned to Rimpar to meet both of them. I found Christian Will to be a man of kindness and great foresight. Christian had never forgotten the destruction of Rimpar's synagogue, when all the sacred objects and books were thrown out into the street. As in other endeavors, I was looking for a way to transform the tragedy wrought by anti-Semitism into something meaningful and healing.

Our family's enthusiastic interest in our ancestral birthplace, coupled with Roland's discoveries, put wind in the sails of Rimpar officials. Roland was tireless in assuring the success of the reunion. The town's leaders understood how important it was that a key part of the initiative come from the town itself. While I was preparing lists for invitations to 250 Lehmans, Roland inspired both the mayor and the Town Council of Rimpar to create a permanent exhibition honoring their former Jewish residents. This was to include not only the Lehmans who had set down in the New World, but also those Rimpar residents who had died in the Holocaust.

On May 3, 1996, the Rimpar Town Council unanimously approved Roland's proposal for an exhibit. They even allocated monies for the display and for the reunion's reception. Christian Will designed and paid for the plaque to be placed on my ancestral home, giving it landmark status. Though he was busy, Roland Flade regularly visited the Rimpar Town Council to help them overcome any last-minute misgivings. Mayor Kutt invited all family members to Rimpar for the permanent exhibition as I tried to give deposits to the hotels for an ever-changing number of attendees. Organizing the affair was complex, but well worth it.

Once we sent out an announcement about the forthcoming reunion, a tremendous ripple effect occurred in the Jewish press worldwide. Coincidentally, we discovered that the Würzburg high school was a "sister" to the Edith Lehman High School in Dimona, Israel (the Israeli school had been named for Herbert Lehman's wife). The Würzburg Gymnasium had set up the exchange without any knowledge of the Lehman connection to Rimpar. There was a program between the two schools where selected German students lived in Israel for part of the year while the Israelis studied in Germany. I contemplated this exchange in contrast to the massacre of eleven Israeli athletes at the Munich Olympic Games in 1972. I believe it shows how extraordinarily far the efforts toward understanding have come since that awful event.

Mother didn't want to know about her ancestors—they were foreign to her. This is not too different from other children of immigrant families. They don't want their parents or grandparents to speak a foreign language in their new land, and they don't want to dwell on their heritage. They're looking to assimilate.

On May 17, 1996, Mother passed away. She had been sick for some time from emphysema, so we all had thought we were reconciled to her death, but it was a shock. *The New*

York Times published a very kind and gracious obituary, which noted Mother's diplomatic and charitable work. They quoted her as once saying, "One thing I had in my mind, I'm never going to be the richest person in the cemetery."[124]

The Rimpar Reunion gave me yet another family gathering in which to celebrate Mother's life, and to grieve. The circle of mourners was widening. I was already in London when I connected with Ruth Thalheimer Nelkin, Leo's daughter, who had read about the reunion in the local press. She was Seligman Lehman's great-granddaughter. I urged her to come, but as she had been born in Würzburg and escaped with her parents under very traumatic circumstances, she was fearful of facing that place again. Ruth agonized over the decision; her husband thought she should stay home. But at the eleventh hour she decided that she would regret not sharing this experience with us and came with her daughter, Amy. In the village of *Veitshöchheim*, Martina Edelman traced Ruth's family tree, going all the way back to the eighteenth century. Ruth returned to the house of her birth and to the synagogue in Würzburg that the Thalheimer family had originally built, now restored, for services. I attended Shabbat services there and invited members of the congregation to our reunion, which many attended.

On June 17, fourteen members of our family and a small group of other invited guests including my lady friend at the time, Karen McGowan, congregated in Rimpar. Karen, like myself, found genealogy a fascinating hobby. The congregation was there for the dedication of the plaque and a first glimpse of the exhibit at the Grumbach Castle. Those who made

Karen McGowan with myself and the late David Rockefeller, who was a friend of mine for over fifty years. His memoir features fascinating family relationships.

Here, Mayor Kutt and I have just unveiled the Lehman plaque. I am seeing the description on the plaque for the first time. What a thrill!

This is the Lehman plaque as it appears at the front door of what is now a pharmacy, but was once the Rimpar home of our ancestors, the Abraham Lehmanns.

Built in 1600, Rimpar's Grumbach Castle towers high above the street where our Lehman ancestors lived. The castle, now the Town Hall, houses city records and the Lehman family exhibit.

This photo of Dr. Roland Flade, Mayor Anton Kutt and me was shot on June 16, 1996, just outside the pharmacy on Niederhoferstrasse in Rimpar. The pharmacy building had been the home of my ancestors, Abraham and Eva Lehmann, in the mid-1800s before three of their sons, Henry, Emanuel and Mayer, my great-grandfather, emigrated to America. A memorial plaque about the Lehman family had been unveiled, and I am holding its covering.

I thanked Hugo Shuster warmly for his gracious permission to let the Lehman plaque be placed at the door of his pharmacy.

Pictured in the room that holds the Lehman exhibit in the Grumbach Castle are, left to right, Mayor Anton Kutt, me, German minister for telecommunications Dr. Wolfgang Bötsch and Dr. Roland Flade.

Pictured here is Duke Max of Bavaria, whose ancestors were kings in power when my ancestors lived in Rimpar.

I was touched when a group of Rimpar students sang for the visiting Lehman family. A few years later, one of the choir members interviewed me about the family reunion.

the sacrifices knew that this was no ordinary family gathering. It was not only a historic journey, but also a ceremony of healing on a global level. The first event of that day was the viewing of the plaque. Dedicated to my Great-Uncle Herbert, my Great-Grandfather Mayer and his father, it was mounted on my ancestral home with the permission of Hugo Shuster, the pharmacist and current proprietor.

IN MEMORIAM HERBERT H. LEHMAN 1878 – 1963
GOUVENEUR-SENATOR
IM U.S.-BUNDESSTANT NEW-YORK DESSEN VATER
MAYER LEHMAN
SOHN DES ABRAHAM LEHMANN
STAMMT AUS DIESEN HAUSE DAS
UM 1850 DIE HAUS NR 2021½ HATTE 17 JUNI 1996

In his speech, Christian Will emphasized the importance of speaking out. "We are the last generation that actually witnessed the Kristallnacht and expulsion of the Jews," he said. He called for "the acceptance of all humans' dignity . . . to stand like a milestone which helps us to make steps in each other's direction." In addition to our family group, a crowd of bystanders had gathered from the town. Their faces were solemn

My cousin, Lord William Goodhart, came from London to join us for the Rimpar Reunion. William was a solicitor who wrote the constitution for the Liberal Democratic Party.

I shared a good laugh with Lady Celia Goodhart over a remark made by her witty husband, Lord William Goodhart, one of the speakers at the reunion.

and stern as they watched us. They did not seem happy—or perhaps they simply didn't know what it all meant—for us to come back.* "How moving, how ironic, how strange" I wrote, "that the citizens of Rimpar were honoring a Jewish family unknown until today."[125]

Permanently housed in Rimpar's Grumbach Castle, the town's exhibit features a display of Governor Herbert Lehman and the Lehman family, as well as homage to the nine Jewish residents who died in the camps.† It also extols the four Rimpar Jews who died for their fatherland during World War I, as well as Rimpar's Jewish doctor, who ran a hospital for everyone during that war.

A very moving part of the exhibit highlights the life of Julie Lassmann, daughter of the town's cantor, born in 1905. A licensed language teacher, Julie stayed in Rimpar to care for her elderly parents. She remained in Rimpar, where she taught piano, sang and staged theatrical productions. A writer and poet, Julie Lassmann was taken to Auschwitz with the last remaining Lower Franconian Jews on June 17, 1943. Sadly, there were no Jews left in Rimpar. Fifty-three years later to the day, she would receive

---

* Though the officials and our hosts were warm and gracious, the townspeople didn't seem very pleased that we were there. Everyone knew that Roland Flade was helping with the reunion, and not one of his colleagues at the newspaper mentioned a single thing about it to him.

† Jewish records from Germany being what they are, some sources claim it was twelve.

a place of honor side by side with the Lehman family. Julie's plight, along with the fate of the Six Million, was best expressed in the words of Israeli poet Yehuda Amichai, born in Würzburg:

> *The worst has happened and nobody must ever forget it. . . . To forget is human and also inhuman. We want to forget and have to remember. We want to remember and have to forget. To us all, this is a matter of survival and of healing.*[126]

The entire visit released a flood of emotion inside of me. The day before, we had visited the cemetery of *Heidingsfeld*, where most of our ancestors are buried. I had placed a stone on the grave of Ben Zion Lehmann, Seligman's son, and on those of Mayer Lehman's in-laws and Babette's parents, Isaak and Friederike Neugass. I couldn't help thinking of Mother. I wrote in the *Jewish Post* of "how proud she had been of her family and their record of accomplishment—to which she has added a most notable page."[127]

Mother would certainly have responded to an international event where letters from President Bill Clinton and Chancellor Helmut Kohl were read amid the moving speeches of German officials welcoming our return to Rimpar. "Bringing with them little more than their wits, their energy and their belief in the American Dream," President Clinton wrote, "members of the Lehman family emigrated to the United States more than 150 years ago. . . . Since that time family members have found success in America and helped to shape its destiny."[128]

Chancellor Kohl wrote,

> *Dear Members of the Lehman and Loeb families, dear citizens of Rimpar:*
>
> *Today's ceremony is unique. The descendants of a family that left home one and a half centuries ago congregate in the village where their ancestors had lived and worked for a long time. It is an American family with German-Jewish roots, a family that cherishes the memory of its past in the knowledge that human rights, democracy and freedom determine Germany's present and future.*
>
> *Thus, [may your] hours spent together in Rimpar combine reflection and joy.*[129]

Kohl commended Rimpar for setting an example that would be recognized "far beyond their village."

In my opening speech to our hosts, the municipal council and Christian Will, I called it

> *a mark of the spirit now alive in Germany that the house of an unknown Jewish resident of Rimpar, Abraham Lehmann, who lived here some two hundred years ago, should be given landmark status, and that the history of the Jewish community of Rimpar, and the fate of its members who were victims of the Holocaust, should be memorialized in your beautiful town hall.*

At the ceremony I greeted such notables as Duke Max of Bavaria, whose great-great-grandfather had been king of Bavaria when my great-great grandfather lived in Rimpar. I did not know at the time that Max's family, of the ancient house of Wittelsbach, had opposed the Nazis. The whole family had fled their palaces and lands and hid in Budapest. When the Germans invaded Hungary in 1944, they were arrested and placed in concentration camps like Oranienburg and Dachau, from which they were liberated by the U.S. Third Army. A composer and talented zither player, Duke Max loved Bavarian folk music, which provided a welcome addition to the ceremonies, along with a children's choir singing songs in the native Franconian. Years later, I sent Duke Max a copy of *Lots of Lehmans*, and he wrote back that the reunion was "an unforgettable experience."[130]

Hermann Leeb, the Bavarian minister of justice, acknowledged that "Germans had incurred a burden of guilt beyond measure," and he urged his people "to stand up to any attempt that would prove an assault on their democratic culture." Dr. Wolfgang Bötsch, the German minister for telecommunications, spoke of a "transatlantic bridge" that had carried Germany in many important moments of its history. He acknowledged that the American presence in Europe after World War II had "made it possible for the Western part of our country to grow in accordance with the ideals of Western democracy, the sharing of powers, and human rights."[131] My thoughts also turned to Arthur (Lehman) Goodhart, who, as part of the Judge Advocate's Office, had played a role in shaping the Treaty of Versailles. And to Carl Joachim Friedrich, my German-born professor at Harvard, who served as the constitutional and governmental affairs advisor for the de-Nazification of Allied-occupied Germany.

Fourteen members of our extended family of 250 Lehmans were able to attend, and I introduced each Lehman one by one: Lord William Goodhart, vice chairman of the Human Rights Institute and cofounder of the Liberal Democratic Party of the UK; Wendy Lehman Lash; William Bernhard, son of my aunt Dorothy, foundation executive and a member of the International Council of MOMA, whose mother, Dorothy Bernhard, had run the Mayer Lehman Charity Fund during the war; composer William Mayer; psychiatrist Terry Asiel; investment banker Orin McCluskey; Cynthia Rubinfien, a writer for the *Philadelphia Inquirer*; Ruth Thalheimer Nelkin and her daughter, Amy; my nephews Charles Chiara, Judy's son and a Hollywood filmmaker who made ten videos during the four-day reunion, and Richard N. Beaty Jr., director of the Dianetic Center in New Jersey. Ruth was the only person at the reunion who had been born in the region, so this return was particularly challenging for her. The original invitees were descendants of Mayer Lehman, but a number of his brother Emanuel's family also came. His brother Seligman was represented by Ruth Thalheimer Nelkin and her daughter.

Among our non-Lehman guests were Louise Stern, the wife of Rabbi Malcolm Stern, whose 1960 book *Americans of Jewish Descent* was a major source for Stephen Birmingham's books *Our Crowd* and *The Grandees*. Rabbi Stern's obituary in *The New York Times* described him as the premier genealogist of American Judaism and noted that his book was considered a "milestone in the study of American Jewish genealogy."[132] His greatest interest was in Jews with Sephardic roots, especially in the Western Hemisphere. Stern's works revolutionized Protestant and Catholic separatism by showing that a good portion of the most prominent American families had Jewish ancestry. The vivacious Louise was a genealogist and writing talent in her own right who made valuable contributions to her husband's work. Malcolm's third edition, published in 1991, was entitled *First American Jewish Families* and included fifty thousand names.

Departing for our homes again, we felt new ties to this community that we expected would not slip away but rather move into future generations. Both in Germany and America, through the press, our reunion opened up new interest in missing Lehmans and in the town of Rimpar. A woman wrote that her husband had also been born in the house that Abraham Lehmann inhabited and sent a photograph. An American soldier sent a 1946 photo of Würzburg in ruins after being heavily bombed because of its proximity to the Schweinfurt plant.

Verna Herbert, who had been a young girl in the choir that sang folk songs to us, later wrote her social studies senior thesis about the impact of the Rimpar Reunion on the town population, not all of whom were eager to face the past. She was equally interested in the family members who had attended it. Although there were no longer any Jews in Rimpar, our family name was now known to the whole town. Verna had an interesting question in mind for the American and British Lehmans. Having returned to Rimpar, how much did the Lehman family feel related to that Bavarian village and that part of the family tree? Do Lehmans believe they were influenced by their German roots?

I was sorry Mother wasn't around to answer her. Verna's question reminded me of a letter Mother wrote to my older sister, Judy, on the question of "why" or "whether" or "in what way" we were Jewish:

> In almost every generation there has been . . . an outbreak of hatred against the Jews. . . . But this has happened to other religious sects . . . to the Huguenots in France, the Puritans in England and to the Quakers.
>
> This is what I believe. That we are just plain people with both good and bad within us. If you look back at history you will see that the plain Jewish people mingled with their countrymen and became an integral part of that country. I believe that German Jews are more German than Jewish . . . the English Jews more English and in the United States they are more American. . . .
>
> You are not a part of any other race but those who have come together on this continent to make a new world and worship any God they believe in. You are an American.[133]

The Lehman descendants who came to Rimpar experienced transformations that only those who made the actual journey could claim. For each of us, it was different. My cousin William Mayer summed up his sentiments beautifully in a letter to Dr. Flade when he returned to New York:

> I had always thought of the Lehman family as charmed and protected from the misfortunes that befell so many other Jewish families. The account of Eva Thalheimer exploded that myth, as did the reference to other family members whom Herbert Lehman could not save. I had always thought of the Holocaust as some remote horror that I was looking down at from a safe distance away. But for the forced journey of the younger Lehman brothers to another country, I might well have been a Holocaust victim along with so many others.

As I wrote in an article for the *Jewish Post* about the event,

> The citizens of Rimpar were honoring a Jewish family that was unknown to them until today . . . our relatives buried in the lovely Jewish cemetery of Heidingsfeld, now part of Würzburg, rest in immaculately tended grounds.

Pictured here at the left is Dr. Karlheinz Müller of Würzburg University, telling one of the Rimpar Reunion attendees the story of the broken Jewish headstones that had been salvaged from buildings in Würzburg. Dr. Müller had done extensive research on them and later published a scholarly book about them.

> *As I listened to the words of praise, of regret, of warning, I thought how much fate and circumstances played in our lives and how lucky I was that my great-grandfather had the good sense and the ambition to emigrate to the United States.*

Sadly, the same year that I learned about all of this undiscovered family I had scattered around the world, I lost the two anchors of my own world: my mother in May, and then my father that December.

After Thanksgiving that year, it got very cold, and Father traveled with my sister Judy down to Lyford Cay in Nassau, the Bahamas, where he had a beautiful vacation home. He actually had been working up to eight weeks before he died; he was also managing all the family affairs until he went off to Nassau. He called me in New York to reveal how sick he was.

"John, this is serious," he said.

"Is there anything I can do?" I asked.

"No," he said. And he hung up.

A day later he came back to New York by hospital plane, but as per his request, Judy refused to bring him to the hospital. At Father's Upper East Side apartment, Dr. Smithen reiterated that he should go into the hospital, but again Father refused. He had stopped eating, and they started to feed him intravenously. Dr. Michael Rosenbluth said this was a sign that his body was just turning off. Despite the doctors' recommendations, Father stayed put.

I came to his apartment in the late afternoon every day that week and would stay with him through dinner. He'd just woken up, looking great, and we'd eat and watch the news together. Father was thin, as always, and he looked healthy, with a full head of hair turning gray at the fringes. There was another round of discussions when Dr. Smithen tried to persuade him to go to the hospital, but Father would not.

That Friday, his friend Al Gordon came to visit. Al was a famous Harvard man (known as "Mr. Harvard") who believed in exercise, always walking from his home on the Upper East Side to his Wall Street office. (He would run his first marathon at age 81 and die at the ripe old age of 107.) Father was wearing a robe, looking elegant, when I arrived for my daily visit. He was there drinking champagne with Al and talking about Wall Street business. Father said he had had dinner already and that he was tired and didn't want to watch TV. It was the last time I would see him.

On Sunday morning, December 8, 1996, I got a call from Dr. Rosenbluth to tell me that Father had passed during the night. I came to his apartment and saw Father lying there in bed. I went over and kissed his forehead; then I sat down next to him and let it all wash over me. Mother had said a number of times that we'd all be happier when they were both dead. But that moment, sitting next to my father's body, only six months after Mother had died, I really didn't feel that way. I felt I was left with a giant gap where my parents had once been.

Soon the undertakers arrived to wrap Father up and take him away. I was taken aback by such a definitive act: it drove home to me that both of my parents were really gone. I began to focus on what I was going to say at the service at Temple Emanu-El, the same kind that Mother had that past May. Although my mother contemplated divorce the day after their wedding, they remained married for almost seventy years and died about six months apart.

As the days went on, I indeed began to feel a kind of relief. Mother was right. I felt liberated. It wasn't just because I was an heir; all of us siblings were financially well-off independently of Mother and Father. I began to feel a release for the first time from both of my extraordinary parents. They had both been such an overwhelming presence, and none of us had been able to break out from their pull and their shadows. I think I felt it the most, as someone who had worked with Father, shared a name with him (and was sometimes confused with him). I often felt stifled by him in my own growth and business matters.

I was sixty-six years old, and fully and finally my own man.

A fall day with Sharon at Ridgeleigh, our country home in Purchase, New York.

CHAPTER TWENTY-ONE

"When Harry Met Sally" (The Story of John and Sharon)

THE VERY BEGINNING

I met Sharon casually in 1980, but she did not re-enter my life for good until almost twenty years later, in 1999. Sharon has observed that Rob Reiner's classic 1989 comedy *When Harry Met Sally* is more than a little evocative of our own romance. Like the movie protagonists', our romance caught fire slowly. It was only after several years of chance meetings that we became good friends, and not until a long time after that that we discovered we were deeply in love. The embers that had been burning brightly finally burst into flame.[*]

Like Harry and Sally, we met through a mutual friend, but years passed before we connected again. Our first meeting was in 1980 just before I became an ambassador, which took me overseas for the next two years. Before I left, my longtime friends Audrey Gruss (then Audrey Debuffy) and Carol Marston gave me a fiftieth birthday party, to which they invited Sharon. Sharon remembers that we said no more than two words at that party: "hello" and "good-bye."

Fast forward six years to 1986. One of my dear friends of many years is a lively Portu-

---

[*] Harry and Sally, played by Billy Crystal and Meg Ryan, were two New Yorkers who had a platonic friendship that grew from chance encounters with each other, while suffering romantic woes with other people. Each found the other the most comfortable to be with until, in the end, they discovered that true love had been right there between them all along.

Sharon when I first met her in 1986.

guese woman named Guida de Carvalhosa. We became friends when I was in my twenties. A born philosopher with a great sense of humor, she was fond of saying that husbands and lovers come and go but good friends are for life. (Happily, I can say that I have been fortunate in maintaining warm friendships with most of my past girlfriends.)

It was spring, and I had recently returned from being ambassador to Denmark. Guida called one day to invite me to a very formal dinner party that a close Latin friend of hers was giving in her magnificent townhouse on Manhattan's Upper East Side. Guida asked me to escort one of her pretty international girlfriends to the party—a friend who was back in Manhattan visiting family and friends before she was to return to her business consulting practice in Milan. I agreed. The young woman I went to escort was Sharon.

I cannot overstate the elegance of the hostess's home, the dinner and the guests, including Sharon, who I remember was dressed in an elegant, fitted, black satin gown that showed off her beautiful figure and her beautiful long blonde hair, both of which she maintains to this day. We were all decked out—the women in long gowns, the men in tuxedos. The most stylish of us all was the Countess Aline Romanones, who lived up to her reputation of being a fixture for many years on the International Best-Dressed List.[*] There were a few of us there who had no royal titles, including Cary Grant, Senator Larry Pressler, and Mario D'Urso (an Italian senator whom I have known for many years). It was a very "social evening," and I met for the first time several royals, including Prince Johannes von Thurn und Taxis and Count Jean D'Harcourt.

After a magnificent but somewhat overwhelming formal dinner, Sharon and I, along with several other couples, danced the night away to the music of a full twelve-

---

[*] I first met Aline on an earlier trip through Spain with Felipe Propper. She had married a Spanish nobleman, Luis Figueroa y Perez, the Count of Quintanilla—Count Romanones. The countess was the author of *The Spy Who Wore Red*, a best-selling and imaginative account of her life as a spy during World War II.

piece orchestra. We were all comfortably accommodated in the enormous front hall of the hostess's townhouse.

Although it was a dramatic and memorable start to a relationship, it was not possible to learn much about each other in such a formidable setting. So, about a week later, I invited Sharon for a tête-à-tête dinner at Oleg Cassini's Le Club, where the famous "Patrick" still reigned as maître d'. At the end of a very convivial evening, it was time to say good night. I was so much taller than Sharon that even in her high heels, she had to stand on a step so I could kiss her properly, which left us both laughing. We had time for one more date before she left for Europe— another wonderful evening of dinner and conversation. Sadly, a few days later Sharon returned to Italy, where she remained for the next seven years.

Sharon when we started dating in late 1999.

In the film *When Harry Met Sally*, the protagonists each get involved in a handful of relationships before they both realize that they were a perfect match for each other all along. Sharon and I definitely followed in the footsteps of Harry and Sally.

In 1988, I met and started dating a young lady named Karen McGowan. In 1993, while I was still with Karen, Sharon and I ran into each other in London at a dinner given by another friend, Coco Blaffer.* I was there with Karen, and Sharon was there with her beau, a handsome Virginian who was living in London. We were delighted to see each other, but it had been seven years since our warm kiss on a New York City doorstep, so when the dinner party was over, we went on with our separate lives and loves.

A few months after Coco's dinner in London, I learned that Sharon had moved back

---

* Coco Blaffer, once married to Harvard alumnus John Royall, is a talented artist. Her great-great-grandfather was the Texas oilman who founded the oil firm that became Exxon. I remember I was once at a large dinner party at the Bayou Club in Texas, where Coco's father, the host of the evening, in a memorable toast to his guests declared, "I don't know much about art, but I do like the people who go with it." I am particularly fond of both Coco and her son, my godson, H. Walker Royall. I had the pleasure of hosting the wedding party for him and his bride, Jennifer, when they married in 2005.

to New York for good. One day, we bumped into each other on Park Avenue as I was heading for my daily lunch at the Four Seasons. After exchanging pleasantries, we bid each other a good day and again went our separate ways. When I got back to my office in the Seagram Building later that day, I told Lance Lessman (a good friend of mine who was an investment specialist sharing space in our Loeb family office) that I had bumped into a mutual friend, Sharon Handler. Lance was quick to say, "I think she'd like you. If you ever break up with Karen, you should really get to know her better." Since Karen and I were still a couple, I did not follow up at the time. However, Sharon and I did remain friendly and every now and then we had lunch at the Four Seasons to catch up on our current life stories—just like Harry and Sally.

Then, one day in 1999, about a year after an inevitable breakup with Karen, I belatedly took Lance's advice and called Sharon. Instead of taking her for lunch this time, we went for a long, leisurely dinner at Café des Artistes on the Upper West Side of Manhattan. My breakup with Karen, with whom I had been in a very long relationship, had sent me into a bit of a tailspin. During that difficult year, Sharon became the sunshine and the energy that not only revived me but later brought the best out in me. After dinner that night, when I took her home, I knew I wanted to see more of her, and as I passionately kissed her good night at the door, we both realized that we were no longer "just friends."

Our relationship evolved gradually. I courted Sharon for several months before we became a couple. We then dated for quite a while before she joined me permanently at my East 61st Street townhouse, a move that was triggered by circumstances beyond our control, a story I will tell later in this memoir.

SHARON AND HER ROOTS

It's a good thing that extremely bright women do not intimidate me; if anything, I am *more* attracted to them. While I wasn't daunted by Sharon's impressive academic background, I now joke that perhaps I should have been. She never talked about her academic accomplishments, but I came across her résumé one day and discovered that she had graduated summa cum laude and Phi Beta Kappa from Tufts University, and from Columbia University's School of Law with highest honors (a "Harlan Fiske Stone Scholar"). To this day, I continue to be amazed by her insightfulness, especially when she zeroes in on a topic or project.

Sharon, a native New Yorker, practiced law for several years with Coudert Brothers in New York and Paris. She then moved to Brussels full time to work for the European Economic Community (EEC). There she pursued a yearlong project that concluded with her writing a lexicon in three languages for the EEC titled *La Nouvelle Language Européenne*. Thereafter, for the next eleven years, she worked in Milan, first for SCR, the largest commercial relations firm in Italy, then as an independent business consultant for American clients doing business in Italy and Italian and European clients doing business in the United States. Her background in law and business development and her fluency in French, Italian and Spanish all helped to make those years of work and play financially and socially very productive and wonderfully interesting for her. In fact, she always said she spent a magical decade there. It was only due to the oppressive era of the "Mani Politi," which began in her eleventh year of residing in Italy, that she finally left a country she once thought would be her home for life.[*]

She comes from a family filled with successes. Her grandfather, Maurice S. Handler, arrived in this country at the age of ten, the youngest of eight orphans and the only boy. He went on to become an American Dream success story. He founded Smart Maid, one of America's first women's wear companies. This was a very successful coat and suit manufacturing company established after World War II that had customers throughout the United States. When invited to take the company public, he turned the offer down and instead sold it at a considerable discount to his loyal employees, for whom he had great compassion. Sharon inherited that same spirit of compassion, entrepreneurship and independence. Her grandfather was also one of the founders of the Albert Einstein College of Medicine at Yeshiva University. This college has been prominent among the many philanthropic interests of the Handler family. Yeshiva University awarded Sharon's father, Jerry Handler, an honorary degree for his own philanthropic work with the college.

In his early twenties, Sharon's father brought the Handler money to the table to join Aaron Gural (Jerry's elder by ten years), who brought his real estate business expertise. Along with a third partner, Jack Shanker, the three men cofounded Newmark & Co., which is today one of New York City's largest commercial real estate companies. Jerry, at age fifty, preferring to keep his entrepreneurial independence, kept his interests in

---

[*] Sharon said she had been told that the corruption of the financial and political worlds exploded with one small contractor who was being so badly squeezed on a building project that he went to the magistrates and agreed to name names if they would give him amnesty. This one set of accusations set in motion a domino effect that traumatized high-ranking business and political people in every major city in Italy, with arrests taking place almost weekly. Even Gianni Agnelli, the oldest son of the industrialist and principal family shareholder of the Italian car company Fiat, might have been jailed if the president of Fiat had not been sacrificed in his place. Milan, a city driven by business, came almost to a standstill, both financially and socially.

Newmark while stepping out of the company to found and operate Handro Properties, a family real estate business. He continued to run this company until his death in 2010. Sharon's twin brother, Scott, a graduate in economics from Tulane University, who had worked with his father for years, took over running the business.

Sharon's sister, Dawn, whom Sharon has always said is the "smartest one in the family," attended both Harvard University and the Harvard Graduate School of Design, from which she graduated as a landscape architect. She then went to work for the City of New York. Dawn became a part of the core team that redesigned the Great Lawn of Central Park. During her tenure with the city, Dawn received various appointments, including: Liaison to the Arts Commission of the City of New York for Parks and Recreation, Director of Central Park's Special Projects for the Parks Department, and Deputy Director of Consultant Project Management for the City. Also during Dawn's tenure with the city, Mayor David Dinkins awarded her the prestigious New York City Art Commission Award for Excellence in Design for her successful redesign of Brooklyn's Carroll Park. Thereafter, she was hired away from the city by the internationally renowned architect Robert A.M. Stern, as his senior landscape architect. A couple of years later, she established her own small but successful company. Several years later, at her father's request, she joined the family real estate business.

Sharon's mother, Lyn, is also very talented. She is a portrait artist of some note who, in addition, has had a distinguished career as the host of a long-running AM radio talk show on the arts and culture called *The Lyn Handler Show.* I learned that Lyn is an impressive and charming interviewer, as I had the pleasure of being interviewed by her with regard to my Danish art collection. I can understand where Sharon gets her charm and intellect.

LIFE AS A COUPLE

Getting back to Sharon and me, our mutual friends were unanimously thrilled about our union. I remember how pleased Ambassador Patricia Gates Lynch was when she spotted us holding hands at one of the ambassadorial events she used to host. She wrote me a wonderful note that included the line, "This time you've got it right."* Another ambassadorial stamp of approval came from a great couple, Ambassador Stuart Bernstein

---

* I became good friends with Patricia Gates Lynch through my work with the American Council of Ambassadors. Appointed by President Reagan, Pat was the ambassador to Madagascar and the Federal Islamic Republic of the Comoros. Prior to that, she was a radio journalist and wrote a memoir called *Thanks for Listening: High Adventures in Journalism and Diplomacy.*

Sharon and I on our first summer holiday in my 1936 Chris-Craft on Upper Saranac Lake in the Adirondacks (summer 1999).

and his wife, Wilma.[*] (He was appointed by President George W. Bush to Denmark and served from 2001 to 2005.)

We first bonded with them when they generously hosted us at the U.S. ambassadorial residence in Copenhagen. It was instant friendship and affection among all of us, which has continued to this day. This friendship has really flourished due to our annual summer visits to Aspen, Colorado, to attend the Aspen Brain Lab, which is organized by the Aspen Brain Institute, of which Sharon is the chair.

Stuart recently helped to found a new museum, the United States Diplomacy Center, which will tell the story of the American Foreign Service. He put together a group of a hundred former ambassadors to help finance the project, and I was one of them. Everyone adores Stuart and Wilma, and Sharon and I feel the same way about them. Stuart is a real leader in many areas of business and politics.

My dear friend Eli Evans tells everyone, "Sharon is the best thing that's ever happened in John's life.[†] One of my longest-standing friends from my college days is Richard Feigen, who was an usher at my first wedding. He, too, enthusiastically agrees that Sha-

---

[*] This glamorous couple was among the guests at my seventy-fifth birthday bash at Blenheim Palace. They were among the first couples in the video that was made at the event who spoke to the camera, praising me but acknowledging Sharon as the "Oz behind the curtain."

[†] Eli Evans is known as the greatest historian and author of southern Jewish life. His two most famous books are *The Lonely Days Were Sundays: Reflections of a Jewish Southerner* and *Judah P. Benjamin: The Jewish Confederate* (about the senator from Louisiana who subsequently became the famous secretary of state of the Confederacy).

St. Tropez (summer 1999)

ron and I are perfect for each other.

In 1999, in the early days of my courting Sharon, we were discussing plans for the coming summer. She mentioned that she would be in the South of France attending the July wedding of her friend Carol Asher.* I asked if I could accompany her and we could make a holiday of it after the celebration. "Oh dear," she said, "that would be wonderful, but I have just reserved the last little single room left in all of St. Tropez." She explained that she had a terrible time getting even that because the town was totally booked due to her friend's enormous wedding, with nearly six hundred guests. My "Type A" personality refused to let me leave it at that. I had always viewed the telephone as my sword, and would now and again use it to save the day. "Leave it to me," I said grandly as I picked up the phone. "I'll get us a suite."

After phoning all over St. Tropez with no luck, I almost admitted defeat. The wedding was so large that I could not even find a small room for two, much less a suite. Undaunted and determined, I decided this was a wonderful excuse to charter a yacht—something I had not done in years. It was an inspired idea.

Sharon and I sailed to St. Tropez from Cannes for a glorious extended weekend and the exquisite wedding of Carol and her Italian groom. The yacht was called *The Lady Lex*. The captain was quite a character, an Englishman who liked his cups a little too much. He had previously been the captain of Adnan Khashoggi's grand yacht, *Nabila*, named after Khashoggi's daughter. After that delightful first summer on a boat, my appetite was whetted. For several years after that our summers included a trip on a yacht, always joined by friends and family.

With my typical caution about committed relationships, engendered by my life experiences, I had frequent debates with myself. I was not yet quite able to ask Sharon to move in with me, though I'd been thinking about it a lot. Then fate intervened. A dramatic event provided the nudge I needed. We had literally just returned from a trip to London and had gone to our respective homes to unpack. We had plans that night to go together to a small dinner party friends were giving.

---

* Carol's father was the famous jeweler who created the "Asher Cut" diamond.

About a half-hour before I was supposed to pick up Sharon, she called my house. Renee, who answered the telephone, heard Sharon frantically say in a small nervous voice that there was a fire on her floor of her apartment building and that she was trying to get out. She hung up as suddenly as she called.

Terrified, I dropped everything and rushed over to her Park Avenue building to find her standing in the street, shaken and dazed. There were fire trucks and firefighters everywhere. I took her next door to the Regency Hotel, hoping a cup of tea would help calm her. I then learned the full story. While unpacking and chatting on the phone with a friend, she had heard what she thought was a truck backing up—a strange beeping noise that did not stop. She then realized the sound was coming from the hallway. Not knowing that the building's smoke alarm had gone off, Sharon opened the door of her fifth-floor apartment. Waves of heavy, hot, black smoke hit her in the face. She slammed the door shut as she shouted to her friend that the floor was on fire. She was so startled that her hands slipped and the phone went crashing to the floor, splintering into pieces. She quickly ran to a second phone and called me. Then, remembering something she had seen in a movie, she grabbed her winter coat, doused it in the shower and wrapped it around her shoulders and head. She then took a deep breath, opened her door and dropped down on all fours, as the only clean air was near the floor. She began to crawl down the hallway to the emergency exit. Everything was engulfed in heavy, black smoke.

Me with "the girls." Left to right: Debbie Reuben, Sharon, Susana de la Puente, and happy me! St. Tropez (summer 2004).

After a swim, a hug from my gorgeous wife.

Dinner at the Cala di Volpe Hotel in Sardinia, Italy (summer 2005).

Relaxing on the boat off the Italian coast (summer 2008).

As she moved along the hallway, Sharon suddenly could see the feet of her neighbor's adolescent daughter. As her image cleared, Sharon could see that the girl, with one hand, was trying to hold open the door to her family's apartment, and with the other was tightly clenching the leash of her big, old yellow Lab. The dog was yelping and jumping, trying to get away from the heat and the burning smoke billowing out of their apartment. The daughter was screaming for her mother to come out. The heat was unbearable near the door, but the girl would not let go of it or the dog. Through the dark smoke Sharon could see the flames moving across the neighbor's apartment toward the open door. She stood up and with all her might pried the girl off the door and almost carried her down the stairs, dragging the dog behind them.

When Sharon got downstairs she discovered no one in the lobby was aware there was a fire. Just as she shouted to the doorman to turn off the elevators, she heard the fire trucks arrive. She rushed outside and heard the firefighters shouting to go to the fourth floor. Several men had already entered the building by the time she could get the attention of additional firemen who had arrived. The first men to arrive believed the fire was on the fourth floor and had gone there fruitlessly banging on and breaking open doors looking for flames. Sharon later learned someone from the Regency originally saw the flames and called in the fire, misidentifying the floor.

The hallway on the fifth floor was so black with smoke that Sharon knew the firefighters would not be able to see their way to the guilty apartment. Things were chaotic and everyone was in motion. Sharon, her voice hoarse with smoke, shouted to the men in heavy gear clamoring past her, telling them how to find the fire on the fifth floor.

After the fire was put out and everyone had gotten out safely, the fire team came downstairs. Their captain stopped to tell Sharon that it was one of the worst smoke fires they had dealt with in years. He said that, thanks to her help, they had finally found the right apartment. It turned out that her neighbors, an Indian couple, had been celebrating the Festival of Lights, with candles lit all over the apartment. One or more had toppled onto their flammable Indian curtain fabric, which started the fast-burning fire.

With each sip of tea, while telling her story, Sharon began to gain her composure and the color in her face. When I finally looked at my watch, there was only an hour left before we were supposed to be at a seated dinner. Sharon insisted that we attend. She felt it was too late to cancel on the hosts. Fortunately, she had a dress she had left at my house that she could wear. My brave lady made it through the first course of the dinner, but by the second course her face had begun to redden and her cough worsened. We excused ourselves and I took her directly to the hospital to be treated for smoke inhalation. Gratefully, she was able to come home with me that same night, a little the worse for the wear.

Sharon is one strong woman. She had just been through a major shock, the fright of escaping from the fire and the nearly complete destruction of her home. Even though she was worn out by a long and disappointing next day of trying to salvage her apartment, that evening she donned the one dress that had not been ruined by the stench of smoke and helped me host 350 people at Scandinavia House for a lecture on Danish art given by Professor Robert Rosenbaum. This was followed by a cocktail hour and then a seated dinner at Le Cirque for forty art lovers and collectors, which Sharon had single-handedly organized. She never complained, but instead glided through the entire evening with her usual grace and style. Only her cough gave away her discomfort caused by the events of the night of the fire.

As anyone who has ever experienced a bad fire knows all too well, the stench of residual smoke permeates everything it touches, taking months, if ever, to fade away. Though Sharon had opened her door only twice, everything in her apartment was blackened and reeked of smoke. After several days of trying to save even a few things, she realized it was an exercise in futility. She really could never live in her apartment again comfortably, not only because of the smell, but because of the vivid memories of that terrible night. The time had come for me to stop my "hesitation waltz" and say, "Come live with me and be my love." So I did … and she did.

BIRTHDAY AT BLENHEIM

In 2004, about a year before my seventy-fifth birthday, Sharon and I began to plan for a long-held dream of mine—to hold a birthday party at Blenheim Palace (Winston Churchill's ancestral home in England). It was to be a party to which we would invite friends and family from all over the world. As a child, from the age of nine, I always had been away at school and, because my birthday is in May, it was always too inconvenient to celebrate it at school or at home. Consequently, my family always lumped it in with the twins' (Ann and Arthur) and Mother's birthday celebrations, which took place in September. Now, with Sharon's enthusiasm and help, the child in me could make up for lost time, and do so in grand style.

I knew of Blenheim's importance not only through my study of history but also because of my close association with the Churchill family through the Winston Churchill Foundation. Located an hour outside of London, in Oxfordshire, the palace is a truly majestic, magnificent home. It was built for the Churchill family, in particular John Churchill, the first Duke of Marlborough, who had won the Battle of Blenheim. In England, up until the 1700s, when a man won a great battle, the Crown gave him not only a prestigious title but also a great deal of money, which was often used to build an extraordinary home.

Blenheim is one of the most beautiful palaces in England. Part of Blenheim is still the current Duke of Marlborough's residence, while the rest of it is open to the public. All kinds of events are held on the grounds, including concerts and private parties.

One rainy day in February 2004, while Sharon and I were in London, we drove out to Blenheim. Sharon had never seen the palace and I wanted to show it to her before I asked her to take on this major endeavor. Even in the mist of gray, English weather, Blenheim and its grounds were impressive. At the end of our tour, as we started down the steps of the palace on the way back to the car, I stopped and turned to Sharon, and asked, "What would you think of giving me my seventy-fifth birthday here?" For a moment Sharon was quiet. Her eyes moved across the landscape, and as she turned around to look at the magnificent edifice, she whispered, "Are you serious?" When I nodded yes, without missing a beat, she enthusiastically said, "Yes!" It would be her great pleasure to take on the project. All the way back to London, in the car, we started to lay the foundation for my "dream birthday."

Before we began, I had my annual lunch with Lady Mary Soames, the daughter of Winston Churchill and the lead director on the Board of the U.S. Churchill Foundation.

"WHEN HARRY MET SALLY" (THE STORY OF JOHN AND SHARON)

Blenheim Palace

The party photographer caught Sharon and me as we dashed up the last step into the entrance of Blenheim Palace to receive our 300 guests. Sharon was dazzling in a white satin gown, and I, of course, wore all of my medals.

The library before Sharon got a hold of it . . . and turned it into a grand dining hall.

501

Over dessert I asked, "How would you feel about my having my seventy-fifth birthday celebration at Blenheim?" With a twinkle in her eye she replied without hesitation, "It's a great idea as long as I'm invited!" She was the first to receive an invitation.

In the summer of 2004, Sharon and I started to concretely plan for the event. We selected June 11, 2005, as the date of the party, because June was the month when many of our friends would already be in London. As Sharon dove into the planning, it became a full-time job—a job she embraced with the enthusiasm and creative imagination of a professional party planner. In fact, except for the last two weeks before the event, Sharon, with the help of her loyal, longtime assistant, Gloria Stevens, carried out most of the details of this party single-handedly. She studied and chose every detail: the music, the magnificent flower arrangements and table settings, the layout of the two long tables at which she personally seated our three hundred guests, the fabulous dinner menu, the speakers' introductions and the music that accompanied them to the stage, as well as the band to which we all danced late into the night.

On June 11, 2005, from the moment one arrived at the palace pulling into the

All of my birthday party guests were impressed with the grandeur of Blenheim Palace, even my well-traveled and sophisticated brother, Arthur, who arrived early. We are barely visible in this picture, walking past the twenty-five-piece military orchestra at the left, toward the series of Blenheim steps guarded by the Royal Cavalry.

The Queen's Trumpeter and Household Cavalry...and that impressive long red carpet.

Christopher "Kip" Forbes in front, followed by Demetrios and Liv Diakolios arriving on the red carpet.

Francine LeFrak Friedberg and her husband, Rick.

long driveway, one was bowled over by the grandeur and beauty of the property. The weather was impeccable, and the palace was awe-inspiring in a way that only a historic castle can be.

I had arranged for the Queen's Household Cavalry[*] to participate at the event. Impressively attired in their brilliant red uniforms, shining silver breast plates and glorious beaver hats, they formed an honor guard, lining both sides of the striking, long red carpet Sharon had chosen, which ran right up the palace steps to the entrance of the building. Majestic torches were placed strategically along both sides of the carpet. A twenty-five-piece military band greeted the three hundred guests with music from great classic American Broadway shows such as *South Pacific*, *Oklahoma* and *The Sound of Music*, to name a few. A sight to behold was watching the guests gracefully gliding down the red carpet to the entrance of Blenheim Palace.

---

[*] The Household Cavalry that came to my birthday at Blenheim was made up of two regiments: the Life Guards and the Blues and Royals, collectively known as the Household Cavalry. These are Queen Elizabeth's personal troops. The Household Cavalry who came to my birthday wore Dismounted Review Order: helmet with white plume, red tunic with silver breast plate (cuirass), buckskin breeches and jack boots. (This was exactly the same kit the Life Guards wore when they charged at the Battle of Waterloo, in 1815.)

The entrance to Blenheim Palace is seen behind me as I survey the view that will be seen by the guests arriving for my 75th birthday party. Standing guard on the stairs at each side of the red carpet are members of the Royal Cavalry.

Lady Mary Soames chatting with Isabele Clemente and Sirdar Aly Aziz.

A charming story is told by Damon Wells from Texas (a longtime director of the U.S. Winston Churchill Foundation), who personally accompanied Lady Mary Soames to the party. He recounts that as he helped her step out of the car and she gazed out over the red carpet, flanked by massive lit torches and the Queen's Military Guard, she sighed and said with a touch of nostalgia, "Oh, for the good old days."

Guests came "dressed to the nines"—women in their most beautiful gowns, some with tiaras; and men in white-tie tuxedos, with medals for those who had them. To add to the majesty of the event, after the guests crossed the threshold of the palace entrance, they were announced in royal fashion before greeting Sharon and me on the reception line. To end the cocktail hour, Sharon arranged for two Scottish bagpipers and a drummer, all dressed in full regalia, to march and play along the full length of the Grand Hall, cutting a swath through the three hundred guests who until that moment were enthusiastically chatting away. With a Scottish march and the room in total silence, they led everyone into the palace's library for the start of the meal. As the guests entered the hallway on the way to the library, they were mesmerized by soft lit candles and the smell of fresh jasmine trees with which Sharon had lined the hall.

The entrance to the Grand Hall, where the
cocktail hour was held.

The regal Scottish
pipes and drummer.

The beautiful Susan Fales-Hill in a divine creation.

Another beauty, Audrey Gruss, dancing with
Winston Churchill.

Oh Johnny Boy . . .
my love for you
keeps growing strong.
It's why tonight . . .
I've written you this song.

Oh Johnny Boy . . .
the reasons that
I love you so,
would fill a list
to sing a mile long.

My Johnny Boy . . .
you're kind,
you are a gentleman.
I love your looks,
your intellect,
your mind.

I love your hands . . .
your twinkling eyes,
your old world charm.
My darling John . . .
you are one of a kind.

Oh Johnny Boy . . .
It's 18 years since we first met.
'Twas common friends
who knew we should be one.

Our lives went passed . . .
til we began five years ago.
and from that day,
I knew our love would last.

Dear friends and family
at Blenheim we do celebrate.
John Langeloth Loeb
on this auspicious date.

Please raise your glass
and toast the man that I adore,
my Johnny Boy . . .
a man who's truly great.

— *Sharon Handler*

As a result, the slow entrance into the library was a treat for the senses. Upon entering the library, the scene took their breath away. There stood two long, beautifully set tables, each seating 150 guests. Accenting the tables were cranberry red table cloths, gold-rimmed glassware and china, very large silver candelabras, and crystal candlesticks. The tables were dripping in delicate Italian ivy with dark cherries, along with red and white orchids. The room was magical. The soft music of Spanish guitars greeted the guests as they found their way to their seats.

After dinner, the entertainment was ushered in with the sudden darkening of the room and the flash of a spotlight on the entrance door to the library. Then, out of the dark appeared "Marilyn Monroe." She sashayed her way up to the stage, where she invited me to join her and sexily sang to me "Happy Birthday, Mr. Ambassador" in that iconic breathy voice à la Marilyn Monroe's original serenading of JFK at Madison Square Garden in 1962. I was then overwhelmed by a series of generous and eloquent toasts that brought tears to my eyes.[*]

The guests were also treated to a film about my life, co-written and produced in the realistic style of an A&E *Biography* by Sharon and a professional film editor, with equal parts flattering and tongue-in-cheek narration. The film charmingly closed with the iconic music and image of the Pink Panther scribbling a big "NOT" in front of the words: THE END.

---

[*] Sharon was the M.C. The speakers were: my brother, Arthur Loeb; my English cousin, Lord William Goodhart; my political mentor, the Honorable Richard V. Allen; my longest-standing English friend from our youth in our twenties, Bobby Buxton; the young international entrepreneur Mark Holtzman; my dear friend and former French consul general to Australia, Michel-Henri Carriol; and the great Winston Churchill's grandson, Winston Spencer Churchill.

Lord William Dartmouth, my long-standing friend, generously hosted, at his London home, a dinner party the day after my birthday event.

The Duke of Marlborough, better known to his friends as "Sunny," whom I first met in 1949.

The "icing on the cake," however, was the final toast given by Sharon, stunning in a white satin gown, diamond necklace and emerald earrings. She sang one of my favorite songs, "Danny Boy" with a twist. She had rewritten the words and performed the song as "Johnny Boy." Her words touched my heart and again brought tears to my eyes.

It was such a heartfelt, beautiful performance, and I was so starstruck, that everyone thought I was going to propose to her right then and there. The guests all stood and applauded, and even the Duke of Marlborough, who admitted he usually only stands for the queen, stood with the rest of the enthusiastic guests.

The party was an extraordinary occasion, better than I could have ever imagined, and Sharon deserved all the credit. She spent nearly a year of her life making sure it all came together impeccably. It certainly made up for all the missed or afterthought birthdays of my youth, and then some! Blenheim Palace provided grandeur and a magnificent setting for the party, but in the end it was the people who brought the evening to life – an evening filled with such warmth and friendship and love. I was very blessed that so many of my family and friends were able to attend.

Much to my delight, most of the Churchill family came, including Mary Soames: Winston Churchill's grandson of the same name and his wife, Luce; my long-standing friend the Duke of Marlborough (whom I first met in 1949 on my first trip to London), along with his daughter, Henrietta Spencer-Churchill; and Churchill's granddaughter (and talented artist) Edwina Sandys and her husband, my Harvard classmate Richard Kaplan.

The guests also included the Earl of Dartmouth, the Earl and Countess Dudley, David

Sharon's mother, Lyn Handler, and her father, Jerry, in his dress uniform. He was a Lieutenant General for the National Guard in his later years.

Davies, my cousin Lady Sharon Sondes and her significant other, Geoffrey Thomas, the Honorable Desmond Guinness, and Sir Tobias Clark (the oldest baronetcy in England), as well as Ambassadors Stuart Bernstein and his wife, Wilma; Edward Elson and his wife, Suzie; Henry Kimelman and his wife, Charlotte; Evan Galbraith and his wife, Marie; and the Italian ambassador to the UN, Piero Francesce, and his wife, Marilena.[*]

As for family, in attendance were my daughter, Alexandra, and her husband, Joe Driscoll; my son, Nicholas; my brother, Arthur Loeb (of the famous and much missed Madison Avenue Bookshop); my older sister, Judy Chiara; my youngest sister, Debby, and her husband, James Brice; as well as my first cousin, Billy Bernhard, and his wife, Catherine Cahill; my nephew, Matthew Bronfman, and his then wife, Stacey Kaye Bronfman; and Lyn and Jerry Handler (Sharon's beautiful mother and distinguished father, who was attired in full military dress and decorations).

All these years later, I still have people tell me it was the "Party of the Century."

TYING THE KNOT

Many of my friends have remarked that Sharon has been the best of all the fortunate things that have happened in my fortunate life. I agree wholeheartedly. In my later years, she has become my guiding spirit in the storm of older age. In 2010, we had a year that was an "annus horribilis," as the Queen of England would say. Sharon's mother got sick in January and had surgery. Only three months after her recovery, in April, Sharon's father was diagnosed with pancreatic cancer. He died two months later, in late May. Then I got unexpectedly sick and had to have surgery in June. Then, two months later,

---

[*] Other guests included Mr. and Mrs. Michel David-Weill, Ezra and Cecile Zilkha, Georgette Mosbacher, Audrey and Martin Gruss, Julie and Michel-Henri Carriol, Beth Rudin DeWoody, Anne Hearst and Jay McInerney, Kip and Astrid Forbes, Lorna and Larry Graev, Daisy and Paul Soros, Joanne Herring, Jeanne Lawrence, Elizabeth and Patrick Gerschel, April and Roddy Gow, Donald and Barbara Tober, Victoria and Frank Wyman, Raul Suarez, Gail Hilson, Mary McFadden, Dalia and Larry Leeds, Susan Fales-Hill and Aaron Hill, Dayssi and Paul Kanavos, and Lee and CeCe Black.

in August, my son, Nicholas, was badly injured in a horrific car accident when his car went off a cliff in the hills of Los Angeles.

On top of all this, when two of my sisters died within six months of each other—Judy Loeb Chiara in November 2010 and Ann Loeb Bronfman in April 2011—I felt a terrible sadness. Although Mother and Father had been gone almost fifteen years, it felt like, with my sisters' deaths, our family had ended. I always felt that Judy and Ann were pillars of the family. I could always go to them if I had a problem to discuss or something joyful to share.

My one constant through all of this was Sharon. One morning I woke up and realized the love of my life was there by my side all those years, and so, on her birthday in March 2011, I got down on one knee and asked her to marry me. Sharon had become such a shining light in my life, it only made sense that she become my wife.

We were both thrilled to be getting married. The ceremony took place on January 12, 2012, at Temple Emanu-El on the Upper East Side of Manhattan, in an intimate, elegant ceremony with family, followed by a formal dinner party at the iconic Four Seasons restaurant. Both of our families were members of Emanu-El, and Sharon and I were very fond of the retired senior rabbi, Rabbi Ronald J. Sobel. Happily, he was delighted to come out of retirement to marry us. He performed a lovely traditional Jewish ceremony, which included the customary breaking of the glass under the groom's foot.

Sharon and I have similar backgrounds—she grew up in Scarsdale, fifteen minutes from where I grew up in Purchase. We are both Reformed Jews—and although she's not particularly religious, I have rediscovered my Jewish identity in the years that she has been in my life. She's truly a wonderful companion, friend and wife, and there is a kinship, a feeling of home and contentment when I am with her that I have never experienced in my life. She completely supports and understands my life's work, and her energy, commitment and vision inspire me each and every day.

My other marriages may have begun more romantically, but they fizzled quickly. Fortunately, Sharon and I had been friends for many years before we became seriously involved, which I believe gave us a strong foundation. She's wonderful with my children, Alexandra and Nicholas, as well as my grandchildren. All my friends and family absolutely adore her, particularly my brother, Arthur.

I started in one place and ventured out, exploring other worlds, and I think of my marriage to Sharon as a "returning." I had to go far and wide to find the home and person who has made me feel the happiest and most loved and who most lets me be who I am. Sharon comes from a world that I left behind, a world that, in some ways, I have rediscovered again through her. I love her deeply.

The husband-to-be, waiting patiently.

My bride-to-be on her way to our wedding.

An intimate family wedding in the private chapel at Temple Emanu-El, Fifth Avenue, New York.

We've happily "tied the knot."

Sharon's niece and flower girl, Zoe, accompanied by her escorts, my grandnephews (left to right) Coby Bronfman and Karma Mason—all of them seven years old.

The ringbearer, my lovely granddaughter, Allegra, who was escorted down the aisle by (left to right) Cullum and Finn Brown.

Sharon's twin brother walked her down the aisle.

My best man was my first cousin, William Lehman Bernhard; Sharon's matrons of honor were her sister, Dawn, and her long-standing friend Karin Wyser-Pratte.

Sharon with all her men.

Sharon with her two nephews (left to right) Darell and Jonathan Handler.

The Handler women: Sharon's mother, Lyn; Sharon; her sister, Dawn; and her niece, Dawn's daughter, Zoe.

My beautiful
daughter, Alexandra.

My handsome son, Nick, and my lovely granddaughter,
Allegra, Alexandra's daughter.

The first dance.

A slice of happiness.

The bride and groom, January 12, 2012.

Happy hour took on a new meaning when this little puppy came home with us.

CHAPTER TWENTY-TWO

Thor, the Prince of Purchase (Our Adopted Son)

I never really had a dog of my own. As children, the four Loeb siblings had a series of dogs that we shared with our parents. I particularly remember two dachshunds that were given to us by my parents' German friends who had escaped Nazi Germany. We were told that they were Jewish dogs who were going to be exterminated by the Nazis. Their names were Hansel and Gretel, and they gave birth to three puppies. We called them Winken, Blinken and Nod—and we kept them all.

At the same time, we had a black cocker spaniel that looked very much like FDR's dog, Fala. I can't remember our cocker spaniel's name, but what I do remember is that it mated with my grandmother's boxer, Bubby. By mating they created what dog lovers would come to know as a new breed of dog, called a *cocker-boxer*. We ended up with seven of them, which we gradually reduced to three by giving several of them away.

Because our dogs were everyone's dogs and not really mine, I didn't really focus on them. They were just there, like everything else at Ridgeleigh. There were eight dogs, four children, two parents, seven in help, and ten more people working on the grounds (including my grandfather's adjoining property). Needless to say, I was never lonely.

In my life with Sharon during these past several years, I would generally go out to Ridgeleigh on Thursday night and stay through Monday, coming into the city for business and various social events from Tuesday through Thursday. Sharon would then come out to Ridgeleigh on Friday and go back to the city late Sunday night. Then I started to stay out at Ridgeleigh on some weekdays. Although I would never stop working, gradually I was trying to move my work to Westchester so that I could ultimately move my office to our Ridgeleigh home—which I finally succeeded in doing in May 2016.

Although I still spent some weeknights in the city and Sharon spent some weeknights in the country, her work still required her to be based in New York City. So I started to think more and more about getting a dog.

Over the years, I had bought a couple of life-sized stuffed dogs, which Sharon perched in the corner of our big U-shaped sofa in the living room at Ridgeleigh. I told everyone they were my "training dogs." (Little girls had training bras, I had stuffed training dogs.) I had always been deterred from getting a dog before, because what would I do when I went to the city? Who would look after the dog?

Although Sharon loved dogs, she was resistant to the idea because she thought she would be left with all the responsibilities, which, with our lifestyle, she thought would be unworkable. Ana, our chef and housekeeper at Ridgeleigh, swore she would never take care of a dog.

Then one day I found the solution. My driver, John Cremin (whose family loves dogs

Thor on a Sunday afternoon.

Thor loves his toys.

SNOW DAYS!

Thor today, looking all grown up.

and has three of them), has a very capable, intelligent daughter named Priscilla, who was studying at Manhattanville College, located near our home. She said she'd be happy to be both a dog walker and "babysitter," giving a dog a temporary home during the week when I needed to be in New York City.

Priscilla and I studied where I might go to find a dog and what breed of dog to buy. I'd always liked cocker spaniels. Also, our friends Yaz and Valentin Hernandez (dog lovers, too) had given me a wonderful book that describes, in detail, all the different traits of the different breeds of dogs: their temperament, their personality, whether they are good with children, affectionate, calm and so on. Happily, I could check off all the positive "boxes" for cocker spaniels.

I was also trying to keep in mind the comments Sharon had made over the years about dogs. She always felt that females had a gentler temperament than males, and that it was not a good idea to get a dog that sheds because of the endless cleaning of dog hair off the furniture and clothing. Also, Sharon had been working with the ASPCA for years, so she felt strongly about not shopping for a dog at pet stores, which get their dogs from puppy mills. She preferred to look for a dog at a shelter.

However, on one Saturday when Priscilla came to Ridgeleigh to discuss how we would proceed, we saw an ad for a cocker spaniel breeder associated with a new pet store recently opened in White Plains. We decided to quietly pay the store a visit—to talk with them about breeders, in general, and see if they might give us some leads. I confess that I was hoping they might also have some cocker spaniels on hand to show us. To my delight, they had just received that week a barely two-month-old cocker spaniel. Like a kid in a candy shop, I couldn't wait to see the puppy.

As we stood at the counter, Gary, the store's salesperson, walked out holding the littlest dog I'd ever seen. It fit in the palm of my hand. The pet store had separate rooms for families to go and play with the dogs in, so off Priscilla and I went with Gary and this little fellow. Within moments of Gary's putting the puppy on the floor, this adorable little animal dashed over to me and landed in my lap with a look on his face like he had fallen in love with me at first sight. I certainly had with him. He was the color of champagne, had big brown eyes and big long blond ears, and had the gentlest manner. What was not to love!

But how to get Sharon to agree? I picked up my cell phone and called her at the house. I asked her to join me in White Plains at "a store" I was at. When I confessed I was at a pet shop looking at a dog, she at first resisted meeting me. She really doesn't like puppy mills and she knew she would never be able to say no to a puppy. Fortunately, I sweet-talked her into coming to meet me.

Fifteen minutes later, Sharon arrived at the store. She says now that she will never forget the vision of me as she entered the little visiting room. There I was, sitting spread-eagle on the floor in my blue jeans, sneakers and red shirt, with this adorable blond puppy dancing around in between my very long legs. Sharon sat on a bench nearby, arms and legs tightly crossed, trying hard not to react to this little bundle of joy. But he was so sweet and gentle and happy that she soon found herself unraveled on the floor with me and the puppy.

Then came the moment of truth . . . would we take him home? Sharon was still hesitant—a male dog that sheds *and* comes from a puppy mill—yikes! But when she heard me speaking to Gary—offering to pay for the dog, leave him at the store while we went home to discuss it and make a decision, *and* if we didn't come back to take him home, the store could keep my money—Sharon realized how very much this little dog meant to me. She turned to me and asked, "You really want this puppy, don't you?" She reminds me to this day that I looked at her with the most soulful eyes and declared, "I don't think I'll ever fall in love with another little dog like this one!" Sharon remembers "that suddenly, I saw before my very eyes my reserved 82-year-old husband turn into an excited little boy of 10 . . . and my heart melted."

I was in heaven—this adorable little creature was coming home with us. As we were leaving the store, Sharon turned to me and said, "We have to give him a name." She paused and said, "The puppy is so little and sweet with those gorgeous big blond ears that look like a mane of hair. We should give him a strong, Nordic name. How about Thor, in the spirit of your love of Scandinavia?" I immediately agreed. And so Sharon, Thor and I went home to start a new phase of life together.

That evening, with the puppy in my lap, we turned on the TV to watch a Netflix movie. We chose a film called *The Avengers*, without paying much attention to the story line. Within a few minutes of the opening scene, a handsome hunk of a man with golden, shoulder-length hair flew out of the sky carrying a big black anvil in his hand . . . and his name was Thor! Sharon and I looked at each other and laughed. It was clearly a sign that we had chosen the right name. And as one can see from pictures taken from the time he was just eight weeks old to now—a strapping three-year-old— he's grown into a strong, handsome cocker spaniel who wears his name well.

Ana, who ran our home at the time and who absolutely swore she would *never* take care of a dog for us, became totally and utterly smitten by Thor. She admitted that from the day we brought him home, "it took no time for all of us to fall in love with him." She even said that "most of the time [she] thinks Thor is a person." She certainly treated him like one.

It is true—he is our much beloved little boy.

I am standing in the hallway of my East 61st Street home, next to one of my favorite Vilhelm Hammershøi paintings, *A Woman in an Interior* (1913).

≡

CHAPTER TWENTY-THREE

Art, Homes and Books

ART

I have had a lifelong affinity for fine art, though my attraction to it goes far beyond the aesthetic. Art is a connector among people and nations, cultures and eras. It is a communicator across geography, religions and language. My patronage and philanthropy in the arts always tries to keep these ideas at the forefront. It is the reason I hung American art at Rydhave as ambassador and hang Danish art in my New York homes. I am drawn to how art bridges worlds—both in space and in time.

Collecting great art has been a passion in my family for many years, and my legacies include collectors' genes inherited from all branches of family—the Lewisohns, the Lehmans and the Loebs. The homes of some of my ancestors were almost like museums, which I took for granted as a child. It was almost a given that I would become a collector myself, growing up in a home decorated with the works of Picasso, Renoir and Manet. A reproduction of a Cézanne even hung in my bedroom when I was a child.

Philip Lehman, my mother's cousin, assembled a remarkable collection of Western European masterpieces. When he died in 1947, his son Robert "Bobbie" Lehman followed in his father's footsteps, both as a Lehman Brothers executive and a major art collector. When Bobbie died in 1969, his own huge collection, together with his father's collection, was left to what is now the Lehman Wing of the Metropolitan Museum.* It holds their paintings

---

* Bobbie Lehman was the head of Lehman Brothers after my grandfather Arthur and his father, Philip Lehman, both died. There were some who thought Bobbie was more interested in his art collecting than in business, but he managed to do both very well. Bobbie brought Lehman Brothers safely through the Depression while simultaneously putting together an internationally celebrated art collection.

from the Renaissance, as well as those of Old Masters, Impressionist and Post-Impressionist paintings and drawings, Oriental and Islamic art, rare manuscripts, bronzes, furniture, enamels, majolica (of which I have a few pieces), Venetian glass jewelry and textiles.

My great-grandfather Adolph Lewisohn bought paintings by Cézanne, Picasso, Monet, Degas, Gaugin and Renoir back when they were all avant-garde artists. Most were left to the Metropolitan Museum and the Brooklyn Museum,* thanks to his daughter-in-law, Margaret Seligman Lewisohn, who inherited them from her husband, Sam. Sam was deeply interested in Impressionist art and wrote a book called *Painters and Personality: A Collector's View of Modern Art*.[134] My grandparents on my mother's side were also major art collectors; a slender book by Claus Virch called *The Adele and Arthur Lehman Collection* was published by the Metropolitan Museum of Art in 1965. The book is gorgeous, a "memorial to a rare person" in Adele, who died that very year.[135]

Virch describes their collection as "a very personal one, in which each painting . . . has

Gary Cooper and his wife, known to me as "Rocky" but whose real name was Veronica Balfe. Their daughter, Maria Cooper, is married to the word-renowned concert pianist Byron Janis.

its chosen place in the owners' home, giving pleasure and enhancing their lives."[136] He also notes that "for both the Lehmans the response to painting is a family tradition,"[137] since their forebearers were such renowned collectors. My mother and her two sisters, Dorothy Lehman Bernhard and Helen Lehman Buttenwieser, inherited some of the paintings that Virch describes. Others went to the Metropolitan Museum and the Fogg Museum at Harvard University. Before my grandmother's death, these pictures, along with a variety of tapestries, hung at 45 East 70th street.

My parents continued the family tradition, becoming avid collectors after World War II. Brendan Gill, my parents' good friend and a longtime *New Yorker* columnist, wrote an introduction to a cloth-bound

---

* Some paintings went to their four daughters: Marjorie Lewisohn, Elizabeth Lewisohn Eisenstein, Joan Lewisohn Crowell and Virginia Lewisohn Cahn. According to Marjorie Lewisohn, some went to other family members, including a Renoir to my grandmother Adele Lewisohn Lehman. The Renoir given to Adele is not the Renoir I chose from my parents' collection. My mother found and bought that one while I was with her, and it is the one I now have. It is known as the "Cooper Renoir," because it was owned for many years by the famous actor Gary Cooper.

Great-Grandfather Lewisohn hung his art collection in the library, located on the top floor of his Fifth Avenue mansion. Over a bookcase at the far left is Cézanne's *Portrait of Madame Cézanne*, which my parents bought in 1956.

catalogue of my parents' collection. In it he aptly notes, "During almost seventy years of marriage they found inspiration in a shared predilection for collecting art." Their collection became so impressive that curators and art historians visited their Park Avenue apartment to hold lectures for students. When any work came on the market that had once been included in Grandpa Lewisohn's collection, my parents made every effort to buy it back.* One of these was a Cézanne portrait of his wife titled *Madame Cézanne Seated in a Yellow Chair*. My mother thought Mrs. Cézanne looked sad and bored, but Father was elated to have retrieved it. It wound up being the "keystone in our collection,"[138] Mother wrote.

My parents were good friends and supporters of Jerusalem's longtime mayor and the founder of the Israel Museum, Teddy Kollek. In 1985, they announced that after their deaths, they would donate a painting to the museum, and they gave Kollek carte blanche to choose whichever one he wanted. Kollek chose Camille Pissarro's *Boulevard Montmartre: Spring*. It was considered by one of the museum directors, Martin Weyl, the "best Pissarro we have."[139]†

Over the decades since the end of World War II, art that was stolen by the Nazis has been reclaimed by descendants of the original owners who were killed in the

---

* For this I am so grateful to my parents' faithfulness to our family's tradition of collecting fine art. Something I have done as well, and that I hope to pass on to my children and grandchildren.

† Many of the unclaimed works of art retrieved by the Allies had been allocated to the Israel Museum, and apparently Pissarro's work was especially favored by the discerning Nazis.

Holocaust. In 1999, after a four-month investigation of the claim's validity, *Boulevard Montmartre* was proven to be from the collection of Max Silberberg, a Breslau industrialist who perished in a Nazi death camp. His widowed daughter-in-law, Gerta Silberberg, was acknowledged as the rightful owner. Mrs. Silberberg agreed to leave the painting at the museum as a long-term loan. It was displayed with explanatory text and a label recognizing its provenance, including my parents, who knew nothing of its previous history. After Gerta Silberberg's death, *Boulevard Montmartre* sold at a Sotheby's auction in 2014 for over $32 million, almost five times the previous auction record for the Impressionist master.[140]

When they died in 1996, my parents' will stipulated that their Impressionist and Post-Impressionist paintings were to be sold at auction, with the proceeds going to a foundation to be named the John Loeb Family Charitable Foundation.* The new foundation—to be managed by my siblings and me—was to support education, health, family planning, art and public policy programs. To handle the sale, my siblings and I chose Christie's, whose vice president, Stephen Lash, is the husband of our Lehman cousin Wendy. Stephen had been very helpful in advising Father on art over the years.

Christie's estimated that the sale would bring at least $80 million. It was held on May 12, 1997, and the headline in *The New York Times* the following day read, "Sale of Coveted Art Collection Brings $92 Million" (it was actually $92.7 million). The art critic Carol Vogel wrote that it had been "one of the most important private collections ever to come to auction" and that the total was the second highest ever for a single-owner sale at auction—and it took all of sixty-six minutes.† The Loeb sale was the difference in allowing Christie's to outsell Sotheby's for the year for the first time in its history.

By an agreement with my father prior to his death, before the auction I was allowed to purchase paintings from my parents' collection that equaled the amount of the Matisse that they had given to my sister Debby. I chose a Redon, a Signac, a Degas and a Renoir. Both the Redon (*Head of Buddha*) and the Signac (*St. Tropez*) had originally been

---

* Father gave $7 million to NYU's Institute of Fine Arts, but he put in a legal stipulation that the institute could not be named for him nor anyone else. A few years after Father's death, Arthur and I found out that the Loeb Student Center at NYU, a gift from my father and his siblings, was about to be torn down. Someone suggested that perhaps the Fine Arts Department could be renamed after my father. Because of Father's wishes, this was only possible if his five children agreed. Unfortunately, the five of us could not agree. We believe that Father would feel differently now, since the Loeb Student Center has ceased to be.

† Mother had been right about the Cézanne being the "keystone" in their collection—it was the most expensive picture in the sale and went for $23.1 million.

in my grandmother's collection and had special meaning to me, especially since I love visiting St. Tropez so much. The Degas (*Desiree Musson*) hung in my parents' library at the home I grew up in. The Renoir (*Girl in a White Hat*) had been bought by my mother herself at an auction, and I was with her.

Each of the five Loeb siblings was charged with distributing funds from the newly created Loeb Foundation. But each already had his or her own favorite philanthropic projects, which they now sought to persuade their siblings to fund through our newly established joint foundation. This made for time-consuming and sometimes spirited debates about how the money should be allocated. In the end, Debby suggested a sensible solution: we divided the foundation money by five and used the divided funds to start five individual Loeb foundations.* I had created the John L. Loeb Jr. Foundation as a young man, funding it modestly until I was able to add significantly to it from my share of the proceeds from the Christie's sale.

There is a wonderful comfort in being surrounded in my homes by art that I love. There is also a certain elation that comes from a new "find" to add to my treasured paintings. In addition, there is the gratification that comes from being able to share the collection through exhibits and lending paintings to museums. Collecting possesses an addictive quality that makes it hard to stop. As a boy, I began collecting toy soldiers. I still have a coin collection that my father began and passed on to me. When Adele Lehman died, her grandchildren were allowed to choose something from her home, which is how I began my majolica collection. Besides collecting, I also had some artistic leanings myself. After winning praise for an early artistic endeavor of a sailboat I drew at about the age of seven—having fallen in love with boats and crayons—I was sure I would grow up to be an artist who specialized in ships. At Hotchkiss, I discovered a latent talent in a private sculpture class, and became quite serious about sculpting for the next ten years.

The private class in my teens was an idea that grew out of my goal of getting nothing but good grades. Having a tin ear, I knew I'd do poorly in the required music appreciation class, so I suggested to the faculty that I study sculpture instead, since at the time I was seriously interested in becoming a doctor. Happily, Tom Blagden, the head of the art

---

* As a chair of the family foundation, I was to be given Father's office in the Seagram Building, but once the one foundation turned into five, I ended up with no office at all. In looking for a new office, I discovered parts of the Wall Street area where real estate prices had almost collapsed. The value of the building where Loeb, Rhoades had had its offices—40 Wall Street, one of the great New York buildings—had dropped to an astonishingly low $5 million. (One of Donald Trump's great coups was his purchase of the building at this price.) I discovered a reasonably priced office at 50 Broad Street, where my grandfather C.M. Loeb first founded Loeb, Rhoades. I took an office in the space the Noyes family had taken for themselves.

department, was willing to give me a private sculpture class. I not only loved sculpting, but I was considered to be a rare talent by both my teacher and my classmates and received the coveted highest grade.

After joining Loeb, Rhoades in 1957, there was simply no time for something that required the intense focus of sculpture, and I have never again undertaken a serious piece of work. Since then, collecting has been the outlet for my ongoing passion for art. Though I admired my parents' art collection, it contained works by artists well beyond my pocketbook. Around 1956, I began collecting with a modest purchase of a painting by the Vietnamese artist Vu Cao Dam, a tender picture of a mother and child, which I still have. I found this particular picture at a small dealer's shop in St. Tropez, where the artist lived, and bought it simply for its charm. I was happy to later discover that Vu Cao Dam's contemporary art was becoming increasingly important.

When I became ambassador to Denmark, my purchases soon turned to Danish painting. After returning to New York in 1983, I became even more enamored with that country's art, and by 1990 there were a hundred Danish paintings in my collection. Today, I have 147 Danish works of art, including three sculptures. I still pore over the Rasmussen auction catalogues and make frequent purchases. As I've said, collecting is addictive.

No parent likes to be asked which child is his favorite, and I never have a ready answer when asked which painting I like best. I would say that my twelve works by Vilhelm Hammershøi are undoubtedly the most important. My first Hammershøi purchase in 1984 was *Woman Placing Branches in a Vase on Table*, an absolute gem. I bought it anonymously for $85,000, the highest price ever paid for a Danish work of art. At that time, a Danish newspaper reported the wrath of someone who had also been bidding on it. "Who is the idiot who paid this crazy price?" he complained. "It was one-fifth of this just a year ago. He obviously doesn't know what he's doing." I certainly did. One of my most frequently borrowed paintings for exhibits, it is today probably worth over $2 million. As my Danish art collection expanded, I ran out of wall space to hang all the other pictures I'd been collecting over the years. I sold some of the

The Danish artist Edvard Eriksen made a few replicas of his renowned sculpture, *The Little Mermaid*. One of them graces the patio of my Purchase home.

Vilhelm Hammershøi's painting *Woman Placing Branches in a Vase on Table*.

Portrait of Vilhelm Hammershøi by his brother-in-law, Peter Ilsted. My son, Nicholas, discovered it online and bought it for me as a present.

non-Danish pieces but still have some in storage, primarily screen prints from important contemporary artists such as Warhol and Lichtenstein.

I have had such pleasure in this collection that one of my lifetime goals has become to make the world—especially Americans—aware of the impressive quality of Danish art, which has not achieved the recognition it deserves. Whenever we have been able to advance it, I leap at the chance.[*]

In early 1994, Harvard's Busch-Reisinger Museum offered such an opportunity. Choosing twenty-eight of my paintings, the museum mounted a three-month exhibit called *Danish Paintings of the Nineteenth Century from the Collection of Ambassador John L. Loeb Jr.* The opening reception was elegant in the courtyard of the Fogg Museum, complete with quartet music. My friend Peter Dyvig, then ambassador to the United States, flew up from Washington to be the main speaker.

Peter Nisbet, then the Daimler-Benz Curator of the Busch-Reisinger Museum, who

---

[*] Kerry Greaves noted in the Summer 2013 *Scandinavian Review* that the "international appeal of nineteenth and early twentieth century Danish art has increased considerably over the last 30 years. In this country, the thirst for Danish art was established by a number of important museum exhibitions during the 1980s and 1990s, as well as the efforts of one visionary collector, Ambassador John L. Loeb Jr." (p. 6).

For several years following the Busch-Reisinger exhibit at Harvard, I loaned the museum, under the aegis of Director Peter Nisbet, one of my favorite Hammershøi paintings, *Courtyard Interior at Strandgade 30*.

organized my exhibit, articulated exactly how I feel about Danish art and artists. He wrote in the exhibit's preliminary news release, "Individual achievement in painting by Danish artists has long been eclipsed by the primacy granted to French painters of the nineteenth century." That French "primacy" is gradually changing, and art professionals have assured me that exhibits of my collection are helping.

Two more institutions worked together to present in sequence, from March through June 2005, an exhibit presenting thirty-four of my nineteenth-century Danish paintings. It ran first at the Bruce Museum of Arts and Science in Greenwich, Connecticut, under the skillful oversight of its director, Peter Sutton, and its curator, Nancy Hall-Duncan. It then traveled to Vassar College in Poughkeepsie, New York, where my sister Judy had once been a student. Held at the Frances Lehman Loeb Art Center, it was curated by Dr. James Mundy, the Anne Hendricks Bass Director of the center. The art critic Ben Genocchio reviewed the exhibit for *The New York Times* and noted wonderful insights about the show. He ended his column with words dear to my heart:

> *Danish art suffers not from an absence of talented artists, or lack of a distinguishable sentiment and tone, but rather, more simply, from a lack of familiarity among audiences worldwide. This exhibition goes some way toward redressing this. It is mandatory viewing for anyone concerned with the history of European art.*[141]

I have enjoyed a wonderful relationship with the American-Scandinavian Foundation (ASF), where I have served for many years as a member of its board. Its visionary president, Edward Gallagher, has been eager to help me in my quest to spread the appreciation of Danish art. The first undertakings we organized together were lectures by prominent academic experts on Scandinavian art.

The first such lecture at Scandinavia House was given by the eminent Robert Rosenblum, a professor of modern European art at New York University. I first got to know Robert through my parents when he wrote a brilliant introduction to a book about their collection. I was particularly interested in having Professor Rosenblum lecture because of his book *Transformations in Late 18th Century Art*.[142] An inspired contrarian, Rosenblum postulated that Modernism did not begin at the turn of the twentieth century, as is commonly taught, and that its birth was not a strictly French phenomenon. I heartily endorse his position, feeling as I do about the lack of worldwide appreciation of Danish art. Rosenblum brought new attention to the importance of Vilhelm Hammershøi's work in the 1960s, a fact important enough to be noted in Rosenblum's *New York Times* obituary.

Dr. Patricia Berman has been invaluable to my Danish art collection. Pat is a specialist in Nordic art, an author and the Theodora L. and Stanley H. Feldberg Professor of Art at Wellesley College. Our friendship and collaboration began in 1982 when she assisted Dr. Kirk Varnedoe with a stunning exhibit called *Northern Light: Realism and Symbolism in Scandinavian Painting, 1880–1910*. Held at the Corcoran and Brooklyn Museums, that exhibit helped to raise the profile of Scandinavian art in the United States.

Shortly thereafter, the Danish ambassador Peter Dyvig invited me to speak at the Smithsonian Institute about Danish culture, as part of a series of lectures from experts in various fields from each of the Nordic countries. I told Peter I was very honored to be asked, but I couldn't discuss Danish culture in general, though I could talk about Danish paintings. I was gratified that I was treated as an expert in a field that I had serendipitously fallen into.

Impressed by her work with Dr. Varnedoe, I asked Pat to help me with my presentation. Pat has a unique way of describing art, and she not only helped me get ready for the lecture but also gave me new insights about my own collection. For instance, she once described Hammershøi's subtle use of color by saying, "His brush is dipped in moonstone and smoke." Since our early felicitous teamwork, Pat has not only been a guest lecturer at Scandinavia House several times, but also curated several of its exhibits, including *Luminous Modernism: Scandinavian Art Comes to America*,

Five of us posed outside Vassar's Frances Lehman Loeb Art Center, beneath a huge fabric poster advertising the exhibit. From left to right: Sharon, me, college president Dr. Frances D. Fergusson, my sister Judy, and museum director Dr. James Mundy.

535

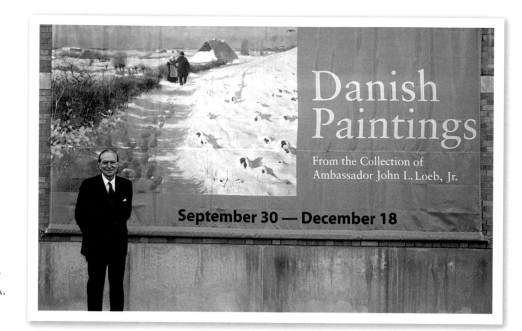

The exhibit poster under which I am standing featured *Winter*, a painting by the Danish artist H.A. Brendekilde.

With my cousin Wendy Lehman Lash and her husband, Stephen Lash, chairman of Christie's.

With my daughter, Alexandra, at my *Danish Paintings* exhibit at Scandinavia House in New York.

Ed Gallagher and Professor Patricia Berman. Ed is president of the American-Scandinavian Foundation, which he has run brilliantly for many years. Professor Berman teaches at Wellesley College and is the world's outstanding expert on the artist Edvard Munch, as well as nineteenth-century Danish Art.

Renowned Scandinavian chef Morten Sohlberg, ASF president Ed Gallagher and Irene and Julian Gingold, at the event/dinner in honor of the exhibition of selected work from my Danish collection, held at Scandinavia House in New York City.

1912, which included six of my paintings. With my instigation and support, she wrote a wonderful book called *In Another Light: Danish Painting in the Nineteenth Century*. She wrote two other well-received books, both about the Norwegian painter Edvard Munch, most famous for his iconic painting *The Scream*.[143]

Twice I flew the Danish art historian Dr. Elisabeth Fabritius from Copenhagen to New York to help with my art projects. Elisabeth provided major research and much of the commentary for the catalogue raisonné of my entire collection, published in 2005. A specialist on the Skagen art colony, she is a brilliant art historian and has an uncanny eye for color, an almost magical ability to never lose the exact visual memory of a painting's colors. Until she came to New York, she had only seen photographs of my collection. After touring my homes and viewing each painting just once, she met with my book designer to check the color of each photograph in the catalogue from memory.

By far the most ambitious exhibit ever undertaken at Scandinavia House was *Danish Paintings from the Golden Age to the Modern Breakthrough*, comprising thirty-seven of my paintings. With help from Dr. Thor J. Mednick, Professor Patricia Berman, Ed Gallagher and his superb staff, they produced a magnificent hardbound catalogue and a series of lectures on Danish art that played to full houses in Scandinavia House's Victor Borge Auditorium.

The exhibit, curated by Dr. Mednick and Professor Berman, attracted unusually large crowds and extremely warm press. *The New York Times* praised the show as "absorbing" and "fascinating."[144] It was the first time that the paper had ever reviewed an exhibition

From October 12, 2013 to January 18, 2014, a hugely popular exhibit (thirty-seven paintings from my collection), *Danish Paintings from the Golden Age to the Modern Breakthrough*, was held at the Scandinavia House in New York City. It was held over for ten extra days because of its popularity.

of Danish art. To be part of such a landmark moment for Danish culture was immensely gratifying for me. David Patrick Columbia's *New York Social Diary* article noted that the art was "serene and soothing . . . it has an emotional power in its beauty that draws me in to want to see more, and to *know*,"[145] which perfectly encapsulates how I feel about it. The show was extended for ten extra days, and the public response reminded me of why I first fell in love with Danish art more than thirty years ago.

I am still in love with Danish art today.

HOMES

Ridgeleigh

There must be as many definitions and concepts of "home" as there are people. The poet Robert Frost wrote, "Home is the place where, when you have to go there / They have to take you in."[146] Johnny Carson once said, "Home is where you keep your stuff." And the humorist Sam Ewing said, "When you finally go back to your old home, you find it wasn't the old home you missed, but your childhood." Fortunately, I don't have to "go back home," because I've never really left Ridgeleigh, the name on the gates of the estate where the home I grew up in is located. But I must admit to the occasional nostalgia for parts of my childhood.

Although Ridgeleigh is my personal definition of home, I spend time in two other residences: one is a historic brownstone in Manhattan, and the other is a London flat, located in the even more historic Eaton Square. Any discussion of homes in my life must also include Gull Bay, the Loeb family summer home located on Upper Saranac Lake in the Adirondacks in upstate New York, which lives warm in my memory. Although I spent two months of every summer from the ages of three to eight in the Lehman cottage at my great-grandfather Lewisohn's Prospect Point estate on Saranac Lake, I spent almost every year thereafter, until I was well into my seventies, at Gull Bay, the property my mother bought when I was seven. (See chapter 1 for more about Gull Bay.)

In the late 1960s, around the time I was to become a co-managing partner of Loeb, Rhoades, Mother offered to lend me part of Ridgeleigh. It was as serendipitous as one could imagine, as Ridgeleigh was always the very definition of home to me. Ridgeleigh is where I find deep peace and comfort, which is why I consider it my real home. In fact, I sometimes wonder why I ever leave it. When something out in the world beckons, and I venture out to tilt at some windmill or other, I always return with relief to Ridgeleigh, my true home from the day I was born.

My sister Judy lived only a few miles from my home in Purchase, so I saw her every weekend, frequently for meals. Having grown up the classic WASP, Judy became something of a bohemian later in life. Her second husband was a younger man, an Italian named Marco Chiara, the son of a famous writer. Judy entirely embraced Italy and Italian culture during her time there. She had a child with Marco named Daniela, who speaks perfect Italian and now lives with her husband half of the year in Venice.

Judy had a wonderfully open spirit; she welcomed everybody and enjoyed everyone, from British royalty—some of whom lived in her basement when they first came to New York—to the poorest of the poor, whom she helped through foundations and organizations like Exponents, the first New York City counseling program to assist AIDS patients. She was also a world traveler, as her son Charlie told me, from the Galapagos Islands to the Himalayas, from South America to Switzerland. She covered the continents with ease and grace.[147]

I was still reeling from Judy's death when Ann passed away, just six months later. It was as though my heart had been ripped out. Ann was beloved as a child, and after her marriage to Edgar Bronfman she became part of one of America's most powerful families. However, she never really embraced the responsibilities that come with such a role, and it likely fractured their marriage, even though Edgar adored her. For whatever reason, Ann never really felt like anyone loved her—although she was always surrounded with loving and caring friends and family. There was a mysterious barrier to happiness inside her.

After almost ten years, Ann wanted a divorce from Edgar, but my parents persuaded her against it. For his part, Edgar couldn't even conceive of a divorce, especially not while

RIDGELEIGH ESTATE: THE HOUSE AND GARDENS WHERE I LIVE NOW

One of Sharon's favorite sculptures, by Ratimir Stojadinović, in front of our house at Ridgeleigh. Inset: John L. Loeb – Friends Welcome – Relatives By Appointment.

Terrace and back of our house, leading to rock garden.

The beautiful pool at Ridgeleigh, where I have been swimming for eighty or more years.

Sunken garden where I was first put in the water and liked it.

The living room as it looked in my bachelor days.

My living room, with Sharon's touch.

Archipenko sculpture in hallway, looking toward living room.

My living room, with a view toward the back patio.

Rock garden with two Chinese soldiers.

View from the swimming pool to the lawn below.

Our rose garden in full bloom.

The freshwater pond where the ducks come to enjoy the spring and summer weather.

RIDGELEIGH ESTATE: THE HOUSE AND GARDENS WHERE I GREW UP

My parents' home where I grew up, built by my grandfather Arthur Lehman in 1928.

Terrace and rear of home. Inset: Our sundial looking out onto the broad sweep of lawns.

Swimming pool at 170 Anderson Hill Road, built by my father to the exact dimensions of the Hotchkiss swimming pool so that I could make the Varsity team—which I did.

The beautiful tennis court at 170 Anderson Hill Road.

Home of our estate manager, Bob Albanese.

his father was alive. Samuel Bronfman considered marriage into the esteemed Loeb-Lehman family as one of his greatest accomplishments. As the years went by, Edgar and Ann became great friends with Senator Philip Hart of Michigan and his wife, Jane Briggs Hart. A couple of years after Sam Bronfman died, in 1971, Ann and Edgar divorced. After Senator Hart died in 1976, Ann and Jane became close and dear friends, which they remained for the rest of their lives.

Grandfather Arthur Lehman purchased the Ridgeleigh estate just after Christmas 1924 for $225,000—a little over $3 million in today's money. At the time, it was a sixty-six-acre property, but by the time I inherited it, in 1996, it encompassed eighty-three acres. It is located on Anderson Hill Road in Purchase, New York, about three miles from White Plains. My grandparents bought Ridgeleigh from Ms. Eva Coleman Davis of Dobbs Ferry, New York. Prior to Ms. Davis's ownership, the estate (spelled "Ridgley" at the time) had been owned by Oliver Harriman Jr., a relative of the Union Pacific railroad mogul E.H. Harriman, and of the diplomat W. Averell Harriman.

The two-story house, unoccupied for nearly six years prior to its acquisition by my grandparents, had a quasi-Georgian architecture, faced with red brick. The estate included a large garage where the chauffeur lived, a gardener's cottage, and a pair of large greenhouses, once called "hot houses." The Arthur Lehmans did a great deal of landscaping, of which my grandmother had a major hand in planning—especially the terraces and the rock garden.

The Arthur Lehmans made major renovations, including turning the attic into wonderfully livable quarters where the grandchildren and their young friends stayed during summers and holidays. With the help and advice of a decorator imported from Chicago, they installed a handsome circular staircase at the left side of the foyer, turned two smaller rooms and a bath on the first floor into a huge living room, and imported paneling from England for both the living room and library.

My cousins the Bernhards spent entire summers in my grandparents' huge house, as did my cousins the Buttenwiesers during World War II. When my grandparents died, they left the house and its immediate acreage to the then-widowed Aunt Dorothy Bernhard. However, the house was large, sprawling and in need of repairs. She decided to raze it, replacing it with a handsome ranch house in the popular style of the 1960s. The one-story house nearly sits on the footprint of the original structure. It is the house where I now live, thanks to my mother having purchased Dorothy's house from my Bernhard cousins. My cousin Billy has remarked that "with its high ceilings, it was almost made for Johnny's six-feet-four inches." Being a card-carrying preservationist, Billy somewhat regrets the razing of that handsome house, once the gathering place of the entire family and the scene of so many wonderful memories. Alas, only one picture of its exterior remains, and none of the interior. Having spent so much time there, Billy remembers well its glittering hall chandelier, the cozy library, the huge drawing room (with a piano nobody played), its large old-fashioned kitchen and its huge pantry.

The name Ridgeleigh encompasses my whole estate, including the house my parents built, which has been renamed Lions Gate to differentiate it from my current home. I now own my house, my parents' house, the caretaker's home, and the peripheral buildings from the original estate, as well as a few acres across the street next to the Century Country Club.

If I were to enumerate the major blessings of my life, I immediately think of Bob Albanese, who found a lifetime career as estate supervisor at Ridgeleigh more than thirty-five years ago, immediately after graduating from Cornell University with a degree in plant science. While serving as a Cornell University trustee, my mother asked one of the professors who taught in Bob's field to post an ad for someone to supervise Ridgeleigh's huge greenhouses. Bob applied and my mother hired him; she quickly recognized his talents and impressive mind. The estate supervisor at the time, Mr. Wilson, had a crew of about ten. When Mr. Wilson died in 1985, Bob was immediately made superintendent. With his impressive management skills, he has been able to pare the estate staff down to himself and one other person. At the same time, Bob has also been my technology guru and patient mentor, guiding me through the constant changes in today's digital world.

At the age of eighteen, Bob and his twin brother studied the stock market and made small investments. Over the years, Bob and I have had deep discussions of investment strategies, and in the next minute worried together about whether the generator would see us through if a snowstorm cut off our main-line electricity. Bob, along with his wife, Mary, and his daughters, Carol Ann and Katie, have become something of a second family to me. I put Katie through four years at NYU; she is certified brilliant, a member of MENSA, an organization exclusively for "geniuses." She is currently finishing her master's degree at Duke University. Carol Ann is a freshman in the business school at Villanova University. The Albaneses live in what was once a cottage on the Ridgeleigh property but is now a beautiful house Bob helped redesign. He is truly "a man for all seasons." His capabilities make it possible for me to feel the peace that I do at Ridgeleigh.

My first real political victory came about through the Ridgeleigh property and as a resident of Purchase. Ron Bianchi, the mayor of Harrison (of which Purchase is a part), had been planning to move the Department of Public Works next door to my Ridgeleigh property, and to acquire land contiguous to my estate (owned by Verizon), which would raise everyone's taxes and cause environmental damage that could not be easily reversed. The plan also called for the widening of Anderson Hill Road and abandoning the local business district. With Bianchi seeking re-election, I drafted a letter detailing the problems with his plan, and joined forces with the Purchase Environmental Protection Association (PEPA) to send the letter to all twelve thousand Harrison residents. Bianchi shot back with a letter of his own arguing against my list, point by point. I also put considerable weight and support behind his challenger, Steve Malfitano, a relative newcomer and Wall Street partner at Cowen and Company. PEPA hosted a "Meet the Candidates Forum" at Manhattanville College, and we drafted a bulletin to the event that emphasized the problems with Bianchi's plan. Malfitano defeated Bianchi in the mayoral race, drowning Bianchi's plans in the water. Bianchi returned to Harrison as a judge, though I've yet to engage in any other battle with him, and hopefully will not need to.

Townhouse

In 1961, I bought a house in Manhattan. I fell in love with a historic brownstone at 237 East 61st Street, which appealed to my attraction to objects of the past. The houses on 61st and 62nd Streets between Second and Third Avenues were built between 1868 and 1876. Mine was one of five built between 1874 and 1875.* At the request of the East Sixties Property Owners Association, these two blocks were officially put under their protective care, designating our blocks as the "Treadwell Farm Historic District."[148] (By 1830, the real estate developer Adam Treadwell had acquired the area originally owned by a colonial farmer named Peter Van Zandt.) The spokesman for the East 61st Street property owners told the commission, "We have no fear of what the commission may do, as far as restricting us in the future. What we do fear is the possible effect in the future of unrestrained economic forces on the neighborhood which has been a pleasant, attractive, charming residential oasis in this city for approximately 100 years." Our current neighborhood group still feels strongly that landmark restrictions are preferable to commercialization.

I've been an active member in the Treadwell Farm Historic Association from the very beginning of my residency at East 61st Street, and have gotten to know many of my neighbors through it. A very special friend has been my next-door neighbor, Helen D. Roosevelt, the widow of John E. Roosevelt, who was a cousin of both Theodore and Franklin. (They bought their house about six months before I bought mine.) Helen is a wonderfully kind

---

* My house on East 61st Street was designed by Florentino Pelletier in a French Second Empire style at an approximate cost of $10,000.

61ST STREET: OUR MANHATTAN TOWNHOUSE

My beloved brownstone, where I have been living for fifty-seven years, part of the Historic Treadwell Farm District.

My beautiful townhouse garden off the formal dining room, thanks to Ray Laufer, our remarkable gardener.

Our ground-floor formal dining room, which opens onto a lovely English garden.

Our first-floor foyer, with stairs on the left leading to the living room and out to the terrace overlooking our private garden.

Sister Parish decorated the library off the first-floor foyer.

The living room off the other side of the first-floor foyer.

and strong person; living cheek by jowl for fifty-four years, we remain very good friends. I arrived too late in the neighborhood to run into the singer Enrico Caruso and actresses Tallulah Bankhead and Gertrude Lawrence, though the actor Montgomery Clift lived only a few doors west of my home. Other well-known previous and current residents include Eleanor Roosevelt, the former CIA director Allen W. Dulles, Beardsley Ruml (the economist who instigated the "pay-as-you-go" tax system), and the writers Clifton Fadiman and Tom Wolfe, who is still a good friend of mine.

I chose the well-regarded Sister Parish as my decorator, having known her casually for some time because her husband was a partner at Loeb, Rhoades. Sister was known for specializing in a styled dubbed "the English country-house look," which suited me perfectly. She was also known for a sharp tongue, and we had our share of words before we finished, but I have to say that the look she achieved was exactly what I wanted. When the house needed renovations a few years ago, I had it replicated even down to the chintz upholstery in the library, one of the hallmarks of the famed decorator. (The chintz had to be specially ordered, because so many years had passed since the days of Sister.) "I try to give permanence to a house," she was quoted in her biography as saying, "to bring out the experiences, the memories, the feelings that make it a home."[149] It is a unique and personal talent, given that the canvas is someone's home; I'm blessed that Sister did her magic upon mine.

Eaton Square

As a certified Anglophile, part of my heart will always belong to England. In December 1985, I purchased a cozy flat in historic Eaton Square, a residential garden square in the Belgravia district in the center of London. Both the stately beauty and the history of the area hold great appeal for me. Whenever in England, I have felt a particular sense of pleasure in staying in my own "digs," as though I'm a denizen of London, not just a visitor passing through.

The Eaton Square houses are managed by the eponymous firm the Grosvenor Group. Back in the late 1600s, the wife of Sir Thomas Grosvenor, Mary Davies, inherited five hundred acres of land north of the Thames. In the 1720s, the Grosvenors began to develop some land that had been mostly meadow. The property was subsequently inherited by a line of aristocratic Grosvenors. Beginning in the 1820s, and with the passage of years, that original property (as well as a lot more acquired over the years by Sir Thomas Grosvenor's heirs) was gradually developed into major residential properties and commercial enterprises worldwide. The Grosvenor Group now oversees and manages all of the vast holdings of the (sixth and current) Duke and Duchess of West-

EATON SQUARE HOME: LONDON

The private garden for those who live in Eaton Square. Across the road is the entrance to my flat, 31 Eaton Square. In another part of this garden is the private tennis court.

This is our beautiful entrance.

As you enter the house, you are greeted by a sun-filled living room that looks out onto Eaton Square's private gardens.

The dining room opens onto a terrace that looks out onto the back of our property, where we have a private garden filled with flowers.

The porch off the dining room captures the unexpected presence of a large tropical palm tree.

Our lovely private garden.

minster, who maintain one of their homes in Eaton Square.*

Eaton Square has been a popular address for fictional characters created by many authors, including Henry James, Anthony Trollope and, recently, Jeffrey Archer. *Downton Abbey* fans will no doubt remember that Lord Crawley's sister, Lady Rosamund Painswick, has an address in Eaton Square, and the Bellamy family of *Upstairs, Downstairs* lived in Eaton Place. As far as I know, no fictional character has lived in my flat, although I have always thought of my life as something out of a novel.

BOOKS

I remember filling out a Social Register form to announce my marriage to Sharon Handler in 2012, and coming to a part that made me smile. I had reached the presumptuous query on the form that requested "Name of yacht," implying that we all had one.[†] Much as I love sailing, I do not even own a sailboat. When writing a check to support a book's publication, I remind myself that seeing a book into print means more to me than any yacht ever could. This is particularly true if the book is related to any of my three passionate pursuits: American Jewish history, genealogy and Danish art.

I cannot write about my love of books without a tribute to my brother, Arthur, whose passion for them surpasses mine by a country mile. He warmed the hearts of Upper East Side Manhattan readers when he founded the intimate Madison Avenue Bookshop in 1973, modeling it after a London carriage bookshop called Heywood Hill. For almost thirty years it supported and championed many New York writers and became an integral part of the community on the Upper East Side, becoming the favorite of such notable neighbors as Joan Didion and John Gregory Dunne.

Arthur hosted a book-reading carriage trade while giving equal attention to any book-hungry reader who wandered in. In 2002, like almost all small, independent bookstores across the country, his store succumbed to the impersonality of e-books and Amazon.

---

* Gerald Grosvenor, sixth Duke of Westminster, is reputed to be the richest property owner in the United Kingdom. In May 1989, I had a wonderful weekend in Fulton, Missouri, at the home of the president of Westminster College, where Winston Churchill delivered his famous "Iron Curtain" speech on March 5, 1946. The school invited the duke to receive an honorary degree and to introduce him. On the campus of Westminster is the Church of St. Mary the Virgin, Aldermanbury, a seventeenth-century church built by Christopher Wren that they moved stone by stone to Missouri.

† In my late teens I learned it was very important among the circles in which I wished to frequent to be listed in the Social Register. While navigating a young lovely through a fox-trot at one of the WASP dance parties, I casually admitted that my parents and I were not listed in it. My dance partner went to the ladies' room and never returned. Lesson learned.

A montage of our books.

My brother, Arthur, began his extremely popular Madison Avenue Bookshop in 1973, and he took personal oversight of every aspect of the business. He appears here in the front of the store in the 1980s.

This night shot shows the first two floors of the five-story building that housed my brother's Madison Avenue Bookshop. Located between 68th and 69th Street the shop drew a great many mourners when it closed in 2002.

After 30 Years, Cozy Bookstore Gets to the End

By DINITIA SMITH

The Madison Avenue Bookshop, the cramped little bookstore that for nearly 30 years has been a literary destination for the carriage trade and for the writers of the Upper East Side, will close on Jan. 10, its owner and manager, Perry Haberman, said yesterday.

The shop, on Madison Avenue between 69th and 70th Streets, is the latest in a long list of independent bookstores that have closed in recent years, many driven out by high rent and the high cost of doing business.

Mr. Haberman, who is also the landlord of the five-story building that houses the store, at 833 Madison Avenue, would not say why he was closing the bookstore, only that it would be replaced by "a retail store."

"I'm too busy to talk right now," Mr. Haberman said in response to questions, as he bustled about today filling orders for books in the tiny space that has always had a bare-bones, all-business air about it. It did not accept credit cards, though house accounts were allowed.

But the Madison Avenue neighborhood between 57th and 63rd Streets has the fastest-rising retail rents in the United States, a recent study by Cushman & Wakefield, the real estate company, found. For the year ending in June, rents for retail space rose 25 percent to an average of $650 a square foot. Rents have also been rising in the area of the bookstore.

In 1997, Upper East Side book lovers lost another favorite store, Books & Co., just five blocks north at Madison Avenue and 75th Street. They reacted with sorrow today.

"I can't believe it," said Nan Kempner, whose book "RSVP," featuring menus and aperçus about entertaining, was displayed in the bookshop window when it was published in 2000.

Ms. Kempner added: "All these years! I just counted on them. They were always wonderful about getting you books out of print. They were so kind about discussing books." Ms. Kempner said she found that helpful because she liked to carefully match gift books with the recipients.

The Madison Avenue Bookshop was founded in 1973 by Arthur Lehman Loeb, a member of the Loeb-Rhodes family. Mr. Loeb and his siblings inherited an estate of some $200 million after the deaths of their parents, John Langeloth Loeb Sr. and Frances Lehman Loeb.

Arthur Loeb said he had wanted to be an English professor but gave up

James Estrin/The New York Times
The Madison Avenue Bookshop, between 69th and 70th Streets, has long been a destination for Upper East Side writers.

his dream to work as a book salesman. In the mid-1980's, he hired Mr. Haberman, a former model, as a stock boy at the store. Mr. Haberman worked his way up to manager. (Mr. Loeb said he never wanted to be manager.)

In 2000, Mr. Loeb gave Mr. Haberman the building and the store and retired.

"Of course I'm unhappy," Mr. Loeb, 70, said of the store's closing. But he didn't ask Mr. Haberman why he was closing the store or what Mr. Haberman intends to do with the space, he said.

"He owns the building, and he can do what he wants," Mr. Loeb said.

Over the years, the bookshop specialized in hand-selling to a high degree and in ferreting out hard-to-find titles for customers. It also held book parties, which were packed with celebrities.

The writer John Gregory Dunne, who with his wife, the essayist and novelist Joan Didion, lives near the store said that ordering books there was cheaper than buying them online because postage and handling was always added onto the online price.

The Madison bookshop would send books over by messenger at no charge, Mr. Dunne said.

The closing of the shop is "like losing a next-door neighbor with whom you have a really close relationship," he said.

MAKE YOUR KITCHEN NEW!
AT LESS THAN THE COST OF FULL REMODELING...
REFACE!
DON'T REPLACE
All New Doors, Hardware and Hinges on Your Old Wood, Metal or Mica Cabinets. We Also Do: New Counters of Sink & Faucets, Add-on Cabinets & Drawers, Appliance/Floor Installation
CALL NOW AND SAVE!
WE DO IT ALL!
CARRA DESIGNS
Nu-facers KITCHENS Since 1981
For Free Estimate CALL NOW
212 426-4160
Visit Our Website: www.nufacers.com
NYCLIC #40564162

The New York Times, Tuesday, December 17, 2002.

My brother, Arthur, and I are pictured here in the hallway of Blenheim Palace at my 75th birthday celebration in 2005. Arthur's toast to me that night is etched in my heart.

The New York Times wrote a fitting tribute to the bookstore upon its closing. During the last weeks, mourning readers came to pay their respects, as though at a wake. Among them was the author and historian Louis Auchincloss, who said about the staff, "You always felt they were more interested in having you read a book than sell you one." Others reminisced nostalgically about book launches and signings from days of yore. It was always in the front window of Arthur's bookstore where the books I launched first saw the first light of day.

Dr. Roland Flade, who discovered all the records of the Lehman family in Germany. He is holding the book he wrote, *The Lehmans: From Rimpar to the New World*. On his right is a portrait of Governor and Senator Herbert Lehman, whose picture now hangs in Rimpar's City Hall.

Always of a scholarly bent (Arthur's academic record at Collegiate, Hotchkiss and Harvard far surpassed mine), my brother had absolutely no interest in joining the family firm. Given his lifelong focus on literature and philosophy, he once thought of becoming an English professor before opting to run the bookstore. When asked by a friend what he thought of the most recent translation of Proust's work, Arthur responded apologetically that he really didn't have an opinion about any Proust translations because "I only read him in French." I think of this chapter as a tribute to my brother, who continues to be a rock and a close confidante in our later years. He gave the most heartening toast at my seventy-fifth birthday party at Blenheim Palace, which touched me deeply. He said,

> *My big brother John is my hero. He is my idea of everything a man should be. Although his many achievements are highly praiseworthy, it is John's spirit that I would most like to honor this evening. At various times in his life, he has suffered the slings and arrows of outrageous fortune, but he has persevered intact with his exuberance, his enthusiasm, his zest for life, and his passionate interest in the interlocking worlds of finance, politics, diplomacy, the fine arts and high society.*
>
> *I feel very lucky and very proud to be part of his life. I would like to wish him a very happy birthday, and many happy returns of the day.*

I asked Arthur a few years afterwards if he meant it all. He looked me square in the eye. "I meant every word," he said.

Mayer Lehman and his wife, Babette Neugass, with children and grandchildren. On the far right is my grandfather Arthur Lehman, in whose home in Purchase I still live.

The background stories about the nine books that I have had published, usually with fervor and funds, are included here, along with some background stories of how they came to be.

The Lehmans:
From Rimpar to the New World: A Family History
By Roland Flade (Würzburg, Germany: Königshausen & Neumann, 1996); second edition, which includes the Rimpar Reunion, published in 1999.

This book was featured in the front window of my brother Arthur's Madison Avenue Bookshop for more than a month after publication. It drew people into the store who had never heard of the Lehmans but were curious about the family story. The book is extensively detailed in the "Family Roots" chapter of this book, which includes the story of the Rimpar Reunion.

Lots of Lehmans:
The Family of Mayer Lehman of Lehman Brothers,
Remembered by His Descendants
Edited and compiled by Dr. Ken Libo; foreword by William J. Bernhard and John L. Loeb Jr.; afterword by June Rossbach Bingham Birge; contributed stories written by fifty-five Lehman family members (New York: Center for Jewish History, 2007).

Three Lehman cousins in front of the portrait of our great-grandfather, Mayer Lehman, one of the three founders of Lehman Brothers. From left: Billy Bernhard, my first cousin; June Rossbach Bingham Birge, a cousin and writer and widow of the well-known congressman Jonathan Brewster Bingham, whose father discovered Machu Picchu; and myself.

"Not on your life," was the instant response of our outspoken and very funny cousin June Rossbach Bingham Birge, an author and playwright, when I suggested that she write a book about Mayer Lehman's descendants.[*] In 2004, at a conference honoring Uncle Herbert, the seed for this book was planted. The Franklin and Eleanor Roosevelt Institute asked my cousins Billy Bernhard and Larry Buttenwieser to solicit Lehman family funds to support a two-day conference about our great-uncle. The event was to be the first in a series about New York State's governors. It was expected to draw around 150 scholars and political science teachers and students to the FDR National Historic Site at Hyde Park and its new Visitor and Education Center.

Uncle Herbert, whose first political post had been as Franklin Roosevelt's lieutenant governor, became New York's governor after FDR became president. Billy Bernhard took on the necessary fundraising and rounded up $100,000 from Lehman-related cousins—five Loebs, three Buttenwiesers and two Bernhards—to make the Lehman conference a reality. I was among the hefty contingent of Lehmans who attended. It was there, surrounded by Lehmans, that the idea for a book about the Mayer Lehman family hit me. It would become a reality, but it took perseverance and funding from Billy, my brother, Arthur, and me.

June's riveting talk about the personal side of Uncle Herbert at the conference brought

---

* June's memoir, *Braided Lives: A 20th-Century Pursuit of Happiness*, is a delightful read.

the house down. Alternately laughing and shedding a tear or two during her presentation, we thought her humorous and candid style was perfect for the book project. But she just wouldn't do it. Billy and I couldn't let the idea of a Lehman book drop, although we knew it would be time-consuming and expensive. We thus persevered, but first we had to find a writer.

I thought of the historian and writer Dr. Ken Libo, who had collaborated with my parents on their memoir, *All in a Lifetime*. Ken had written several articles for various Jewish publications and seemed a good fit for the topic. After Ken agreed to spearhead it, Billy and I persuaded June to come on board to help with the book, and the four of us had a wonderful time working together. Fortunately, though it was put together by committee, it did not turn into a camel. We came up with the idea of a compilation of short memory pieces written by all the living descendants of Mayer and Babette Lehman. Ken would have the considerable task of tracking us all down. Even armed with our cousin Wendy Lehman Lash's list of most recent Lehman addresses, this was an impressive feat.

Ken wheedled, cajoled and sometimes badgered the fifty-five members of our clan to turn in their stories. When they complied, he judiciously edited them all. One small but memorable anecdote proved to be more character-revealing than a whole chapter might have been. June, whose humor is evident throughout the book, came up with the perfect title, *Lots of Lehmans*. In the book, she tells a childhood anecdote about visiting one of our uncles, Judge Irving Lehman, and his wife, Aunt Sissie, while Albert Einstein was also there. Aunt Sissie took little June aside. "June," she said, "you must be very quiet while you are here. Mr. Einstein is thinking."

Dr. Ken Libo, the guiding light of *Lots of Lehmans*, was not only a respected professor of literature and history at Hunter College, but also a prolific author of articles and essays on Jewish history in America.

As June might have said, her "paw tracks" are all over the book. Thanks to Bruce Slovin, the founder of the Center for Jewish History, who saw the book's historical potential, the center became its publisher. Later, Syracuse University agreed to be our distributor. The publication of *Lots of Lehmans* was more than reason enough to see if another family reunion in the form of a book launch would be appropriate. We learned shortly after the launch that our book timing was almost too late. What no one knew during that year was that June was terminally ill; she had never said a word about it.

Eli Evans, to the left of a large poster, and Kathy Plotkin (with her back to the camera), at the book launch of *An American Experience: Adeline Moses Loeb (1876–1953) and Her Early American Jewish Ancestors*, held at the Metropolitan Club on May 5, 2009.

June attended the publication party, which Ken orchestrated, on February 28, 2007, at the Museum of Jewish Heritage, thanks to the instrumental help of Bob Morgenthau, its chairman. June died only six months later, in August. Ken Libo died in late March 2012. In hindsight, I think of the book as a tribute not only to the Lehman clan, but to both June and Ken, whose vision and tireless resolve made this book what it is.

An American Experience:

Adeline Moses Loeb (1876–1953) and Her Early American Jewish Ancestors

Introduction by Eli Evans; contributions by Ambassador John L. Loeb Jr., Kathy Plotkin, Margaret Kempner and Judith Endelman; genealogical charts and city maps by David Kleiman of Heritage Muse (New York: Sons of the Revolution in the State of New York, 2009).

This is a beautifully produced tribute to my southern belle grandmother and the history she helped shape. Half of this book is due to Judith Endelman, who wrote the deeply researched stories. She remarkably traces our family—all in the USA, all Jewish— nine generations back from me to our earliest ancestor in America. He arrived in New Amsterdam (New York) in 1967. His name was Abraham Isaacks. He is my great, great, great, great, great, great-grandfather. Eli Evans wrote the introduction. Kathy Plotkin deserves credit—with the late David Kleiman—for putting the book together. I contributed a foreword to the book, as did Margaret Kempner.

The Levy Family and Monticello, 1834–1923: Saving Thomas Jefferson's House

By Dr. Melvin I. Urofsky (Charlottesville, VA: Thomas Jefferson Foundation, Monticello Monograph Series, 2002).

Something that really ignites my passion is bringing to light cultural contributions to our country made by historic Jewish Americans. Uriah Phillips Levy has been described as brilliant, eccentric and extremely determined when it came to causes he believed in. He became the first Jewish commodore in the U.S. Navy, despite the significant anti-Semitism that still permeated that institution. He is also credited with ending flogging in the Navy, a vicious punishment he found sickening. The beatings were so brutal they ripped into seamen's muscles, ending their naval careers. He became quite unpopular among his fellow officers for helping to end this practice, which naval leaders found useful and even sometimes essential to maintain discipline.

Because of the severe anti-Semitism he experienced throughout his life, Levy was deeply devoted to Thomas Jefferson and his position on religious freedom. Jefferson died on July 4, 1826, deeply in debt. His once elegant plantation, Monticello, was already in great disrepair. Jefferson's widowed daughter was forced to sell the estate to a pharmacist, James Barclay, who greatly destroyed the land by turning it into a silkworm farm. The historic Monticello building rotted into disarray: the cows were housed in the basement, and grain was stored in the parquet-floored drawing room.

Commodore Levy, who became wealthy through prescient investments in New York City real estate, learned of Jefferson's Monticello sinking into disrepair in response to a question asked of him by the Marquis de Lafayette. Levy was in a financial position to buy the estate, and he purchased the house and some acreage in 1834 for $2,700, eight years after Jefferson's death.[150]

Levy immediately started to restore the home and its grounds. He even doffed his uniform to prune shrubs himself when he was home long enough from his naval duties. In his absence, his widowed mother, Rachel Phillips Levy, presided over the early stages of restoration. When she died in 1839, she was buried in the estate's graveyard, not far from the house.

Uriah P. Levy died during the Civil War. In his will, he left Monticello to the U.S. government to be used as an agricultural school for the orphaned children of noncommissioned naval officers. Because the war was absorbing the federal budget, Congress declined the responsibility of restoring and maintaining Monticello. Various members of his family did want the land, and they disputed Levy's will. Monticello ownership was in limbo for several years while remaining under the care of the Levy family. The Civil War ravaged some of the Monticello property. Ultimately, Uriah Levy's nephew Jefferson Monroe Levy, then a congressman from New York, became the legal owner. J.M. Levy continued Uriah's restoration of the plantation.[151] For several years thereafter, Jefferson Levy hosted Monticello receptions for Washington dignitaries, including President Teddy Roosevelt.

J.M. Levy ran into financial difficulties, and, in 1923, he reluctantly sold Monticello to the newly formed Thomas Jefferson Memorial Foundation, which still owns and operates it. Without the Levy family's care, Americans would not have the magnificent and beautifully restored Monticello to visit today. In 1971, I became aware of all that Uriah Phillips Levy and his family did to save Monticello, a story that the general public did not know. I'd read about Levy's stunning life and how he saved Monticello in the several chapters on him in Stephen Birmingham's book *The Grandees*.

I made my very first visit to Thomas Jefferson's home, too long delayed, in early December 1994. I'd just received a CBE (Commander of the British Empire) from Her Majesty Queen Elizabeth II, awarded in a private ceremony by Ambassador Sir Robin Renwick at the UK embassy in Washington, D.C. Since I was already that far south, I went to Charlottesville, Virginia, to visit a dear friend of our family, Felicia Warburg, and to tour Monticello, something I'd long wanted to do. I fell in love with the estate, as all visitors do, but I was dismayed when I asked the docent leading my group about Commodore Levy. She knew nothing of how Levy had saved Monticello or that his mother was buried right there on the grounds. I was shocked and made up my mind to find a way to make sure the story became common knowledge at Monticello and part of Jeffersonian history.

Later that year, I was sitting with Rodney Rockefeller's wife, Sascha, at a dinner. I knew that Rodney, Nelson's oldest son, was on the board of the Monticello Foundation, and I mentioned that I had recently been to Monticello for the first time and was surprised by how little the docent knew about the Levys, including the presence of Rachel's gravesite on the grounds. Sascha said that I should go and speak to Rodney about what I had discovered, so I later called him up. We had a lunch shortly thereafter at a restaurant off Rockefeller Center, where I again mentioned Monticello and the Levys. He was surprised and put me in touch with Dan Jordan, the foundation's director.

It turned out that Jordan had long wanted to focus public attention on the Levy story. Right after his appointment, in 1984, he was accosted by a group of people, including Saul Viener, president of the American Jewish Historical Society, who said, "What are you going to do about the Levy issue?" In response to the pushback, Jordan organized an impressive commemorative ceremony in 1985, held at the grave of Levy's mother. Three people who took part in that ceremony were my former brother-in-law Edgar M. Bronfman (then

A Genesis of Religious Freedom
The Story of the Jews of Newport, RI and Touro Synagogue
INCLUDING WASHINGTON'S LETTER OF 1790

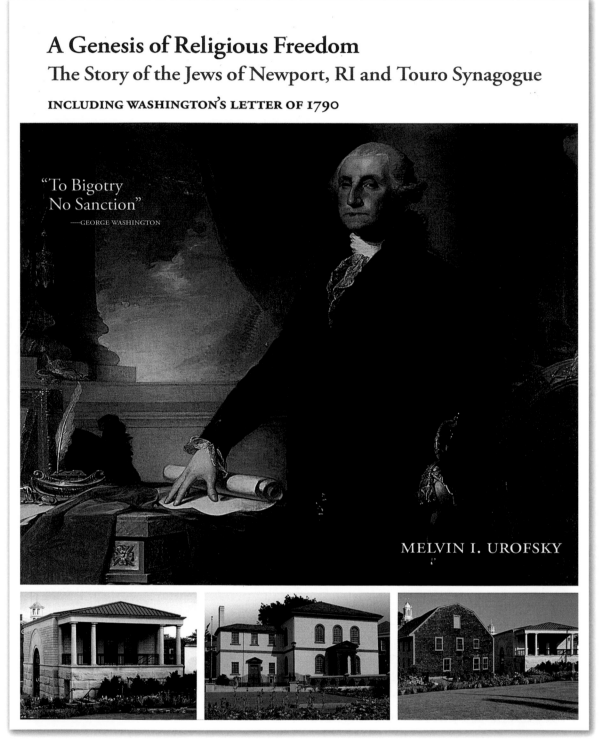

"To Bigotry No Sanction"
—GEORGE WASHINGTON

MELVIN I. UROFSKY

A Genesis of Religious Freedom—the story of Jews who arrived from the Caribbean in the 1600s. By 1763 they were successful enough to be able to build a synagogue, which still stands today. Much of their story comes from the memoirs and diaries of an amazing congregational minister, Ezra Stiles, who learned Latin and Greek and became president of Yale University. The experience of the Jews was remarkable, as evidenced by the fact that they were permitted to build their synagogue in the most prominent part of town, overlooking the harbor and the ocean. One of the first things ships coming into this "new port" saw was the beautiful Touro Synagogue.

president of the World Jewish Congress); Rabbi Malcolm Stern, the genealogist who produced the breakthrough book *Americans of Jewish Descent: 600 Genealogies, 1654–1988*; and Saul Viener. At the seventy-fifth anniversary of the foundation in 1998, there was an event at the Morgan Library in New York. The historian David McCullough gave an impassioned talk. There were some very distant relatives of the Levys there as well, and a whole group, including Saul Viener, pushing the Levy issue.

As is often true of Jewish history, the absence of the Levys' story was not an accident. The Levys were intentionally removed from the Jefferson and Monticello story. Before World War I, a congressman's wife had begun a campaign arguing that Monticello was too important to be in the hands of a single individual (i.e., the hands of a Jew). J. M. Levy didn't want to sell it, but he ran into financial problems and had no choice. Twenty-five percent of those who started the foundation that bought Monticello were Jewish, but because of the whole campaign, they thought it was not a wise idea to promote the Levy story.

Flash forward seventy years—it's an entirely different world, and I am pushing for the story of the Levys to come out, as are others. I had no idea of the campaign to bring the Levys' story to light. I just knew that too many people had no idea of this important piece of history. I suggested that there should be a book about Levy and that I'd be willing to pay for it. We came up with the idea of asking Melvin Urofsky to write it. Jordan knew Mel from the years they had served together in the history department at Virginia Commonwealth University.

As a result of the book's publication, a Jewish philanthropist gave a large donation to the Monticello Foundation, which helped enormously with its fundraising. Thanks to the serendipity of timing and the dedicated work of a number of individuals, along with the coincidental publication of a second book on Levy by the University of Virginia Press, the Levys' role in American history was restored to its proper place. In addition, Dan promised to brief the Monticello docents on the Levys' role in rescuing one of America's most significant homes.

A Genesis of Religious Freedom:
The Story of the Jews of Newport, RI and Touro Synagogue
By Dr. Melvin I. Urofsky; David Kleiman, contributing editor (New York: George Washington Institute for Religious Freedom [GWIRF], with support from the David Berg Foundation, the J.M. Kaplan Fund and Ambassador John L. Loeb Jr., 2013).

After the publication of his book on Uriah Levy and Monticello, I met Mel Urofsky, who became a strong advisor to me on my founding of the George Washington

Dr. Patricia Berman, author and art professor at Wellesley College, has provided major input about my Danish art collection ever since I was invited to speak about the collection at the Smithsonian Institution back in the mid-1990s. Over the years since then, she has curated many of my exhibits and given stimulating lectures about Danish art at the American Scandinavian Foundation.

Institute for Religious Freedom. In fact, he drafted a series of notes briefing me on the historical background of Roger Williams's life in Newport, the granting of the charter from Charles II, and the story of Rhode Island's Jews from the early 1600s to the early 1700s, when they could finally afford to build a synagogue. This synagogue, now known as Touro Synagogue, is the oldest existing synagogue building still standing in the United States.

The notes reached book length, and we decided to publish them. In addition to Mel's entertaining and readable text, we had acquired many stunning images of portraits, maps, documents and photographs that would make a beautiful book. The book is built around a prize-winning design by Gill Fishman Associates and editorial input from the late David Kleiman.

The Ambassador John L. Loeb Jr. Danish Art Collection
Written primarily by Danish art historians Dr. Elisabeth Fabritius and Suzanne
Ludvigsen, with contributions from Mette Thelle, Peter Nisbet and Torben Thim,
and an introduction by Suzanne Ludvigsen (New York: MTM, 2005).

This catalogue was organized by a talented young woman named Benedicte Hallowell, who had been Peter Nisbet's assistant for the Harvard exhibit of my Danish art. Much impressed at the time, I later sought her help with other Danish art issues. Half Danish, Benedicte is the U.S. representative for Bruun-Rasmussen, the Copenhagen auction house from which I have bought almost all of my Danish art. However, the real credit for putting this book together goes to my editorial assistant, Kathy Plotkin.

In Another Light:
Danish Painting in the Nineteenth Century
By Patricia G. Berman (New York, London and Copenhagen:
Vendome Press, distributed by Harry N. Abrams, 2007).

I have had some wonderful collaborations in my lifetime, both in business and in my passionate pursuits, including my Danish art collection. One of my best cooperative ventures had its genesis many years ago, in 1982, when I first met Dr. Patricia Berman while she was working on the *Scandinavia Today* art exhibition with Kirk Varnedoe in 1982.

Ever since I discovered Danish art in the 1980s, I have longed for it to enjoy the worldwide recognition it so deserves and has not yet received. With that goal in mind, I have lent some of my paintings for exhibitions all over the world, sponsored seminars and lectures about Danish art, and given talks about it whenever I'm invited to do

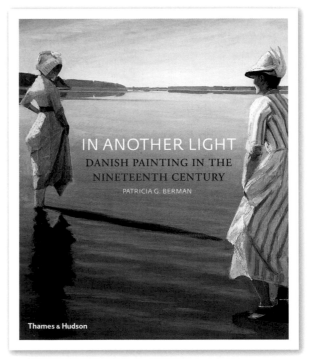

so. One day, I brought an idea to both Alex Gregory and Mark Magowan, co-owner of Vendome Press, a renowned publisher of art books. I proposed that Vendome publish a book by Pat Berman about nineteenth-century Danish art. It didn't take a lot of persuasion, but it did take some time to get it all arranged, especially for Pat to fit writing a book into her busy academic life at Wellesley College, where she chaired the Art Department.

The end result is a large, handsome book published simultaneously in New York, London and Copenhagen, of which I am very proud. In England, it was hailed as among the ten best art books of the year. The *Sunday Times* wrote it "can be wholeheartedly recommended . . . engagingly written, attractively illustrated . . . any art lover would be delighted to be given this book."

Sometime in 2006, I had the germ of an idea for a book about 19th century Danish art. That germ grew into *In Another Light: Danish Painting in the Nineteenth Century*. With my backing, the Vendome Press and I persuaded Dr. Patricia Berman to write the book, which got off to a wonderful start with two book-launching parties in November 2007.

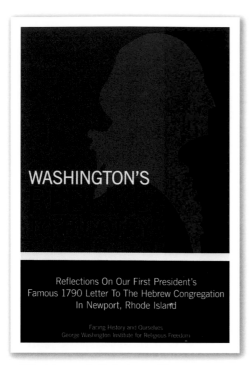

WASHINGTON'S

Reflections On Our First President's
Famous 1790 Letter To The Hebrew Congregation
In Newport, Rhode Island

Facing History and Ourselves
George Washington Institute for Religious Freedom

Washington's Rebuke to Bigotry provides extremely insightful essays about George Washington's short but moving letter to the small Hebrew Congregation in Newport, Rhode Island, in 1790. He happened to be there to congratulate Rhode Island on signing the Constitution, the last colony to do so.

RA Magazine called it "timely and important . . . both scholarly and illuminating." The book was so popular it went back for multiple reprints. Spreading knowledge and appreciation of Danish art has become something of a second career (or third)—and I don't intend to ever retire from it.

Liberty of Conscience and the Growth of Religious Diversity in Early America, 1636–1786

By Carla Gardina Pestana (Providence, RI: John Carter Brown Library, 1986).

Pestana's book, which was co-financed by the John L. Loeb Jr. Foundation, focuses on America's path toward liberty of conscience and was published to honor the 350th anniversary of the founding of Rhode Island. The John Carter Brown Library's director, Norman Fiering, notes in the book that "one of the library's goals has been the publication of a work that would provide historical perspective on an issue that continues to be a source of friction in American society, namely church and state relations." Only twelve hundred copies of the book were originally printed, with three hundred given to schools, colleges and libraries in Rhode Island. (One rare book vendor recently advertised a copy for nearly $1,000.)

Washington's Rebuke to Bigotry: Reflections on Our First President's Famous 1790 Letter to the Hebrew Congregation in Newport, Rhode Island

Edited by Adam Strom, Dan Eshet, and Michael Feldberg
(Brookline, MA: Facing History and Ourselves, 2015).

Washington's Rebuke to Bigotry is a landmark book and one close to my heart. It examines and celebrates George Washington's famous letter to the Newport congregation—"a foundational document of religious tolerance"[152]—through essays from thirty different interdisciplinary writers, including Justice Ruth Bader Ginsburg and the Pulitzer Prize-winning historian Gordon S. Wood. Diane L. Moore of the Harvard Divinity School said that the book "represents some of the most eloquent voices on one of our most confounding challenges." If I am remembered for anything after I'm gone, I hope it's for publicizing and celebrating Washington's important letter and its impact on religious freedom in the nation. The remarkable story of the Loeb Visitors Center at Touro Synagogue and the George Washington Institute for Religious Freedom, which has become one of the most prominent aspects of my life's work, are detailed in the next chapter.

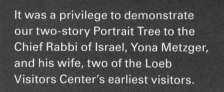

It was a privilege to demonstrate our two-story Portrait Tree to the Chief Rabbi of Israel, Yona Metzger, and his wife, two of the Loeb Visitors Center's earliest visitors.

≡

CHAPTER TWENTY-FOUR

Loeb Visitors Center at Touro Synagogue, Since 2009

In 1915, when my great-grandfather Adolph Lewisohn was asked why he provided the funds to build Manhattan's Lewisohn Stadium on the City College campus, he responded, "Because they asked." That is essentially how I became involved with what ultimately became the Loeb Visitors Center on the campus of the Touro Synagogue National Historic Site in Newport, Rhode Island. Tracing the history that led to the building of the Loeb Visitors Center, it's clear that fate certainly played a role as well. In Yiddish, the term for the sequence of events is *bashert*—something fated or meant to be.

I first became aware of Touro Synagogue and the Colonial Jewish Cemetery in the 1950s while I was a student at Harvard College. I had been invited by a girl I'd been dating to spend a weekend at her parents' home in historic Newport. A history buff, I took a walk by myself around the city and was astounded to find a beautiful synagogue in the center of Newport, a city famous as a summer retreat for wealthy WASPs. (I myself was a guest of WASPs that weekend.) I asked around, but no one seemed to know anything about Touro Synagogue, this center of Jewish life in what I thought of as a WASP oasis.

I've had a great interest in genealogy and Jewish history from early on, so I did more digging and learned that Judah Touro (1775–1854), a distant Loeb relative, was buried in the Colonial Jewish Cemetery in Newport. Judah Touro is considered the first major philanthropist in the United States. Both Judah and his brother, Abraham, contributed generously to Jewish and non-Jewish causes, including Christian churches, the Bunker

Hill Monument and Massachusetts General Hospital. Their father, Isaac Touro, had been the first leader—what we'd now call the rabbi—of the Newport synagogue, then known as the Hebrew Congregation or Yeshuat Israel Congregation. It was under his leadership that the synagogue was built in 1763. It was designed by Peter Harrison, one of America's first great architects. Isaac Touro's two sons became successful businessmen, and when they died, they left a good sum of money to the city of Newport in trust. The income from this endowment helps to support the synagogue building's maintenance and the rabbi's salary. Because of their generosity toward the city, there is now a Touro Park and a Touro Street. In describing the building after receiving the Touro sons' endowment, the city fathers referred to it as "Touro's Synagogue," a name that endures today, with the synagogue being known as "the Touro Synagogue" without the possessive "s." (In New Orleans, where Judah Touro made his great fortune, there is a synagogue where the original name is actually Touro Synagogue.)

Further digging revealed that a good number of my early American Jewish relatives lived and died in Newport and are buried in the Colonial Jewish Cemetery, a few hundred yards up Touro Street from the synagogue building. In fact, the cemetery predates the synagogue. (See the chart in Appendix H, which provides insight into that remarkable old Jewish Cemetery and my connections to it.)

The Revolutionary War caused the majority of my ancestors, their families and their friends to leave Newport. Among the few members still living there in 1790 was the congregation's lay leader, my cousin Moses Seixas. When the recently elected president George Washington came up from New York to visit Newport in 1790, Seixas welcomed him on behalf of the town's dwindling Hebrew Congregation, which no longer had a rabbi.

Seixas's address, which noted that Jews had a history of being deprived of equal citizenship and legal rights, elicited a magnificent response from President Washington. His response, four days later, would go on to become part of American history. His letter is now known as "George Washington's Letter to the Hebrew Congregation in Newport, Rhode Island of 1790," or more simply as the "George Washington Letter."* The historian and author Ron Chernow, in Washington's Pulitzer Prize–winning biography *Washington: A Life*, writes that the letter "ranks as his most beautifully enduring statement on religious toleration."

---

* The letter is reprinted in the Appendix C.

Learning about my ancestral Newport forebears was the start of my emotional connection to Touro Synagogue. I learned that my four-times-great-grandparents, Jacob Phillips and Hannah Isaacks, were married in Newport in 1785. Because they were observant Jews and Hannah had been born and reared in Newport, the wedding almost certainly took place in the Touro Synagogue. The more I searched, the more I discovered roots that ran through Newport and the closer I felt connected to the city.

Several years after my first trip to Newport, I was asked to contribute to "John F. Kennedy Peace Forest," the John F. Kennedy memorial in Israel. The memorial included fifty concrete pylons—one for each U.S. state—listing the names of individual American contributors. New York was already taken so I chose Rhode Island, drawn to the idea of my name representing a state that had been such an integral part of my ancestors' story in America.

In 1974, when I was about to run for Congress, having a campaign event in Newport seemed like a wise idea. I wanted the support of the Jewish community, which operates as a network across state and national boundaries. That occasion, with supporters such as Senator Claiborne Pell and John Kennedy Jr. appearing on my behalf, further cemented my warm feelings toward Newport and, by extension, the Touro Synagogue. On a trip to Israel in the 1980s, I observed with interest and surprise that in the Diaspora Museum in Tel Aviv, Israel, the only evidence of American Jews at the time—the *only* symbol of America at all—was a replica of the Touro Synagogue.

In 1996, things came to a memorable full circle in terms of my own recognition and appreciation of the importance of my Jewish ancestry—both European and American. It was in that year that I traveled to Rimpar, Germany, to reunite with Lehmans from across the world. I met relatives whom I had never known and heard stories about a few who had perished in the Holocaust. That was a significant and emotional journey for me.

It was also the year I lost both of my parents, who had led fascinating lives and contributed so much to their communities. Their passing left a profound void in the continuity of family life. But an experience I was to have in Newport gave me buoyancy and deepened my appreciation of my American Jewish ancestors and especially, along with that, the fortunate happenstance of birth as a citizen of this great American country.

I was accorded a great honor from Touro Synagogue Foundation (TSF), which worships at Touro Synagogue, to be the reader at their annual celebration of the George Washington Letter. In August of each year, on the Sunday closest to the date of Wash-

Left to right: Touro Synagogue, Patriots Park and the Levi-Gale House. I commissioned the design and installation of the garden in Patriots Park, including the Ambassador John Loeb Jr. Gate, which separates the park from the synagogue. To the right of the park and down the steps is the Loeb Visitors Center.

Roger Williams, the founder of Rhode Island, landing among the Narragansett Indians following his expulsion from Boston.

ington's visit, the synagogue invites one public figure to read Seixas's address and another to read Washington's letter. As I noted, the letter had already become part of my consciousness; because of my anti-Semitic experiences at Hotchkiss, it had touched me profoundly. I was almost moved to tears that day reciting Washington's words of promise that the "government of the United States gives to bigotry no sanction, to persecution no assistance." Remembering my own experiences of bigotry as a child, I felt that I was helping to spread the essential message that Washington had iterated in that letter.

Standing up there among residents of a city that claimed my ancestors, a place intricately linked to my Jewish heritage, I felt a purpose slowly shift into place. Washington's letter was not nearly as well known as it should have been; and I was in a unique position to change that. I decided to work to spread knowledge of that letter, along with America's foundational belief in the separation of church and state.

In the process, I became even more focused in my study of the history of anti-Semitism and increasingly aware of the importance of the separation of church and state, especially after I studied the life of Roger Williams, the founder of Rhode Island. I learned the background of his heroic efforts to establish that principle in the colony as early as 1636. It's extraordinary to me that I can find no record from the seventeenth or eighteenth centuries of how influential Roger Williams was in helping to establish the separation of church and state in this country. It was not until the late nineteenth and early twentieth centuries that Williams received his due, partly from a book by Oscar Straus called *Roger Williams: The Pioneer of Religious Liberty.*

In 1986, the John Carter Brown Library in Providence, Rhode Island, asked me to help finance a book by Carla Gardina Pestana called *Liberty of Conscience and the Growth of Religious Diversity in Early America, 1636–1786.* The book taught me more about the significance of the George Washington Letter by also emphasizing its *timing.* Washington wrote the letter, proclaiming religion as an "inherent natural right," a year *before* the Bill of Rights was adopted. Washington and Thomas Jefferson had been campaigning throughout the thirteen original states to get the Constitution ratified. The reason that Washington, Jefferson and an entourage of other federal officials made that historic trip to Newport in 1790 was that, by the narrowest of margins, the Rhode Island legislature had finally ratified the Constitution. The Union of all thirteen states was now complete. Why had I not learned all this at my expensive boarding schools? I began to wonder if American students anywhere were being taught about the letter or the principle of religious freedom it proclaims.

Although not religiously observant, I became a lifetime member of Congregation Jeshuat Israel in Newport, the successor congregation to Yeshuat Israel that originally built the synagogue in 1763. I wanted to show my support for the current group, which was struggling to survive with fewer than one hundred families as members. But I also thought it might help to reaffirm my identity as a Jew. I had been a member of Temple Emanu-El in Manhattan for many years—as had my nonobservant parents—but membership there was more habit than anything. It was another thing I inherited from my parents, and I hadn't put much conscious thought into it. My Jewish identity was something I carried without really ever holding—it was with me, though I didn't recognize its importance. That would all come later.

In 1997, Bernard Wax, a former executive director of the American Jewish Historical Society,

Anne Hutchinson, a follower of Roger Williams, a founder of Newport. Years later, Anne Hutchinson and her ten children were killed by Indians while living in upstate New York. The Hutchinson River Parkway is named after her.

The rear of the Loeb Visitors Center, which includes "the old Barney House," which is the annex to the Loeb Visitors Center.

contacted me on behalf of Congregation Jeshuat Israel. He told me that two pieces of property abutting the Touro Synagogue campus had come up for sale. The small congregation did not have the funds yet, but they had long hoped to buy the properties in order to build a visitors center. Would I consider making the property purchase for them?

Bernie was extremely persuasive, pushing all the right buttons by telling me how a small visitors center could tell the integral story of the role of religious freedom in the early years of our country. It could also tell about how all religions were welcomed into this *new port*, allowing a young town to boom and, by extension, a new country to grow. Visitors could learn how one of the first important Jewish communities in America developed in tolerant Newport, and how it built a synagogue right in the center of the town. At the time, the view from the center of town was panoramic, with an extraordinary view of the water. The first ships that entered Newport immediately saw the synagogue, as opposed to in most European cities, where Jewish houses of worship were mostly hidden out of sight.

The timing of Bernie Wax's proposal was yet more *bashert*, fate. It had been a year since my parents' death and a few months after the Christie's auction of their art collection that netted enough money for each of the five Loeb children to set up foundations of their own. I had already been thinking long and hard about what might be the most meaningful contribution I could make with my new foundation's money. Spent properly, that money could go a long way. The congregation estimated that $500,000 would be enough to buy the two properties and build the center. I was being asked to buy the two properties, but the money to actually build the center was intended to come from other donors from the congregation, including its president, David Bazarsky. Though not in writing, there was a mutual understanding that this would be the case.

In my innocence, I had always thought that what philanthropists like my parents did was sign a check, wield a shovel at the ground-breaking and be invited back for a ceremony to dedicate a new building. To paraphrase Shakespeare wrote, "the more fool I." The purchase of the two properties adjacent to the synagogue had problems from the start. For one thing, there was no one in the congregation able or willing to undertake oversight of the purchase. I stepped in reluctantly, enlisting my real estate attorney Richard Wiener to advise me. The congregation planned to raze one of the properties, a nondescript building called the Gray Typewriter Building, to make room for the center. The other building, the Barney House, was a landmark structure protected by the Newport Historic District Commission. The Barney House could be used as the center's annex and developed to contain an auditorium and a gift shop.

In 2002, I made an outright gift to the congregation of the two buildings and the land under them. It was not until a decade later that I learned something staggering:

Richard Wiener has been not only my attorney for many years, but a close friend as well. He has been my strong right arm for many of my undertakings. Without his assistance and support, the Loeb Visitors Center could never have been built.

Gilbert Stuart's portrait of Sarah Lopez and her son, Joshua. Her husband, Aaron Lopez, was a merchant of great eminence.

Congregation Jeshuat Israel does not own Touro Synagogue, the building in which it worships. The synagogue is legally held in trust for the benefit of the Jews of Newport by Congregation Shearith Israel in New York City, the oldest Jewish congregation in the United States.

Why did a congregation in Manhattan own a building almost two hundred miles away in Newport, Rhode Island? The story goes like this: When Touro Synagogue had been built in 1763, there was no such thing as a nonprofit corporation, so the building was not owned by the congregation. Three Jewish families, members of the congregation, had purchased the land, retained architect Peter Harrison to design the building, and paid workers to erect and furnish it. These were the families of Jacob Rodriguez Rivera, Moses Levy and Isaac Hart.

Twenty years later, the American Revolution left Newport's economy in tatters, and it would take decades to recover. Gradually, over the next fifty years, the Jewish families in Newport left for New York City, with the last group leaving in 1822. Most of them, including the three families mentioned above, joined Congregation Shearith Israel (currently located on the Upper West Side of Manhattan.) These three families transferred their deed to the leaders of Congregation Shearith Israel, who were to hold it on behalf of the Jewish community of Newport—should it ever reemerge—and ownership could then be transferred to a resurrected congregation. Had I known the history and status of the building's ownership in 2002, I might have made other arrangements for the proposed visitors center. After all, what if, by some remote chance, Shearith Israel decided to expel its "tenant"?

With David Bazarsky's guidance, I personally bought both the Barney House and the Gray Typewriter Building. Subsequently, I came to the conclusion with Richard Wiener, as my attorney, that I alone was going to be privately responsible for the building of the visitors center. Overseeing the project would be a time-consuming undertaking, one that would divert attention from family, business and other philanthropic commitments, but neither Richard nor I could orphan the project. Neither of us had ever been directly involved in building a museum (or any building at all).

In 2004 the John L. Loeb Jr. Foundation entered into a formal agreement with Congregation Jeshuat Israel (CJI) and the Touro Synagogue Foundation (TSF) to build the Loeb Visitors Center at the Touro Synagogue National Historic Site. TSF is a nonprofit organization formed in 1947 to maintain the synagogue as a national historic site, the first American religious building so designated. After hiring Newport Collaborative Architects to design the visitors center, we would have to win approval

Henry Wadsworth Longfellow, a poet, for many summers was a resident of Newport. He wrote the poem, "The Jewish Cemetery at Newport."

Emma Lazarus, a poet, also a summer resident of Newport, became a great friend of Longfellow's. The author of the "The New Colossus" also wrote "In the Jewish Synagogue at Newport."

from the Historic District Commission, the Zoning Board of Review and the Newport Planning Board.

Throughout this process, a Jewish family living across the street from the synagogue tried to block us at every turn, protesting our plans at each public hearing. The family eventually filed a lawsuit in the Supreme Court of Rhode Island to try to stop us. Though their suit failed, their resistance held us up for almost a year. We would eventually learn that their problem was that the building's construction had become too loud for their taste and comfort. Everyone else, both Jewish and Christian, was enthusiastic about what we were doing. It was ironic that the only real opponent we encountered in building the center was this one Jewish family. If Father had been alive, he would have said I was slightly crazy to try to build a visitors center on the site of an Orthodox synagogue in a town I knew nothing about. He would not have been wrong.

The area that links the synagogue and the visitors center was an indifferently landscaped area called Patriots Park, which commemorates a Jewish patriot from each of

What we know about Jewish life in Newport in the late 1700s is due to Congregationalist minister Ezra Stiles, who was at the opening and consecration of the synagogue. His extraordinary diary is the basis of how we created the exhibits at the Loeb Visitors Center. He was president of Yale University from 1778–1795.

the thirteen original colonies. We all agreed that the park would need beautification to match the other upgrades, so I offered to pay the first $400,000 toward the landscaping of the park. The congregation and foundation pledged to provide any additional funding that might be required, but my foundation ended up covering the full cost, as well as another $500,000 to restore the synagogue.

In early 2007, we retained H.V. Collins as general contractor, and after a few more delays, we were ready to break ground—after nine years. Avi Decter of History Now was hired as the exhibition designer. His work would be based on an extensive report I'd commissioned, much of it based on an extraordinary diary from a Newport resident, Congregationalist minister, Hebrew scholar and future president of Yale named Ezra Stiles. My good friend Professor Melvin I. Urofsky produced an almost book-length report on the history of religious freedom in Rhode Island and the important role that Jews played in that story. In fact, this report was turned into a book published in 2013 by the George Washington Institute for Religious Freedom (to be discussed in the next chapter) titled *A Genesis of Religious Freedom: The Story of the Jews of Newport, RI and Touro Synagogue.* Due to the book's popularity, a second edition has been printed.

Decter brought in RBH Media for the cutting-edge digital elements, Charles Mack for design of the graphic elements, and Final Push Construction for fabrication and installation of the exhibits. Though brilliant, Decter was difficult to work with and eventually left the project. Steven Sitrin, the new executive director of the Touro Synagogue Foundation, stepped into Decter's role and worked smoothly and cooperatively toward completion of the project.

In 2008, I learned that the congregation had failed to pay the real estate taxes on the two properties and that the City of Newport was going to put the sites up for tax sale. I donated funds to help the congregation meet its tax obligations, but I was now clearly aware of the congregation's precarious financial status. In November, TSF began laying off staff members and falling behind on its bills. In order to stem the tide, my foundation agreed that it would provide TSF with money to pay its construction bills. In February 2009, just months before we were scheduled to open the visitors center, some harsh exchanges occurred between TSF and Richard and me after TSF claimed we had agreed to pay the salary of the visitors center's manager.

Realizing that my patience had worn thin, TSF chairman Keith Stokes came to visit me in Purchase. I reassured Stokes of my commitment to the project, and he had a deeper understanding of how much I had done for the congregation and his organization. He then wrote a letter to all members of the Board of Trustees of CJI and the Board of Directors of TSF, reminding them of my generosity of both money and time: after all, I was stepping into the breach by agreeing to run the visitors center on a daily basis, although that had never been my intention. He called on the congregation and the foundation to openly express their support and gratitude.

Everything was completed in time for the grand opening of the Ambassador John L. Loeb Jr. Visitors Center at the Touro Synagogue National Historic Site on August 2, 2009. It was one of the proudest, happiest days of my life. Despite the headaches and backslides, all of the work had gone toward something significant: a place where visitors can come to learn about, examine and celebrate the legacy of religious freedom in America. As far as I know, the Loeb Visitors Center ("the LVC") is the first freestanding visitors center erected for an active house of worship. Its presence has helped to

The Ambassador Loeb Gate connects the Loeb Visitors Center and Patriots Park with the synagogue.

587

Inside Touro Synagogue.

stimulate the steady upgrading of Newport's Old Quarter, the colonial district whose scale and antiquity stand in fascinating contrast to Newport's Gilded Age oceanfront mansions. Rhode Island's leading architecture critic, David Brussat, wrote a major review of the Loeb Visitors Center:

> *It is obviously a classical building, yet it is unlike any other. No work of classicism could possibly depart from canon with greater dignity, hence no building could possibly fit onto a historic street with greater distinction. Embedded in this otherwise ancillary building is the spirit of civic congeniality embodied by George Washington's famous words. In tapping its spirit, the Loeb Visitors Center succeeds admirably. The brave new building seems at home in old Newport.*

While the Loeb Visitors Center is modest in size, it contains a wealth of historical information presented in innovative ways. When visitors enter the building, they are greeted by a welcome video featuring yours truly as host. In it, I explain that Newport is the home of American religious freedom and that Touro Synagogue is a powerful

High above the Loeb Visitors Center entrance we see the brightly lit Touro Synagogue.

symbol of that value. From the time Roger Williams established the Rhode Island colony, persons of every faith were welcome to live there, conduct business and worship—or not worship—as they chose. In 1663, King Charles II of England granted the colony a charter proclaiming, "No person within the said Colony, at any time hereafter, shall be any wise molested, punished, disquieted, or called in question, for any differences in opinion, in matters of religion, who does not actually disturb the peace of our said Colony; but that all and every person and persons may, from time to time, and at all times hereafter, freely and fully have and enjoy his own and their judgments and consciences, in matters of religious concernments."

To the left of the welcome video, a panel tells this foundational story in greater detail. To the right of the video is a longer panel titled "Philanthropy, Faith and History." It tells the story of early Jewish life in Newport through the biographies of some of its most important Jewish residents. Among those featured are Moses Seixas, Abraham and Judah Touro, Aaron Lopez, Moses Michael Hays and Emma Lazarus.

The most unusual element in the visitors center stands in the far left corner of the first floor: the Early American Jewish Portrait Gallery (the "Portrait Tree"), an array of ten vid-

On the left is the Portrait Tree and on the right in the front is the large table that holds the interactive vignettes also seen below. In the distance are portraits of Roger Williams and Reverend John Clarke, who founded Rhode Island.

Also on the center's second floor are audio-video vignettes depicting the daily lives of Newport's 18th-century residents.

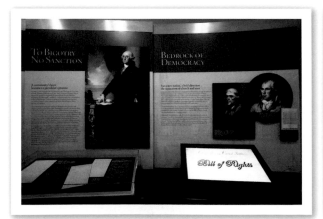

In President Washington's 1790 Letter to the Hebrew Congregation in Newport, he promises that our country will not countenance religious bigotry. These words can never be read too often.

Newport's leading Jewish citizens and the part they played in the 18th and 19th centuries are featured on the first floor of the Loeb Visitors Center.

The first-floor windows of the Loeb Visitors Center face Spring Street, with its entrance just a few steps off the street.

The second-floor portico on the rear side of Loeb Visitors Center offers a view of Patriots Park.

eo screens rising two stories high. In random rotation, the screens display more than two hundred digital images from the Loeb Jewish Portrait Database. Four touch screens allow visitors to access the database for more information about the portraits' subjects through brief biographies. Many of those included on the Portrait Tree lived in Newport or were connected to its Hebrew Congregation.

Adjacent to the Portrait Tree is a curving grand stairway to the second floor. (The center also has an elevator for those who cannot climb stairs.) At the top of the stairway, visitors are greeted by a portrait of Reverend Ezra Stiles, the Congregationalist minister who lived in Newport and was a close friend of *hazzan* Isaac Touro, Aaron Lopez and other members of the Hebrew Congregation. Much of what we know about Jewish life in early Newport comes from Stiles's diary, which has detailed accounts of the consecration of the synagogue in 1763 and of his social and intellectual exchanges with the Reverend Isaac Touro and Lopez, among others. Like many other educated Christians in colonial America, Stiles learned Hebrew so he could read the Bible in its original language. Stiles would later leave Newport to become president of what is now Yale University.

The gaze in Stiles's portrait draws our attention to the center of the room and an exhibit titled *Colonial Newport's Multicultural Townscape*. As one of America's busiest seaports, early Newport attracted a wide variety of individuals and groups who lived in mutual harmony. In addition to the Baptist followers of Reverend John Clarke, who settled Newport after leaving Providence, the community included Quakers, Catholics, Jews, African Americans (both free and slave) and a variety of mariners and traders from around the world.

Through a series of filmed vignettes performed by actors (based on accounts in Stiles's diary), visitors can learn about relationships between Newport's early Christian and Jewish neighbors, early commerce and trade, the status of African Americans, freedom of the press and other aspects of Newport life.

Beyond the townscape is a video exhibit on the architecture of Touro Synagogue and the biography of its architect, Peter Harrison. This screen and accompanying wall text explain how the understated, dignified architecture of Touro Synagogue reflects the lack of ostentation of Newport's houses of worship in deference to the spirit of equality among all faiths in the city.

The final exhibit is, to me, the most important. At its center is a large reproduction of Thomas Sully's portrait of Washington and facsimiles of the original letters between Moses Seixas and George Washington in August 1790. An interactive touch screen allows visitors to learn the history of the two letters and explore their importance.

This center exhibit is flanked to the left by a panel titled "The Lively Experiment," which tells the story of John Clarke's and Roger Williams's decade-long effort to receive the 1663 Rhode Island charter from King Charles II that stipulated religious toleration for everyone. To the right of the letters is "Bedrock of Democracy," a panel that explains how the political leaders Thomas Jefferson and James Madison incorporated religious freedom—the bedrock of democracy—into the nation's fundamental laws.

The late David M. Kleiman played major roles in preparing the Loeb Visitors Center for its opening. David was its curator at the time of his death in January 2014.

The Loeb Visitors Center has attracted an average of close to 15,000 visitors annually since the first full year of its opening, most of them in the summer months. But the spring and fall also bring public school groups from Rhode Island and religious school groups from New York. During the winter months, the center is open on Sunday afternoons in conjunction with tours of the synagogue.

Before we opened the center, the late David Kleiman recruited and trained a first-rate group of docents to answer questions and help visitors prepare for their guided tour of the Touro Synagogue. His wife, Kate, was also an invaluable, behind-the-scenes part of getting the center running. Through 2016, we have already hosted more than 110,000 visitors from dozens of countries around the world, many of them students. Both Kleimans deserve enormous credit and gratitude for their instrumental contributions to the Loeb Visitors Center.

Chuck Flippo and Mary Jo Valdes were part of the first team of docents we hired when the Loeb Visitors Center opened in 2009. Today, Chuck serves as site manager and Mary Jo as assistant manager. Both of them are highly knowledgeable about Newport history and particularly about the Jews of Newport. They also do an admirable job of training the docent team and making visitors feel welcome at the center.

Thanks to the cooperation of the leaders of Congregation Jeshuat Israel and the Touro Synagogue Foundation, the Loeb Visitors Center's docents have been able to develop a close relationship with the guides who lead tours of Touro Synagogue itself. The docents and guides often fill in for one another at their respective institutions. Meryle Cawley, the executive director of the Touro Synagogue Foundation, coordinates schedules and training with Chuck and Mary Jo. And Asa Montgomery has, from the first, kept the center, the synagogue and Patriots Park in tip-top shape. I am grateful to all of the above, and to the officers and boards of the synagogue and the foundation, who are working diligently to preserve and perpetuate this great historic site.

I feel that the building is an apt metaphor for what I have tried to do in my philanthropic and educational work: harmonize with the community, respect the history and honor the values that I have to come to believe in so strongly. While the building cost me far more in effort, time and money than I had anticipated, it was all worth it. Perhaps, like the pangs of motherhood, the joy of the result has overtaken the memory of what it took to deliver. I have said on more than one occasion that if I have a legacy, I hope it will be the Ambassador John L. Loeb Jr. Visitors Center—my tribute to my Newport ancestors to reducing anti-Semitism, and my most enduring contribution to teaching and celebrating the history of religious freedom for all in America.

For more information about the Loeb Visitors Center, go to www.loebvisitors.org.
For more information about Touro Synagogue, go to www.tourosynagogue.org.
For more information about the Ambassador John L. Loeb Jr. Database of Early American Jewish Portraits, go to www.loebjewishportraits.com.

Our first president, author of the historic Letter to the Hebrew Congregation in Newport, Rhode Island, of 1790. Gilbert Stuart, *George Washington*, the "Munro-Lenox Portrait," c. 1800. (Collection of Judith and Michael Steinhardt, courtesy of Richard L. Feigen)

≡

CHAPTER TWENTY-FIVE

THE LOEB INSTITUTE FOR RELIGIOUS FREEDOM AT THE GEORGE WASHINGTON UNIVERSITY, Since 2016
and the George Washington Institute for Religious Freedom, 2009–2016

One capstone of my philanthropic and educational endeavors was the opening of the Loeb Visitors Center at Touro Synagogue in 2009. Given my age, it might well have been enough. As it turned out, the event marked a new beginning rather than an endpoint. Little did I suspect how much more I would undertake and accomplish in the years since then.

I consider the second capstone of such endeavors to be the 2016 creation of the **Loeb Institute for Religious Freedom ("the Loeb Institute")** at the George Washington University (GWU), located in our nation's capital.

How did this come about?

In October 2014, Dr. Ben Vinson III, dean of the Columbian College of Arts & Sciences at the George Washington University (GWU), reached out to the **George Wash-**

Dr. Ben Vinson III, dean of the Columbian College of Arts & Sciences, with me, is making history founding the Loeb Institute at the George Washington University.

ington Institute for Religious Freedom (GWIRF), which I had founded in 2009, after the opening of the Loeb Visitors Center.

After fruitful meetings and discussions, the establishment of the Loeb Institute was announced on January 27, 2016. The academic resources that we have sponsored and the relationships that we have forged with our civic education partners through GWIRF now have a bright future and a permanent home at GWU. I endowed the Loeb Institute, which operates within the university's Columbian College of Arts & Sciences.

After the creation of the Loeb Institute was announced, I held a luncheon on March 2, 2016, at the Knickerbocker Club to inform board members, advisory board members and major donors of this exciting affiliation. There, Dean Vinson cited the importance of the Loeb Institute in light of the current epidemic of religious violence abroad and heated debates over the place of religion in U.S. politics:

> *Religious freedom is the concern of all humanity. . . . We live in a world that is enduring rapid and furious change; a world where critical questions of peace, security and tolerance are being challenged. As such, it is incumbent upon universities to both train the minds that will help engineer future change, but also help understand what's happening to us as we move in bold new directions. And we must do it, not alone, but as a community of knowledge, where institutional and university partners around the globe reach out and help each other, as we guide our students to mature into the lives they were meant to have, as they mature into the global citizens that we desperately need to push human society forward. . . . Today, I celebrate, I toast, and I salute the ways in which the **Ambassador John L. Loeb Jr. Institute for Religious Freedom** will catapult us forward in our most noble, institutional mission.*

Even in its brief existence to date, the Loeb Institute is having a transformational impact on the GWU campus and around the globe. Endowed by me, the new Loeb

Dr. Michael Feldberg, the executive director of the George Washington Institute for Religious Freedom, is pictured here with me. Michael, a former director of the American Jewish Historical Society, has been a major figure from the very beginning of GWIRF's formation.

Institute is attracting participation from numerous departments in the George Washington University's Columbian College of Arts & Sciences, as well as the university's Schools of Law and Medicine.

Dean Vinson foresees the Loeb Institute's synergy with the rigorous scholarship occurring in GWU's departments of religion, peace studies, history, political science and other disciplines. Vinson envisions that the leadership of the institute will develop educational programs on and off campus, work with faculty across disciplines, leverage relationships with embassies, develop new programmatic initiatives, plan conferences and events and engage the broader community to further the Loeb Institute's agenda.

The institute will manage academic, curricular and co-curricular programs, publications, collaborations and activities with organizations, scholars, students, educators and the public engaged in the mission of the institute. It will also continue the ambassa-

This seal depicting George Washington was designed to use as the GWIRF logo on its newsletters and other publications.

Pictured at the GWIRF symposium, left to right, are Judith W. Ringer, executive director of the John L. Loeb Jr. Foundation, me, and my good friends Peter and Jessica Tcherepnine. Peter is one of my financial advisors and was an advisory board member of GWIRF. Judith is the overseer of fund allocations from my personal foundation and, as such, helped to develop and manage GWIRF.

dorial outreach program established by the George Washington Institute for Religious Freedom (GWIRF), which was the forerunner of the Loeb Institute at GWU.

To my delight, Professor Sam Goldman was named the inaugural director of the Loeb Institute. He is a scholar of the theological sources of political ideas and an assistant professor of political science at GWU's Columbian College of Arts & Sciences. Professor Goldman will work with Dean Vinson to advance the Loeb Institute's work in fostering dialogue on religious understanding and the separation of church and state.

I am honored and gratified that our successful work at GWIRF will be continued at such a remarkable, appropriate institution, named for the author of the 1790 Letter to the Hebrew Congregation in Newport. Disseminating the message of that famous document, along with the imperative of our moving beyond tolerance to respect and acceptance of others regardless of faith and background, has become my most fervent passion. I hope that my efforts toward that objective will become my most enduring legacy.

You may wonder what is the linking thread between the Loeb Visitors Center (chapter 24) and the establishment of the Loeb Institute. My friend Lee Pollock, executive director of the Churchill Centre, had been working with a number of people at GWU to create the National Churchill Library and Center, which recently opened on the campus.

In the course of developing the National Churchill Library and Center, Lee approached me as chair of the Winston Churchill Foundation of the United States. (The Winston Churchill Foundation sends fifteen brilliant science graduate students to spend a year at Churchill College, Cambridge, England. See chapter 19 for the story of the foundation.) From me, Lee learned about the famous Washington Letter and GWIRF.

Lee spoke to the leadership at the George Washington University about the Washington Letter and GWIRF. He was thinking about the possibility of the university's exploring a connection with GWIRF, considering the parallel of names and ideals between GWU and GWIRF.

GEORGE WASHINGTON INSTITUTE FOR RELIGIOUS FREEDOM

Four months after the opening of the Loeb Visitors Center, having already received ten thousand visitors, we decided to go further. Why not reach out to high school students and teachers across the United States? I started actively searching for ways to take Washington's message of religious freedom to a national audience. The outgrowth of that impulse became the George Washington Institute for Religious Freedom (GWIRF), an organization I founded in 2009 to disseminate the message of Washington's letter worldwide. The Loeb Visitors Center told this important story, but only in one place. GWIRF would extend the story beyond the confines of the Loeb Visitors Center and the synagogue. GWIRF could launch education, interaction and discussion about Washington's profound idea, which was part of the foundational groundwork of this great nation.

My specific objective was to make the letter the starting point of a fruitful and meaningful dialogue between teachers and students on religious freedom and respect for religious diversity. I cannot help but believe that my young Hotchkiss classmates were suffering from ignorance and social conditioning rather than any inborn callousness. The more that religious freedom is taught to young people as a central tenet, perhaps the central tenet, of the American way of life, the more we can uproot the bigotry and bullying that I—and so many others—faced as a youth.

Washington's letter was specifically addressed to the Jews of Newport, but it was surely intended as—and remains now—a universal message. It resonates across Jewish, Christian, Muslim, Hindu, Buddhist and atheist lines. Long before it was an established nation, America was first and foremost an idea. A fundamental element of that idea was that the government would neither champion nor degrade any particular religion. Americans would be forever free to believe and practice what most weren't allowed to in their previous homelands. For so many generations, religious liberty has been the motivating force that brought them here. We need only picture the courage to do such a thing—and the difficulty of such a trip—to imagine how much that idea must have meant, and continues to mean, to those persecuted for their religion.

We live in a world that is increasingly wracked by wars, terror attacks and social breakdown justified by religious doctrines. GWIRF's agenda is to promote a powerful text, Washington's letter, from which individuals and groups of different faiths and backgrounds can begin, instead, to seek common ground and understanding. It is my hope that societies will go beyond mere tolerance and reach a true sense of reciprocal respect and community.

It is incumbent on all of us to feed this idea to others. The world will not change until we all embrace it. GWIRF is playing its part in pushing this idea along. My wife, Sharon, is as involved in the project as I am. She suggested we call the nonprofit the George Washington Institute for Religious Freedom. It achieved public charity status quickly. The historian Michael Feldberg, whom I had known for many years when he ran the American Jewish Historical Society, became our education consultant and then, in 2011, our executive director.

Through my interaction with high school teachers, administrators and education experts, I learned that many public school teachers consider classroom discussion of anything even tangential to religion a "third rail," too dangerous to touch. The fear is that such talks could be interpreted as advocacy for a particular religion, violating the principle of separation between church and state. Some teachers also fear that they might be misinterpreted as disparaging a particular religion, or religion in general, potentially offending students or parents. GWIRF faced a challenge: helping teachers and students feel free to discuss religious freedom while still respecting the "inherent natural right" of all to believe in a particular religion, or, equally important, to believe in none.

With its historical basis and our most unassailable Founding Father as its author,

Juniors & Seniors

You'll be receiving a letter from George Washington on his 278th birthday - Feb. 22.

"The history behind Washington's letter gives us insight into two fundamental tenets of American democracy: the separation of church and state, and the right of individuals to believe in and practice their religion. The George Washington Institute for Religious Freedom is particularly thrilled to work with the Rhode Island Department of Education and the Governor's Office in Rhode Island, the birthplace of religious liberty in America."

Ambassador John L. Loeb, Jr.
The George Washington Institute for Religious Freedom
Educating Students across America on the Importance of Religious Liberty
www.gwirf.org

the letter provides a nonthreatening way to begin classroom discussions of religious freedom in every school. After all, if our first president could promise religious freedom to a small group of Jews in Rhode Island, then it must be safe, over two hundred years later, to discuss the principle in our classrooms. At a minimum, thousands of students across the nation could be exposed to the letter, interact with it, perhaps even let it simmer in their impressionable and burgeoning minds. It seemed a valuable exercise that could impress the key tenet of religious freedom onto future generations.

True, I already had some experience bringing Washington's letter into a high school. In 1992 I began funding an annual prize at Hotchkiss for the best essay on tolerance written by a rising senior, stipulating that the essays be based on the study of the George Washington Letter. First called the "Loeb Essay on Tolerance and Mutual Respect," but recently renamed the "George Washington Letter Award," the essays that students have written are remarkable, touching and profoundly meaningful to me. Today's Hotchkiss students seem to grasp how Washington's thoughts on religious freedom can be extended to issues of difference in other realms of life.

Encouraged by the impact that the essay contest was having at Hotchkiss, I decided to extend the competition to two public high schools: Rogers High School in Newport, Rhode Island, and Harrison High School, close to my home in Purchase.

I had come to understand that writing essays about the contemporary relevance of the George Washington Letter was a very meaningful way for students to explore and reflect on religious freedom—perhaps one of the most significant tenets of America's Founding Fathers. This principle's impact has reverberated down the generations for more than two centuries.

I then asked Judith W. Ringer, the executive director of the John L. Loeb Jr. Foundation, to help further my outreach to the First Freedom Center in Richmond, Virginia, a national organization with the mission to "advance the fundamental human rights of freedom of religion and freedom of conscience." The First Freedom Center recognizes in its very name that the very first right enumerated in the Bill of Rights is religious liberty. First Freedom's most ambitious activity is its annual national high school essay contest, which reaches seventy-five thousand high school teachers and hundreds of thousands of their students in grades nine through twelve across three hundred school districts. Students are invited to compete for awards by submitting an essay or video production on an aspect of religious freedom.

We had convinced Isabelle Kinnard Richman, then vice president for education at First Freedom, to let my foundation fund the contest in the 2008–2009 academic year and shift its focus directly to Washington's letter, a natural topic. More than 2,500 student essays made it to the national judging round in that first year's contest. A prestigious panel from the worlds of academia, law, clergy and government was chosen to select the winners. I also invited the top winner and his teacher to be my guests at the August 2009 annual reading of Washington's letter at Touro Synagogue in Newport.

GWIRF again funded First Freedom Center's annual national high school essay contest with this same topic in 2012–2013. (First Freedom Center recently merged with The Valentine, a venerable art and history museum that opened in 1898 in Richmond, Virginia.)

I decided that the next big step should be taken in Rhode Island, where Roger Williams established the first political entity that fully separated the church from the state—and, of course, home of the historic exchange between Seixas and Washington. (King Charles II of England memorably approved Williams's charter by calling it a "lively experiment.") In 2010, with the help of GWIRF's dedicated staff, spearheaded by the late, talented David Kleiman, a public relations firm and my dear friend Kitty Cushing (a GWIRF board member and a Rhode Island resident), we distributed thirty thousand copies of the Seixas and Washington letters to all junior and senior high school students across Rhode Island. We included an introductory essay and information for teachers and administrators on how to conduct a classroom reading or school assembly on the topic of religious freedom. To maximize the program's impact, we arranged for Rhode Island elected officials to appear at ten of the state's high schools. I had the pleasure of spending the morning with Rhode Island's then attorney general, Patrick Lynch, at St. Raphael Academy, and the afternoon with Providence's mayor, David Cicilline (now Congressman Cicilline), at the Met School. We were gratified by how engaged the students were and received similar reports of success at other schools that day.

The Rhode Island experiment whetted my appetite, and my dream is that one day these events will be held all over the United States. We decided that the best way to obtain national—and even international—recognition was to partner with other nonprofit civic education organizations to create teacher training programs, enabling them to use Washington's letter in their classrooms.

In 2010 we approached the Bill of Rights Institute in Arlington, Virginia. The Bill of Rights Institute had been founded by the philanthropist Charles Koch to help teachers more effectively engage their students in exploration of the Constitution. The outgrowth of our partnership was a workbook, *Religious Liberty: The American Experiment*, and a series of workshops for middle school and high school teachers. To date, the Bill of

Rights Institute has trained more than two thousand teachers across the country to conduct and stimulate classroom discussion through a reading of Washington's letter.

My Boston cousin, Dr. Paul Buttenwieser, then suggested that I meet Margot Stern Strom, founder and executive director of Facing History and Ourselves in Brookline, Massachusetts. Margot started teaching about the Holocaust as a teacher in Memphis, Tennessee, and then in the Brookline public schools. No longer focused solely on the Holocaust, Margot's organization asks students both to explore their own identity and to become "upstanders," rather than bystanders, whenever they encounter someone becoming a victim of bigotry or prejudice for their identity, be it religious, gender, racial or ethnic. Over almost four decades, she built Facing History into an international educational powerhouse across North America and beyond, with overseas offices in England, Northern Ireland, Israel, Rwanda, South Africa and China. Facing History engages three million students annually through its network of more than thirty thousand educators around the world.

Margot and I hit it off famously. She was raised in Memphis, Tennessee, so we share a love of the finer aspects of southern culture. Margot had been looking for a vehicle to extend Facing History's engagement with religious pluralism and diversity. Washington's letter seemed ideal for laying the groundwork to explore religious democracy in the contemporary world.

In 2010, GWIRF provided Facing History with a three-year grant to establish Give Bigotry No Sanction, an initiative to create educational materials and training pro-

At the Facing History symposium, John Sexton, then president of New York University, made a dramatic apology for the demise of the Loeb Student Center at NYU. Behind me is my cousin Michael Kempner; smiling from the audience is my daughter, Alexandra.

grams for teachers about religious freedom and the separation of church and state. In 2011, Facing History launched the initiative with a grand symposium at New York University, hosted by NYU president John Sexton, which attracted an audience of more than six hundred, including over a hundred high school teachers.

Facing History has since brought Washington's letter to the attention of tens of thousands of students, teachers and community leaders by offering a series of public symposia, teacher training workshops and webcasts in the United States, Europe and South Africa. The organization has developed a free e-book for teachers titled *Religious Freedom and Democracy: Teaching George Washington's Letter to the Hebrew Congregation in Newport, Rhode Island.*

In time for Washington's Birthday in 2015 (when he would have been a spry 283), Facing History published a collection of essays, *Washington's Rebuke to Bigotry: Reflections on George Washington's Famous 1790 Letter to the Hebrew Congregation in Newport, Rhode Island.* It contains more than thirty essays by a distinguished international group of scholars, jurists, educators and writers, including Justice Ruth Bader Ginsburg; the Pulitzer Prize–winning historian Gordon S. Wood; Princeton philosopher Kwame Anthony Appiah; and Martha Minow, then dean of the Harvard Law School. Writers from the United States, France, England, India and Israel, with specialties such as neurobiology, sociology, education and journalism, make the book an enormously important contribution.

In 2012 and 2013, GWIRF was fortunate to be given several opportunities to disseminate Washington's message of religious inclusion in new ways. The first was through a grant from the Peter Jay Sharp Foundation. My good friend and Hotchkiss schoolmate Dan Lufkin serves as one of three trustees of this foundation, established from the estate of a classmate from our Hotchkiss years. Peter Jay Sharp's legacy supports worthy projects that advance environmental conservation, education, medical research and the arts. The foundation had repeatedly funded GWIRF early on with generous grants that propelled GWIRF's ability to develop educational resources on our own and to collaborate with our civic education partners. Dan then persuaded his board colleagues to fund GWIRF's Future Teachers Initiative.

The idea sprung from a simple idea: What if we could reach high school faculty in their pre-service years, while they were still training to become teachers? It would be more efficient to make the letter part of their teaching repertoire from the start than to ask them to absorb it later on. GWIRF has worked to disseminate the curriculum to educators at colleges and universities across the United States.

This article referred to the Texas State Board of Education considering students learn that the U.S. is a Christian nation.

LET
IN RESPONSE TO

Founding Father?

It's easy to scoff at a state that would consider letting a dentist determine its history curriculum. But what do we expect, given the poor quality of history instruction in our schools? In science and math classes, we give students a series of puzzles to solve. But we present history as a set of "facts" rather than as a set of debates and arguments about them.

Nobody in Russell Shorto's article suggests that students should be required to examine the religious ideas of the founding fathers and come to their own conclusions about them. And until that happens, Americans will remain ignorant about the real nature of historical thinking. Adults disagree — often vehemently — about the American past. Why do we pretend otherwise when the kids are in the room?

JONATHAN ZIMMERMAN *Professor of Education and History*
New York University, New York

For the answer to the question "How Christian were the founding fathers?" one can turn either to Christian activists or to the founders themselves. James Madison, the primary author of the Constitution, spoke of "almost 15 centuries" during which Christianity had been on trial: "What have been its fruits? More or less in all places, pride and indolence in the clergy, ignorance and servility in the laity, in both, superstition, bigotry and persecution." The Constitution has no mention of Christianity, and the presidential

oath of office mandated by the Constitution has no mention of God. Thomas Jefferson compared the story of the virgin birth of Jesus to a Roman fable and prohibited the teaching of religion to undergraduates at the University of Virginia. Finally, in 1797, the Senate unanimously ratified the Treaty of Tripoli, which contained the words "As the government of the United States of America ... is not, in any sense, founded on the Christian religion." The founders were there at the time. The Christian activists were not.

KENNETH J. KAHN *Long Beach, N.Y.*

The educational system's position seems to be that man needs only a sanitized form of enlightenment. This approach fails to recognize that man is a spiritual being. No wonder we have bred an increasing number of "sociopaths." Children need moral guidance — denying that continues to show the unfettered ignorance of those responsible for teaching and higher learning.

MICHAEL RODRIQUEZ *Novato, Calif.*

It would come as a surprise to George Washington to learn that the Texas State Board of Education is considering requiring students to learn that the United States is a Christian nation founded to advance Christian ideals.

In his letter to the Hebrew Congregation in Newport, R.I., of 1790, Washington described our nation as one in which "all possess alike liberty of conscience and immunities of citizenship." Washington went further: "It is now no more that toleration is spoken of, as if it was by the indulgence of one class of people, that another enjoyed the exercise of their inherent natural rights," he said. "For happily the government of the United States, which gives to bigotry no sanction, to persecution no assistance, requires only that they who live under its protection, should demean themselves as good citizens ... while every one shall sit under his own vine and figtree, and there shall be none to make him afraid."

The Texas State Board of Education should note that Washington invoked this phrase from the Bible (Micah 4:4) to extend religious diversity, not to favor any particular religion.

AMBASSADOR JOHN L. LOEB JR.
Former U.S. Ambassador to Denmark
Chairman of the George Washington Institute for Religious Freedom
New York

Shorto's cover story to be flippant and offensive. I doubt the editors and art directors involved would have the physical — not just moral, but physical — courage to try that approach when dealing with icons of a certain religion popular in the Mideast. Christians — and Catholics in particular — seem to be a favorite topic for

the timorous New
...ists-in-residence
...itically acceptable
...e who enjoy
...up of which they

North Port, Fla.

E-MAIL letters to *magazine@nytimes.com*. All letters should include the writer's name, address and daytime telephone number. We are unable to acknowledge or return unpublished letters. Letters may be edited for length and clarity. The address of The New York Times Magazine is 620 Eighth Avenue, New York, N.Y. 10018.

MONTAGE BY CARIN GOLDBERG

MOST POPULAR LETTERS TOPIC: "FOUNDING FATHER?" BY RUSSELL SHORTO

8

My response to the article "How Christian Were the Founders?" appeared in a later edition of *The New York Times Magazine*.

I also arranged for an initiative in which Harvard University's undergraduates, graduate students and faculty may receive financial support for research into the impact of religious freedom on the cultural, social, political and economic development of societies. The somewhat long title of the effort is the "Ambassador John L. Loeb Jr. Initiative on Religious Freedom and Its Implications."

Here's the story behind the initiative. In 1967, Loeb, Rhoades contributed $100,000 to the Harvard business school, originally intended to fund an annual award to the top student in finance. Nearly forty years later, in 2004, the dean of the Harvard Business School, Kim Clark, told me that the original endowment of $100,000 had grown to $2.5 million, and the business school was paying out unusually high amounts to awardees. He also revealed that the Business School now grants its student awards on the basis of need, not merit, which defeated the original purpose of the Loeb, Rhoades prize.

Dean Clark asked whether there was some other purpose to which I would like to see a portion of the available funds directed. I proposed, and Dean Clark accepted, that the majority of the endowment would go to a project I'd been contemplating—a campus-wide initiative to explore the differences between countries that provide for freedom of religion and those that restrict or deny it. I was interested in the way religious freedom influenced the larger picture and wanted, in particular, to study the impact of a country's degree of religious freedom on its financial and social development. Admittedly, I was hoping to find evidence of what I intuitively believe—nations that accommodate religious diversity are more likely to be socially stable and economically productive.

The initiative has evolved through a process of trial and error. In 2005, the logical Harvard academic unit in which to house the Loeb Initiative on Religious Freedom and Its Implications appeared to be the Harvard Divinity School. We negotiated an agreement with the Divinity School to provide fellowships for students whose research touched on the intersection of religious freedom and cultural, social, political and economic outcomes. In any event, only a handful of the school's students were taking that approach to the study of religion. Fair enough—most students at a school of divinity tend to study theology, not sociology.

After reviewing the topics that the Divinity School awardees had submitted in the first three years of Loeb Initiative support, I attempted to reconnect with Dean Clark, but he had left to become president of Brigham Young University-Idaho. I had wanted to express my disappointment in the fit between my intentions and the well-meaning, thoughtful, but off-topic papers submitted by the Divinity School's students. Ralph

This picture includes the symposium panel and my wife, Sharon, who continues to be a key player, as she was in the early days of GWIRF, even providing its name. Left to right are Shaykh Dr. Yasir Qadhi, Sharon, me, Reverend J. Brent Walker, Rabbi Angela W. Buchdahl and Professor Henry Louis Gates Jr.

James, who was the executive director of external relations at the Harvard Business School, was very kind and helpful.

Hannah Peters, the associate dean for development and external relations at the Divinity School, contacted me to suggest that the optimum recipient and manager of the funds would be the Center for American Political Studies (CAPS) under its director and professor of government, Daniel Carpenter. Given the many debates over the meaning of religious freedom and church-state separation in American politics, it seemed that CAPS, within the Faculty of Arts and Sciences, might be a better fit to grant the excess funds from the Loeb, Rhoades fellowships.

From 2013 to 2015, CAPS used the funds to provide fellowships to undergraduate and graduate students studying the relationship between religious freedom and a nation's cultural, social, economic and/or political progress. In addition to research grants and fellowships, the new initiative used the funds to conduct seminars and public programs for a general audience interested in the issue and impact of religious freedom.

To bring maximum visibility for the Loeb Initiative within the Harvard community,

CAPS and GWIRF held a major public kickoff event. I asked Dan Carpenter to meet with Harvard's well-known Professor Henry Louis "Skip" Gates Jr. to ask if Gates could make time in his busy schedule to moderate a symposium. Because of my great interest in genealogy, I had become aware of the charismatic Gates through the PBS series *Finding Your Roots.* To my delight, the famous scholar said yes.

The Symposium on Religious Freedom and Its Implications took place on May 1, 2014. Three additional distinguished panel participants took part, one from each of the Abrahamic religions: Shaykh Dr. Yasir Qadhi, dean of academic affairs at the AlMaghrib Institute in Memphis; Reverend J. Brent Walker, executive director of the Baptist Joint Committee for Religious Liberty in Washington, D.C.; and Rabbi Angela Buchdahl, senior rabbi at Central Synagogue in New York City—the world's only Korean American female rabbi. The room was packed, the conversation stimulating, and the Loeb Initiative was finally relaunched as successfully as I'd originally hoped.

As with so much else in life, events took an unexpected turn. Dan Carpenter was subsequently appointed director of research at the prestigious Radcliffe Institute at Harvard; CAPS was absorbed into the Government Department; and I was retasked to find another appropriate unit at Harvard to use the surplus Loeb, Rhoades endowment funds to promote the virtues of religious freedom and the message of Washington's Letter to the Hebrew Congregation.

As of the writing of this memoir in 2017, I believe I have found the appropriate vehicle at Harvard to achieve my goals. Working closely with David N. Hempton, dean of the Divinity School since 2012, and the aforementioned Hannah Peters, I have redirected the funds to Harvard's Committee on the Study of Religion, a joint program of the Divinity School and the Faculty of Arts and Sciences. Under the guidance of the committee's members, who represent a variety of disciplines, the funds are to be used first and foremost to support student research on the influence of religious freedom or its absence on the success of nations. The annual balance may be used to support public programs, publications and conferences at Harvard that address this issue.

As a vice chair of the Council of American Ambassadors, I long had the dream of placing Washington's letter in the hands of every sitting U.S. ambassador abroad, with the hope that they would find an appropriate opportunity to read the letter at a public event at their embassy. We developed a packet of materials that included Seixas's and Washington's letters and an essay explaining the background, along with a cover letter encouraging the ambassadors to consider using them. In 2014 we mailed the packet to every American ambassador. Their responses were gratifying. To date, we have received

Here I am at the GWIRF symposium with two dear friends. Pictured, left to right, are Richard Allen, actor John Lithgow and me.

more than twenty expressions of appreciation and commitments to read the letter at a public event. Some of the ambassadors' responses can be read on the GWIRF website.

Another exciting opportunity to spread Washington's message of religious freedom came through the Aspen Institute's Inclusive America Project. The Inclusive America Project's aims are to "increase respect for diverse religious identities in the public sphere, foster positive interfaith interactions and form productive partnerships among people of different faiths in the service of the common good." In 2011 the Aspen Institute convened a conference cochaired by former secretary of state Madeleine Albright and David Gergen, a former advisor to four presidents and now a professor at Harvard's Kennedy School of Government. The meeting generated commitments from some of the nation's leading youth and educational organizations to work collaboratively with the Aspen Institute.

The Aspen Institute's Justice and Society Program's director, Meryl Justin Chertoff, under whose aegis the Inclusive America Project took place, had heard about our work from Greg Epstein, the Humanist Chaplain at Harvard University. She invited GWIRF to join with a select group of civic educational organizations to develop leadership and staff training programs for the national Boys & Girls Clubs and the YMCA of the United States, which together serve nine million children and their family members. Many of their local clubs are working to integrate and accommodate the needs of the members of minority groups—especially religious minorities—coming to their facilities. Typically, their staff members are college students or other young persons who work part time at these clubs; often, their exposure to non-Christian peoples and religions is minimal. How should a young, white Christian lifeguard respond to a Somali Muslim girl who says her parents have told her that she can't swim in the same pool with boys, even Somali Muslim boys? How can local YMCAs and Boys & Girls Clubs make sure that immigrant children and their families don't feel unwelcome at an event because the only food served violates their religious restrictions?

Working with other advisory groups, we helped the Inclusive America Project develop training materials and programs and identify pilot sites where they could test the effectiveness of the training. This project is another example of our trying to bring real-world, on-the-ground training to those who deal with religious plurality on a daily basis.

My good friend Victoria Hughes, who was executive director of the Bill of Rights Institute when GWIRF partnered with that organization, approached me when she accepted a senior position with the Ashbrook Center, an independent center at Ashland University in Ohio. The center restores and strengthens the capacities of the American people for constitutional self-government and is focused on training teachers in American history.

GWIRF provided support to help the Ashbrook Center develop content ideas for website materials on "Religion in American History and Politics," an interactive online exhibit that the center created. In May 2015, educators and web developers assembled by the Ashbrook Center met in Newport at the Loeb Visitors Center and visited Touro Synagogue in order to develop recommendations for the new website.

GWIRF's success was hallmarked not only by the work that GWIRF undertook itself, but also by the results of its collaborations with the marvelous organizations mentioned above. These civic educational institutions provided the well-honed expertise that enabled them to further embed the historic Washington letter in the public conscience.

GWIRF'S first and foremost obligation will always be to assure that the Loeb Visitors Center in Newport continues to operate at its current high level. To that end, I have committed to provide funds for the operation and maintenance of the Loeb Visitors Center during my lifetime and established an endowment that will become operational upon my death to guarantee the center in perpetuity.

GWIRF will also maintain its website, *www.GWIRF.org*, which is a significant educational tool, to inform teachers, students and the public about George Washington's historic letter. Visitors to the website may freely download the Educators Classroom Kit, which contains information about key concepts, learning modules, letter-reading programs and essay contests. In order to reach a wide, diverse audience, the Washington and Seixas letters are translated into nine languages.

This journey that I have taken over the last two decades through the creation of the Loeb Visitors Center, The George Washington Institute For Religious Freedom (GWIRF), and, finally, the Loeb Institute has been the most thoughtful and gratifying trip that I have ever undertaken to help "make the world a better place." I hope that these endeavors will, indeed, help to accomplish that goal.

For more information about the Loeb Institute for Religious Freedom at the George Washington University, go to https://loeb.columbian.gwu.edu. *For more information about the George Washington Institute for Religious Freedom, go to* www.GWIRF.org.

My wife, Sharon, and I at the Emma Lazarus Statue of Liberty Award in 2015.

CHAPTER TWENTY-SIX

Receiving the Emma Lazarus Statue of Liberty Award, 2015

On November 11, 2015, the American Jewish Historical Society honored me with the prestigious Emma Lazarus Statue of Liberty Award. I was particularly pleased because my late brother-in-law, Edgar Bronfman, had received this award, as had former secretary of state Henry Kissinger, former secretary of state George Shultz and Elie Wiesel, among other well-known recipients.

My family and I have been supporters of the American Jewish Historical Society for nearly four decades. The society was the first, and for many years the only, organization to give importance to the fact that Jews settled in America in New York City. In those days, New York City was called New Amsterdam and was controlled by the Dutch. In 1664, the King of England gave New Amsterdam to his brother, the Duke of York, with the mission of taking control of the city—hence the name became New York.

The Emma Lazarus Award meant a great deal to me for several reasons. First, it was named after one of my family's most fascinating ancestral cousins, Emma Lazarus. She was a well-known minor poet. Sadly, she had a very short life, but she wrote many wonderful poems, including the famous one engraved on the base of the Statue of Liberty, titled "The New Colossus." The most well-known, powerful words are:

"Give me your tired, your poor,

Your huddled masses yearning to breathe free,

The wretched refuse of your teeming shore.

Send these, the homeless, tempest-tost to me,

I lift my lamp beside the golden door!"

THE EMMA LAZARUS AWARD EVENING

My son, Nicholas, and the Honorable Richard V. Allen, who introduced me that night.

Jamie and Peter Gregory

Laura Hunt, Somers Farkas (cochair of the gala) and Susan Fales-Hill

With Sharon, Vera Wang, and Nick.

John Rosenwald, Sharon, Zoe Harbart (Sharon's niece), Alexandra Munroe and Chuck Scarborough

Rabbi Schneier opened the evening with a beautiful prayer.

Susan Fales-Hill, Sharon and Hunt Slonem

Jackie Weld Drake and
Amy Fine Collins

Dayssi de Kanavos and
Prince Dimitri of Yugoslavia

Geoffrey Bradfield and
Adrienne Vittadini

Emma's father was a neighbor of Henry Wadsworth Longfellow in Newport, Rhode Island. This was before the Civil War and at a time when, for all intents and purposes, there was no anti-Semitism in Newport. Previously, Longfellow, who was one of Harvard's great professors, had been surprised to see a cemetery in Newport with Spanish/Sephardic names. He wrote a magnificent poem titled "The Jewish Cemetery at Newport." It was a beautiful but sad poem that implied that the Jews were disappearing from history. Ironically, that was just the period when Jewish thinkers and philosophers, mainly in Eastern Europe, were starting to write and talk about the re-creation of the State of Israel after two thousand years.

The second, and equally important, reason the award was meaningful to me was that Nicholas, my son, not only attended the event but also gave a beautiful speech that touched me deeply. He spoke just before the evening's guest speaker, my good friend Richard V. Allen (Reagan's first national security advisor).

Nick began by saying, "So, other than a toast, I have been given several letters from some very important people that I am to read tonight, so I picked the best one":

Dear John:

Barbara and I send our personal congratulations and respects, as you are appropriately honored by the American Jewish Historical Society with the prestigious Emma Lazarus Statue of Liberty Award. When we think of you, we think of honor, decency and integrity. We think about tireless advocacy for religious freedom. We think about service to others and we think about friendship. Your life's mission has been to "do your part." The list is long—the impact immeasurable. This wonderful recognition of your many contributions is another milestone in your accomplished career and we salute you and thank you. Congratulations again on this well-deserved honor.

Warmest personal regards,

George Bush

Nick then went on to say:

> As an American, I cannot think of anyone more suited to be honored in the name of Emma Lazarus than my father—and not because he is my father—and not because of the accomplishments he is noted for here tonight—but because of what he stands for and what drove him to carry her torch.
>
> You know, America has come a long way in our history and we have offered a worldwide welcome to live in a country that separates church and state, empowers the exiled and huddled masses. Maybe today, more than ever, we need education to remind us of why our families came to America and what this country stands for.
>
> Now, although my father's experience motivated him to build foundations to educate generations to come, what truly is inspirational here is that he did not back down in fear, he did not hide with humiliation, he did not segregate himself into being a Jewish American or a German American. But instead, he knocked down that boy from school. He stood up and proudly proclaimed, "I am an American and just American first before all others."
>
> Dad, this is what I am most proud of. Because if we could get back to this, as a country, and the people who started coming here could still feel like that, we could begin again to build that wall which is now America's "conquering limbs astride from land to land." You have set this as an example and this is what makes you a true leader, and I say this because I am your son and I learned this from you.

And thirdly, the award itself recognizes American Jews who have contributed significantly to our country. I feel so honored to be included among those distinguished individuals.

As a last note, the American Jewish Historical Society gave me the Emma Lazarus Statue of Liberty Award, but my extraordinary and beautiful wife, Sharon, really put the entire event together. She took the lead, with the help of her office and mine, to bring over two hundred friends and family to the Roosevelt Hotel in New York City to celebrate this unique evening for me. Under her guidance, the Roosevelt Hotel never looked more glorious, and she, her family and other dear friends were significant contributors to making the event a great success. (Even Sharon's eleven-year-old niece, Zoe Harbart, made it a special evening. She helped open the evening by impeccably reading the entire Emma Lazarus poem "The New Colossus" without missing a beat.)

EPILOGUE

—————

Reflections

Back before the age of computers, cell phones and instant communication, my mother and father kept in touch the old-fashioned way: they wrote the most wonderful letters to each other. They were passionate and funny, barbed and wry and honest. I recently came across a letter that my mother wrote to my father while she was still a student at Vassar in the 1920s. She wrote,

> *Do you ever play a game where you pretend to yourself just where and what you'd like to be at this precise moment if you were given your choice? I'd like to be down south somewhere where it's warm and starry. I'd be wearing a beautiful white evening dress and we'd be sipping champagne . . .*

I admit to having played this game, though I might never consider it to be one. It seems to me more like a test, or an inventory of sorts. It's a way of stepping back and checking in. And I always come up with the same answer: *right here, right now.*

As I write this I am sitting on the porch of my home looking out over the beautiful landscape. I can see ten miles out to Long Island Sound and farther, a clear shot to the horizon; in front of me unfolds a gorgeous rock garden and a beautiful pool. I can hear my beloved wife, Sharon, and adorable dog, Thor, nearby. Only one place in the world looks and sounds and feels like this to me: This is Ridgeleigh, a place I loved as a child, and a home that has only grown closer to me as it and I age. I can honestly say I have never been happier or more relaxed in my life. For one thing, I no longer feel the need to compete any-more. That is a game for the young, and I have wisely decided to leave it to them.

I'm eighty-seven now and people seem to give me a pass on everything: I am no longer compared to others, free from the race, the push and pull, the who's up and who's down of the modern world. The world is kinder to the aged, as though we have earned our place. I've even found that—quite extraordinary in New York City—women stop to open the door for me, though I don't need it. I'm always shocked when it happens, because I still feel young. I don't feel inside myself the same way I must appear to the world. As the Scottish poet Robert Burns wrote,

> *And would some Power give us the gift*
> *To see ourselves as others see us!*
> *It would from many a blunder free us,*
> *And foolish notion:*
> *What airs in dress and gait would leave us,*
> *And even devotion.*[153]

Everybody has a story to tell. It's what makes us human. We have ancestors, parents, a family narrative, a context for how we got here, roots that stretch back and tie us to a larger history. "The mariner's bound to tell of his story / to tell his tale wherever he goes," Coleridge wrote in *The Rime of the Ancient Mariner*. Perhaps I feel a duty as well. Gone is Lewisohn Stadium, gone is The Loeb Student Center at NYU, gone is the Herbert Lehman Children's Zoo (as the children's zoo in New York's Central Park was once called), gone are Lehman Brothers, Loeb, Rhoades, and Seagram's. I've done my best in these pages to capture a world that doesn't exist anymore, a period of life that has faded like so many pic-tures, and the story of one man who both made and was made by his time.

I was both the beneficiary and the victim of two very accomplished and, some would argue, overbearing parents, whose oil portraits have been looking over me in the Ridge-leigh dining room where I've been writing these memoirs.

A man's desk often tells the story of who he was, who he is and who he imagines himself to be. On my desk I have pictures of my family, of course, as well as awards and honors I've received over the years. I also have two personal items that hold particular significance to me. One is a poem written by Kalidasa, a fifth-century poet, considered to be Sanskrit's greatest writer:

Listen to the Exhortation of the Dawn!
Look to this Day!
For it is Life, the very Life of Life.
In its brief course lie all the
Verities and Realities of your Existence.
The Bliss of Growth,
The Glory of Action,
The Splendor of Beauty;
For Yesterday is but a Dream,
And Tomorrow is only a Vision;
But Today well lived makes
Every Yesterday a Dream of Happiness,
And every Tomorrow a Vision of Hope.
Look well therefore to this Day!
Such is the Salutation of the Dawn![154]

The poem is something of a call to arms, something of a pocket of inspiration. It is a gift from Albert Edelman, a wonderful man I had known for years. Albert was a partner at Jacob Javits's law firm, which had an office in the same building as Loeb, Rhoades. I became friendly with his son Tom, a Hotchkiss graduate and then board member; the younger Edelman looked up to me before going on to build an enormous fortune in oil. After my father died, Tom was looking for an office and I rented out Father's old office to him.

Around this time, I was engaged in a lawsuit against a Pakistani man who had tried to bilk me out of a fortune he and a partner had made—with my help—in gas wells in Pakistan. He had brought me on to grease the wheels with their government and ours in order to secure the contract. When they won it, he tried to freeze me out. During one of countless exhausting meetings about this with my lawyers, who did little but compound my difficulties, I grew angry. Tom must've heard me raising my voice through the walls. When he came by to ask if I was all right, I told him about the terrible time I was having with the suit. He suggested I get in touch with his father.

I took Albert to lunch, and he took over the suit soon after. He was a maestro—he came in, settled the case, got me my money back and charged me virtually nothing. Albert and I became great friends; we had lunch every couple of weeks—talking about life, liberty, pursuits of happiness. He was thirteen years older than I was, but that didn't matter to either of us: we had a growing relationship that transcended age, time and all other matters.

One day in 2003, Albert had a stroke while working at the office and died before the ambulance came. It was a terrible blow and I lost a great friend. Albert had given me the Kalidasa poem as a gift. I framed it and placed it above my desk, where it remains to this day. A few years later I wrote to Tom asking for a picture of his dad. After he sent it, I wrote him back a thank-you message, which included the poem. "It starts my day on a positive note," I wrote. I've always firmly believed that entering into a new venture, new challenge—or even just a new day—with a positive and bold mindset can accomplish great things.

The other notable item on my desk is a picture of Bill Mulligan, another lawyer. I never would've made it without Bill, who represented me in the lawsuit against my second wife, Meta, who was bipolar and seeking custody of Nicholas. Meta had hired a big gun to represent her in the divorce, and I needed someone who could win such a fight. Bill was an Irish Catholic graduate of Harvard Law School, and a Son of the American Revolution. We bonded over a common background and a common cause, perhaps the most important fight of my life. He also spent an afternoon with my parents, who were not on my side in the custody hearing; by the end of Bill's visit, he had completely turned them around. Because he saved Nicholas for me, I owe a debt of gratitude to him that can never be repaid. Who knows where Nicholas or I would be without him?

Two of my closest friends who were not lawyers were English. I met Bobby Buxton in 1956. He died recently and I miss him terribly. I mention him, and have a picture of him, in "The Moses-Loeb Story" in Part One.

Bobby introduced me to Toby Clarke (Sir Tobias Clarke, Bt), and Toby and I also became very great friends. He is related to the American Roosevelts, and he is a cousin of my next-door neighbor, Helen Roosevelt.

Both Bobby and Toby were at Sharon's wonderful party at Blenheim for my seventy-fifth birthday. Then, as a kind of birthday present for me, they put me up for Whites. Whites is the oldest and grandest English club. It still has enormous cachet and prestige, and it usually takes years to become a member. At a certain age, they make exceptions. In any case, within a year after Blenheim I became a member of Whites.

I used to go to England every year, but I am not doing so now. However, Bobby and Toby's present touched me deeply.

When I was young I had three ambitions in life. First, I wanted to be married with a family, and make enough money that my standard of living wouldn't go down. Since I had grown up under a high standard, this was a considerable goal. My dream was to live somewhat along the same standard of living as my parents.

The second ambition I had was to be the head of Loeb, Rhoades, the company that bore my name and my father's and grandfather's name. In some sense I thought of it as my legacy, in the manner of kings or, perhaps, the Rothschilds. Alas, it was not to be, but with age I have been given perspective. I remember talking to my daughter, Alexandra, when she was thirteen, around the time I was distraught about being unceremoniously pushed out of the firm. It never occurred to me that a father, much less a *Jewish* father, would push his son out of what essentially was a family business.

Alexandra was a very bright young girl, sensitive and caring, so I talked to her about this. She said something that stuck with me. "Dad, you know," she said, "everybody should do their own thing. Maybe it's *better* that you do something else." She was quite insightful at a young age—and she was absolutely right.

The third goal was to be important in politics. I knew early on that I'd never be president; I was Jewish, and when I was already thirty years old the idea of a Catholic running for president was still considered nearly taboo. But I had dreams of perhaps being a senator like my uncle Herbert Lehman, or maybe a diplomat.

To some extent, I have met all these goals: I am living on my grandfather's property, I got to be a U.S. ambassador and, for a brief time, I was the senior partner of Loeb, Rhoades. I have even recaptured the company name, and made myself chairman—a nod to the roots that tie me back to C.M. and my father. I think of holding onto the company as a keepsake more than anything, a sentimental strand that links me with the past.

Life is funny: it's not the goals themselves but the paths and detours I've taken toward achieving them that have given me a fruitful life. We learn so many things along the way, most of which come from not sticking to the plan. I've always been a cautious man, one who takes into account the whole before acting, but even I know that serendipity, fate and *bashert* have played as much of a role in my life as any blueprint has.

I once thought of calling my memoir *The Education of John L. Loeb Jr.* after the historian Henry Adams's account of his life. It seems to me that one's life is indeed an education—or should aspire to be one. I've certainly had many opportunities to learn and grow in many fields, the most recent being genealogy. My interest in genealogy has come about through a curiosity about the world that gave birth to my own, as well as the mystery of what my people contributed to that world. The historian Edward Gibbon, famous for his *The History of the Decline and the Fall of the Roman Empire*, wrote about how going back in history gives us the sense of extending our lives. This sounds right to me: history as immortality.

As I wrote in a letter to a friend about my late-life passion,

> *Genealogy is also giving me a sense of where I fit in this very complex world. It gives me a kind of serenity and peace which I don't get from religion as I am not sure what I believe in. My father called himself a humanist—deeds, not words. And I think maybe that is what I am.*

At one point early in life, I thought about becoming a teacher, an ambition that my father once held as well. I like to think that maybe I have come full circle. Thanks to GWIRF, the Visitors Center at Touro Synagogue, the Loeb Institute for Religious Freedom at the George Washington University, my Danish art collection, my publishing ventures, genealogy and fatherhood, I am now the history teacher that I once wanted to be. In the end, I can see that I opted to share rather than to compete, to extend rather than to hoard. I believe things multiply that way, for one. And this is certainly the only way our contributions will carry on without us.

FORTUNE

April 1963

Wherever You Look,
There's Loeb, Rhoades

by T. A. Wise

Reprinted solely for the information of
the staff of Carl M. Loeb, Rhoades & Co.

© 1963 TIME INC.

Wherever You Look, There's Loeb, Rhoades

By T. A. Wise

Brokerage income	$27 million
Institutional income	$3 million
Foreign income	$3 million
Underwriting volume	$100 million
Investment-management funds	$500 million
Venture capital	$350 million

1962, estimated

The good name of Carl M. Loeb, Rhoades & Co., an extremely well-to-do and rising young investment-banking firm, was involved in three of the biggest front-page business stories of the last year—about three more than the traditional banking house would be likely to relish. With heavy holdings in Twentieth Century-Fox, Loeb, Rhoades demanded an accounting from a management that was unable to cope with Elizabeth Taylor's costly antics in the production of *Cleopatra*, and provoked an executive upheaval that rocked Hollywood. The firm moved in on the venerable Curtis Publishing Co., backed a new executive team that is fighting to reverse the tide of losses in a fiercely competitive industry, and thus risked its prestige not only in banking terms but before the advertising industry and the readers of the *Saturday Evening Post* and the *Ladies' Home Journal*. And it lent early backing to Edward M. Gilbert, the wonder boy who frantically tried to merge Celotex Corp. into his E. L. Bruce Co., only to be caught short in last May's market crash and fly off in panic to Brazil—returning five months later to face charges of fraud.

Each of these involvements has deepened Wall Street's curiosity about the house that appears to be "in the middle of everything," and each sheds some light on Loeb, Rhoades' far-reaching operations. Taken together, they are public evidence of the quality of unorthodox adventure and daring that has resulted in hundreds of less publicized and more successful undertakings. And this quality, in turn, is but a part of the combination of shrewdness, diversity, and immense wealth that has enabled Loeb, Rhoades to establish itself firmly among New York's venerable financial houses in the relatively short span of thirty-two years.

Loeb, Rhoades' twenty-three partners grace the boards of over sixty major and medium-sized corporations. It has memberships on seventeen securities and commodities exchanges. It has over 1,000 employees, a large number for an organization with but fourteen offices of its own. Its $12,500,000 in stated capital ranks it among the top firms in the Street.

Its brokerage income runs to $27 million annually and is solidly based on a network of twenty-two correspondent firms, stretching into 140 cities in the U.S. and Canada. In this relationship Loeb, Rhoades performs the traditional services of a clearinghouse in executing and clearing orders and delivering shares (for a fee that runs as high as 40 per cent). But there is far more to it than that. Many of its correspondent firms are the leading houses in their respective areas (e.g., Piper, Jaffray & Hopwood in Minnesota, Boettcher & Co., in Denver, Sutro & Co. in California, H. C. Wainwright & Co. in Boston). So Loeb, Rhoades, the broker, has a ready-made network serving Loeb, Rhoades, the underwriter (with an annual volume of $100 million), in the distribution of new issues—while the correspondent firms also feed promising underwriting deals into New York. In addition, the firm nets $3 million from private placement with, and management of, institutional accounts, and manages investment funds totaling $500 million.

This handsomely paired underwriting-brokerage operation is harnessed to Loeb, Rhoades' capital resources, conservatively estimated at $350 million, a figure that the partners admit could be revised sharply upward if the need or opportunity arose. The capital pool represents the fruits not only of profitable past investments, but also of strategic marriages and mergers (see page 9), which have brought into the firm's orbit the Bache, Lehman, and Bronfman fortunes. And it is the vast supply of risk capital that has enabled Loeb, Rhoades to undertake a wide variety of enterprises ranging from the creation of one of the world's largest shipping fleets and financing young scientists in the development of new electronic equipment to quietly becoming the largest stockholder in a large, established oil company by purchasing its shares on the open market.

There are larger brokers (Merrill Lynch), bigger underwriters (Morgan Stanley), and investment houses with more prestige (Lehman Brothers) than Loeb, Rhoades, but no other investment-banking house on the Street matches this rich mix of venture capital, underwriting, and brokerage. It is this combination that has carried the firm to its present position in a single generation. It is also this combination that has contributed to the aura of mystery that surrounds it, because while it operates publicly in the traditional functions, it can act privately, with great wealth, in many situations that the public does not, and perhaps cannot, understand. Rarely are Loeb, Rhoades' deals simple and straightforward. They frequently are geared to long periods of time, and have been known to skip gracefully through the business complexities of a half-dozen countries before culminating, with considerable effect, in a major coup that involves control of an American corporation. Even Wall Street sophisticates are often puzzled and intrigued by what goes on at 42 Wall.

DEALS ARE SET IN CONCRETE

What goes on there largely reflects the talent, instincts, and personality of one man, John Langeloth Loeb, sixty. John Loeb founded the firm with his father in 1931 and has always been its dominant force. Few men claim to know him well. Those who do discern a prevailing warmth, charm, and quiet good humor. From even a slight distance, however, he appears to be "the aristocrat of autocrats," courteous, quiet-spoken, attentive in one mood, yet glacial, enigmatic, acid in the next— with the moods subject to change sharply and swiftly.

He can, as business requires, exercise enduring patience, but here too he is beyond prediction. In prolonged discussions, even his close associates cannot determine his position until he has voiced it. "He will listen attentively to a proposition, nodding his head all the while, and then say no," says one who has sat across from him frequently. This is particularly discouraging to suitors who have just completed a long, involved presentation and cannot for the life of them begin to know on which of many points he might be willing to bargain or negotiate. Once a deal is set, though, it is set in concrete so far as he is concerned, and he expects others to stand by it. On one occasion Loeb spearheaded negotiations on an important underwriting for a major corporation, a good customer. All the essential details had been worked out to everybody's apparent satisfaction. When the moment came for signing the papers the corporate president, well known for turning tough and negative in negotiations, began to seek additional concessions. Loeb turned abruptly to his colleagues and suggested that they go back to their offices to handle the work piling up. Tempers blazed and pulses pounded, but John Loeb walked out. It was a ticklish affair and Loeb, Rhoades fully expected to lose its relationship with the corporation. But, as Loeb knew, the corporation *did* need the money, and soon was ready to sign on the basis of the original terms.

The qualities that give John Loeb such confident control are an almost uncanny sense of timing (he completed the sale of the firm's major Cuban holdings the day before Fidel Castro took over), and an ability to pick talented and often diverse types to operate in the several areas of the business. Like many big banking partnerships, Loeb, Rhoades takes care to educate the proper number of relatives and sons-in-law who may inherit partnership interests. But with this duty served, John Loeb chooses his prospective partners not so much for the capital they can bring in as for the talents they will be able to apply to the company's affairs. If the types are diverse in outlook, so much the better for discussion at the weekly partners' luncheon meetings under the gleaming ormolu chandelier in the eighth-floor private dining room. And so much the better for the company, as experience has richly proved.

"THE GREAT STEDMAN-ERPF CONFLICT."

Nothing so firmly established Loeb, Rhoades in the brokerage world as a running conflict during the inflationary Fifties between two partners, which can be described in textbook terms as "the struggle between the value concept and the growth theory of investing." It was no academic exercise. In other times or other places such diversity of outlook might have been fatal, but in Loeb, Rhoades' case it kept the firm itself out ahead in its awareness of changing trends, caught the attention of the financial community, and provided Loeb, Rhoades correspondents with precise and profitable advice on growth areas that gave them a leg up on their competitors. In personal terms the debate was known as "the great Stedman-Erpf conflict," and its protagonists were Armand Erpf, now sixty-five, and the late Samuel Stedman.

Erpf is, and has been for many years, one of the legendary analysts of Wall Street. He is recognized as one of the nation's top investment men with the ability to combine a keen grasp of domestic and international economic forces with a talent for the hard, detailed work of breaking down balance sheets and income statements to create a solid base for his investment decisions. He was, for example, a pioneer among analysts in emphasizing the importance of "cash flow" in determining the actual earning power of a company and making comparisons in corporate financial reports. A measure of Erpf's ability and eminence is the regularity with which the Scottish investment trusts, oldest and canniest of the institutional investors, seek his counsel when making commitments in U.S. securities.

As director of Loeb, Rhoades research, Erpf drummed away at the idea of offering investors a broad group or spectrum of securities selling at deflated values. This was the policy of the firm during the Thirties when it usually recommended stocks of mining companies and heavy industry.

Sam Stedman was a Missourian who graduated from the Harvard Business School. He joined Bache & Co. in 1937, when Jules Bache himself had the controlling interest. Stedman was at that time, in the words of an associate, "a pleasant, lighthearted young man who although a sharp, alert analyst really seemed to have little interest in making money."

After World War II things changed. Stedman came back from the Army, followed Clifford Michel, a Bache partner, to Loeb, Rhoades and went to work as a junior analyst. He became more serious, more intent in his security studies, more interested in making money. The definite turn in his career came one day when John Loeb walked into a meeting of analysts and began firing questions. Most of the analysts double-talked and sparred for time while trying to figure out what Loeb was up to. Stedman, though, responded by giving him a twenty-minute rundown of all the major industries, with details on the conditions prevailing in each industry, and recommendations on the best stock in each group. Loeb left the room and ordered that recommendations be prepared for the correspondent firms on Stedman's twenty best buys. The correspondents were delighted. A short time later Stedman took charge of correspondent relations.

Stedman had been working out an investment concept of his own and in the early Fifties he began to put it to use. He summed it up in the observation that "there would be more people with more money and more time to spend it." This discretionary spending Stedman believed would benefit that part of industry based on convenience, education, or recreation. To qualify as a true "growth" company under Stedman's definition, a company had to be in the consumer-goods field and have at least one of three types of franchise: strong patents (Polaroid), distinctive marking methods (Avon Products' door-to-door selling), or superb management (General Foods). Also, the company had to show sustained increases in per share earnings and a potential for increasing them over a five- or ten-year period. Stedman believed that the number of true "growth stocks" in any market is very few, and in fact his reputation was made on his recommendations of no more than a dozen or so (e.g., Polaroid, Diners' Club, Fairchild Camera, Brunswick Corp.). Stedman contributed somewhat to his own forecasting accuracy by persuading institutional investors to accept growth stocks; for once a stock had been recognized as suitable for investment by institutions, its price-earnings multiple changed dramatically.

As Stedman's ideas and personality began to infiltrate the correspondent system, a subtle but significant change took place. The routine analyses of the research department under Erpf were more or less taken for granted, and correspondents came to seek Stedman's more exciting recommendations.

In 1969 Stedman was at the peak of his fame and influence, having run up a personal fortune estimated at approximately $10 million in seven years. Late that year he was stricken with cancer of the stomach. Eight months after his death came the market collapse, which put a dampener on the whole growth-stock theory. If Stedman had lived, would he have seen the signs of the break and warned his followers in time? Most of them think so, and blame his successors, rather than Stedman, for losses suffered because of the big sell-off (although Loeb, Rhoades' market letters in late 1961 began to point out that the market was too high). In any case, Erpf's ideas regained the ascendancy; the firm is now re-emphasizing basic values and special situations that more or less conform to Erpf's definition of growth.

THE PROFITABLE INTERCONNECTION

While the clash in investment philosophies had yielded Loeb, Rhoades a net profit in status and acceptance, John Loeb's sense of timing told him not to try it again; it was, he decided, high time to reorganize so that future conflict would be settled within the four walls. Inevitably in the reorganization the easy, informal method of doing business began to vanish. More and more decisions were fed up to the key group, consisting of Loeb, Erpf, Mark Millard, head of the new-business department, and Cliff Michel, a reserved, self-effacing individual who is closest to John Loeb and virtually his second-in-command.

John Loeb's reorganization, far from walling off the functions of brokerage, underwriting, and personal investment, was designed to get the most out of their interconnection. Lesser partners were established two deep in each area; the second man in research, for example, is the first in correspondent relations, and the first man in research is the No. 2 man in dealing with correspondent firms. Loeb made the most of his strong foreign connections, handed down from his father's day, by placing Europe in the hands of three capable and widely known partners, W. Palmer Dixon, an Eton boy who was his contemporary at Harvard, Hubert Simon, a German-born banker who became a British citizen during World War II, and Hans Widenmann, a German-born specialist in central banking.

Thus the total organizational pattern was set to reinforce Loeb, Rhoades' ability to move effectively in several profitable directions at once. The firm's new-business department, for example, is on the prowl for young corporations that need new or fresh capital in the equity market, while it is also seeking more embryonic situations that require large supplies of venture capital, where the risks—and rewards—are greater. Similarly, the partnership has always used its private capital to round up investment-banking business.

Since World War II only two houses, Merrill Lynch, Pierce, Fenner & Smith and Dean Witter, have pushed into the front rank of underwriters. Loeb, Rhoades will probably be the third. In the bread-and-butter business of participating in syndications it has, since 1961, insisted that it will take only a major position in a syndicate, and made it stick. A large part of this success is due to the ability of Mark Millard to dig up new situations. These are fed to the underwriting department, headed by John Loeb's handpicked syndicate manager, J. Howard Carlson, who came over to the firm in 1956 after handling eastern syndications for Halsey, Stuart & Co., the dean of bond underwriters. But rapid acceptance of a new underwriting firm in such a select circle is not that easily explained; some underwriters feel that Loeb, Rhoades is slipping into the front ranks with the tacit acquiescence of other major firms, which are aware that Loeb, Rhoades aspires to step into underwriting participations passed up by Kuhn, Loeb, which has been less than aggressive lately in defending its historic and established position. In any case, Loeb, Rhoades has proved its stature by being co-manager or first-line participant in such issues as Brunswick Corp., the Great Atlantic & Pacific Tea Co., Joseph E. Seagram & Sons, and a long list of oil and gas offerings.

Loeb, Rhoades, however, is still in the second rank of the prestigious business of originating major deals, largely for lack of old, established connections with major corporations. "We've had to dig, scratch, and invent our investment-banking business," says one of the partners. Yet newness can be turned to advantage. The management of the Korvette discount stores would have preferred Lehman Brothers as its underwriter, but Lehman declined because of old ties to some of the nation's large department-store chains. Korvette went to Loeb-Rhoades.

PUSHING $10,800,000 TO $320 MILLION

The profits and possibilities of the troika-like operation never showed to better advantage than in the series of operations that parlayed an investment of $10,800,000 into a $320-million merger. In 1948 Loeb, Rhoades put $800,000 into Texas Natural Gas Co., producer of liquefied petroleum gas, and in 1954 $10 million into Union Sulphur Co., then diversifying heavily into oil and gas. In 1960, with both companies growing rapidly, Loeb, Rhoades promoted a merger to create a single corporation, the Union Texas Natural Gas Co. No sooner had this merger been worked out than another deal popped up. Stockholders in Anderson-Prichard Oil Corp. wanted to liquidate their company, one of the largest integrated independents. Loeb, Rhoades spilt Anderson-Prichard into two parts, sold its producing properties to Union Texas, and set up a separate company, Apco Oil Corp., to operate the marketing and refining assets. The Anderson-Prichard shareholders, whose shares had been selling at around $25 per share, received $49.58 in the liquidation; Union Texas shareholders enjoyed an increase in assets. To top things off, some untested acreage from the deal proved to have enough oil to offset completely the cost to Union Texas of the Anderson-Prichard properties.

The climax of this fourteen-year exercise in creative capitalism came when Allied Chemical Corp. stepped up with an offer to buy out the whole operation of Union Texas for 6,300,000 shares of Allied common, representing 24 percent of the outstanding shares and valued at $318 million. Loeb, Rhoades' original investment of $10,800,000 had returned a profit of over $65 million by 1962, while the underwriting department had benefited by the floating of three different issues.

John Loeb's sense of touch and timing showed again to advantage in the ring-around-the-hemisphere performance that wound up by making Loeb, Rhoades a potentially dominant stockholder in Cities Service. It began in 1956 when John Loeb saw promise in the Cuban Atlantic Sugar Co., the largest sugar-producing enterprise in Cuba, which was selling below net-current-asset value. Loeb, Rhoades acquired about 20 percent of the stock. After a management shuffle, Cuban Atlantic earned $6 million in 1957. Uneasy about political conditions, Loeb began negotiating the sale of the mills and refinery—known as the Hershey properties—to Julio Lobo, the Cuban sugar king, who was rapidly gaining control of the island's refined-sugar output (FORTUNE, September, 1958). Lobo agreed to buy the property for $24,500,000. Despite vigorous protests from other stockholders and directors Loeb closed the sale at midnight on December 31, 1958. As the New Year broke, Batista pulled out of Havana and Castro took over.

The chief remaining assets were the company's plantation operations, which were folded into a producing subsidiary 50 percent owned by the Loeb interests. When Castro blocked exchange transactions with the U.S., the company declared a $2-million dividend payable in shares of Meeres & Co., a specially created Panamanian subsidiary.

The scene shifts. On Mark Millard's hunch, Loeb, Rhoades had worked out a deal with the Argentine Government under which the firm would assume all the expense and risk of looking for oil in return for a percentage of profit. To handle this operation Loeb, Rhoades formed the L. R. Development Corp., its main asset being a two-thirds interest in this contract with the government. The Signal Oil Co. and Loeb, Rhoades-controlled Union Texas Natural Gas took the remining one-third. Meeres & Co., of Panama, heir to the blocked Cuban pesos that Loeb, Rhoades could not transfer to the U.S., was a major stockholder in L. R. Development.

There was a certain amount of eyebrow raising in both Buenos Aires and Washington over some of the political pressure tactics involved in the Argentine arrangement. In any case, no major explosions resulted, and by July, 1961, L. R. Development was showing profits at a rate of $2,500,000 a year. At this point Loeb, Rhoades agreed to sell its two-thirds interest to Cities Service for $8,800,000 in notes and 124,709 shares of Cities Service common. The Cities Service common (then selling around $54) represented pure profit to the Loeb, Rhoades group. Moreover, John Loeb's timing was still good; no sooner had Cities Service bought into the Argentine deal than a series of political upheavals led to the ousting of President Arturo Frondizi by the military.

There is a postscript—as always. Last fall Cities Service decided to add a chemical company to its petroleum operations, and chose Tennessee Corp., controlled by the Bache estate through partner Cliff Michel. If the acquisition goes through—Antitrust is threatening to block it—Loeb, Rhoades interests might well emerge as the largest single group of stockholders in Cities Service.

THE GILBERT AFFAIR

Loeb, Rhoades has never had a tauter risk or luckier timing than in the case of Eddie Gilbert. When Gilbert began buying control of E. L. Bruce Co., the Memphis plywood producer, Loeb, Rhoades was his major broker. His great coup was cornering Bruce stock—the first time that a corner had developed on a regulated exchange since the early Twenties. Bruce common was suspended on the American Exchange, and suspended stock cannot be carried at full value on a broker's books.

Loeb, Rhoades was not troubled by this development although many a smaller firm caught in this position, with its net worth endangered, would have had to ask the client to take the shares elsewhere or put up more cash. Gilbert appreciated Loeb, Rhoades' support. Later he invited Loeb, Rhoades to place a director on his board and also offered an option on 50,000 shares of Bruce common at $10 a share. The firm accepted the option, later exercising it, and sent Henry Loeb to become a Bruce director in 1960.

In preparing for his next move Gilbert began some unorthodox trading and borrowing in his account to a degree that upset Loeb, Rhoades. In July, 1961, at the very time Gilbert was laying the groundwork to move in on Celotex, Loeb, Rhoades forced him to sign an agreement severely curbing his trading account. By its terms he was required to liquidate within thirty days some securities in a special account to repay a loan. And both the initial margin (for new investments) and the maintenance margin (on old investments) were raised. For all practical purposes Gilbert's trading through Loeb, Rhoades slowed to a trickle thereafter although the account remained there until the following April, when it was shifted to the First National Bank of Chicago—ostensibly because Gilbert was quietly preparing for a divorce and wanted his assets outside of New York.

A CALL FROM RUBEROID

Gilbert was cockily confident that he could repeat his Bruce coup in getting control of Celotex Corp. To finance this scheme he borrowed against his personal Bruce holdings; since U.S. law permitted only a 30 percent margin, he patronized European banking houses, particularly the Swiss, who were willing to give him as much as 75 percent margin. He also built a close relationship with Lazard Frères which invested more than $2,750,000 in Bruce shares and debentures.

As Gilbert's lunge for control of Celotex set the price of both Celotex and Bruce soaring, Lazard twice expressed concern that the Bruce common was overpriced. Both times Gilbert boldly offered personally to purchase the convertible debentures. Both times Lazard agreed and the second deal was consummated at 10:00 a.m., May 28. By 3:30 p.m. of that day of the great sell-off Gilbert was more than $1 million poorer.

In early June, Gilbert desperately tried to raise cash and offered to sell out his position in 150,000 shares of Celotex to Ruberoid at $36 per share. Ruberoid had wanted control of Celotex and indicated serious interest but wanted a little time. Gilbert meanwhile was already dipping into Bruce's corporate funds to meet margin calls. Although Henry Loeb was on the Bruce board, the first he learned of Gilbert's use of Bruce money was on Monday, June 11, at the City Midday Club during a luncheon with Gilbert, Robert West of Shearman & Sterling, the Bruce lawyer, Gilbert's father, who was also a Bruce director, and several others. They were discussing action to be taken at the board meeting the next day, including the proposal to sell Celotex shares

REFLECTIONS, MEMORIES AND CONFESSIONS

to Ruberoid. West interrupted to say that Eddie had used Bruce cash improperly. Loeb, surprised, asked why the directors had not been informed. Gilbert asked what difference it would have made if Henry Loeb had known. What would he have done? Henry replied that he would have called his lawyer. And when Henry returned to the office that is exactly what he did do.

At the start of the next day's board meeting, Gilbert was calm and confident. He indicated he would repay the corporation, apparently banking on the sale to Ruberoid to restore his funds. A call from Ruberoid interrupted the meeting with the news that it was not interested in purchasing the Celotex shares at $36 per share. There was no further discussion. E. L. Bruce, presiding as chairman, made a motion to accept Gilbert's resignation. Although Gilbert's father was also present, there was no dissenting vote and no discussion. Gilbert fled to Brazil that night and the Celotex situation was left up in the air. Ruberoid then came forth and announced it sought 350,000 shares of Celotex common, but now at a price of $25 per share. Jim Walter, the shell-house pioneer (FORTUNE, April, 1962), whose original financing was underwritten by Loeb, Rhoades, dropped in on his old friend John Loeb and asked his help in gaining control of Celotex. Loeb, Rhoades knew where some of the large blocks of Celotex were and by offering $30 a share quickly amassed some 300,000 shares, including the 70,000 shares held by Bruce.

Gilbert returned to the U.S. in October to face back federal taxes of $3,300,000 and a charge of fraud. There was some talk in investment circles that Loeb, Rhoades might have forestalled trouble by exercising tighter control over him earlier in the game. What is not generally known is just how early and how drastically Loeb, Rhoades did act—a fact that lifted the firm well out of the way when trouble came. One of Gilbert's closest associates in the Celotex move, a man who lost heavily in the venture, is vaguely unhappy about the role of the U.S. investment houses, but centers his real fire on the European bankers who, in his view, "lured Eddie to the top of a treacherous sandpile by making too much easy credit available to him."

THE POWERS OF *CLEOPATRA*

Loeb, Rhoades' headline connection with the Twentieth Century-Fox affair came through a determined effort to protect a big investment on behalf of both partners and clients. Fox stock was selling around $30 when analysts detected an asset value of $70 a share based primarily on some valuable Beverly Hills real estate. Loeb, Rhoades partners and clients acquired an estimated 250,000 of Fox's 2,500,000 shares, and a Loeb, Rhoades New York correspondent, Peter Treves & Co., acquired another 150,000 for its own clients. When the losses from film production threatened to wipe out real-estate profits, stockholder anguish was heard in stereophonic sound. John Loeb and Milton Gould, a lawyer representing Treves, were invited to join a board that was already badly divided. Old Spyros Skouras, the wily Greek who had been in unchallenged command for twenty years, wanted to remain in power or at least pick his successor. Most of the other directors, including Robert Lehman, the amiable senior don of Lehman Brothers, were agreed that Skouras had to go but divided on who should replace him.

Things got worse in late 1961 as shooting went forward in Rome on the second attempt to produce *Cleopatra*. A prime reason for the costly foreign production was to satisfy Miss Taylor's desire to have a tax-free capital gain for her Swiss company. Under the contract her company is to get 10 percent of the picture's gross above $7,500,000, quite apart from the $8,000-a-day working salary she received—when she worked. As she dallied, the costs mounted to epochal proportions and the pressure on the board became intense. With John Loeb heartily concurring, Skouras was fired as chief executive officer and a committee of six directors appointed to seek out candidates for the presidency. Several candidates were put forward but only one, Darryl Zanuck, was well equipped to fight for the job. Zanuck, sixty, one of the founders of Twentieth Century and operating boss of Twentieth-Century Fox from 1935 to 1956, was the largest individual stockholder, with 110,000 shares of the common. Zanuck presented himself before the directors' selection committee, Loeb coolly noted that Zanuck's productions in the last five years had lost over $6 million for the company. "Mr. Zanuck," said Loeb, in a scene Hollywood would have paid much to watch, "I see nothing here that convinces me you are the right man to head this company."

The directors committee never did submit a report favoring any particular candidate. But Zanuck retained lawyer Louis Nizer and prepared for a proxy fight. At the next board meeting on July 25, Skouras, matching his 100,000 shares with Zanuck's 110,000, proposed Zanuck for the presidency. Attention focussed on Bobby Lehman. If he voted against Zanuck, and with Loeb, it might signal an all-out proxy fight. If he voted for Zanuck, he might offend his friend John Loeb and strain the family business ties that bound them. Lehman, however, was convinced that none of the other candidates could match Zanuck's experience, so he voted for Zanuck. The majority of other directors followed his lead.

Loeb and Gould resigned the next day. Lehman's vote was taken in good grace, but Lehman's appraisal of Zanuck did not change John Loeb's mind, and Loeb, Rhoades soon began selling out its position in Twentieth Century-Fox. It remains to be seen which house showed the shrewder judgment. At the year's end Zanuck predicted the company would lose $30 million in 1962. Then with his *The Longest Day* well launched, he announced that Fox would spend another $3 million to $5 million on the production of *Cleopatra* to give it a few more spectacular battle scenes, which in his opinion it needed to ensure its box-office appeal when it opens in June.

ON TO THE ANTIPODES

Defeat is generally taken stoically at Loeb, Rhoades, its sting balmed by the knowledge that there are countless other opportunities waiting to be seized—or created. Even as its interest in Fox was being reduced, the partnership was expanding its holdings in a major oil company; the acquisition of $22 million of assets of Bush Terminal Buildings Co. was commanding John Loeb's attention; the new-business department was working on an underwriting of industrial properties from a wealthy estate; in partnership with the Cabot interests of Boston it was financing experimental work on a process to make liquid natural gas transportable in tankers. In the foreign field Loeb, Rhoades began trimming its interests in Latin America and stepping out of its role as adviser to the New York Capital Fund, a nonresident-owned Canadian fund specializing in Canadian and foreign securities. The firm's sharpest eyes were turned, instead, toward the investment potential of Australia and New Zealand.

This unceasing search for new ways to put capital to work will be accelerated at 42 Wall Street as long as John Loeb continues to have his way. He made that clear recently at the close of a luncheon in the private dining room, when, surrounded by his partners, he outlined the firm's working philosophy:

"Since father and I founded our firm, really to look after our own affairs, we've sought to build a sound investment-banking and brokerage business. If we ran our business on a strict cost-accounting basis, some phases of it might not turn out profitable. But you can't measure this investment business that way. It's the whole mix that makes us what we are. But if we didn't get any fun out of it and if what we do is to be constantly suspect, it would be easier to shut up and go back to the job of investing our own money."

All of which is another way of saying that so long as Carl M. Loeb, Rhoades & Co. is under its present management it intends to be very much in the middle of everything.

Of Men, Money, And Marriage

The prodigious success of Carl M. Loeb, Rhoades & Co. derives from the three M's of men, money, and marriage—in approximately that order.

The founder, Carl Morris Loeb, was born in 1875, the son of a Frankfurt drygoods merchant. As a youngster, he broke away from the retail business to go to work as an office boy for one of Germany's leading metal-fabricating firms, Metallgesellschaft. He was seventeen when the company sent him off to its U.S. trading subsidiary, American Metal Co., and he was billeted to American Metal's branch office among the wealthy German-Americans in St. Louis. Carl Loeb quickly established himself as a young man with an uncannily retentive memory and an instinctive feel for commodity values; within three years he was manager of the St. Louis office.

The serious, energetic young immigrant was eminently eligible in solid St. Louis, and his choice of a bride was to have interesting reverberations in the world of high finance. Adeline Moses was the daughter of Alfred Huger Moses, the head of one of the more prominent Jewish families of the South. As a merchant banker in Montgomery, Alabama, Alfred Moses had lost heavily in a luckless attempt to finance development of hydroelectric power at Muscle Shoals, Alabama (later the heart of the TVA system). Though he was working in St. Louis in the insurance and real-estate business in an effort to get on his financial feet, the important point, in history's eye, is that the Moses family was well known to the three Lehman brothers, the Montgomery drygoods merchants whose cotton and banking interests ultimately led to the establishment of one of the most influential banking houses in the U.S. (see "The Bustling House of Lehman," FORTUNE, December, 1957). In 1896, at twenty-one, Carl Loeb married Adeline Moses.

Thirty years later their eldest son, John, married Arthur Lehman's youngest daughter, Frances.

The news of Carl Loeb's driving genius traveled eastward to Jacob Langeloth, the president of American Metal. In 1905, Langeloth brought Loeb, at thirty, to New York as vice president. Ten years later Loeb was the new president of American Metal. A hard, strong-willed man, he drove American Metal into a new era of development after it was split off from German ownership at the close of World War I. Loeb, for example, pushed the firm into ownership of mining, smelting, and refining facilities. Later, he committed American Metal to help finance production of molybdenum through a separate company. This was the origin of the Climax Molybdenum Co., which merged with American Metal in 1957.

Gradually, however, a split developed between Loeb and his board of directors. Loeb became increasingly annoyed at what he regarded as the board's interference in his management of the company. Although the particular issue that brought the feud to a head has been lost to history, the break came in June, 1929. He offered his resignation, it was accepted, and at fifty-four Carl M. Loeb for the first time in thirty-eight years was jobless—but wealthy. Providentially, as part of the resignation settlement, the board agreed to buy his 80,000 shares of A.M.C. common at the price quoted at the time of resignation. Six months later the stock plunged to half that price in the great crash.

John Langeloth Loeb, the eldest of Carl and Adeline Loeb's three boys, grew up in the easy patrician elegance of the well-to-do New York German-Jewish community. He graduated from Harvard in 1924 to serve a brief apprenticeship with American Metal. But investment banking beckoned after his marriage in 1926 to Frances Lehman. (Frances Lehman's two older sisters also married investment bankers. Dorothy married Richard Bernhard, a partner in Wertheim & Co.; their son is now a partner in Lehman Brothers. And Helen married Benjamin Buttenwieser, a limited partner in Kuhn, Loeb.*) Father Lehman took a hand in John Loeb's training, and John was put to work at Wertheim in 1929.

John's own father, meanwhile, had taken a fling at leisure with a world cruise, and then put in his time puttering around with his own investments. This state of unemployment got to be too much for John's mother. "Do something about your father," she begged John in 1931. "I'd do anything to get him out of the house." John's idea of "doing something" was to propose that they buy a seat on the big board. Carl asked but one

---

* The Loebs of Loeb, Rhoades have no family connections with Kuhn, Loeb & Co., co-founded by Solomon Loeb in 1867, or with Gerald Loeb, partner of E. F. Hutton & Co. and one of the nation's best-known brokers and counselors.

question. Did John think he could run an investment firm? John said he could, and that he had a young friend, a cashier at Wertheim, Ted Bernstein, who was willing to come along to handle the back-office work.

A SILVER LINING

The new firm was launched on January 31, 1931. The Loebs made no dramatic killing at the start. Most of the time was spent investing the funds that Carl himself had accumulated and those of the friends of the family.

The first great coup came in 1932 when Franklin Roosevelt, courting the cooperation of western Senators, agreed to support the price of silver. Silver went wild. With excellent international contacts in London, Bombay, and Shanghai, the Loebs began an international business in silver. At one point the young partnership was doing almost 50 percent of all the silver futures trading on the New York Commodity Exchange. But this dreamy situation came to an abrupt end in late 1933, when the federal government slapped a seigniorage tax of 50 percent on all silver transactions.

To fill the void in activity, the senior Loeb turned his attention to rubber. Assembling a group of experts in the rubber market, Loeb became a major dealer in rubber futures, a business that was to reach a peak during the Korean war.

Meanwhile the firm was building a network of correspondent firms to support an aggressive trading and underwriting program. The correspondent business had walked in on John Loeb during 1937 in the person of Everett Cady, the then senior partner of Rhoades & Co. Founded in 1898 with many members of old New York families in the firm, Rhoades had been hard hit in the early days of the depression. It had recovered but was on shaky legs. When the business began to turn down again in 1937, Cady sought a way to keep it alive.

His solution to his problem was straightforward. One weekend he took home the Stock Exchange directory and studied each firm in it. He wanted a merger that would benefit both parties, and the more he looked the more he was certain that Loeb and Rhoades needed each other. Loeb was a fine Jewish firm with a list of good clients, and Rhoades was a fine old Christian firm with another list. Loeb had interests in the same cities where Rhoades had correspondents. And, most important from Cady's viewpoint, Loeb had capital and Rhoades needed it.

Despite his father's coolness to the idea, John Loeb saw some advantages from his point of view and the merger was made. Cady stayed with Loeb, Rhoades until 1952, when he wearied of the work and travel involved in servicing correspondents, and retired to a partnership in Cady, Roberts, a much smaller house. He still believes the merger "was one of the greatest on the Street because the conception was very sound."

AN ALLIANCE WITH CANADA

Mergers of another kind were providing the firm with a broad capital foundation. With Loeb-Lehman money in hand, an alliance was made with the Bache millions when Clifford Michel joined as a partner in 1945. Michel is married to one of the granddaughters of the late Jules Bache, whose Bache & Co. is today second only to Merrill Lynch in brokerage business. (Another Bache granddaughter is married to F. Warren Pershing, son of General John J. Pershing of World War I and head of Pershing & Co., a brokerage house that also specializes in handling correspondent firms.)

The most recent fortune to fall under Loeb, Rhoades influence is Canadian in origin. On January 10, 1953, John Loeb's daughter, Ann Margaret, married Edgar Bronfman, elder son of Samuel Bronfman, founder and chief executive of Distillers Corp.–Seagrams, Ltd. Sam Bronfman is undoubtedly one of the wealthiest men in the Commonwealth. His money is not formally part of the capital of Loeb, Rhoades, but, as one member of the firm puts it, "he's a kind of partner who is awfully important." Bronfman money, in fact, meets Loeb money and Bache holdings to constitute the largest single group of stock in New York's Empire Trust Co., with assets of approximately $270 million. (Edgar Bronfman joined Empire's board in February.) Bache interests are also strong in Tennessee Corp. and in Canada's Dome Mines and Dome Petroleum.

Thus the third generation at Loeb, Rhoades has made an auspicious start of its own in the two M's of money and marriage. As ever, the third M of "men" is governing. The new ranks of Loebs, their kin, and non-Loebs are promising, but have yet to be thoroughly tested.

≡

David Patrick Columbia's New York Social Diary

THE BIRTHDAY CELEBRATION AT BLENHEIM PALACE, JUNE 13, 2005

I came over to London, arriving last Friday morning to make a seventy-fifth birthday party organized by **Sharon Handler** for her great and longtime friend and companion, **Ambassador John Loeb** at Blenheim Palace on Saturday. I had no idea what to expect, and although I'd never been there, Blenheim is a very grand place and a place therefore, for a very grand party.

Blenheim resonates for me personally because of a close friendship I had with the late **Lady Sarah Churchill** who moved there when her father succeeded her grandfather and became the **10th duke of Marlborough** (her brother is the current Duke) when she was twelve. In fact, there is no one who ever had a friendship with Lady Sarah who doesn't connect her enormous and powerful (and at times controversial) personality with Blenheim. Her long after recollections of first moving into this, the world's largest private palace (covering seven acres of ground with courtyard), were of something over-sized, overwrought and frightening. I think Sarah's memories were not unusual. I found a passage about Blenheim written by the Canadian writer **Marian Fowler** in her book *Blenheim—Biography of a Palace*:

> *I felt awed, ant-like, apprehensive, as I gazed on Blenheim's huge baroque mass, its fearful symmetry, its threatening roofscape of ferocious lions and plunging swords, its trumpeting central portico and tremendous trailing wings. House and courtyards cover seven acres. This is a dragon of a house which once breathed fire and was turned to stone by some terrible curse. Blenheim sprawls like a petrified dinosaur*

or beached whale, completely out of scale with the little blue folds of hills that lap it round. Surely the huge stones of its walls were quarried by giants; how they reached the site in the days before cranes and lorries is a mystery as awesome as how the Egyptians built their pyramids.

When **George III** first saw Blenheim, astonished by its grandeur, he is alleged to have said something like: "But we don't have anything like this!" And indeed, old King George didn't, and never would.

It was England's gift under the reign of **Queen Anne** to **General John Churchill** who defeated the armies of **Louis XIV** in 1703 at Blenheim. Churchill was made the first duke of Marlborough and his wife **Sarah, the first duchess** (actually he was first made **Earl of Marlborough**). It began with a gift of land and then monies to build the house which began in 1705 and was sort of completed in 1722 after acrimony and many other problems. The Churchills, both husband and wife were formidable figures and never without controversy. **Jonathan Swift** wrote of the first Sarah: of the *"three furies that reigned in her heart, sordid Avarice, disdainful Pride, and ungovernable Rage."*

But that bit of a large history will have to be continued at another time for there is John Loeb's 75th birthday celebration that is at hand in today's Diary.

On Saturday afternoon, the invitation instructed, guests without cars were to meet at Claridge's at 5:15 on Brook Street where buses (the British call them coaches) were waiting to transport us to Blenheim, about an hour and a half ride from London. The coaches were all seats of four with tables. Once aboard and off, a stewardess served champagne (or water depending on your preference), and we were off for the ride outside London through the beautiful English countryside.

About an hour and a half later we arrived at the gates of Blenheim—an imposing yellow stoned monument leading to a long driveway through a park by a lake, around a bend until before us was this great looming, stately palace with a long driveway leading directly to its front door. In Lady Sarah's early days, this driveway was lined with great elms that had been planted more than a century before but had all been destroyed by blight in the 1940s or 50s.

There was, as you can see, a long red carpet which led to the steps of the entrance to the palace, which were lined by "guards" in red uniforms. Everyone immediately seemed to muster their noblesse oblige for the trip. The immense theatricality that we were presented with immediately put everyone in an other-worldly (and very good) mood.

Once inside we were in the Great Hall with its 67-foot-high ceiling and stone enrich-

The Queen's Household Cavalry, shown here in London, lined the red carpet at my birthday party at Blenheim.

ments carved by **Grinling Gibbons** which portray the arms of Queen Anne. On its ceiling, which was painted in 1716 by **Sir James Thornhill**, there is a scene of John Churchill, the victorious Marlborough, with the battle order of Blenheim spread before him.

There we gathered, very patiently waiting as at the other end of this vast hall, Sharon Handler, dressed simply and elegantly in a long white satin dress and Ambassador Loeb in white tie and tails and decorations, received each of the guests who then passed into the Saloon.

In keeping with the times, there were several photographers and cameramen shooting the arrivals and the reception line. A man with a mike came along with a cameraman to ask us who we were and how we happened to be there—they were making a record of the party for the host and hostess. This exercise was an excellent device for uniting everyone as a guest, plain and simple and was also an interesting way to enter the party with its large (350) guest list of all kinds of people from all over the world—Europe, the US, Australia and Vietnam.

The Saloon, where cocktails were served, is one of the most photographed of the rooms at Blenheim. This is used as the state dining room and the photographs of it never articulate its vastness. Its walls are covered with magnificent frescoes and a ceiling, all painted by **Louis Laguerre** which includes a caricature of the painter.

Drinks served were wine, cocktails or water along with hors d'oeuvres. The enormous room was very crowded and everyone was very excited to be in this—for most of us—very elegant and exotic setting. From there at the appointed time—a man in a red uniform with a handmike, announced that dinner would be served in the Long Library.

The trip required moving down a hallway to the west, by the room (open to see) where Sir Winston Churchill was born on November 30, 1874. Sir Winston's father Randolph, was the second son of the 8th duke and brother of the 9th duke who was the grandfather of the current duke.

We moved through the three apartments known as the First, Second and Third State Rooms, the walls of which are hung with tapestries of Marlborough's military campaigns as well as bronzes and elegant furniture of 18th-century French and Italian. In the Red Room there was a photographer waiting to photograph each of us. It was here that I got a shot of **Jonathan Farkas and Somers White** posing for their portrait. This room contains the huge **John Singer Sargent** portrait of the 9th duke and his wife, the former **Consuelo Vanderbilt** and their two children **Lord Ivor** and **John, the Marquess of Blandford**, father of the present duke.

From there we moved through the 2nd and 3rd State rooms into the Long Library with its more than 150-foot length, set with four long tables covered in red cloth and lit by candelabra. This room was originally designed by Blenheim's original architect vanBrugh as a picture gallery. The 8th duke (who was also married to an American) installed The Willis organ at one end in 1891 and his successor, the present duke's grandfather (the man in the Sargent portrait) made it into a library of books largely collected by him. The room contains coronation robes, liveries, uniforms and the coronets of the present Duke and Duchess which are displayed in a central by along with a cap which belonged to Queen Anne, Blenheim's benefactress.

It was an amazing sight—all of these men and women dressed so formally for the occasion in this truly palatial setting with its centuries old relationship to British and European history. The room was entirely candlelit—except for the light from the dais as well as the video screen placed strategically in different quarters of the room which ran a series of black and white photos of John Loeb from infancy through and up to the present.

I had the privilege of being seated to the right of **Mary, Lady Soames** who is a daughter of Sir Winston and **Clementine, Lady Churchill**. Lady Soames accompanied her father to Washington during the Second World War when Churchill came to consult with **FDR**, and they stayed at the White House more than sixty years ago. Lady Soames has published several books about her parents and is currently working on her memoir.

Sitting next to this woman who was witness to the Anglo-American alliance of six decades ago, I couldn't resist asking her what it was like to be with the **Roosevelts** in the

White House. I realized that she might tend to be very discreet or even be wary of divulging to another writer what her property is. She did tell me that Roosevelt at the end of the day liked to put business aside and enjoy himself with company and conversation and cocktails, whereas **Eleanor Roosevelt**, although Lady Soames admired her very much, was always all-business. I made a comparison between the personalities of the two and the personalities of Mr. and Mrs. Clinton. Lady Soames seemed unimpressed by my comparison.

After the dessert, there was much milling about as people wanted to see who was there. There were several ambassadors who served in the Administrations of **Ronald Reagan** (when John Loeb was US Ambassador to Denmark) and **George H.W. Bush**, as well as the Duke of Marlborough, his daughter **Lady Henrietta Spencer Churchill**, his cousin, Winston Churchill's granddaughter **Edwina Sandys** and her husband **Richard Kaplan; the Earl of Dartmouth, the Earl and Countess Dudley, M. and Mme. Michel David-Weill, Ezra and Cecile Zilkha** and their daughter **Donna Zilkha**; John Loeb's siblings, **Arthur Loeb** (who founded the famous and much missed Madison Avenue Bookshop) and **Judith Chiara, Sharon Sondes** (with **Geoffrey Thomas**), **Bill Bernhard and Catherine Cahill** (Bernhard's mother and Loeb's mother were sisters); his son **Nick Loeb** and daughter **Alexandra Driscoll, Julie and Michel-Henri Carriol** from Australia; **Beth DeWoody, Anne Hearst, Kip Forbes, Lee and CeCe Black, Daisy and Paul Soros, Joanne Herring, Jeanne Lawrence, Elizabeth and Patrick Gerschel, Bobby Pressman and Mallory Samson, April and Roddy Gow, Linda Silverman, Donald and Barbara Tober, Victoria and Frank Wyman, Raul Suarez, Gail Hilson; Tito Guadier** from Barcelona, **Desmond Guinness, Lorna and Larry Graev, Mary McFadden, George and Carol McFadden, Dariah and Larry Leeds, Susan Fales-Hill and Aaron Hill, Gail Hilson, Dayssi and Paul Kanavos, Denise Rich, Luce and Winston Churchill II**, and more luminaries than I can remember at this moment.

After dinner, our hostess took the podium and introduced the ambassador's brother and his sister, his cousin and several of John's friends who spoke about him. What emerged for those of us who may not have known was his history and his achievements. There were letters read from **Nancy Reagan**, both **Presidents Bush**, and a video of **Richard Allen**. He was born on May 2, 1930 to **Frances Lehman** and **John Loeb**, the grandson of Carl Loeb who founded the great Wall Street banking house of Carl M. Loeb, Rhoades.

He grew up in an economically privileged life where much was expected of him. He attended Hotchkiss, Harvard and Harvard Business School. (The Loebs donated $150 million to Harvard on their deaths.) He entered public life in the family business and later became involved in political and community affairs. His parents were people of high expectations. Their son went into the family business and later, through his interest in politics (fund-raising for the Republican party and Ronald Reagan whom he met in the mid-1970s when few thought the former movie actor and California governor had much of a political future). In his many incarnations, he also became a wine-maker (the Sonoma-Loeb private reserve, which was served, naturally, at dinner) and among many other things, the head of the Winston Churchill Foundation.

The party at Blenheim he explained grew out of the lifelong fact that from childhood, being the eldest, his birthday was rarely celebrated because he was away at school. And because of his association with Churchill, he once told Sharon he wanted to celebrate his 75th birthday at Blenheim.

After the speeches and encominums and a brilliant video which Sharon Handler produced in the style of A&E biography (it looked very real) covering the ambassador's entire life and ending with graphics of the *Pink Panther* at The End, where the Pink Panther scribbled a big "NOT" over "The End," we were treated to a **Marilyn Monroe** look-a-like who came out of nowhere to sing, or rather, coo: "Happy Birthday, Mr. Am-bass-a-dor" à la MM's original serenading of **JFK** at Madison Square Garden in 1962. And when she left, ("so Happy Birthday, Sugah, and toodle-oo") the Ambassador came up to the podium where Ms. Handler surprised him and everyone else with a specially written rendition which she sang of "Danny Boy" (*"Oh Johnny boy, I love you so..."*). It brought tears to the eyes of the stately ambassador, and when it was over, he took the podium to thank his partner for the wonderful party she had made for him, and to thank his friends and his family for attending.

After dinner, the guests retired to the Great Hall for dancing and dessert and champagne and a tour, if they wished of Blenheim's staterooms. At about one-thirty guests started thinking of the trek back to London although the champagne and music and dancing continued the distraction in this great private palace.

We got into a coach at about quarter to two, hardly the last of the stragglers, and were back in London by 3:30 a.m. I crawled into my very comfortable bed at the fabulous Lanesborough about quarter to four thinking how amazing life was that I would have the immense pleasure of visiting Blenheim for the first time in my life at a very grand party full of very grand people for a man of great accomplishments and friendship who was celebrating his 75th birthday. It was one of those thoughts where there's nowhere else to go in one's mind except... to sleep. A brilliant night behind me.

=

LONDON WEEKEND, JUNE 15, 2005

We returned from John Loeb's birthday party at Blenheim at a quarter to four Saturday night/Sunday morning. Dead tired. I slept until quarter to two the following afternoon. I don't remember when I last slept that long; maybe it was jet lag.

My room (or I should say rooms—a double has a sitting room plus the bedroom) here at the Lanesborough is so quiet and comfortable. And with its fourteen-foot ceilings, heavy mahogany door and window frames, it's very English and reassuring, and of course just this side of grand—which is a treat if you're going to be away from your own home and hearth. I think it's the first time I've ever stayed at a hotel where it seemed like a perfect, cozy Sunday afternoon just staying in my hotel room.

The Sunday papers were waiting outside my door, of course, and so I dawdled Sunday-style, reading. After an hour of that I began thinking I should get up and get out and have a look at the world, so I shaved, showered and went downstairs for something to eat.

The main dining room is a glassed-over solarium style room with a décor which reminds me of the Brighton Pavilion. They were not serving breakfast or much else at that hour, however (3:30), just finishing up lunch and preparing for the dinner hour. So I went across the lobby to the big sitting room off the bar with its comfy sofas and chairs with small round tables nearby. There you can take a table for yourself, with your paper, and order just about anything you'd want. I ordered the roasted turkey club. Second time; creature of habit (or no imagination). And a cappuccino.

It was a grey London day and I was actually hoping for some rain just because it was London. Looking out the window, however, I could see the double decker sightseeing buses rounding Hyde Park corner, with their passengers riding on top in the open air.

At about 7 o'clock I took a taxi over to the house of the Earl of Dartmouth who was holding a cocktail and buffet reception for **Ambassador Loeb**. Drinks were called for seven with dinner at 8:30. By the time I got there about seven-fifteen there were many in the receiving line just inside the front door. Waiters in white jackets were holding trays of water, orange juice or white wine for the taking.

The earl is a very friendly, bright-faced individual who greeted scores of people he may very well had never seen before, and directed them upstairs to the piano nobile where they were congregating for drinks. I'd never met him before but he evidently has scores of friends in New York which he visits often. He looks American.

The second Earl of Dartmouth, also **William Legge**, was a British statesman who is most remembered in English history for his part in the government before and during the American Revolution. For **King George III**, Legge was the 2nd Secretary of State for the Colonies, serving from 1772 to 1775. To Americans his most important role was his donation to a trust which financed the founding of Dartmouth College, which was created to educate the children of the natives and of "English youth" in the New Hampshire wilderness. Dartmouth College obviously is named in his honor.

Meanwhile, back to the 2nd earl's descendant, the French doors of the reception room were open and many were out on the terrace overlooking Bayswater Road with its enormous old trees tenting the road and surrounding the blocks of white townhouses.

Everything about the place from this New Yorker's perspective is just different enough to intrigue. For here I am in one of the world's greatest cities where the language spoken is the same as my city—although the accent can make it seem almost foreign to these ears. The energy of the people seems different, however. I'm not sure what it is. Perhaps it's because there's a quieter, less intense quality to this city. Perhaps it's because so many of the buildings are lower and boulevards wider and so there is more sky. However, my taxi driver coming over from the hotel was complaining about the Sunday traffic and how heavy it was. I could only think of Manhattan any day of the week—this was nothing.

Although Mr. Dartmouth's house is spacious enough, there were many from the night before, at least more than a hundred and so it was one of those crowded cocktail parties (the British say "drinks parties") where you'd find yourself talking to anybody.

About eight-thirty, someone announced the buffet was ready. There was couscous, sliced beef, salad, cold poached salmon, bread and biscuits. I took my plate and went up the stairs to another room where there were several tables and chairs set up. I sat with **Sharon** (**Lady Sondes**), who is a cousin of the guest of honor (her mother was a Lehman), and **Geoffrey Thomas**, **Raul Suarez**, **Joanne Herring** from Texas, and **Kooki Fallah**, an Englishwoman I met years ago when she'd come to New York to stay with our mutual friend the late **Judy Green**. Kooki has a relatively new business here in London teaching people how to play bridge.

After dinner there were more speeches in the reception room about the Ambassador who then took the floor to thank everyone for joining him and **Sharon Handler** in sharing this fantastic birthday celebration.

It was about ten-thirty as the guests began making their way out to Bayswater Road looking for taxis. I hitched a ride with **Lee and Cece Black** who dropped me off at Park Lane and Piccadilly. I wanted to walk a bit over to the Lanesborough so that I could get a shot at night of Apsley House, the residence that the British nation gave to the **Duke**

of Wellington after his victory over **Napoleon** at the Battle of Waterloo. Known to the British as "Number One London" (because it was the first house passed when one entered London through the toll gate from the countryside). No more countryside there, however. For just across the way from Number One, on the opposite corner is the Lanesborough, waiting to welcome me back after the end of a brilliant London weekend.

George Washington's Letter to the Hebrew Congregation in Newport, Rhode Island

Gentlemen:

While I received with much satisfaction your address replete with expressions of esteem, I rejoice in the opportunity of assuring you that I shall always retain grateful remembrance of the cordial welcome I experienced on my visit to Newport from all classes of citizens.

The reflection on the days of difficulty and danger which are past is rendered the more sweet from a consciousness that they are succeeded by days of uncommon prosperity and security.

If we have wisdom to make the best use of the advantages with which we are now favored, we cannot fail, under the just administration of a good government, to become a great and happy people.

The citizens of the United States of America have a right to applaud themselves for having given to mankind examples of an enlarged and liberal policy—a policy worthy of imitation. All possess alike liberty of conscience and immunities of citizenship.

It is now no more that toleration is spoken of as if it were the indulgence of one class of people that another enjoyed the exercise of their inherent natural rights, for, happily, the Government of the United States, which gives to bigotry no sanction, to persecution no assistance, requires only that they who live under its protection should demean themselves as good citizens in giving it on all occasions their effectual support.

It would be inconsistent with the frankness of my character not to avow that I am pleased with your favorable opinion of my administration and fervent wishes for my felicity.

May the children of the stock of Abraham who dwell in this land continue to merit and enjoy the good will of the other inhabitants—while every one shall sit in safety under his own vine and fig tree and there shall be none to make him afraid.

May the father of all mercies scatter light, and not darkness, upon our paths, and make us all in our several vocations useful here, and in His own due time and way everlastingly happy.

G. Washington

Letter from the Hebrew Congregation in Newport, Rhode Island to President George Washington

Sir:

Permit the children of the stock of Abraham to approach you with the most cordial affection and esteem for your person and merits — and to join with our fellow citizens in welcoming you to Newport.

With pleasure we reflect on those days — those days of difficulty, and danger, when the God of Israel, who delivered David from the peril of the sword — shielded Your head in the day of battle: and we rejoice to think, that the same Spirit, who rested in the Bosom of the greatly beloved Daniel enabling him to preside over the Provinces of the Babylonish Empire, rests and ever will rest, upon you, enabling you to discharge the arduous duties of Chief Magistrate in these States.

Deprived as we heretofore have been of the invaluable rights of free Citizens, we now with a deep sense of gratitude to the Almighty disposer of all events behold a Government, erected by the Majesty of the People — a Government, which to bigotry gives no sanction, to persecution no assistance — but generously affording to all Liberty of conscience, and immunities of Citizenship: deeming every one, of whatever Nation, tongue, or language equal parts of the great governmental Machine:

This so ample and extensive Federal Union whose basis is Philanthropy, Mutual confidence and Public Virtue, we cannot but acknowledge to be the work of the Great God, who ruleth in the Armies of Heaven, and among the Inhabitants of the Earth, doing whatever seemeth him good.

For all these Blessings of civil and religious liberty which we enjoy under an equal benign administration, we desire to send up our thanks to the Ancient of Days, the great preserver of Men beseeching him, that the Angel who conducted our forefathers through the wilderness into the promised Land, may graciously conduct you through all the difficulties and dangers of this mortal life: And, when, like Joshua full of days and full of honour, you are gathered to your Fathers, may you be admitted into the Heavenly Paradise to partake of the water of life, and the tree of immortality.

Done and Signed by order of the Hebrew Congregation in NewPort, Rhode Island August 17th 1790.

Moses Seixas   Warden

THE AMBASSADOR JOHN L. LOEB, JR. INSTITUTE FOR RELIGIOUS FREEDOM AT THE GEORGE WASHINGTON UNIVERSITY   LOEB.COLUMBIAN.GWU.EDU

The Story Behind the George Washington Letter to the Hebrew Congregation in Newport, RI, August 1790

Ambassador John L. Loeb, Jr.

Back in 1789, the Constitution that we Americans today take so for granted had still not been ratified by each of the states forming "these United States." Nor had the First Amendment to the Constitution, with its guarantees of religious freedom and separation of church and state, been adopted. George Washington, recently elected to the presidency, decided to tour the New England states in the fall of 1789, with the exception of Rhode Island. Some scholars believe that he bypassed Rhode Island because the state had not yet ratified the new Constitution.

In June 1790, the Rhode Island legislature finally ratified the Constitution, in large part because the proposed First Amendment would guarantee religious freedom. After Congress adjourned in early August of 1790, President Washington decided to pay a goodwill visit to Rhode Island after all. He brought Secretary of State Thomas Jefferson, New York Governor George Clinton and several other federal officials with him. They sailed from New York City (then the American capital) in a small packet ship to Newport, RI, arriving early Tuesday morning, August 17. There the group was treated to a day and night of town celebrations, including a formal dinner toasting the new Constitution and President Washington.

The next morning, August 18, a handful of city officials and representatives from various civil and religious groups had the honor of presenting messages of welcome to the president. Among them was the lay leader of Newport's tiny Jewish congregation, Moses Seixas.

When he read the congregation's message to Washington, Seixas poured out his heart full of gratitude to George Washington for the president's leadership in war and the establishment of the new nation. Seixas expressed the congregation's hope that the nation would accord all of its citizens respect and tolerance, whatever their background or religious belief. He reminded Washington that for centuries Jews had suffered at the hands of hostile governments, but that the United States had the opportunity to create a new birth of religious freedom for all.

Seixas's address moved the president. A few days later, Washington responded in a letter assuring the congregation that "every one shall sit in safety under his own vine and figtree and there shall be none to make him afraid." He promised that, under his leadership, the United States would be a nation that would not discriminate on religious grounds. A copy of the entire letter that he wrote is enclosed for you to read, along with the address that Moses Seixas read to Washington.

Beginning in 1789, George Washington wrote letters to a number of American religious organizations, including:

· On May 10, 1789, he wrote to the United Baptist churches in Virginia;

· That same month, he wrote to the General Assembly of Presbyterian churches;

· In September of 1789, he wrote to the annual meeting of the Quakers;

· In March 1790, he wrote to the Roman Catholics;

· And in August of 1790, he sent his deservedly famous letter to the Hebrew Congregation in Newport.

The tone of this last message was different from the others—it was declarative, assertive and unusually crisp compared to Washington's ordinary style. The Letter to the Hebrew Congregation in Newport, RI has become a clarion call promising more than mere tolerance, but full liberty of conscience to every American no matter what his or her religious belief. In the moment, Washington was throwing his personal weight behind the proposed First Amendment, which would be added to the Constitution on December 15, 1791. In the long run, he set the standard of religious inclusiveness that each of his successors has had to emulate.

Some of the words in George Washington's letter never fail to move me: "It is now no more that toleration is spoken of as if it were by the indulgence of one class of people that another enjoyed the exercise of their inherent natural rights." He then notes, "For, happily, the Government of the United States, which gives to bigotry no sanction, to persecution no assistance, requires only that they who live under its protection should demean themselves as good citizens in giving it on all occasions their effectual support." He concludes by looking forward to a time when "every one shall sit in safety under his own vine and figtree and there shall be none to make him afraid."

American historian Melvin Urofsky has written:

Although this letter carries with it a unique and cherished significance for American Jewry, in many ways it is a treasure of the entire nation. America, as de Tocqueville (a French political thinker and historian who visited America in the early 1800's) famously wrote, had been 'born free,' unfettered by the religious and social bigotries of medieval Europe. The United States, although initially founded by people from the British Isles, had well before the Revolution become a haven of many peoples from continental Europe seeking political and religious freedom and economic opportunity. The new nation recognized this diversity for what it was, one of the country's greatest assets, and took as its motto *E Pluribus Unum*—Out of Many, One... The separation of church and state, and with it the freedom of religion enshrined in the First Amendment to the Constitution, has made the United States a beacon of hope to oppressed peoples everywhere.

THE AMBASSADOR JOHN L. LOEB, JR. INSTITUTE FOR RELIGIOUS FREEDOM AT THE GEORGE WASHINGTON UNIVERSITY   LOEB.COLUMBIAN.GWU.EDU

David Brussat: Newport's Deft New Touro Jewel

This Sunday, on the grounds of Touro Synagogue, in Newport, the new Loeb Visitors Center is to open. Newport's first Jewish congregation, Jeshuat Israel, founded in 1658, remains established on this hallowed terrain. In 1790, it addressed to George Washington its congratulations, eliciting the new president's epistolary declaration that religious freedom in the new nation would protect all faiths, not just rival sects of Christianity.

Any building erected to introduce visitors to this proud history requires a venerable design.

The visitors center sits amid the most astonishing set of colonial buildings in America. Many cities can claim some number of houses built before the revolution, but only the City by the Sea boasts such a large number of civic, commercial and ecclesiastical buildings from the colonial era. The Touro Synagogue (finished in 1763) was designed by Peter Harrison, reputedly America's first professional architect. His Market House (1772) sits at the other end of Washington Square, and his Redwood Library (1750) is up the hill. Colony House (1739) and the neo-colonial County Courthouse (1926) frame the view from Washington Square of the new Ambassador John L. Loeb Jr. Visitors Center.

It was with a great sense of relief that I learned, on a trip to Newport last Saturday, that the Loeb more than fills the need for a venerable building.

Word of a new building always sends shivers of concern up my spine, especially if it is to go up amid the beauty of a historical setting. In this case, it was already up. Even in Newport, historic preservationists and other professionals who ought to know better embrace the idea that new buildings in historic districts should avoid seeming as if they might belong there. At best, in this childish view, a visitors center should appear to be an alien spacecraft on a mission to intimidate the locals. Championing new architecture that fits into historical settings is as vital an aspect of preservation as protecting old buildings, but it is rejected by professional preservationists nearly everywhere. Fortunately, with a very few exceptions, Newport has kept the aliens at bay.

It seems that my fears were almost realized. The Newport Historical District Commission had urged that the visitors center be contemporary in style. Its leading sponsor, Ambassador Loeb, and Holly Grosvenor, its chief designer at Newport Collaborative Architects, toyed diplomatically with the notion and then brushed it off in favor of the far more appropriate edifice scheduled to open this Sunday.

Ambassador Loeb discovered that he has ancestors among the congregation that addressed President Washington (including warden Moses Seixas, who wrote it), and that he has 10 blood relatives buried in the congregation's cemetery. He insisted that the visitors center be classical in style but that it not compete with the synagogue itself.

The Loeb Visitors Center hugs a corner of the Touro compound opposite the synagogue, across the newly renovated Patriot Park, and next to the Barney House. The latter was built as early as 1702 by a neighboring landowner, and is being restored as an annex to the visitors center.

The new building reflects the Palladian influences central to Peter Harrison's architecture while deferring to that of his synagogue. A building meant to introduce visitors to another building of greater importance mustn't be more imposing than that building. The Loeb Center commits no such impropriety. And yet its design departs rather boldly from canonical aspects of classical style—doffing its cap, one imagines, to the departure of Touro's congregation from colonial America's religious orthodoxy.

For example, the four columns of the visitors center's porch hover between regular classical spacing and that of tightly matched pairs. And their capitals flout the canon by pulling in rather than edging out from under their architrave. In the hands of a lesser practitioner, such departures might be deemed canonical errors of the sort that drive many orthodox classicists batty. The innovations will be studiously ignored by modernists eager to insist, blindly, that the Loeb "copies the past." The Touro congregation is orthodox; its visitors center is not.

Yet unlike modern architecture whose features revel in the spirit of contradiction, the Loeb Center's primary aesthetic features all conspire to express their unorthodoxy in ways that help the building fit into its colonial context. Its rusticated Indiana limestone, its arched Palladian fenestration of mahogany, its gently pitched roof all proclaim its embrace of Newport's architectural community. It is obviously a classical building, yet it is unlike any other. No work of classicism could possibly depart from canon with greater dignity, hence no building could possibly fit onto a historic street with greater distinction.

Embedded in this otherwise ancillary building is the spirit of civic congeniality embodied by George Washington's famous words. In tapping its spirit, the Loeb Visitors Center succeeds admirably. The brave new building seems at home in old Newport.

≡

The Story of How the Danes Rescued Their Jews
Including My Cousin Oscar Lewisohn's Story

Given my Danish family connections, and my experience as the U.S. ambassador to Denmark, I believe the following short reprise of an awesome piece of Danish history bears retelling in my memoir. Once well known worldwide, the story is now fading from public memory, and I find myself wondering if those younger than baby boomers are familiar with this amazing example of Danish bravery.

A Note: My cousin Oscar Lewisohn helped to get translated into English a book called *Nothing Much to Speak Of: Wartime Experiences of the Danish Jews 1943–1945*, about the rescue of the Jewish community in Copenhagen in 1943, and it has been a source of details for me.

THE DANES RESCUE THE JEWS

The story begins on an early April morning in 1940, when the futile six-hour resistance to the Nazis by Denmark's small but brave army ended, and the five-year occupation of Denmark started. In November 1942, Dr. Werner Best, a leading member of the SS, was sent to be the sovereign German authority in Denmark, a command he held until the official end of World War II in 1945. Best soon met a fellow German, Georg F. Duckwitz, who would become his colleague and confidant. Duckwitz had lived in Copenhagen as an executive of a German shipping company since 1928, but he had become Germany's Copenhagen maritime attaché in 1939. He spoke fluent Danish, had many friends in Denmark, and though a member of the Nazi Party, he was its occasional critic and, according to the writer Eric Silver, "drifted away" from it.[*] Even with Duckwitz's lukewarm attitude toward the Nazi Party, Best made him a member of his staff.

At the outset of the occupation in 1940, the Germans dealt with the Danes relatively leniently (compared with other countries they occupied, that is), and they allowed the Danish king, Christian X, to remain on the throne until mid-September 1943.[†] Up to that point there had been no major harassment of Copenhagen's Jewish community by the Nazis. However, with the war beginning to turn against Hitler,[‡] and the subversive Danish resistance movement becoming increasingly effective, a tightening of the Nazi grid was ordered. On August 28, Best ordered the arrest of Copenhagen's chief rabbi, Dr. Max Friediger, plus a dozen other prominent Jews and a hundred dissident Danes thought to be dangerous to the Reich. The day after those arrests, the Danish government resigned en masse, providing a good excuse for Best to wire Berlin on September 8, stating that measures should be taken to "solve the Jewish problem" in Denmark. Adolf Eichmann, who was in overall charge of the Nazi strategy on this subject, had long advocated such action, and Berlin swiftly agreed. Best confided to Duckwitz on September 11 that there would be a raid on October 1 to round up all of Denmark's Jews and deport them—to the death camps, of course. Shocked and furious, Duckwitz threatened to resign his post, but Best disingenuously told him that he agreed with his views, and then asked, "What can we do but obey orders?" Simmering, Duckwitz flew immediately to Berlin to urge passionately that the order be rescinded. But it was too late; the wheels of Jewish deportation had been set relentlessly in motion. Back in Copenhagen, he wrote in his diary on September 19, "I know what I have to do."

With no time to spare, he quickly manufactured a business trip to Stockholm, but

---

[*] Oscar Lewisohn has brought to my attention a good deal of material about this period of Danish history, and I have been particularly impressed with a wonderful book, *The Book of the Just: The Unsung Heroes Who Rescued Jews from Hitler*, by Eric Silver (New York: Grove Press, 1992). It has provided me with many more details about Duckwitz's heroism than I had known before.

[†] There is a lovely myth that all during the occupation, King Christian wore a yellow Star of David to show solidarity with the Jews, which in fact he did not. Nevertheless, it is true that the Danish king (unlike Norway's collaborator, the minister-president Vidkun Quisling) was very favorably disposed to Denmark's Jewish population. My friend Gordon Zacks, an advisor in several arenas to President George H.W. Bush, writes of the Danish king's attitude toward the Nazis, and the defense of them by Christian X is cited in his book *Defining Moments, Stories of Character, Courage and Leadership* (New York: Beaufort Books, 2006).

[‡] Among other bad news for the Axis powers, Italy had just conceded defeat on September 7, 1943.

in reality to a meeting in the home of Sweden's prime minister, Per Albin Hansson, arranged by a Swedish diplomat. There, Duckwitz pleaded for a favorable Swedish reception of Jewish refugees if they could escape across the Øresund, the strait between Denmark and Sweden. In Hansson he had a friendly ear, and he was told that official Swedish assurances would come "soon," but that even if there was not an immediate governmental announcement, the Swedes would not be surprised or upset if boatloads of Jews arrived on their coast. Eventually, the promise of welcome for the Jews came, but for Duckwitz it was not soon enough. He then took a third step, well knowing that helping Jews escape was punishable by death. He met secretly with Copenhagen's Socialist Democrats to tell them that the surprise roundup would start October 1. Hans Hedtoft, the head of the Social Democrats, contacted the acting chief rabbi, Dr. Marcus Melchior,* who alerted the Jewish congregation in the Great Synagogue in Krystalgade on September 30. He told them why there would be no service the next day, and that "by nightfall we must all be in hiding."

C.B. Henriques, the chairman of the Danish Jewish Community, was also notified. Henriques was stunned and at first didn't take the warning seriously. He reflected the mindset of many, especially Denmark's Jewish elite. Even after the resignation of the Danish government just days earlier, many refused to believe they were at risk. Hadn't Dr. Best just that week announced that all Jews were safe, and that all this talk about a roundup was nothing but a rumor? But now, with the Duckwitz warning, they had no choice but to believe, hide and flee when they could.

The Danes had just three days from the warning they'd received on September 28 until the eve of Rosh Hashanah to bring about a miracle. The daunting task was to alert, hide and arrange the escape of almost eight thousand Danish Jews. The entire populace rose in solidarity. Farmers, businessmen, professors, students, secretaries, waitresses, mechanics and teenagers—all worked as though organized by a single entity. Some worked totally on their own. One enterprising taxi driver took it upon himself to phone the homes of every name in the phone book that sounded even vaguely Jewish. Hospitals released Jewish patients and readmitted them under Christian names. Ambulances spirited Jews away until a hiding place or passage on a ship was secured. Some volunteers found fishermen who would risk not only their boats and their livelihoods, but also their lives, by sneaking the refugees across the Nazi-patrolled open water. These amazing Danish Gentiles kept Jews in their own attics and basements, or

---

* The chief rabbi, Dr. M. Friediger, had been arrested a day earlier and was under house arrest.

≡

Genealogy,
Including Sons of the Revolution and Lord of the Manor

SONS OF THE REVOLUTION

The origins of my passionate interest in genealogy in general, and our family's history going back before the American Revolution in particular, was inspired by a certificate three feet wide and two feet high in my father's bedroom. It was a kind of diploma that he received from the Sons of the American Revolution stating that he was able to join that organization because he was a descendent of Jacob Phillips. This certificate was probably three times as big as my father's diploma from Harvard.

We know that Jacob Phillips served in the South Carolina Militia. He may have gone into battle, or he may have watered the horses, but he "served."

Because of various quarrels and personalities in the state of New York, there are now two Sons of the American Revolution in New York City, as well as one of the Sons of the Revolution. One major difference between the three organizations is that the Sons of the Revolution in the State of New York (SRNY) has a building known as Fraunces Tavern, a picture of which is included on the next page.

Fraunces Tavern is located at 54 Pearl Street, close to Wall Street. A small portion of it dates back to the early part of the eighteenth century. A man by the name of Samuel Fraunces owned the tavern. He was reputed to be from the West Indies. Taverns at that time were not only places to eat and drink, but also places to do business. With the help of a tavern, Alexander Hamilton formed the Bank of New York. When I worked in London in the 1950s, messengers on the floor of the London Stock Exchange were

Fraunces Tavern was a historic eighteenth-century tavern, a convivial colonial gathering place, and is now owned by the Sons of the Revolution in the State of New York (SRNY). It was in this tavern that General George Washington bade an emotional farewell to his officers in December 1783.

Fraunces Tavern includes a museum, a restaurant and several galleries. A portrait of my grandmother, Adeline Moses Loeb, a Daughter of the American Revolution, hangs in a gallery named in her honor.

still called "waiters." Fraunces Tavern has become well known because it was in this tavern that General George Washington, who later became our first president, said farewell to his first officers in a very emotional ceremony.

On January 24, 1975, the Armed Forces of Puerto Rican National Liberation (known as FALN) detonated bombs in the area, which devastated one side of Fraunces Tavern. I took the lead financially to help restore the building. As a result, the Board of Managers of Fraunces Tavern designated a small gallery named in honor of my grandmother, Adeline Moses Loeb, who was already a Daughter of the American Revolution.

In 1993 I was given the Sons of the Revolution Distinguished Patriot Award, and in 2009 the Board of Managers made me an Honorary President of the Sons of the Revolution.

For more information, see the book *An American Experience: Adeline Moses Loeb (1876–1953) and Her Early American Jewish Ancestors*, which is discussed in chapter 23.

LORDSHIP OF THE MANOR OF BRINSLEY

My interest in genealogy went so far that it led me to buy the Lordship of the Manor of Brinsley years ago for £5,000. The title "Lordship of the Manor" was actually part of the land, and therefore under English law the title "Lordship of the Manor" is considered property. The Lordship of the Manor of Brinsley belonged originally to the Seventh Duke of Newcastle. Because he had no male heirs, his title to Brinsley, as well as many other titles, went to his general estate.

The reason there are Lordships of the Manor still available goes back to William the Conqueror. Originally, his colleagues were happy with the title of Lordship of various manors, but over the years those titles became unimportant and other titles took their place, such as baron, marquis, duke, and so on.

The Lordship of the Manor of Brinsley belonged to the Most Noble Henry Pelham

Archibald Douglas, Seventh Duke of Newcastle, who died May 30, 1928. The duke had no children or heirs. When I visited Brinsley, the community was extremely welcoming. They not only missed having a Lord of the Manor, but they were also willing to accept me even though I was American, Jewish (although not religious) and had paid for the lordship. For example, in the attached newspaper article you will see where it says "He [me] paid a visit to *his* Parish" (emphasis added).

EVENING POST Friday 19th September, 1997 No 572 Vol 98

American Lord of Manor drops in on Brinsley

A CENTURIES OLD title has been brought back to life and with it a transatlantic friend for Brinsley.

American businessman, John Loeb, bought the title Lord of the Manor of Brinsley some time ago from a manorial society.

He paid a visit to his parish at the weekend when he was so impressed by his welcome and the activities of the village carnival committee who were holding their annual dance, he pledged funds for a recreation project.

Chairman Tony Chettle was "over the moon" with the gift of £2,500 to the carnival committee.

"The money is the balance outstanding needed to convert the portable buildings on the recreation ground into changing accommodation."

Sponsors already include the carnival committee (£500), Warburtons bakery (£100) and accountants AF Butler (£50).

"His generosity has made a pleasant weekend into an exceptional weekend to the benefit of the community," said Mr. Chettle.

Mr. Loeb, a former US diplomat, has been a self-confessed Anglophile for almost 50 years.

As well as an honorary CBE from the Queen he has long-standing connections with Cambridge University and with the Churchill Association in America.

He revealed that the weekend's trip to Brinsley was the second time he had visited the parish.

The first was kept under wraps by local civic leaders.

At the weekend he was hosted by Maurice and Christine Styles and taken on a tour of the area by parish council chairman Coun Norman who introduced Mr. Loeb to as many local groups as his busy schedule allowed.

The "meet the people: exercise left Mr. Loeb bowled over by the warmth of his welcome.

My lasting memory of this trip will be of the friendliness and hospitality of people in the parish.

He added that when the opportunity arose to purchase the title he had been attracted by the name of Brinsley. He did not know of the parish but had a broad awareness of the area and its associates with DH Lawrence.

Count Norman said he felt it important "Mr. Loeb meet villagers and get a feel for life in Brinsley."

"I think he liked what he saw and was most impressed by the casual and friendly way in which he was welcomed. It seems a great pity the council were not aware of his first visit and that we had in fact got a Lord of the Manor."

"1996 was important in the history of Brinsley Parish Council and I am sure John would have liked the opportunity to join in the centenary celebrations," he added.

"John showed a genuine interest in Brinsley, particularly its history, and I feel the village has earned itself a good and lasting friend," Coun Norman, who explained that the recreation project would entail multi-use changing accommodation, extra car parking as well as landscaping.

Numerous people were given a further chance to meet the 'Lord' at a Sunday afternoon reception hosted by the White Lion.

Parish councilor Stan Cooke presented Mr. Loeb with one of his own paintings of the original Brinsley headstocks as a momento of his visit and Coun Norman also presented him with a framed centenary print of the village.

Prior to returning to his London home, Mr. Loeb said he was already looking forward to his next visit which hopefully would coincide with the annual carnival.

"It was mainly through the carnival that this latest visit came about. When I leaned that this year was likely to be Tony Chettle's last, I felt I had to come and meet him."

"He really is a most remarkable man and I'm only sorry I wasn't able to be here for the event itself."

APPENDIX G

≡

The Social Register

Specific to the United States, the **Social Register** (**SR**) is a directory of names and addresses of prominent American families who are claimed to be from the social elite. Inclusion has historically been limited to members of polite society, members of the American upper class[*] and "the establishment," and those from "old money" or white Anglo-Saxon Protestant (WASP) families, within the *Social Register* cities. The *Social Register* cities are Baltimore, Boston, Chicago, Cleveland, New York, Philadelphia, Pittsburgh, Portland, Providence, San Francisco, Seattle, St. Louis, and Washington, D.C., as well as various "Southern Cities." In European countries, similar directories for the perceived upper class, such as those published by Burke's Peerage in the United Kingdom, have been published for centuries.

Historically, the social elite was a small closed group. The leadership was well known to the readers of society pages, but in larger cities it was impossible to remember everyone, or to keep track of the new debutantes, the marriages, and the obituaries. The solution was the *Social Register*, which listed the names and addresses of the families who mingled in the same private clubs, attended the right teas and cotillions, worshipped together at prestigious churches, funded the proper charities, lived in exclusive neighborhoods, and sent their daughters to finishing schools and their sons away to prep schools.

One of the earliest social registers in the United States was the *Cleveland Social Directory*, later known as the *Cleveland Blue Book*. Its first publication appeared in 1880 and was described by its publisher as a "Ladies Visiting List and Shopping Guide" for

---

[*] The *Social Register* has always included a few elite Jewish families, such as the Lehmans and Loebs. It now includes a much wider group of Jewish families, as well as African Americans—Barack and Michele Obama are now in the *Social Register*.

Cleveland society. A volume called *The List: A Visiting and Shopping Directory* was published in New York City in 1880 by Maurice M. Minton; it included lists of prominent New York families, with their addresses. The original *New York Social Register* first was published in 1886 by Louis Keller, a German American of wide social acquaintance, who combined the "visiting lists" of a number of fashionable ladies. Initially, it consisted largely of the descendants of Dutch or English settlers, the "Knickerbocker" merchant class who had built New York City.

One's entry in a *Social Register* was not guaranteed to be permanent. People were removed from the ranks for various scandals or peccadillos, or simply for pursuing "undesirable" careers, such as the theater. One example concerns an actress, Jane Wyatt, a descendant of the prominent Van Rensselaer family. Wyatt was believed to have been removed from inclusion because of her profession, but in fact she was still listed until her death in October 2006, at the age of 96. Jane Wyatt's article states that she was restored to the register after her marriage. Charles Black, a partner of Lehman Brothers, was dropped from the *Social Register* in 1950 for marrying the former child star Shirley Temple.

While the *Social Register* helped define high society decades ago, its day has passed. *The New York Times* stated in 1997:

"Once, the *Social Register* was a juggernaut in New York social circles. . . . Nowadays, however, with the waning of the WASP elite as a social and political force, the register's role as an arbiter of who counts and who doesn't is almost an anachronism. In Manhattan, where charity galas are at the center of the social season, the organizing committees are so studded with luminaries from publishing, Hollywood, and Wall Street, that the perceived importance of family lineage is almost irrelevant."

A successor publication, *The Social Register*, is released annually as a single national directory, published in winter and summer editions from New York by *Forbes* magazine. Those aspiring to be listed must be sponsored by at least five individuals currently appearing in its pages. Those sponsored are reviewed by an advisory committee that makes the final decision regarding inclusion. Approximately 5 percent of nominated names are added each year. The committee also arrives at additions on its own and sends the potential listees "blanks," or forms to fill in their information.

"The Fortune 500 list is infinitely more valuable" said Nan Kempner, the late famous Park Avenue hostess and cousin of mine. "The *Social Register* has never been on my mind."

Blaine Trump, a former sister-in-law of President Donald Trump, and a super socialite and fundraiser, said she had never read or even seen the *Social Register*. "I'm sorry, is that some sort of a directory?" she asked. "It's just not a point of reference for me."

Colonial Jewish Cemetery— Newport, Rhode Island

Moses Alvarez (b. –d. 1766)

Myer Benjamin (1723–1776)

Mrs. Phila Elcon (b. –d. 1820)

Catherine Hays (1776–1854)

Judah Hays (1770–1832)

Moses Michael Hays (1739–1805)

Rachel *Myers* Hays (1738–1810)

Rebekah Hays (1769–1802)

Slowey Hays (1779–1836)

Benjamin Levy (1692–1787)

Bilah Levy (1742–1781)

Mrs. Judith Levy (1700–1788)

Moses Levy (1704–1792)

Sarah Ann Levy (1808–1809)

Aaron Lopez (1731–1782)

Mrs. Abigail *Lopez* Lopez (1726–1762)

Mrs Abigail Lopez (b. –d. 1792)

Isaac Lopez (b. –d. 1763)

Jacob Lopez (1755–1764)

Jacob Lopez (1750–1822)

Moses Lopez (1706–1767)

Moses Lopez (1739–1830)

Mrs. Rachel *Lopez* Lopez (1758–1789)

Mrs. Rebecca Lopez (b. –d. 1854)

Abraham Minis (1788–1801)

Mrs. Maratha Moravia (b. –d. 1787)

Isaac Polock (1700–1764)

Isaac Jacob Polock (1746–1782)

Mrs. Rebecca Polock (b. –d. 1764)

Abraham Rodriguez Rivera (d. 1765)

Jacob Rodriguez Rivera (1717–1789)

Mrs. Rachel Rodriguez Rivera (b. –d. 1761)

Edwin Rosenstein (b. –d. 1866)

Isaac Mendes Seixas (1708–1780)

Isaac Seixas (1779–1786)

Moses Seixas (1744–1809)

Abraham Touro (1777–1822)

Judah Touro (1775–1854)

Mrs. Reyna *Hays* Touro (1743–1784)

(Names in blue are my relatives.)

APPENDIX I

≡

I Remember

I REMEMBER, I REMEMBER RIDGELEIGH.

WE STILL LIVE THERE, BUT IT IS NOT THE SAME. WE USE THE TENNIS COURT NOW AND OUR OWN POOL. THE POOL IS VERY NEW AND VERY BEAUTIFUL AND VERY WHITE, AND THE WATER IS WARMER THAN MY GRANDMOTHER'S. WE USED TO USE MY GRANDMOTHER'S POOL. THE YEARS HAVE SHADED IT BY HUGE SLUMPING ELMS AND IVY HAS GROWN THICK ON THE WALLS AROUND IT. THE POOL IS COOL AND AT THE SHALLOW END IS A SMALLER POOL WHERE THE WATER IS VERY COLD. WE WOULD FORCE OURSELVES INTO THIS SMALLER ONE FIRST AND THEN DIVE QUICKLY INTO THE LARGER POOL SO THAT BY COMPARISON IT WOULD BE WARM.

WE STILL STROLL OVER THE SOFT, WIDE LAWNS, THE GENTLE RISES IN THE LAND, BUT IT IS NOT THE SAME. WE HAVE GROWN UP NOW, AND THE NOISE FROM THE PLAYROOM IS JAZZ. THE SCREAMS, THE TEARS AND LAUGHTER OF CHILDREN, TIN TOYS CLANGING AGAINST THE TOYS ARE GONE, AND ONLY THE FEW SCRATCHES ON THE WALLS AND FLOORS ARE SIGNS THAT THEY WERE EVER THERE.

RIDGELEIGH IS A QUIET PLACE. I SUPPOSE IT ALWAYS WAS. I LOVE IT FOR ITS PEACE, SO APART FROM REALITY. I LOVE THE LAND, MOIST IN SPRING, CAKED HARD UNDER A FRINGE OF GRASS BY THE FIRST FROSTS OF WINTER, AND I LOVE IT BEST WHEN I AM ALONE. WHEN I AM ALONE AND LOOK BACK TO THE TIME WHEN WE LIVED THERE AND FROM ONE END OF THE YEAR TO ANOTHER HAD NEVER HEARD OF BOARDING SCHOOL, RIDGELEIGH IS MINE. I OWN IT WITH MEMORIES.

RIDGELEIGH IS THE NAME OF MY GRANDPARENTS' HOME, AND WHEN MY MOTHER MARRIED, MY GRANDFATHER GAVE HER PART OF IT AND BUILT HER A HOUSE THERE. I HAVE ALWAYS CALLED THE WHOLE PLACE RIDGELEIGH ALTHOUGH OUR PLACE DOES NOT EVEN HAVE A NAME. MY GRANDFATHER IS DEAD NOW. HE DIED WHEN I WAS FIVE YEARS OLD. THE ONLY THING I CLEARLY REMEMBER ABOUT HIM WAS THE HONEY AND TOAST HE WOULD GIVE US WHEN WE CAME OVER TO SEE HIM ON SUNDAY MORNINGS.

I REMEMBER THE LITTLE THINGS -- THE ROCK BENCH ON THE HILL THAT HAS LONG SINCE CRUMBLED, A WONDERFUL FEELING OF HOME WHEN WE WERE FORCED INSIDE BY THE RAIN. DURING THE SUMMER THERE WERE ALWAYS SIX OR SEVEN COUSINS OF ALL AGES LIVING AT MY GRANDMOTHER'S. WE SPEND THE HOT, HEAVY DAYS, HALF NAKED, ROAMING LIKE BANDITS ON OUR BICYCLES OVER THE BACK ROADS AND FOREST PATHS OR PLAYING FOX AND HOUNDS FOR HOURS IN THE POOL. WE LEARNED EVERY HIDING PLACE, EVERY STUMP, EVERY FALLEN TREE AND THICKET ON RIDGELEIGH. IN WINTER WHEN THE SNOW BECAME TOO CRISP TO SLEIGH-RIDE AND THE RUNNERS WOULD STICK, WE WOULD TAKE OUT OUR PANS AND TRAYS AND SPIN CRAZILY DOWN THE HILL.

* * * * * *

I HAVE A BABY SISTER NOW. SHE IS ONLY THREE. IT IS AS IF WE WERE IN ANOTHER GENERATION. I WONDER, SEEING HER PLAY WITH HER NURSE IN THE SANDBOX, WHAT RIDGELEIGH WILL BE TO HER.

This short essay was written by me for my freshman English class at Harvard in the fall of 1948.

APPENDIX J

Presidents Who Have Known Me

Dwight D. Eisenhower (1953–1961)
John F. Kennedy (1961–1963)
Lyndon B. Johnson (1963–1969)
Richard M. Nixon (1969–1974)
Gerald R. Ford Jr. (1974–1977)
James E. Carter Jr. (1977–1981)
Ronald W. Reagan (1981–1989)
George H.W. Bush (1989–1993)
William J. Clinton (1993–2001)
George W. Bush (2001–2009)
Donald J. Trump (2017–)

Stories about each of them will be in the second, revised edition of my memoir.

Endnotes

THE LEHMAN STORY

1   Stephen Birmingham, *"Our Crowd": The Great Jewish Families of New York* (New York: Harper & Row, 1967), p. 1.

2   Roland Flade, *The Lehmans: From Rimpar to the New World: A Family History* (Königshausen & Neumann, 1996), p. 58.

3   Ibid.

4   All of Herbert Lehman's papers are collected at Columbia University in the Herbert H. Lehman Collection section of the Rare Book and Manuscript Library.

5   Flade, *The Lehmans*, p. 66.

6   Interview with John Durr's granddaughter-in-law, Virginia Foster Durr.

7   Using the Consumer Price Index provided by measuringworth.com.

8   The collection of Judaica at Temple Emanu-El in New York that became the Herbert & Eileen Bernard Museum of Judaica was donated by Irving Lehman.

9   Computed from *Comparing the Purchasing Power of Money in the United States (or Colonies) from 1665 to 2002*, EH.net Calculator, using consumer price index.

10 American Council of Learned Societies, *Dictionary of American Biography*, Vol. 11, Supplements 1 and 2 (New York: Scribner's, 1958).

11 Frances Lehman Loeb's unpublished memoir, p. 6.

12 Susan Heller Anderson, "Helen Buttenwieser, 84, Lawyer and Civic Leader," *The New York Times*, November 23, 1989.

THE LEWISOHN STORY

13 Much of what I now know about my great-grandfather—especially from the time before my birth in 1930—has been gleaned from thousands of articles about him and his family in the venerable *The New York Times*. I also have his unpublished autobiography as a source, as well as an abundance of family lore passed on from my mother, Frances Lehman Loeb, and my grandmother Adele Lehman Lewisohn. (In his autobiography he wrote, "Such books [autobiographies] often turn out to be more fiction than fact and not of great interest to their readers. I confess that I often avoid them when I can, so why should I bring to others what I do not like very much myself?" I can almost hear his heavy German accent reading those lines.) Additional stories have come from conversations with his granddaughters Dr. Marjorie Lewisohn and Joan Lewisohn Crowell, as well as from *Never a Dull Moment* by Virginia Kahn, his youngest granddaughter.

14 Walter Schwartz, "The Life and Legacy of Adolph Lewisohn," *Westchester Historian* 91, no. 3 (Summer 2015), p. 75.

15 An entire chapter of Stephen Birmingham's book *Our Crowd* is entitled "der Reiche Lewisohn."

16 *The Citizenship of Adolph Lewisohn: An Autobiography* (unpublished), chapter XI.

17 American Council of Learned Societies, *Dictionary of American Biography*, Vol. 11, Supplements 1 and 2 (New York: Scribner's, 1958), p. 383.

18 *The Citizenship of Adolph Lewisohn: An Autobiography*, p 47.

19 Birmingham, *Our Crowd*, p. 259.

20 Schwartz, "The Life and Legacy of Adolph Lewisohn," p. 70.

21 *The New York Times*, July 29, 1916, obituary of Mrs. Adolph Lewisohn.

22 Frances Lehman Loeb, *For My family: A Memoir* (unpublished, 1982), p. 29.

23 John Langeloth Loeb and Frances Lehman Loeb, with Kenneth Libo, *All in a Lifetime* (privately published), p. 39.

24 Conversation with Joan Lewisohn Crowell, Nov. 16, 2005.

25 Harvey H. Kaiser, *Great Camps of the Adirondacks* (Jaffrey, NH: David R. Godine, 1982).

26 Birmingham, *Our Crowd*, p. 358.

27 *The New York Times*, May 29, 1930.

28 *The New York Times*, May 28, 1938.

29 *The New York Times*, January 1, 1921.

30 Conversation with Dr. Marjorie Lewisohn, August 24, 2005.

31 Ibid.

32 Virginia Kahn, *Never a Dull Moment* (privately published, 2007), p. 3.

33 Taped conversation with Joan Lewisohn Crowell, November 16, 2005.

34 Birmingham, *Our Crowd*, p. 356.

35 *The Citizenship of Adolph Lewisohn*, p. 185.

36 Letter to the *Brooklyn Daily Eagle*, July 7, 1929.

37 Ibid, p. 191.

38 Interview with Marjorie Lewisohn.

39 Jonathan Stern, "Music for the (American) People: The Concerts at Lewisohn Stadium, 1922–1964" (PhD diss., City University of New York, 2009).

40 *The New York Times*, August 19, 1938.

THE MOSES-LOEB STORY

41 In a small book she calls an "album" titled *Old Family Things*, my cousin Judith Alexander Weil Shanks reveals much more of The Oaks's history. The plantation was given in 1680 as a "warrant" to Edward Middleton by the British Lords Proprietors. The plantation had 328 acres of cleared land and 389 acres of woodland.

42 Theodore Rosengarten and Dale Rosengarten, *A Portion of the People: Three Hundred Years of Southern Jewish Life* (University of South Carolina Press, 2002).

43 Quoted from *Rebecca's Things*, a family history by Judith Alexander Weil Shanks, my third cousin.

44 Margaret Loeb Kempner, *Recollection* (unpublished), p. 5.

45 "Sheffield," *Northern Alabama, Historical and Biographical* (Birmingham, AL: Smith and De Land, 1888), p. 409.

46 Margaret Loeb Kempner, *Recollection*.

47 For a more complete story of my grandmother and her forebears, see the book *An American Experience: Adeline Moses Loeb (1876–1953) and Her Early American Jewish Ancestors*, published by the Sons of the Revolution in the State of New York (www.sonsoftherevolution.org) in 2009.

48 Letter from Jacob Langeloth, American Metal Co. Ltd., to Carl Loeb, dated February 9, 1895.

49 Letter from Carl Loeb to Jacob Langeloth, American Metal Co. Ltd., dated February 12, 1895.

50 Margaret Loeb Kempner, *Recollection*, p. 18.

51 Hans Widenmann, *Carl M. Loeb, Rhoades & Co. 1931–1945* (unpublished, 1945).

52 Ibid.

CHAPTER 1

53 Loeb and Loeb, *All in a Lifetime.*

54 Frances Lehman Loeb, *For My Family, A Memoir* (unpublished, 1982), p. 78.

55 Ibid, p. 140.

56 From my essay about Ridgeleigh, written for a freshman English class at Harvard.

57 Loeb and Loeb, *All in a Lifetime*, p. 154.

58 Loeb and Loeb, *All in a Lifetime*, pp. 95–96.

59 From Harvard essay about Ridgeleigh.

60 Loeb, *For My Family: A Memoir*, p. 96.

61 Ibid.

62 Ibid, p. 103.

63 I have written much more about her in *Adeline Moses Loeb and Her Early American Jewish Ancestors.*

64 Quoted from Paul Buttenwieser, *Their Pride and Joy* (New York: Delacorte Press, 1987).

CHAPTER 2

65 Loeb and Loeb, *All in a Lifetime*, p. 106.

CHAPTER 3

66 Birmingham, *Our Crowd*, p. 372.

67 Letter from Al Silberman to Robert A. Oden Jr., Hotchkiss headmaster, May 25, 1993.

68 Obituary of John Hersey, *The New York Times*, March 25, 1993.

69 Anne Roiphe, *1185 Park Avenue, a Memoir* (New York: Touchstone, 1999), p. 147.

CHAPTER 4

70 Sex and dating at Harvard were covered in Arianne R. Cohen's "Love Nesting 101" and "Open Door, Three Feet on the Floor," *Harvard Magazine*, July–August 2002.

71 The real quote is "A chiel's amang ye takin' notes, and faith, he'll prent [print] it," from "On Captain Grose's Peregrinations through Scotland" by Robert Burns.

CHAPTER 6

72 Letter from John L. Loeb Jr. to Dorothy Bernhard, January 26, 1955.

73 Letter from John L. Loeb Jr. to Aunt Dorothy, February 28, 1955.

74 Letter from John L. Loeb Jr. to Ann McKinstry, Newbegin's Book Shop, San Francisco, September 22, 1955.

CHAPTER 7

75 John L. Loeb Jr. letter responding to phone call of June 12, 1956.

76 Harold Epstein transcript of November 14, 1990, p. 9.

77 Ibid, p. 3.

CHAPTER 8

78 T.A. Wise, "Wherever You Look, There's Loeb, Rhoades," *Fortune Magazine*, April 1963.

79 Carl M. Loeb, Rhoades & Co., press release, June 8, 1960.

80 Loeb and Loeb, *All in a Lifetime*, p. 181.

81 Birmingham, *Our Crowd*, p. 379.

82 Loeb and Loeb, *All in a Lifetime*, p. 197.

83 Leon Levy, with Eugene Linden, *The Mind of Wall Street: A Legendary Financier on the Perils of Greed and the Mysteries of the Market* (New York: Public Affairs, 2002), p. 89–90.

84 Loeb and Loeb, *All in a Lifetime*, p. 162.

85 Ibid.

86 Ibid.

87 "Impressionist Masterpiece by Manet to Be Auctioned by Sotheby's," Art Daily.com, http://artdaily.com/news/37961/Impressionist-Masterpiece-by-Manet-to-Be-Auctioned-by-Sotheby-s.

88 Edited excerpt in the *Financial Times*, January 1, 2009, from a book by Philip Hook, *The Ultimate Trophy: How the Impressionist Painting Conquered the World* (London: Prestel Publishers, 2009).

89 London's *Daily Express*, front page, October 16, 1958.

90 Using oanda.com's conversion rate.

CHAPTER 9

91 "John L. Loeb Jr., A Name of His Own," *Forbes*, May 15, 1968, p. 79.

92 John L. Loeb Jr., letter to his father, August 9, 1971, p. 2.

93 "The Michel Move," *The New York Times*, November 28, 1971.

94 "Wall Street's Environment's Upsetting the Animals," *The Economist*, June 30, 1973.

95 Charles Geisst, *The Last Partnerships: Inside the Great Wall Street Money Dynasties* (New York: McGraw Hill, 2001), p. 74.

96 Ehrlich and Rehfeld, *The New Crowd*, p. 159.

97 Sandy Weill and Judah S. Kraushaar, *The Real Deal: My Life in Business and Philanthropy* (New York: Warner Business Books, 2006), p. 95.

98 Ibid, p. 96.

99 Ehrlich and Rehfeld, *The New Crowd*, p. 9.

100 Ehrlich and Rehfeld, *The New Crowd*, p. 158.

CHAPTER 10

101 Kelly Killoren Bensimon, "Nick Loeb Chats Onion Crunch and Building a Brand," *amNewYork*, August 7, 2014, http://www.amny.com/lifestyle/nick-loeb-talks-onion-crunch-and-building-a-brand-1.8991517.

CHAPTER 12

102 "Iran Releases American Hostages as Reagan Takes Office," *The New York Times*, January 20, 1981.

CHAPTER 14

103 "Notes on People," *The New York Times*, March 27, 1982.

CHAPTER 15

104 Elizabeth Drew, "Politics and Money," *The New Yorker*, December 13, 1982, p. 79.

CHAPTER 19

105 Interview with Harold Epstein, April 1, 2011.

106 Emma Bazilian, "Calling Mr. Hathaway: Saks and Fairchild's 'Footwear News' revive David Ogilvy's eye patch icon," *Advertising Age*, September 21, 2011.

107 Colville's close personal relationship with Churchill and the Churchill family was revealed in his diaries, *The Fringes of Power: 10 Downing Street Diaries 1939–1955* (New York: Norton, 1985).

108 Ambassador John L. Loeb Jr. speech at the W. Averell Harriman Award ceremony.

109 Ibid.

110 Ibid.

111 Jeanine Stein, "Reagan Receives Churchill Award," *Los Angeles Times*, May 19, 1989.

112 George H.W. Bush, "Remarks Upon Receiving the Winston Churchill Award from Queen Elizabeth II of the United Kingdom," May 14, 1991, http://www.presidency.ucsb.edu/ws/?pid=19578.

113 Julian Aronson, *Valeria: The Story of Jacob Langeloth and His Legacy* (small booklet, privately published, 1963), p. 10.

114 Valeria Langeloth Bonham, *Utopia in the Hills, The Story of Valeria Home and Its Founding* (New York: Robert M. McBride & Company, 1948).

115 Ibid.

116 Ibid.

117 *Boston Evening Transcript*, Aug. 31, 1914.

118 Letter from Adam Hochschild, December 15, 2011.

CHAPTER 20

119 Georgia Dullea, "Lehman Wingding in Lehman Wing," *The New York Times*, June 16, 1989.

120 Ibid.

121 Ibid.

122 Roland Flade, "Family History & Its Meaning for Today: The Case of the Lehmans," *Journal of German-Jewish Genealogical Research*, published by the Leo Baeck Institute, Summer 2006.

123 Ibid.

124 Lawrence Van Gelder, "Frances Loeb, 89, Lifesaver to Foreign Diplomats," *The New York Times*, May 19, 1996.

125 Ambassador John L. Loeb Jr., in an article published in the *Chicago Sentinel*, September 12, 1996.

126 From Yehuda Amichai's speech upon receiving and accepting the 1981 Kulturpreis in Würzburg.

127 Ambassador John L. Loeb Jr., "There Are No Jews in Rimpar," *Jewish Post*, June 19, 1996, http://www.jewishpost.com/archives/news/there-are-no-jews-in-rimpar.html.

128 President Bill Clinton, The White House, June 12, 1996.

129 Chancellor Helmut Kohl, June 3, 1996.

130 Letter from Duke Max to Ambassador John L. Loeb, June 14, 2007.

131 Flade, *The Lehmans*, p. 130, footnote 18.

132 http://americanjewisharchives.org/publications/fajf/.

133 Letter written by Frances Lehman Loeb to her oldest daughter, Judy, on the question "Why Am I a Jew?" Most likely written in the late 1930s or early 1940s.

CHAPTER 23

134 From a conversation with Dr. Marjorie Lewisohn in her apartment, where a Picasso hung in her hallway and a Manet over her living room sofa, August 24, 2005.

135 Claus Virch and James J. Rorimer, "Introduction," in *The Adele and Arthur Lehman Collection* (New York, Metropolitan Museum of Art, 1965), p. 7.

136 Ibid, p. 9.

137 Ibid, p. 9.

138 Frances Lehman Loeb's unpublished memoir, p. 111.

139 *The Jerusalem Report*, August 2, 1999.

140 Armenpress, February 6, 2013.

141 Ben Genocchio, "The Light Is 19th Century, but the Sensibility Is Modern," *The New York Times*, April 3, 2005.

142 Robert Rosenblum, *Transformations in Late 18th Century Art* (Princeton, NJ: Princeton University Press, 1967).

143 Kynaston McShine, ed., *Edvard Munch: the Modern Life of the Soul* (with essays by Reinhold Heller, Elisabeth Prelinger and Edvard Munch; New York: Museum of Modern Art, 2006); and Patricia G. Berman and Pari Stave, *Munch/Warhol and the Multiple Image* (New York: American-Scandinavian Foundation, 2013).

144 Ken Johnson, "Desire and Prudery, Wrestling to a Draw," *The New York Times*, December 5, 2013.

145 "Gala Pickin'," *New York Social Diary*, October 10, 2013, http://www.newyorksocialdiary.com/social-diary/2013/gala-pickin.

146 "Death of a Hired Man," by Robert Frost (1914).

147 E-mail from Charlie Chiara to John Loeb, January 2016.

148 According to the minutes of the December 13, 1967, Landmarks Preservation Commission meeting.

149 Apple Parish Bartlett and Susan Bartlett, *Sister: The Life of the Legendary American Interior Decorator Mrs. Henry Parish II* (New York: St. Martin's Press, 2000).

150 http://www.monticello.org/site/house-and-gardens/uriah-phillips-levy.

151 Stephen Birmingham, *The Grandees: The Story of America's Sephardic Elite* (New York: Harper & Row, 1971).

152 https://www.facinghistory.org/nobigotry/washingtons-rebuke-press-release.

EPILOGUE

153 Excerpt from "To A Louse, On Seeing One on a Lady's Bonnet at Church," by Robert Burns, 1786.

154 English version by W. S. Merwin and J. Moussaieff Masson; found in Old Saint Paul's Church, Baltimore, dated 1692.

ADDITIONAL NOTES

p. 246 From *The Economist*, June 30, 1973, ©1973 The Economist. All rights reserved. Used by permission and protected by the Copyright Laws of the United States. The printing, copying, redistribution, or retransmission of this Content without express written permission is prohibited.

p. 287 From *The New York Times*, November 1, 1971, ©1971 The New York Times. All rights reserved. Used by permission and protected by the Copyright Laws of the United States. The printing, copying, redistribution, or retransmission of this Content without express written permission is prohibited.

p. 349 From *The New York Times*, March 27, 1982, ©1982 The New York Times. All rights reserved. Used by permission and protected by the Copyright Laws of the United States. The printing, copying, redistribution, or retransmission of this Content without express written permission is prohibited.

p. 396 From *The New York Times*, February 10, 1984, ©1984 The New York Times. All rights reserved. Used by permission and protected by the Copyright Laws of the United States. The printing, copying, redistribution, or retransmission of this Content without express written permission is prohibited.

p. 560 From *The New York Times*, December 17, 2002, ©2002 The New York Times. All rights reserved. Used by permission and protected by the Copyright Laws of the United States. The printing, copying, redistribution, or retransmission of this Content without express written permission is prohibited.

p. 608 From *The New York Times*, February 14, 2010, ©2010 The New York Times. All rights reserved. Used by permission and protected by the Copyright Laws of the United States. The printing, copying, redistribution, or retransmission of this Content without express written permission is prohibited.

p. 609 From *The New York Times*, February 28, 2010, ©2010 The New York Times. All rights reserved. Used by permission and protected by the Copyright Laws of the United States. The printing, copying, redistribution, or retransmission of this Content without express written permission is prohibited.

pp. 629-646 ©1963. Time Inc. All rights reserved. Translated from *FORTUNE* Magazine and published with permission of Time Inc. Reproduction in any manner in any language in whole or in part without written permission is prohibited.

Index

Page numbers in **boldface** indicate that the indexed item is in the subject of an illustration or photograph.